# MARYLAND SCHOOL LAW DESKBOOK

## 2007 – 2008 School Year Edition

Stephen C. Bounds
John R. Woolums
Judith S. Bresler
Rochelle S. Eisenberg
Edmund J. O'Meally

Editors-in-Chief:
Stephen C. Bounds & John R. Woolums

Maryland Association of
Boards of Education

# We invite your comments on this publication

*Send us your feedback and receive a discount
on your next purchase.*

Just complete and fax or mail the survey located in the back of this book.

## QUESTIONS ABOUT THIS PUBLICATION?

For CUSTOMER SERVICE ASSISTANCE concerning replacement pages, shipments, billing, reprint permission, or other matters,

please call Customer Service Department at 800-833-9844
email *customer.support@lexisnexis.com*
or visit our interactive customer service website at *www.lexisnexis.com/printcdsc*

For EDITORIAL **content questions** concerning this publication,

please call 800-446-3410 ext. 7447
or email: *LLP.CLP@lexisnexis.com*

For **information on other LEXISNEXIS MATTHEW BENDER publications**,

please call us at 800-223-1940
or visit our online bookstore at *www.lexisnexis.com/bookstore*

ISBN: 1-4224-4155-5

This publication is designed to provide accurate and authoritative information in regard to the subject matter covered. It is sold with the understanding that the publisher and authors are not engaged in rendering legal advice or services. If legal advice is required, the assistance of a school board attorney or other competent professional should be sought.

Matthew Bender & Company, Inc.
Editorial Offices
P.O. Box 7587
Charlottesville, VA 22906-7587
800-446-3410
www.lexisnexis.com

Product Number 2760011

# PUBLISHED IN COOPERATION WITH

## Maryland Association of Boards of Education (MABE)

621 Ridgely Avenue, Suite 300
Annapolis, MD 21401-1087
Telephone: (410) 841-5414
Fax: (410) 841-6580
Website: www.mabe.org

### Executive Staff

Carl W. Smith
*Executive Director*

Steven P. James
*Deputy Executive Director*

Stephen C. Bounds
*Director of Legal and Policy Services*

John R. Woolums
*Director of Government Relations*

**Maryland Association of
Boards of Education**

# CONTENTS

# FOREWORD

## by Dr. Carl W. Smith

## Maryland Association of Boards of Education

The challenges facing school leaders today are far more complex and nuanced than was the case even a decade ago. Many factors have contributed to the complexity of those challenges. Being well educated is essential to success in this era of electronic communication. The skills and knowledge that students need to be successful go well beyond anything required of previous generations. The result has been increasing expectations for student performance at all levels of our society. Those expectations coupled with a framework of strict accountability—symbolized by No Child Left Behind—have added layers of legal and procedural requirements to the mix.

Educational issues and challenges aside, parents and students have increasingly diverse expectations not only for themselves but for schools and school personnel. Those demands add to the pressure on school leaders to respond effectively and within the framework of the law. As laws change and new laws are enacted both in Maryland and at the federal level, so do procedural and other requirements. The actions and decision of the State Board of Education which more often than not have the force of law add to the ongoing challenge school leaders face when they make decisions affecting students, parents, and staff.

To date, Maryland has not had a legal primer for school leaders that lays out in practical language the parameters within which they must act or face the potential for serious unintended consequences. This book provides that framework and belongs on the desk of every single school administrator and school board member in Maryland. It will be an invaluable tool for those who teach educational law to prospective school administrators.

We are very pleased to be offering this legal primer in partnership with LexisNexis as an invaluable reference for school leaders in Maryland. We are also gratified by the outstanding response from Maryland Educators and board members to this new resource first published in 2006. Finally, I wish to acknowledge the leadership of Steve Bounds and John Woolums, of the MABE staff, in bringing this project to fruition.

August 2007

# FOREWORD

## by Dr. Nancy S. Grasmick
## Maryland State Superintendent of Schools

Legal issues complicate the work of educators throughout our state. It has become increasingly difficult for education leaders to know where to turn when a legal issue arises, and these situations turn up with regularity. One of the key questions confronting educators is this: How do we keep legal issues from becoming full-blown legal problems?

There are no easy answers, of course. As I visit with education leaders throughout Maryland, they are concerned about maintaining order in the classroom and the school campus, while offering the best possible instruction so that real learning takes place. To do this, it helps to stay out of the courtroom and away from unwelcome and unwanted publicity.

The legal issues facing administrators, teachers, and policymakers are more complex than ever before. The federal No Child Left Behind Act added a new layer to a system that already confused most educators, many of whom have had minimal legal training. There is little doubt that many education statutes have helped change schools for the better, but the myriad of laws also have kept many of our best administrators up at night, wondering how to respond to a new situation or nagging problem.

Current, easy-to-understand legal information can help educators steer clear of danger. *The Maryland School Law Deskbook* put together by the Maryland Association of Boards of Education, is the first and only guide I know of that is designed to help educators at the school and district level as they consider legal matters and their consequences. The information contained in this book is intended to keep educators out of the courtroom and in the schoolhouse where they can best help students achieve great things.

August 2007

# ABOUT THE AUTHORS

**Stephen C. Bounds** is an attorney and is currently the Director of Legal and Policy Services for the Maryland Association of Boards of Education, and is the administrator of the Maryland Legal Services Association. Steve provides education law and policy information, training and assistance to Maryland school board members and school system staff throughout the state. Steve served on the Howard County Board of Education from 1994-2000, including as its chairman and vice-chairman. Steve is also an adjunct graduate instructor in school law with McDaniel College and Towson University. Steve received his B.A. from Furman University in 1977 and his J.D. from the University of Maryland in 1980. Steve is a member of the state and national Council of School Attorneys.

**John R. Woolums** is the Director of Governmental Relations with the Maryland Association of Boards of Education. He has been responsible for conducting the Association's state and federal lobbying activities on behalf of Maryland's twenty-four boards of education since 2001. John is a 1995 graduate of the University of Maryland School of Law and is a member of the Maryland Bar, Maryland State Bar Association, and national and Maryland Council of School Attorneys. John is a 1987 graduate of Miami University in Oxford, Ohio. After graduation from Miami University, John worked for five years as a legislative aide to U.S. Senator Barbara Mikulski. Upon graduating from law school, he worked with a Washington, D.C. law firm in 1996 and as committee counsel to the Maryland House of Delegates' Environmental Matters Committee in 1997. Prior to joining the Maryland Association of Boards of Education, John was the associate director of the Maryland Association of Counties from 1998 to 2001.

**Judith S. Bresler** is a partner at the law firm of Reese & Carney, LLP and an adjunct professor, teaching school law, at Johns Hopkins University and Goucher College. She received her undergraduate degree from the College of Education, University of Maryland, and her *juris doctor* degree from Washington College of Law, American University, in Washington, D.C. She is a frequent speaker on school law issues and chair of the Maryland Council of Local School Board Attorneys as well as a member of the National Council of School Board Attorneys.

**Rochelle S. Eisenberg** is a member of the Maryland law firm of Hodes, Pessin & Katz, P.A. A graduate of the University of Maryland, College of Education, and the Washington College of Law of The American University, where she was a member of *The Law Review*, she has practiced education and employment law in the public and private sectors since 1977, representing school systems and employers throughout the State of Maryland. She is a past President of the Maryland Council of School Attorneys, has taught at colleges and universities, and has provided over 250 seminars on school and employment law. She regularly handles cases involving all areas of education and employment law, including special education, student issues, collective bargaining, wage and hour laws, and employment discrimination.

**Edmund J. O'Meally** is a member of the law firm of Hodes, Pessin & Katz, P.A., and teaches school law at Johns Hopkins University, Goucher College, and McDaniel College. A 1984 graduate of the University of Maryland School of Law where he served as Executive Editor of the *Maryland Law Review*, Mr. O'Meally clerked for the judges of the United States Court of Appeals for the Fourth Circuit upon his graduation. Since 1986, Mr. O'Meally has represented school boards and superintendents in collective bargaining negotiations, employee discipline matters, discrimination litigation, First Amendment issues, special education hearings and litigation, construction and procurement issues, Public Information Act and Open Meetings Act compliance, sports injury litigation, student suspensions and expulsions, sexual harassment, and Title IX.

# ACKNOWLEDGMENTS

I would like to thank my lovely and strong wife, Linda, and my above average children, Matt, Rachel and Andrew, for all their support and encouragement during the many hours of research and writing that went into this labor of like. Perhaps the great American novel will be next.

**Stephen C. Bounds**


I would like to thank my wife, Jenni, and our boys, Calder and Sean, for their patience and encouragement during the early and late hours I spent on the home computer.

**John R. Woolums**


I thank the students, educators, and parents of Maryland for teaching me about educating students with disabilities and hope that this book will have a positive impact on all.

**Rochelle S. Eisenberg**

# LIST OF COMMON ACRONYMS AND ABBREVIATIONS

**ACBM:** Asbestos-Containing Building Materials

**ACLU:** American Civil Liberties Union

**ADA:** Americans with Disabilities Act

**ADD/ADHD:** Attention Deficit Disorder/ Attention Deficit Hyperactivity Disorder

**ADEA:** Age Discrimination in Employment Act

**A/E:** Architecture and Engineering

**AED:** Automated External Defibrillator

**AHERA:** Asbestos Hazard Emergency Response Act

**ALJ:** Administrative Law Judge

**ALT-MSA:** Alternate Maryland State Assessment

**AMO:** Annual Measurable Objective

**APC:** Advanced Professional Certificate

**ASME:** American Society of Mechanical Engineers

**AYP:** Adequate Yearly Progress

**BIP:** Behavior Intervention Plan

**BPW:** Board of Public Works

**CART:** Communication Access Real-Time Translation

**CDC:** Center for Disease Control

**CIP:** Capital Improvement Program

**CMP:** Comprehensive Maintenance Plan

**CNA:** Child Nutrition Act

**COLA:** Cost of Living Adjustment

**COMAR:** Code of Maryland Regulations

**CSP:** Charter School Program

**DGS:** Department of General Services

**DHMH:** Department of Mental Health and Hygiene

**DHR:** Department of Human Resources

**DLLR:** Department of Labor, Licensing and Regulation

**EAA:** Equal Access Act

**EEEP:** Extended Elementary Education Program

**EEOC:** Equal Opportunity Employment Commission

**ELL:** English Language Learners

**EPA:** Environmental Protection Agency

**ESEA:** Elementary and Secondary Education Act

**ESOL:** English for Speakers of Other Languages

**ESY:** Extended School Year

**FAPE:** Free Appropriate Public Education

**FBA:** Functional Behavioral Assessment

**FERPA:** Family Educational Rights and Privacy Act

**FLSA:** Fair Labor Standards Act

**FMLA:** Family and Medical Leave Act

**FMNV:** Foods of Minimal Nutritional Value

**FPCO:** Family Policy Compliance Office

**FTE:** Full Time Equivalent

**GAAFR:** Government Accounting, Auditing and Financial Reporting

**GAAP:** Generally Accepted Accounting Principles

**GASB:** Government Accounting Standards Board

**GCEI:** Geographic Cost of Education Index

**GFOA:** Government Finance Officers Association

**GFSA:** Gun-Free Schools Act

**GSA:** Gay-Straight Alliance

**GTB:** Guaranteed Tax Base

**HOUSSE:** High Objective Uniform State Standard of Evaluation

**HSA:** High School Assessment

**IAC:** Interagency Committee on School Construction

**IAES:** Interim Alternative Educational Setting

**IAQ:** Indoor Air Quality

**IBB:** Interest Based Bargaining

**IDEA:** Individuals with Disabilities Education Act

**IDEIA:** Individuals with Disabilities Education Improvement Act

**IEE:** Independent Educational Evaluation

**IEP:** Individualized Education Program

**IPM:** Integrated Pest Management

**IPT:** IDEA® Proficiency Test

**LEA:** Local Education Agency

**LEP:** Limited English Proficient

**LRE:** Least Restrictive Environment

**MAS:** Maryland Adolescent Survey

**MHRC:** Maryland Human Relations Commission

**MIEMSS:** Maryland Institute for Emergency Medical Services Systems

**MOE:** Maintenance of Effort

**MOSHA:** Maryland's Occupational Safety and Health Act

**MSA:** Maryland School Assessment

**MSBE:** Maryland State Board of Education

**MSDE:** Maryland State Department of Education

**MSPAP:** Maryland School Performance Assessment Program

**MSRM:** Maryland Student Records System Manual

**MSSA:** Maryland Science Supervisors Association

**NAEP:** National Assessment of Educational Progress

**NBC:** National Board Certification

**NCES:** National Center for Education Statistics

**NCLB:** No Child Left Behind Act

**NHTSA:** National Highway Traffic Safety Administration

**NIH:** National Institutes of Health

**NLRB:** National Labor Relations Board

**OAH:** Office of Administrative Hearings

**OCR:** United States Department of Education Office for Civil Rights

**OLA:** General Assembly's Office of Legislative Audits

**OSHA:** Occupational Safety and Health Administration

**PAYGO:** Pay-As-You-Go

**PGU:** Participating Governmental Unit

**PLOP:** Present Levels of Performance

**PPRA:** Protection of Pupil Rights Amendment

**PSCP:** Public School Construction Program

**QZABs:** Qualified Zone Academy Bonds

**RFRA:** Religious Freedom Restoration Act

**ROTC:** Reserve Officer Training Corps

**RTC:** Resident Teacher Certificate

**SAFE:** School Accountability Funding for Excellence

**SEA:** State Education Agency

**SES:** Supplemental Education Services

**SPC:** Standard Professional Certificate

**SPD:** Severely & Profoundly Disabled

**TANF:** Temporary Assistance for Needy Families

**UMIRS:** Uniform Management and Information Reporting Systems

**USC:** United States Code

**USCO:** Unsafe School Choice Option Non-Regulatory Guidance

**USDE:** United States Department of Education

**VSC:** Voluntary State Curriculum

**YRBSS:** Youth Risk Behavior Surveillance System Survey

**YTS:** Youth Tobacco Survey

# INTRODUCTION

Hardly a day goes by when the news fails to contain a story about decisions made by educators that lead to significant and seemingly unexpected adverse legal consequences. The authors of this book firmly believe that such incidents are often avoidable with the possession of a basic understanding of school law and a healthy dollop of common sense. While no book can help with the latter, except to encourage more thoughtful decision-making, a basic understanding of school law is within the reach of every Maryland educator. This book will be a success if those that study it become equipped to educate our children without stepping on legal landmines along the way, and instead, engender news stories that demonstrate outstanding educational leadership.

Prior to the publication of this book, there was no text that focused on Maryland school law, and the many ways that it varies from other states. Within these covers you will find simple explanations of complex school law concepts, and more importantly, practical advice for the application of those concepts to the everyday demands of educating our children. The most frequently posed questions from school based and central office administrators and those that aspire to those positions, as well as, board of education members, state and local government officials, and even school law attorneys are dealt with in an easy to follow question and answer format. The annual updates that follow will also provide insight into the latest school law issues and keep you abreast of the latest changes in state and federal law and regulations.

Without question, there are more gray areas in school law than areas of absolute certainty, but a clear understanding of some basic school law concepts can help those in the education community to address the myriad of issues within these pages with a renewed sense of confidence. No book can serve as a substitute for competent legal counsel, but it is our sincere hope that this text will result in less time and resources being spent in the courtroom and instead remaining in the classroom where the maximum benefit can be accomplished in this era of growing expectations for student achievement.

Stephen C. Bounds
John R. Woolums
Authors and Editors-in-Chief
August 2007

# 1. Local School Board Roles and Responsibilities

## 1:1. What is a board of education?

The hallmark of American public education is local control, and that local control expresses itself in local boards of education. Each board of education is made up of a group of local citizens whose selection is determined by state law. Nationally, there are nearly 15,000 local school districts ranging in size from districts with several dozen students to districts with several hundred thousand students.

In Maryland, there are 24 local school systems, one in each county and one in Baltimore City (Md. Code Ann., Ed. Art. § 3-102) and they range in size from the smallest, Kent County Public Schools, with less than 2500 students to the largest, Montgomery County Public Schools, with more than 140,000 students. In each such county school system there is a local county board of education (Md. Code Ann., Ed. Art. § 3-103). It should be noted that the legal definition of "county" and "county board", specifically include Baltimore City (Md. Code Ann., Ed. Art. § 1-101(c) and (d)).

Each county board of education is a corporate body in Maryland, and as such has perpetual existence and may sue or be sued in a court of law (Md. Code Ann., Ed. Art. § 3-104).

## 1:2. What is the board of education role in public school governance?

A local board of education is charged with administering the operation of the schools within the boundaries of their district. A local board of education has tripartite jurisdiction and is thus charged with carrying out all three of the primary functions in the American system of government, namely executive, legislative and judicial roles.

Each county board of education in Maryland is placed in control of educational matters within their county, and is directed to seek ways to promote the interests of the schools within their counties (Md. Code Ann., Ed. Art. § 4-101).

## 1:3. How is a board of education formed?

Title 3 of the Education Article of the Annotated Code of Maryland, in separate Subtitles and Sections, contains the provisions for the establishment of each local board of education, including how board members are selected, the size of each board, and various other matters ranging from board officers and student members to board meetings and board member compensation.

**1:4. What are the duties and responsibilities of a board of education?**

There are four broad categories of duties for a county board of education set forth in § 4-108 of the Education Article of the Annotated Code of Maryland, including:

1. To the best of its ability carry out the applicable provisions of this article and the bylaws, rules, regulations, and policies of the State Board;

2. Maintain throughout its county a reasonably uniform system of public schools that is designed to provide quality education and equal educational opportunity for all children;

3. Subject to this article and the applicable bylaws, rules, and regulations of the State Board, determine, with the advice of the county superintendent, the educational policies of the county school system; and

4. Adopt, codify, and make available to the public bylaws, rules, and regulations not inconsistent with State law, for the conduct and management of the county public schools.

Among the major responsibilities of a county board of education is to establish curriculum guides and courses of study for the schools in their county, including appropriate programs for students with disabilities (Md. Code Ann., Ed. Art. § 4-111). Another of the most significant responsibilities of a county board is the appointment of a county superintendent of schools (Md. Code Ann., Ed. Art. § 4-201). Each county board is also required to prepare and publish an annual report on the condition, current accomplishments, and needs for improvement of the schools as well as a statement of the business and financial transactions of the county board, which is to be published before the end of the calendar year (Md. Code Ann., Ed. Art. § 5-111).

**1:5. Are board of education members elected or appointed?**

While the vast majority of local boards of education in the United States are elected rather than appointed, in Maryland, up until the mid-1990's, there was an equal division between elected and appointed boards with 12 of each. In recent years, the trend has clearly been toward elected boards with 18 of 24 currently in the elected category (as of the 2008 elections), including the following county boards; Allegany, Calvert, Carroll, Cecil, Charles, Dorchester, Frederick, Garrett, Howard, Kent, Prince George's, Montgomery, Queen Anne's, St. Mary's, Somerset, Talbot, Washington, and Worcester (Md. Code Ann., Ed. Art. § 3-114). The remaining appointed county boards include, Anne Arundel, Baltimore City, Baltimore, Caroline, Harford, and Wicomico. In five of the six appointed county boards, the Maryland Governor makes the appointment of a county resident (Md. Code Ann., Ed. Art. § 3-108), and in Baltimore City, the Governor and the Mayor of Baltimore City jointly appoint from a list of qualified individuals submitted by the State Board (Md. Code Ann., Ed. Art. § 3-108.1). Effective July 1, 2007, members appointed in Anne Arundel will emerge from a formal nominating process and will be required to stand for a retention election during the next general election where they will need to secure a majority vote to continue in office (Md. Code Ann., Ed. Art. § 3-108). During the 2007 Maryland legislative session, multiple bills were introduced to modify the selection process for several of the remaining appointed boards. Among the new proposals aimed at appointed boards were attempts to broaden and mandate a specific nomination process, modify existing appointment authority, establish subsequent retention elections, and to create hybrid "blended" boards with both elected and appointed members.

## 1:6. Are board of education elections partisan or non-partisan?

In Maryland, county boards of education are elected on a non-partisan basis. Thus, any registered voter may vote for county board members in primary elections regardless of party affiliation or lack thereof, and candidates for county boards of education elections file their candidacy and appear on the ballot without party affiliation (Md. Code Ann., Elect. Art. § 8-802).

## 1:7. What are the qualifications of a board of education member?

Subtitle 2 through Subtitle 14 of Title 3 of the Maryland Annotated Code, Education Article, provide for the qualifications of elected county boards on a county-by-county basis. In all counties, an adult board of education member is required to be a resident of the county in which they seek to serve, as well as a registered voter of that county. Among the qualifications that are set forth for various counties, but not necessarily others, are being a qualified voter and/or county resident for a certain minimum time, being a resident of a specific district or the county at large, not exceeding term limits, and nomination by registered voters. If at any time, a county board member ceases to live within that county or within a specific district of the county from which they were selected, then they are not permitted to continue their service on the county board.

## 1:8. How many members serve on a board of education?

The general rule (Md. Code Ann., Ed. Art. § 3-105) is that school systems with less than 50,000 students will have five members on the county board, these include Allegany, Calvert, Caroline, Carroll, Cecil, Garrett, Kent, Queen Anne's, St. Mary's, and Somerset. Exceptions with less than 50,000 students include Dorchester with six; Charles, Frederick, Harford, Howard, Talbot, Washington,

Wicomico, and Worcester with seven. School systems with between 50,000 and 100,000 students will have seven members on the county board; this includes Anne Arundel, and Baltimore City is an exception with nine members. Finally, school systems with over 100,000 students will have nine members on the county board; this includes Prince George's. Montgomery with seven members and Baltimore County with eleven members are exceptions among the largest category of school systems.

In some counties, County Commissioners or County Council members serve as nonvoting, ex officio members of the county board (Md. Code Ann., Ed. Art., Title 3).

### 1:9. May current school system employees serve on a board of education?

Nearly always the answer is no. An individual that is subject to the authority of a county board may not be appointed in the six counties that appoint members (Md. Code Ann., Ed. Art. § 3-108(b)(2)). As far as elected county boards are concerned, someone subject to the authority of a county board is likewise ineligible (Md. Code Ann., Ed. Art. § 3-114(b)), except that school bus contractors are allowed to serve in Worcester County only (Md. Code Ann., Ed. Art. § 3-1401(c)(3)).

### 1:10. May retired school system employees serve on a board of education?

Yes, there is no prohibition against a former school system employee serving on a county board; in fact, it is not an uncommon occurrence. Such former employees may need to occasionally abstain from voting on a matter that is of direct benefit to them as retirees.

### 1:11. Are there student members on boards of education?

Yes, but the selection methodology and authority of such student members, who are charged with advising county boards on the interests of students, vary widely and are set forth in Annotated Code of Maryland, Education Article, Title 3. Anne Arundel County currently boasts the only student board member in the United States with full voting rights on all matters. They may be called student members or student representatives depending upon the specific county. Most serve in a non-voting capacity, although several are permitted to cast opinion or preference votes that are recorded in the minutes but do not count as official votes. There are also several student board members that have limited voting rights; among those limitations may be votes on budgets, boundary lines, collective bargaining, student and teacher discipline, personnel matters, appeals, and closed session participation.

A number of counties also place qualification restrictions on their student members, including grade level, grade point average, good attendance and behavior records, and in the case of Worcester County the three student representatives each are chosen from one of the three county high schools.

## 1:12. May a person who holds another public office serve on a board of education?

No, Article 35 of the Declaration of Rights of the Maryland Constitution provides, "That no person shall hold, at the same time, more than one office of profit, created by the Constitution or Laws of this State…" An office is to be considered public when it involves the exercise of government responsibility in an ongoing, rather than occasional, nature. An office of profit includes any office that results in the receipt of fees, a salary or other compensation, but the reimbursement of expenses alone does not trigger the prohibition.

## 1:13. What is the term of office for a board of education member?

In five of the six counties with appointed boards, terms are for a period of five years, except Baltimore City, which has a three-year term. All of the appointed boards are limited to a total of two terms. Conversely, in 17 of the 18 counties with elected boards, terms are for a period of four years, except Kent County, which has a six-year term. Notably, only two of the elected boards have any term limitation, Cecil (two-term limit) and Talbot (three-term limit) (Md. Code Ann., Ed. Art., Title 3).

## 1:14. Do board of education members have staggered terms of office?

The six counties with appointed boards all have the terms of their members staggered on an annual basis. Conversely, 17 of the 18 counties with elected boards have the terms of their members staggered on a two-year cycle to correspond with both presidential and state/non-presidential election cycles, except that Charles County elects all seven of their board members in the same (state/non-presidential) election year (Md. Code Ann., Ed. Art., Title 3).

## 1:15. What officers does a board of education have?

Each county board of education selects their own officers, and 18 county boards have a President and a Vice President. The remaining 6 county boards have a Chair or Chairman and a Vice Chair or Vice Chairman (Md. Code Ann., Ed. Art., Title 3). The county Superintendent of schools (Chief Executive Officer in

Baltimore City and Prince George's County) serves as the executive officer, secretary, and treasurer of each county board (Md. Code Ann., Ed. Art. § 4-102).

### 1:16. Are board members legally considered to be local or state officials?

In Maryland county board members are considered to be state officials. While local school districts are not considered to be state agencies in a majority of states, in Maryland, local school systems have been considered by both the Maryland Court of Appeals and Maryland Federal District Court, in a number of cases, including *Jones v. Frederick County Board of Education*, 689 F. Supp. 535 (D. Md. 1988), to be state agencies.

### 1:17. Do board of education members take an oath of office?

Yes, before taking on the duties of a board member, the following oath of office from the Maryland Constitution, Article I, Section 9 must be taken:

> I, name of person, do swear or affirm, that I will support the Constitution of the United States; and that I will be faithful and bear true allegiance to the State of Maryland, and support the Constitution and Laws thereof; and that I will, to the best of my skill and judgment, diligently and faithfully, without partiality or prejudice, execute the office of Board of Education member, according to the Constitution and Laws of this State.

### 1:18. Must a board of education adopt ethics provisions?

Yes, all county boards in Maryland have adopted ethics policies and regulations pursuant to the requirements of State Government Article §§ 15-811 to 15-815. Each county board is required to submit such ethics provisions and any amendments to the State Ethics Commission for review and approval (Md. Code Ann., St. Gov't Art. § 15-815). Two model regulations, a long version and a shorter, more concise, version are provided as samples for county boards pursuant to the Code of Maryland Regulations (COMAR), Title 19A, Subtitle 05.

### 1:19. Are board of education members subject to conflict of interest restrictions?

Yes, the ethics provisions adopted by a county board must contain conflict of interest regulations that are similar to the State Ethics Law, but which may be modified in order to establish relevance to the prevention of conflicts of interest in that local school system (Md. Code Ann., St. Gov't Art. § 15-812).

## 1:20. What are some examples of prohibited conflicts of interest?

Prohibited conflicts of interest identified by county boards include: participating in a matter in which they, a relative, or affiliated business, have a direct financial interest; engaging in employment that interferes with their duties or embarrasses the school system; representing on a paid basis a party bringing a claim against the school system; or soliciting or accepting a gift that exceeds a set dollar amount or could appear to impair the impartiality of the board member.

## 1:21. Are there any other ethics provisions applicable to board of education members?

Yes, the ethics provisions adopted by a county board must regulate the lobbying of its members by those who would seek to influence any official action of the board through the provision of food, entertainment or gifts (Md. Code Ann., St. Gov't Art. § 15-814).

## 1:22. Must board of education members disclose personal financial interests?

Yes, the ethics provisions adopted by a county board must require annual financial disclosure by board members of matters such as landholdings within the county; interests in, debts to, or gifts from entities that do business with the county school system; and whether someone in the immediate family of the board member is employed by the county school system (Md. Code Ann., St. Gov't Art. § 15-813).

## 1:23. May a spouse or other relative of a board of education member be employed by the school system?

Yes, provided that such employment is disclosed, that the board member does not participate in a matter that would provide a direct financial benefit to said spouse or relative, or that such employment is not prohibited in the respective county. For example, in Frederick County, an individual who is married to a teacher or administrator of the county school system is not eligible to serve on the county board (Md. Code Ann., Ed. Art. § 3-5B-02).

## 1:24. May a board of education member resign from office?

Yes, and when a county board member resigns from an appointed board, a replacement to serve out the remaining term of office is appointed by the same method as an initial appointment. In the case of a resignation from an elected board, the method for choosing a replacement differs county by county, from appointment by the governor, various county government officials or government bodies, or by the remaining county board members (Md. Code Ann., Ed. Art., Title 3).

### 1:25. May a board of education remove one of its members?

No, a board of education does not have the authority to remove one of its own members. The authority to remove a local board member rests with the State Board of Education in the case of elected boards, except that the Governor must concur in Charles and Prince George's County and the removal authority in Montgomery County rests with the county council. The authority to remove a member of an appointed board rests with the State Superintendent upon approval of the Governor, and for Baltimore City, with the approval of the Mayor as well (Md. Code Ann., Ed. Art., Title 3).

### 1:26. What are the grounds for removal of a board of education member?

There are four primary grounds for the removal of a member of an elected board; immorality, misconduct in office, incompetency, or willful neglect of duty. In addition, in Calvert, Cecil, Dorchester, Talbot, and Worcester County, a member may also be removed for failing, without good cause, to attend at least 75 percent of the scheduled meetings of the county board in any one calendar year, and/or missing three consecutive scheduled meetings. The same four primary grounds for removal also apply to appointed boards and a fifth is added, that of failure to attend without good cause, at least half of the scheduled meetings of the board in any one calendar year. Finally, whether elected or appointed, a member that ceases to meet the residency requirements or is otherwise removed is to be replaced in the same manner as set forth above in **1:24** (Md. Code Ann., Ed. Art., Title 3).

### 1:27. What is the process for removing a board of education member?

Regardless of whether a board member serves on an elected or appointed board, and regardless of where the authority for removal rests (see **1:24**) before being removed, a local board member must receive essentially the same due process. The entity with removal authority is required to send the member a copy of the charges against them and give the member an opportunity within 10 days to request a hearing before said entity. If the member requests a hearing, one must be held before the entity with removal authority with an opportunity to be heard publicly in the member's own defense, either in person or by counsel. A member so removed also has the right of an appeal to the Circuit Court of their county (Md. Code Ann., Ed. Art., Title 3).

**1:28. May a board of education member be censured or reprimanded?**

A county board of education is without power to discipline its members, but an Attorney General Opinion states that a county board is free to pass a resolution, without any formal legal effect as a sanction, that expresses the county board's disapproval of the action of a board member (Op. Att'y Gen. No. 65-347 (1980)).

**1:29. Can board of education members be paid for their services as board members?**

Yes, under Maryland law, local board members may receive compensation and/or expense reimbursement for their services. The compensation varies widely by county, and ranges from minimal compensation up to approximately $20,000.00 per year in Montgomery and Prince George's County, with most county boards being in the $3000.00 to $6000.00 range. The available amount for reimbursement of expenses varies from a low of less than $1000.00 per year to a high of $7000.00 per year, with most county boards being in the $2000.00 to $4000.00 range. A relatively recent trend has been for a few county boards to become eligible for health insurance and/or other fringe benefits provided to other county school system employees (Md. Code Ann., Ed. Art. § 4-107 and Title 3). In those counties with board member terms of four years or less (see **1:13**) Article III Section 35 of the Constitution of Maryland prohibits an increase or decrease in salary or compensation during the board member's term of office, but does not prohibit such an increase or decrease for any subsequent new term of office.

**1:30. What are the powers of a board of education?**

As has already been set forth in **1:4** above, a county board is responsible for the creation of educational policies regarding the conduct and management of a uniform system of public schools designed to provide a quality and equal educational opportunity for all children (Md. Code Ann., Ed. Art. § 4-108). Each county board is also placed in control of educational matters within their county, and is directed to seek ways to promote the interests of the schools within their counties (Md. Code Ann., Ed. Art. § 4-101).

**1:31. What are some examples of powers of a board of education?**

Among the specifically enumerated powers of a county board are: establishing curriculum guides and courses of study (Md. Code Ann., Ed. Art. § 4-111); taking a census of the school age children in the county (Md. Code Ann., Ed. Art. § 4-113); holding title to school system property (Md. Code Ann., Ed. Art. § 4-114); acquiring land for school sites and contracting for facility construction (Md. Code Ann., Ed. Art. § 4-115); employing architects (Md. Code Ann., Ed. Art. § 4-117);

accepting donations (Md. Code Ann., Ed. Art. § 4-118); bringing condemnation proceedings to acquire needed land (Md. Code Ann., Ed. Art. § 4-119); arranging for the transportation of students (Md. Code Ann., Ed. Art. § 4-120); designating "drug free school zones" (Md. Code Ann., Ed. Art. § 4-124); appointing a county school superintendent and setting their salary and related expenses (Md. Code Ann., Ed. Art. §§ 4-201, 4-202, and 4-203); preparing and submitting the annual school system budget (Md. Code Ann., Ed. Art. §§ 5-101 and 5-102); providing an annual financial audit (Md. Code Ann., Ed. Art. § 5-109); making all reports required by the State Board and State Superintendent (Md. Code Ann., Ed. Art. § 5-111); approving school system purchases in excess of $25,000.00 (Md. Code Ann., Ed. Art. § 5-112); developing and implementing a comprehensive master plan for student and school accountability (Md. Code Ann., Ed. Art. § 5-401); employing school system personnel (Md. Code Ann., Ed. Art. § 6-201); suspending or dismissing school system personnel (Md. Code Ann., Ed. Art. § 6-202); negotiating with employee organizations (Md. Code Ann., Ed. Art. §§ 6-408 and 6-510); selecting and purchasing textbooks (Md. Code Ann., Ed. Art. § 7-106); and authorizing public charter schools (Md. Code Ann., Ed. Art. § 7-103).

### 1:32. What are some examples of powers that a board of education does not have?

Unlike boards of education in many other states, Maryland boards have no taxing authority or ability to conduct bond issues, and are thus fiscally dependent entities. They also lack the power to reduce the number of school days and hours required (Md. Code Ann., Ed. Art. § 7-103) and implement corporal punishment (Md. Code Ann., Ed. Art. § 7-306). In addition, county boards are prohibited from carrying a negative fund balance without statutory corrective matters being triggered (Md. Code Ann., Ed. Art. § 5-114).

### 1:33. What is the executive role of a board of education?

As with any executive role in government, the county board is charged with leading the county school system. This leadership does not extend to the day-to-day operations as that is the responsibility of the local superintendent, but the board oversees the superintendent and thus administers the work of the school system. The executive role in government typically also includes appointment authority, and the county board has the power to appoint the superintendent and professional staff. Another executive function of a county board is the oversight and approval of the expenditure of school system funds. Finally, the county board is responsible for implementing, supporting and enforcing the applicable federal, state, and local laws and the policies of the county board, which govern the operation of the school system.

## 1:34. What is the legislative role of a board of education?

While county boards do not pass laws, they do adopt policies that govern and guide the operation of the county school system. The policy role of the board is potentially their most important role, and local board policy provides the principles and rules under which the school system operates. Local board policy insures continuity, clarifies expectations, directs the superintendent, informs the public, and secures the board's position. County board policy formation is more fully explored in **1:72** hereafter.

## 1:35. What is the quasi-judicial role of a board of education?

County boards are empowered to hear and decide appeals under three separate sections of Maryland law. The suspension and dismissal of professional personnel falls under Md. Code Ann., Ed. Art. § 6-202, and an individual facing such action is given 10 days to request a full evidentiary hearing before the county board of education. Student suspensions and expulsions likewise may be appealed to the county board under Md. Code Ann., Ed. Art. § 7-305, within 10 days of imposition, and the penalty is not stayed pending the results of the full evidentiary hearing.

Finally, nearly any decision of the local superintendent may be appealed to the county board within 30 days pursuant to Md. Code Ann., Ed. Art. § 4-205. This last type of appeal usually does not require an evidentiary hearing and may instead be decided on the written record alone, although appeals involving a property or liberty interest may require an evidentiary hearing. In any of these types of appeals, the county board has the option of assigning the case to a hearing officer of the board's choosing to hear the case and submit a transcript of proceedings and exhibits, findings of fact, conclusions of law, and recommended action to the county board which will render a decision after oral argument from the parties.

In all of these cases, the action of the county board may be appealed to the State Board within 30 days of the issuance of the county board's written decision. The county board is not required to accept appeals that are filed late. An evidentiary hearing before the county board is not equivalent to a trial in court and the formal rules of evidence do not apply. Finally, under Maryland law, the board's holding of a full evidentiary hearing cures any failures of due process that may have occurred before a case reaches the county board (*Tanya Johnson v. Baltimore City Board of School Commissioners*, MSBE Op. No. 03-19 (2003)).

**1:36. What is the method by which a board of education must take official actions?**

A county board may only take action in public session by an affirmative vote of a majority, meaning more than half of the board members considered to be present, and who usually must be physically present at the meeting in order to have the right to vote (Md. Code Ann., Ed. Art., Title 3). A motion fails if the vote results in a tie. A "proxy" authorizing someone else to vote in the place of an absent board member is not allowed due to its fundamental incompatibility with the proper functioning of a deliberative body. The agenda for a meeting only becomes official when it is adopted by the board at the beginning of the meeting, and any board member may move to amend the agenda. While it is common practice for the superintendent and board president/chair to propose a meeting agenda, it has no finality until it is adopted by the board. Generally, most county boards operate according to Robert's Rules of Order, or some variation on Robert's Rules, but county boards are free to establish the procedures under which they operate and conduct their business, provided that the rules generally adopted by deliberative bodies are observed (COMAR 13A.02.01.01). See **Appendix 1-1** for a chart of common motions showing how they are made, whether debatable, amendable, and the vote required to pass the motion.

**1:37. Is an unauthorized action by a board of education valid?**

No, if a county board takes action that is not within their authority granted by law, such action is said to be "ultra vires", a Latin term meaning "beyond powers." Such an unauthorized action would have no legal force or effect.

**1:38. Do individual board of education members have any authority to take official action on the board's behalf?**

No, a county board of education is only empowered to act as a corporate body, and no individual board member has any authority to take official action on the board's behalf. It is normal for boards to appoint one member as a representative of the county board to some other organization or entity, but the member so appointed derives no individual independent authority as a result of their representative status. It is common for a county board to designate someone, usually an officer, to act as spokesperson for the board, but the positions espoused are to be those of the majority.

**1:39. May boards of education have committees?**

Yes, larger county boards in particular often establish committees and find that it helps to manage the extensive workload that can face a board in a large school system. Some examples of subject areas that have been referred to committees among Maryland county boards include audit, budget, capital planning, communication, legislative, policy, personnel, strategic planning, and technology.

Additionally, each county board is required to establish at least one citizen advisory committee to advise the county board and to assist with the programs and activities of the school system (Md. Code Ann., Ed. Art. § 4-112).

### 1:40. Do board of education committees have any authority to take official action on the board's behalf?

No, while committees can help to handle the background work and planning, it is still necessary for the entire board to take any action required by a majority vote in open session.

### 1:41. May boards of education appoint a superintendent of schools?

Yes, one of the most important jobs of a county board is the selection of a local superintendent. The selection of a superintendent is conditioned on approval of the State Superintendent, who is charged with ensuring that the proposed local superintendent meets the state qualifications to hold such office (Md. Code Ann., Ed. Art. § 4-201).

### 1:42. May boards of education remove or otherwise discipline a superintendent?

No, there is no provision of authority for a county board to discipline a local superintendent. Furthermore, only the State Superintendent can remove a local superintendent during the term of their four-year contract with a county school system. A local superintendent may be removed for the following grounds: (i) immorality; (ii) misconduct in office; (iii) insubordination; (iv) incompetency; or (v) willful neglect of duty, and must be provided with basic due process (Md. Code Ann., Ed. Art. § 4-201(e)).

### 1:43. May boards of education extend a superintendent's contract?

Yes, but only during the time established by law, which is the period from February 1st until June 30th, during the final year of the superintendent's existing contract. Initially, the superintendent is legally required to advise the county board if they wish to be a candidate for reappointment by February 1st, and thereafter the board has until March 1st to reappoint the incumbent superintendent. If a superintendent is not in place by July 1st of any year, or if a vacancy otherwise occurs, the county board must appoint an interim superintendent to serve until the window for selecting a superintendent arrives again the following February 1st (Md. Code Ann., Ed. Art. § 4-201(b) and (d)).

### 1:44. May boards of education retain an attorney?

Yes, a county board has the authority to retain an attorney in order to represent the board in a wide range of matters, including personnel, discipline, construction, contracts, policy, special education, litigation and board governance matters. Legal services in some counties may be provided through the office of county attorney or city solicitor (Md. Code Ann., Ed. Art. § 4-104).

### 1:45. Can actions of a board of education be challenged?

Yes, most actions of a county board may be appealed to the State Board within thirty days after a formal decision of the county board is made (Md. Code Ann., Ed. Art. §§ 4-205(c), 6-202, and 7-305).

### 1:46. What are the methods to challenge the actions of a board of education?

In addition to appeals to the State Board, described in the preceding answer, an aggrieved party may proceed to file suit challenging the action of a county board under some limited circumstances. In actions where the appropriate avenue of appeal is to the State Board, the doctrine requiring the exhaustion of administrative remedies demands that such administrative appeals be fully completed before an aggrieved party may proceed to court (*Board of Education v. Hubbard*, 305 Md. 774 (1986)).

### 1:47. May appellate bodies substitute their judgment for that of the board of education?

No, the standard of review for appeals from actions of a county board are limited to specific areas that do not simply allow the appellate body to substitute their judgment in the event that they disagree with a county board decision (COMAR 13A.01.05.05A).

### 1:48. May newly raised facts and issues be considered in an appeal from a board of education action?

Generally no, facts and issues must first be considered by the county board in order for them to be considered upon appeal. Typically, if a new fact or issue is first raised on appeal it will not be considered by the appellate body. Occasionally, when an appellant seeks to submit additional evidence on appeal, the State Board considers whether the proffered evidence is material and that there were good reasons for the failure to offer the evidence before the county board, and based on those matters, the State Board may: remand to the county board for their reconsideration in light of the additional evidence; or decide to receive the evidence (COMAR 13A.01.05.04).

### 1:49. What is the standard of review in appeals of actions of the board of education?

The legal standard for reversing the county board in an appeal is that the action of the county board is considered prima facie correct, and can only be overturned if arbitrary, unreasonable, or illegal. In order for an action to be considered arbitrary or unreasonable, it would need to be contrary to sound educational policy, or that a reasoning mind could not have reasonably reached the conclusion of the county board. An illegal action permitting an appellate reversal would be one or more of the following: unconstitutional; exceeding the statutory authority or jurisdiction of the county board; misconstruing the law; results from an unlawful procedure; is an abuse of discretionary powers; or is affected by any other error of law (COMAR 13A.01.05.05).

### 1:50. What constitutes a meeting of a board of education?

A meeting of a public body, which includes a county board of education, occurs when a quorum of the public body is convened for the consideration or transaction of public business (Md. Code Ann., St. Gov't Art. § 10-502(g)).

### 1:51. What types of meetings are held by a board of education?

Each county board is required to hold an annual meeting at which the board officers are to be selected; these meetings are typically held in July for appointed boards, and in December or January for elected boards. In addition to the statutorily required monthly or twice monthly meetings (Md. Code Ann., Ed. Art., Title 3 and § 4-107), county boards also sometimes meet to conduct work sessions, public hearings, public forums, joint meetings with county officials, quasi-judicial hearings, and retreats.

### 1:52. Must board of education meetings be held within the school district?

There is no specific statutory requirement that all county board meetings be held within the school district, but as a practical matter, only occasional retreats are held at out-of-county locations by most county boards. On the other hand, there is a requirement that nearly all county board meetings be conducted in sessions that are open to the public (Md. Code Ann., Ed. Art., Title 3), and thus, holding public meetings outside of the county could be challenged as not providing reasonable public access, as the general public is entitled to attend (Md. Code Ann., St. Gov't Art. § 10-507).

### 1:53. May boards of education hold telephone or electronic meetings?

Once again, the requirement that nearly all county board meetings be conducted in sessions that are open to the public (Md. Code Ann., Ed. Art., Title 3), would thus render telephone or electronic meetings as likely to be challenged for not providing reasonable public access, as the general public is entitled to attend (Md. Code Ann., St. Gov't Art. § 10-507).

County boards are free to adopt local procedures allowing individual board members to participate in public meetings of the county board either by telephone or electronically, under certain specific circumstances, although there is no right to participate by such methods absent county board approval. Generally, such accommodations must be conducted in a fashion where all participating board members can speak, hear, and interact contemporaneously as if they were all physically present in order to protect the deliberative process.

### 1:54. What type of notice is required to hold a board of education meeting?

Before a county board meets in open or closed session, reasonable advance notice of the meeting must be given to the public. In order to be reasonable, such notice must be in writing and contain the date, time and place of the session, and if appropriate, include a statement that all or part of the meeting may be conducted in closed session. The appropriate methods for giving such notice include: notification of the news media who regularly report on county board meetings; by posting the notice at a previously identified convenient public location; or by any other reasonable method. Finally, the county board must keep a copy of the notice for each meeting for at least one year after the session (Md. Code Ann., St. Gov't Art. § 10-506). In fact, the failure to give proper notice of an open session could result in the action taken at the meeting being declared to be void (*Community & Labor United for Baltimore Charter Committee v. Baltimore City Board of Elections*, 377 Md. 183 (2003)).

### 1:55. Is a board of education required to hold a certain number of meetings?

In addition to their annual meeting, county boards may hold any other meetings that their duties and business require, but most boards are required to meet either once or twice per month (Md. Code Ann., Ed. Art., Title 3 and § 4-107).

## 1:56. What constitutes a quorum for a board of education meeting?

A quorum is defined as the majority of the members of the public body (Md. Code Ann., St. Gov't Art. § 10-502(k)). For county boards of five members, three constitute a quorum; if six or seven members, four constitute a quorum; if eight or nine members, five constitute a quorum; if ten or eleven members, six constitute a quorum; and if twelve members, seven constitute a quorum (COMAR 13A.02.01.01). It should be noted that for some county boards, the number required for a quorum may vary depending on whether the issue is one for which the student member is allowed to cast an official vote, and thus be counted among the members for determination of a quorum. If, during the course of a meeting, a quorum ceases to be present, no further action on substantive matters is permitted.

## 1:57. Must boards of education keep public minutes of its meetings?

Yes, the local superintendent or their designee must keep accurate minutes of each meeting of the county board. Said minutes are to be duly approved at the first subsequent session of the county board, and thereafter maintained as a public record (COMAR 13A.02.01.02). The minutes of a county board must include: each item that the board considered; the action that was taken on each item; and each vote that was recorded (Md. Code Ann., St. Gov't Art. § 10-509(c)(1)). The minutes of an open meeting must also include the time, place and purpose of any closed meeting along with the information required to be included in the written statement of the closed meeting described in **1:59**.

## 1:58. Are board of education meetings open to the public?

Yes, when a county board meets in open session, the public is entitled to attend (Md. Code Ann., St. Gov't Art. 10-507 and Md. Code Ann., Ed. Art., Title 3). Since a meeting of a county board of education only occurs when a quorum of the public body is convened for the consideration or transaction of public business (Md. Code Ann., St. Gov't Art. § 10-502(g)), a quorum of the county board is not prohibited from coming together by a chance encounter, social gathering, or other occasion that is not intended to circumvent the public's entitlement to attend county board meetings (Md. Code Ann., St. Gov't Art. § 10-503(a)(2)).

## 1:59. When may a board of education hold a meeting that is not open to the public?

County boards may meet in closed session in order to consider certain specific matters pursuant to the Open Meetings Act, Title 10, Subtitle 5, of the State Government Article, Annotated Code of Maryland. The Open Meetings Act does not apply to county boards when they are carrying out administrative or quasi-judicial functions (Md. Code Ann., St. Gov't Art. § 10-503(a)(1)). County boards may also carry out administrative functions (formerly executive functions) in non-public sessions under a 2006 change in the Act.

In order to meet in closed session, a county board must take a recorded vote in open session to close a meeting under one of fourteen exceptions under the Open Meetings Act, including: specific personnel matter; protection of personal privacy on a matter unrelated to public business; acquisition of real property; proposed business relocation or expansion; investment of public funds; marketing of public securities; obtaining legal advice from counsel; consulting about pending or potential litigation; collective bargaining; public security; scholastic, licensing, or qualifying examinations; criminal investigations; requirement to close a meeting imposed by other law; or preliminary discussion of procurement matters. The county board must also prepare a written statement of the reason for closing the meeting, including the citation of authority and a list of topics to be discussed, persons present, and each action taken during the meeting, and such statement becomes a matter of public record that must be maintained for at least one year after the date of the session (Md. Code Ann., St. Gov't Art. § 10-508).

### 1:60. Are board committee meetings open to the public?

Yes, committees established by a county board are open to the public; even when they do not include a quorum of the board, they are considered to be public bodies that are subject to the Open Meetings Act (Md. Code Ann., St. Gov't Art. § 10-502). The Open Meetings Act does not apply to committees established by the local superintendent alone, and does not apply to meetings of school system staff.

### 1:61. Does the public have a right to speak at a board of education meeting?

No, but most if not all county boards provide some type of public comment period during their regular business meeting. The method and rules for conducting public comment sessions are set by the county board and may be included in board policy or operating procedures. Typically, the time for comments and number of speakers may be limited, and matters such as complaints about staff and students are not usually allowed to name specific staff or students for privacy reasons.

### 1:62. Does the public have the right to audiotape or videotape a board meeting?

No, the general public probably does not have a right to audiotape or videotape a board meeting, although the public is entitled to attend. While the news media may have the right to film a board meeting, they do not have the right to disrupt a board meeting, and clearly could be excluded if a disruption was caused. A number of county boards already televise their meetings on local cable channels for the benefit of the interested public.

### 1:63. Is the chair/president of the board entitled to make motions and vote?

Yes, although some county boards have local protocols that have the chair/president speak last on an issue, there is no parliamentary requirement that the board chair/president refrain from making motions or voting.

### 1:64. May boards rescind an action previously taken at a board meeting?

Yes, although if a board desires to reconsider an action at the same meeting in which the action was taken, the motion to reconsider can only be made by a board member who voted in the majority in the first place. The rescinding of an action taken at a previous board meeting requires a simple majority vote provided that prior notice of the proposed rescission is given, without prior notice, a two-thirds majority is required for such rescission.

### 1:65. May boards take actions that extend beyond their term of office?

In some cases, yes, and in others, no, the county board may or may not take actions that extend beyond their term of office. Since most of the terms of county board members are staggered, some members will always be in a position to leave office before the completion of a four-year term of a local superintendent that they voted to hire or retain, or during the term of a school bus contract that they voted to approve. On the other hand, it would be potentially inappropriate and unenforceable for a county board to lock their school system into a long-term contract for services or products that a subsequent board might desire to change.

### 1:66. Are board of education records subject to public disclosure and inspection?

Yes, county boards are covered under the Maryland Public Information Act (Md. Code Ann., St. Gov't Art. § 10-611 to § 10-628). This law provides for public access and public inspection of existing originals or copies of government records, which include: cards; computerized records; correspondence; drawings; films or microfilms; forms; maps; photographs or photostats; recordings; or tapes (Md. Code Ann., St. Gov't Art. § 10-611(g)). Under the law, there is a presumption that favors broad disclosure of such records (Md. Code Ann., St. Gov't Art. § 10-613). The custodian of the county board records must grant or deny such a records request within thirty days of receipt, and denials must be written (Md. Code Ann., St. Gov't Art. § 10-614).

**1:67. Are there any restrictions on who may access board of education records?**

No, any person or government agency may access county board records at any reasonable time (Md. Code Ann., St. Gov't Art. § 10-613). It is important to note that reasonable fees for the time and expense of searching and preparing such records and copying the records may be charged (Md. Code Ann., St. Gov't Art. § 10-621).

**1:68. What types of records are not subject to public access?**

Restriction of public access to records that are otherwise protected from being released by state law or regulation, federal statute or regulation, or court order or rule is required. There is also an affirmative duty to deny access to county board records that are legally confidential such as pursuant to lawyer-client privilege (Md. Code Ann., St. Gov't Art. § 10-615). The law additionally provides for required denial for personnel files, letters of reference, retirement records, or individual student records (Md. Code Ann., St. Gov't Art. § 10-616). Other required denials are for medical and psychological records, home addresses and telephone numbers of employees, individual financial records, records of information system security, and individual occupational and professional records (Md. Code Ann., St. Gov't Art. § 10-617). Finally, a county board may deny access to records where disclosure would be contrary to the public interest, such as, investigation records, security records, testing records, and real estate appraisals while acquisition is pending (Md. Code Ann., St. Gov't Art. § 10-618).

**1:69. What penalties exist for wrongfully denying access to public board records?**

A county may be ordered to pay all expenses incurred to secure the records including: attorney fees; court costs; and actual damages for the wrongful failure to disclose a properly requested public record (Md. Code Ann., St. Gov't Art. § 10-623). In addition to such civil penalties, the willful and knowing violation of the Maryland Public Information Act may constitute a misdemeanor and result in criminal fines up to $1,000.00 for each violation (Md. Code Ann., St. Gov't Art. § 10-627).

**1:70. Are there any restrictions on the destruction of board of education records?**

Yes, pursuant to Md. Code Ann., St. Gov't Art. §§ 9-1007 and 10-632, and according to the regulations set forth in COMAR, Title 14, Subtitle 18, State Archives, county boards are required to adopt records retention and disposal schedules with regard to both written and electronic records, and must comply with said regulations with respect to the destruction of county board records. The Federal Rules of Civil Procedure, which govern procedural process of cases brought in the federal court system, on December 1, 2006, underwent major changes in regard to the handling of electronic data discovery issues and the destruction of such data. School districts will face significant new challenges in determining what electronic data will need to be preserved in light of potential litigation threats as these new and somewhat vague rules are interpreted and enforced over the coming years (FRCP 16, 26, 33, 34, and 37).

### 1:71. Do board of education members have access to employee and student records?

County board members only have access to individual employee or student records when required for carrying out their quasi-judicial responsibilities or for some other legally appropriate board purpose.

### 1:72. What is a policy?

The simplest and possibly most accurate description of county board policy is that it answers the "what" and "why" questions, with regard to the board's setting of a course of action for the county school system. Board policies establish a framework or guideline for the operation of the school system, and inform the public of the board's position, clarify expectations, and insure continuity. The county board, within a well-defined process, creates policy and only the county board has the authority to modify their policy. Policy helps the board and school system to operate efficiently by providing guidance that applies to a multitude of situations.

### 1:73. What is a regulation or procedure?

Having answered the "what" and "why" questions through the adoption of board policy, the "how" question is determined by regulations or procedures established by the local superintendent and school system staff. Whether a county school system refers to them as regulations or procedures, they describe in detail the mechanics for how policies will be implemented. They also contain important details, assign specific responsibility for tasks, and provide step-by-step instructions. The local superintendent can change regulations and procedures as needed, and while the county board does not normally approve them; the board to ensure that the intent of the policy is being carried out reviews them.

### 1:74. What are the main problem areas when considering board policy?

The most frequently identified problems in the policy arena are: blurring the line between policy and regulation/procedure; misalignment between policy, regulation/procedure, and actual school system practice; failure to keep policies and regulations/procedures up to date; failure to communicate changes to staff; and inadequate training of staff regarding key policies.

### 1:75. Must boards of education maintain policy manuals?

While all county boards once relied solely on their rather massive policy manuals, sometimes several volumes, the majority of county boards now maintain their policies online. Some school systems are phasing out the printed manuals, which are difficult to keep up to date, although they continue to exist in many school systems.

### 1:76. Who serves as the secretary of the board of education?

The local superintendent serves as the secretary, treasurer, and executive officer of each county school system. Unless the extension of their contract, salary, or the administration of the office of the local superintendent is under consideration by the county board, the local superintendent or their designee must attend all meetings of the county board and its committees (Md. Code Ann., Ed. Art. § 4-102).

### 1:77. How is the local superintendent of schools selected?

The county board, pursuant to the time frame described in **1:43**, above, appoints a local superintendent. The appointment of a local superintendent is not valid unless approved in writing by the State Superintendent (Md. Code Ann., Ed. Art. § 4-201(c)(2)); and the State Superintendent must give written reasons for disapproval to the county board, in the event that an appointment is disapproved (Md. Code Ann., Ed. Art. § 4-201(c)(3)).

### 1:78. What are the qualifications of a local school superintendent?

An individual may only be appointed as a local superintendent if they: are eligible to be issued a certificate for the office; are a graduate from an accredited college or university; and have completed two years of graduate work including public school administration, supervision, and methods of teaching (Md. Code Ann., Ed. Art. § 4-201(c)).

### 1:79. What are the roles and duties of a local school superintendent?

A local superintendent is charged with carrying out the following: laws relating to the schools; applicable enacted and published by-laws of the State Board; policies of the State Board; rules and regulations of the county board; and policies of the county board (Md. Code Ann., Ed. Art. § 4-204). A local superintendent has many duties under Maryland law, and among the main duties are included: interpreting school laws and State Board requirements; deciding all controversies and disputes involving the county school system; approval of contracts; assignment of personnel; providing for the professional development of teachers; visiting schools and advising principals; evaluating the program of instruction in the county school system; recommend curriculum and courses of study; selecting textbooks, materials of instruction, school supplies, and school furniture and equipment; preparing and presenting the annual school budget and securing funds from local authorities; and making recommendations regarding school system buildings and land (Md. Code Ann., Ed. Art. § 4-205).

### 1:80. What is the responsibility of the superintendent regarding the submission of school system reports?

In the local superintendent's capacity as executive officer of the county board, the superintendent is required by Md. Code Ann., Ed. Art. § 4-205(e) to: conduct all correspondence; receive all reports from administrators and teachers; and see that all reports are made and submitted properly. A local superintendent must also prepare and submit to the county board for adoption the following: all reports required from the county board by the State Board or State Superintendent and the annual report to the people of the county required by Md. Code Ann., Ed. Art. § 5-111.

### 1:81. How many years are the terms of local school superintendents?

The term of office of a local superintendent is four years, commencing July 1st, and continuing until a successor is appointed and qualifies (Md. Code Ann., Ed. Art. § 4-201(b)).

### 1:82. How is a local school superintendent removed from office?

Only the State Superintendent can remove a local superintendent during the term of their four-year contract with a county school system. A local superintendent may be removed for the following grounds: (i) immorality; (ii) misconduct in office; (iii) insubordination; (iv) incompetency; or (v) willful neglect of duty, and must be provided with basic due process (Md. Code Ann., Ed. Art. § 4-201(e)).

**1:83. What is the role of local government in public school governance?**

The role of local government in public school governance is primarily limited to the provision of funds, both operating funds for the day-to-day operation of the school system, and capital funds for the construction and systemic improvement of school system facilities. The precise details of said funding relationship will be more fully spelled out in Chapter 4. In some counties, County Commissioners or County Council members serve as nonvoting, ex officio members of the county board (Md. Code Ann., Ed. Art., Title 3). The latest skirmishes over the control of local school systems have centered around the mostly urban phenomenon of mayoral takeovers. A number of major U.S. city school systems are now under the control of mayors, including most notably New York and Chicago, legal wrangling over such takeovers is currently ongoing in Los Angeles and Washington, D.C., and the trend is even spreading to smaller urban venues such as Albuquerque. Such proposals to turn floundering urban districts over to non-educators raise questions about whether motivations are more focused on student achievement or the control of what may be as large as billion dollar school budgets.

**1:84. How are conflicts over authority and duties in public education resolved?**

While the source of the conflict may effect the response, generally, local superintendents have the primary responsibility for resolving such disputes, although those decisions may be appealed to the county board, State Board, and through the state court system in turn (Md. Code Ann., Ed. Art. § 4-205(c)(2) and (3)).

# Appendix 1-1. Parliamentary Procedure Chart

| Action desired: | What is stated: | Interrupt speaker? | Second required? | Debatable? | Amendable? | Vote required? |
|---|---|---|---|---|---|---|
| Adjourn meeting | I move to adjourn | No | Yes | No | No | Majority |
| Recess meeting | I move to recess | No | Yes | No | Yes | Majority |
| Make complaint re: temperature, noise, etc | I raise a point of privilege | Yes | No | No | No | Chair decides the complaint |
| Require the agenda to be followed | I move for the orders of the day | Yes | No | No | No | None |
| Suspend action | I move to table | No | Yes | No | No | Majority |
| End the debate on a motion | I move the previous question | No | Yes | No | No | Two-thirds majority |
| Limit or extend debate | I move that debate be limited/extended | No | Yes | No | Yes | Two-thirds majority |
| Postpone consideration | I move to postpone this matter to | No | Yes | Yes | Yes | Majority |
| Refer to a committee to study | I move we refer this matter to a committee | No | Yes | Yes | Yes | Majority |
| Amend a pending motion | I move to amend the motion by | No | Yes | Yes | Yes | Majority |
| Postpone a motion indefinitely | I move the motion be postponed indefinitely | No | Yes | Yes | No | Majority |
| Make a main motion | I move that | No | Yes | Yes | Yes | Majority |

| Action desired: | What is stated: | Interrupt speaker? | Second required? | Debatable? | Amendable? | Vote required? |
|---|---|---|---|---|---|---|
| Procedural objection | Point of order | Yes | No | No | No | None |
| Appeal decision of the chair | I appeal from the decision of the chair | Yes | Yes | Yes | No | Majority |
| Take up a matter out of scheduled order | I move we suspend rules and consider | No | Yes | No | No | Two-thirds majority |
| Objection to an improper matter | I object to consideration of | Yes | No | No | No | Two-thirds majority |
| Divide the motion into parts | I move to divide the question | No | Yes | No | Yes | Majority |
| Parliamentary issue | Parliamentary inquiry | Yes | No | No | No | None |
| Request information | Point of information | Yes | No | No | No | None |
| Verify an actual vote count | I call for a division of the house | Yes | No | No | No | None |
| Take up motion previously tabled | I move we take from the table | No | Yes | No | No | Majority |
| Cancel a prior action taken | I move to rescind | No | Yes | Yes | Yes | Majority/ Two-thirds majority without notice |
| Reconsider motion already considered | I move to reconsider the vote on | No | Yes | No/ Yes, if prior motion was debatable | No | Majority |

# 2. State Role in Public Education

## 2:1. Where does Maryland get the authority to provide public education?

Maryland's Constitution, adopted in 1867, mandates that the General Assembly "shall by Law establish throughout the State a thorough and efficient System of Free Public Schools; and shall provide by taxation, or otherwise, for their maintenance" (Md. Const., Art. VIII, § 1). Section 3 further provides that "The School Fund of the State shall be kept inviolate, and appropriated only to the purposes of Education."

Under these Constitutional directives, the General Assembly has enacted statutes throughout the years that have established a State school finance system, and created and delegated authority to the State Board of Education, the office of the State Superintendent, the Maryland State Department of Education (MSDE), and each of the 24 local boards of education and offices of local superintendents.

More recently, the federal government has asserted itself into the historically local and state prerogative of public education through federal legislation regarding special education, programs targeting low-income students, and the creation of the U.S. Department of Education. State education agencies are typically authorized to receive federal funds and monitor and enforce local compliance with federal education requirements.

## 2:2. What does it mean to provide a "thorough and efficient System of Free Public Schools"?

The courts and legislature have periodically endeavored to define the scope of this constitutional provision, generally focusing on one of the two major concepts in education funding, "equity" and "adequacy."

In 1983, the Court of Appeals rejected an "equity" challenge to the state's education finance system, in *Hornbeck v. Somerset County Board of Education*, 295 Md. 597 (1983), holding that the State Constitution did not mandate equality in per-pupil spending among the state's school districts. However, the court also held that the education clause of the Maryland Constitution embodies a right to "an adequate education measured by contemporary educational standards" (see **14:6**).

In 1994, the American Civil Liberties Union (ACLU), on behalf of Baltimore City school children, sued the State alleging that the children of Baltimore are not receiving an "adequate" education as required under the State constitution. In September, 1995, Baltimore City also filed suit against the State Superintendent of Schools and other State officials claiming that the State had failed to fulfill its duty to provide a "thorough and efficient" education for children as provided in the

State Constitution. The *Bradford* case, which remains open to this day, prompted 1997 legislation to abolish and restructure the Baltimore City board of education and launch several years of significant increases in annual State funding for the City's school system. *Bradford* laid the foundation for the "Thornton" Commission's statewide adequacy analysis, subsequently enacted funding increases under the Bridge to Excellence Act, and has firmly established the scope of the constitutional mandate to include quantifiable per pupil funding amounts.

### 2:3. What is the governance framework of Maryland's public school system?

Public education enjoys a prominent place in the overall structure of Maryland State government, in large part due to the State constitutional mandate to establish the public school system, and in light of the additional State constitutional protection of education funding and the payment of debt service as the two top budget priorities (65 Op. Att'y Gen. 45 (1980)).

In addition to these constitutional priorities, Maryland's public education system is organized under a comprehensive school reform enacted in the early Twentieth Century; a reorganization based on the recommendations included in *Public Education in Maryland: A Report to the Maryland Educational Survey Commission* by Abraham Flexner and Frank P. Bachman, known as the *Flexner Report*. In 1916, the Maryland General Assembly enacted the statute recommended by the *Flexner Report*, including the creation of the appointed local boards of education and the centralization of authority in the appointed State Board and office of the State Superintendent. The statutory framework adopted in 1916 remains largely in place today.

In accordance with the recommendations of the *Flexner Report*, Maryland's public school system is governed by a State Board of Education appointed by the governor, which in turn hires a State Superintendent to administer the State's Department of Education, which develops and recommends for the State board's approval, education policies and regulations ("*Public Education in Maryland: A Report to the Maryland Educational Survey Commission*", Abraham Flexner and Frank P. Bachman (1916)). Local boards of education and their local superintendents, similarly develop and adopt local education policies and procedures, as well as carry out state requirements.

## The Governor and General Assembly

### 2:4. What is the role of the Governor regarding public school governance?

The Governor has no direct role in the governance decisions or policies adopted by the State Board of Education or local boards. In fact, a hallmark of the *Flexner Report* was the separation of public education governance from partisan politics and the election cycle. Thus, unlike many other States, Maryland's Governor does not have the authority to appoint a Secretary of Education, or in Maryland's case, the State Superintendent of Schools. Maryland's State Superintendent does not serve as an appointee of the Governor, but rather as an employee of the State Board of Education. The power to appoint members of the State Board represents a potential means for a Governor to effect decisions regarding public school governance.

Interestingly, also unlike virtually all other States, the Governor is solely authorized to appoint all members of six of the State's 24 local boards of education. Local processes vary from county to county regarding the nominating of board candidates, but for appointed boards the appointment decision is the Governor's. An exception to this rule is the appointed board of the Baltimore City School Commissioners, which is appointed jointly by the Governor and the Mayor of Baltimore City. In addition, many appointed boards have been and continue to be converted to elected boards.

### 2:5. What is the role of the Governor regarding public education generally?

A primary role or function of the Governor is to develop and propose the annual operating and capital budgets, including all State operating funding for public education. Maryland is rather unique in vesting in the Governor the authority to draft a budget to which the General Assembly may not add. Referred to as an "executive budget", Maryland's process lends considerable weight to the Governor's positions on school funding issues. Lastly, the Governor, as represented by the State's Attorney General, decides the State's legal position on State and federal litigation.

### 2:6. What is the role of the Maryland General Assembly regarding public school governance?

The General Assembly, comprised of 141 delegates and 47 senators, passes all laws necessary for the welfare of the State. Counties, municipalities, and school systems are statutory creations of the General Assembly, as opposed to established in the State Constitution. Therefore, the powers and duties of school boards and superintendents are subject to the statutes compiled in the Annotated Code of Maryland. With regard to governance issues, an important function of the General Assembly is to determine whether a local board is appointed by the Governor or locally elected. In addition, by virtue of being creatures of the State, local boards may be abolished and reconstituted by State statute; most recently occurring in Prince George's County.

In the extreme, the federal No Child Left Behind Act authorizes State education agencies to select methods of restructuring certain persistently low-performing school systems, including abolishing the local education agency (NCLB § 1116(c)(10)(c)). In Maryland, such action would require legislation.

## 2:7. What are the duties and responsibilities of the General Assembly in education?

Generally, the legislature may enact all laws affecting the general welfare of the State, determine how State funds are to be allocated, and adopt amendments to the State Constitution, subject to ratification by the voters. Bills may be introduced in either house and when passed by both houses may become law by being signed, vetoed, or allowed to pass without signature, by the Governor. The General Assembly may override a veto by a three-fifths majority.

The General Assembly's primary roles regarding public education are twofold: to establish a state school funding system under the constitutional mandate, and to enact laws concerning the operation of the State Department of Education and local school systems. Yet another role of the legislature is to confirm the Governor's appointees to the State Board of Education.

With regard to education policy, the legislature has delegated considerable authority to the MSDE and the State Board (see **2:33**). Local boards, including their composition, terms of appointment or election, terms for removal, and compensation, are creations of State statute under the control of the legislature and the Governor. Every legislative session of the Maryland General Assembly includes the introduction of proposed legislation on education-related issues ranging from curriculum to collective bargaining to the conversion from an appointed to an elected school board in a given county. Thus, a natural tension has developed between the legislature's desire to enact laws effecting education policy, and the response from the State Board, MSDE, and local school systems that legislative action is not appropriate since this authority has been delegated to the State Board.

The General Assembly, in coordination and consultation with the Executive Branch, is responsible for adopting the annual budget for Maryland State government, including all education funding. The Constitution specifies that it is the responsibility of the Governor to present the annual budget to the General Assembly within five days of the beginning of each legislative session. The Constitution also requires that the budget is balanced by not exceeding anticipated revenues (Md. Const., Art. III, § 52). This constitutional requirement prevents deficit spending and accounts in large part for the excellent bond rating enjoyed by the State; a bond rating that contributes to the State's robust school construction funding program.

## 2:8. What are some examples of the education powers exercised by the General Assembly?

The General Assembly may impose conditions or limitations on an appropriation relating to the expenditure of State funds (*Bayne v. Secretary of State*, 283 Md. 560 (1978)). For example, state funding may be contingent on a local matching contribution, and other reporting requirements. In addition to statutory reporting requirements, the General Assembly may formally request certain actions and reports, as it does at the conclusion of each annual legislative session through the Joint Chairmen's Report. This report is issued by the House Appropriations and Senate Budget and Taxation Committees and includes reporting "requests" to State agencies, including the Maryland State Department of Education (MSDE). In 2007, MSDE is requested to hold five regional public hearings on the High School Assessment program, and to report on the hearings and program status by January 1, 2008 (*Joint Chairmen's Report-Operating Budget, pp. 157-158* (2007)).

Legislation establishing new funding formulas also requires annual master plans and new auditing requirements. Failure to comply with the new auditing requirements may result in the State withholding installments of State aid (Md. Code Ann., Ed. Art. §§ 5-114 and 5-213).

## 2:9. What is meant by the State's "preemption" of local laws regarding education?

State law may preempt local law in one of three ways: (1) preemption by conflict; (2) express preemption; or (3) implied preemption. A local law is preempted by conflict when it either prohibits an act permitted under State law, or permits an act that is prohibited under state law. (*Worton Creek Marina, LLC v. Claggett*, 381 Md. 499 (2004)).

State legislation in the field of education has been found to be so pervasive as to demonstrate the "occupation of the field" and, under the theory of implied preemption, prohibits a local government from adopting local legislation which interferes with the State's statutory and regulatory framework (*McCarthy v. Board of Education*, 280 Md. 634 (1977)). However, this constraint may not apply to local legislation to establish certain programs, such as a "voluntary, non-binding grant program that also rewards school performance, as long as the program does not infringe on the discretion of State or local education authorities" (81 Op. Att'y Gen. No. 26 (1996)).

**2:10. Has the General Assembly ever enacted legislation to reverse a State Board of Education decision?**

Yes, in 2006 the General Assembly responded directly to a recent State Board decision by enacting legislation, and overriding the Governor's veto, to prohibit the State Board and the State Superintendent from imposing a major restructuring of the governance arrangement for schools in the Baltimore City public school system, and prohibiting the removal of a public school from the direct control of the Baltimore City Board of School Commissioners (House Bill 1215, Chapter 59, 2007 Session Laws of Maryland; Md. Code Ann., Ed. Art. § 4-309).

**2:11. How often does the Maryland General Assembly meet and for how long?**

Since 1970 the General Assembly has met annually for 90 calendar-day sessions beginning on the second Wednesday of each January. In addition to these "regular" sessions, the General Assembly may be convened by the Governor for "special sessions." Article III, Section 15, of the Maryland Constitution provides:

> (1) The General Assembly may continue its session so long as in its judgment the public interest may require, for a period not longer than ninety days in each year. The ninety days shall be consecutive unless otherwise provided by law. The General Assembly may extend its session beyond ninety days, but not exceeding an additional thirty days, by resolution concurred in by a three-fifths vote of the membership in each House. When the General Assembly is convened by Proclamation of the Governor, the session shall not continue longer than thirty days, but no additional compensation other than mileage and other allowances provided by law shall be paid members of the General Assembly for special session.

**2:12. Where are the education laws promulgated by the General Assembly found?**

A separate volume of the Annotated Code is the "Education Article" and contains numerous "Titles" which include provisions establishing the State Board of Education, the duties of the State and local superintendents, all local boards, the State's school financing system and formulas, collective bargaining and other personnel provisions, special education, charter schools, and other related concerns.

## 2:13. Does public education play a prominent role in the General Assembly session?

Yes, during each annual legislative session the General Assembly considers approximately 2,500 pieces of legislation of which approximately 250 typically relate directly to elementary and secondary public education.

The prominent place of public education on the legislative agenda is, in part, a function of the often polarizing policy debates generated by bills dealing with issues such as school safety, student health and nutrition, charter schools, and school vouchers. However, a major factor in the role public education plays during the session is that State aid to local school systems constitutes approximately 75 percent of the total State aid to local governments, and more than 22 percent of the total operating budget. The magnitude of this annual State investment consistently warrants a prominent place on the agenda relative to other priorities (see *"Fiscal Briefing"*, Department of Legislative Services Office of Policy Analysis, January 22, 2007; *http://mlis.state.md.us/2007rs/budget_docs/ALL/2007_Fiscal_Briefing.pdf*).

## 2:14. What are some recent examples of education laws enacted by the General Assembly?

In addition to the operating and capital budgets which provided significant increases in State funding, in 2007 the General Assembly passed and the Governor signed to law several education related measures which:

- Raise indoor air quality standards for relocatable classrooms;

- Require a local superintendent to notify the local board of education of criminal charges brought against the superintendent; and

- Raise licensing standards for speech language pathologists and audiologists.

## 2:15. Are all Maryland education laws found in the Education Article?

The Education Article of the Maryland Annotated Code contains the vast majority of laws pertinent to the operation of the State and local school systems. However, examples of other Articles of the Code directly impacting school systems include:

- The Open Meetings Act, State Government Article

- School bus requirements, Transportation Article

- Integrated pest management, Agriculture Article; and

- Prohibitions of weapons on school property, Criminal Law Article.

# State Board of Education

### 2:16. What is the Maryland State Board of Education?

Created by statute under Section 2-201 of the Education Article, the State Board is a 12 member body appointed by the Governor with the duties and responsibilities outlined in Section 2-205 of the Education Article, including functioning as the head of the State Department of Education and appointing the State Superintendent of Schools.

### 2:17. How is the State Board of Education selected and what are the qualifications of a member?

The State Board consists of 11 regular members, and 1 student member, appointed by the Governor with the advice and consent of the Senate. The 11 regular members of the State Board are appointed to four-year terms by the Governor. In making appointments to the State Board, the Governor is required by statute to appoint members from the general public and consider representation from all parts of this State; and "areas of this State with concentrations of population or unique needs" (Md. Code Ann., Ed. Art. § 2-202(b)). The Governor may not appoint a member who is subject to the authority of the Board, the Governor, or the State Superintendent.

### 2:18. Is there a student member of the State Board of Education?

Yes. The student member is selected by the Governor from a list of 2 persons nominated by the Maryland Association of Student Councils and must be a regularly enrolled student in good standing in a public high school in the State. The student member is a voting member and is allowed to attend and participate in an executive session of the Board, but may not vote on any matter that relates to the following issues:

- The dismissal of or other disciplinary action involving personnel;
- Budget; or
- Appeals to the State Board under Sections 2-205, 4-205, or 6-202 of the Education Article (Md. Code Ann., Ed. Art. § 2-202(c)).

### 2:19. What is the term of office for a State Board of Education member?

Each regular member of the State Board serves for a term of 4 years and until a successor is appointed and qualifies. These terms are staggered as required by the terms of the members serving on the State Board as of July 1, 1989. A member is eligible for reappointment but may not serve for more than two full 4-year terms.

The student member serves for a term of 1 year. A student member is also eligible for reappointment but may not serve more than two full 1-year terms (Md. Code Ann., Ed. Art. § 2-202(d)).

## 2:20. Are State Board of Education members compensated for their service?

No. Members of the State Board serve without compensation but are entitled to reimbursement for certain expenses in accordance with the State's Standard State Travel Regulations (Md. Code Ann., Ed. Art. § 2-204(d)).

## 2:21. What officers does the State Board of Education have?

The State Board members annually elect a president and vice-president from among its members. In addition, similar to the governance structure of local boards, the State Superintendent serves as the chief executive, secretary, and treasurer of the State Board (Md. Code Ann., Ed. Art. § 2-204(b) and (c)).

## 2:22. Who serves as the Chief Executive, Secretary and Treasurer of the State Board?

The State Superintendent is designated as the Chief Executive, Secretary, and Treasurer of the State Board, and may advise the Board on any question under consideration, but may not vote. The Superintendent is required to attend each meeting of the Board and of its committees, except when the tenure, salary, or the administration of their office are under consideration.

## 2:23. What is the process for removing a State Board of Education member?

Only the Governor may remove a member of the State Board, and any removal must be based on one or more of the following causes:

- Immorality;
- Misconduct in office;
- Incompetency; or
- Willful neglect of duty.

Members are guaranteed due process protections including notice of the charges and the opportunity to request a public hearing before the Governor in his own defense, in person or by counsel. Upon request, the Governor must promptly hold a hearing. If a member of the State Board is removed, the Governor must file in the office of the Secretary of State a complete statement of all charges, the

Governor's findings, and a complete record of the proceedings (Md. Code Ann., Ed. Art. § 2-203).

### 2:24. What is the procedure for filling vacancies on the State Board of Education?

In order to fill a vacancy on the State Board, the Governor appoints a new member to fill any vacancy for the remainder of that term and until a successor is appointed and qualifies (Md. Code Ann., Ed. Art. § 2-202(d)).

### 2:25. Is the State Board of Education required to hold a certain number of meetings?

Yes. At a minimum, the State board is required by statute to hold a meeting in July and at least three other regular meetings. In addition, the State Board is authorized to hold other special meetings as necessary (Md. Code Ann., Ed. Art. § 2-204(a)).

### 2:26. How often does the State Board of Education actually meet?

Traditionally the State Board meets monthly on the fourth Tuesday and Wednesday of each month, excluding November, for one full day (9:00 a.m. to 5:00 p.m.) on Tuesday and a half-day (9:00 a.m. to 12:00 p.m.) on Wednesday.

### 2:27. Are State Board of Education meetings open to the public?

Yes. As a public body the State Board is subject to the State's Open Meetings Act and attendant provisions governing open and closed meetings, public notice, permissive subjects for closed meetings, and the definition of meetings to perform administrative functions which are outside the purview of the Open Meetings Act (Md. Code Ann., St. Govt' Art. § 10-508).

### 2:28. When may the State Board of Education hold a meeting that is not open to the public?

The State Open Meetings Act defines the criteria for conducting closed meetings, in executive session, for a limited array of topics. The State Board routinely meets in executive session through the middle of the day during the Tuesday monthly Board meeting, and at the closing of the Wednesday meeting. In addition, the Open Meetings Act provides an exception to the Act's requirements for certain meetings to perform administrative functions (Md. Code Ann., St. Govt' Art. § 10-502).

## 2:29. Does the public have a right to speak at a State Board of Education meeting?

No. However, the State Board has adopted the practice at its monthly meetings of including a limited opportunity for public comment. The Board limits public comment to no more than 10 speakers for no more than 3 minutes each, and requires advanced notice to the executive director to the Board regarding the speaker's identification and subject matter.

## 2:30. What are the duties and responsibilities of the State Board of Education?

The broad outline of the State Board's authority includes:

- Determining the elementary and secondary educational policies of this State;

- Enforcing the provisions of the Education Article that are within its jurisdiction;

- Explaining the true intent of the Education Article and deciding all controversies;

- Appointing the State Superintendent to administer the State Department of Education;

- Adopting bylaws, rules, and regulations for the administration of the public schools;

- Developing and proposing to the Governor the annual State budget for public education; and

- Recommending any legislation it considers necessary.

## 2:31. What is the method by which the State Board of Education must take official actions?

The affirmative vote of the majority of the members of the State Board is required for any action by the Board (Md. Code Ann., Ed. Art. § 2-204(e)). In practice, the State Board typically approves proposed departmental regulations for publication in the *Maryland Register* as a consent agenda item at the outset of each monthly meeting. During the meeting, action items are identified on the agenda and may be voted on at any time. The Board's legal opinions, also determined by a majority vote, are signed by all members of the Board, including any dissents, and typically issued following the monthly meeting.

**2:32. What types of decisions are the State Board authorized to make?**

The functions performed by the State Board of Education include the administrative functions of overseeing the operation of the State Department of Education and the office of the State Superintendent, the quasi-legislative function of adopting bylaws and regulations which have the force and effect of law, and the quasi-judicial function of deciding disputes regarding the intent of provisions of the education article as well as deciding cases on appeal from local school systems.

**2:33. What is the scope of the State Board's decision-making authority?**

The courts have consistently found that Section 2-205 of the Education Article confers comprehensive "visitatorial power" upon the State Board. This "visitatorial power" has been recognized for more than century, and is typically described in the same manner prescribed by Maryland's highest court in a recent decision, *Board of Education v. Heister*, 392 Md. 140 (2006):

> The totality of [the Education Article] provisions has been described as a visitatorial power of such comprehensive character as to invest the State Board "with the last word on any matter concerning educational policy or the administration of the system of public education." The broad sweep of the State Board's visitatorial power has been consistently recognized and applied since the principle was first enunciated in 1879 in Wiley v. School Comm'rs, 51 Md. 401.

The court, in *Heister*, went on to explain the scope and purpose of the State Board's visitatorial power:

> We think it beyond question that the power of visitation vested in the State Board is one of general control and supervision; it authorizes the State Board to superintend the activities of the local boards of education to keep them within the legitimate sphere of their operations, and whenever a controversy or dispute arises involving the educational policy or proper administration of the public school system of the State, the State Board's visitatorial power authorizes it to correct all abuses of authority and to nullify all irregular proceedings.

**2:34. What are the limitations on the State Board's decision-making authority?**

The courts have said the State board may not exercise its visitatorial power fraudulently, in bad faith, or in breach of trust (*Wilson v. Board of Education*, 234 Md. 561 (1964)). In addition, the State Board may not exercise its visitatorial power in contravention of statute (*Zeitschel v. Board of Education*, 274 Md. 69 (1975)).

## 2:35. What are some examples of administrative decisions of the State Board?

The State Board is responsible for specifying the information required to be reported by local boards, school administrators and teachers, including financial records and annual budget, and all educational records (Md. Code Ann., Ed. Art. § 2-205(o)). The State Board is charged with the responsibility of submitting an annual report to the Governor describing the functions of the Department and a plan for elementary and secondary education in the State (Md. Code Ann., Ed. Art. § 2-205(p)). The Board must forward a proposed budget to the Governor including appropriations for the department and State aid to the counties for operating and capital expenses (Md. Code Ann., Ed. Art. § 2-205(j)). In addition, the Board routinely approves departmental budget adjustments, and meets in executive session to discuss appointments and assignments of departmental staff. These duties arise from the Board's role as head of the State Department of Education and are carried out with the advice of the State Superintendent.

## 2:36. What is the scope of the quasi-legislative authority of the State Board?

Section 2-205(c)(2) of the Education Article provides that the State Board's "bylaws, rules, and regulations have the force of law when adopted and published." The State Board does not have the authority to enforce local school system compliance with a model policy or guidance not formally adopted as a bylaw or regulation (76 Op. Att'y Gen. No. 220 (1991).

## 2:37. Where are regulations promulgated by the State Board of Education found?

Title 13A of the Code of Maryland Regulations (referred to as COMAR) includes all regulations promulgated by the State Board of Education pertaining to pre-kindergarten through twelfth grade public education. Just as the statutes regarding elementary and secondary education are not confined to the Education Article, pertinent regulations may be found in other Titles of the Code of Maryland Regulations, such as Transportation (Title 11), Agriculture (Title 15), and State Retirement and Pension System (Title 22).

**2:38. What are some examples of quasi-legislative decisions of the State Board?**

The State Board's authority to adopt regulations and bylaws that have the force of law is exercised routinely at its monthly meetings through the process of approving proposed regulations for publication, receiving public comment, and approving the final regulations. Recent examples of regulations promulgated by the Board include the adoption of new statewide standardized tests, the Maryland School Assessments (MSAs), in accordance with the federal No Child Left Behind Act (COMAR 13A.01.04.05); and the adoption of new High School Assessments (HSAs) as graduation requirements beginning with the graduating class of 2009 (COMAR 13A.03.02.09).

**2:39. What is the scope of the Board's quasi-judicial authority?**

Courts recognize both the original jurisdiction of the State Board to decide statewide issues it enumerates, and its appellate jurisdiction to hear appeals from local school board decisions. Section 2-205(e) of the Education Article enumerates the following powers and duties of the State Board:

> (1) Without charge and with the advice of the Attorney General, the State Board shall explain the true intent and meaning of the provisions of:
>
>> (i) This article that are within its jurisdiction; and
>>
>> (ii) The bylaws, rules, and regulations adopted by the Board.
>
> (2) The Board shall decide all controversies and disputes under these provisions.
>
> (3) The decision of the Board is final.

The Board has been found to lack the authority to determine purely legal questions, in contrast with its broad decision-making authority regarding the administration of the public education system. A recent example of a question on appeal from the State Board that the court determined to be "purely legal" involved whether the three essential elements of a valid and enforceable liquidated damages clause were satisfied (*Board of Education v. Heister*, 392 Md. 140 (2006)).

**2:40. What are some examples of quasi-judicial decisions of the State Board?**

The State Board routinely issues opinions deciding issues on appeal from local board decisions regarding a broad array of issues. Examples of disputed local decisions include:

- The termination of a teacher's employment;

- The denial of a student transfer request;

- The change in the school attendance boundary;

- The granting of a waste management contract;

- The denial of charter school applications; and

- The determination of the adequacy of funding provided to charter schools.

## 2:41. What is the process for appealing a local board's decision to the State Board?

The general procedures, hearing procedures, standard of review, and other provisions relating to appeals to the State Board are found in State regulations under COMAR 13A.01.05. An appeal from a local board decision may be taken within 30 days of the local decision. In addition, a party may seek a declaratory ruling on the interpretation of law or regulation that is material to an existing case or controversy (COMAR 13A.01.05.02D).

## 2:42. What is the standard of review used by the State Board in reviewing local board decisions?

Regarding appeals involving a decision of the local board relating to a local policy, the local board's decision is considered prima facie correct, and the State Board may not substitute its judgment for that of the local board unless the local board decision is arbitrary, unreasonable, or illegal (COMAR 13A.01.05; *Chesapeake Charter, Inc. v. Anne Arundel County Board of Education*, MSBE Op. No. 03-09 (2003)).

Regarding appeals from local board decisions regarding student suspensions and expulsions, the State Board in *Lynn v. Anne Arundel County Board of Education*, MSBE Op. No. 04-20 (2004), opined that:

> It is well established that the decision of a local board of education with respect to a student suspension or expulsion is considered final. *See* Md. Code Ann., § 7-305. Therefore, the State Board's review is limited to determining whether the local board violated State or local law, policies, or procedure; whether the local board violated the due process rights of the student; or whether the local board acted in an otherwise unconstitutional manner. COMAR 13A.01.01.03E(4)(b).

## 2:43. What constitutes an "arbitrary or unreasonable" decision of a local board?

State regulations provide that "a decision may be arbitrary or unreasonable if it is one or more of the following: (1) It is contrary to sound educational policy; or (2) A reasoning mind could not have reasonably reached the conclusion the local board or local superintendent reached" (COMAR 13A.01.05.05B).

## 2:44. What constitutes an "illegal" decision of a local board?

State regulations provide that "a decision may be illegal if it is one or more of the following:

(1) Unconstitutional;

(2) Exceeds the statutory authority or jurisdiction of the local board;

(3) Misconstrues the law;

(4) Results from an unlawful procedure;

(5) Is an abuse of discretionary powers; or

(6) Is affected by any other error of law (COMAR 13A.01.05.05C).

## 2:45. On what basis may the State Board dismiss an appeal from a local decision?

**Waiver:** The State Board may determine that the right to an appeal has been waived, and has consistently done so where issues have not been reviewed initially by the local board (*Craven v. Board of Education of Montgomery County*, 7 Op. MSBE 870 (1997) (failure to challenge suspension before local board constituted waiver); and *Hart v. Board of Education of St. Mary's County*, 7 Op. MSBE 740 (1997) (failure to raise issue of age discrimination below constituted waiver on appeal)).

**Timeliness:** State law and regulation require appeals of local board decisions to be filed with the State Board within thirty days of the local board decision (Md. Code Ann., Ed. Art. § 4-205(c)(3) and COMAR 13A.01.05.02B(1)(a)). The 30 days run from the later of the date of the order or the opinion issued explaining the decision (COMAR 13A.01.05.02B(1)(b)). The State Board strictly adheres to time limitations as generally mandatory, and not to be overlooked except in extraordinary circumstances such as fraud or lack of notice (*Schwalm v. Montgomery County Board of Education*, 7 Op. MSBE 1326 (1998)).

**Standing:** The State Board adheres to the general rule on standing which requires that "for an individual to have standing, even before an administrative agency, he must show some direct interest or 'injury in fact, economic or otherwise'" (*Bellotte v. Anne Arundel County Board of Education*, MSBE Op. No. 03-08 (2003)).

**Mootness:** The State Board may determine that an appeal is moot if "there is no longer an existing controversy between the parties, so that there is no longer any effective remedy which the courts [or agency] can provide" (*In Re Michael B.*, 345 Md. 232, 234 (1997); and *Becker v. Carroll County Board of Education*, MSBE Op. No. 03-01 (2003)).

**Jurisdiction:** The State Board has found that it lacks jurisdiction to hear certain appeals arising from a local board's exercise of its quasi-legislative authority; concluding that such local decisions are not appealable through the § 4-205(c) appeals process (*Montgomery v. Howard County Board of Education*, MSBE Op. No. 04-35 (2004), a case involving the local board's decision not to permit age waivers for early entry into kindergarten).

### 2:46. What is the role of the Office of Administrative Hearings (OAH) regarding appeals to the State Board?

The State Board may, at its discretion, refer a case to the Office of Administrative Hearings (OAH) for review and recommended outcome. The OAH review results in a decision rendered by the Administrative Law Judge (ALJ), that includes proposed, or recommended, findings of fact and conclusions of law. The State Board may rely on the ALJ's decision for the basis of its final ruling, but must also identify and state reasons for any changes to the ALJ's decision (see Md. Code Ann., St. Gov't Art. § 10-216(b)). The State Board must give deference to the ALJ's demeanor-based witness credibility findings unless there are strong reasons present that support rejecting the assessments (*Reese, et al. v. Prince George's County Board of Education*, MSBE Op. No. 06-18 (2006); citing *Department of Health & Mental Hygiene v. Anderson*, 100 Md. App. 283 (1994)).

### 2:47. Can actions and decisions of the State Board of Education be challenged?

Yes. State regulations provide that "a party aggrieved by the decision rendered in an appeal may file a request for reconsideration within 30 days, or appeal the decision to the circuit court of the jurisdiction where the appellant resides" (COMAR 13A.01.05.10 and .11).

### 2:48. What standard is applied to a request for reconsideration?

The State Board's discretion to reconsider its final decision is limited to cases in which there is "sufficient indication in the request that: (1) The decision resulted from a mistake of law; or (2) New facts material to the issues have been discovered or have occurred subsequent to the decision" (COMAR 13A.01.05.10D).

### 2:49. What standard of review does the circuit court apply to appeals from actions of the State Board?

Generally, courts review the decisions of the State Board of Education in accordance with the standard of review applied to other administrative agencies. Because the State Board is an administrative body, specifically created by statute to administer the public education system in a comprehensive fashion, its decisions are afforded great deference (Md. Code Ann., Ed. Art. § 2-201); and *Hurl v. Board of Education of Howard County*, 107 Md. App. 286, 299 (1995)). When examining the factual findings of an agency, the court is "limited to determining if there is substantial evidence in the record as a whole to support the agency's findings and conclusions" (*United Parcel v. People's Counsel*, 336 Md. 569 (1994)). However, on questions of law, the court "may substitute its judgment for that of the [administrative agency]" (*Gray v. Anne Arundel County*, 73 Md. App. 301 (1987)).

Regarding appeals from State Board decisions, the courts have extended even greater deference, finding that the State Board's decisions regarding the administration of Maryland's public schools are "beyond judicial interference" unless they are contrary to law or arbitrary or capricious, or the State Board "exercised its power in bad faith, fraudulently, or in breach of trust" (*Hurl v. Board of Education of Howard County*, 107 Md. App. 286 (1995)). Maryland's highest court has distinguished its standard of reviewing appeals from decisions of the State Board, finding that "the paramount role of the State Board of Education sets it apart from most administrative agencies" (*Montgomery County Education Association v. Board of Education of Montgomery County*, 311 Md. 303 (1987)).

### 2:50. When may the court apply less deference, or greater scrutiny, to the State Board's decision?

The court has identified the following "four instances" where judicial scrutiny of State Board decisions may be more expansive:

(1) The matter involves a purely legal question;

(2) The State Board has contravened state statute;

(3) The State Board exercised its power in bad faith, fraudulently, or in breach of trust; or

(4) The State Board exercised its power arbitrarily or capriciously.

(*Board of Education v. Heister*, 392 Md. 140 (2006), citing *Hurl v. Board of Education of Howard County*, 107 Md. App. 286, 299, 667 A.2d 970, 977 (1995)).

**2:51. May the courts substitute their judgment for that of the State Board of Education?**

The courts have consistently distinguished between the State Board of Education's broad authority to interpret the education laws of the State in furtherance of the proper administration of the State's public school system, and limitations on this authority, such as the court's responsibility to determine purely legal questions. Therefore, the court should not substitute its judgment on the merits of a specific Board decision, but rather determine whether the Board exceeded its authority, or identify and resolve a purely legal question outside the Board's jurisdiction. A recent example of a court finding that the State Board acted arbitrarily or capriciously involved the Board definition of "commensurate funding" under the Charter School Act (*Prince George's County Board of Education v. Lincoln Public Charter School, Inc.*, Circuit Court of Prince George's County, 05-10496). An example of the court exercising more expansive review of a State Board decision on a "purely legal question" involved the question of whether the forfeiture provision included in the State's public school teachers' employment contract is a valid and enforceable liquidated damages clause or an unenforceable penalty (*Board of Education v. Heister*, 392 Md. 140 (2006)).

**2:52. What role does the District Court of Maryland play in public education matters?**

Generally, District Courts function as small claims courts and have jurisdiction over non-juvenile criminal matters, such as trespass or failure to stop for a school bus. In Montgomery County, the District Court serves as the juvenile court. In all other Maryland jurisdictions, the Circuit Court has jurisdiction over juvenile cases (see Md. Ann. Code, Cts. & Jud. Proc. Art. § 3-801(i)). The District Court may also administer programs such as the Truancy Reduction Pilot Program established under Subtitle 8C of the Courts and Judicial Proceedings Article.

**2:53. What role does the Maryland Court of Special Appeals play in public education matters?**

Appeals from circuit court decisions are made to the Court of Special Appeals, the highest court to which an appellant has an automatic right to appeal. The court has held that, "Under Maryland law, when the Court of Special Appeals is reviewing an appeal originating out of an administrative agency, the role of the appellate court is 'precisely the same as that of the circuit court.' We examine the decision for errors of law, a nondeferential review ..., and to determine if substantial evidence exists to support the conclusion, a deferential review." (*Bragunier Masonry Contractors, Inc. v. Maryland Commissioner of Labor and Industry*, 111 Md. App. 698 (1996)).

**2:54. What role does the Maryland Court of Appeals play in public education matters?**

Maryland's highest court may, at its discretion, issue a *writ of certiorari* to hear appeals from a final decision of the Court of Special Appeals, or it may intervene and decide cases prior to the lower Court's final decision. In either case, the Court of Appeals' decision to hear a case is discretionary.

# The State Superintendent of Schools

**2:55. What is the role of the State Superintendent of Schools?**

Generally, the State Superintendent is responsible for the administration of the Maryland Department of Education (MSDE) and has the powers provided in Subtitle 3 of the Education Article (Md. Code Ann., Ed. Art. § 2-103). The powers and duties of the State Superintendent of Schools are outlined in Section 2-303 of the Education Article. In addition to the powers specifically conferred in this section, Section 2-104 describes the responsibilities for appointing and overseeing departmental employees, and the State Board's powers and duties outlined in Section 2-205 also include several specific references to the role of the Superintendent.

Beyond the statutory framework, as noted in Question **2:4**, Maryland's State Superintendent is the only cabinet level agency head who does not serve at the pleasure of the Governor, but rather by appointment by the State Board of Education. This autonomy has contributed to the notably long tenure of many of Maryland's State Superintendents, and to the State Superintendent's prominent leadership role in developing and advocating positions on fiscal and policy issues, and in crafting major educational reforms.

**2:56. What are the major powers and duties of the State Superintendent?**

The Superintendent wields considerable influence over the State's education system, in large part due to the statutory framework that stipulates that the State Board's "general control and supervision over the public schools and educational interests" must be exercised through the State Superintendent (Md. Code Ann., Ed. Art. § 2-205(g)(2)). Similarly, the statute requires the State Board to "establish basic policy and guidelines for the program of instruction for the public schools ... with the advice of the State Superintendent" (Md. Code Ann., Ed. Art. § 2-205(h)).

The broad array of powers assigned directly to the State Superintendent include carrying out the educational policies of the State Board and enforcing the provisions of the Education Article and the bylaws and regulations adopted by the State Board (see Md. Code Ann., Ed. Art. § 2-303(b) and (c)). The State

Superintendent performs these duties through the employees and divisions within the Maryland State Department of Education (MSDE). While Section 2-102 of the Education Article designates the State Board as the "head of the Department", Section 2-103(a) provides that the State Superintendent, "acting under the bylaws, rules, and regulations of the State Board ... is responsible for the administration of the Department and has general supervision of all professional and clerical assistants of the Department."

### 2:57. How does the State Superintendent enforce the education laws and regulations?

The State Superintendent has the authority to respond to a violation of any of the provisions of the Education Article, by an educational institution or local school system, by requiring the State Comptroller to withhold from that institution or board "all or any part of an appropriation made by the General Assembly; and all or any part of any other payment from funds budgeted by the State" (Md. Code Ann., Ed. Art. § 2-303(b)(2)).

### 2:58. Does the State Superintendent have a role in the State's school construction program?

Yes. The State Superintendent has a major role in overseeing the State school construction program. All contracts for school construction projects must be approved by the State Superintendent to be valid, and the Superintendent is responsible for approving or disapproving each of the following:

- Proposals for the purchase or sale of any ground, school site, or building;

- Plans or specifications for the remodeling of a school building if the remodeling costs more than $350,000;

- Plans or specifications for the construction of a new school building; and

- Change orders that cost more than $25,000 for the remodeling, restoration, or construction of a school building (Md. Code Ann., Ed. Art. § 2-303(f)).

In addition, the State Superintendent is designated by statute to be the chair of the Interagency Committee on School Construction (IAC), the body responsible for developing the projections and recommendations for school construction projects (Md. Code Ann., Ed. Art. § 5-302)).

## 2:59. Does the State Superintendent have a role in the operation of local school systems?

The Superintendent is charged with the responsibility of "certificating" the professional personnel within the local school systems. Therefore, in this instance, the State Superintendent is not overseeing a local program and compliance with State standards, but is instead administering a program concerning the employees of each of the 24 local school systems (Md. Code Ann., Ed. Art. § 2-303(g)).

## 2:60. Does the Superintendent's authority extend to State agencies other than the Department of Education?

Yes. The State Superintendent is also responsible for approving and overseeing the educational program of instruction provided in conjunction with the services offered through the following agencies:

- The Department of Juvenile Services;

- The Developmental Disabilities Administration, or Mental Hygiene Administration of the Department of Health and Mental Hygiene;

- The Department of Public Safety and Correctional Services; or

- The residential school located within the Institute of Psychiatry and Human Behavior of the University Hospital (Md. Code Ann., Ed. Art. § 2-303(h).

## 2:61. How is the State Superintendent selected?

The State Board is authorized to appoint the State Superintendent in accordance with the qualifications outlined in Section 2-302(c) of the Education Article.

## 2:62. What is the term of office for the State Superintendent?

The State Superintendent is appointed by the State Board to a term of 4 years beginning on the first day of July after the appointment and serves until a successor is appointed and qualifies.

## 2:63. What are the qualifications of the State Superintendent?

Statute requires that the State Superintendent be an experienced and competent educator; a graduate of an accredited college or university; have at least 2 years of special academic and professional graduate preparation in an accredited college or university; and have at least 7 years of experience in teaching and administration (Md. Code Ann., Ed. Art. § 2-302(c)).

## 2:64. How is the salary of the State Superintendent established?

The State Board sets the salary of the State Superintendent on a four-year schedule in conjunction with the beginning of the Superintendent's term (Md. Code Ann., Ed. Art. § 2-302(b)).

## 2:65. What is the process for removing the State Superintendent?

The State Board is solely authorized to remove the State Superintendent from office for the following causes: immorality; misconduct in office; insubordination; incompetency; or willful neglect of duty. The Superintendent is afforded the due process protections of notice of the charges, the opportunity to request a hearing, and representation by counsel (Md. Code Ann., Ed. Art. § 2-302(d)).

## 2:66. What is the procedure for filling a vacancy in the office of State Superintendent?

The State Board must appoint a new State Superintendent to fill a vacancy for the remainder of the unexpired term (Md. Code Ann., Ed. Art. § 2-302(e)).

# State Department of Education

## 2:67. What is the State Department of Education?

The Maryland State Department of Education (MSDE), is one of several agencies of State government established by statute, and is the principal department of the State government for the purpose of exercising "authority over: (1) Matters of elementary and secondary education that affect this State; and (2) The general care and supervision of public elementary and secondary education" (Md. Code Ann., Ed. Art. §§ 2-101 and 2-106).

MSDE is organized under the State Board of Education and administered by the State Superintendent of Schools. The Office of the Deputy Secretary for Instruction and Academic Acceleration oversees the Divisions of Early Childhood Development, Instruction, Student and School Services, Special Education, Career Technology and Adult Learning, and Correctional Education. The Office of the Deputy Secretary for Administration oversees the Divisions of Business Services, Assessment and Accountability, and Certification and Accreditation. In addition, the Office of Administration oversees the Human Resources, Audit, and Equity Assurance Offices. Other offices and divisions include the Office of the Deputy Superintendent for Academic Policy, and the Divisions of Leadership Development, Library Services, and Rehabilitation Services.

**2:68. What is the role of the State Department of Education in public school governance?**

The Maryland State Department of Education (MSDE) comprises the State Board, State Superintendent, and the staff responsible for administering and enforcing the directives of the Board and Superintendent. In this sense, it is the State Department which is invested with the broad "visitatorial" powers referred to in this Chapter.

**2:69. What is meant by the term "State Education Agency" (SEA)?**

The Maryland State Department of Education (MSDE) is Maryland's State Education Agency (SEA), the term used by the federal government to refer to a State board of education or agency primarily responsible for the supervision of public elementary and secondary schools in a State. **Chapter 3** provides a detailed description of the federal role in public education.

# 3. Federal Role in Education

### 3:1. What role does the federal government play in Maryland's education system?

The federal government in multiple ways—by the U.S. Constitution and various Amendments, by numerous federal statutes, by multiple federal cabinet level departments and federal agencies, and by the decisions of federal courts—impacts Maryland's education system.

### 3:2. Does the U.S. Constitution make specific provision for an education role?

The provision of public education is not mentioned in the U.S. Constitution or any of the twenty-seven Amendments thereto.

### 3:3. What is the effect of the Tenth Amendment on a federal role in education?

Since there is no power over public education delegated to the federal government by the U.S. Constitution, the Tenth Amendment clearly reserves to each state, including Maryland, the power to control public education. The Tenth Amendment provides, "The powers not delegated to the United States by the Constitution, nor prohibited by it to the States, are reserved to the States respectively, or to the people."

### 3:4. What are the cited foundations for a federal role in education?

States accepting federal funds provided by the U.S. Congress, by authority of the General Welfare Clause of the U.S. Constitution, are obliged to comply with accompanying federal regulations. Federal regulations promulgated by authority of the Commerce Clause of the U.S. Constitution, and tied to the provision of federal funds; provide a second avenue of federal control over certain aspects of public education. Finally, Maryland and other states are bound by the decisions of federal courts enforcing and interpreting the provisions of the U.S. Constitution and federal statutes.

### 3:5. What part does the General Welfare Clause play in the federal role in education?

Article I, Section 8, of the U.S. Constitution gives the federal government the authority to tax and spend for "the General Welfare of the United States…". The

Supreme Court, in *Helvering v. Davis,* 301 U.S. 619 (1937), has held that the use of this power of the purse is not limited to specifically granted federal powers, but can be extended to other general welfare purposes, among which education has been included during the years since. Thus, the federal government can only establish educational requirements in conjunction with the appropriation of funds. The state must have the choice to accept the federal funds with the accompanying requirements, or to turn down the federal funds without subjecting the state to the accompanying federal educational requirements. The state thus retains its right to control educational decision-making.

### 3:6. What part does the Commerce Clause play in the federal role in education?

Article I, Section 8, of the U.S. Constitution also gives the federal government the power to "regulate Commerce with foreign Nations, and among the several States …". The broad scope of federal authority under the Commerce Clause has been most commonly applied in the educational arena to matters relating to transportation, health and safety requirements, and labor relations. In an education law case, dealing with the limits of the Commerce Clause, the Supreme Court in *United States v. Lopez,* 514 U.S. 549 (1995), found the Gun-Free School Zones Act of 1990 to exceed the authority of Congress under the Commerce Clause because the statute was not tied to the provision of federal funds. Note that the Gun-Free Schools Act of 1994, which did tie its regulatory provisions to the acceptance by states of federal funds, remains in place today.

### 3:7. What part does the Supremacy Clause play in the federal role in education?

Article VI, Section 2, of the U.S. Constitution states, "This Constitution, and the Laws of the United States which shall be made in Pursuance thereof;… shall be the supreme Law of the Land; and the Judges in every State shall be bound thereby; any Thing in the Constitution or Laws of any State to the Contrary notwithstanding." The Supremacy Clause means that a federal statute, adopted under valid authority, takes precedence over a state statute that is in direct conflict. The Supreme Court issued an opinion defining such valid authority in the case of *Alden v. Maine,* 527 U.S. 706 (1999).

### 3:8. What role does the U.S. Department of Education play in education?

The Department of Education was created in 1980, and the Secretary of Education sits on the President's cabinet. The Department of Education promulgates regulations that implement the statutes passed by Congress to provide funding for public education; states must agree to implement those regulations to secure the accompanying federal funds. Congress reviews the regulations administered by the Department of Education in well over 200 varied program areas to ensure that the legislative intent is properly carried out. The programs administered by the Department of Education run the gamut from Advanced Placement Tests and Bilingual Education to Vocational Education and Women's Educational Equity.

### 3:9. Do other U.S. Cabinet Level Departments play a role in education?

Yes. The Department of Agriculture regulates school milk; the Department of Defense regulates military recruiters; the Department of Health and Human Services regulates school wellness and safety issues; the Department of Labor regulates wage and hour laws; and the Department of Transportation regulates school bus safety standards, to name just a few.

### 3:10. Do other federal agencies play a role in education?

Yes. The Equal Opportunity Employment Commission (EEOC) and the Office of Civil Rights (OCR) both regulate and investigate claims of discrimination in the public school setting. The Environmental Protection Agency (EPA) regulates storage of fuels, use of pesticides, and asbestos abatement programs. The Center for Disease Control (CDC) provides guidance in matters ranging from autism to youth suicides. Other federal agencies playing a role in public education include the National Labor Relations Board (NLRB), the Occupational Health and Safety Administration (OSHA), and the National Institutes of Health (NIH).

### 3:11. What role does the U.S. Congress play in education?

Congress passes laws that affect schools under the broad power granted under the General Welfare Clause and the Commerce Clause, and Congress appropriates funds for public education that offer federal funds to the states while requiring the acceptance of federal regulations in order to secure those funds. Federal funds for public education typically provide between 6 and 7 percent of the annual budget of a local school system. The Senate also must approve the President's appointment of the U.S. Secretary of Education.

### 3:12. What are some main examples of federal statutes that impact education?

The federal statutes that have the largest impact on public education today include the No Child Left Behind Act (NCLB) (see **Chapter 8**); the Individuals with Disabilities Education Act (IDEA) and Section 504 of the Rehabilitation Act of 1973 (see **Chapter 15**); the Equal Access Act (see **Chapter 13**); Title VII of the

Civil Rights Act of 1964, the Age Discrimination in Employment Act, and the Family and Medical Leave Act (see **Chapter 6**); Title IX of the Education Amendments of 1972 and the Equal Educational Opportunities Act (see **Chapter 14**); and the Family Educational Rights and Privacy Act (see **Chapter 10**).

### 3:13. To what extent are state education agencies given immunity under the Eleventh Amendment?

In the context of state education agencies, the Eleventh Amendment limits the power of federal statutes to impose liability and claims for monetary damages against state education agencies. Such immunity does not permit a state to violate applicable provisions of the U.S. Constitution or federal statutes that are applied to a state on a valid constitutional basis. The Supreme Court addressed the issue of Eleventh Amendment state immunity in the case of *Alden v. Maine,* 527 U.S. 706 (1999).

### 3:14. How are state education agencies defined with respect to Eleventh Amendment immunity?

While local school districts are not considered to be state agencies in a majority of states, in Maryland, local school systems have been considered by both the Maryland Court of Appeals and Maryland Federal District Court, in a number of cases, including *Jones v. Frederick County Board of Education*, 689 F. Supp. 535 (D. Md. 1988), to be state agencies for the application of immunity under the Eleventh Amendment.

### 3:15. What are the effects of the Fourteenth Amendment on public education?

The Fourteenth Amendment provides in pertinent part:

> No State shall make or enforce any law which shall abridge the privileges and immunities of citizens of the United States; nor shall any State deprive any person of life, liberty, or property, without due process of law; nor deny to any person within its jurisdiction the equal protection of the laws.

Three separate aspects of the Fourteenth Amendment are the basis for a significant number of claims against public schools. First, the Supreme Court, in *Gitlow v. New York,* 268 U.S. 652 (1925), held that the Fourteenth Amendment makes the liberties granted under the Bill of Rights applicable to the states. Thus, the first ten amendments, which were specifically directed at Congress and the federal government, have made the states, and thus local school systems, equally responsible to protect the freedoms found in the First, Fourth, Fifth and Ninth Amendments.

Second, the Due Process Clause of the Fourteenth Amendment prohibits states, and thus local school systems, from depriving citizens of life, liberty, or property without due process of law. Students have a property right to attend public school as a result of compulsory attendance laws and thus must be provided with due process before being denied school attendance (see **Chapters 10** and **11**). Teachers have a property interest in continued employment as a result of teacher tenure laws and thus must be provided with due process before their employment can be negatively affected (see **Chapters 6** and **7**).

Finally, the Equal Protection Clause of the Fourteenth Amendment prohibits states, and thus local school systems, from denying to any person the equal protection of the laws. In the public school setting, individuals are protected against discrimination based upon race, national origin, gender, and disability (see **Chapters 14** and **15**).

### 3:16. What are the effects of the First Amendment on public education?

Applicable to state agencies, and thus local school systems via the Fourteenth Amendment, the First Amendment is the best known and possibly most often litigated portion of federal constitutional law in the public school setting. There are three primary areas of concern within the First Amendment which states:

> Congress shall make no law respecting an establishment of religion, or prohibiting the free exercise thereof; or abridging the freedom of speech, or of the press; or the right of the people peaceably to assemble, and to petition the Government for a redress of grievances.

The initial area of potential conflict under the First Amendment is the always challenging interaction between the Establishment Clause, which provides that local school systems may not favor or advance any particular religion; and the Free Exercise Clause, which provides that local school systems may not abridge an individual's right to carry out their sincerely held religious beliefs. The vast majority of public school religion cases, involve to some degree a clash between these two First Amendment mandates. A detailed explanation of all the factors to be considered in navigating the sea of public school religion cases is found in **Chapter 13**.

A second portion of the First Amendment that generates more than its share of disputes in the school setting are the guarantees of freedom of speech and of the press. In **Chapter 12** and to a lesser extent in **Chapter 7**, you will learn much more about the rights of students and teachers to express themselves in public school. For now, it is sufficient to note that free expression rights are not as great in the school setting as they are outside the school setting, the referenced chapters will provide the basic parameters under which decisions about speech and press matters may be addressed in public schools, while minimizing legal challenges.

Finally, the right to peaceably assemble has generated litigation from areas as diverse as student clubs to teachers' rights to form associations and engage in collective bargaining. These issues are addressed in **Chapters 6** and **13**, where important questions pertaining to the right to assemble and associate will be considered for public schools.

### 3:17. What are the effects of the Fourth Amendment on public education?

The Fourth Amendment, applicable to public schools via the Fourteenth Amendment, is a key constitutional basis that comes into play in the area of discipline in the school setting, whether for students or teachers, stating in pertinent part, "The right of the people to be secure in their persons, houses, papers, and effects, against unreasonable searches and seizures, shall not be violated...". The standard for conducting searches and the reasonable expectation of privacy for lockers, backpacks, cars, and clothing in the school setting for students is addressed in **Chapter 11**, and with respect to teachers is addressed in **Chapter 7**.

### 3:18. What are the effects of the Fifth Amendment on public education?

The portion of the Fifth Amendment that occasionally arises in the school setting, once again under the Fourteenth Amendment, states in pertinent part, "No person ... shall be compelled in any criminal case to be a witness against himself, nor be deprived of life, liberty or property, without due process of law; nor shall private property be taken for public use, without just compensation."

The Due Process Clause of the Fourteenth Amendment is the traditional vehicle for challenging alleged substantive or procedural due process violations, because it is specifically applicable to state agencies and thus local school systems. The Fifth Amendment prohibition against self-incrimination has been cited from time to time by teachers under investigation by school administrators, and is touched on in **Chapter 7**. The occasional practice of taking land for school use under eminent domain laws also involve Fifth Amendment issues and is briefly addressed in **Chapter 5**.

### 3:19. What are the effects of the Ninth Amendment on public education?

The Ninth Amendment, via the Fourteenth Amendment, is another provision of the Bill of Rights that may come into play in the public school arena. It states:

> The enumeration in the Constitution, of certain rights, shall not be construed to deny or disparage others retained by the people.

Teachers have sometimes based their claim of privacy rights outside of the classroom setting on the unenumerated rights provided under the Ninth Amendment, and this is briefly discussed in **Chapter 7**. Public school policies and regulations pertaining to personal grooming also have been the subject of occasional Ninth Amendment challenges and are briefly addressed in **Chapter 12**.

### 3:20. What is the role of the federal court system with respect to public education?

Article III, Section 1, of the U.S. Constitution states in pertinent part, "The judicial Power of the United States, shall be vested in one supreme Court, and in such inferior Courts as the Congress may from time to time ordain and establish." It is possible to classify federal court cases into one of two categories; cases arising from disputes between citizens of different states, and cases arising from disputes pertaining to federal statutes or the U.S. Constitution. The federal courts play three primary roles with respect to public education. Federal courts are called upon to resolve public school disputes by applying applicable federal law to the facts of a particular case. Statutory interpretation is another role of federal courts, as they are frequently called upon to construe federal laws that have applicability to public education. Finally, federal courts are charged with the determination of whether statutes or school actions or policies are constitutional, although federal courts will nearly always decide cases on other grounds if possible, and thus not decide constitutional issues unless there is no alternative.

See **Appendix 3-1** for a U.S. map depicting the structure of the federal court system (Title 28, U.S.C. Part I, Chap. 3, § 41). All federal judges are nominated by the President, and after approval of the Senate, are appointed to lifetime judicial terms.

### 3:21. What role does the Federal District Court play in public education matters?

The Federal District Courts are the trial level courts in the federal court system, where judges and juries hear specific disputes that arise within their judicial venue in cases that meet the above criteria for federal jurisdiction. There is at least one federal district within each state and approximately half of the states have between two and four federal districts. The number of judges within a federal district varies from a low of one in several federal districts with small populations to a high of twenty-eight in the Southern District of New York.

In Maryland, there is only one federal district, the District of Maryland has ten active judges and two court locations in Baltimore and Greenbelt.

### 3:22. What role does the Circuit Court of Appeals play in public education matters?

Decisions of the federal district courts may be appealed as a matter of right to the court of appeals for the circuit in which the district court is located. There are thirteen federal courts of appeals; one with national jurisdiction to hear specific categories of cases such as patents and copyrights, one for the District of Columbia, and eleven that consist of numbered geographic groupings of states. Of the numbered circuits, the First Circuit Court of Appeals has the least number of active judges with six, and the Ninth Circuit Court of Appeals has the greatest number of active judges with twenty-eight.

Circuit courts of appeal are not trial courts and thus do no fact finding; they instead review cases in order to determine whether the applicable law was properly applied to the facts of a particular case. Circuit courts of appeal also rule on matters of statutory interpretation and constitutionality as described above. Cases are normally heard by three judge panels that make decisions on a majority basis (*i.e.*, 3-0 or 2-1). On rare occasions in matters of significant importance, a circuit court of appeals may agree to permit a case to be heard by all judges within the circuit, these are referred to as en banc appeals. Upon hearing an appeal, a circuit court of appeals may affirm the district court, reverse the district court, or remand the case for further proceedings consistent with the appellate courts instructions about the law to be applied.

Maryland is located in the Fourth Circuit along with Virginia, West Virginia, North Carolina and South Carolina. The Fourth Circuit Court of Appeals is located in Richmond, Virginia and has fifteen active judges from the various states that make up the circuit.

### 3:23. What role does the U.S. Supreme Court play in public education matters?

The Supreme Court of the United States is the highest court in the nation. The vast majority of cases that come before the Supreme Court arrive pursuant to a writ of certiorari, which is Latin for "to be informed of". The writ of certiorari is an order from a superior court to an inferior court, directing that the record of a particular case be forwarded to the superior court for consideration of whether there were errors made by the inferior court. Interestingly, only four of the nine Supreme Court Justices are required to issue a writ of certiorari, but ultimately a majority of the court; or five Justices must agree on some level in order to decide a case. Every year, Supreme Court review is sought in thousands of cases, but only about two hundred are accepted annually by the high court. A denial of certiorari has the effect of leaving the lower court decision intact. The Supreme Court can affirm the lower court, reverse the lower court, or remand the case to the lower court to apply the correct legal standard as directed. There is no appeal from a decision of the U.S. Supreme Court.

## 3:24. What occurs when federal courts reach different results in similar cases?

Lower courts are required to follow the decisions of appellate courts that have revisory authority over them. For example, the District Court for Maryland is bound by any appellate decision rendered by the Fourth Circuit Court of Appeals, even if the case originated in another state within the Fourth Circuit. Likewise, the District Court of Maryland and the Fourth Circuit Court of Appeals are bound by any appellate decision rendered by the U.S. Supreme Court, even if the case originated in another judicial circuit. Decisions of the U.S. Supreme Court also are binding on all state level courts including the Maryland District Courts, Circuit Courts, Court of Special Appeals, and the Court of Appeals (see **Chapter 2**).

On the other hand, the District Court for Maryland and the Fourth Circuit Court of Appeals are not bound by a decision reached in another judicial circuit, although they are free to adopt the rationale used by the court of a different circuit if it is found to be persuasive. It is not rare for different judicial circuits to rule in conflicting ways on educational issues that come before them, and thus the law to be applied by a public school may vary depending on the geographic circuit in which it is located. If the Supreme Court were to decide such a case where there is disagreement between the judicial circuits, a decision of the Supreme Court would settle the issue for all judicial circuits, and thus for all public schools, regardless of the geographic circuit in which they are located.

## 3:25. What is the importance of precedent in deciding public education cases?

The Latin term "stare decisis" means to abide by or to adhere to, and the modern term precedent essentially means that courts should decide current cases based upon the rulings in prior cases that were identical or substantially similar. This doctrine has the effect of giving some degree of certainty to local school systems as they create policies and take actions using existing court decisions to guide current practice. If every judge were to be free to decide each case without the constraints of precedent, then no public school decision maker could ever have any degree of confidence that they were able to act within the safety of established law.

While it is generally the duty of the highest court addressing a matter to follow its own prior decisions, a court that is not bound by the decision of a higher court, may decide that its own prior decision was wrong and unjust, and thus is free to reach a different conclusion. Courts should only rarely depart from precedent if they determine that the injury to the legal system will be greater by continuing the precedent than the injury that will result from reversing the established case law.

When no binding precedent exists, a court is free to formulate a decision based upon that court's determination of the proper law to be applied to the facts of a particular case.

### 3:26. What is the importance of actual controversy in deciding public education cases?

Article III of the U.S. Constitution permits federal courts only to decide cases where an actual controversy exists, they are not to decide hypothetical cases or cases in which the parties are friendly and nonadversary. The controversy must be definite in nature and must be susceptible to being resolved in a judicial forum. Federal courts likewise do not issue advisory opinions, partially for fear that the advice, if rejected, would adversely affect the court's authority; and partially to prevent the federal courts from exercising greater power than their constitutional mandate.

### 3:27. What is the importance of mootness in deciding public education cases?

Article III of the U.S. Constitution prevents federal courts from deciding cases that are moot. Mootness exists when a decision in a case can have no practical effect on the controversy before the court. This can occur if the law has changed, or the actual controversy no longer exists. In the public education setting, this can easily occur if the student bringing the case graduates, and is no longer subject to the school policy or action complained of.

### 3:28. What is the importance of premature actions in deciding public education cases?

Just as a case cannot be maintained after it is too late, or moot, a case cannot be maintained if it is brought too early, or prematurely. Article III of the U.S. Constitution also requires a federal court to determine whether a case is ripe for judgment; the controversy must have sufficient existence and immediacy to justify the court's agreement to adjudicate the matter. In the public education setting, cases are often found not to be ripe if the established system of administrative appeals available to the aggrieved party has not been completed; this is the doctrine requiring the exhaustion of administrative remedies.

### 3:29. What is the importance of standing in deciding public education cases?

In order for a party to have standing to bring a public education case before a federal court, they must be personally adversely affected by the school policy or action complained of. If the party bringing the action is not injured by the challenged policy or action, the court will not accept an otherwise proper matter for its consideration. Standing is an issue of proper jurisdiction, unrelated to the merits of a case. If the same case were brought by a proper litigant, then standing would not be a bar to consideration of the case.

### 3:30. What is the importance of injunctions in deciding public education cases?

In the public school setting, if a federal court finds that a party is subject to irreparable injury from a public school, and there is no adequate remedy that can be provided otherwise, the court may issue injunctive relief. An injunction typically either directs a party to take some specific action or prohibits a party from taking some specific action.

### 3:31. Is the growing federal role in public education being challenged in the courts?

At the present time, several states and several educational advocacy groups are challenging the No Child Left Behind Act (NCLB) as an under-funded mandate and as undermining the rights of a state to adopt and carry out its own system of accountability for educational results (see **Chapter 8**). Another portion of the No Child Left Behind Act (NCLB) that is generating legal controversy is the requirement that schools must provide to military recruiters the same access to students and student information that colleges and employers are provided. Despite sizable organized protests at a number of Maryland schools, no formal legal challenge to the requirement has as yet been brought. It should be noted though that the Supreme Court in the case of *Rumsfeld v. Forum for Academic and Institutional Rights*, 547 U.S. ___ (2006), ruled 8-0 on the constitutionality of a federal law requiring institutions of higher education receiving federal funds to provide equal campus access to military recruiters. While no suit has been filed to date, another common area of complaint regarding federal funding that could eventually lead to such a challenge relates to the Individuals with Disabilities Education Act (IDEA), where the promised 40 percent federal contribution to the extra cost of provision of services for special education students has barely reached one-third of that amount, which was to be in place more than two decades ago.

# Appendix 3-1. Number and Composition of United States Judicial Circuits

## United States Code

## Title 28. Judiciary and Judicial Procedure

## Part I. Organization of Courts

## Chapter 3. Courts of Appeals.

**Sec. 41. Number and composition of circuits.** The thirteen judicial circuits of the United States are constituted as follows:

| Circuits | Composition |
| --- | --- |
| District of Columbia | District of Columbia |
| First | Maine, Massachusetts, New Hampshire, Puerto Rico, Rhode Island. |
| Second | Connecticut, New York, Vermont. |
| Third | Delaware, New Jersey, Pennsylvania, Virgin Islands. |
| Fourth | Maryland, North Carolina, South Carolina, Virginia, West Virginia. |
| Fifth | District of the Canal Zone, Louisiana, Mississippi, Texas. |
| Sixth | Kentucky, Michigan, Ohio, Tennessee. |
| Seventh | Illinois, Indiana, Wisconsin. |
| Eighth | Arkansas, Iowa, Minnesota, Missouri, Nebraska, North Dakota, South Dakota. |
| Ninth | Alaska, Arizona, California, Idaho, Montana, Nevada, Oregon, Washington, Guam, Hawaii. |
| Tenth | Colorado, Kansas, New Mexico, Oklahoma, Utah, Wyoming. |
| Eleventh | Alabama, Florida, Georgia. |
| Federal | All Federal judicial districts. |

**Source:** June 25, 1948, ch. 646, 62 Stat. 870; Oct. 31, 1951, ch. 655, Sec. 34, 65 Stat. 723; Pub. L. 96-452, Sec. 2, Oct. 14, 1980, 94 Stat. 1994; Pub. L. 97-164, title I, Sec. 101, Apr. 2, 1982, 96 Stat. 25.

# Geographic Boundaries
## of United States Courts of Appeals and United States District Courts

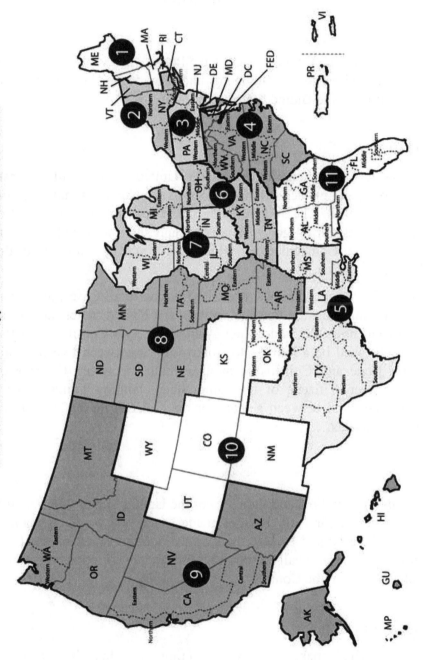

# Appendix 3-2. Selected Provisions of the United States Constitution

## Article I

Section 8. [1] The Congress shall have Power To lay and collect Taxes, Duties, Imposts and Excises, to pay the Debts and provide for the common Defence and general Welfare of the United States; ...

## Article III

Section 1. The judicial Power of the United States shall be vested in one supreme Court, and in such inferior Courts as the Congress may from time to time ordain and establish. The Judges, both of the supreme and inferior Courts, shall hold their Offices during good Behaviour, and shall, at stated Times, receive for their Services a Compensation, which shall not be diminished during their Continuance in Office.

Section 2. [1] The judicial Power shall extend to all Cases, in Law and Equity, arising under this Constitution, the Laws of the United States, and Treaties made, or which shall be made, under their Authority; ... to Controversies to which the United States shall be a Party;—to Controversies between two or more States;—between a State and Citizens of another State;—between Citizens of different States;—between Citizens of the same State claiming Lands under Grants of different States, and between a State, or the Citizens thereof, and foreign States, Citizens or Subjects....

## Article VI

[2] This Constitution, and the Laws of the United States which shall be made in Pursuance thereof; and all Treaties made, or which shall be made, under the Authority of the United States, shall be the supreme Law of the Land; and the Judges in every State shall be bound thereby, any Thing in the Constitution or Laws of any State to the Contrary notwithstanding.

## Amendment I [1791]

Congress shall make no law respecting an establishment of religion, or prohibiting the free exercise thereof; or abridging the freedom of speech, or of the press; or the right of the people peaceably to assemble, and to petition the Government for a redress of grievances.

## Amendment IV [1791]

The right of the people to be secure in their persons, houses, papers, and effects, against unreasonable searches and seizures, shall not be violated, and no Warrants shall issue, but upon probable cause, supported by Oath or affirmation, and particularly describing the place to be searched, and the persons or things to be seized.

## Amendment V [1791]

No person shall be ... compelled in any criminal case to be a witness against himself, nor be deprived of life, liberty, or property, without due process of law; nor shall private property be taken for public use, without just compensation.

## Amendment VIII [1791]

Excessive bail shall not be required, nor excessive fines imposed, nor cruel and unusual punishments inflicted.

## Amendment IX [1791]

The enumeration in the Constitution, of certain rights, shall not be construed to deny or disparage others retained by the people.

## Amendment X [1791]

The powers not delegated to the United States by the Constitution, nor prohibited by it to the States, are reserved to the States respectively, or to the people.

## Amendment XIV [1791]

Section 1. All persons born or naturalized in the United States, and subject to the jurisdiction thereof, are citizens of the United States and of the State wherein they reside. No State shall make or enforce any law which shall abridge the privileges or immunities of citizens of the United States; nor shall any State deprive any person of life, liberty, or property, without due process of law; nor deny to any person within its jurisdiction the equal protection of the laws.

# 4. Budget and Finance

### 4:1. How are public schools funded in Maryland?

Public schools in Maryland, like all public schools in the nation, rely on the combined contributions of federal, state, and local revenues. Major federal funding programs include Title I (aid targeted for low-income students), the federal school lunch program (subsidizing daily school lunches for low-income students), special education (targeting funding for federally mandated services), and impact aid (targeting funding for school systems serving children living on federal lands and military bases).

Maryland's State education aid programs are funded through formulas allocating per pupil funding to local school systems based on general enrollment, and the numbers of special education, limited English proficient, and low-income students. Maryland does not have any designated revenue source for education funding, such as the state lottery. However, the State property tax is the designated source of funding for debt service, including the State's substantial share of capital debt payments for public school construction projects.

Local funding for public schools is provided by the 23 county governments and Baltimore City from revenue sources including local property and income taxes. Local contributions are subject to an annual maintenance of effort requirement.

Supplementing these government funds are private sources of funding which vary from large grants from foundations, such as the Gates Foundation, to the modest funds routinely raised by school-based parent/teacher groups.

## Federal Funding

### 4:2. What is Title I?

This federal program provides financial assistance through State educational agencies (SEAs) to local educational agencies (LEAs) with public schools with high numbers or percentages of children from low-income families to help ensure that all children meet State academic content and student academic achievement standards. The program requires LEAs to target Title I funds to public schools with the highest percentages of children from low-income families. Schools enrolling at least 40 percent of students from poor families are eligible to use Title I funds for school-wide programs that serve all children in the school. Under Title I, local educational agencies (LEAs) are also required to provide services for eligible private school students, as well as eligible public school students.

## 4:3. Is federal funding provided for the federal No Child Left Behind Act (NCLB)?

Yes, in that the major component of NCLB is Title I. However, a common criticism of NCLB is that federal funding has not been increased commensurately with the scope of new requirements NCLB imposes on states and local school systems. Following the enactment of NCLB in 2002, Congress made an initial effort to put significantly more money into Title I, which is NCLB's main funding source. But for fiscal year 2004, funding was increased by just 5 percent. Funding was then increased by 3 percent for FY 2005 and was cut slightly for FY 2006. The FY 2007 funding amount was not increased, and the President's proposed FY 2008 budget would provide $24.6 billion in funding for NCLB programs, the highest level of funding in NCLB's history, but still $14.8 billion less than specifically authorized.

In light of the federal funding scenario, Maryland's local school systems have been relatively fortunate to be receiving the significant funding increases under the State's Bridge to Excellence Act during the same years in which NCLB is being implemented. See **Chapter 8** for a detailed discussion of the No Child Left Behind Act.

## 4:4. Is federal funding provided for the Individuals with Disabilities Education Act (IDEA)?

Yes, in part. In 1975, Congress enacted the Individuals with Disabilities Education Act (IDEA) which guarantees all disabled students a "free, appropriate public education" (20 U.S.C. § 1400 *et seq.*). Overall the program serves more than 10 percent of the public school population. Because federal special education legislation resulted in additional costs to the public schools to provide special services, the legislation included the goal that the federal government would provide 40 percent of the extra costs. The federal government has never achieved this goal, providing approximately 15 to 20 percent. State and local governments must, therefore, fund the balance of mandated special education services.

Congress reauthorized IDEA in 2004, as the Individuals with Disabilities Education Improvement Act (IDEIA), and issued final regulations in 2006. The amended law authorizes significant funding increases which, if appropriated, would achieve the 40 percent goal by 2011. In addition, the amended law makes several changes to funding provisions, including:

- Establishes new formulas for determining the maximum amount a state can receive based on certain factors and a new formula for allocating any increase in appropriations over the previous fiscal year, based on a state's relative population of children with disabilities and based on the relative population of children with disabilities who are living in poverty;

- Establishes risk pools for local school systems to provide additional funding for the education of high-need students and the new enrollments of students with disabilities;

- Caps the amount of funds that may be used for administration at the fiscal year 2004 level and allows states to retain an increased portion for other required state level activities; and

- Authorizes local school systems to reduce expenditures on certain programs below the prior year's levels, up to an amount equivalent to 50 percent of new federal special education funding each year, as long as an equivalent amount of local funds is used for activities authorized under NCLB.

### 4:5. What is the federal school lunch program and how is it funded?

The federal government administers the National School Lunch and Breakfast Programs. The School Lunch Program is intended to ensure access for all students to a nutritious lunch. This program also offers afterschool snacks in sites that meet eligibility requirements. The Breakfast Program provides nutritious breakfasts to promote learning readiness and healthy eating behaviors.

Schools receive federal funds for each lunch served, provided that the meal meets established nutrition standards. The federal government and states provide additional funds to schools for each meal served to children who qualify because of family income, for free or reduced-price meals.

Congress reauthorized the Child Nutrition and WIC Reauthorization Act in 2004, which includes the national school lunch and breakfast programs (42 U.S.C. §§ 1751, 1760, 1779 *et seq.*). The amended law makes several policy and funding changes. A major policy change is the requirement that each local school system adopt new comprehensive school wellness policies. Funding provisions include the continuation of the requirement that school districts audit only 3 percent of student applications for free and reduced-price lunches to verify the families' financial eligibility. In addition, the law strengthens the household income verification process by requiring targeted audits of free and reduced-price lunch recipients in order to ensure their financial eligibility, rather than using random samples for audits.

### 4:6. What is "impact aid"?

Many local school districts across the United States include within their boundaries parcels of land that are owned by the federal government or that have been removed from the local tax rolls by the federal government, including military installations and Indian lands. Because such property is exempt from local property taxes, the primary source of local public education funding, local school systems often confront a major challenge of funding public education with less local revenue than is available to other school districts.

Since 1950, Congress has provided financial assistance to local school districts through the Impact Aid Program (20 U.S.C. § 7703). Approximately half of Maryland's 24 school systems receive some Impact Aid, with Anne Arundel and St. Mary's Counties receiving the majority of these funds. School districts use Impact Aid for a wide variety of expenses, including the salaries of teachers and teacher aides; purchasing textbooks, computers, and other equipment; after-school programs and remedial tutoring; advanced placement classes; and special enrichment programs. Payments for Children with Disabilities must be used for the extra costs of educating these children.

Impact aid was the subject of a recently decided Supreme Court case addressing the question of whether the methodology used by the U.S. Department of Education in determining whether New Mexico's state funding system is equalized is based on a permissible interpretation of the Impact Aid statute. The Court rejected the local school district's claim that it was entitled to significantly more funding on a per pupil basis than the state distributed statewide on a district basis (*Zuni Public School District No. 89 v. Department of Education*, 550 U.S. ___ (2007)).

## State Funding

### 4:7. What role does the Maryland Constitution/Declaration of Rights play regarding public school funding?

Article VIII, Section 1, of the Maryland Constitution mandates that the General Assembly "shall by Law establish throughout the State a thorough and efficient System of Free Public Schools; and shall provide by taxation, or otherwise, for their maintenance." Section 3 further provides that "The School Fund of the State shall be kept inviolate, and appropriated only to the purposes of Education."

### 4:8. What is the "general state school fund"?

Maryland statute broadly defines the "general state school fund" as all money appropriated by the General Assembly to aid in support of public schools, with limited exceptions.

The State Comptroller shall charge against and, as provided in this section, pay from the General State School Fund annual appropriations for the following:

- The Maryland State Department of Education, State Board, and office of the State Superintendent;

- The Maryland Teachers' Retirement System;

- The education of disabled children;

- Subsidized or free feeding programs;

- Career and technology education;

- Physical education and recreation;

- Case and guidance service for individuals with disabilities who need vocational rehabilitation;

- Equivalence examinations;

- Public libraries;

- Adult education;

- The State share of the foundation program;

- Student transportation;

- School building construction aid;

- State funding for compensatory education;

- State funding for students with limited English proficiency;

- State funding for special education; and

- The Guaranteed Tax Base program.

## 4:9. How is State funding disbursed to local school systems?

The Education Article provides for bi-monthly installments of State aid to be paid by the State Comptroller to each local school system per the certification of the State Superintendent. On receipt of the warrant of the State Comptroller, the State Treasurer pays the amount due to the treasurer of each county board. Payments are disbursed ten days before the end of July, September, November, January, March, and May (Md. Code Ann., Ed. Art. § 5-212(a)). Payments include the portion of the annual State share of funding for education programs outlined above.

## 4:10. What is the difference between an operating budget and capital budget?

The operating budget supports the day-to-day operation of the school system, including the provision of salaries and benefits for teachers and other staff; textbooks, supplies and other materials; and other operational needs of schools and administrative offices. The capital budget supports school construction and other major projects related to school facilities, such as additions, renovations, roof replacements, and the purchase and/or relocation of portable classrooms. This chapter focuses exclusively on operating budget issues; capital budget issues are covered in **Chapter 5**.

## 4:11. How is the state's education budget prepared?

Each year, the Maryland State Department of Education (MSDE) prepares its budget requests to the Governor in the form of three separate budgets corresponding to funding for the administration of the department (Headquarters), state aid to the 24 local school systems (Aid to Education), and grants to numerous institutions to supplement their educational functions (Aid to Educational Organizations). The State Board typically approves the department's budget proposal in late summer in advance of the State's budget.

## 4:12. What is included in the State Aid to Educational Organizations budget?

The State budget annually funds grants administered by MSDE to over 30 institutions that provide educational services, such as the Chesapeake Bay Foundation and the Baltimore Zoo.

## 4:13. What other public education programs are funded by the State?

In addition to the public schools operated by local school boards, and the aid to education organizations described above, the state funds allocated to MSDE include funding for correctional education and vocational rehabilitation for the disabled. The State also funds the Maryland School for the Deaf and the Maryland School for the Blind. The School for the Deaf is responsible for the education and personal development of deaf school-age children residing in the State and in attendance at the school. The Maryland School for the Blind, which is a private, nonprofit organization that serves students who are blind or visually impaired, receives most of its operating funds from a State grant. In 2006, legislation approved the creation of a new state boarding school for at-risk youth to be administered by MSDE.

## 4:14. What is meant by "wealth equalization" of state education funding?

The State's share of education funding, which is calculated and distributed on a per pupil basis, is adjusted according to the county's taxable wealth, so that school systems with relatively smaller tax bases receive proportionally more state aid. For example, Maryland's wealthiest counties receive thousands of dollars less per pupil than the least wealthy counties.

One of the recommendations of the Commission on Education Finance, Equity and Excellence was to increase the percentage of State aid that is wealth equalized. The Commission sought to increase the overall percentage of State aid that is wealth equalized from 65 percent in fiscal 2002 to 80 percent in fiscal 2007.

## 4:15. What is meant by "local wealth"?

For the purpose of calculating state education aid, a county's wealth is calculated as the sum of the county's: net taxable income; 100 percent of the assessed value of the operating real property of public utilities; 40 percent of the assessed valuation of all other real property; and 50 percent of the assessed value of personal property (Md. Code Ann., Ed. Art. § 5-202(a)(14)).

## 4:16. What is the *Hornbeck* decision and how has it affected school funding?

In 1983, the Court of Appeals rejected an "equity" challenge to the state's education finance system, in *Hornbeck v. Somerset County Board of Education*, 295 Md. 597 (1983), holding that the state constitution did not mandate equality in per-pupil spending among the state's school districts. However, the court also held that the education clause of the Maryland constitution embodies a right to "an adequate education measured by contemporary educational standards." Thus, Maryland's highest court upheld the constitutionality of the state's system of public school funding.

Maryland's highest court, in *Montgomery County v. Bradford*, 345 Md. 175 (1997), characterized the *Hornbeck* decision as follows:

> While *Hornbeck* teaches that the Maryland constitutional provision does not mandate uniformity in per pupil funding or require that the system operate uniformly in every school district, it does require that the General Assembly establish a Statewide system to provide an adequate public school education to the children in every school district.

## 4:17. What is the *Bradford* decision and how has it affected school funding?

In December 1994, the American Civil Liberties Union (ACLU), on behalf of Baltimore City school children, sued the State in the Baltimore City Circuit Court alleging that the children of Baltimore are not receiving an adequate education as required under the State constitution. In September 1995, Baltimore City also filed suit in Circuit Court against the State Superintendent of Schools and other State officials claiming that the State had failed to fulfill its duty to provide a "thorough and efficient" education for children as provided in the State Constitution. The State responded by filing to include Baltimore City officials as defendants in the ACLU lawsuit. The State claimed that if the children of Baltimore are not receiving an adequate education, it is a result of poor management by the Baltimore City Public Schools. The State called for a total restructuring of the management of the city school system. The Circuit Court for Baltimore City brokered a Consent

Decree, signed by all parties, agreeing that $254,000,000 of state funding "shall be provided" to the Baltimore City Schools over a five-year period.

The *Bradford* case, which remains open to this day, prompted 1997 legislation to abolish and restructure the Baltimore City Board of Education and launched several years of significant increases in annual State funding for the City's school system. The *Bradford* plaintiffs returned to court in 2000, and the circuit court declared that the state "is still not providing the children of Baltimore City . . . a constitutionally adequate education," and had failed to comply with the 1996 Consent Decree. The court ordered the state to provide "additional funding of approximately $2,000 to $2,600 per pupil" in 2001 and 2002. *Bradford's* impact extends beyond Baltimore City in that it laid the foundation for the statewide adequacy analysis and funding increases that would follow.

### 4:18. What is meant by the Baltimore City "partnership" or "remedy plan"?

The *Bradford* lawsuit resulted in a consent agreement between the State and the City that called for Baltimore City to receive $254 million in new State aid over the next five years. The Consent Decree's funding agreement was conditioned on the creation, in statute, of a partnership between the State and the Baltimore City School System. The provisions of the consent agreement were incorporated into 1997 legislation providing Baltimore City with an additional $30 million in aid in fiscal 1998 and $50 million annually in fiscal 1999 through fiscal 2002 (Senate Bill 795, Chapter 105, Laws of Maryland, 1997). The partnership grants were extended by subsequent legislation, expiring after the final 2006 grant of $14,093,016.

The "Baltimore City partnership" also included provisions requiring additional funds to be used to improve the educational performance of schools with a high percentage of students living in poverty and targeting schools eligible for reconstitution. Personnel initiatives included the goal of teacher salary parity with Baltimore County, and the use of a new performance-based, system-wide evaluation system for teachers, principals, and administrators.

Statewide provisions of the "partnership" bill included increased funding for a new targeted poverty program, limited English proficiency grants, Aging Schools Program grants, the Extended Elementary Education Program, teacher mentoring, magnet schools, and gifted and talented programs.

### 4:19. What is the "Thornton Commission"?

The Commission on Education Finance, Equity, and Excellence, commonly referred to as the "Thornton Commission" for its chairman, Dr. Alvin Thornton, was created by the General Assembly in 1999. The 27-member commission was charged with reviewing the State's public school finance system and accountability measures and making recommendations: (1) for ensuring adequacy of funding for students in public schools; (2) for ensuring equity in funding for students in public schools; (3) for ensuring excellence in school systems and student performance; (4) providing for a smooth transition when current educational funding initiatives sunset at the end of fiscal 2002; (5) regarding the issue of whether it is more effective to provide additional State aid in the form of targeted grants or by increasing funding through the base formula; and (6) for ensuring that local property tax policies do not affect the equitable allocation of funding for students in public schools.

The Commission contracted with Augenblick and Myers, a Colorado-based firm nationally recognized for its education adequacy analysis and involvement in litigation, to conduct analyses and make recommendations regarding the adequacy and equity of Maryland's school finance system. The Commission issued an interim report in December 2000 and a final report in January 2002; the final report was the basis for the Bridge to Excellence in Public Schools Act of 2002 (*Commission on Education Finance, Equity, and Excellence – Final Report* (*Final Report*) (2002), available at *http://mlis.state.md.us/other/education/final/contents.pdf*).

### 4:20. What is meant by the term "equity"?

Generally, the goal of "equity" in education funding refers to the belief that educational opportunities should not depend on a jurisdiction's relative ability to raise revenue from local sources, and the corresponding need for adjustments in the allocation of State aid. The Thornton Commission and Bridge to Excellence Act adhere to Maryland's longstanding public policy establishing a State school funding system that wealth-equalizes education aid so that per pupil State aid in less wealthy jurisdictions is greater than per pupil State aid in more wealthy jurisdictions.

### 4:21. What is meant by the term "adequacy?

The Thornton Commission recommendations and Bridge to Excellence Act are premised on the belief that there should be a direct link between what is expected of school systems in terms of student performance and the level of State funding that school systems receive. Thus Maryland has adopted a State school finance system that defines "adequacy" as the total projected costs associated with meeting State performance standards, including the additional costs associated with providing services to students with special needs, *e.g.*, special education, limited English proficient, and economically disadvantaged (*Final Report*, p. 13).

## 4:22. How did the Thornton Commission determine adequacy?

The Commission contracted with Augenblick and Myers to conduct a two-pronged adequacy study using the "professional judgment" and the "successful schools" approaches. Both methods work under the theory that adequacy has two components: (1) a base cost per pupil common to all districts (the parameter that could be used to establish the per student aid amount that is distributed under Maryland's foundation program); and (2) a series of adjustments to the base to reflect the cost pressures associated with different pupils, different programs, or different characteristics of school districts.

The professional judgment approach used multiple panels of educators to determine the kinds of resources needed to achieve a particular set of objectives in prototypical elementary, middle, and high schools. The resources identified by the panels were then "priced out" based on salary levels and other factors to determine the per pupil costs. The successful schools approach examined the basic spending of schools meeting performance objectives established by the State.

## 4:23. What role does county funding have in achieving "adequacy"?

The Thornton Commission acknowledged that State funding increases alone will not achieve funding adequacy. Therefore, the Bridge to Excellence Act is premised on the expectation of significant increases in county funding for education through 2008. The Commission estimated that if counties provide future increases in education funding comparable to the increases provided between 1997 and 2000, most school systems would meet or exceed the adequacy goals. While the Commission recognized that reaching adequacy by FY 2008 will require additional local funding, the Act did not enhance the statutory minimum maintenance of effort (MOE) requirement that counties maintain per pupil funding levels from one fiscal year to the next.

## 4:24. What is meant by a "standards-based" school finance system?

Generally, aligning the allocation of state education aid with goals and objectives for student performance is broadly referred to as a "standards-based" approach to school financing. According to the final report of the Thornton Commission and its primary consultant, Augenblick & Myers: "the primary obligations of a State in a standards-based education system are to: (1) establish performance standards for students, schools, and school systems; (2) ensure that schools and school systems have adequate funding necessary to meet the State's performance standards; and (3) hold schools and school systems accountable for making progress toward, and ultimately meeting, the State's performance standards" (*Final Report*, p. 59).

## 4:25. What is the Bridge to Excellence in Public Education Act?

In 2002, Maryland adopted the Bridge to Excellence in Public Schools Act, which was based on the recommendations of the Commission on Education Finance, Equity, and Excellence, and intended to align the allocation of state education aid with goals and objectives for student performance. This approach is broadly referred to as a "standards-based" approach to school financing.

## 4:26. What is foundation aid?

The Bridge to Excellence Act redefined not only state funding calculations for three special needs categories (compensatory, special education, and limited English proficient), but also the per pupil amount for the remaining, or general, education student population. This general "foundation" per pupil amount, previously referred to as the basic current expense amount, is the basis on which all state funding is calculated. Statute sets the foundation amount ($4,124) and applies various formulas to this amount to determine the annual increases mandated by the Bridge to Excellence Act, and the increased per pupil amounts for each of the three special needs categories.

## 4:27. Is state education aid adjusted for inflation?

The U.S. Commerce Department calculates the implicit price deflator for state and local governments as a measure of inflation that is based on the set of goods and services that state and local governments typically purchase. The Thornton Commission utilized the implicit price deflator to develop its projected FY 2007 adequacy costs and began to apply the implicit price deflator as an inflation adjustment in FY 2003. Beginning in FY 2009, following the FY 2003 through FY 2008 increases mandated by the Bridge to Excellence Act, increases in state education aid will be determined in accordance with the implicit price deflator for state and local governments (Md. Code Ann., Ed. Art. § 5-202(a)(13)).

## 4:28. What is compensatory aid?

A local school system receives enhanced, or weighted, per pupil state aid for each student eligible for compensatory education aid. To be eligible for compensatory aid, a student must have been eligible for free or reduced price meals for the prior fiscal year. The increased compensatory education per pupil amount is defined as 97 percent more than the annual per pupil foundation amount calculated under Section 5-202 of the Education Article multiplied by the State share of compensatory education funding. "Eligible for free or reduced price meals" means eligible for free or reduced price meals based on eligibility requirements established by the United States Department of Agriculture. This supplemental state aid is wealth equalized, and the State per pupil amount may not fall below a certain minimum amount (Md. Code Ann., Ed. Art. § 5-207).

### 4:29. What is limited English proficient aid?

A local school system receives enhanced, or weighted, per pupil state aid for each "limited English proficient" (LEP) student. The additional LEP per pupil amount is defined as 99 percent more than the annual per pupil foundation amount calculated under Section 5-202 of the Education Article multiplied by the State share of LEP funding. "Limited English proficiency" is defined under the reporting requirements established by MSDE. This state aid is wealth equalized, and the State per pupil amount may not fall below a certain minimum amount (Md. Code Ann., Ed. Art. § 5-208). Again, this results in a per pupil allocation for LEP students that is double the foundation amount.

### 4:30. What is special education aid and how is it funded?

Federal law requires states to provide an education to all students with disabilities through age 20 who are found to be in need of special education services. Services must begin as soon as the child can benefit from them, regardless of whether the child is of school age. Federal funding supplements the significant State and local expenditures to provide the enhanced services required to ensure a free and appropriate public education (FAPE) for each identified disabled student.

Most students receive special education services through their county school system. However, if required services are not available through the public schools, students may be placed in appropriate nonpublic programs.

A local school system receives enhanced, or weighted, per pupil state aid for each "special education student" requiring services defined in the federal Individuals with Disabilities Education Act. The increased special education per pupil amount is defined as 74 percent of the annual per pupil foundation amount calculated under Section 5-202 of the Education Article multiplied by the State share of special education funding. This state aid is wealth equalized, and the State per pupil amount may not fall below a certain minimum amount (Md. Code Ann., Ed. Art. § 5-209).

### 4:31. How are services funded for special education students enrolled in nonpublic facilities?

The State and the counties share in the cost of educating children with disabilities in nonpublic programs under Section 8-406 of the Education Article. The county contribution is three times the basic per pupil amount, representing the sum of the local share of the basic cost and an additional amount equal to 200 percent of the basic cost. In addition, the county is responsible for an amount not to exceed 20 percent of the approved cost or reimbursement in excess of this sum. The State is thereby responsible for 80 percent of the costs exceeding the total local contribution (Md. Code Ann., Ed. Art. § 8-415).

## 4:32. What is the guaranteed tax base program?

The Thornton Commission recommended, and the Bridge to Excellence Act established, a Guaranteed Tax Base (GTB) program to provide local governments in low-wealth counties with a financial incentive to fund public schools. The Bridge to Excellence Act allocated funding for the GTB program based on local wealth and local education tax effort.

Section 5-210 of the Education Article defines and mandates state funding for GTB program grants for a local board of education if the county's additional education effort is greater than zero; and local wealth per pupil is less than the guaranteed wealth per pupil. "Additional education effort" is defined as a county's additional education appropriation divided by the county's wealth, rounded to seven decimal places. And, "additional education appropriation" means the difference between a county's education appropriation for the prior fiscal year and the county's local share of the foundation program calculated under Section 5-202 of the Education Article. "Guaranteed wealth per pupil" means 80 percent of the statewide wealth per pupil. "Local wealth per pupil" means a county's wealth divided by the county's full-time equivalent enrollment. "Statewide wealth per pupil" means the sum of the wealth of all counties divided by the statewide full-time equivalent enrollment.

The GTB per pupil amount is defined as the lesser of 20 percent of the annual per pupil foundation amount calculated under Section 5-202; and the product of a county's additional education effort and the difference between guaranteed wealth per pupil and local wealth per pupil (Md. Code Ann., Ed. Art. § 5-210).

## 4:33. What is the Geographic Cost of Education Index?

The Thornton Commission recommended that State aid be adjusted to reflect differences in the cost of providing educational services in different jurisdictions. The Commission used the Geographic Cost of Education Index (GCEI) prepared for the National Center for Education Statistics (NCES) as the best existing estimate of these differences. The GCEI is referred to as a "hedonic" cost index that estimates the different costs of hiring personnel in different geographic areas based on cost of living differences as well as the desirability of intangible factors present in the region that may influence employment decisions, such as crime rate and weather. The Bridge to Excellence Act used the NCES index and called for MSDE to develop a Maryland-specific index to be used beginning in fiscal 2005.

Unfortunately, despite the index being developed, adopted in statute, and determined to warrant more than $100 million in additional foundation aid, the Attorney General has opined that this provision of the Act is not mandatory and neither the Governor or legislature has ever included GCEI funding in the State budget (Md. Code Ann., Ed. Art. § 5-202(f)).

### 4:34. How is State funding calculated for student transportation?

The Bridge to Excellence Act established 2003 "base grant amounts" for each county and mandates annual increases to this amount and to each subsequent year's amount based on enrollment growth, and also the percentage increase in the private transportation category of the Consumer Price Index for all urban consumers, for the Washington-Baltimore metropolitan area, as of July of the fiscal year preceding the year for which the amount is being calculated. The increase in the amount of a base grant for student transportation that is based on the increase in the private transportation category of the Consumer Price Index may not be less than 3 percent nor more than 8 percent of the amount of the grant for the previous year (Md. Code Ann., Ed. Art. § 5-205).

The statute also allows a local school system to carry over any unexpended transportation funds, while prohibiting any transfer of these carried-over funds from the student transportation category to any other category.

### 4:35. Is additional per pupil funding provided for the transportation of disabled students?

Yes. In addition to the base grant for student transportation, beginning in fiscal 2008, a $1,000 disabled student transportation grant is required to be distributed to each county board. The amount of the grant to each board is based on the number of disabled students requiring special transportation services who are transported by the county board in the previous fiscal year (Md. Code Ann., Ed. Art. § 5-205(d)).

### 4:36. How is mandated full-day kindergarten funded?

The Thornton Commission recommended that full-day kindergarten be mandated in all local school systems by fiscal 2007. The implementation deadline was extended to the 2007-2008 school year by the Bridge to Excellence Act, which adopted the funding mechanism of incrementally increasing the 0.5 kindergarten full time equivalent (FTE) count by 0.1 each fiscal year, arriving at a full 1.0 FTE count by the end of the implementation period in fiscal 2008.

Unfortunately, the incremental increase in state per pupil funding not only lags behind the need to meet the 2007-2008 deadline, but also failed to provide the necessary capital funding to expand facilities to accommodate new classrooms as schools expanded half-day programs to full-day.

### 4:37. How is mandated targeted pre-kindergarten funded?

State law requires that, by the 2007-2008 school year, every school system provide full-day kindergarten for all eligible students and pre-kindergarten programs for all economically disadvantaged four-year-old children. After fiscal 2007, the law eliminates special funding for the Extended Elementary Education Program (EEEP) and replaces the program's funding with enhanced formula funding for at-risk students through the compensatory aid program.

## Local Funding

### 4:38. What are the major expenses for a public school system?

Employee salaries and benefits typically represent 80 to 90 percent of a school system's total operating budget. Benefits funded in the school system budget include health insurance, life insurance, retirement contributions, social security taxes, workers compensation, and unemployment insurance. The remainder of the budget represents expenditures for textbooks and other instructional supplies, "non-public placement" tuition for special education students who must attend private schools, utilities such as electricity and natural gas, food for school lunches, and school buses and bus fuel. In addition, school system operating and capital budgets include funding for school facility maintenance, renovations, and construction.

### 4:39. Do school boards in Maryland have taxing authority?

No. Unlike the vast majority of the 15,000 local school boards throughout the nation, Maryland's 24 local boards do not have any authority to determine and collect *ad valorem*, Latin for "according to the value," property taxes for the operation of the school system. Most school systems outside of Maryland identify the amount of money needed in the upcoming fiscal year and identify the corresponding property tax rate needed to generate that amount. Whether and to what extent the approval of local residents is required to enact the increased rate varies among districts. Maryland's school systems are entirely fiscally dependent on revenues collected by county, state, and federal governments.

### 4:40. What is the role of county government in funding public education?

Although local school boards enjoy significant autonomy, the county governments establish the overall level of funding for the public schools. School boards must submit their budgets to the county governing body. The budget submission includes revenues and expenditures by major category, as established by State law and the State Board of Education. The county governing body reviews, modifies, and approves the budget. Any reductions are made by major category. The high degree of county government control regarding the school system budget is a function of the dominant role of local funding as percentage of the total school budget. Because state funding is wealth equalized, local funding in a wealthier county can represent 60 to 70 percent of the operating budget. Correspondingly, local funding may represent 30 to 40 percent of the budget in a less wealth county.

## 4:41. Does the State or local government control the school system budget process?

Local boards "are subject to the county, not the State, budget process" and must justify their budget requirements to county governments, which, "subject to certain limitations and requirements, have ultimate approval power over" annual school budgets (*Chesapeake Charter, Inc. v. Anne Arundel County Board of Education,* 358 Md. 129 (2000)). In addition, the local board is to follow county budget procedures not inconsistent with State law (68 Op. Att'y Gen. No. 236 (1983)).

## 4:42. What are the sources of local revenue for public education?

Local property taxes and local "piggy-back" income taxes are the primary sources of revenue for county governments and, therefore the primary sources of revenue for the county share of education funding. Local property taxes represent the largest single source of county revenue and are generating an increased share of local revenues as assessments have climbed in recent years. Local income tax rates also have risen. Prior to 1993, counties had the authority to levy a local income tax at a rate between 20 percent and 50 percent of the state income tax rate. Since 1993, counties have been authorized to raise their rates above 50 percent.

## 4:43. Are counties required to levy taxes for public education?

Yes. County governments are required to levy and collect local income taxes, property taxes, and other revenues which will "produce the amounts necessary to meet the appropriations made in the approved annual budget of the county board" (Md. Code Ann., Ed. Art. § 5-104(a)).

## 4:44. What is the timeline for the development and adoption of the local school system's budget?

Each local school system begins to craft the next fiscal year's budget even as the current budget year is concluding. The fiscal year begins on July 1 and ends on June 30; requiring the initial development of the next year's budget no later than the fall. During the fall, the board of education may hold public meetings or conduct other community engagement strategies to identify and communicate priorities for the coming year. The local superintendent typically presents to the board a recommended budget between November and January, followed by local board hearings and deliberations in work sessions. The local board adopts its final budget in late winter/early spring in order to provide the opportunity for review, amendment, and approval by the county government. Importantly, throughout this timeline the school system is often engaged in negotiations with multiple employee unions regarding the salaries and benefits that constitute the overwhelming majority of the budget being developed.

The deadline by which a local board must submit its budget to the county government is prescribed in statute as "not less than 45 days before the date for levying local taxes or an earlier date on or after March 1 as may be requested by the county fiscal authority" (Md. Code Ann., Ed. Art. § 5-102(b)(2)).

## 4:45. What is the role of the local superintendent in the budget process?

Local superintendents are required by statute to prepare, and advocate for adequate local funding for, the school budget. "The county superintendent shall: (1) Take the initiative in the preparation and presentation of the annual school budget; and (2) Seek in every way to secure adequate funds from local authorities for the support and development of the public schools in the county" (Md. Code Ann., Ed. Art. § 4-205(k)).

## 4:46. What is the role of the local board of education in the budget process?

With the advice of the local superintendent, the local board is responsible for preparing the school system budget in accordance with the state statutory and regulatory requirements for submitting its budget to the county government (Md. Code Ann., Ed. Art. §§ 5-101 and 5-102). In addition, the local board sets the parameters for employee compensation and other terms of the pending collective bargaining agreements; identifies educational goals and objectives for the superintendent to implement; and engages the public in the process of identifying budget priorities.

### 4:47. Is the local board's budget process open to the public?

A local board may choose to conduct its budget formulation process in public, and must conduct its budget consideration process in public pursuant to the state's Open Meetings Act (Md. Code Ann., St. Gov't Art. §§ 10-501 to 10-512). Maryland's Open Meeting Compliance Board has opined that the local board of education's budget process is subject to a distinction in the Open Meetings Act between "budget formulation" and "budget consideration" (Open Meetings Compliance Board Opinion 00-01(2000)). Recognizing that local boards perform legislative, quasi-judicial, and executive functions, the Compliance Board concluded that the local board's development of the budget is an executive function, not subject to the Open Meetings Act, and the consideration and approval of the proposed budget is a legislative function subject to the Act.

### 4:48. How are funds appropriated to the local board of education?

Generally, federal, state, and local funding received by the local school system is passed through the county government and disbursed to the treasurer of the local school system, which is the local superintendent. A school system may receive federal grants, private grants, and other funds directly from other public or private sources.

### 4:49. What are the budget categories?

Each local school system is required by statute to classify all expenditures by one of 14 major categories. Categories correspond to the purpose of expenditures, allowing for consistent comparisons among districts according to each type of expenditures. The local government in each county allocates funds to public schools by category totals and the local board is required to allocate funds within each category total. Section 5-101 of the Education Article defines the budget categories as follows:

### Operating Budget Categories

Current Expense Fund (Part I)

(1) **Current expense fund, estimated receipts**:

(i) Revenue from local sources;

(ii) Revenue from State sources;

(iii) Revenue from federal sources;

(iv) Unliquidated surplus;

(v) Revenue from all other sources with identification of the source.

(2) **Current expense fund, requested appropriations**:

(i) Administration, which means those activities associated with the general regulations, direction, and control of the county board, including:

    1. Executive administration;

    2. Business support services; and

    3. Centralized support services;

(ii) Mid-level administration, including:

    1. The office of the school principal; and

    2. Staff providing administration and supervision to the school instructional programs;

(iii) Instructional salaries, which means those activities which deal directly with teaching students, including:

    1. Teachers;

    2. Aides;

    3. Psychological personnel;

    4. Guidance counselors; and

    5. Library personnel;

(iv) Textbooks and classroom instructional supplies;

(v) Other instructional costs;

(vi) Special education with subcategories and items budgeted in this category to be determined by the State Board with the advice of the county board;

(vii) Student personnel services;

(viii) Health services;

(ix) Student transportation;

(x) Operation of plant and equipment;

(xi) Maintenance of plant;

(xii) Fixed charges;

(xiii) Food services; and

(xiv) Capital outlay.

## Capital Budget Categories

School Construction Fund (Part II)

(3) **School construction fund, estimated receipts:**

(i) Revenue from local sources;

(ii) Sale of bonds;

(iii) State General Public School Construction Loan;

(iv) Revenue from State sources;

(v) Revenue from federal sources;

(vi) Unliquidated surplus, the actual from the previous fiscal year and the estimated for the current fiscal year, whether accrued from revenues or expenditures; and

(vii) Funds from all other sources, with identification of the source.

(4) **School Construction Fund, requested appropriations:**

(i) Land for school sites;

(ii) Buildings and the equipment that will be an integral part of a building by project;

(iii) School site improvement by project;

(iv) Remodeling by project;

(v) Additional equipment by project; and

(vi) Debt service.

### 4:50. May a school system transfer money from one category to another?

After approval of the budget, transfers between major expenditure categories must be submitted in writing and approved by the county governing body. If the county fails to act on transfer requests within 30 days, they are considered approved. Similarly, the expenditure of non-local funds received by the school board after the adoption of the budget requires notice to the county government and its approval of the funding source and manner of spending (Md. Code Ann., Ed. Art. § 5-105(c)).

## 4:51. What happens if a local board fails to notify the county government of a transfer?

A county governing body may notify MSDE that a local board has not complied with one or more reporting requirements or expenditure limitations and if the State Superintendent determines that a violation has occurred without reasonable justification, for the next fiscal year following the final determination of a violation, the county board may not make a category expenditure, as defined by the Maryland Board of Education reporting manual, in excess of the category expenditure in the operating budget approved by the county governing body without the prior approval of the county governing body (Md. Code Ann., Ed. Art. § 5-113).

## 4:52. Must the county council accept the county executive's budget amendments?

In jurisdictions with a county executive, the executive reviews the budget submitted by the local board first, and may amend it before submitting it to the county council. However, with the exception of Baltimore County, the council may restore any reductions made by the county executive to the proposed school board budget. Note that this distinction does not apply to the majority of the counties which have a commissioner form of government that combines the executive and legislative functions in one body.

## 4:53. What is maintenance of effort?

There is a county maintenance of effort requirement in State law. To receive an increase in State foundation aid and compensatory aid, a local government must appropriate at least as much funding per pupil to the local board of education as it appropriated in the previous fiscal year. The total amount of the county's appropriation to the school operating budget in the prior fiscal year is presumed to be the baseline amount for the maintenance of effort requirement (76 Op. Att'y Gen. No. 91-013 (1991)). The statute further prohibits any shifts between a county operating budget and a county school operating budget intended to artificially satisfy this statutory provision (Md. Code Ann., Ed. Art. § 5-202(d)(2)). Certain non-recurring costs (see **4:56**) may be excluded from the maintenance of effort if approved by the State Board. In addition, the State Board may grant a county government experiencing fiscal problems a temporary or partial waiver of the maintenance of effort requirement.

**4:54. How is the maintenance of effort requirement enforced?**

State education aid is, in part, conditioned on the county government's satisfying the following requirements. To be eligible to receive the State share of the foundation program, a county governing body must:

- levy an annual tax sufficient to provide an amount of revenue for elementary and secondary public education purposes equal to the local share of the foundation program; and

- appropriate local funds to the school operating budget in an amount no less than the product of the county's full-time equivalent enrollment for the current fiscal year and the local appropriation on a per pupil basis for the prior fiscal year (Md. Code Ann., Ed. Art. § 5-202(d)(1)).

**4:55. Are all operating budget allocations include in the calculation of the next year's maintenance of effort amount?**

No. Counties may fund certain "non-recurring cost" items without that expenditure increasing the annual operating budget figure that determines the next year's minimum maintenance of effort requirement. Since 1984, counties must exclude from the calculation of the county's highest local appropriation to its school operating budget for the prior fiscal year:

- A nonrecurring cost that is supplemental to the regular school operating budget, if the exclusion qualifies under regulations adopted by the State Board; and

- A cost of a program that has been shifted from the county school operating budget to the county operating budget.

**4:56. What are non-recurring costs and how are they treated differently?**

Qualifying non-recurring costs are defined in statute (Md. Ann. Code, Ed. Art. § 5-202(d)(6)) as including, but not limited to:

- Computer laboratories;

- Technology enhancement;

- New instructional program start-up costs; and

- Books other than classroom textbooks.

State Board regulations, COMAR 13A.02.05.03, expand the statutory definition of non-recurring costs as follows:

2) Qualifying nonrecurring costs shall be limited to:

(a) Costs to establish new computer laboratories that include the cost for equipment, furniture, wiring, hardware, software, space renovations, and the initial up-front cost for staff development, and training but not ongoing costs such as maintenance, staff salaries, staff development, and training;

(b) Costs for new technology that include the cost for equipment, furniture, wiring, hardware, software, space renovations, and the initial up-front cost for staff development, and training but not ongoing costs such as maintenance, staff salaries, staff development, and training;

(c) New instructional program start-up costs that include the cost for equipment, furniture, wiring, hardware, software, space renovations, textbooks, manipulatives, staff development, and training;

(d) Books other than classroom textbooks to establish a new library collection and new books required in new and renovated schools;

(e) Capital items with a useful life of 5 years or more that include the cost to acquire fixed assets other than land and buildings; and

(f) Other unique one-time costs that the local board and county mutually agree to be one-time expenditures.

### 4:57. What is the penalty for failing to satisfy maintenance of effort?

Section 5-213(a) of the Education Article provides that "after notification from the State Superintendent that a county is not complying with the provisions of the State program of public education, the State Comptroller shall withhold any installment due the county from the General State School Fund." The State Board must certify the determination of noncompliance and upon receipt of certification the Comptroller shall suspend, until notification of compliance is received, payment of any funds due the county for the current fiscal year, as provided under Section 5-202 of the Education Article, to the extent that the State's aid due the county in the current fiscal year exceeds the amount which the county received in the prior fiscal year.

**4:58. What effect can a local tax or revenue cap have on education funding?**

Five charter counties (Anne Arundel, Montgomery, Prince George's, Talbot, and Wicomico) have amended their charters to limit property tax rates or revenue growth. The impact of these provisions on local education funding is limited to the extent they impede funding in excess of maintenance of effort, which remains the statutory funding floor. In addition, the Guaranteed Tax Base Program is designed to reward low-wealth counties demonstrating a high level of education effort which, in turn, depends on the robust investment of local revenues.

**4:59. Does the State have the authority to override local revenue/tax caps?**

In 1977, the Court of Appeals held that the area of public education has been preempted by the State and that local governments lack the authority to enact laws regarding public education (*McCarthy v. Board of Education of Anne Arundel County*, 280 Md. 634 (1977)). Under the State's constitution, charter amendments that impose tax restrictions, like any other charter amendment, are subject to the General Laws of the State. Therefore, the State has the authority to enact legislation that overrides tax restrictions in a county's charter. The State also has the authority to enact legislation that establishes procedures that would allow a county to exceed a tax restriction for the purpose of funding public schools (79 Op. Att'y Gen. No. 94-057 (1994)).

In 1992, the Court of Appeals held that, even in the absence of State law that expressly supersedes a tax cap, a local tax cap may be found invalid if it prevents a county from performing its duties under State law (*Board v. Smallwood*, 327 Md. 220 (1992)). The Thornton Commission's final report in 2002 noted that while a tax restriction may begin to inhibit a jurisdiction's ability to raise local revenue and adequately fund education, three of the four counties that had tax restrictions in place from fiscal 1997 to 2002 increased funding for education at a rate that was equal to or greater than the State average (*Final Report*, pp. 46-48).

**4:60. Do municipalities have any role in funding public education?**

No. Maryland's municipal governments, other than Baltimore City which also functions as that jurisdiction's "county" government, have no statutory obligation or role in generating or allocating revenues for the provision of public education. Costs incurred by a municipal government may include transportation and other local infrastructure costs related to school facilities within their boundaries.

# Fiscal Accountability

## 4:61. What is meant by "fiscal accountability"?

State statute includes an array of fiscal accountability requirements for local school systems. Section 2-205(c) of the Education Article requires the State Board to adopt bylaws, rules, and regulations that govern the administration of the public school systems in Maryland and Section 2-205(o) empowers the State board to direct the local collection and reporting of financial records. Section 5-101 establishes the operating and capital budget categories and references the *Financial Reporting Manual for Maryland Public Schools*. Section 2-303 authorizes the State Superintendent to withhold funding if a school system violates the legal requirements identified in the laws, bylaws, and State board rules and regulations. Section 5-109 prescribes a uniform method of reporting receipts, expenditures, and balances of the operations and activities of the public schools. Pursuant to Section 5-109, the Code of Maryland Regulations further defines the Annual School Budget and Annual School Financial Report (COMAR 13A.02.01.02).

## 4:62. What accounting standards apply to a local school system?

Maryland's local school systems are required to maintain their accounts in accordance with the "generally accepted accounting principles", or GAAP, that are recognized by the American Institute of Certified Public Accountants and the Association of School Business Officials. GAAP for state and local governments are set by the National Council of Governmental Accounting, a group sponsored by the Government Finance Officers Association (GFOA). GFOA issues the publication, *Government Accounting, Auditing and Financial Reporting* (GAAFR), which provides practical guidance for implementing GAAP standards and is commonly referred to as "the blue book." In addition, the Government Accounting Standards Board (GASB) has incorporated these standards into its *Codification of Governmental Accounting and Financial Reporting Standards*.

Pursuant to the accounting standards referenced above, local school systems are required to use fund accounting, and the fund categories described in GAAFR. A fund is defined as a "fiscal and accounting entity with a self-balancing set of accounts recording cash and other financial resources, together with all related liabilities and residual equities or balances, and changes therein, which are segregated for the purpose of carrying on specific activities or attaining certain objectives in accordance with special regulations, restrictions, or limitations."

## 4:63. What is the State Financial Reporting Manual?

Section 5-101 of the Education Article establishes the budget categories and references the *Financial Reporting Manual for Maryland Public Schools* as the source for identifying additional budgetary details which the county fiscal authorities may request of the local board of education. The *Manual* was first developed and adopted by the Maryland State Board of Education in 1963 in response to the need for a uniform system of budgeting and reporting Maryland public school financial data. To provide uniform reporting at both the federal and state levels, the Manual was based upon the federal Handbook II, Financial Accounting for Local and State School Systems, issued by the U.S. Office of Education in 1957. The Manual has been updated several times, most recently in 1996, and another revision is ongoing.

Maryland's local school systems are required to adhere to the definitions and terms of the Manual when submitting expenditure information to MSDE. Failure to comply with the definitions and other requirements is a violation of State Board regulations and may be the basis for withholding State Aid in accordance with Sections 2-303(B) and 5-205(a) of the Education Article.

### 4:64. May a local school system carry a budget deficit?

No. The Fiscal Accountability Act of 2004 added a prohibition on deficit spending by a local board of education by prohibiting a local school system from carrying a deficit as reported in its annual audit. The Act defines "deficit" as "a negative fund balance in the General Fund of 1 percent or more of General Fund revenue at the end of the fiscal year" (Md. Code Ann., Ed. Art. § 5-114).

### 4:65. What happens if a local school system has a deficit?

If a local school system has a deficit, the State Superintendent shall immediately notify the Governor, the General Assembly, the Department of Legislative Services, and county governing body and shall require the local school system to:

(i) Develop and submit for approval a corrective action cost containment plan within 15 days;

(ii) File monthly status reports with the State Superintendent and county governing body demonstrating actions taken to close the deficit and the effect of the actions taken on the deficit; and

(iii) Include information on the corrective action cost containment plan, actions taken to close the deficit, and status of the deficit in the biannual financial status reports filed with the State Superintendent and county governing body (Md. Code Ann., Ed. Art. § 5-114).

## 4:66. What is the State's role in overseeing the finances of local school systems?

The State Superintendent and MSDE are required to monitor the financial status of each local school system and report on a biannual basis the financial status of each local school system to the Governor and General Assembly.

## 4:67. What are the responsibilities of a local school system regarding financial accountability?

Each local superintendent or chief executive officer of a local school system is required to file a biannual report on the financial status of the local school system with the superintendent and county governing body on or before April 30 and December 31 of each fiscal year and attest to the accuracy of each biannual report when the report is submitted to the superintendent and county governing body.

## 4:68. What are the audit requirements for local school systems?

Each local board is required to provide for an annual audit of its financial transactions and accounts. The audit must be made by a certified public accountant or a partnership of certified public accountants licensed by the State Board of Public Accountancy and approved by the State Superintendent. The audit must be made in accordance with the standards and regulations adopted by the State Board (Md. Code Ann., Ed. Art. § 5-109).

## 4:69. Are audit results available to the public?

Yes. The results of the audits of local school systems, including the letter of recommendation submitted by the auditor, are a matter of public record. In addition, the results must be reported within 3 months after the close of the fiscal year to the State Superintendent; the county government; the General Assembly's Joint Audit Committee; Senate Budget and Taxation Committee; Senate Education, Health, and Environmental Affairs Committee; House Appropriations Committee; and House Ways and Means Committee.

## 4:70. May a county government conduct an independent financial audit of its local school system?

Yes. In addition to the audit provided by the local school board, as required by under Section 5-109 and described above, the county commissioners or county council may conduct a financial audit using auditors employed by the county (Md. Code Ann., Ed. Art. § 5-109(d)).

## 4:71. What is the penalty for failing to comply with audit/reporting requirements?

If a local school system does not file the annual audit results in a timely manner with the State Superintendent as required by Section 5-109 of the Education Article, the State Superintendent must immediately notify the Department of Legislative Services, the county governing body; and the local board and local superintendent or chief executive officer of the local school system, and order that the audit report be filed within 10 days.

If a local school system fails to comply with the statutory auditing and reporting requirements, the State Superintendent has the authority, with the approval of the State Board of Education, to notify the State Comptroller. Upon notification, the State Comptroller must withhold 10 percent of the next installment and each subsequent installment due the local school system from the General State School Fund until the State Superintendent notifies the Comptroller that the local school system is in full compliance with the requirements.

## 4:72. What is a performance audit?

A performance audit is defined as "an assessment of an entity's or program's practices to determine whether the entity or program is operating economically and efficiently and whether corrective actions for improving its performance are appropriate" (Md. Code Ann., Ed. Art. § 5-110(a)). Local school boards and county governments may agree on the need for a performance audit and share the costs. In the absence of an agreement and at the request of the county government, MSDE must conduct the performance audit. The cost of the MSDE audit is shared equally between the county government and local board. Interestingly, performance audits are prohibited from assessing or evaluating the local board's "efforts to meet the standards of the Maryland School Performance Program" (Md. Code Ann., Ed. Art. § 5-110).

## 4:73. What do the audits being conducted by the State legislature include?

The scope of the audits being conducted by the General Assembly's Office of Legislative Audits (OLA) include the following areas: general/planning, revenues and billing cycles, grants, procurement and disbursement cycles, human resource functions, inventory control and accountability (non-food or transportation related), information technology issues, physical plant, student transportation services, food service operations, school board operations and oversight, and other financial controls and miscellaneous issues.

The audit focuses on specific objectives under each of these areas. For example, the objectives for the audit of revenues and billing cycles include:

- Are the LEA's policies and procedures adequate to ensure that revenues are collected, processed, recorded and promptly deposited, and all available revenues are maximized?; and

- Do the LEA's billing and accounts receivable processes make sure that all monies owed are billed and collected timely?

# Procurement

### 4:74. What rules apply to bids?

Local boards must draft specifications for, and advertise, bids for goods or commodities if the cost is more than $25,000. 2006 legislation raised the minimum bid threshold from $15,000 to $25,000. Bid requirements include the following:

- The county board shall draft specifications that provide a clear and accurate description of the functional characteristics or the nature of an item to be procured, without modifying the county board's requirements.

- Specifications that use one or more manufacturer's product to describe the standard of quality, performance, or other characteristics needed to meet the county board's requirements, must allow for the submission of equivalent products.

- A contract for the school building, improvements, supplies, or other equipment shall be awarded to the lowest responsible bidder who conforms to specifications with consideration given to:

  - The quantities involved;

  - The time required for delivery;

  - The purpose for which required;

  - The competency and responsibility of the bidder;

  - The ability of the bidder to perform satisfactory service; and

  - The plan for utilization of minority contractors.

- The county board may reject any and all bids and readvertise for other bids (Md. Code Ann., Ed. Art. § 5-112).

### 4:75. What advertising requirements apply to bids?

If the cost of any school building, improvement, supplies, or equipment is more than $25,000, the county board, at least two weeks before bids are to be filed, must advertise for bids in a medium accessible to the general public, which includes: a newspaper of general circulation in the region; the Maryland Contract Weekly or comparable State publication; or an electronic posting on a bid board and physical posting on the local school system bid board (Md. Code Ann., Ed. Art. § 5-112).

### 4:76. Does the State's general procurement law apply to local boards of education?

No, school system procurements are governed by the provisions of the Education Article outlined in **4:74** above. Local boards are not defined as units of state government within the meaning of the State General Procurement Law and therefore service contracts entered into by county school boards are not subject to State general procurement law or to the jurisdiction of the State Board of Contract Appeals (*Chesapeake Charter, Inc. v. Anne Arundel County Board of Education*, 358 Md. 129 (2000)).

However, local school systems are required to comply with certain State procurement regulations and requirements of the Maryland State Interagency Committee for School Construction (IAC), which is subject to the Maryland State Board of Public Works.

### 4:77. May a school system participate in a buying consortium?

Maryland statute authorizes local boards of education, other educational institutions, and county governments, to enter into agreements to establish and participate in "the cooperative or joint administration of programs." Agreements made under this section may include the cooperative or joint administration of programs that relate to: purchasing, personnel, accounting, data processing, printing, insurance, building maintenance, and transportation. Agreements are subject to the approval of the county government and review by the Attorney General (Md. Code Ann., Ed. Art. § 4-123).

If an agreement establishes a separate administrative entity to conduct or administer the joint or cooperative undertaking with power to employ persons, receive and spend money, or receive and spend federal or State grants and appropriations, the agreement must specify, in part: "the manner of financing the joint or cooperative undertaking and of establishing and maintaining its budget, including the manner for receiving, holding, and disbursing federal and other grants and appropriations, and the responsibilities of each cooperating unit of government involved for the payment of the share of the employer in any pension, retirement, or insurance plan administered by any of the participants."

# Personnel Costs

**4:78. How are teachers' and other employees' salaries and benefits paid?**

The local board of education determines the qualifications, tenure, and compensation of all school system employees. The local superintendent develops the school system budget, of which 80 to 90 percent may represent employee salaries and benefits.

The rate of salaries and benefits of teachers and most other school system employees are determined by collective bargaining agreements with the respective employee unions. Separate unions typically represent different categories of employees, *e.g.*, teachers and other professionals, supporting services employees, and principals and other supervisors.

**4:79. What effect does collective bargaining have on school system budgets?**

Board of education employees in all counties are able to engage in collective bargaining. Employee salaries and benefits represent the vast majority of a school system's operating budget and are the primary subject of the collective bargaining negotiations between the school system and its respective unions. In this light, collective bargaining has a pivotal role regarding the school system budget (see **6:25** to **6:29**). By State law, all public employees must be covered by unemployment insurance. All counties and the larger municipalities offer their employees some form of health insurance.

All the counties and some municipalities and special districts provide retirement benefits to their employees. These benefits are provided either through participation in the State employee retirement and pension systems or through retirement plans operated by individual governments. The State provides retirement benefits for professional staff and school clerks in the local boards of education, some library employees, and the professional and clerical staff of community colleges. These employees participate in the State teachers' retirement and pension systems. The vast majority of all local employees participate in Social Security. The exceptions are a few very small municipalities and some law enforcement agencies.

**4:80. Who pays for teacher and school system employee retirement benefits?**

The State pays all of the required employer pension contributions for members of the teachers' retirement and pension systems, however, these payments do not account for the entire burden of providing retirement benefits to school system employees. Some school system, and local government, employees are not members of teachers' retirement or pension system but are members of the state's employee pension system. These employees are referred to as employees of a "participating governmental unit", or PGU. The school system is responsible for paying the employers' share of retirement contributions for their employees in the state's employee pension system.

### 4:81. Who pays the licensing fees for professional staff?

Generally, a local school system may decide, or agree through the negotiation of a collective bargaining agreement, to pay the professional licensing fees of employees, such as school nurses, psychologists, or audiologists. Specifically, legislation enacted in 2006 requires local boards of education to reimburse audiologists and speech-language pathologists for their licensing fees if they: (1) provide audiology and speech-language services on a third-party billing basis in schools; and (2) are licensed by the State Board of Audiologists, Hearing Aid Dispensers, and Speech-Language Pathologists (Md. Code Ann., Ed. Art. § 6-112.1).

### 4:82. Who pays the costs of the employer contribution for Social Security?

County governments have been required to fund the employer contributions to the federal Social Security system since 1993. Prior to 1993, Social Security costs were covered by the State.

### 4:83. Who is responsible for paying the costs of retiree health care benefits?

Each of the 24 boards of education provide for varying levels of health benefits for retired school system employees. Funding for these programs is included in the school system budget, except in Baltimore City where the City government funds these benefits separately.

### 4:84. What is "GASB 45" and how does it impact retiree health care benefits?

In 2004, the Government Accounting Standards Board (GASB) issued Statement 45, "Accounting and Financial Reporting by Employers for Post-Employment Benefits Other Than Pensions", which requires public agencies, including local school systems, to report their projected costs and obligations for retiree healthcare benefits. GASB 45 imposes a new and significant mandate on school systems to calculate and report these projected costs as an expense and liability on their financial statements beginning in FY 2008.

The immediate challenges posed by GASB 45 involve the new responsibility and expense of the actuarial services to quantify and evaluate the scope of the future benefits costs in order to report these costs in annual financial statements.

However, all government entities impacted by GASB 45 recognize that additional challenges will follow, including decisions to begin to appropriate funding in advance, as pensions are funded, and the need to assess how the new accounting rules may effect bond ratings.

# Generally

### 4:85. How are charter schools funded in Maryland?

The Charter School Act requires a local board to "disburse to a public charter school an amount of county, state, and federal money for elementary, middle, and secondary students that is commensurate with the amount disbursed to other public schools in the local jurisdiction" (Md. Code Ann., Ed. Art. § 9-109(a)). The Act also allows the State Board or local board to give surplus educational materials, supplies, furniture, and other equipment to a public charter school" (Md. Code Ann., Ed. Art. § 9-109(b)). Other sources of funding could include private donations, or additional local, state, or federal funding (see **Chapter 16** for a more detailed description of charter school funding issues).

### 4:86. Do private schools receive public funding in Maryland?

Yes. For example, Maryland operates a program that provides state funding for the purchase of nonreligious "textbooks or computer hardware and software and other electronically delivered learning materials as permitted under Title IID, Section 2416(b)(4), (6), and (7) of the No Child Left Behind Act for loan to students in eligible non–public schools with a maximum distribution of $60 per eligible non–public school student" (Section R00A03.04 Aid to Non–Public Schools, House Bill 50 (2007)). This program provides funding for those nonpublic schools where tuition does not exceed the average per-pupil expenditures of public schools.

In addition, nonpublic schools may participate under any contracts for goods or commodities that are awarded by county boards, other public agencies, or intergovernmental purchasing organizations, if the lead agency for the contract award follows public bidding procedures (Md. Code Ann., Ed. Art. § 5-112(e)).

### 4:87. Are any restrictions imposed on funding for parochial schools?

The annual capital budget bill typically includes funding for parochial or religiously affiliated schools in the form of matching grants to support projects such as roof replacements, and improvements to HVAC and fire protection systems. However, the FY 2007 capital budget bill imposes the following conditions on such funding (Uncodified Section 10, House Bill 51 (2007)):

SECTION 10. AND BE IT FURTHER ENACTED, That, no portion of the proceeds of a loan or any of the matching funds provided for a project funded under this Act may be used for the furtherance of sectarian religious instruction, or in connection with the design, acquisition, construction, or equipping of any building used or to be used as a place of sectarian religious worship or instruction, or in connection with any program or department of divinity for any religious denomination. Upon the request of the Board of Public Works, a recipient of the proceeds of a loan under this Act shall submit evidence satisfactory to the Board that none of the proceeds of the loan or any matching funds has been or is being used for a purpose prohibited by this Act.

### 4:88. What is meant by a "school voucher"?

School vouchers are government-sponsored tuition assistance grants made available to parents to enhance their ability to choose a nonpublic and/or parochial school for their child. The constitutionality of school vouchers was contested for many years, and generally rejected by the public education community, until the U.S. Supreme Court found the Cleveland, Ohio, school voucher program constitutional in *Zelman v. Simmons-Harris*, 536 U.S. 639 (2002). While many state legislatures responded to *Zelman* by enacting school voucher programs, Maryland's General Assembly has not considered legislation on this specific issue.

### 4:89. What is a "tuition tax credit"?

Tuition tax credit programs provide a significant tax credit for private contributions to authorized entities for the purpose of distributing tuition assistance grants, *i.e.*, vouchers. In 2007, Maryland's legislature considered, but did not adopt, legislation to create a tuition tax credit system modeled on a program in Pennsylvania. The legislation would have created a tax credit for 75 percent of the contributions made by a business to an eligible nonprofit organization that either: (1) provides scholarships to eligible nonpublic school students, *e.g.*, vouchers, or scholarships to teachers at a nonpublic school; or (2) provides grants to public schools to support innovative educational programs that are not part of the regular public education program (see Fiscal and Policy Note for SB 265, available at *http://mlis.state.md.us/2007RS/fnotes/bil_0005/sb0265.pdf*).

### 4:90. Do parent/teacher associations receive any state funding?

A new state aid program was enacted in 2007 creating a Parent-Teacher Association Matching Fund Pilot Program to encourage parent-teacher associations (PTAs) to raise funds for public high schools and to provide additional State funds to high schools (House Bill 1017, 2007 Session Laws of Maryland). Each high school PTA in Baltimore City and Prince George's County is eligible to receive a dollar-for-dollar match from the State for private donations made to the school's PTA, up to a maximum of $125,000 for each school system divided by the number of public high schools in the system. The total amount expended for the program may not exceed $250,000. The Fiscal and Policy Note for the bill estimates that the 34 high schools in Baltimore City could each generate $3,676 in State matching funds; and the 23 high schools in Prince George's County could each generate up to $5,435 in additional State funds.

# 5. School Facilities, Student Transportation, and Health and Safety

## School Facilities: Roles and Responsibilities

### 5:1. Under what authority does the state exercise control over the construction of public schools?

Legislation enacted in 1971 established a state school construction program and funding system which, for the first time, shifted a substantial amount of the funding burden for Maryland's public schools to the state. At that time, the General Assembly also authorized the Board of Public Works to adopt rules, regulations, and procedures for the administration of the school construction and capital improvement program (see Md. Code Ann., Ed. Art. §§ 5-301 to 5-302). The Board of Public Works, comprised of the Governor, State Comptroller, and State Treasurer, has since 1971 been granted final authority over public school construction in the state, and has adopted rules, regulations, and procedures for the administration of the program by the Interagency on School Construction (IAC) (Md. Code Ann., Ed. Art. § 5-301 (a)(1)).

Maryland's laws, regulations, rules, and procedures regarding school facilities reflect the state's development over the past four decades of a robust and highly centralized program of school facility planning, design, construction, and financing. Due to the complex and highly specialized nature of the state public school construction program (PSCP), those interested in more detailed programmatic information should contact the PSCP directly at: *http://www.pscp.state.md.us*. The statutory framework for the Maryland Public School Construction Program has been aptly described as "sparse" (see *Review of Public School Construction Rules and Procedures*, MD Dept. of Legislative Services, Dec. 18, 2003). In addition, until very recently, the rules and procedures governing the program were not included in the Code of Maryland Regulations, thus limiting public access to the program's many definitions and requirements. The General Assembly enacted the School Facilities Act of 2004, which included the direction to the Board of Public Works to adopt regulations in accordance with the Administrative Procedures Act by July 1, 2005. The Board of Public Works approved final regulations on April 17, 2007. This chapter highlights key provisions of the newly adopted regulations, which are effective as of May 21, 2007.

**5:2. What is the scope of the Board of Public Works' authority regarding school construction?**

Statute confers to the Board of Public Works, through its regulations regarding the school construction program, full authority over the State Board of Education, the State Superintendent, the county governments, the local boards of education, and all other state or local governmental agencies. The statute stipulates that the Board's authority also includes "sites for school buildings" (Md. Code Ann., Ed. Art. § 5-301(g)(1)).

The Board of Public Works essentially holds both the purse strings and authority over the standards and procedures by which school facilities must be planned, approved, and constructed. The Board approves all state payments for school construction projects, and state payment extends only to projects in compliance with the Board's rules.

Statute provides that any conflict between the policies and procedures adopted by the Board of Public Works and any other unit of government is to be resolved in favor of the Board of Public Works (Md. Code Ann., Ed. Art. § 5-301(g)(2)).

Through these provisions, and additional authority granted to the General Assembly, State Board of Education, and State Superintendent, the state has assumed a significant degree of control over the construction standards and finance system for public school construction in Maryland.

**5:3. What is the role of the Interagency Committee on School Construction (IAC)?**

The Interagency Committee on School Construction (IAC) administers the public school construction program (PSCP) on behalf of the Board of Public Works. Historically, the IAC consisted of three individuals including the State Superintendent of Schools, Secretary of the Department of Planning, and Secretary of Department of General Services. In 2005, in response to growing concerns regarding the scope of the Governor's control over an IAC of which two out of three members were appointed by the Governor, the General Assembly added two members of the public to be appointed by the House and Senate, respectively (Md. Code Ann., Ed. Art. § 5-302).

When state regulations refer to the "IAC or its designee" this means a member of the IAC, or IAC staff member, including the designated staff of the Departments of Education, General Services, or Planning (COMAR 23.03.01.B.20). Also, whereas the PSCP Guidelines referred to the state agency as the PSCP, the newly adopted regulations refer instead to the IAC.

## 5:4. What is the role of the State Board of Education regarding school construction?

Notwithstanding the broad authority conferred upon the Board of Public Works, the State Board of Education is charged with the responsibility for adopting standards and guides for planning and constructing school building projects, per the recommendations of the State Superintendent. These standards are applied by the State Superintendent in the review and approval of locally developed school construction plans and specifications. The State Board is further required to maintain a school construction planning service to assist in the development and review of preliminary and final plans and specifications; collect, publish, and distribute to the local boards information on school construction procedures, methods, and materials; and assist local school systems and advise them on the suitability of plans based on educational effectiveness, construction, and cost efficiency (Md. Code Ann., Ed. Art. § 5-205 (l)).

In addition to its oversight and assistance role, the State Board is solely responsible for developing and forwarding to the Governor the annual State public school budget, which, according to statute, includes state aid for the construction of public school buildings (Md. Code Ann., Ed. Art. § 5-205 (j)). In practice, the State Board of Education does not play an active role in developing recommendations regarding the state school construction budget. The Governor's capital budget, including the amount allocated for school construction, and any additional funds provided by the General Assembly, are applied to the projects approved by the IAC and Board of Public Works.

## 5:5. What is the role of the State Superintendent regarding school construction?

Maryland's State Superintendent of Schools plays multiple roles in the school construction process, serving as the chief administrator of the Maryland State Department of Education (MSDE) in conjunction with the State Board of Education (Md. Code Ann., Ed. Art. § 2-303(f)); and also as the chair of the Interagency Committee on School Construction (IAC); which is accountable to the Board of Public Works (Md. Code Ann., Ed. Art. § 5-302 (a)(3)).

The State Superintendent's powers and duties include the sole authority to approve or disapprove each:

- Proposal for the purchase or sale of any ground, school site, or building;

- Plan or specification for the remodeling of a school building if the remodeling costs more than $350,000;

- Plan or specification for the construction of a new school building; and

- Change order that costs more than $25,000 for the remodeling, restoration, or construction of a school building (Md. Code Ann., Ed. Art. § 2-303(f)(1)).

The State Superintendent's disapproval of a project must include a written statement providing the reasons for the disapproval, is binding on any pending construction by a local board, and renders any contract for work not approved by the State Superintendent invalid (Md. Code Ann., Ed. Art. § 2-303(f)(2)).

### 5:6. What is the Maryland Department of Education's role?

The State Department of Education reviews the educational specifications and schematic drawings for each project approved by the Board of Public Works to ensure that the design of the proposed facility is reasonable in terms of scope and capacity. MSDE also reviews local comprehensive maintenance plans. In addition, MSDE headquarters also houses the offices of the Public School Construction Program.

### 5:7. What is the Governor's role in the school construction process?

In September of each year, the Governor advises the IAC of the budget that will be proposed for public school construction. The Governor establishes the total amount of the capital budget based on the advice and recommendations of the Capital Debt Affordability Committee regarding the available short-term and long-term bond financed funding.

### 5:8. What is the General Assembly's role?

The General Assembly receives the Governor's proposed capital budget, including school construction funding, as an Administration bill introduced by the Speaker of the House and President of the Senate. The capital budget bill is considered by the General Assembly's respective House Appropriations and Senate Budget and Taxation Committee. An important distinction between the capital budget bill and the state operating budget bill is that the General Assembly may add to the total capital budget bill contingent on identifying revenue sources. The General Assembly's capital budget decisions are also informed by the Capital Debt Affordability Committee's recommendations.

### 5:9. What is the role of Capital Dept Affordability Committee?

The Capital Dept Affordability Committee (CDAC), was established in 1978, and is charged with reviewing the size and condition of State tax supported debt, and advising the Governor and General Assembly each year regarding the maximum amount of new general obligation debt that prudently may be authorized for the next fiscal year. Members of the CDAC include the State Comptroller, Treasurer, Secretary of Transportation, Secretary of Budget and Management, and one member of the public. Since its creation in 1978, the CDAC's charge was expanded by the Public School Facilities Act of 2004 to include examination and recommendations for potential means of funding the State's share of school construction needs (Chapters 306, Laws of Maryland 2004, uncodified Section 11).

The CDAC is required to review the size and condition of the state debt on a continuing basis and to submit to the Governor, by September 10 of each year, an estimate of the total amount of new state debt that prudently may be authorized for the next fiscal year. The CDAC recommendations and reports are not binding; the Governor is required to give "due consideration" to the Committee's findings in determining the total authorizations of new State debt and in preparing preliminary budget allocations for the next fiscal year. Although the Committee's estimates are advisory only, the Committee is required to consider:

- The amount of State tax supported debt that will be outstanding and authorized but unissued during the next fiscal year;

- The capital program and the capital improvement and school construction needs during the next five fiscal years;

- Projected debt service requirements for the next ten years;

- Criteria used by recognized bond rating agencies to judge the quality of State bond issues;

- Other factors relevant to the ability of the State to meet its projected debt service requirements for the next five years or relevant to the marketability of State bonds; and

- The effect of new authorizations on each of the factors enumerated above (Md. Code Ann., St. Fin. & Proc. Art. § 8-104).

### 5:10. Do other State agencies have a role in the school construction process?

The Maryland Department of Planning and the Department of General Services have certain specific responsibilities pertaining to the Public School Construction Program. The Maryland Department of Planning reviews requests for capital improvement to determine eligibility for State funding. Staff also analyzes educational facility master plans, requests for property acquisitions and dispositions, and local enrollment projections.

The Department of General Services (DGS) reviews design development and construction documents for each project to ensure that the facility meets industry design standards and certain State safety standards (*e.g.*, fire safety standards). The

DGS review must be completed before the school system solicits bids for the construction contract. In addition, DGS is responsible for conducting the maintenance inspections of 100 public schools throughout the State each year.

### 5:11. What is the local board of education's role regarding school construction?

Local boards of education are vested with the authority to establish public schools, subject to the approval of the State Superintendent and in accordance with applicable bylaws, rules, and regulations of the State Board of Education (Md. Code Ann., Ed. Art. § 4-109(a)). With the advice of the local superintendent, local boards establish the geographical attendance areas for each public school in their jurisdiction (Md. Code Ann., Ed. Art. § 4-109(c)).

Subject to the approval of the State Superintendent, and in accordance with the State Board's rules and regulations, local boards may purchase or otherwise acquire, land, school sites or buildings; and rent, repair, improve, or build school buildings and approve contracts (Md. Code Ann., Ed. Art. § 4-115).

With regard to a specific school construction project, the local school system is responsible for competitively bidding and awarding the construction contracts to the lowest responsive and responsible bidders. The *Rules and Regulations* provide that the local board has the sole responsibility for bidding a project within the State and local allocations (*Rules and Regulations*, Section 9(c)). In addition, the IAC requires that each local board submit one-year and five-year capital improvement plans for school construction by the date specified by the IAC.

### 5:12. What is the role of county government regarding school construction?

Generally, the school construction process, including the planning and funding of projects, requires the continuous collaboration of state, county, and school system officials. County governments have historically transitioned from being solely responsible for school construction, to the adoption of the State school construction program in 1971 which featured the provision of 100 percent State funding coupled with the state's assumption of the planning and approval process, to the current system that preserves the State's authority and maintains the state and local cost share system adopted in 1987. In this way, local governments must provide the funding beyond the eligible costs provided by the state. County governments must approve the Capital Improvement Plan (CIP) developed by the local board of education (COMAR 23.03.02.03).

In addition, school property determined by the local board as no longer needed, reverts to the county government for sale, lease or other purpose (Md. Code Ann., Ed. Art. § 4-115(c)).

**5:13. What is the federal government's role, if any, regarding school construction?**

**Charter Schools:** The federal Credit Enhancement for Charter School Facilities program provides grants assistance to charter schools to meet their facility needs. Under this program, funds are provided on a competitive basis to public and nonprofit entities, and consortia of those entities, to leverage other funds and help charter schools obtain school facilities through such means as purchase, lease, and donation. Grantees may also use grants to leverage funds to help charter schools construct and renovate school facilities (20 U.S.C. § 7223).

**QZABs:** In recent years, Qualified Zone Academy Bonds (QZABs) have facilitated Maryland's investment in school improvements and renovations. The federal government created the Qualified Zone Academy Bonds in the Tax Reform Act of 1997 as a new type of debt instrument to help finance certain types of education expenditures. Financial institutions, insurance companies, and investment houses were authorized to purchase the bonds, which provide for a federal tax credit instead of interest earnings. A school is eligible to receive funding from the issuance of Qualified Zone Academy Bonds if it is located in an enterprise or empowerment zone, or at least 35 percent of the school's students qualify for free and reduced price meals. In addition, the funding is contingent on the local school system generating private sector matching contributions equal to 10% of each QZAB grant. Maryland has applied the proceeds from the QZABs for renovations or repairs to existing public schools. Eligible projects included asbestos and lead paint abatement, fire protection systems and equipment, painting, plumbing, roofing, heating, ventilation and air conditioning systems, site redevelopment, wiring schools for technology, pre-kindergarten facilities, and renovation projects related to education programs and services.

**Impact Aid:** The federal Impact Aid program disburses Impact Aid payments to local school systems that are financially burdened by federal activities, such as military installations and Indian Lands, from which no property tax revenue is generated. Federal impact aid has historically included limited financial assistance for school facility costs.

# School Facilities: Rules and Regulations

**5:14. Where are the state regulations governing the state school construction program located?**

The statutory framework governing public school construction broadly delegates to the Board of Public Works the responsibility to adopt rules and regulations establishing the state school construction program. Section 5-301 of the Education Article provides the primary statutory basis for State financial participation in public school construction. Section 5-302 establishes the

Interagency Committee on School Construction (IAC), Section 5-303 provides guidance on renovation of existing school buildings, and Section 5-308 provides for county reimbursement of State debt under certain circumstances. All other requirements relating to the state's Public School Construction Program (PSCP) are found in the newly adopted state regulations (COMAR 23.03.01 - .05).

### 5:15. What is included in the regulations recently adopted by the Board of Public Works?

The regulations include major sections on Terminology (COMAR 23.03.01), Administration (COMAR 23.03.02), Construction Procurement Methods (COMAR 23.03.03); Project Delivery Methods (COMAR 23.03.04); and Alternative Financing (COMAR 23.03.05). The stated purpose of the regulations is:

> "to formalize into law the Administrative Procedures Guide of the Public School Construction Program that establishes the operation and administration of the Program. The regulations also implement the Public School Facilities Act of 2004 which includes among its provisions the authority for counties to finance construction and renovation of public school facilities using alternative financing methods; the authority for counties to engage in procurement methods such as unsolicited proposals and quality-based selection in certain circumstances; and a requirement that the counties implement comprehensive maintenance plans" (*Maryland Register*, Vol. 34, Issue 4, February 16, 2007).

## School Facilities: Planning and Construction

### 5:16. How are school construction projects planned?

The Maryland Public School Construction Program (PSCP), which administers the planning, design, and construction of all school facilities in the state, has adopted a project development system consisting of three phases: programming, planning, and construction. In the programming phase, the educational facilities master plan is developed, a capital improvement program is devised, architects are selected, and sites are approved. The planning phase describes the steps in the planning process, the individuals involved, the development of an educational specifications document, and the schematic review process. The design and construction phase describes in detail the design development review, construction document review, bidding and change orders. Also included are the procedures for financial operations and alternative construction methods.

The new regulations replacing the PSCP Administrative Procedures Guide thoroughly outline major program requirements. However, in many instances the *PSCP Guide* continues to provide more detailed descriptions and therefore is referenced for this purpose.

### 5:17. What is the Local Educational Facilities Master Plan?

Each school system must annually adopt and submit an educational facilities master plan to the IAC by the date specified by the IAC (COMAR 23.03.02.02). The master plan must include:

- Educational goals, standards, and guidelines;

- Community analysis;

- An inventory and evaluation of existing school buildings;

- Current and projected enrollment data; and

- Analysis of future school facility needs.

### 5:18. How are local master plans reviewed, approved, and enforced?

The IAC or its designee reviews each master plan and notifies the local school system in writing of any objections or exceptions to the plan. The locally adopted plan together with any locally adopted amendments and comments by the IAC or its designee constitute the "plan of record" (COMAR 23.03.02.02). In addition, the IAC may recommend to the Board of Public Works the disapproval of any school construction project that is not consistent with the current master plan of record.

### 5:19. What are educational specifications?

Educational specifications, commonly referred to as "ed specs," describe in detail the proposed educational activities for a particular school facility and the corresponding school facility architectural and design requirements to facilitate those activities. The PSCP "*Outline for Educational Specifications*" recommends components such as project rationale, educational plan, project design factors, activity areas, and summaries of spatial relationships (*PSCP Guide*, Appendix D).

Schools are designed and constructed pursuant to educational specifications addressing the distinct functions and educational objective of elementary, middle and high schools. Broad elements of a school's specifications may include general classrooms, planning areas, special education, science labs, media centers, technology education, physical education, health rooms, cafeterias, auditoriums, teacher lounges, and others. Within these broad categories, educational specifications typically include very detailed requirements regarding square footage per teacher and student, and furniture and equipment requirements for classrooms and other programs, *e.g.*, science classroom: 28 students, 1200 sq. ft., and 3 storage units including 1 lockable unit for hazardous chemicals.

Local boards must be cognizant of the cost implications as they develop and approve school-specific educational specifications; and balance competing interests in providing certain services, such as a larger auditorium, with the availability of state funding for narrowly defined eligible costs and local funding beyond this amount.

### 5:20. What is a Capital Improvement Program (CIP)?

Generally, a capital improvement program is developed to guide the development of public facilities over a number of years. A CIP organizes projects in a sequential, priority order and includes estimated costs and anticipated methods of funding for each project.

In Maryland, each local school system must submit to the IAC a capital improvement program for the next fiscal year and a capital improvement program for the 5 years following the next fiscal year (COMAR 23.03.02.03). The IAC compiles these local CIPs to create the state CIP. State regulations provide a detailed outline of CIP requirements applicable to Local Submissions (COMAR 23.03.02.03.A), IAC Review (COMAR 23.03.02.03.B), Preliminary State Capital Improvement Program (COMAR 23.03.02.03.C), Final State Capital Improvement Program (COMAR 23.03.02.03.D), and Revisions (COMAR 23.03.02.03.E).

### 5:21. Does the IAC prioritize individual projects?

Yes. The IAC evaluates the merits of each request for planning approval contained in the local capital improvement program using the following factors (COMAR 23.03.02.03.B(1)(a) – (k)). The IAC ranks the requests on a statewide basis using the five factors described below in items (a) through (e).

(a) State educational priorities;

(b) Enrollment projections, that is, the extent to which 7-year enrollment projections exceed the State-rated capacity for the applicable schools;

(c) Average age of the building;

(d) The State's policy set forth in State Finance and Procurement, § 5-7B-07, Annotated Code of Maryland, that emphasizes projects that target the rehabilitation of existing schools to ensure that facilities in established neighborhoods are of equal quality to new schools;

(e) The number of students who receive special education services, who are eligible for free and reduced price meals, or who are English language learners;

(f) Analysis of the feasibility studies required for projects in which an LEA seeks to abandon an existing school building or demolish more than 50 percent of the gross square footage;

(g) Adequacy of maintenance programs;

(h) Justification for the transfer of a school building in the same geographic area by a local board to the county government because the property was determined no longer needed for school purposes;

(i) Progress on previously approved projects;

(j) Statewide needs measured against the potential for future capacity for State funding; and

(k) Other factors considered appropriate.

## 5:22. How does the IAC evaluate funding requests?

The IAC evaluates requests for funding approval using the factors outlined in COMAR 23.03.02.03.B.(2):

(a) Enrollment projections;

(b) Adequacy of maintenance programs;

(c) Adequacy of project description;

(d) Adequacy of project cost estimate;

(e) Progress on project design and anticipated bid date;

(f) Statewide needs measured against the capacity for State funding;

(g) For relocatable facilities, the review criteria in Regulation .16 of this chapter;

(h) Progress on previously approved projects;

(i) Recurring or unresolved audit exceptions; and

(j) Other factors considered appropriate.

## 5:23. How are enrollment projections calculated?

Enrollment projections and enrollment capacities for individual schools are developed by the local school system. Projecting future enrollment levels involves analyses of new housing patterns, changes in household composition, and past enrollment changes. The results of these local studies are subject to the review and acceptance of the IAC. In addition, Maryland's Department of Planning operates the Maryland State Data Center which conducts independent analyses of enrollment projections and school capacities.

### 5:24. What is meant by "state-rated capacity"?

State-rated capacity is defined as the number of students that the IAC or its designee determines that an individual school has the physical capacity to enroll (COMAR 23.03.02.04). The approved capacities for elementary and secondary school classrooms are:

- Prekindergarten classroom—20;

- Kindergarten classroom—22;

- Grades 1 through 5 classroom—23;

- Grades 6 through 12 classroom—25; and

- Special education classroom—10.

Similarly, state-rated capacities apply to schools, calculated by multiplying the number of classrooms in each grade by the approved capacity for that grade. The total school calculation also includes features such as laboratories, career technology rooms, music rooms, art rooms, consumer science rooms, and gymnasiums.

### 5:25. May a local school system appeal the IAC's preliminary recommendations?

Following notice of the IAC's preliminary recommendations, a local school system is provided an opportunity to "present information pertaining to projects that were not recommended for approval by the IAC staff for inclusion in the State capital improvement program" (COMAR 23.03.02.03.B.(3)).

### 5:26. What is the "preliminary state capital improvement program"?

By December 31 of each year the IAC must submit to the Board of Public Works its preliminary capital improvement program for the following fiscal year that:

(a) Identifies new construction projects, renovation projects, systemic renovation projects, and relocatable classrooms recommended for planning approval and funding approval;

(b) Recommends a maximum state construction allocation for each project; and

(c) Totals at least 75 percent of the anticipated school construction capital budget.

The IAC may not recommend a systemic renovation project that has been solicited. The Board of Public Works reviews the IAC recommendation, modifies it as appropriate, and approves the preliminary state CIP (COMAR 23.03.02.03.C).

### 5:27. What is the "final state capital improvement program"?

After the state capital budget is finalized for the following fiscal year, the IAC must submit to the Board of Public Works a final state CIP that recommends a maximum state allocation for projects recommended for planning and funding approval, including new construction projects, renovation projects, and relocatable classrooms. The IAC recommendations included in the final CIP must take into account the preliminary CIP, additional information provided by the local school system, any increases to the final allocation of funds or funds added from the statewide contingency account, requirements included in the capital budget bill, and other information deemed appropriate by the IAC (COMAR 23.03.02.03.D).

### 5:28. May the final state CIP be revised?

Yes, the Board of Public works may revise the final state CIP, but only based on the review and recommendation of the IAC (COMAR 23.03.02.03.E).

### 5:29. How does the IAC indicate a specific project's rank?

The IAC reviews the requests for planning and funding approval included in each CIP and assigns a status to each project as follows:

- "A": Project approved by the IAC and recommended to the Board of Public Works;

- "B": Project has met all technical requirements but has not yet been approved by the IAC, or is recommended for deferral due to fiscal constraints:

- "C": Project has technical issues that must be resolved before staff can proceed to recommend for approval by the IAC; and

- "D": Project which is not recommended for approval.

**5:30. What is the timeline for developing and approving a Capital Improvement Program (CIP)?**

**Public School Construction Program**

**Capital Improvement Program (CIP) Time Line**

*July 1 ............................... LEA submits Educational Facilities Master Plan. (10 year review and analysis)

July 10 .............................. Materials/Instructions distributed for preparation of CIP.

August 25 .......................... Governor establishes tentative budget figure for next fiscal year.

Prior to September 15 ....... Preliminary figure sent to each LEA.

*October 15 ....................... Annual and five-year CIP submitted by Board of Education. Comprehensive Maintenance Plan submitted.

October 18/November 3 .... Meetings held with each LEA to review and discuss the CIP requests.

November 9 ....................... Staff recommendations sent to: the IAC, school system, and local government.

*December 7 ..................... Deadline for the submission of (a) amendments to the CIP, (b) local government approval letter in support of the board of education's request.

December 13 ..................... IAC hearing for board of education appeals on the staff recommendations. IAC submits recommendations to the BPW, notifies LEA and local government.

January 22 ......................... Governor submits the capital budget (single line total budget for PSCP).

January to March .............. Legislative Budget Committee hearings on Capital Budget and Pay-Go.

January 30 ......................... BPW hearing for board of education appeals on the IAC recommendations. BPW approves specific projects recommended by the IAC. Material submitted at hearing held until final budget approved.

April 8 ............................. Legislature approves the budget (operating "Pay-Go" and capital) Single line for total amount of budget.

May 9 ............................. BPW reconvenes to approve additional projects in response to the appeals presented in January (based upon funds available).

*June 1 ............................. Funding for projects approved to be funded with bond proceeds available.

*July 1 ............................. Funding for projects approved to be funded with "Pay-Go" funds as available.

* These dates remain constant each fiscal year. All others are subject to change but are on or about the same date each year (Source: Maryland Public School Construction Program).

## 5:31. What is the typical timeline for a school construction project?

### Public School Construction Program

### Typical Time Line for an Elementary School Construction Project

July 1, 2007 ....................... LEA submits its educational facilities master plan to the IAC

September 15, 2007 .......... IAC informs LEA of estimated capital funds for next fiscal year

October 7, 2007 ................. Submittal of request for planning approval in FY 2008 CIP

January 2008 ..................... Approval of local planning by BPW

March 2008 ....................... LEA begins development of Educational Specifications

June 2008 .......................... LEA selects architect for project

July 2008 ........................... Architect begins design process

September 1, 2008 ............ LEA submits schematic designs to IAC for review and approval

October 15, 2008 .............. Submittal of request for State funding in FY 2009 CIP

November 1, 2008 ............. LEA submits design development documents to IAC for review and comment

January 2009 ..................... Approval of State funding by BPW

April 2009 ........................ LEA submits construction documents

May 2009 ......................... Project is bid

June 2009 ......................... Construction begins (12 – 15 months)

September 1, 2010 ........... Project completed – school occupied

(Source: Adapted from a 2004 PSCP outline).

### 5:32. What is meant by a "systemic renovation" to a school facility?

The PSCP defines a "systemic renovation" as "the repair or replacement of a major system of a properly maintained facility thereby extending the useful life of the facility or component thereof for a minimum of 15 years" (*PSCP Guide*, Section 401.1, p. 4-2). Generally, projects with total costs under $100,000 are not eligible for state funding. However, state funding for small systemic renovations costing between $50,000 and $100,000 is available for systems with no major systemic renovation requests. Systemic renovations include the repair or replacement of the following:

- Structural: roofs, walls, floors, ceilings;
- Mechanical: heating, ventilation, air conditioning;
- Plumbing: water supply, sanitary system;
- Electrical;
- Fire Safety: sprinklers, fire detection and alarms;
- Conveying system: elevators.

## School Facilities Funding

### 5:33. How are school facility projects funded?

The state and county governments share public school construction costs approved by the state, with the exception of certain costs (*e.g.*, site acquisition, architectural and engineering fees, off-site infrastructure improvements) which are ineligible for state funding, and therefore borne entirely by county governments. The state's share of construction costs is wealth equalized according to the county's taxable wealth so that jurisdictions with smaller per pupil tax bases receive proportionally more state aid. The sources of revenue for both the state and counties include bond financed funding and pay-as-you-go operating funding. Federal funding and private contributions contribute a very small share of school facility funding.

For each approved project, the IAC establishes a maximum project budget that the State will participate in funding. The project budget is derived from the average statewide cost per square foot of school construction, established square footage allowances per student, and approved student capacity. Importantly, the state budget is limited to the "eligible costs" for the project. The state share, or percentage, for the county is then applied to the maximum eligible project budget to determine the maximum state funding amount for the project.

The limited state funding available for approved projects necessitates close collaboration of school system and county government officials in developing the Capital Improvement Program (CIP), prioritizing local projects, and identifying sufficient local revenues to supplement state funds in order to complete approved projects.

## 5:34. What is meant by an "eligible cost"?

State regulations (COMAR 23.03.02.11) define certain types of capital improvements and related expenditures as eligible for state funding through the state/local cost share formula. Eligible costs include:

A. New construction, as follows:

    (1) Construction of a new school facility, that is, work necessary to construct a new school facility, including building and site development;

    (2) Additions to an existing facility, that is, work necessary to increase space at an existing school facility, including:

        (a) Building and site development; and

        (b) Work to physically integrate the addition into the existing school;

    (3) Replacement of a building or building portion, that is, work necessary to reconstruct a school facility that cannot be economically repaired or renovated, including building and site development; and

    (4) Modular construction, that is, factory-fabricated structures that have the same quality systems and materials as used for permanent school construction and that meet the standards of the COMAR 05.02.04;

B. Renovation, that is, work necessary to restore and modernize an existing school facility or a portion of a facility that is 16 years old or older;

C. Systemic renovations as set forth in Regulation .15 of this chapter;

D.  State-owned relocatable classrooms as set forth in Regulation .16 of this chapter;

E.  Temporary facilities, including utilities and relocatable classrooms, that are necessary on-site during construction of a State-funded project;

F.  Built-in equipment and furnishings as defined by the IAC;

G.  Off-site development costs required by local, State, or federal agencies; and

H.  Emergency repairs as set forth in Regulation .17 of this chapter.

## 5:35. What is an ineligible cost?

State regulations (COMAR 23.03.02.12) define certain types of capital improvements and related expenditures as ineligible for state funding through the state/local cost share formula, including:

A.  Site acquisition;

B.  Offsite development costs except those listed as eligible in Regulation .11G of this chapter;

C.  Architecture, engineering, or other consultant fees, except as permitted by Regulation .10 of this chapter;

D.  Master plans, feasibility studies, programs, educational specifications, or equipment specifications;

E.  Ancillary construction costs such as:

    (1) Permits;

    (2) Test borings;

    (3) Soil analysis;

    (4) Bid advertising;

    (5) Water and sewer connection charges;

    (6) Topographical surveys;

    (7) Models;

    (8) Renderings; or

    (9) Cost estimating;

F.  Leasing or purchasing school facilities except as provided in COMAR 23.03.05;

G.  Construction inspection services;

H.  Relocation costs for site occupants;

I.  Salaries of local employees;

J.  Construction of administrative or support facilities, including regional or central administrative offices, warehousing, resource, printing, vehicle storage, and maintenance facilities;

K.  Movable equipment, furnishings, and artwork as defined by the IAC;

L.  Maintenance; and

M.  Temporary storage.

## 5:36. What is the State's process for annually approving projects and funding amounts?

In September of each year, the Governor advises the IAC of the budget that will be proposed for public school construction. The IAC provides this information to the local school system and requests that each system submit one-year and five-year capital improvement plans for school construction by October 15. During the period from October 15 to early November, IAC staff reviews local project requests, meets with each system to discuss its capital improvement program, and determines the eligible projects, including those projects that should be funded. In November the staff presents recommendations to the IAC. The IAC then holds a hearing in mid December and compiles a list of eligible projects and determines which of those projects should be recommended to the Board of Public Works for approval.

Beginning in 1998, the IAC has employed the practice of initially allocating approximately 75 percent of the proposed school construction budget to specific projects in the event that the full amount of the proposed funding is not ultimately appropriated by the General Assembly. The Board of Public Works at a meeting in January hears appeals from the LEAs and acts on the IAC's recommendations. The Program is incorporated into the State's capital budget. The Board's approved Program and any supplemental requests made by the Governor to change the Program funding level are submitted to the General Assembly for approval.

This process of assigning 75 percent of the Governor's initial allocation, coinciding with the annual session of the General Assembly, has resulted in contentious interactions between the Governor, General Assembly, counties, and local school systems, regarding the selection of projects to benefit from the remaining 25 percent of the Governor's initial allocation, and any additional funding that may be added by the General Assembly through the routine capital budget process or by the Governor through his supplemental budget.

## 5:37. How are the state and local cost sharing formulas determined?

Historically the formulas were adopted in the rules and regulations developed by the IAC and adopted by the Board of Public Works. More recently, the General Assembly adopted the Public School Facilities Act of 2004, including the following state/local shared cost formulas which will be in effect for fiscal years 2006, 2007, and 2008 (Source: PSCP website: *http://www.pscp.state.md.us/GI/gicost.htm*). The new state regulations require the IAC to review and, if appropriate, recommend revisions to the formulas beginning in FY 2009 and every three years thereafter (COMAR 23.03.02.05.C).

| County | State/Local Formula FY 2006 through FY 2008 |
|---|---|
| Allegany | 90% |
| Anne Arundel | 50% |
| Baltimore City | 97% |
| Baltimore County | 50% |
| Calvert | 69% |
| Caroline | 89% |
| Carroll | 65% |
| Cecil | 70% |
| Charles | 70% |
| Dorchester | 77% |
| Frederick | 72% |
| Garrett | 70% |
| Harford | 65% |
| Howard | 58% |
| Kent | 50% |
| Montgomery | 50% |
| Prince George's | 75%/69% * |
| Queen Anne's | 70% |
| St. Mary's | 72% |
| Somerset | 97% |
| Talbot | 50% |

| County | State/Local Formula FY 2006 through FY 2008 |
|---|---|
| Washington | 65% |
| Wicomico | 81% |
| Worcester | 50% |

\* In Prince George's County, the State cost share percentage for approved projects is 75% of the eligible costs up to and including $35 million, and for funding above $35 million the State funds 69% of eligible costs.

## 5:38. What is meant by bond financing?

State general obligation bonds are bonds that are backed by the full faith and credit of the State, and are authorized and issued to provide funds for State-owned capital improvements as well as to provide grants to local governments and nonprofit organizations for capital projects that serve a public purpose.

## 5:39. Are counties authorized to issue bonds to finance school construction projects?

Yes. Since the 2004 adoption of Section 5-602 of the Education Article, any county may issue bonds to finance any or all of the costs of construction or improvement of public schools in the county in accordance with the requirements of the State Finance and Procurement Article. Under Section 5-602, "construction or improvement" is defined as the planning, design, engineering, alteration, construction, reconstruction, enlargement, expansion, extension, improvement, replacement, rehabilitation, renovation, upgrading, repair, or capital equipping, of a school facility. The statute further requires that bonds must be authorized by a resolution of the governing body of the county

## 5:40. What is meant by PAYGO funding?

The term "Pay-Go" or "PAYGO" is derived from "pay-as-you-go" and refers to revenues available in the current fiscal year for immediate payment for goods or services. The General Assembly and/or Governor have at times allocated significant amounts of PAYGO funds toward school facilities projects. Similarly, county governments may finance school facilities projects through a combination of bond financing and PAYGO funds.

### 5:41. Are projects that will be used cooperatively by non-school system groups eligible for State funding?

Yes. The *PSCP Rules and Regulations* recognize and even encourage cooperative arrangements for sharing facilities among two or more school systems, among educational and non-educational governmental agencies, and for the use of school facilities for community and recreational purposes shall be encouraged. The IAC shall determine what part of the cost of constructing or improving such facilities is fairly assignable for educational purposes and, accordingly, eligible for State payment. In addition, the IAC may provide State funding for up to 3,000 square feet, per project, for space to support recreational, health and other community programs that would serve school children and other members of the community. Initiatives eligible for such funding must be coordinated with appropriate State and local agencies, satisfy regulations on the use of bond proceeds, and may include programs such as school-based health centers, parks or recreation programs, day care facilities, parenting and volunteer programs, multipurpose community programs, social services, and public library programs and services.

### 5:42. Who is responsible for hiring the architects and engineers?

All plans, specifications, and related documents for each construction project must have been developed under the supervision and responsibility of an architect or engineer who is licensed or registered in the State of Maryland. The selection of the architect or engineer must be made by the local board, which must notify the IAC of the architect selected, and file a copy of the approved A/E Agreement with the IAC (COMAR 23.03.02.14).

### 5:43. What is the Architecture and Engineering (A/E) Agreement required to include?

The Architecture and Engineering (A/E) Agreement is required to include, as terms of the contract, provisions for cost control, life cycle costing, energy conservation, a fixed limit of construction cost, and the agreement to submit to IAC review and/or approval of the schematic, design development, and construction documents (COMAR 23.03.02.14).

### 5:44. May the State funding be used to purchase land?

No. Statute provides that the "cost of acquiring land may not be considered a construction or capital improvement cost and may not be paid by the State" (Md. Code Ann., Ed. Art. § 5-301 (a)(2)).

**5:45. Does the state or local government have condemnation authority to acquire land on which to build a school?**

Yes. A local board of education may bring condemnation proceedings to acquire land for any school purpose, if the county is unable to contract with the owner of the land for purchase based on fair valuation (Md. Code Ann., Ed. Art. § 4-119).

**5:46. Are school construction contracts subject to competitive bidding requirements?**

Yes, generally. However, alternative finance provisions enacted in 2004 provide that "in order to finance or to speed delivery of, transfer risks of, or otherwise enhance the delivery of public school construction" a county may:

- engage in competitive negotiation, rather than competitive bidding, in limited circumstances, including construction management at-risk arrangements and other alternative project delivery arrangements, as provided in regulations adopted by the board of public works;

- accept unsolicited proposals for the development of public schools in limited circumstances, as provided in regulations adopted by the board of public works; and

- use quality-based selection, in which selection is based on a combination of qualifications and cost factors, to select developers and builders, as provided in regulations adopted by the board of public works (Md. Code Ann., Ed. Art. § 4-126(b)).

**5:47. What procurement laws and regulations apply to public school construction projects?**

Generally, all public school contracts in amounts in excess of $25,000 must be advertised for the bids and the contract awarded to the lowest responsible bidder who conforms to the specifications (Md. Code Ann., Ed. Art. § 5-112(b)). In addition, several sections of the State Finance and Procurement Article apply specifically to school facilities projects.

Sections 14-301 through 14-308 define the requirements for minority business participation. These sections are applicable to local boards of education when state PSCP funding is utilized. Each board must approve and implement a minority business enterprise procedure to attempt to achieve the results that minimum of 10 percent of the total dollar value contracted or expended is made directly or indirectly from minority business enterprises (Md. Code Ann., St. Fin. & Proc. Art. §§ 14-301 to 308).

Local bid documents must include prevailing wage rates when state funds are used for the construction, the project cost including state and local funding will exceed $500,000, and the state share are to be used to provide 50 percent or more of the construction cost (Md. Code Ann., St. Fin. & Proc. Art. §§ 17-201 through 17-226).

Contractors for construction contracts exceeding $50,000 must furnish a performance and payment bond which becomes binding upon award of the contract. The contractor may provide the equivalent in cash or other security satisfactory to the public body awarding the contract (Md. Code Ann., St. Fin. & Proc. Art. §§ 17-101 through 17-110).

A person convicted for bribery, attempted bribery, or conspiracy to bribe is disqualified from entering into a contract with any county or other subdivision of the state (Md. Code Ann., St. Fin. & Proc. Art. § 16-201).

### 5:48. How do "prevailing wage" requirements impact school construction projects?

Maryland's prevailing wage law is based on the Davis-Bacon Act of 1931, which requires contractors or their subcontractors to pay workers employed directly on the work site, no less than the locally prevailing wages and fringe benefits paid on projects of similar character. Prevailing wage applies to school construction projects if the project is over $500,000 and the State is paying at least 50 percent of the construction costs. Title 17, Subtitle 2 of the State Finance and Procurement Article outlines the requirements of Maryland's prevailing wage law. The prevailing wage law regulates hours, wages, and employment conditions of contractors and subcontractors for public works in Maryland. Currently, construction projects for elementary and secondary schools with construction costs of at least $500,000 and for which the State funds 50 percent or more of the construction costs are subject to the prevailing wage law.

During the 2000 legislative session, the General Assembly passed legislation amending provisions of the prevailing wage law that required 75 percent or more of an elementary or secondary school construction project to be funded by the State in order for the prevailing wage law to apply and adopted the current 50 percent threshold.

### 5:49. What is meant by "alternative financing"?

Legislation enacted in 2004 attempted to promote and facilitate the practice of employing "alternative financing methods" to school construction and renovation projects. "Alternative financing methods" are defined as including:

(1)  Sale-leaseback arrangements, in which a county board agrees to transfer title to a property, including improvements, to a private entity that simultaneously agrees to lease the property back to the county board and, on a specified date, transfer title back to the county board;

(2)  Lease-leaseback arrangements, in which a county board leases a property to a private entity that improves the property and leases the property, with the improvements, back to the county board;

(3)  Public-private partnership agreements, in which a county board contracts with a private entity for the acquisition, design, construction, improvement, renovation, expansion, equipping, or financing of a public school, and may include provisions for cooperative use of the school or an adjacent property and generation of revenue to offset the cost of construction or use of the school; and

(4)  Performance-based contracting, in which a county board enters into an energy performance contract to obtain funding for a project with guaranteed energy savings over a specified time period; and

(5)  Design-build arrangements, that permit a county board to contract with a design-build business entity for the combined design and construction of qualified education facilities, including financing mechanisms where the business entity assists the local governing body in obtaining project financing (Md. Code Ann., Ed. Art. § 4-126(a)).

## 5:50. Do any different standards apply to alternatively financed school projects?

Yes. A project that qualifies for alternative financing methods must meet requirements demonstrating the advantages of the project to the public, including provisions addressing:

(1)  the probable scope, complexity, or urgency of the project;

(2)  any risk sharing, added value, education enhancements, increase in funding, or economic benefit from the project that would not otherwise be available;

(3)  the public need for the project; and

(4)  the estimated cost or timeliness of executing the project (Md. Code Ann., Ed. Art. § 4-126(c)).

In addition, a county board may not use alternative financing methods without the approval of the county governing body (Md. Code Ann., Ed. Art. § 4-126(f); see COMAR 23.03.05).

### 5:51. What is the "Aging Schools Program"?

The Aging Schools Program is administered by the IAC and provides funds to local school systems for improvements, repairs, and deferred maintenance of aging public school buildings. Eligible program expenditures include small grants for asbestos and lead paint abatement; the upgrade of fire protection systems and equipment; painting; plumbing; roofing; the upgrade of heating, ventilation, and air conditioning systems; site redevelopment; wiring schools for technology; and renovation projects related to education programs and services.

The program was initially established by the Baltimore City-State partnership legislation, which provided $4.4 million for the program and specific allocations for local school systems. The following year, the School Accountability Funding for Excellence (SAFE) legislation increased the annual funding level by $6.0 million to $10.4 million, the same as the current statutory funding level. The fiscal 2007 State budget included $10.4 million for the mandated statutory formula plus $1.1 million for the hold harmless grants and an additional $3.651 million to be distributed in proportion to each county's share of the mandated statutory amount. In 2007, the General Assembly amended the funding allocation for the Aging Schools Program by making approximately half of the FY 2008 state funding contingent on the more stringent requirements of the Qualified Zone Academy Bond (QZAB) program. See **5:13** for a description of the QZAB program.

### 5:52. What role do transfer taxes play in school construction financing?

Transfer taxes are collected by the State and county governments based on a percentage of the assessed value of property at the time the title is transferred. Many but not all of Maryland's county governments have been authorized by state statute to levy a local transfer tax and counties typically designate all or part of this stream of revenue to school construction costs.

### 5:53. What role do impact fees play in school construction financing?

Impact fees may be collected from new home purchasers and used to defray the costs of public infrastructure, such as schools and roads, arising from the development of the new home. Impact fees may be structured as a single payment due at the time of home purchase or as a charge spread out over a number of years. In Maryland, an impact fee may be as high as $15,000 per residence. However, legal limitations imposed on impact fees include the requirements that the government must be able to demonstrate the quantifiable impact of a particular development, the fees must be used to pay for infrastructure in the vicinity of the development from which it is collected, and impact fee revenue may not be used for new program improvements such as class size reduction, but only to offset development impacts.

## 5:54. What role do excise taxes play in school construction financing?

Excise taxes may be collected from property owners and are not subject to the limitations of impact fees described above. For example, in 2002, Charles County replaced existing impact fees with a new excise tax to fund new school capacity. The new excise tax was referred to as the Fair Share School Construction (FSSC) Excise Tax. The excise tax is levied on all new residential development at the time of the Use and Occupancy permit approval. Homeowners make payments to the county to be paid over 10 years at level amortized payments financed at the County's interest rate. In addition, the County has the authority to issue school construction bonds to be serviced by the homeowner payments (see *Local Funding Strategies for School Construction*, Lisa Rawlings, University of Maryland School of Public Affairs (2004)).

# School Facilities: Standards

## 5:55. What is meant by an "adequate" school facility?

The Task Force to Study Public School Facilities was established by the Bridge to Excellence Act of 2002 and conducted a comprehensive survey of local school facilities in order to identify "fundamental elements necessary for an adequate school facility" (*Final Report of the Task Force to Study Public School Facilities, "Final Report"*, 2002). The Task Force, through an advisory panel, approved the assessment of the adequacy of local school facilities based on fundamental school facility standards in the following 31 areas:

| 31 Fundamental Elements of School Facility Adequacy ||
|---|---|
| Air Quality | General Secondary Classrooms |
| Fire Safety | Special Education |
| Building Systems, Materials, or Conditions | Instructional Resource Rooms |
| Security | Secondary Science Labs |
| Potable Water | Library/Media Centers |
| Lavatories | Technology Education |
| Communications Systems | Fine Arts |
| Comfort | Health Services |
| Acoustics | Food Services |
| Lighting | Auditoriums/Theaters |

| 31 Fundamental Elements of School Facility Adequacy | |
| --- | --- |
| Accessibility | Administration |
| Telecommunications | Guidance |
| Student Capacity | Itinerant Services |
| Pre-K/K Classrooms | Site Layout |
| | Teacher Planning |

### 5:56. What is the comprehensive maintenance plan required by the IAC?

Local boards are required to annually develop and approve a comprehensive maintenance plan (CMP) which describes strategies for maintaining public school facilities. The CMP includes descriptions of all scheduled, unscheduled, and deferred maintenance activities. State regulations provide that the CMP must be compatible with the local educational facilities master plan and the local capital improvement program. The IAC reviews the plan, notifies the school system of concerns and recommendations, and the school system is to "resolve the IAC's issues to the reasonable satisfaction of the IAC or its designee" (COMAR 23.03.02.18).

The purpose of the CMP is described as supporting the "delivery of educational programs in safe and healthy physical environments", with objectives that include:

- Maintaining a positive learning environment;

- Maintaining the asset value of the property;

- Eliminating or reducing the number and scope of fires, accidents, and other safety hazards on the property;

- Providing that buildings function at top efficiency;

- Providing continuous use of facilities without disruptions to the education program; and

- Conserving energy.

In addition, the *PSCP Guide* indicates that the "local government will appropriate, as part of its annual operating and/or capital budget, funds to implement the CMP (*PSCP Guide*, Section 802.1 - .4).

### 5:57. Who inspects schools for compliance with facility standards?

The IAC is responsible for annually surveying the condition of public schools. The IAC surveys are conducted by the staff of the Department of General Services

(DGS). PSCP annually inspects the condition of approximately 100 school buildings to identify maintenance needs, highlight the importance of effective maintenance programs, and increase awareness of and support for sound maintenance programs among school personnel and local boards of education. Approximately 100 schools are surveyed each year; due to time and staffing constraints not all of the state's approximately 1500 public school facilities can be surveyed annually. The IAC reports the survey results to the Board of Public Works, as well as the General Assembly and Governor (Md. Code Ann., Ed. Art. § 5-310).

The IAC maintenance surveys are performed in accordance with a carefully developed procedure that has been refined over the last 23 years. Each year staff from MSDE selects schools to be inspected based on the size of the school district, proposed renovation or construction schedules, and any special circumstances.

At the school the inspector evaluates the condition or performance of 34 systems or components and gives each a rating from "superior" to "poor." The inspector applies weighting factors to determine an overall score and completes an itemized list with written observations that is provided to the school system. If any serious hazards or deficiencies are identified, the school system is asked to submit a written plan outlining how and when the deficiencies will be corrected.

In addition, the General Assembly enacted legislation in 2004 adding the requirement that MSDE adopt regulations that provide for periodic surveys of the condition of all public school facilities in Maryland at least every 4 years. The regulations adopted by the State Board of Education outline the requirements for state and local surveys of the condition, adequacy, and costs to improve school facilities. However, the regulations provide that such surveys are contingent on the provision of state funding (COMAR 13A.01.02.04).

### 5:58. Does the State provide any funding to address emergency repairs?

Yes. In 2004, the General Assembly directed the Board of Public Works and the IAC to establish "an emergency repair fund to finance renovations and improvements to public schools that resolve deficiencies that present an immediate hazard to the health or safety of the students or staff of the schools," as certified by local education agencies and approved by the Interagency Committee on School Construction (see uncodified Section of the School Facilities Act of 2004, Chapter 306, Laws of Maryland (2004)).

### 5:59. What health and safety standards apply to school facilities?

School systems are responsible for ensuring that school facilities comply with an array of health and safety standards and requirements. Major health and safety issues include emergency repairs, indoor air quality, lead paint, asbestos, pesticide use, occupational health and safety protections for employees, and emergency preparedness planning, among others.

### 5:60. Do state and/or federal Occupational Health and Safety Act requirements apply to schools?

The federal Occupational Safety and Health Administration (OSHA) adopts and enforces standards dealing with occupational safety and health in the federal government and private sector. However, OSHA does not have jurisdiction over State and local government employees, including those in public schools. Section 18 of the Occupational Safety and Health Act allows States to develop OSHA-approved State plans; giving the State regulatory and enforcement responsibilities for occupational safety and health within its borders. Section 18 requires state plans to include standards for enforcement that are identical to (or at least as protective as) Federal OSHA standards. The state plans are also required to extend their coverage to all State and local government workers, including those in public schools.

Maryland's Occupational Safety and Health Act (MOSHA) covers every Maryland employer in a business, trade, commercial or industrial activity, who has one or more employees, including State and local governments.

### 5:61. How does the Americans with Disabilities Act (ADA) apply to school facilities?

Public schools are required to comply with Title II of the ADA (42 U.S.C. § 12101 *et seq.*) which covers all public entities. Public schools must provide program access in an integrated setting unless separate programs are necessary to ensure equal benefits or services. For existing facilities, school systems are required to operate each program so that, when viewed in its entirety, the program is readily accessible to and usable by individuals with disabilities. Acceptable methods of making programs accessible include: reassignment of services to an accessible location; the purchase, redesign, or relocation of equipment; assignment of aides; and structural changes to eliminate barriers. School districts are not required to take any action that would result in a fundamental alteration of the nature of the program or activity or in undue financial and administrative burdens. However, public schools must take any other action that would not result in a fundamental alteration or undue burden but would ensure that individuals with disabilities receive the same benefits and services offered to others without disabilities.

School facilities are designed, constructed and renovated in accordance with ADA as well other codes and standards, including the International Building Code

(IBC), the Americans with Disabilities Act Accessibility Guidelines (ADAAG), and the Architectural Barriers Act (ABA) Guidelines for Buildings and Facilities.

In Virginia, the Richmond school board settled a lawsuit in 2006 that claimed it failed to comply with state and federal disability laws, including ADA. The board admitted its failure to comply and agreed to develop a plan to make its facilities accessible. The cost of the school-wide modifications is indicated by board's development of a three-year, $17.1 million, plan.

## 5:62. May a school rely on well water or a septic system?

Yes. Nothing in state statute or regulation prohibits the reliance on a septic system for waste water, or well water as a source of potable water, at a school facility. However, school facility planning is impacted by Maryland's "Smart Growth" program, which imposes restrictions on state funding for infrastructure projects outside designated priority funding areas. The program, enacted in 1997, is intended to deter projects in areas not served by public water and sewer services (Md. Code Ann., St. Fin. & Proc. Art. § 5-7B-01-10). The statute provides that: "it shall be the policy of the state that the emphasis of funding for public school construction projects shall be to target the rehabilitation of existing schools to ensure that facilities in established neighborhoods are of equal quality to new schools." However, the Act also states that "this section may not be construed to prohibit the provision of school construction funding outside a priority funding area" (Md. Code Ann., St. Fin. & Proc. Art. § 5-7B-07).

## 5:63. What is Integrated Pest Management (IPM)?

Since 1998, School systems have been required to comply with Department of Agriculture standards and criteria for the application of pesticides in school facilities and on school grounds, including the development and implementation of an integrated pest management program. "Integrated pest management" is defined as:

> … a managed pest control program in which methods are integrated and used to keep pests from causing economic, health related, or aesthetic injury through the utilization of site or pest inspections, pest population monitoring, evaluating the need for control, and the use of one or more pest control methods including sanitation, structural repair, nonchemical methods, and, when nontoxic options are unreasonable or have been exhausted, pesticides in order to: (i) Minimize the use of pesticides; and (ii) Minimize the risk to human health and the environment associated with pesticide application. (Md. Code Ann., Agric. Art. § 5-208.1(a)(6)).

### 5:64. What is "indoor air quality" (IAQ) as it relates to school facilities?

"Indoor air quality" (IAQ) refers to the adequacy of ventilation, absence of mold and other irritants and/or pollutants, and other facets of maintaining a healthy respiratory environment for school students and staff. The federal government, through the U.S. Environmental Protection Agency (U.S. EPA) has developed the IAQ "Tools for Schools Kit" that provides detailed guidance as well as links to other information resources to help design new schools as well as repair, renovate and maintain existing facilities. Maryland's General Assembly has considered and rejected legislation to mandate the adoption of the EPA program by local school systems.

In 2007, the General Assembly responded to concerns about indoor air quality in relocatable classrooms by directing the Board of Public Works to adopt standards for newly constructed, purchased, or leased units (House Bill 164, Chapter 223, 2007 Laws of Maryland). The standards require each relocatable classroom to:

- include appropriate air barriers to limit infiltration;

- be constructed in a manner that provides protection against water damage by using proper materials and drainage systems;

- provide continuous forced ventilation when the unit is occupied;

- include a programmable thermostat;

- be outfitted with an energy efficient lighting and heating and air conditioning system; and

- be constructed with building materials that contain low amounts of volatile organic compounds (Md. Code Ann., Ed. Art., § 5-301(b-1)).

### 5:65. What, if any, energy efficiency standards apply to school facilities?

In 2004, the General Assembly directed the PSCP to "develop design guidelines and provide financial incentives, such as supplemental design funds or additional construction funding, for school construction projects that use innovative building techniques or include energy conservation, sustainable building, or green architecture design features" (see uncodified Section 7 of the School Facilities Act of 2004, Chapter 306).

The *PSCP Guide* stipulates that school construction projects financed with the assistance of the State must be designed "in a manner which will minimize the initial construction cost to the State and the consumption energy resources used in the operation and maintenance of the building." Therefore, school systems must conduct an analysis conforming with the Department of General Services,

*Procedures for the Implementation of Life Cycle Cost Analysis and Energy Conservation* (*PSCP Guide*, Appendix G, p. G-1).

## 5:66. What standards apply to boilers in schools?

Maryland's Department of Labor, Licensing and Regulation (DLLR) administers the Boiler and Pressure Vessel Safety Inspection unit, which adopts and enforces standards for boilers and pressure vessels (Md. Code Ann., Pub. Saf. Art., §§ 12-901 through 12-919). Boilers and pressure vessels include a range of devices including large building boilers, smaller hot water heaters, and steam cookers in school cafeterias. Any boiler or pressure vessel to be installed in Maryland must be built to a standardized nationwide construction code (American Society of Mechanical Engineers (ASME) Boiler and Pressure Vessel Code). Through periodic inspections and close monitoring of all repair work, the unit ensures the safe operation of boilers and pressure vessels.

Legislation enacted in 2005 created a new State Board of Stationary Engineers and mandated significant changes to the licensure requirements for school system employees responsible for operating and maintaining boilers in schools (House Bill 1589, 2005 Laws of Maryland). The state regulations regarding boiler standards and stationary engineers are found in the DLLR regulations in Title 9 of COMAR.

## 5:67. What must school systems do regarding asbestos in schools?

The Asbestos Hazard Emergency Response Act (AHERA) was enacted in 1986 and mandates the U.S. Environmental Protection Agency (EPA) to promulgate rules regarding asbestos hazards in schools (15 U.S.C. § 2651). EPA promulgated the Asbestos-Containing Materials in Schools Rule, which requires all private and public non-profit elementary and secondary schools to inspect their schools for asbestos-containing building materials (ACBM), develop a plan to manage the asbestos in each school building, notify parents and staff regarding the management plan, provide asbestos awareness training to school maintenance and custodial staff, and implement timely actions (repair, encapsulation, enclosure, removal) to address dangerous asbestos situations. The federal regulations, 40 C.F.R. Part 763, Subpart E – Asbestos-Containing Materials in Schools, apply to both public and nonpublic schools.

The following is an outline of several additional required actions by local school systems under AHERA:

- Assign and train a designated person to oversee asbestos activities and ensure compliance with AHERA requirements.

- Provide maintenance and custodial staff with two-hour asbestos awareness training.

- Conduct an initial inspection to identify ACBM in all school buildings.

- Conduct periodic surveillance, at least every six months, in buildings that contain ACBM.

- Conduct reinspections every three years by a certified inspector/management planner.

- Provide annual notifications regarding asbestos inspections and response actions to workers, occupants and legal guardians.

- Post warning labels adjacent to ACBM located in routine maintenance areas.

- Maintain documentation of inspections, reinspections, surveillance, response actions and training.

The Maryland State Department of Education (MSDE) provides technical assistance for the public and private schools that are subject to the 1987 Asbestos Hazard Emergency Response Act (AHERA). The schools are required to have their facilities inspected for asbestos-containing building materials and develop a management plan for handling these materials. MSDE also conducts compliance inspections in these schools and EPA Region III provides enforcement (COMAR 26.11.21.00).

### 5:68. Does asbestos continue to be used in construction materials?

Yes, and the U.S. EPA continues to highlight the need to ensure that materials used in schools do not contain asbestos. For example, Maryland's local school systems recently received a letter from the EPA alerting them to potential compliance actions regarding reliance on Material Safety Data Sheets (Letter of Henry Daw, Chief, Pesticides/Asbestos Programs & Enforcement, Region III EPA (September 5, 2006)). The letter states:

> Recently, EPA Region III became aware that many LEAs in the states of Maryland and West Virginia have been using information included in Occupational Safety and Health Administration (OSHA) Material Safety Data Sheets (MSDS) to determine whether school building material is regulated as asbestos-containing material. According to 40 C.F.R. §763.85, LEAs are required to visually inspect school buildings to identify the locations of all suspected ACBM. These regulations further require LEAs to either assume suspect building material to be regulated as ACBM or sample and analyze such material in accordance with 40 C.F.R. §§763.86 and 763.87. As described at 40 C.F.R. §763.93, school management plans must include not only the location, quantity, and condition of all ACBM but also descriptions of sampling protocols and results of

laboratory analyses. Neither AHERA nor EPA's regulations specify OSHA MSDS as a method to determine whether school building material is regulated as ACBM. If you have used MSDS to determine whether school building material is ACBM in any school under your jurisdiction, you are in violation of federal requirements and must come into compliance immediately.

## Student Transportation

### 5:69. Where are the laws and regulations regarding student transportation located?

Section 5-205(f) of the Education Article authorizes the State Board to "adopt rules and regulations that provide for the safe operation of the student transportation system of each county board of education" (Md. Code Ann., Ed. Art. § 5-205(f)). This statute also sets the base grant amounts and disabled student grants for student transportation for each local board. Pursuant to Section 5-205, the State Board has adopted regulations under COMAR 13A.06.07. The State Board's regulations incorporate by reference several federal regulations regarding bus driver qualifications, as well as cross-referencing numerous provisions of the Maryland Department of Transportation's regulations regarding school vehicles and drivers.

The state's regimen of student transportation standards reflects the state's strong interest in ensuring student safety and the federal government's corresponding regulation of commercial transportation including school vehicles. On the local level, school systems must not only comply with all state and federal safety requirements, but also adopt bus routes, stops, loading zones, and schedules. In this way student transportation presents local boards with myriad, daily operational challenges.

### 5:70. What state agency sets the safety standards for school buses?

Maryland's Motor Vehicle Administration, with the advice of the Maryland State Department of Education (MSDE), is required to adopt and enforce rules and regulations governing the safe operation of all school vehicles.

### 5:71. What is the local board's role in setting transportation policies?

With regard to transportation safety, state regulations provide that the local school system is responsible for the safe operation of the student transportation system, must comply with all state procedures and guidelines, and may adopt policies and procedures which exceed the state's minimum requirements (COMAR

13A.06.07.03). With regard to local administration and operation of the student transportation system, state regulations require that each local system employ a local supervisor of student transportation, and prescribe numerous operational and reporting requirements for the hiring of school vehicle driving instructors, employment qualifications for bus drivers, bus inspections, and routing and scheduling.

### 5:72. What federal requirements apply to student transportation?

The federal Department of Transportation is responsible for adopting safety standards for school buses and school bus equipment manufactured in, or imported into, the United States (49 U.S.C. § 30125(b)). Standards include minimum performance requirements for: emergency exits; interior protection for occupants; floor strength; seating systems; crashworthiness of body and frame (including protection against rollover hazards); vehicle operating systems; windows and windshields; and fuel systems.

The National Highway Traffic Safety Administration (NHTSA), part of the U.S. Department of Transportation, is authorized to issue and enforce Federal motor vehicle safety standards (FMVSSs) applicable to all new motor vehicles, including school buses.

### 5:73. What types of vehicles may be used to transport students?

A "school vehicle" as defined in statute is either a Type I or Type II school vehicle. Type I school vehicles are a conventional style school bus that has a gross vehicle weight of more than 15,000 pounds (Md. Code Ann., Transp. II Art. § 11-173). Type II school vehicles are a van-conversion style school bus that has a gross vehicle weight of 15,000 pounds or less (Md. Code Ann., Transp. II Art. § 11-174). Local school systems use primarily Type I school vehicles to transport children. Only Type I or II school vehicles may be used to transport students to and from school and related activities, unless the vehicle is a taxicab or a commercial motor vehicle, only one student is transported, or special approval has been granted by the State Superintendent (COMAR 13A.06.07.10B).

### 5:74. Who owns and operated school buses?

School buses may be purchased and operated by a local school system or purchased and operated by a private entity contracting services to the local school system. Similarly, school bus drivers may be employees of the school system or employees of the independent contractor.

**5:75. What is the maximum number of years of operation for a school bus?**

Generally, a school vehicle may be operated for no more than 12 years. However, the General Assembly recently extended the time period to 15 years for buses operating since prior to July 1, 2004; and for all buses operating in Somerset, Wicomico and Worcester Counties (Md. Code Ann., Ed. Art. § 7-804)

**5:76. What qualifications apply to school bus drivers?**

School systems are prohibited from permitting a person from operating a school vehicle who satisfies certain "disqualifying conditions" relating to criminal charges including:

- Child abuse or neglect;
- Contributing to the delinquency of a minor;
- A state or federal controlled dangerous substance offense;
- Driving any vehicle under the influence of drugs or alcohol (COMAR 13A.06.07.06A).

**5:77. How is eligibility for bus ridership determined?**

Local school systems are responsible for adopting policies determining the maximum distance from a school within which school bus service will not be provided.

**5:78. May students be required to cross a road to reach the school bus?**

Yes. However, on four-lane highways students must be picked up and discharged on the same side of the road as they reside (COMAR 13A.06.07.12D)

**5:79. May a student be transported by taxicab?**

Yes. However, regulations provide that the use of taxis must be kept to a minimum "and restricted to those times when transportation by a school vehicle is not feasible" (COMAR 13A.06.07.12E).

**5:80. May a school system use passenger vans to transport students?**

The laws regarding the use of large passenger vans for student transportation are confusing, in that the law holds dealers selling the vans, and the school systems purchasing them, to different standards. Federal requirements regulate new vehicles that carry 11 or more persons that are sold for transporting students to or from school or school related events. Those vehicles are required to meet all federal safety standards applicable to school buses. These standards require that school buses have stop arms along with many other safety features over and above those of other passenger vehicles. Under 49 U.S.C. § 30101 *et seq.*, a vehicle is regarded as being sold for use as a school bus if, at the time of sale, it is evident that the vehicle is likely to be significantly used to transport students to or from school or school related events. This statute applies to school buses sold to public as well as parochial schools. Thus, it the responsibility of the dealer selling a new 15-passenger van to be used for school transportation to ensure that the van is certified as meeting school bus standards.

Federal regulations do not prohibit the use of vans by schools, but require any van (with a capacity of more than 10) sold or leased for use as a school bus to meet the safety standards applicable to school buses.

### 5:81. May public school buses be used to transport nonpublic school students?

Yes. For example, state statute authorizes the Calvert County Board of Education to provide transportation to nonpublic students (Md. Code Ann., Ed. Art. § 7-801(c)).

### 5:82. Why aren't seatbelts required on school buses in Maryland?

According to the National Highway Traffic Safety Administration (NFTSA), whereas seat belts have been required on passenger cars since 1968, school buses are different by design and use a different kind of safety restraint system that works extremely well. NHTSA describes large school buses as heavier and distribute crash forces differently than do passenger cars and light trucks. Because of these differences, the crash forces experienced by occupants of buses are much less than that experienced by occupants of passenger cars, light trucks or vans. NHTSA decided that the best way to provide crash protection to passengers of large school buses is through a concept called "compartmentalization." This requires that the interior of large buses provide occupant protection such that children are protected without the need to buckle-up. Through compartmentalization, occupant crash protection is provided by a protective envelope consisting of strong, closely-spaced seats that have energy-absorbing seat backs.

NHTSA guidance indicates that small school buses (with a gross vehicle weight rating of 10,000 pounds or less) must be equipped with lap and/or lap/shoulder belts at all designated seating positions. Since the sizes and weights of small school buses are closer to those of passenger cars and trucks, seat belts in those vehicles are necessary to provide occupant protection (see NHTSA guidance at *www.nhtsa.dot.gov*).

Maryland statute and regulations do not require seatbelts on school vehicles, but do require that a motor vehicle used by nursery schools, camps, day nurseries, or day care centers for retarded children to transport children, and which is not regulated as a school bus, must be equipped with seat belts for each seat in the vehicle (COMAR 11.13.09.02).

### 5:83. When must a driver stop for school bus, and what are the penalties for failing to do so?

If a school vehicle has stopped on a roadway and is operating alternately flashing red lights, the driver of any other vehicle meeting or overtaking the school vehicle must stop at least 20 feet from the rear of the school vehicle, if approaching the school vehicle from its rear, or at least 20 feet from the front of the school vehicle, if approaching the school vehicle from its front. In addition, if a school vehicle has stopped on a roadway and is operating alternately flashing red lights, the driver of any other vehicle meeting or overtaking the school vehicle may not proceed until the school vehicle resumes motion or the alternately flashing red lights are deactivated. Violators may be assessed three points and are subject to a maximum $1000 penalty under the Maryland Vehicle Law. Drivers who elect not to contest the violation are subject to a $275 pre-pay penalty. These requirements do not apply to the driver of a vehicle on a divided highway, if the school vehicle is on a different roadway (Md. Code Ann., Transp. II Art. § 21-706).

## Student Health and Safety

### 5:84. What is the local board's role regarding the health of students?

Local boards of education are required, with the assistance of the county health department, to provide "adequate school health services" and "instruction in health education, including the importance of physical activity in maintaining good health" and "a healthful school environment" (Md. Code Ann., Ed. Art. § 7-401(a)). In addition, each local board must designate a school health services program coordinator.

### 5:85. What is the state's role regarding the health of students?

State law directs the Maryland State Department of Education (MSDE) and Department of Health and Mental Hygiene (DHMH) to (1) jointly develop public standards and guidelines for school health programs, and (2) offer assistance to the county boards and county health departments in their implementation (Md. Code Ann., Ed. Art. § 7-401(b)). MSDE is required to conduct at least two meetings annually with all school health services program coordinators.

In addition, much of the state's role is derived from its obligations to enforce federal requirements regarding nutrition, which are discussed under **5:92** through **5:94**.

### 5:86. What is the role of the school health coordinator?

School health coordinators may be employees of the local health department or the school system and, in general, are responsible for the school system's compliance with the adopted Maryland State School Health Services Guidelines. The state legislature enacted a new law in 2006 to require each local board of education to designate a school health services program coordinator. The law further defines the duties of the coordinator to include: (1) implementing state and local health policies in the public schools, (2) ensuring that public schools adhere to local health guidelines, and (3) communicating health policies to the parents and guardians of public school students. The law goes so far as to direct school systems to "grant the school health services program coordinator the authority to carry out the provisions of this subsection" (Md. Code Ann., Ed. Art. § 7-401(c)).

Interestingly, the legislation was motivated, at least in part, by the concern that students were not being permitted to apply sunscreen before recess, and includes an uncodified provision stating:

> [E]ach school health services program coordinator shall ensure that public schools in the county adhere to the Maryland State School Health Services Guidelines issued in 2001 by the State Department of Education, the Department of Health and Mental Hygiene, and the Maryland State School Health Council entitled "Guidelines for Protecting Students and Staff from Overexposure to the Sun."

### 5:87. What are the Maryland State School Health Services Guidelines?

The Maryland State School Health Services Guidelines include a series of separate guidelines on the subjects listed below. The guidelines are available on the MSDE website at: *http://www.marylandpublicschools.org/MSDE/divisions/ studentschoolsvcs/studentservices_alt/school_health_services/shsguidelines.htm.*

- Acquired Immune Deficiency Syndrome (AIDS)/HIV Infection
- Asthma
- Anaphylaxis
- Body Fluids

- Certified Nursing Assistant Training
- Chain of Survival
- Confidentiality
- Communicable Diseases
- Delegation of Nursing Functions

- Dental Resource Guide
- Diabetes Mellitus
- Do Not Resuscitate
- Documentation of School Health Records
- Emergency Planning for School Nurses
- Emergency Care in Maryland Schools
- Facility and Design Guide for School Systems
- Hemophilia
- Hearing and Vision

- Laws that Impact School Health Services Programs
- Medication in Schools
- Nursing Appraisal/Assessment of Students
- Oxygen Dependent Student
- Overexposure to the Sun
- Private Duty Nurses
- Role of the School Health Services Staff
- Skin Cancer Prevention

## 5:88. Are schools required to provide hearing and vision screenings?

Yes. However, it is the responsibility of the county health department, not the public school system, to fund and provide hearing and vision screenings for all students in the public schools and licensed private schools. (Md. Code Ann., Ed. Art. § 7–409(a)). Screenings are required for all students in the year that a student enters a school system, enters the fourth, fifth, or sixth grade, and enters the ninth grade.

## 5:89. What restrictions apply to dispensing prescription drugs in schools?

The state guidelines provide that all prescription medication to be given in a school must be ordered by a person authorized to prescribe medication (*Administration of Medication in Schools*, Maryland State School Health Services Guideline (Jan. 2006)). In Maryland an authorized prescriber is defined as physician, nurse practitioner, certified midwife, podiatrist, physician's assistant or dentist (Md. Code Ann., Hlth. Oc. Art. § 12-101(b)). The guidelines describe the recommended approved medication administration/authorization form, which must be signed by the authorized prescriber and the parent/guardian. The guidelines outline the responsibilities of the school nurse to administer narcotics, over the counter, and homeopathic and herbal medications. The guidelines also address the process of determining when a student may self-administer a medication, and when the school nurse may delegate authority to dispense medication to another staff person.

**5:90. Who other than a school nurse may dispense medication?**

In the absence of the school nurse, the guidelines provide that in all cases the person to whom the administration of medications is delegated should be trained and supervised in accordance with the School Health Medication Administration Training Program and meet criteria set forth in COMAR 10.27.11 and COMAR 10.39.01, which provide that:

- In the judgment of the nurse, the task delegated can be properly and safely performed by the unlicensed individual or certified nursing assistant without jeopardizing the client's welfare; and

- That the person is competent to perform the task assigned.

**5:91. When may a student self-administer medication?**

Yes. The Maryland General Assembly enacted a new law in 2005 which requires each local school system to adopt a written policy that authorizes a student to possess and self-administer an asthma inhaler or other emergency medication used to relieve an airway-constricting disease while in school, at a school-sponsored activity, or on a school bus (Md. Code Ann., Ed. Art. § 7-421).

The statute provides that in order to self-administer medication, a student must annually provide a written order from a health care provider and written approval from the student's parent or guardian. A student's parent or guardian must obtain written confirmation from the student's health care provider that the student has the knowledge and skills necessary to safely administer the treatment, and a school nurse must assess the student's ability to demonstrate the skill level necessary to ensure effective self administration. A student may be subject to disciplinary action if the treatment is not administered in a safe and proper manner.

**5:92. What is the federal role in promoting student health?**

The federal government's role in directing state and local policies is generally derived from its power to place conditions on the provision of federal funding, and significant amounts of funding are provided by the Richard B. Russell National School Lunch Act (42 U.S.C. § 1751 *et seq.*) and the Child Nutrition Act of 1966 (42 U.S.C. § 1771 *et seq.*). Through such legislation, federal requirements are playing an increasing role in state and local laws, regulations, policies and practices regarding student health.

A primary example of this trend is the 2004 reauthorization of the federal Child Nutrition Act (CNA) which requires all local school districts to put comprehensive wellness programs in place by the beginning of the 2006-2007 school year. The CNA requires school systems to appoint wellness councils, which must include students, teachers, community members, and representatives of the district's food-service program. The wellness councils are responsible for developing plans to be adopted by local boards of education to address the types of food sold in schools, physical education, and nutrition. School districts are also required to appoint monitoring officers to ensure compliance.

The Act includes in the preamble the following: "Congress recognizes that schools play a critical role in promoting student health, preventing childhood obesity, and combating problems associated with poor nutrition and physical inactivity."

## 5:93. What is required to be included in the locally developed school wellness policy?

Federal law requires that school wellness policies include the following:

- Goals for nutrition education, physical activity and other school-based activities that are designed to promote student wellness in a manner that the local educational agency determines is appropriate;

- Sample policy language, existing state and local policies, implementation tools, and resources are available for: nutrition education, physical activity, and other school-based activities designed to promote wellness;

- Nutrition guidelines selected by the local educational agency for all foods available on each school campus under the local school system during the school day with the objectives of promoting student health and reducing childhood obesity;

- A plan for measuring implementation of the local wellness policy, including designation of one or more persons within the local educational agency or at each school, as appropriate, charged with operational responsibility for ensuring that each school fulfills the district's local wellness policy; and

- Community involvement, including parents, students, and representatives of the school food authority, the school board, school administrators, and the public in the development of the school wellness policy.

## 5:94. What are the federal statutes addressing school nutrition?

Maryland regulations (COMAR 13A.06.01.01) incorporate by reference the following list of applicable federal statutes and regulations:

(1) National School Lunch Program, 42 U.S.C. §§ 1751—1760 and 1779, and 7 C.F.R. Part 210;

(2) Special Milk Program, 42 U.S.C. §§ 1772 and 1779, and 7 C.F.R. Part 215;

(3) School Breakfast Program, 42 U.S.C. §§ 1773 and 1779, and 7 C.F.R. Part 220;

(4) Summer Food Service Program, 42 U.S.C. §§ 1758, 1761, and 1762a, and 7 C.F.R. Part 225;

(5) Child and Adult Care Food Program, 42 U.S.C. §§ 1758, 1759a, 1762a, 1765, and 1766, and 7 Part C.F.R. 226;

(6) Nutrition Education and Training Program, 42 U.S.C. § 1788, and 7 C.F.R. Part 227;

(7) Eligibility for Free and Reduced Price Meals and Free Milk in Schools, 42 U.S.C. §§ 1751—1752, 1758, 1759a, 1760, 1772—1773, and 1779, and 7 C.F.R. Part 245; and

(8) Food Distribution Program, 42 U.S.C. §§ 1751, 1755, 1758, 1760—1762a, and 1766, and 7 C.F.R. Part 250.

### 5:95. Does the state set additional school nutrition standards?

Yes. The State Board of Education has approved detailed policy guidance intended to ensure that schools promote a healthy school environment in regard to foods and beverages available to students during the school day (see *MSDE School and Community Nutrition Programs Branch Management and Operations Memorandum Number 12*, March 2005 (MOM 12)). The state guidance outlines all federal and state regulations that apply to serving foods and beverages in schools and facilities that participate in the School Nutrition Program. The policy addresses four components, including:: Nutrition Policy, Foods of Minimal Nutritional Value, Nutrition Guidelines, and Nutrition Integrity Teams.

### 5:96. How may vending machines be used in schools?

Federal law provides that in order to receive funding through the school nutrition programs, local school systems must sign written agreements to deny students access to vending machines that sell foods of minimal nutritional value before the end of the final lunch period of the day. Maryland's General Assembly frequently considers legislation regarding school nutrition standards, including expanding restrictions on access to "junk food", referred to as "foods of minimal nutritional value" (FMNV). Most recently, the General Assembly enacted the requirement that by August 1, 2006, vending machines in public schools must have and use a timing device to automatically prohibit or allow access to vending machines in accordance with the nutrition policies established by the county board (Md. Code Ann., Ed. Art. § 7–423).

Local policies on vending machines are addressed in MOM 12, which is the state policy setting minimum requirements and providing guidance for local school systems electing to set policies which go beyond those contained in the memorandum. Regarding vending machines, MOM 12 states: "The sale of all items on the list of foods of minimal nutritional value as outlined in Attachment A is prohibited from 12:01 a.m. until the end of the last lunch period. *School Food Authorities are strongly encouraged to extend this restriction on the sale of these foods until the end of the standard school day*" (emphasis added). This language reflects the State Board's decision to not mandate, but rather encourage, that vending machines selling FMNVs be turned off until after the school day.

### 5:97. What is a "food of minimal nutritional value"?

U.S. Department of Agriculture regulations (Appendix B of 7 C.F.R. Part 210), incorporated by reference in Maryland regulations and restated in MOM 12, define foods of minimal nutritional value (FMNV) as:

(1) Soda Water;

(2) Water Ices;

(3) Chewing Gum;

(4) Certain Candies;

    (i)   Hard Candy;

    (ii)  Jellies and Gums;

    (iii) Marshmallow Candies;

    (iv) Fondant;

    (v)  Licorice;

    (vi) Spun Candy; and

    (vii) Candy Coated Popcorn.

Interestingly, the federal regulations provide a detailed list of foods of minimal nutritional value, by manufacturer and commercial product name, which are exempted from the restrictions on availability to students.

### 5:98. What are the state requirements for school health education programs?

State regulations (COMAR 13A.04.18.02) outline detailed requirements of Maryland's comprehensive health education program and curriculum, which "shall provide for the diversity of student needs, abilities, and interests at the early, middle, and high school learning years, and shall include all of the following goals and subgoals" (*subgoals omitted*):

A. To gain knowledge and skills that lead to an understanding about self and one's relationships with others;

B. To acquire and apply knowledge of tobacco, alcohol, and other drugs and the consequences of their non-use, use, and abuse;

C. To adopt sound personal health practices and make appropriate use of health care products, services, and community resources;

D. To understand the value of achieving a healthy lifestyle through the development and application of responsible nutritional and fitness behaviors;

E. To develop an understanding of behavior and skills that promote safe living in the home, school, and community;

F. To recognize the family as a basic unit of society that perpetuates life and promotes healthy growth and development; and

G. To acquire knowledge of disease and methods for prevention and control and to analyze their effects on the individual, family, and society.

### 5:99. What are the state requirements for physical education programs?

State law (Md. Code Ann., Ed. Art. § 7–409(a)) provides broad discretion to local school systems to establish physical education programs, as follows:

"(a) Each public school shall have a program of physical education that is given in a planned and sequential manner to all students, kindergarten through grade 12, to develop their good health and physical fitness and improve their motor coordination and physical skills."

State Board adopted regulations further require yearly physical education instruction for all students in grades kindergarten through 8, and elective classes for students in grades 9 through 12. In addition, State regulations require one semester of physical education in grades 9 through 12 for high school graduation. Regulations require that physical education programs provide an "individualized, developmentally appropriate, and personally challenging instructional program that advances the student's knowledge, confidence, skills, and motivation to engage successfully in a lifelong healthy and active lifestyle" (COMAR 13A.04.13.01). COMAR also requires each school system to develop physical education curriculum guides for the elementary and secondary schools under its jurisdiction.

Maryland's state legislature has frequently considered and rejected proposals to mandate minimum numbers of minutes per day or week of physical education in elementary schools. The proposed minimum standard is typically based on the adopted standards of the National Association for Sport and Physical Education, which call for instructional periods totaling 150 minutes per week in elementary grades and 225 minutes per week in middle and high school grades.

## 5:100. What are examples of safety related laws affecting public schools?

School safety includes a wide variety of public policy issues which may be generally grouped into three categories. First, school safety issues arise in the daily operation of school facilities and services such as buses, science labs, kitchens, and boiler rooms. Second, school safety issues arise in the daily administration of school discipline policies and procedures, including the suspension and expulsion of students for disruptive behavior. Third, school safety issues arise as school systems develop plans to respond to natural and man-made disasters such as tornadoes, hurricanes, floods, industrial accidents, and criminal acts including acts of terrorism.

Many of the federal, state, and local laws, regulations, and policies relating to school safety have been discussed in the facilities and transportation sections of this chapter. Student and staff disciplinary issues are addressed in **Chapters 11 and 7**. The federal No Child Left Behind Act, discussed in **Chapter 8**, also includes provisions relating "persistently dangerous" schools as well as the federal Gun-Free Schools Act. Additional safety issues are discussed below.

## 5:101. How is school safety defined?

While the terms "safe school" or "school safety" are not defined in state law or regulation, state regulations (COMAR 13A.01.04.03) do address the need to ensure a safe school environment for students:

> All students in Maryland's public schools, without exception and regardless of race, ethnicity, region, religion, gender, sexual orientation, language, socioeconomic status, age, or disability, have the right to educational environments that are:
>
> A. Safe;
>
> B. Appropriate for academic achievement; and
>
> C. Free from any form of harassment.

## 5:102. How are safety issues addressed in the school curriculum?

Each public school is required to have a program of safety education that is organized and administered under the bylaws, rules, and regulations of the State Board of Education (Md. Code Ann., Ed. Art. § 7–410).

## 5:103. What is an example of a safety education program?

One example is the Maryland Science Safety Manual, which is a comprehensive set of safety guidelines for use by local school systems and schools in providing safe classroom instruction in science. The manual was a joint project of the Maryland Science Supervisors Association (MSSA) and the Maryland State Department of Education (MSDE), and is available on the MSDE website at: *http://www.mdk12.org/instruction/curriculum/science/safety/contents.html*.

## 5:104. Are schools required to have emergency management plans?

The federal No Child Left Behind Act requires that all local school systems receiving federal funding under Title IV, Part A, Safe and Drug-Free Schools and Communities, which includes all 24 school systems in Maryland, provide an assurance that they have a crisis management plan in place to respond to crisis and emergency situations on school grounds.

Maryland regulations (COMAR 13A.02.02.01 – .04) require the adoption, implementation and annual certification of local school system emergency plans as follows:

A. In consultation with other health and safety officials in the local community, each local school system school shall develop an emergency plan for each public school and central administration office under its jurisdiction that:

(1) Deals with the contingencies of man-made, technological, and natural hazards; and

(2) Conforms to the requirements of this chapter.

B. Each public school emergency plan shall be on file in each public school system.

C. Each local school system shall develop and implement an annual schedule of drills for each school within the system.

An emergency plan is defined as a plan for each school system and each public school within the school system that addresses mitigation, preparation, response, and recovery to an emergency including responding to: (a) Violent or traumatic events on school grounds during regular school hours or during school-sponsored activities; or (b) Events in the community that affect normal school functioning.

### 5:105. Are schools required to have routine fire drills?

Yes, each public school must conduct fire drills at least ten times each school year and at least once every 60 days (Md. Code Ann., Ed. Art. § 7–408).

### 5:106. Are schools required to have automated external defibrillators (AEDs)?

Legislation enacted in 2006 requires local school systems to develop and implement an automated external defibrillator program, in accordance with the requirements of § 13-517 of the Education Article, for each high school in the county. An AED program must ensure that an AED is provided on-site, and that an individual trained in the operation and use of an automated external defibrillator is present at all school-sponsored athletic events (Md. Code Ann., Ed. Art. § 7–425).

An AED is a defined as a medical heart monitor and defibrillator device that:

    (i)   Is cleared for market by the federal Food and Drug Administration;

    (ii)  Recognizes the presence or absence of ventricular fibrillation or rapid ventricular tachycardia;

    (iii) Determines, without intervention by an operator, whether defibrillation should be performed;

    (iv) On determining that defibrillation should be performed, automatically charges; and

    (v)  1.  Requires operator intervention to deliver the electrical impulse; or

          2.  Automatically continues with delivery of electrical impulse (Md. Code Ann., Ed. Art. § 13-517).

State regulations promulgated by the Maryland Institute for Emergency Medical Services Systems (MIEMSS) apply to all approved AED programs, including public school programs (COMAR 30.06.01). In addition, the 2006 legislation requires MSDE, in consultation with the Department of Health and Mental Hygiene, the Maryland State School Health Council, and the Maryland Institute for Emergency Medical Services Systems, to adopt regulations that establish guidelines for periodic inspections and annual maintenance of the automated external defibrillators in high schools.

# 6. Employee Relations and Rights

## 6:1. Who is the "Public School Employer"?

The "Public School Employer" is the local board of education (Md. Code Ann., Ed. Art. §§ 6-401(e); 6-501(g)).

## 6:2. Who is a "Public School Employee"?

For certificated employees, under Md. Code Ann., Ed. Art. § 6-401(d), the term "public school employees" is defined to include all employees holding a professional certificate issued by the Maryland State Department of Education— see COMAR 13A.12, *et seq.,* setting forth Maryland certification requirements for teachers (13A.12.02), guidance counselors (13A.12.03.02), media specialists (13A.12.03.03), pupil personnel workers (13A.12.03.04), reading specialists (13A.12.03.05), reading teachers (13A.12.03.06), psychometrists (13A.12.03.07), school psychologists (13A.12.03.08), speech pathologists (13A.12.03.09), occupational and physical therapists (13A.12.03.10), and administrators and supervisors (13A.12.04)—with the exception of the Superintendent or a person acting in a negotiating capacity (*e.g.,* a member of the local board's negotiations' team). Specific provisions in this section of the statute add additional employees to the ranks of public school employees on a county-by-county basis as follows: Montgomery County (certificated and non-certificated substitute teachers and home and hospital teachers); Baltimore County (school nurses and supervisory non-certificated employees); Frederick County (social workers); Prince George's County (home and hospital teachers and Junior ROTC instructors); and Charles County (Junior ROTC instructors).

For non-certificated employees, under Md. Code Ann., Ed. Art. § 6-501(f), the term "public school employees" is defined to include any "noncertificated individual who is employed for at least 9 months a year on a full-time basis by a public school employer." Here, it is important to note that the term "full-time basis" is *not* defined and is subject to interpretation (or negotiation) on a county-by-county basis.

## 6:3. Are all employees of the local board "Public School Employees"?

No. Following from the definitions discussed above, not all employees of the local board of education are considered "public school employees". The distinction is critical, because only "public school employees" are included within employee bargaining units for collective bargaining purposes. For example, one county may define "full-time" as being 40 hours per week, while another county may define "full-time" as being a much lesser number of working hours, such as 25 hours per week. The significance is that those counties that define "full-time" as being a lesser number of working hours will have many more employees counted as "public school employees" who are thus included within one of the non-certificated employee units (*Carroll Association of School Employees v. Carroll County Board of Education*, MSBE Op. No. 04-41 (2004)).

### 6:4. What is the impact when an employee of the local board does not meet the definition of a "Public School Employee"?

If an employee of a local board does not meet the definition of a "public school employee", the employee cannot be a member of a "specified unit" (commonly referred to as a "bargaining unit") of certificated or non-certificated employees. All "public school employees" must be included within one of the specified units (Md. Code Ann., Ed. Art. §§ 6-404(d), 6-505(d)).

### 6:5. What is a bargaining unit?

Although it is clear that public sector employees have a First Amendment right to associate and peaceably assemble into unions and other labor organizations (*Smith v. Arkansas State Highway Employees, Local 1315*, 441 U.S. 463 (1979); see also discussion at **3:16**), the First Amendment does *not* create a right to public sector collective bargaining. Such a right is created under State law. Md. Code Ann., Ed. Art. §§ 6-404(b) and 6-505(b) require the local board to determine the composition of specified units of certificated or non-certificated employees after "negotiation with any employee organization that requests negotiation concerning the composition of the unit." The unit may, or may not, have an "exclusive bargaining representative" which is typically an organized association or union that represents members of the bargaining unit in all matters involving wages, salaries, benefits, and working conditions (see *Charles County Supporting Services Employees Local 301 v. Board of Education of Charles County*, 48 Md. App. 339 (1981) (local board is under no obligation to recognize an exclusive bargaining representative for a specified unit)).

### 6:6. How many bargaining units can a local board designate?

A local board, with the exception of the Board of Education of Baltimore County, may recognize up to five distinct bargaining units—three units for non-certificated employees and two units for certificated employees (see Md. Code Ann., Ed. Art. § 6-404(c) (two unit limit for certificated employees); Md. Code Ann., Ed. Art. § 6-505(c) (three unit limit for non-certificated employees)). By statute, Baltimore County may recognize up to three certificated units for a total of six distinct bargaining units, provided that one of the three certificated units covers school nurses and another covers both certificated and non-certificated supervisors (Md. Code Ann., Ed. Art. § 6-404(c)(2)).

## 6:7. May certificated and non-certificated employees be in the same bargaining unit?

Unless there is a specific statutory provision particular to the local board providing otherwise, as with Baltimore County (see **6:6**), certificated and non-certificated employees are prohibited from being in the same bargaining unit. Similar legislation was passed for Carroll County during the 2007 session of the Maryland General Assembly providing for non-certificated administrators and supervisors to become members of the same bargaining unit as certificated administrators and supervisors.

## 6:8. May supervisory and non-supervisory employees be in the same bargaining unit?

For certificated employees, supervisory and non-supervisory employees may be in the same bargaining unit. For example, directors, supervisors, principals, and assistant principals may be in the same bargaining unit with teachers and other certificated employees. For non-certificated employees, however, the statute clearly provides that "a unit may not include both supervisory and nonsupervisory employees" (Md. Code Ann., Ed. Art. § 6-505(c)(1)). A supervisory non-certificated employee is defined as an "individual who responsibly directs the work of other employees, as determined by the public school employer in negotiation with an employee organization that requests negotiation on the issue."

## 6:9. Who determines the composition of the bargaining unit?

The public school employer (*i.e.,* the local board) determines the composition of the bargaining unit in negotiation with the exclusive bargaining representative for the unit, if any (Md. Code Ann., Ed. Art. §§ 6-404(b); 6-505(b)). For non-certificated employees, if there is no recognized exclusive bargaining representative, but one or more associations or unions seek recognition as the exclusive bargaining representative of a newly created or potential bargaining unit, then the public school employer should first determine if it will allow exclusive representation at all (see *Charles County Supporting Servs. Employees Local 301 v. Board of Education of Charles County*, 48 Md. App. 339, 348-349 (1981) (reasoning that the requirement to negotiate unit composition "is not triggered so as to impose a present imperative duty unless and until the public [school] employer first decides that it will allow exclusive representation among its noncertificated employees")). If it chooses to do so, it should then negotiate the composition of the bargaining unit with the applicable associations or unions (*Carroll Association of*

*School Employees v. Carroll County Board of Education*, MSBE Op. No. 04-41 (2004)).

### 6:10. If the local board and the association or union do not agree with the composition of the bargaining unit, who has the final say?

The public school employer (*i.e.,* the local board) has the obligation to negotiate in good faith but, ultimately, has the final say on the composition of the bargaining unit.

### 6:11. Must the local board recognize an exclusive bargaining representative for a bargaining?

For certificated employees, Md. Code Ann., Ed. Art. § 6-404(a) states that the Board "*shall* designate ... which employee organization, if any, shall be the exclusive representative of all public school employees in a specified unit" (emphasis added). For non-certificated employees, the Board has more discretion, since Md. Code Ann., Ed. Art. § 6-505(a) provides that the Board "*may* designate ... which employee organization, if any, shall be the exclusive representative of all public school employees in a specified unit" (emphasis added) (see discussion at **6:9**).

### 6:12. What is the process for recognizing an association or union as the "exclusive bargaining representative"?

An employee organization that certifies to the local board that it has membership enrollment of at least thirty percent of the total employees within a specified unit as of June 1 of the year in which certification is made may seek recognition as the exclusive representative of all public school employees within that specified unit. An election is *not* required if (1) no other organization certifies that it has membership enrollment of at least ten percent of the specified unit, (2) the employee organization does not request an election, and (3) the employee organization certifies that it has membership of a *majority* of the public school employees within the specified unit (Md. Code Ann., Ed. Art. §§ 6-405(b)(e); 6-506(b)(e)).

### 6:13. If there are multiple associations or unions seeking to represent the same bargaining unit, how is an "exclusive bargaining representative" recognized?

If there is another employee organization that certifies membership of at least ten percent of the total employees within a specified unit as of June 1, there shall be an election whereby employees will be allowed to choose which organization, *if any*, they wish to represent the specified unit (Md. Code Ann., Ed. Art. §§ 6-404(c); 6-505(c)).

### 6:14. Once an association or union is recognized as the "exclusive bargaining representative", are employees required to join that association or union and pay dues?

No. Employees are never required to join an association or union even when such an entity is recognized as the "exclusive bargaining representative" for the unit in which the employee is a member (the one exception is with respect to non-certificated employees in Prince George's County, where, pursuant to Md. Code Ann., Ed. Art. § 6-504(c), "the County Board shall negotiate an organizational security provision, commonly known as 'agency shop', with employee organizations"). However, by statute, members of the bargaining units in some counties may be required to pay a "representation fee" even though they have elected not to become dues paying members of the association or union. The representation fee is sometimes referred to by associations and unions as "fair share" since they are required to represent all members of the bargaining unit in collective bargaining negotiations even if the bargaining unit members are not dues paying members of the association or union.

Md. Code Ann., Ed. Art. § 6-407(b) provides, for certificated employee organizations, that an "employee organization designated as an exclusive representative shall represent all employees in the unit fairly and without discrimination, whether or not the employees are members of the employee organization." Of note, there is no comparable language for non-certificated employees. Moreover, even though this language does not provide any limitations with respect to the words "*shall* represent", it appears that the employee associations take the view that representation of non-members within the bargaining unit is confined to the negotiations process only and does not include the representation of non-members in grievances, appeals, or litigation.

### 6:15. In which counties are public school employees required to pay a representation fee?

There are statutory provisions for the negotiation of "a reasonable service fee" for certificated employees in Montgomery, Prince George's, Baltimore City, Baltimore County, Allegany, Charles, Garrett, Washington, and Anne Arundel Counties (see Md. Code Ann., Ed. Art. § 6-407(c)(1) (Montgomery and Prince George's Counties and Baltimore City), § 6-407(c)(5) (Baltimore County), § 6-407(d) (Allegany, Charles, Garrett, and Washington Counties), § 6-407(f) (Anne Arundel County)). In each of these jurisdictions, the statute provides that the local board "may negotiate" such fees. For non-certificated employees, the statutory provisions provide that the local board "shall negotiate" the payment of a "reasonable service fee" in Montgomery, Allegany, and Charles Counties and in Baltimore City, and that the local board "may negotiate" the payment of such fees in Anne Arundel and Baltimore Counties (see Md. Code Ann., Ed. Art. § 6-504(b) (Montgomery, Charles, and Allegany Counties), § 6-504(e) (Baltimore City), § 6-504(d) (Anne Arundel and Baltimore Counties); see **6:11** regarding the mandatory "agency shop" for non-certificated employees in Prince George's County)). Legislation adopted during the 2007 session of the General Assembly for Howard County would allow negotiation of a "reasonable service fee" for certificated employees and would require such negotiations for non-certificated employees.

### 6:16. Must a public school employer negotiate with an association or union recognized as the "exclusive bargaining unit"?

Yes. The local board is required to negotiate in good faith "on all matters that relate to salaries, wages, hours, and other working conditions" (see Md. Code Ann., Ed. Art. § 6-408(b)(1) (for certificated employees), § 6-510(b)(1)). These topics are "mandatory" subjects of collective bargaining.

### 6:17. Are all matters negotiable?

No. There are illegal subjects of collective bargaining. Any item that is precluded by statute (*e.g.*, school calendar or class size) or is statutorily within the exclusive authority of the superintendent or local board is an illegal subject of collective bargaining (see Md. Code Ann., Ed. Art. § 6-408(b)(3) (for certificated employees), § 6-510(b)(3); see, *e.g.*, *Kent County Board of Education v. Kent County Teachers' Association*, MSBE Op. No. 05-12 (2005), *aff'd*, Case No. 14-C-05-0063689 (Cir. Ct. Kent Co. Nov. 4, 2005) (decision to assign IEP chair duties to principals within the Superintendent's statutory duty to assign and transfer personnel under Md. Code Ann., Ed. Art. § 6-201(b)); *Harford County Board of Education v. Harford County Educational Services Council*, MSBE Op. No. 05-24 (2005) (holding that the Superintendent's statutory authority under Md. Code Ann., Ed. Art. § 6-201(c) to appoint non-certificated staff includes a substantive, non-negotiable authority to determine the cause for discipline and discharge); *Allegany County Teachers Association v. Allegany County Board of Education*, MSBE Op. No. 05-27 (2005) (reasoning that if a provision in a negotiated collective bargaining agreement "can affect the outcome of the transfer decision, the provision is illegal as transfer and assignment are precluded from negotiation by statute")). In *Calvert County Board of Education v. Calvert Education Ass'n.*, MSBE Op. No. 07-05 (2007), the State Board recently held that budgetary matters were non-negotiable as a matter of law and that, accordingly, a dispute over the use of moneys placed in a health insurance "Rate Stabilization Reserve Fund" was not arbitrable as a matter of law because the dispute concedrned the Board's budgetary authority.

### 6:18. What are the differences between mandatory, permissive, and illegal subjects of collective bargaining?

Prior to the enactment of amendments to the collective bargaining statute in 2002, there was no such thing as "permissive" subjects of negotiation. Topics were either mandatory subjects of collective bargaining (*i.e.,* salaries, wages, hours, and other working conditions) or illegal subjects. If the topic did not clearly fall within one of the mandatory areas, a two-part test was used to determine whether a subject was a lawful matter for negotiations or an illegal subject: First, if the matter was precluded from negotiations by statute, it was an illegal subject of collective bargaining. Second, if the matter was not precluded by statute a balancing test was utilized to determine if the subject had a greater impact upon educational policy or the administration of the school system than it did over working conditions. If so, it was also an illegal subject of negotiations (*Montgomery County Education Association v. Board of Education of Montgomery County*, 311 Md. 303, 309-310 (1987)).

In 2002, the General Assembly amended the collective bargaining law to provide for the negotiation of "permissive" subjects (see Md. Code Ann., Ed. Art. § 6-408(b)(2) (for certificated employee organizations), § 6-510(b)(2) (for non-certificated employees)). Both sections provide that the local board and the employee organization "may negotiate" on "matters that are mutually agreed to by the employer and the employee organization." The only difference between the two provisions is that in Section 6-510(b)(2) there is the additional provision for the permissive negotiation of "due process for discipline and discharge" for non-certificated employees. In *Harford County Board of Education v. Harford County Educational Services Council*, MSBE Op. No. 05-24 (2005), the State Board held that this language allowed for the permissive negotiation of due process procedures but did not divest the superintendent's substantive statutory authority to determine cause for non-certificated employee discipline and discharge and that such decisions were appealable under Md. Code Ann., Ed. Art. § 4-205(c), but not subject to arbitration (*accord Livers v. Charles County Board of Education*, 6 Op. MSBE 407 (1992), *aff'd*, 101 Md. App. 160, *cert. denied*, 336 Md. 594 (1994) (similar decision prior to 2002 amendments)).

Permissive subjects would include items that are not precluded from negotiations by statute or items that are not within a statutory delegation of authority to the Superintendent or the Board. The nature of "permissive" subjects is that if either side declines to negotiate the permissive subject, it is off the table. If the matter is not negotiated, it may not be the subject of an impasse between the parties (Md. Code Ann., Ed. Art. §§ 6-408(b)(4), 6-510(b)(4)).

**6:19. Is there a particular process that must be followed in collective bargaining negotiations?**

Although there is an overriding requirement that parties negotiate in "good faith", there is no prescribed methodology for collective bargaining unless such a methodology is negotiated as a "permissive topic" and made a part of the collective bargaining agreement. In addition, it is typical for the negotiated agreement to prescribe when negotiations will take place for a successor agreement or if there is a need for negotiations on topics that may arise during the term of an existing collective bargaining agreement.

There are several examples of collective bargaining methodologies: The traditional approach involves an exchange of bargaining positions back and forth at the collective bargaining table—usually with chief negotiators leading the discussions for their respective negotiations teams—until an agreement is reached through a process of compromises and trade-offs. In addition, there are several "collaborative" approaches—including "Getting to Yes" and "Interest Based Bargaining" or "IBB"—where there is more of a collaborative approach to negotiations, and the interests of the parties are discussed in an effort to build consensus.

**6:20. Who has the authority to determine whether an impasse has occurred?**

The Maryland State Superintendent of Schools is the only person with authority to officially declare an impasse. Either the local board or the employee association or union may ask the State Superintendent to declare an impasse. Often, the request for an impasse is made jointly after both parties agree that they have reached a juncture in negotiations where they are unable to reach agreement on their own (Md. Code Ann., Ed. Art. §§ 6-408(d), 6-510(d)). The State Superintendent has the discretion to refuse to declare an impasse and direct the parties to resume negotiations on their own.

**6:21. Once the State Superintendent determines that an impasse exists, what process is followed to resolve the impasse?**

Typically, the local board and the employee association or union agree to the appointment of a panel consisting of a representative of each party (often, the chief negotiators) and a neutral (often, a mediator chosen from a list provided by the American Arbitration Association or the Federal Mediation and Conciliation Service). In addition, "the assistance and advice of the State Board may be requested" (Md. Code Ann., Ed. Art. §§ 6-408(d), 6-510(d)). In the typical impasse, the neutral mediator will assist the teams in reaching a compromise that both sides can accept.

## 6:22. If the parties are unable to reach an agreement in the impasse mediation, what responsibilities does the impasse mediator have?

If a mediated settlement is not reached, the mediator will issue a written report and recommendation within thirty days.

## 6:23. Is the impasse mediator's report and recommendation binding?

Maryland does not have binding impasse arbitration. It is important to note that the mediator's *recommendation* is just that and is not binding on either party.

## 6:24. Since the impasse mediator's recommendation is not binding, what authority does the local board have?

Ultimately, the local board has the statutory authority to impose its "final determination as to matters that have been the subject of negotiation" (see Md. Code Ann., Ed. Art. §§ 6-408(d)(7) (certificated employees), 6-511(d)(7)). In other words, even if the parties are unsuccessful in reaching an agreement, the local board has the final authority to *impose* its final position on the employee organization without a formal collective bargaining agreement.

Any final determination reached by the local board, with or without a formal signed collective bargaining agreement, is subject to the fiscal relationship between the local board and the county government (see Md. Code Ann., Ed. Art. §§ 6-408(d)(7) (certificated employees), 6-511(d)(7)). It must always be remembered that local boards are not self-funding entities. Accordingly, even if the local board signs a formal collective bargaining agreement, if it later finds that it cannot meet the terms of that agreement due to a lack of funding from the county government, the local board is not bound by the agreement (see Md. Code Ann., Ed. Art. §§ 6-408(d)(7) (certificated employees), 6-511, 6-511(d)(7)). This is an important point when one considers that although local boards often negotiate multi-year collective bargaining agreements with employee organizations, they only get an annual budget from the county government as well as from the State and federal governments.

## 6:25. Are employee associations or unions permitted to strike?

No. An employee association or union "may not call or direct a strike" (Md. Code Ann., Ed. Art. §§ 6-410(a), 6-513(a)). Even if the word "strike" is not used (*e.g.,* an organized "sick out"), it is still considered an illegal strike. If an employee association or union calls or directs a strike, then the local board is required to revoke the organization's designation as the "exclusive representative" for a period of at least two years and shall stop making payroll deductions for employee dues for a period at least one year (Md. Code Ann., Ed. Art. §§ 6-410(a), 6-513(a)).

### 6:26. What is a "work to rule"?

A "work to rule" is a concerted job action whereby participating employees express their displeasure with the local board by strictly adhering to their contractual duties and refrain from performing any work beyond the contractual duty day. A "work to rule" is not an illegal strike but, rather, is a legal action designed to demonstrate how often public school employees perform services beyond their contractual duties. On occasion, employees participating in a "work to rule" will refuse to volunteer at school events and may even refuse to write letters of reference for students. Employees working to rule may not, however, refuse to perform duties for which they may be contractually obligated. For example, a teacher who has agreed to an extra-pay for extra-duty coaching position would not be allowed to stop coaching during the term of the extra-duty assignment.

### 6:27. What is the role, if any, of the county government in school system collective bargaining?

As discussed above (see **6:24**), local boards of education in Maryland are not self-funding entities and are entirely dependant upon federal, state, and county governments for funding the school system's budget. Since most federal and state funds are earmarked for specific programs, the county government funding is where the local board obtains most of its funding for such items as salary increases and other negotiated benefits. Although the county governments do not participate in collective bargaining negotiations with public school employee bargaining groups, the local boards must be careful in developing their budgetary requests so that they are able to fund the negotiated collective bargaining agreements. Very often, local boards find themselves negotiating with employee bargaining groups on the one level while "negotiating" budgetary priorities with the county government on yet another level. This is an important point when one recognizes that the county governments set the categorical totals in the local boards' budgets (see Md. Code Ann., Ed. Art. § 5-102(c) (counties with county executive), § 5-102(d) (Baltimore City), § 5-103(c) (counties with commissioner or county council form of governments)). Accordingly, even if the overall budget may provide enough money to fund a negotiated collective bargaining agreement, it is important to see that the appropriate budget categories have the appropriate funding as well. For example, if the overall budget is sufficient to fund the negotiated collective bargaining agreement, but the category for "instructional salaries" is insufficient to fund negotiated salary increases, there would be a short-fall necessitating either a budget transfer between categories (which requires county approval; see Md. Code Ann., Ed. Art. § 5-105(b)(2)) or re-negotiation of the collective bargaining agreement.

**6:28. What are the local board's options if it is unable to fund a collective bargaining agreement?**

As discussed earlier (see **6:24**), if a local board is unable to fund a negotiated collective bargaining agreement, it has the ability to impair the existing collective bargaining agreement and renegotiate with the employee bargaining groups.

**6:29. What is meant by the term COLA?**

COLA stands for "cost of living adjustment". It is somewhat of a misnomer because it is rarely tied to the consumer price index or any other recognized indicator of the "cost of living." For example, even in years without any inflation, employee bargaining groups still referred to their requests for salary increases as a COLA. As a result, the negotiated COLA is the percentage increase that is most recognized in collective bargaining negotiations for employee salary increases.

**6:30. What are steps?**

Steps are built into negotiated salary schedules and are based upon employee longevity and experience. Many, but not all, steps provide for additional salary increases. Salary schedules are often set for a comparatively long period of time lasting on occasion for many successive contracts. In years of budget difficulties, however, employees are occasionally "frozen on step". Moreover, if a superintendent rates a teacher or principal's certificate as "second class", that employee may not receive a step increase (Md. Code Ann., Ed. Art. § 6-301).

**6:31. What are ranges or lanes?**

Ranges or lanes are also built into the negotiated salary schedules and are usually based upon attaining an advanced degree or graduate credits or advanced certification. Each progressive range or lane typically contains a higher pay rate. Accordingly, as an example, a teacher who attains a masters degree may get a salary increase based upon a move from one lane to another, plus an increase in salary based upon a longevity-based step, as well as the negotiated COLA increase.

**6:32. What is the difference between a re-classification and a transfer?**

A transfer or re-assignment is when the Superintendent or his/her designee moves an individual from one existing position to another existing position (Md. Code Ann., Ed. Art. § 6-201(b)(2)). A re-classification is when an existing position is changed to a newly created position, or the position is moved to a different range, lane, or step. The re-classified position may or may not result in different duties and may or may not carry a different rate of pay. Neither re-classifications nor transfers are subject to collective bargaining or the grievance/arbitration process (for re-classifications, see, *e.g.*, *Montgomery County Education Association v. Board of Education of Montgomery County*, 311 Md. 303 (1987); *Washington County Education Classified Employees Association v. Board of Education of Washington County*, 97 Md. App. 397 (1993); for transfers, see, *e.g.*, *New Board of School Commissioners of Baltimore City v. Public School Administrators & Supervisors Association*, 142 Md. App. 61 (2002); *Hurl v. Board of Education of Howard County*, 107 Md. App. 286 (1995); *Kent County Board of Education v. Kent County Teachers' Association*, MSBE Op. No. 05-12 (2005), *aff'd*, Case No. 14-C-05-0063689 (Cir. Ct. Kent Co. Nov. 4, 2005) (decision to assign IEP chair duties to principals within the Superintendent's statutory duty to assign and transfer personnel under Md. Code Ann., Ed. Art. § 6-201(b)); *Allegany County Teachers Association v. Allegany County Board of Education*, MSBE Op. No. 05-27 (2005) (reasoning that if a provision in a negotiated collective bargaining agreement "can affect the outcome of the transfer decision, the provision is illegal as transfer and assignment are precluded from negotiation by statute")). An example of a re-classification might be when the Superintendent decides to eliminate the position of "instructional assistant" and create a variety of "para-educator" positions at different levels based upon duties, educational level, and "highly qualified" status in accordance with the No Child Left Behind Act (see **Chapter 8**).

### 6:33. What is a contract "opener"?

All collective bargaining agreements cover a set period of time and require re-negotiation for a successor contract prior to the expiration of the contract term. Sometimes, the parties negotiate a multi-year contract but provide for periodic contract "openers" whereby the parties meet during the term of the contract to re-negotiate specific provisions but not the contract as a whole. For example, the Board and the Association may negotiate a three year contract, but, due to funding uncertainties, provide for an opener on salary for the second and third years. Contract openers allow the parties to maintain the benefit of a multi-year agreement without being locked in on certain specific provisions. On occasion, the contract may also provide for a limited number of "non-specified openers" whereby either party may seek negotiation on an additional item of the party's choice (for a discussion of contract openers, see *Harford County Board of Education v. Harford County Educational Services Council*, MSBE Op. No. 05-24 (2005)).

### 6:34. What is a grievance and arbitration clause?

Negotiated agreements typically contain a grievance and arbitration clause whereby employees or the employee organization may seek resolution of a dispute centered on the interpretation and application of the negotiated agreement. Typically, the grievance and arbitration clause will require the employee or employee organization to seek resolution at the lowest possible level before moving to higher levels or to binding arbitration. For example, the negotiated agreement may provide that the first step is the school principal, the second step is the director of human resources, the third step is the superintendent, and the fourth step is binding arbitration through the American Arbitration Association. The grievance and arbitration clause will also specify the timelines for filing a grievance and for moving the grievance from step to step and for responding to the grievance. Unless waived by mutual agreement of the parties, these timelines will be strictly construed. The actual provisions in the grievance and arbitration clause are, of course, subject to negotiation between the parties.

### 6:35. Are all disputes grievable or arbitrable?

No. The grievance and arbitration process must be distinguished from the administrative appeals process set forth in Md. Code Ann., Ed. Art. § 4-205(c) (concerning disputes and controversies arising under state education laws and regulations, local board policies, and the administration of the school system) and in Md. Code Ann., Ed. Art. § 6-202(a) (concerning the suspension or termination of certificated employees). Grievances and arbitrations are limited to negotiable matters set forth within the collective bargaining agreement. Matters that fall within the Board or Superintendent's authority are neither negotiable nor subject to grievance or arbitration (see discussion at **6:17, 6:18**).

For example, in *Board of Education of Carroll County v. Carroll County Education Association*, 53 Md. App. 355 (1982), the Court of Special Appeals of Maryland held that the Board's statutory authority to grant or deny tenure under Md. Code Ann., Ed. Art. § 6-201(f) could not be delegated away to an arbitrator. In *Livers v. Charles County Board of Education*, 6 Op. MSBE 407 (1992), *aff'd*, 101 Md. App. 160, *cert. denied*, 336 Md. 594 (1994), the State Board and the Court of Special Appeals ruled that "just cause" language for the discipline and discharge of non-certificated employees is an illegal subject of collective bargaining and arbitration (*accord Harford County Board of Education v. Harford County Educational Services Council*, MSBE Op. No. 05-24 (2005) (re-affirming *Livers* decision based upon holding that the 2002 amendments to the collective bargaining provisions of Md. Code Ann., Ed. Art. § 6-510(b)(2) permitting "permissive" negotiations in certain areas did not divest the superintendent's substantive statutory authority to determine cause for non-certificated employee discipline and discharge and that such decisions were appealable under Md. Code Ann., Ed. Art. § 4-205(c), but not subject to arbitration)). In *New Board of School Commissioners of Baltimore City v. Public School Administrators & Supervisors Association*, 142 Md. App. 61 (2002), the State Board and the Court of Special Appeals held that the statutory authority to re-assign principals and other employees to lower pay positions under Md. Code Ann., Ed. Art. § 6-201(b) was not an arbitrable issue (*accord Kent County Board of Education v. Kent County Teachers' Association*, MSBE Op. No. 05-12 (2005), *aff'd*, Case No. 14-C-05-0063689 (Cir. Ct. Kent Co. Nov. 4, 2005) (decision to assign IEP chair duties to principals within the Superintendent's statutory duty to assign and transfer personnel under Md. Code Ann., Ed. Art. § 6-201(b)); *Allegany County Teachers Association v. Allegany County Board of Education*, MSBE Op. No. 05-27 (2005) (reasoning that if a provision in a negotiated collective bargaining agreement "can affect the outcome of the transfer decision, the provision is illegal as transfer and assignment are precluded from negotiation by statute")).

### 6:36. Who determines whether or not a dispute is grievable or arbitrable?

In *Board of Education of Dorchester County v. Hubbard*, 305 Md. 774 (1982), the Court of Appeals of Maryland held that the Maryland State Board of Education—and not arbitrators or the courts—has the primary jurisdiction to determine whether disputes are subject to the administrative appeals process or to the grievance and arbitration process (commonly referred to as "scope of bargaining disputes"). This "primary jurisdiction" is critically important because, otherwise, an arbitrator would make a decision on the question of arbitrability. In the event that a Demand for Arbitration is filed by an employee organization over a matter that a local board believes is inarbitrable as a matter of law, the local board will typically file a Petition for Declaratory Ruling with the Maryland State Board of Education. Unless the employee organization voluntarily agrees to stay the arbitration pending the State Board's ruling, the local board will be required to seek a stay of the arbitration in the circuit court pending the State Board's determination of the arbitrability issue. Such a process was followed in *Harford County Board of Education v. Harford County Educational Services Council*, MSBE Op. No. 05-24 (2005), and *Kent County Board of Education v. Kent County Teachers' Association*, MSBE Op. No. 05-12 (2005), *aff'd*, Case No. 14-C-05-0063689 (Cir. Ct. Kent Co. Nov. 4, 2005). Unless the local board seeks a stay of the arbitration in the circuit court, the arbitration will move forward unless *both* the local board and the employee organization agree to the stay.

### 6:37. If a dispute is not grievable or arbitrable, how may the dispute be resolved?

Each county superintendent is required to explain the "true intent and meaning" of the public school laws and the State Board's regulations, and the superintendent is further obligated to decide all "controversies and disputes" arising under the county board's policies and regulations and the proper administration of the school system (Md. Code Ann., Ed. Art. § 4-205(c)(1)(2)). Accordingly, a dispute that is not properly the subject of arbitration is most likely subject to an appeal to the superintendent. If an employee is dissatisfied with the decision rendered by the superintendent or the superintendent's designee, the dispute may be appealed to the local board (Md. Code Ann., Ed. Art. § 4-205(c)(3)). If the employee is still dissatisfied with the local board's decision, the dispute may be appealed to the State Board. If the employee is dissatisfied with the State Board's decision, the dispute is subject to an appeal to the courts.

### 6:38. When a dispute is arbitrable, how is the dispute resolved?

Although the process utilized for submitting disputes to arbitration is subject to the provisions in the negotiated collective bargaining agreement, the typical process is for the parties to submit a "Demand for Arbitration" to the American Arbitration Association. In addition to the American Arbitration Association, some school systems use the services of arbitrators provided by the Federal Mediation and Conciliation Service or contract for arbitrators privately. The arbitrator will conduct an evidentiary hearing and will render a binding decision.

### 6:39. How is the arbitrator selected?

After the Demand for Arbitration is filed, the American Arbitration Association will provide to the parties a list of potential arbitrators, along with the arbitrators' curriculum vitae. The parties then engage in a process of elimination whereby they "strike" a certain number of arbitrators from the list. From the arbitrators not stricken by either party, the American Arbitration Association then selects an arbitrator. The arbitrator is a neutral party who will then try the arbitration case in a manner similar to a judge; however, the rules of evidence are more relaxed. The arbitrator may or may not request that the parties submit written memoranda. Eventually, the arbitrator will render a written decision (called an "award") that is binding upon the parties.

### 6:40. Is the arbitrator's decision binding?

Yes. The arbitrator's decision is binding and is not subject to an "appeal."

### 6:41. Under what circumstances may an arbitrator's decision be vacated?

The arbitrator's decision may, however, be "vacated" by a circuit court if the arbitrator's decision involved an illegal subject of collective bargaining (for example, if the arbitrator made an award concerning class size or the school calendar) or if the decision was the subject of fraud or irregularity. An argument that the arbitrator's decision was "wrong"—either as a matter of fact or of law—will not suffice as grounds for vacating an arbitrator's decision.

### 6:42. Other than the collective bargaining agreement, do public school employees have any other contracts with the public school employer?

Yes. Teachers and other certificated professional employees must sign either the "regular" or the "provisional" contract on the forms set forth in COMAR 13A.07.02.01. This section provides in paragraph A as follows: "All contracts with certificated professional employees shall be in writing and on contract forms prescribed by the State Board of Education." Non-certificated employees do not sign either the regular or the provisional contract.

### 6:43. What is the "Regular Teacher's Contract"?

The "Regular Teacher's Contract" is set forth verbatim in COMAR 13A.07.02.01B and is for all "employees who hold professional certificates." No other contract other than that prescribed in this section of COMAR will be recognized.

### 6:44. What is the difference between a "regular" contract and a "provisional contract"?

The "provisional contract" set forth in COMAR 13A.07.02.02C is for "employees who hold conditional or resident teacher certificates ... and no others shall be recognized."

### 6:45. What is the duration of a "regular contract"?

Among other things, the "regular contract" provides for a probationary period of employment whereby the non-tenured employee may be terminated by the Board without cause by May 1 (June 15 if the certificated employee was hired after January 1) of the first, second, or third year. Otherwise, the "contract shall continue from year to year" subject to termination for the specified reasons set forth in Md. Code Ann., Ed. Art. § 6-202(a) (*i.e.,* immorality, misconduct in office, insubordination, incompetency, or willful neglect of duty) or "if the employee ceases to hold a professional certificate."

### 6:46. What is the duration of a "provisional contract"?

The term of the "provisional contract" is for a maximum of one school year and expires automatically on June 30 following the execution of the contract. If the employee ceases to have a conditional or resident teacher certificate, then the contract ends automatically. However, if the employee obtains a professional certificate, then the Board may offer the employee a "regular contract" after June 30, and the employee's time under the "provisional contract" shall count towards tenure.

### 6:47. What is "tenure"?

Tenure is a contractual and statutory expectation to continued employment that rises to the level of a constitutionally protected "property" interest in that continued employment subject only to termination for cause after the opportunity for a hearing (see *Board of Regents v. Roth*, 408 U.S. 564 (1972); *Perry v. Sinderman*, 408 U.S. 593 (1972); see also *Parker v. Board of Education of Prince George's County*, 237 F. Supp. 222 (D. Md.), *aff'd*, 348 F.2d 464 (4th Cir. 1965), *cert. denied*, 382 U.S. 1030 (1965) (non-renewal of teacher for using book *Brave New World* in class after being told not to); see generally **3:15** (discussing the effects of the Fourteenth Amendment on public education)). A "probationary" certificated employee in the first or second year of employment cannot have tenure in Maryland. In addition, a probationary period may be extended for a third year (Md. Code Ann., Ed. Art. § 6-202(b)).

### 6:48. Who is eligible to achieve tenure?

Only professionally certificated employees are eligible for tenure (Md. Code Ann., Ed. Art. § 6-202(b)). Non-certificated employees, even those holding professional degrees such as accountants, engineers, and in-house legal counsel, are not eligible for tenure.

### 6:49. How does a certificated employee achieve tenure?

At a minimum, the certificated employee must be employed by the local board of Education for a period of two years. There is also the possibility of a third probationary year. If the certificated employee is hired before January 1, then a decision to not renew the employee's contract or to place the employee on a third probationary year must be communicated to the employee in writing no later than May 1 of the second year of employment. If the certificated employee is hired after January 1, then a decision to not renew the employee's contract or to place the employee on a third probationary year must be communicated to the employee in writing no later than June 15 of the second year of employment (COMAR 13A.07.02.01). These deadlines are mandatory. Failure to give the employee timely written notice by these deadlines will result in the employee achieving tenure (see, e.g., *Powell v. Montgomery County Board of Education*, MSBE Op. No. 01-04 (2001), at 3 (reasoning that, "under State Board regulation, for probationary certificated employees, the only process due the individual is written notice by May 1 of the decision not to renew the probationary contract"); *Resnick v. Board of Education of Howard County*, 7 Op. MSBE 123 (1995) (nonrenewal notice deposited in United States mail on May 2 is untimely)).

### 6:50. Does a certificated employee obtain tenure in a particular school or position?

No. The certificated employee holds tenure in the school system only—not in a particular school or in a particular position. Moreover, tenure is not transferable from school system to school system. Accordingly, if a veteran teacher resigns from one county to take a position in another, the employee becomes a non-tenured employee once again. Of course, most school systems will place the employee on the salary scale based upon the employee's experience from the other county.

### 6:51. Do administrators and supervisors obtain tenure as administrative employees?

No. Administrators and supervisors, including principals and assistant principals, do not hold tenure in their administrative position. As with teachers, they are tenured only as certificated employees of the local Board of Education (see **6:62**; *Jackson-Nesmith v. Charles County Board of Education*, 7 Op. MSBE 1320 (1998)).

### 6:52. Is the superintendent required to demonstrate cause prior to denying tenure or deciding to not renew a non-tenured certificated employee's contract?

No. The Superintendent is never required to give a reason or demonstrate cause for a non-renewal (*Board of Regents v. Roth*, 408 U.S. 564 (1972); *Melton v. Talbot County Board of Education*, MSBE Op. No. 00-38 (2000)).

### 6:53. May a certificated employee appeal a non-renewal decision?

Yes. A non-renewal decision may be appealed to the Superintendent, then to the local Board of Education, and then to the State Board under Md. Code Ann., Ed. Art. § 4-205(c). There is no right to an evidentiary hearing on such an appeal. In *Bricker v. Board of Education of Frederick County*, 3 Op. MSBE 99, 101 (1983), the State Board reasoned that, "probationary teachers' legal rights are not required by law or constitutional right to be determined after an agency hearing." The State Board went on to reason that although a former probationary employee may, as was done in this case, "appeal a dispute or controversy under Section 4-

205(c), their only right is to have that appeal accepted by the State Board for review." Thereafter, the State Board's decision may be appealed to the courts.

### 6:54. Who has the burden of proof on an appeal of a non-renewal decision?

The employee challenging the non-renewal decision has the burden of proof under Md. Code Ann., Ed. Art. § 4-205(c).

### 6:55. What is the standard of review on an appeal of a non-renewal decision?

In order to be successful on an appeal from a non-renewal decision, the certificated employee must demonstrate that the decision was discriminatory or otherwise illegal (*Melton v. Talbot County Board of Education*, MSBE Op. No. 00-38 (2000)).

### 6:56. What is the standard for termination or suspension of a non-tenured certificated employee?

There is a distinction between non-renewal, on the one hand, and termination or suspension, on the other hand. As discussed earlier (see **6:52**), there is no need to demonstrate cause for a non-renewal. There is a much different standard for termination or suspension without pay of a non-tenured certificated employee. Such employees are entitled to the same rights as are tenured employees and may only be suspended without pay or terminated for immorality, misconduct in office, insubordination, incompetency, or willful neglect of duty pursuant to Md. Code Ann., Ed. Art. § 6-202(a). On such an action, the superintendent has the burden of proof in a full evidentiary hearing before the local Board of Education, and the local Board of Education's decision is subject to a *de novo* appeal to the State Board. Unlike with other decisions appealed to the State Board where the State Board must give deference to the local Board of Education's decision, the State board can substitute its judgment for that of the local Board of Education (see **7:10**).

### 6:57. Are non-certificated employees ever eligible for tenure?

No. Tenure is only for certificated employees (see **6:48**).

### 6:58. If non-certificated employees do not achieve tenure, what is the effect of a "probationary" period for non-certificated employees?

The local Boards of Education may, by policy or through negotiated provisions in their collective bargaining agreement, provide additional procedural protections to their non-certificated employees after the expiration of a probationary term (see Md. Code Ann., Ed. Art. § 6-510(b)(2) (providing for the negotiation of due process for discipline and discharge as a permissive subject of collective bargaining with non-certificated bargaining groups)). Such provisions provide a fundamentally fair process; however, they do not create tenure under Maryland law (see **7:1**).

### 6:59. Are "re-hired retirees" eligible for tenure?

No. Re-hired retirees are hired for a one-year term only (COMAR 13A.07.02.05).

### 6:60. Who has the authority to assign and transfer employees?

The Superintendent has the broad statutory authority to assign certificated and non-certificated employees to their positions within the schools and to transfer or re-assign these employees "as the needs of the schools require" (Md. Code Ann., Ed. Art. § 6-201(b)). Very often, the Superintendent will delegate that authority to designated employees who are under the Superintendent's authority. For example, a Superintendent may delegate to a principal the authority to assign teachers within the principal's school.

### 6:61. Are there any limits on the superintendent's authority to assign and transfer staff?

The only limit on the Superintendent's authority to assign and transfer staff is the employee's right to file an appeal to the local Board of Education under Md. Code Ann., Ed. Art. § 4-205(c) (see **6:65**).

### 6:62. If a principal or other administrator is re-assigned to a lower pay position, is that considered a 'demotion" or an involuntary transfer/re-assignment?

It is considered a transfer or re-assignment. The word "demotion" is not found in the Education Article to the Annotated Code or in COMAR Title 13A. Pursuant to Md. Code Ann., Ed. Art. § 6-201(b), the Superintendent always has the authority to re-assign administrative or supervisory employees to other positions "as the needs of the schools require"—even if the position carries a lower rate of pay (see, e.g., *New Board of School Commissioners of Baltimore City v. Public School Administrators & Supervisors Association*, 142 Md. App. 61 (2002) (affirming decision to re-assign a number of principals to positions with less authority and less pay); *Hayes v. Board of Education of Carroll County*, 1 Op. MSBE 719, 723 n.1 (1978)).

## 6:63. If a principal or other administrator is transferred/re-assigned to a lower pay position, is he or she otherwise entitled to the same rate of pay?

No. A principal or other administrator may be transferred or re-assigned to a position with a lower rate of pay. The only limitation on the Superintendent's authority to make such re-assignments is that "if the transfer be made during the school year or after the opening of the school for any year, the salary shall not be reduced for the remainder of the year." This language is contained within the Regular Contract as set forth in COMAR 13A.07.01B. The Regular Contract further provides that the "term 'school year' as used in this contract means the period of time the certificated employee is obligated to perform duties (teaching and nonteaching) under his or her assignment for a local school system." Accordingly, if a Superintendent were to re-assign a principal to a ten-month teaching position, the principal would be entitled to his or her same rate of pay through June 30, which is the end of the fiscal year for the school system and, hence, the end of the duty year for twelve-month employees.

## 6:64. Do coaches or persons holding other extra-duty positions have tenure in these assignments?

No. There is no tenure in a coaching or other extra-duty assignment. Such positions are subject to assignment on an annual basis, and, although disputes over such assignments are appealable, they are not grievable or arbitrable (*Education Association of St. Mary's County v. Board of Education of St. Mary's County*, 7 Op. MSBE 683 (1997)).

## 6:65. If an employee is unhappy about a transfer or assignment decision, is the dispute subject to grievance and arbitration or the administrative appeals process?

As discussed above at **6:61**, an employee may always appeal a transfer or assignment decision pursuant to Md. Code Ann., Ed. Art. § 4-205(c). A dispute over a transfer or assignment decision is *never* grievable or arbitrable (see **6:35**; see also *Kent County Board of Education v. Kent County Teachers' Association*, MSBE Op. No. 05-12 (2005), *aff'd*, Case No. 14-C-05-0063689 (Cir. Ct. Kent Co. Nov. 4, 2005) (decision to assign IEP chair duties to principals within the Superintendent's statutory duty to assign and transfer personnel under Md. Code Ann., Ed. Art. § 6-201(b)); *Allegany County Teachers Association v. Allegany County Board of Education*, MSBE Op. No. 05-27 (2005) (reasoning that if a provision in a negotiated collective bargaining agreement "can affect the outcome of the transfer decision, the provision is illegal as transfer and assignment are precluded from negotiation by statute")).

### 6:66. Who has the burden of proof, and what is the standard of review, in an appeal involving a transfer or assignment dispute?

On such appeals, as with other appeals under Md. Code Ann., Ed. Art. § 4-205(c), the employee has the burden of proof and must demonstrate that the assignment or transfer decision was arbitrary, unreasonable, or illegal.

### 6:67. If an employee wishes to contest a classification or re-classification decision, is that dispute subject to grievance and arbitration or the administrative appeals process?

Classification and re-classification decisions are appealable, but they are not grievable or arbitrable (*Montgomery County Education Association v. Board of Education of Montgomery County*, 311 Md. 303 (1987); *Washington County Education Classified Employees Association v. Board of Education of Washington County*, 97 Md. App. 397 (1993); *Baltimore Teachers Union v. City Board of School Commissioners*, MSBE Op. No. 03-34 (2003)).

### 6:68. Who has the burden of proof and what is the standard of review in an appeal involving a classification or re-classification dispute?

On such appeals, as with other appeals under Md. Code Ann., Ed. Art. § 4-205(c), the employee has the burden of proof and must demonstrate that the classification or re-classification decision was arbitrary, unreasonable, or illegal.

### 6:69. What laws protect employees against discrimination in the work place?

There are a variety of federal and state laws protecting employees against discrimination in the work place including Title VII of the Civil Rights Act of 1964, as amended, 42 U.S.C. § 2000e, Section 504 of the Rehabilitation Act of 1973, 29 U.S.C. § 794, the Americans with Disabilities Act, 42 U.S.C. § 12132, the Family and Medical Leave Act, 29 U.S.C. § 2601, and Article 49B of the Annotated Code of Maryland (see **3:12**).

It should be noted that the provisions of the Age Discrimination in Employment Act of 1967, 29 U.S.C. §§ 621-634 ("ADEA"), are inapplicable to State agencies, such as Maryland local boards of education (see *Adams v. Calvert County Public Schools*, 201 F. Supp. 2d 516, 520-522 (D. Md. 2002) (holding that Maryland school boards are State agencies and are immune from liability under the Age Discrimination in Employment Act); *Kimel v. Florida Board of Regents*, 528 U.S.

62 (2000) (holding that, in enacting the ADEA, Congress did not validly abrogate the State's sovereign immunity and that Congress was without the requisite Constitutional authority to make the ADEA applicable to the States or to State agencies)).

### 6:70. What is the difference between the Equal Employment Opportunities Commission and the Maryland Commission on Human Relations?

The Equal Employment Opportunity Commission ("EEOC") is the federal agency charged with the primary responsibility of investigating charges of employment discrimination arising under Title VII of the Civil Rights Act of 1964, the Americans with Disabilities Act, and the Equal Pay Act. The Maryland Human Relations Commission ("MHRC") is a state agency with a work sharing agreement with the EEOC pursuant to which it also can investigate charges of employment discrimination. In addition, the MHRC will investigate allegations of discrimination arising under Article 49B of the Annotated Code of Maryland—for example, discrimination on the basis of sexual orientation. Both agencies offer mediation services to employers and employees in addition to their authority to investigate charges of discrimination and to ascertain whether or not probable cause exists to determine if a violation occurred.

### 6:71. What is meant by the term "exhaustion of administrative remedies"?

The term "exhaustion of administrative remedies" means that a party is required to follow a prescribed administrative procedure before bringing suit in court.

### 6:72. What is the administrative exhaustion requirement?

Under Title VII of the Civil Rights Act of 1964, a charging party has 180 days to file a charge of discrimination unless the party resides in a state with an agency workshare agreement, such as in Maryland, in which case the time is extended to three hundred days.

In Maryland, an employee must file a charge of discrimination with the EEOC or MHRC within three hundred days of the last act of discrimination and await the agency investigation and issuance of a "Notice of Right to Sue" before filing a complaint in either federal or state court. In addition, a charging party may file a Complaint under Article 49B in state court upon the passage of one hundred eighty (180) days from the filing of the charge with the MHRC.

The Supreme Court's recent decision in *Ledbetter v. Goodyear Tire & Rubber Co., Inc.*, ___ U.S. ___ (2007), illustrates the need for careful adherence to the strict statutory timeline for exhaustion of administrative remedies. In *Ledbetter*, the

Plaintiff alleged that several supervisors had given her poor evaluations because of her sex and that, as a result, her pay was not increased as it would have been had she been evaluated fairly. Significantly, the discriminatory evaluations occurred well prior to 180 days before the Plaintiff filed her charges of discrimination with the EEOC. Nonetheless, the past pay decisions continued to affect Plaintiff's pay such that, at the time of her retirement, she was paid significantly less than her male coworkers. Although a jury found the evaluations were discriminatory and awarded damages to the Plaintiff, the United States Court of Appeals for the Eleventh Circuit reversed, and the Supreme Court affirmed the reversal on the grounds that the Plaintiff should have filed her charge within 180 days of the discriminatory evaluation. According to the Supreme Court, the paychecks that Plaintiff received during the 180 days prior to filing her charge of discrimination with the EEOC were not discriminatory acts even though they had the effect of perpetuating the earlier discriminatory evaluations. Accordingly, the paychecks did not extend the filing period for discrimination based upon the earlier evaluations.

### 6:73. Does Maryland law cover any areas not protected by federal anti-discrimination laws?

Yes. For example, discrimination based upon sexual orientation is covered under Article 49B of the Annotated Code of Maryland but is not covered under Title VII of the Civil Rights Act of 1964.

### 6:74. What remedies are available under federal and Maryland anti-discrimination laws?

Under Title VII of the Civil Rights Act of 1964, a party may be entitled to reinstatement, back pay, front pay, damages of up to three hundred thousand dollars ($300,000.00), and attorneys' fees. Under *current* Maryland law, a party may only receive reinstatement and back and front pay but not damages. However, as a result of legislation passed during the 2007 session of the General Assembly, effective October 1, 2007, administrative law judges will be authorized to award compensatory damages up to three hundred thousand dollars ($300,000.00) against employers for violations of Article 49B of the Annotated Code of Maryland. However, an April 23, 2007, letter from the Attorney General to the Governor points out that the General Assembly failed to provide "a fully effective waiver" of the State's sovereign immunity and also failed to provide "a mechanism to appropriate funds to satisfy judgments against state agencies with respect to the enhanced remedies." Since Maryland boards of education already have a partial waiver of sovereign immunity under Md. Code Ann., Ed. Art. § 4-105 and Md. Code Ann., Cts. & Jud. Proc. Art. § 5-518 (see **9:15**), it remains to be seen whether the Attorney General's concerns will have any impact on local boards of education.

**6:75. What are the types of sexual harassment prohibited under Title VII of the Civil Rights Act of 1964?**

Title VII of the Civil Rights Act of 1964 prohibits sexual harassment in the workplace under both the *quid pro quo* (*i.e.,* an exchange of benefits for sexual favors) and hostile environment varieties.

**6:76. What is the difference between "hostile environment" harassment and "quid pro quo" harassment?**

Hostile environment harassment is very broad and includes any *unwelcome* act or gesture of a sexual nature including, but not limited to, staring, stalking, telling dirty jokes, sending pornographic e-mails, and repeatedly asking a person out for a date despite being told "no". Hostile environment harassment may be between co-workers of like or different status as well as harassment by vendors, parents of students, and students themselves. *Quid pro quo* harassment implies an offer of an exchange of "services" for "benefits" and is typically between a supervisory employee and a subordinate employee.

**6:77. Does it matter that the alleged harasser did not intend to cause harm?**

No. The focus must always be on the impact to the victim rather than the intent of the harasser (*Meritor Savings Bank, FSB v. Vinson*, 477 U.S. 57 (1986)).

**6:78. Does it matter if the alleged harasser is of the same gender as the victim?**

No. Sexual harassment may be male on male, female on female, female on male, and male on female (*Oncale v. Sundowner Offshore Services, Inc.*, 523 U.S. 75 (1998)).

**6:79. Are school systems required to protect employees against harassment by non-employees?**

Yes. For example, a school system would be required to take prompt and effective remedial action to prevent a parent from engaging in pervasive sexual harassment of a teacher.

**6:80. What steps should a school system take in an effort to help prevent sexual harassment in the work place and to respond to it if it occurs?**

The school system should employ the following pro-active and re-active steps in an effort to prevent harassment and in an effort to respond when harassment occurs:

1.  Each school system should have a clear, well-written policy prohibiting harassment and explaining how and to whom a report of harassment should be made.

2.  Each school system should conduct mandatory in-service training for all staff and volunteers to make sure that all employees and volunteers understand the harassment policy and further understand that they are encouraged to report allegations of harassment. Taking attendance at the in-service presentations is important.

3.  Each school system should conduct prompt, thorough investigations of all allegations of harassment in as confidential a manner as possible.

4.  Each school system should take prompt, effective, remedial action in every case. The range of remedial action will be dependent upon the outcome of the investigation, the seriousness of the allegations, and whether there were repeat occurrences.

Accord *Burlington Industries, Inc. v. Ellerth*, 524 U.S. 742 (1998); *Farragher v. City of Boca Raton*, 524 U.S. 775 (1998) (standing for the proposition that the employer may be able to avoid liability by demonstrating that it exercised reasonable care to prevent sexual harassment in the workplace and that it has a practice of taking prompt, effective remedial action when it becomes aware of such harassment).

### 6:81. How does a school system minimize liability in the area of sexual harassment?

By scrupulously following each of the above steps, a school system will greatly reduce its risk of liability for sexual harassment.

### 6:82. What laws protect employees with disabilities?

Section 504 of the Rehabilitation Act of 1973, 29 U.S.C. § 794, and the Americans with Disabilities Act ("ADA"), 42 U.S.C. § 12101, *et seq.*, protect qualified individuals with a disability against discrimination in the workplace and require an employer to make reasonable accommodations to such an employee in an effort to help the employee perform the essential functions of the job.

### 6:83. What entities are covered under Section 504 of the Rehabilitation Act of 1973?

Section 504 covers both public and private institutions that are recipients of federal funds.

## 6:84. What entities are covered under the Americans with Disabilities Act?

The ADA covers public and private entities with at least 15 employees but exempts religious institutions. So, for example, a parochial school that receives federal funds for free and reduced meals would be subject to Section 504 of the Rehabilitation Act of 1973 but would not be subject to the Americans with Disabilities Act.

## 6:85. Who is considered a "qualified individual with a disability"?

A qualified person with a disability is one who can perform the essential functions of the job with or without reasonable accommodations. For example, a blind teacher who can perform the essential functions of the job of a teacher but needs a para-educator to work with him to help read the students' written work would be considered a qualified individual with a disability. The provision of the para-educator to assist the blind teacher would be considered a reasonable accommodation to assist the teacher perform the essential functions of the job. Conversely, a teacher who misses an excessive number of days from work may not be considered a "qualified individual with a disability" because the absences prevent the teacher from performing the "essential functions of the job" of a teacher (*Tyndall v. National Education Centers, Inc.*, 31 F.3d 209, 213 (4th Cir. 1994)).

## 6:86. What is meant by the "essential functions of the job"?

An "essential" job function is one that is central to the satisfactory performance of the job. For example, an essential function of a teacher's job is that the teacher be present in the classroom so as to instruct students. Accordingly, if the teacher's disability is such that it prevents the teacher from coming to school to teach the students, that teacher would not be considered a qualified person with a disability.

## 6:87. What types of accommodations are required under the ADA and/or Section 504?

The ADA and Section 504 requires the employer to provide *reasonable* accommodations. The types of accommodations that would constitute *reasonable* accommodations are many and varied and are based upon the particularities of each case. The employer, however, is not required to provide a requested accommodation that would work an *undue* hardship for the employer. Examples of reasonable accommodations might be changing a work location or schedule, re-assigning a person to a job not requiring heavy lifting, providing telephone amplification equipment, etc. The ADA also requires the removal of architectural barriers within buildings and the making of modifications to facilitate access.

**6:88. Are all employers expected to provide the same level of accommodations?**

Not necessarily. What might be a reasonable accommodation for any Maryland public school system might be an undue hardship for a small private school. Each case is fact specific.

**6:89. Which employees are eligible for over-time pay under federal and state wage and hour laws?**

Under the Federal Fair Labor Standards Act, 29 U.S.C. § 207, *et seq.*, and Maryland's Wage and Hour Law, Md. Code Ann. Lab. & Empl. Art. § 3-415, an employee is eligible for time and a half overtime pay (*i.e.,* 150 percent of regular hourly rate) for all hours worked in excess of forty hours in a designated work week unless the employee is exempt under *both* the salary test and the duties test. Although the Maryland law is generally read in a manner consistent with the federal law, it is doubtful that it applies at all to local boards of education because Sections 6-411(b) and 6-514 of the Education Article specifically, albeit awkwardly, provide that "[t]his subtitle does not make the State labor laws in Titles 3 and 7 of the Labor and Employment Article apply to public school employment."

**6:90. What is the salary test under the Fair Labor Standards Act?**

In order to be exempt from the overtime provisions of the Fair Labor Standards Act, the employee must be paid on a salary basis of no less than $455 per week. For certain computer professionals, the employee may be paid an hourly wage of at least $27.63 and still be exempt.

**6:91. What is the duties test under the Fair Labor Standards Act?**

The employee must be primarily employed in an occupation that falls under one of the following categories: executive, administrative, professional, or outside sales. For example, most certificated employees of a school system (such as teachers, speech pathologists, or guidance counselors) would fall under the category of a professional. School system administrators, whether certificated or not, would fall under the administrative exemption. Note: clerical employees, such as secretaries, do not count as administrative employees, and paraeducators do not constitute professionals—even if they are paid on a salary basis.

**6:92. If a non-exempt employee holds two jobs for the school system and, although neither job exceeds forty hours in the work week, the combined hours exceed forty hours, is the school system responsible for overtime pay?**

Yes. If the two rates of pay are different, the employer must pay overtime based upon either the blended rate of pay or based upon the pay rate of the position on which the overtime was worked.

**6:93. Are non-exempt employees eligible for "compensatory time" in lieu of overtime pay?**

Under the Fair Labor Standards Act, non-exempt employees (*i.e.,* employees eligible for overtime pay) may receive compensatory time from a governmental employer in lieu of overtime pay if there is a written agreement or written "understanding". Compensatory time must be awarded at the rate of time and a half. Of concern, however, is the omission of a compensatory time provision under Maryland's wage and hour law.

Although there are no reported Maryland cases on this point, there is always a risk that a court might find that the absence of a compensatory time provision in the Maryland law prohibits the use of compensatory time in lieu of overtime pay despite the fact that it is allowed under federal law.

**6:94. If an employee works additional hours without permission, is entitlement to overtime waived?**

No. It is the employer's responsibility to keep track of the hours worked by all non-exempt employees. If a non-exempt employee works beyond forty hours in a work week, the employer is deemed to have "suffered" the employee to work those additional hours, and the employer must still pay the overtime pay. An employee who works beyond forty hours in a work week without permission may be disciplined for doing so, but the employee must be paid the overtime nonetheless.

**6:95. Who is responsible for keeping track of the hours worked by employees?**

The employer is always responsible for keeping track of non-exempt employee hours. Merely providing a schedule for the employee does not suffice to meet the employer's record keeping requirements.

**6:96. Under what circumstances can a non-exempt employee "volunteer" to work additional hours for the school system without entitlement to overtime pay?**

Ordinarily, a non-exempt employee is prohibited from volunteering for the employer without being owed payment. Exceptions would be when the non-exempt employee volunteers for a position unrelated to the employee's regular duties. For example, a custodian may serve as a volunteer assistant football coach if, in fact, the custodian is truly an unpaid volunteer. Under these circumstances, the non-exempt employee can only be reimbursed for expenses and not paid a stipend, wage, or fee. Such incidents should be extremely rare because COMAR requires that certificated teachers be assigned coaching positions if possible.

**6:97. Is it possible for the school system to forfeit the exempt status of certain employees?**

Yes. If the employer treats exempt employees as though they were non-exempt hourly employees by "docking" (*i.e.*, by reducing pay on an hourly basis for working less than a full work week or for being late), then the employer will essentially negate the salary basis of the employees resulting in the loss of the exempt status. The law presumes that a salaried exempt employee will receive a consistent salary for each work week regardless of the quantity or quality of the work performed. As such, an employee may work sixty hours one week and thirty hours in another week. Accordingly, if a salaried exempt employee takes off early one day for whatever reason, the employer may not "dock" the employee on an hourly basis.

# 7. Employee Discipline and Dismissal

### 7:1. Is there a distinction between certificated and non-certificated employees when it comes to employee discipline?

Yes. There are several important distinctions between certificated and non-certificated employees when it comes to employee discipline. The Superintendent hires non-certificated employees and may suspend them and terminate them. Unless more procedural due process is negotiated for non-certificated employees and placed in the collective bargaining agreement, the non-certificated employee is entitled only to notice of the allegations and an opportunity to respond prior to the imposition of discipline, coupled with a post-disciplinary appeal to the Board of Education under Md. Code Ann., Ed. Art. § 4-205(c) (see *Harford County Board of Education v. Harford County Educational Services Council*, MSBE Op. No. 05-24 (2005) (non-certificated employees are subject to discipline by the local superintendent, and they may appeal to the local board but not demand arbitration); see also *Livers v. Charles County Board of Education*, 6 Op. MSBE 407 (1992), *aff'd*, 101 Md. App. 160, *cert. denied*, 336 Md. 594 (1994) (school custodian terminated for drug activity off school property may appeal but not pursue arbitration); *accord Cleveland Board of Education v. Loudermill*, 470 U.S. 532 (1985) (establishing minimum due process standards for classified employees as pre-termination notice of offense and opportunity to respond coupled with post-termination appeal)). For certificated employees (who are appointed by the local board), the local superintendent cannot terminate or suspend without pay (as the ultimate action) but may only *recommend* such action to the local board pursuant to Md. Code Ann., Ed. Art. § 6-202(a).

### 7:2. What are the specific grounds for the suspension or dismissal of a certificated employee?

Under Md. Code Ann., Ed. Art. § 6-202(a), the local board of education may suspend without pay or terminate a certificated employee only for immorality, misconduct in office, insubordination, willful neglect of duty, or incompetency.

### 7:3. What is meant by the term "immorality"?

The term "immorality" is subject to the standards of the local board of education in the particular county where the certificated employee is employed. Accordingly, an act deemed to rise to the level of "immorality" and grounds for termination in one county might merit a lesser degree of discipline in another. An act of immorality is generally one that is abhorrent to the mores and values of the community (see, *e.g.*, *Gaither v. Baltimore City Board of School Commissioners*, 6 Op. MSBE 777 (1994) (teacher terminated for immorality and misconduct, despite nineteen years of satisfactory service, because he was purchasing, using, and selling illegal drugs); *Hayhurst v. Garrett County Board of Education*, 7 Op. MSBE 441 (1996) (in affirming the local board's dismissal of teacher for immorality and misconduct for use of marijuana, the State Board reasoned that a teacher's "repeated and deliberate violations of the drug laws compromised her ability to effectively discourage students from abusing drugs")).

### 7:4. What is meant by the term "misconduct in office"?

The term "misconduct in office" includes an act contrary to express and implied rules of conduct for employees (see, *e.g.*, *Resetar v. State Board of Education*, 284 Md. 537, *cert. denied,* 444 U.S. 838 (1979) (teacher terminated for misconduct for referring to junior high school students as "jungle bunnies"); *Kearns v. Carroll County Board of Education*, 6 Op. MSBE 714 (1994) (veteran teacher terminated for misconduct as a result a prolonged pattern of verbal abuse whereby she directed "humiliation, ridicule and sarcasm" at her fifth grade students); *Murray v. Anne Arundel County Board of Education*, MSBE Op. No. 04-11 (2004) (experienced guidance counselor terminated for misconduct as a result asking explicit questions about female student's sexual practices during counseling session)). Among other offenses, the failure to report suspected child abuse or neglect is specifically included in the statute as an act of misconduct that can lead to termination (see **7:33**, discussing possible loss of teaching certificate for failing to report suspected abuse or neglect). Although the statute speaks to misconduct *in office*, there are numerous examples of when an employee engages in misconduct that takes place outside of the duty day or away from school that would suffice for termination. Employee use of illegal drugs would be an example (*Gaither v. Baltimore City Board of School Commissioners*, 6 Op. MSBE 777 (1994)). In such cases, the conduct of the employee has clearly impaired the employee's effectiveness in the performance of his or her duties and as a role model for students.

### 7:5. What is meant by the term "willful neglect of duty"?

An act of "willful neglect of duty" would include situations where the employee intends an act of neglect of duty but perhaps may not intend the consequences of the act. Actions of deliberate indifference would rise to willful neglect. For example, an employee charged with the responsibility of watching school children on the playground but who, nonetheless, goes inside for a cup of coffee while leaving the children unattended has committed an act of "willful neglect of duty" (see, *e.g.*, *Wiggins v. Board of School Commissioners of Baltimore*

*City*, MSBE Op. No. 04-44 (2004) (failure to report to work constitutes an example of willful neglect of duty)).

### 7:6. What is meant by the term "insubordination"?

Insubordination includes the failure to follow direct instructions from a supervisory employee or taking steps, outside of the grievance or appeal process, to undermine the authority of a supervisory employee (see, *e.g.*, *Gordon v. Prince George's County Board of Education*, MSBE Op. No. 06-12 (2006) (termination for insubordination based in part upon teacher's failure to meet with principal as directed to develop an improvement plan, failure to respond to memorandum sent by assistant principal, failure to cover a class as directed, and failure to call a parent as directed)).

### 7:7. What is meant by the term "incompetency"?

Incompetency is the inability to perform one's duties in a competent manner for whatever reason. Typically, a person terminated for incompetency has had several years of unsatisfactory evaluations coupled with plans of assistance and, perhaps, a placement on a second class certificate (see, *e.g.*, *Beck v. Montgomery County Board of Education*, MSBE Op. No. 04-13 (2004) (demonstrating the Herculean efforts that a school system will take before terminating a teacher for incompetency); see also **7:45** for a discussion of "second class" certificates). However, even if an employee is capable of satisfactory performance, the employee may, nonetheless, be technically incompetent due to the inability to perform the essential functions of the job, despite the provision of reasonable accommodations, as a result of extended illness or disability (see, *e.g.*, *Kimble v. Board of Education of Montgomery County*, MSBE Op. No. 02-27 (2002) (reasoning that an employee may be dismissed for incompetency due to medical reasons that prevent the employee from performing essential job functions)).

### 7:8. Are there specific statutory grounds for the suspension or dismissal of non-certificated employees?

The Education Article of the Annotated Code of Maryland does not prescribe specific grounds for the suspension or dismissal of non-certificated employees. Such grounds are left to local board policy or the discretion of the local superintendent. Although the provision of due process procedures for the suspension or dismissal of a non-certificated employee is a permissive subject of negotiations under Md. Code Ann., Ed. Art. § 6-510(b)(2), the determination of the causes for non-certificated employee discipline and discharge rests with the superintendent (see *Harford County Board of Education v. Harford County Educational Services Council*, MSBE Op. No. 05-24 (2005); **6:18**).

**7:9. Can a certificated or non-certificated employee be disciplined for conduct committed during non-duty time away from school?**

Yes. Any conduct committed during non-duty time that undermines the effectiveness of the employee would be grounds for discipline (see, *e.g.*, *Conlan v. Montgomery County Board of Education*, MSBE Op. No. 01-25 (2001) (non-certificated employee with twenty-nine years experience terminated for providing alcoholic beverages to two 17-year-old former students who were visiting with him at his beach house); *Livers v. Charles County Board of Education*, 6 Op. MSBE 407 (1992), *aff'd*, 101 Md. App. 160, *cert. denied*, 336 Md. 594 (1994) (school custodian terminated for drug activity off school property)).

**7:10. What process must be followed for the suspension without pay or dismissal of a certificated employee?**

The process for the dismissal or suspension without pay of a certificated employee under Md. Code Ann., Ed. Art. § 6-202(a) is such that certificated employees have a great deal of due process under the Fourteenth Amendment to the United States Constitution (see **3:15**, **6:46**, **6:48**).

First, unlike with non-certificated employees, the local superintendent can only *recommend* to the local board that the certificated employee be suspended without pay or dismissed. For non-certificated employees, the local superintendent has the authority to suspend without pay or terminate (*Harford County Board of Education v. Harford County Educational Services Council*, MSBE Op. No. 05-24 (2005)).

Second, the certificated employee has the right to a full evidentiary hearing before the local board where the local superintendent has the burden of demonstrating that the employee committed an act of immorality, misconduct, insubordination, incompetency, or willful neglect of duty (Md. Code Ann., Ed. Art. § 6-201(a)(2)(i)).

Third, if the local board upholds the superintendent's recommendation and dismisses or suspends the certificated employee without pay, then the employee is entitled to a *de novo* appeal to the State Board. The State Board follows the following process under COMAR 13A.01.05.05F:

1. It will refer the matter to an administrative law judge ("ALJ") at the Maryland Office of Administrative Hearings for an evidentiary hearing. The ALJ may issue subpoenas for witnesses and documents.

2. The ALJ will issue a *proposed decision* to the State Board.

3. The State Board will allow the parties to submit memoranda and will provide the parties an opportunity for brief oral argument on whether it should accept, reject, or modify the ALJ's proposed decision.

4. Unlike with other appeals, the State Board need not give deference to the local board but "shall exercise independent judgment on the record before it in determining whether to sustain the suspension or dismissal of a certificated employee" (COMAR 13A.01.05.05F(2)).

5. The local board has the burden of proof at the hearing by a preponderance of evidence (COMAR 13A.01.05.07F).

## 7:11. Does the superintendent have the authority to suspend a certificated employee prior to action by the local board?

Yes, but only if the suspension is "with pay". In addition, the local superintendent has the authority to suspend *without* pay if he or she makes a recommendation of dismissal to the local board (see 63 Op. Att'y Gen. 256 (1978)).

## 7:12. Is there a difference between "administrative leave" and a "suspension"?

No. The term "administrative leave" is commonly used but is not found in the statute. An administrative leave is the same as a suspension with pay, and it is usually used while an investigation is being conducted.

## 7:13. Who has the burden of proof in a hearing before the local board on a recommendation for suspension without pay or dismissal of a certificated employee?

The local superintendent has the burden of demonstrating by a preponderance of evidence that the employee committed an act of immorality, misconduct, insubordination, incompetency, or willful neglect of duty.

## 7:14. Is the local board bound by the superintendent's recommendation?

No. The local board may accept, reject, or modify the superintendent's recommendation. In modifying the recommendation, it should be noted that the local board may impose a more stringent punishment than that recommended by the superintendent (see, *e.g.*, *Hayhurst v. Garrett County Board of Education*, 7 Op. MSBE 441 (1996) (affirming the local board's dismissal of teacher for immorality and misconduct for use of marijuana despite the fact that the superintendent only recommended a thirty-day suspension)).

**7:15. What appeal rights does the certificated employee have if he or she is dissatisfied with the local board's decision?**

As discussed in **7:10**, the certificated employee has the right to a *de novo* appeal to the State Board.

**7:16. What is meant by the term "de novo" review?**

The term *de novo* technically means "from the beginning". Essentially, what this means is that the State Board has the authority to review the entire record before it and exercise its own judgment without being required to give any deference to the local board's decision (see *Board of Education v. Waeldner*, 298 Md. 354 (1984) (upholding the State Board's authority to modify a local board's decision from termination to suspension)).

**7:17. What is the standard of review on an appeal to the State Board from a local board's decision on the dismissal or suspension without pay of a certificated employee, and who has the burden of proof?**

As discussed in **7:10**, the State Board exercises independent judgment when reviewing appeals concerning the dismissal or suspension without pay of a certificated employee. This is a significant distinction from the more deferential standard of review exercised by the State Board in other appeals where the State Board views the local board's decision as being *prima facie* correct and only looks at whether the local board's decision was arbitrary, unreasonable, or illegal. Accordingly, for example, the State Board could overturn a local board's decision to dismiss an employee for immorality based on a different view of prevailing mores and community values from a state-wide perspective.

**7:18. What is the role of the administrative law judge in an appeal from a local board's decision on the dismissal or suspension without pay of a certificated employee?**

As discussed in **7:10**, the administrative law judge (ALJ) conducts an evidentiary hearing on behalf of the State Board and issues a proposed decision to the State Board for its review. It is important to note that the ALJ has the power to issue subpoenas to compel the attendance of witnesses and the production of documents. This is a significant tool when one considers that local boards do *not* have subpoena power. Accordingly, witnesses who were unavailable or unwilling to testify before the local board may be compelled to testify in the hearing before the ALJ.

**7:19. Is the State Board bound by the administrative law judge's recommended decision?**

No. The State Board may accept, reject, or modify the ALJ's proposed decision.

**7:20. Does the State Board provide any additional hearings beyond that conducted by the administrative law judge?**

As discussed in **7:10**, the State Board will conduct oral arguments (*i.e.,* not an evidentiary hearing) whereby the parties or their counsel will have an opportunity to argue to the State Board itself why the State Board should accept, reject, or modify the ALJ's proposed decision.

**7:21. What process must be followed for the suspension without pay or dismissal of a non-certificated employee?**

The procedures discussed above for certificated employees do *not* apply to non-certificated employees. For non-certificated employees, including those non-certificated employees holding professional level positions, the local superintendent has the authority to suspend without pay or dismiss without making a recommendation to the local board (see, *e.g.*, *Venter v. Howard County Board of Education*, MSBE Op. No. 05-22 (2005)). This authority is derived from the local superintendent's authority to appoint non-certificated employees without local board approval pursuant to Md. Code Ann., Ed. Art. § 6-201(c) (*Harford County Board of Education v. Harford County Educational Services Council*, MSBE Op. No. 05-24 (2005)).

**7:22. Is the non-certificated employee entitled to appeal the superintendent's decision on suspension or dismissal to the local board?**

For non-certificated employees, the only review that the local board has over the local superintendent's employment decisions is where an appeal is filed pursuant to Md. Code Ann., Ed. Art. § 4-205(c).

**7:23. Is the non-certificated employee entitled to grieve the superintendent's decision on suspension or dismissal or take the matter to arbitration?**

No. Although non-certificated employee suspensions and dismissals are appealable, they are not grievable or arbitrable (see, *e.g.*, *Harford County Board of Education v. Harford County Educational Services Council*, MSBE Op. No. 05-24 (2005) (although *procedural* due process is a *permissive* subject of collective bargaining for non-certificated employees, the substantive decision making authority rests with the superintendent subject to an administrative appeal to the local board and the State Board but never to arbitration); *Livers v. Charles County Board of Education*, 6 Op. MSBE 407 (1992), *aff'd*, 101 Md. App. 160, *cert. denied*, 336 Md. 594 (1994) (school custodian terminated for drug activity off school property may appeal but not pursue arbitration)).

## 7:24. Who has the burden of proof in a hearing before the local board on an appeal of the superintendent's decision to suspend or dismiss a non-certificated employee?

On such an appeal, the burden is on the employee to demonstrate that the local superintendent's decision was arbitrary, unreasonable, or illegal (*accord* COMAR 13A.01.05.05A (setting forth the State Board's standard of review); see *Cone' v. Carroll County Board of Education*, MSBE Op. No. 99-31 (1999) (affirming that non-certificated employee has the burden of proof on appeal to the local board)).

## 7:25. Is the local board bound by the superintendent's decision?

No; however, the local board should give deference to the local superintendent's decision.

## 7:26. What appeal rights does the non-certificated employee have if he or she is dissatisfied with the local board's decision?

The non-certificated employee has the right to appeal a local board's decision on a dismissal or suspension without pay to the State Board pursuant to Md. Code Ann., Ed. Art. § 4-205(c).

## 7:27. What is the standard of review on an appeal to the State Board from a local board's decision on the dismissal or suspension of a non-certificated employee, and who has the burden of proof?

Under COMAR 13A.01.05.05A, the non-certificated employee has the burden of demonstrating that the local board's decision was arbitrary, unreasonable, or illegal.

## 7:28. Is the State Board required to grant a hearing to the non-certificated employee who is appealing from a dismissal or suspension?

No. The State Board rarely holds hearings on non-certificated employee appeals.

**7:29. Is the State Board required to give deference to the local board's decision on the suspension or dismissal of a non-certificated employee?**

Under COMAR 13A.01.05.05A, the State Board must give deference to the local board's decision and consider it *prima facie* correct.

**7:30. Why is it that certificated employees are entitled to more due process before the local board and State Board than is accorded to non-certificated employees?**

The distinction reflects the value placed by the General Assembly on positions requiring professional certifications and that certificated employees hold contracts giving them a protected property interest during the contract term (if non-tenured) and indefinitely (if tenured) (*accord* **3:15**).

**7:31. Are certificated and/or non-certificated employees entitled to appeal decisions by the State Board through the judicial process?**

Yes. Both certificated and non-certificated employees may appeal from the State Board to the courts under the Maryland Administrative Procedure Act, Md. Code Ann., St. Gov't Art. § 10-201 *et seq.*

**7:32. Are certificated and/or non-certificated employees entitled to by-pass the administrative process and proceed directly to court to contest an alleged "wrongful dismissal"?**

No. Since the employees have an adequate remedy under the Education Article to the Annotated Code of Maryland, and because that remedy is "primary", there is no remedy based upon a wrongful discharge theory (see *Makovi v. Sherwin-Williams Co.*, 316 Md. 603 (1989) (no remedy for wrongful discharge when there is an existing statutory remedy)).

**7:33. Are there any offenses that might also lead to the revocation or suspension of a certificated employee's certificate?**

Yes. There are several situations in which a professional employee's certificate from the Maryland State Department of Education may be suspended or revoked.

A certificate may be suspended for up to 365 days under COMAR 13A.12.05.2B if the certificated employee resigns from a local board without first obtaining permission after July 15. Such a suspension is designed to deter employees from putting school systems in a bind shortly before the beginning of the school year. Obviously, when a teacher resigns in the weeks shortly before the school year begins, the school system needs to scramble to hire a replacement. In addition, a teacher will forfeit any of his/her ten-month salary held back for "summer pay" (*Board of Education of Talbot County v. Heister*, 392 Md. 140 (2006)).

In addition, an employee's certificate "shall be suspended or revoked" if the certificate holder pleads guilty or *nolo contendere*, is convicted, or receives a probation before judgment on a criminal offense contributing to the delinquency of a minor, a criminal offense involving moral turpitude that bears on the individual's fitness to teach, or a controlled dangerous substance offense (COMAR 13A.12.05.02C(1)). Moreover, under COMAR 13A.12.05.02C(2), a certificate "shall be suspended or revoked" if the certificate holder "willfully and knowingly" makes a material misrepresentation or concealment of information on the application for a certificate, files a false report or record about a material matter in the certificate application, commits a violation of test security and data reporting policy and procedures, fraudulently or deceptively obtains a certificate, knowingly fails to report suspected child abuse, is dismissed or resigns after notice of allegations of misconduct involving a student in *any* school system or *any other* minor, is dismissed or resigns after notice of allegations of misconduct involving *any* cause for suspension or revocation of a certificate, or has had a certificate suspended, revoked, or surrendered in another state for a reason that would be grounds for suspension or revocation of a Maryland certificate.

Finally, COMAR 13A.12.05.02D provides that a certificate "shall be revoked" if the certificate holder pleads guilty or *nolo contendere*, is convicted, or receives a probation before judgment on a criminal offense involving child abuse or neglect, a crime of violence, or comparable crimes in another state, or if the certificated employee is dismissed or resigns after notice of allegations of sexual child abuse.

## 7:34. What process is required for the revocation or suspension of a certificate?

Under COMAR 13A.12.03, the local superintendent is required to notify the State Superintendent of any offense set forth in **7:33** above (with the exception of a late resignation, where the seeking of a suspension is optional by the local superintendent) if the certificate holder was employed by the local board at the time the conduct occurred or the conduct is reported to the local school system in a criminal background investigation. Of course, a superintendent may (and probably should) also report any information that comes to light regarding a current employee even if the offense occurred *prior* to the person's employment with the school system. For example, if it is just learned that a current employee committed an act of child abuse prior to his employment with the school system, that is a matter that a prudent superintendent should report to the State Superintendent.

Upon receipt of the notification from the local superintendent, the State Superintendent will send the certificate holder a copy of the charges and advise the certificate holder that he or she has ten days to request a hearing in writing. If the certificate holder does not request a hearing, the State Superintendent shall suspend or revoke the certificate. If a hearing is timely requested, one will be provided by an Administrative Law Judge ("ALJ") from the Maryland Office of Administrative Hearings in accordance with COMAR 13A.12.05.04.

In a hearing on a proposed certificate suspension or revocation, the ALJ is charged with the responsibility of determining whether the charges against the certificate holder are supported by a preponderance of the evidence. Here, it is important to note that the focus is *only* on the charge leading to the suspension or revocation of the certificate—not the guilt or innocence of the certificate holder on the underlying offense. For example, in a situation where a certificate may be revoked because an employee resigned upon being notified of an allegation of sexual child abuse, the ALJ will not determine whether or not the employee actually committed the abuse but whether or not the employee resigned upon receipt of notice of the allegation of abuse.

At the conclusion of the hearing, the ALJ will render a proposed decision to the State Superintendent. The parties may file written exceptions to the ALJ's proposed decision. If exceptions are filed, the State Superintendent shall allow the parties to make a brief oral argument limited to 15 minutes per side.

### 7:35. Who has the final say on the suspension or revocation of a certificate?

The State Superintendent has the final say on the suspension or revocation of a certificate (COMAR 13A.12.05.06).

### 7:36. Does the local superintendent have any discretion in reporting to the State Superintendent on a matter that calls for a possible suspension or revocation of a certificate?

As discussed in **7:34**, the local superintendent has discretion in requesting a suspension for a "broken contract"—*i.e.*, when a certificated employee resigns without permission after July 15. Moreover, the provisions of COMAR do not mandate that a superintendent report a matter that occurred before the certificate holder was employed by the local board unless it is disclosed on a criminal background check. Otherwise, there is absolutely no discretion in the local superintendent's reporting obligation to the State Superintendent.

**7:37. What is the standard of review on a suspension or revocation of a certificate, and who has the burden of proof?**

If the certificate holder was or is an employee of the local board, the local board has the burden of demonstrating by a preponderance of evidence that the certificate holder committed the offense triggering the suspension or revocation.

**7:38. Are decisions by the State Superintendent involving the suspension or revocation of a certificate appealable?**

The State Superintendent's decision is "final"; however, the party aggrieved by the decision may seek judicial review. In addition, the aggrieved party may ask the State Superintendent for reconsideration under COMAR 13A.12.05.07 within thirty days of the suspension or revocation decision. Moreover, under COMAR 13A.12.06.08, if a suspension or revocation is based upon a conviction, plea, or probation that is subsequently overturned in a judicial proceeding, a request for reinstatement of the certificate may be filed and will be reviewed by a Reinstatement Review Panel.

**7:39. Are school systems allowed to proceed with the termination or suspension without pay of certificated or non-certificated employees who are subject to criminal charges?**

Technically, yes. However, criminal prosecutions take primacy over employee disciplinary actions. In the case of child abuse investigations involving employees, the Attorney General has cautioned that school systems should not commence even a personnel investigation until *after* the alleged abuse has been reported and the local law enforcement agency and Department of Social Services have given the school system permission to proceed (76 Op. Att'y Gen. 220 (1991)). Accordingly, it is very important for the school system to coordinate with local law enforcement agencies and the state's attorney's office to make sure that a disciplinary proceeding does not impair the prosecution efforts. Such coordination often means that the school system keeps the employee on administrative leave or suspension with pay pending the outcome of the criminal proceedings.

When there is an employment investigation into matters that may also involve criminal charges, an employee may assert the Fifth Amendment right against self-incrimination (see **3:18**). However, the Fifth Amendment privilege does not usually extend to protect an employee from inquiries regarding professional competence (see, *e.g.*, *Beilan v. Board of Public Education*, 357 U.S. 399 (1958) (upholding termination for incompetency arising out of teacher's refusal to answer superintendent's questions regarding loyalty and affiliation with allegedly subversive organizations); *Childs v. McCord*, 420 F. Supp. 428 (D. Md. 1976) (engineer's compelled immunized testimony in criminal proceeding may be used against him to revoke or suspend professional license)).

### 7:40. What are the requirements for school system employees when it comes to reporting suspected child abuse or neglect?

Under the Family Law Article to the Annotated Code of Maryland, individual school system employees must report suspected child abuse or neglect as soon as possible to either the local Department of Social Services or the appropriate local law enforcement agency and follow up in writing within 48 hours by filing a written report to the local Department of Social Services with a copy to the local State's Attorney if there is suspected abuse (Md. Code Ann., Fam. Law Art. § 5-704).

### 7:41. Does an employee meet his/her reporting obligation by simply reporting the matter to a supervisory school official?

No. Although it is always a good idea to *also* advise a supervisory employee when a report is being made, each employee has an independent and mandatory reporting obligation. That obligation is *not* met by simply reporting to a supervisory employee. As noted in **7:4** above, the failure to report suspected child abuse is an act of misconduct that would justify termination or suspension in accordance with Md. Code Ann., Ed. Art. § 6-202(a).

### 7:42. Are school systems allowed to regulate staff/student relations even when those relationships are not "abusive"?

Yes. Every school system should have a policy prohibiting inappropriate staff/student relations—even when such relations are not abusive or otherwise illegal. It is imperative for teachers and other school system employees to maintain a level of professional separation from students and to not place themselves in a situation that could get out of control or compromise their integrity.

### 7:43. Is there a specific procedure for issuing oral or written reprimands?

The procedures for issuing oral and/or written reprimands vary from school system to school system and are a matter of personnel policy. Typically, oral reprimands are issued before more formal written reprimands are put into an employee's file.

**7:44. Are oral or written reprimands subject to the grievance/arbitration process, or are they subject to the administrative appeals process?**

Since oral and written reprimands are a matter of educational and personnel policy, they are neither grievable nor arbitrable, but they are subject to the administrative appeals process set forth in Md. Code Ann., Ed. Art. § 4-205(c).

**7:45. What is meant by the term "second class certificate"?**

Under Md. Code Ann., Ed. Art. § 6-102(a), there are two classes of teachers' certificates: First and Second class. The local superintendent is required to rate a certificated employee's certificate every two years. As the State Board discussed in *Jackson v. Dorchester County Board of Education*, MSBE Op. No. 04-15 (2004), "the local superintendent is to consider the teacher's scholarship, executive ability, personality, and teaching efficiency" in rating the certificate. If the certificate is rated as second class by the local superintendent, then the employee is frozen on step and may not receive an experience based pay increase (see Md. Code Ann., Ed. Art. § 6-103 (providing that a teacher *or principal* who has a second class rating "may not receive a salary increment based on experience")). Usually, such a move is after a certificated employee receives an unsatisfactory rating and is being considered for a possible termination in the subsequent year. Often, a certificated employee who is placed on a second class certificate is given a mentor and an improvement plan.

**7:46. May an employee appeal or grieve/arbitrate a decision placing the employee on a "second class certificate"?**

Yes. Such a decision is appealable under Md. Code Ann., Ed. Art. § 4-205(c). The certificated employee has the burden of demonstrating that the local superintendent's decision was arbitrary, unreasonable, or illegal. The decision would not, however, be the subject of a grievance because employee discipline is not grievable or arbitrable.

**7:47. May an employee appeal or grieve/arbitrate an unsatisfactory evaluation?**

A certificated employee may appeal only if the employee receives "an overall rating of unsatisfactory" on an evaluation, but such matters are not grievable or arbitrable (COMAR 13A.07.04.04). Although there is no comparable COMAR provision concerning evaluations of noncertificated employees, it is presumed that such matters could be the subject of an appeal under Md. Code Ann., Ed. Art. § 4-205(c) since the appointment and continued employment of these employees is determined by the Superintendent under Md. Code Ann., Ed. Art. § 6-201(c). The employee challenging the evaluation has the burden of proof.

### 7:48. May an employee appeal or grieve/arbitrate an observation report?

An employee may appeal an unsatisfactory observation report only if it is a "component of unsatisfactory evaluation" and there is an appeal of the evaluation (*Strother v. Board of Education of Howard County*, 96 Md. App. 99 (1992); COMAR 13A.07.04.04B; see *Bodaghi v. Prince George's County Board of Education*, MSBE Op. No. 06-11 (2006)). Observation reports are never subject to a grievance or arbitration.

### 7:49. Are temporary employees such as substitute teachers entitled to any due process rights prior to or after the imposition of any employee discipline?

Such employees have no legitimate expectation of continued employment and are, rather, employees at-will who may be terminated with or without cause. Such employees have no protected "property interest" in their positions and, as such, are not entitled to due process prior to a termination decision. At best, such employees would be entitled to a post-termination appeal under Md. Code Ann., Ed. Art. § 4-205(c).

### 7:50. Do employees working at a charter school have the same rights as employees working in other public schools?

Yes. Employees working at a public charter school are employees of the local board and have the same rights as other board employees. The only exception would be for employees working directly for the charter school rather than the local board who hold unique positions (*e.g.,* a karate instructor) that would not ordinarily be held by board employees (see Md. Code Ann., Ed. Art. § 9-108(a) (stating that employees of a public charter school are "public school employees"); see also **6:2** (defining "public school employee")).

### 7:51. Do public school system employees have the right to freedom of speech?

Yes. Employees of public school systems have First Amendment rights and do not shed these rights "at the schoolhouse gate" (*Tinker v. Des Moines Independent Community School District*, 393 U.S. 503, 506 (1969)). In *Pickering v. Board of Education of Township High School District 25*, 391 U.S. 563 (1968), a teacher was terminated after writing a letter critical of a proposed tax increase and the manner in which the board of education and superintendent had handled fiscal matters. In reversing in favor of the teacher, the Supreme Court held that "in a case such as this, absent proof of false statements knowingly or recklessly made by him, a teacher's exercise of his right to speak *on issues of public importance* may not furnish the basis for his dismissal from public employment" (*Pickering* at 574 (emphasis added)). Accordingly, when a teacher or other public school system employee speaks out on a matter of true public concern, the employee has the same First Amendment expressive rights as any other citizen (see generally discussion at **3:16** and **3:19**).

**7:52. Can public school system employees be disciplined for their speech and speech related activities?**

Yes. Notwithstanding a public school employee's right to speak out on matters of public concern, the expressive rights of public school employees are curtailed to a significant extent by virtue of the employment relationship. This is so because the school district, as a governmental employer, has legitimate goals of operating effectively and efficiently; accordingly, when a person employed for the very purpose of furthering those goals undermines those goals through speech or speech related conduct, the employee may be disciplined (see, *e.g.*, *Connick v. Myers*, 461 U.S. 138 (1983) (assistant district attorney not engaged in "protected speech" when circulating survey critical of office policies); *Waters v. Churchill*, 511 U.S. 661 (1994) (discharge of nurse overheard complaining "how bad things are" in her department); *Garcetti v. Ceballos*, ___ U.S. ___, 126 S. Ct. 1951 (2006) (upholding allegedly retaliatory transfer of attorney who had written a memorandum complaining of purported government misconduct); *Boring v. Buncombe County Board of Education*, 136 F.3d 364 (4th Cir. 1998) (teacher does not have a First Amendment right to choose curriculum or select a play for student dramatic performance); *East Hartford Education Association v. Board of Education*, 562 F.2d 838 (2d Cir. 1977) (upholding faculty dress code as not violating First Amendment "symbolic speech" right or Fourteenth Amendment liberty interest)).

In *Garcetti*, the Supreme Court recently explained that governmental restriction of employee speech on matters that fall short of a genuine "public concern" "does not infringe any liberties the employee might have enjoyed as a private citizen" ( ___ U.S. at ___, 126 S. Ct. at 1960). Rather, the ability of the governmental employer to impose such restrictions "simply reflects the exercise of employer control over what the employer itself has commissioned or created". Similarly, in *Gisriel v. Washington County Board of Education*, 7 Op. MSBE 971, 974 (1998), the State Board held that an employee "underground" newspaper containing information on personnel related issues and other controversial issues was not "protected speech" under the First Amendment:

> In balancing the rights of the parties involved, it is important to note
> that personal grievance, complaints about conditions of

employment, or expressions about other matters of personal interest do not constitute speech about matters of public concern that are protected by the First Amendment. Rather, these are matters more immediately concerned with the self-interest of the speaker as employee, and, therefore, can be grounds for dismissal or other disciplinary action.

Accordingly, to the extent that neither students nor employees "shed their constitutional rights to freedom of speech or expression at the schoolhouse gate" (*Tinker*, 393 U.S. at 506), the expressive rights of public school system employees *as employees* are not nearly as extensive as those enjoyed by students, parents and other who exercise their rights only *as citizens* (see, *e.g.*, *Lee v. York County School Division*, 484 F.3d 687 (4th Cir. 2007) (holding that public school teacher does not have First Amendment right to post religious materials on bulletin boards, as the bulletin boards were an extension of the curriculum); *Mayer v. Monroe County Community School Corporation*, 474 F.3d 477 (7th Cir. 2007) (teacher does not have a First Amendment right to advocate her personal antiwar viewpoints during instructional time to a captive audience of students in classroom setting)).

### 7:53. Do public school system employees have the right to be free from unreasonable searches?

Public school system employees enjoy protection under the Fourth Amendment to the United States Constitution from unreasonable searches and enjoy a reasonable expectation of privacy with respect to personal items and spaces kept at the workplace (see **3:17**). That said, as with searches of students (see **Chapter 11**), school system employees are not held to the same standard as law enforcement officers and do not need a search warrant or probable cause before executing a search (*O'Connor v. Ortega*, 480 U.S. 709 (1987)). What constitutes a "reasonable" search depends upon the circumstances under which the search occurs and requires a balancing of the employee's expectation of privacy against the school system's legitimate need for maintaining control and supervision in the school. Accordingly, if an employee's interest in privacy is relatively slight and the school system's interest is great, the search is clearly reasonable—for example, a search of a locked custodian's closet for weapons or drugs. Similarly, where a public sector employee holds a "safety sensitive" position, the Supreme Court has held that the Fourth Amendment is not violated as a result of random or suspicion-based urinalysis drug testing (*National Treasury Employees Union v. Von Raab*, 489 U.S. 656 (1989); *Skinner v. Railway Labor Executive Association*, 489 U.S. 602 (1989)). In Maryland, the Court of Appeals has held that a drug testing program for police and firefighters does not violate the Fourth Amendment (*City of Annapolis v. United Food and Commercial Workers, Local 400*, 317 U.S. 544 (1989)). Moreover, all school systems in Maryland maintain a drug testing program for school vehicle operators that involves pre-hire, post-accident, reasonable suspicion, and random urinalysis drug testing (see COMAR 13A.06.07.09; *accord Reed v. Carroll County Board of Education*, MSBE Op. No. 00-4 (2000) (upholding de-certification of school vehicle driver who had a positive random drug test after eating cookies laced with marijuana)). Although there are no published Maryland decisions regarding the urinalysis drug testing of public school system employees other than school vehicle drivers, the United States Court of Appeals for the Eleventh Circuit upheld the termination of a teacher who refused to submit to a urinalysis drug test after marijuana was found in her vehicle following an alert by a drug detecting dog. In that case, *Hearn v. Board of Public Education*, 191 F.3d 1329 (11th Cir. 1999), the Court found that the requirement of a drug test under these circumstances was not an unreasonable search under the Fourth Amendment and did not violate her Fifth Amendment right to refrain from self-incrimination (*accord* **7:39**).

## 7:54. Do employees in the non-public schools have similar rights to public school employees?

There are some similarities and many differences between employees in public and private schools. The greatest distinction is that private school employers are not subject to constitutional restrictions. Employees of private schools are subject to a variety of laws, such as Title VII of the Civil Rights Act of 1964 and the Fair Labor Standards Act, to the same extent as public school employees. However, none of the rights accorded to public school employees set forth in the Education Article to the Annotated Code of Maryland are applicable to employees of private schools. Accordingly, employees of private schools have no "tenure" unless such is provided by virtue of a contract. Moreover, although employees of private schools have collective bargaining rights, such rights are set forth in the National Labor Relations Act rather than under the Education Article.

# 8. The No Child Left Behind Act

## 8:1. What is the No Child Left Behind Act?

The No Child Left behind Act (NCLB) is the most recent version, or reauthorization, of the federal Elementary and Secondary Education Act (ESEA), which was first enacted in 1965. The thrust of the intent of NCLB is the new federal mandate that each State must define what constitutes adequate yearly progress (AYP) in increasing student achievement in reading and mathematics toward the goal of all students reaching proficient levels on uniform state assessments in these subjects by 2014.

The core components of NCLB include an array of new federal mandates. NCLB requires that State and local education agencies (LEAs) test all students using assessment tools aligned to state learning objectives; adopt "research-based" curricula; define and achieve adequate yearly progress for all student subgroups; hire highly qualified teachers, principals, and paraprofessionals; and institute corrective actions in schools and school systems consistently failing to meet AYP (Pub. L. 107-110 (January 8, 2002); 20 U.S.C. § 6301 *et seq.*). Regulations issued pursuant to NCLB are found in the Code of Federal Regulations at 34 C.F.R. § 200. In addition, the U.S. Department of Education (USDE) has issued non-regulatory guidance and policy guidance further explaining major provisions of the Act.

NCLB is scheduled for reauthorization in 2007 and, accordingly, the President, Congress, and education organizations have been advocating for and against a wide variety of revisions to the Act. As of the date of publication of this volume, the NCLB reauthorization had not been enacted. Therefore, to avoid any undue confusion, proposed changes to the Act are not described in detail in this chapter.

## 8:2. How does NCLB relate to other educational initiatives in Maryland?

In Maryland's context, NCLB was signed on January 8, 2002, coinciding with the Visionary Panel for Better Schools report "Achievement Matters Most", which was released a week later. The State Board adopted the Maryland State Department of Education's (MSDE's) strategic framework in May 2002, including the Visionary Panel's recommendations. At the same time, the Maryland General Assembly passed the Bridge to Excellence in Public Schools Act of 2002. This legislation not only mandated significant increases in education aid, but also prescribed new accountability requirements including an annual comprehensive master plan for student achievement.

The State Board subsequently reviewed and approved MSDE's long-range strategic plan, which was remodeled to seamlessly integrate NCLB and the goals and objectives of the Visionary Panel report and the Bridge to Excellence Act. For example, the local master plan mandated by the Bridge to Excellence Act was developed to include not only the anticipated state components, but also to serve as the local accountability plans and annual reports required under NCLB.

### 8:3. How may the federal government enforce compliance with NCLB?

The federal government's authority to enforce compliance with NCLB is grounded in the authority to define criteria and conditions for eligibility for federal education aid. Thus the most contentious deliberations between the states and the federal government regarding NCLB ultimately hinge on whether the state is willing to forego its annual allocation of federal education aid.

### 8:4. Has any State challenged NCLB?

Yes. For example, the State of Connecticut, through its attorney general, has pursued litigation against the U.S. Department of Education premised on the claim NCLB illegally imposes millions of dollars in unfunded federal mandates on Connecticut, in violation of the Unfunded Mandates Provision of NCLB (20 U.S.C. § 7907(a)). The National Education Association has been joined by school districts in Pontiac, Michigan; Laredo, Texas; and Rutland, Vermont, in litigation based on the same claim, which is that Section 9527(a) of NCLB (20 U.S.C. § 7907(a)) imposes a prohibition against requiring states or school districts to spend their own funds for NCLB compliance. Notably, several states and the American Association of School Administrators filed amicus briefs supporting this claim.

Other challenges include more symbolic protests, such as Virginia's House of Delegates passing a resolution in 2004 calling on Congress to exempt from NCLB any "states such as Virginia that have successfully increased student achievement through their own standards and accountability reforms" (House Joint Resolution 192, Virginia (2004)).

A recent challenge from the Fairfax County, Virginia, school district involved the district's refusal to administer the NCLB mandated student assessments in reading and math to students not proficient in English. The district was, instead, assessing student progress toward English proficiency. The U.S. Department of Education responded by threatening to withhold the district's $17 million in Title I funds, and the district acquiesced by directing schools to follow all federal testing rules.

## 8:5. How may the State enforce local compliance?

Again, as for the federal government, the state's primary enforcement tool is the threat of withholding funding. In Maryland, § 2-303 of the Education Article provides that:

> (b) (1) The State Superintendent shall enforce the provisions of:
>
> > (i) This article that are within his jurisdiction; and
> >
> > (ii) The bylaws, rules, and regulations of the State Board.
>
> (2) If an educational institution or county board violates any of these provisions, the State Superintendent, by written notice, may require the State Comptroller to withhold from that institution or board:
>
> > (i) All or any part of an appropriation made by the General Assembly; and
> >
> > (ii) All or any part of any other payment from funds budgeted by the State.

In 2007 the General Assembly repealed § 5-401(k) of the Education Article, which authorized the State Board to withhold funding from a local board if the school system fails to make adequate yearly progress or to develop a satisfactory master plan (see Senate Bill 907, Chapter ___, 2007 Laws of Maryland).

# Student Performance Goals

## 8:6. What are the educational goals and objectives required by NCLB?

NCLB establishes the following five performance goals, which are accompanied by more specific performance indicators.

- *Performance Goal 1*: By 2013-2014, all students will reach high standards, at a minimum attaining proficiency or better in reading/language arts and mathematics.

  (Indicator: The percentages of students, in aggregate and by subgroup, at or above the proficient level in these areas)

- *Performance Goal 2*: All limited English proficient (LEP) students will become proficient in English and reach high academic standards, at a minimum attaining proficiency or better in reading/language arts and mathematics.

  (Indicators: The percentage of LEP students who have attained proficiency by the end of the school year; and the percentage of LEP students attaining reading/ language arts and math proficiency under Goal #1)

- *Performance Goal 3*: By 2004-2005, all students will be taught by highly qualified teachers.

  (Indicators: the percentage of classes taught by "highly qualified" teachers in the aggregate and in "high poverty" schools; the percentage of teachers receiving "high quality" professional development; and the percentage of qualified paraprofessionals.)

- *Performance Goal 4*: All students will be educated in learning environments that are safe, drug free, and conducive to learning.

  (Indicator: The number of "persistently dangerous" schools, as defined by the State.)

- *Performance Goal 5*: All students will graduate from high school.

  (Indicators: The percentage of students who graduate with regular diploma disaggregated by race, ethnicity, gender, disability status, migrant status, English proficiency, and economic status; and the percentage of students who drop out of school, also disaggregated.)

## 8:7. What are the comprehensive master plans?

The Bridge to Excellence Act of 2002 mandated new five-year master plans to be developed by each local school system. The plans must include:

- Goals and objectives that are aligned with State performance standards and local performance standards;

- Implementation strategies for meeting goals and objectives;

- Methods for measuring progress toward meeting goals and objectives;

- Time lines for implementation of the strategies for meeting goals and objectives;

- Time lines for meeting goals and objectives;

- A description of the alignment of the county board's budget with goals, objectives, and strategies for improving student achievement;

- The impact of the proposed goals, objectives, and implementation strategies on public school facilities and capital improvements that may be needed to implement the plan; and

- Any other information required by the State Superintendent (Md. Code Ann., Ed. Art. § 5-401(c)).

Legislation was enacted in 2007 to extend the master plan requirement beyond the original five-year period which spanned the 2002-2003 to 2007-2008 school years. The legislation requires local boards of education to continue submitting updates to their existing master plans in 2008 and 2009, and to submit new five-year master plans by October 15, 2010. In addition, the annual updates beginning in 2011 must cover a five-year period, thereby extending the planning requirement in perpetuity. (Senate Bill 907, Chapter 652, 2007 Laws of Maryland).

### 8:8. Has Maryland changed its educational performance standards to conform with NCLB?

Yes. Maryland revised its "public school standards" under the Code of Maryland Regulations (COMAR) 13A.01.04.05 to reflect the new NCLB standards that apply to the required student performance areas. In addition to student achievement rates, the regulations also define the high school graduation rate and attendance rate that factor into NCLB reporting and accountability requirements.

### 8:9. What are the academic content standards required by NCLB?

States were required to adopt academic content standards for reading/language arts and mathematics for grades 3 through 8 by March 2003 (*U.S. Department of Education, Standards and Assessments Non-regulatory Draft Guidance*, March 10, 2003, at 2) ("*Standards and Assessments Guidance*"). The Act maintained the existing requirement for content standards in reading/language arts and mathematics for grades 10 through 12.

### 8:10. What is the timeline for implementing NCLB?

The Act's timeline for adopting content standards include the following: By the 2005-2006 school year, states must have content standards for grade spans 3 through 5, 6 through 9, and 10 through 12. In addition, states must adopt achievement standards in reading/language arts and mathematics for grades 3 through 8. By the 2007-2008 school year, states must develop content and student achievement standards in science for grade spans 3 through 5, 6 through 9, and 10 through 12.

### 8:11. What are the core academic subjects required under NCLB?

NCLB, rather than mandating instruction in specific content areas, mandates student assessments in reading/language arts, mathematics, and science. Student performance on assessments in reading/language arts and mathematics determines whether individual schools and school systems achieve adequate yearly progress

(AYP) and thereby determine whether certain sanctions may be imposed by the State. The science assessment will become mandatory in 2008.

### 8:12. Has Maryland changed its content standards to conform with NCLB?

Yes. Maryland, as all other states, has undertaken a dramatic revision of content standards in the core subject areas of mathematics, reading/language arts, and science.

### 8:13. Does NCLB impact Maryland's limited English proficiency (LEP) standards?

Yes. Maryland has revised its English proficiency standards to be aligned with the State academic content and student academic achievement standards in reading/language arts and mathematics. The Maryland LEP standards are aligned with the Maryland Voluntary State Curricula in the four core content areas of mathematics, reading, science, and social studies. The LEP Standards demonstrate the connection between learning the correct forms of English and the functional application of that knowledge to the content areas of reading/language arts, math, science, and social studies. They focus on the development of academic language proficiency by identifying the forms and functions of English that LEP students need in order to access, comprehend, and participate successfully in the classroom setting.

### 8:14. What is Maryland's voluntary state curriculum (VSC) and how does it relate to the NCLB content standards?

The VSC is the document that aligns the Maryland Content Standards and the Maryland Assessment Program. State regulations define Maryland content standards as "measurable statements of what students should know and be able to do within a content area as defined in the Voluntary State Curriculum" (COMAR 13A.06.02.02).

The VSC includes definitions of what students should know and be able to do at grade level, pre-K through grade 8, in each of the following subject areas: mathematics, reading/ English language arts, English language proficiency, science, social studies, health and physical education, fine arts, foreign language, and technology.

In addition, MSDE may order a local school system to "institute and fully implement a new curriculum aligned with the Voluntary State Curriculum that is based on State and local academic content and achievement standards" as one optional form of corrective action (COMAR 13A.01.04.08B).

## 8:15. Has NCLB required or resulted in the purchase new textbooks?

Not directly, but indirectly NCLB's emphasis on instructional methodologies that are developed in accordance with "scientifically based research" has significantly impacted the textbook market and purchasing activity (20 U.S.C. § 6361).

## 8:16. What is "scientifically based research"?

NCLB defines scientifically based research as follows:

(A) means research that involves the application of rigorous, systematic, and objective procedures to obtain reliable and valid knowledge relevant to education activities and programs; and

(B) includes research that:

(i) employs systematic, empirical methods that draw on observation or experiment;

(ii) involves rigorous data analyses that are adequate to test the stated hypotheses and justify the general conclusions drawn;

(iii) relies on measurements or observational methods that provide reliable and valid data across evaluators and observers, across multiple measurements and observations, and across studies by the same or different investigators;

(iv) is evaluated using experimental or quasi-experimental designs in which individuals, entities, programs, or activities are assigned to different conditions and with appropriate controls to evaluate the effects of the condition of interest, with a preference for random-assignment experiments, or other designs to the extent that those designs contain within-condition or across-condition controls;

(v) ensures that experimental studies are presented in sufficient detail and clarity to allow for replication or, at a minimum, offer the opportunity to build systematically on their findings; and

(vi) has been accepted by a peer-reviewed journal or approved by a panel of independent experts through a comparably rigorous, objective, and scientific review (20 U.S.C. § 7801(37)).

# Testing

### 8:17. What student assessment requirements are imposed by NCLB?

The Act required that by the 2004-2005 school year, states administer annual assessments in reading/language arts and mathematics at least once in grades 3 through 5, 6 through 9, and 10 through 12 (20 U.S.C. § 6311(b)(3)(C)(v)(I)). Student assessments must be aligned with the State's rigorous academic standards and provide coherent information about student achievement of those standards (20 U.S.C. § 6311(b)(3)(C)(iii)).

By the 2005-2006 school year, states were required to administer annual assessments in reading/language arts and mathematics in each of grades 3 through 5, at least once in grades 6 though 9, and at least once in grades 10 through 12 (20 U.S.C. § 6311 (b)(3)(C)(vii)). Beginning in the 2007-2008 school year, states must administer annual assessments in science at least once in grades 3 through 5, 6 through 9, and 10 through 12 (20 U.S.C. § 6311 (b)(3)(C)(v)(II)).

### 8:18. Has Maryland changed its student assessment requirements to conform to NCLB?

Yes. Prior to the passage of NCLB, the Maryland School Performance Assessment Program (MSPAP) was administered from 1993 through 2002. Following passage of NCLB, the State Board adopted the Maryland School Assessment (MSA) in 2003 and it was initially administered in reading and mathematics in grades 3, 5, 8, and 10, and included the Alternate MSA (ALT-MSA) for students with severe cognitive disabilities.

In 2004, tests were added for students in grades 4, 6, and 7, and an Alt-MSA was developed for students in those grades as well. Science will be added to the assessment requirement in grades 3, 5, and 8 beginning in the 2007-2008 school year in accordance with the NCLB requirement. In addition, Maryland's High School Assessment (HSA) program includes the two high school level assessments in reading (English 2) and math (Algebra) required by NCLB.

Passage of NCLB, and the adoption of the MSAs, has also resulted in the elimination of the Maryland Functional Test.

### 8:19. What was the Maryland School Performance Assessment Program (MSPAP)?

In 1990, the State Board of Education approved student learning goals for the year 2000. MSPAP was the accountability system developed to assess progress toward achievement of those learning outcomes. More specifically, the MSPAP was a criterion-referenced performance test in reading, mathematics, writing, language usage, science, and social studies administered to 3rd, 5th, and 8th grade students. The MSPAP was aligned with Maryland's learning outcomes, scored by teams of Maryland educators, and results were reported through five proficiency levels. School performance was rated by district and statewide on the school performance index.

## 8:20. What were the Maryland Functional Tests?

Since 1990, a graduation requirement for all students was passage of the Maryland Functional Tests in reading, writing, and mathematics. Maryland abolished the longstanding functional tests in 2003 as the State Board restructured the student assessment system in response to NCLB. The graduating class of 2004 was the last class of students required to pass the Maryland Functional Tests to earn a diploma.

## 8:21. What are the Maryland School Assessments (MSAs)?

The Maryland School Assessments (MSAs) are the uniform State assessments adopted by the State Board to comply with NCLB. The MSAs require students in grades 3 through 8 to demonstrate what they know about reading and math and grade 10 students in reading. It is also given in algebra after students complete a high-school algebra course. The MSA tests measure basic as well as higher level skills, and include both multiple-choice and short-essay questions. The test is intended to describe how well students master the reading and math content specified in the Maryland Content Standards. Science will be added to the assessment requirement in grades 3, 5, and 8 beginning in the 2007-2008 school year in accordance with the NCLB requirement. Each student receives a score in each content area that categorizes their performance as basic, proficient, or advanced, based on scores adopted by the State Board of Education.

## 8: 22. When will Maryland begin administering an MSA in science?

Maryland revised its science content standards for pre-K through grade 8 and in the 2006-07 school year Maryland field tested the Science Maryland School Assessments (MSA) in grades 5 and 8 and added a science component to its ALT-MSA assessments in those grades. The State board must establish the basic, proficient, and advanced student performance levels for the science assessments by September 1, 2008 (COMAR 13A.01.04.05).

**8:23. How are the "basic, proficient, and advanced" levels of student performance defined?**

MSDE develops the minimum "cut scores" for the proficient and advanced levels, based on the input of panels of experts.

**8:24. How are student assessment results used?**

The MSAs are administered in March, with results provided to school administrators by late summer. MSA results are intended to inform instructional decisions in the coming school year.

**8:25. Must every student participate in the MSAs?**

A minimum of 95 percent of the student population must participate in reading/language arts and mathematics assessments. In addition, 95 percent of the students in each of the identified student subgroups must participate in these tests (20 U.S.C. § 6311(b)(2)(I)(ii)).

**8:26. What is the participation requirement in Maryland?**

According to Maryland's Accountability Plan submitted to the USDE, Maryland takes a two-pronged approach to requiring and monitoring local compliance with the 95 percent participation rate for schools and LEAs in state assessments. When calculating the performance level for a school or school system, all enrolled students are included, and a "basic" performance level is assigned to any student absent for the mathematics or reading assessment or make-up administration of these assessments.

The Plan provides that the participation rate will be computed for each subgroup, and in the aggregate, for each of the reading and mathematics assessments by dividing the number of students present in each testing group by the number of enrolled students in that group. The participation rate will be calculated for each subgroup and for the aggregate separately in each of reading and mathematics assessments where a group includes at least:

1. 30 students for schools with one grade tested,

2. 60 students for schools with two or more grades tested, or

3. 60 students for LEAs.

Groups not meeting the minimum criteria listed above will not be checked for participation rate. MSDE indicated to the federal government that this procedure "should ensure that subgroups are appropriately included in the participation check while protecting schools and LEAs from the effects of the absences of a few students in very small subgroups (see *Consolidated State Application Accountability Workbook*, MSDE (revised May 2006)).

### 8:27. Must students with disabilities take the MSAs?

Yes, however an alternative assessment is available for students with the most severe cognitive disabilities. The Alternate Maryland School Assessment (ALT-MSA) is the Maryland assessment in which students with disabilities participate if through the IEP process it has been determined they cannot participate in the Maryland School Assessment (MSA) even with accommodations (COMAR 13A.03.04.01A(4)). The ALT-MSA assesses and reports student mastery of individually selected indicators and objectives from the reading and mathematics content standards or appropriate access skills. A portfolio is constructed of evidence that documents individual student mastery of the assessed reading and mathematics objectives. Eligible students participate in the ALT-MSA in grades 3-8 and 10. The statewide performance standards reflecting three levels of achievement: Basic, Proficient, and Advanced are reported for the ALT-MSA.

According to the state accountability plan submitted to USDE, Maryland "fully intends to revise or add policies in accordance with any new U.S. Department of Education guidance on the development of alternative and modified assessments" following the reauthorization of the Individuals with Disabilities Education Act (IDEA) (*Consolidated State Application Accountability Workbook*, MSDE (revised May 2006)). The plan further provides that:

> All students with disabilities are tested. Students pursuing a course of study based on Maryland content standards participate in the administration of Maryland School Assessments and the end-of-course algebra/data analysis and English 2 exams. Students pursuing an alternate course of study based on their IEP participate in Maryland's alternate assessment, Alt-MSA. Beginning in 2006-2007, Maryland will implement the modified assessments for students with disabilities. The proficient scores from the modified assessments will be capped at 2% of the total tested population. Participation rates and performance levels of students with disabilities on MSA, Alt-MSA, and the modified assessments are included in AYP determinations. Maryland's alternate achievement standards and modified achievement standards are aligned with the State's academic content standards.

**8:28. How have the reauthorization of IDEA in 2004 and the regulations issued in 2006 affected NCLB testing requirements?**

NCLB's mandate that all students with disabilities be tested involved significant amendments to IDEA and Title I regulations. Subsequently, Congress enacted a comprehensive reauthorization of IDEA in 2004, followed by regulations issued by USDE in 2006. Until recently, federal Title I regulations allowed the use of an alternative assessment subject to a cap of 1 percent of all students assessed at the state and local levels, limited to students with significant cognitive disabilities. Therefore, the amended regulations published in the *Federal Register* in 2007 revise and increase the cap provisions and more broadly authorize states to adopt alternative academic achievement standards and develop alternative assessments for disabled students (72 FR 17748, April 9, 2007). According to USDE, "Since those regulations were published, the experiences of many States, as well as recent research, indicate that, in addition to students with the most significant cognitive disabilities, there is a small group of students whose disability has precluded them from achieving grade-level proficiency and whose progress is such that they will not reach grade-level proficiency in the same time frame as other students" (*Modified Academic Achievement Standards Non-Regulatory Guidance (Draft)*, USDE, April 2007).

**8:29. How may students with disabilities be included in the State assessment system?**

The assessment options for students with disabilities include the following:

- Participation in a general grade-level assessment.

- Participation in a general grade-level assessment with accommodations.

- Participation in an alternate assessment based on grade-level academic achievement standards.

- Participation in an alternate assessment based on modified academic achievement standards (up to 2 percent of all proficient and advanced scores may count towards AYP).

- Participation in an alternate assessment based on alternate academic achievement standards (up to 1 percent of all proficient and advanced scores may count towards AYP).

**8:30. What is the 2 percent cap and how is it implemented?**

Under the final regulations on modified academic achievement standards, when measuring AYP, States and local school systems have the flexibility to count the proficient and advanced scores of students who take alternate assessments based on modified academic achievement standards provided that the number of those proficient and advanced scores does not exceed 2 percent of all students in the grades assessed at the local and state levels.

The regulations impose no limit on the number of students who may take an alternate assessment based on modified achievement standards. However, the proficient and advanced scores of students who take these assessments may only count under the 2 percent cap, with additional test scores above the 2% cap considered "non-proficient" scores (72 FR 17748, April 9, 2007).

## 8:31. Who determines the method of assessing students with disabilities?

A student's individualized education program team (IEP Team), which includes the student's parent, determines how the student will participate in the State assessment system and what, if any, accommodations are needed for the student to take the general assessment.

## 8:32. What is a modified academic achievement standard?

A modified academic achievement standard is an expectation of performance that is challenging for eligible students, but is less difficult than a grade-level academic achievement standard. Modified academic achievement standards must be aligned with a State's academic content standards for the grade in which a student is enrolled. Thus, only the academic achievement standards are modified, not the content standards on which those modified academic achievement standards are based. USDE explains that "although the assessment and modified academic achievement standards for a particular grade must be challenging for eligible students, they may be less difficult when compared with the general test and grade-level academic achievement standards" (*Guidance (Draft)*, USDE, April 2007).

## 8:33. What is an alternative academic achievement standard?

Alternate academic achievement standards, on the other hand, are based on a very limited sample of content that is linked to grade-level content standards but may not fully represent grade-level content and may include substantially simplified content. USDE emphasizes that modified academic achievement standards are not based on academic content standards that have been modified or restricted.

## 8.34. Must limited English proficient students take the MSAs?

Yes. Under NCLB, limited English proficient (LEP) students must be included in a state's assessment of academic achievement in reading/language arts and mathematics, and must receive appropriate accommodations and, to the extent practicable, native language assessments. LEP students must also be assessed annually for their proficiency in English in the modalities of listening, speaking, reading, and writing (34 C.F.R. § 200.6(b)). Students who have been identified for participation in a language instruction educational program are tested for their knowledge of English using the IDEA® Proficiency Test (IPT), published by Ballard and Tighe. Students are tested not later than 30 days after the beginning of the school year. Students who enroll in school after the first 30 days must be tested within two weeks of the child being placed in a language instruction educational program. Student results on the proficiency test are evaluated, and the student is designated as: (1) Beginner; (2) Intermediate; (3) Advanced; or (4) Proficient. Students identified as (1) Beginner have no or very minimal English language proficiency.

### 8:35. How do the LEP students' reading and math results factor into adequate yearly progress?

Students identified as limited English proficient and in their first year of enrollment in U.S. schools can use the English Language Learner Test (IPT) rather than the MSA reading assessment or English 2 to meet adequate yearly progress (AYP) participation requirements. These students are not included in AYP calculations for the reading MSA. All other LEP students must take the MSA and their scores will be included in the calculation of AYP.

However, all LEP students, regardless of their enrollment date, must take the math assessment. Only the scores of LEP students enrolled for less than one full calendar year will not be included in the calculation for AYP. Students participating in the math assessment are eligible to receive appropriate accommodations as determined in their LEP Plan.

In order to capture the gains made by students exiting active LEP services, the school's AYP calculation for the LEP student group will continue to include their scores on the reading and math MSAs for two years following their exit from active LEP services (34 C.F.R. § 200.6(b)).

### 8:36. How are student assessment results reported in Maryland?

The Maryland School Performance Report/Maryland Report Card reports detailed information on Maryland and its 24 school systems.

# Accountability

### 8:37. What is adequate yearly progress (AYP)?

Under NCLB, adequate yearly progress (AYP) is the measure of the extent to which students, schools, and school systems, demonstrate proficiency in at least reading/language arts and mathematics toward the goal of all students demonstrating proficiency in these core subjects by the end of the 2013-2014 school year.

Each state has developed its own definition of AYP, and these definitions have been approved by the U.S. Department of Education and are available in the state's accountability plan as required under 20 U.S.C. § 6311 (see *Consolidated State Application Accountability Workbook*, MSDE (revised May 2006)). Maryland's plan, and all other state plans, may be found on the U.S. Department of Education website: *http://www.ed.gov/admins/lead/account/ stateplans03/index.html*.

### 8:38. Is student performance the only factor in achieving adequate yearly progress?

No. AYP must also measure the progress of schools based on other academic indicators, such as the graduation or school attendance rate.

### 8:39. What is an annual measurable objective (AMO)?

Annual measurable objectives (AMOs) are the specific performance targets established for each student subgroup. Each group must meet the AMO for reading and the AMO for mathematics (20 U.S.C. § 6311(b)(2)(I)); 34 C.F.R. § 200.18). The "All Students" group in an elementary or middle school must meet the AMO for the attendance rate, the other academic measure for that school. The "All Students" group in a high school must meet the AMO for the graduation rate, the other academic measure for high schools. There are a total of 19 different targets for a school, depending on the subgroups represented in the enrollment. In Maryland, the nine student groups are:

1. All Students

2. Special Education Students

3. Limited English Proficient Students

4. Students Receiving Free/Reduced Price Meals

5. American Indian/Native American Students

6. Asian/Pacific Islander Students

7. African-American Students

8.  White Students (not of Hispanic Origin)

9.  Hispanic Students.

### 8:40. How is AYP determined in Maryland?

NCLB requires each State to administer student assessments in reading/language arts and mathematics (beginning in 2003) and science (beginning in 2008) and achieve progressively higher rates of proficiency on these assessments toward the goal of achieving 100 percent proficiency by 2014. Adequate yearly progress (AYP) describes the minimum level of improvement in student performance that schools and school systems must achieve annually (see *MSDE Consolidated State Application Accountability Workbook, "State Workbook"*, revised, May 2006).

### 8:41. What is "disaggregated" data?

Disaggregated data is data from schools or school districts which has been broken down according to categories of different groups of students, such as by race and gender.

### 8:42. What is a student "subgroup" as defined by NCLB?

NCLB requires that states and school districts collect and report student assessment results disaggregated by student subgroups according to race, ethnicity, gender, disability status, migrant status, English proficiency, and status as economically disadvantaged (20 U.S.C. § 6311(b)(2)(C)(v)). The Act requires each state to identify its major racial or ethnic groups that will constitute defined categories of students. The designation allows a state to determine the composition and number of distinct groups. Maryland has identified eight student subgroups, including African American, American Indian, Asian/Pacific Islander, Hispanic, White, limited English proficiency, free and reduced-price meal recipients, and special education students.

### 8:43. How many students may constitute a subgroup?

NCLB does not specify the size or range of sizes for a student subgroup for purposes of calculating AYP.

### 8:44. How many students constitute a subgroup in Maryland?

Maryland selected the minimum subgroup size of 5. Maryland has received national attention for selecting the smallest "N" value in the nation. The "N" value in other states ranges from 15 to 60. The implication of Maryland's small "N" value appears to be that it subjects a Maryland to a very high, albeit self-imposed, standard with regard to making AYP given the reliance on the satisfactory performance of such small numbers of students. MSDE explains the merits of using the "N of 5" in two ways. First, the rationale is provided that Maryland is, in fact, committed to assessing school and school system performance on the individual student assessments of even the smallest subgroup. Second, MSDE points to its application of a statistical tool referred to as a confidence interval; a tool that serves to balance the desire for inclusive testing and achieving adequate yearly progress based on the performance of all student subgroups, even when the groups contain very few students.

### 8:45. What is a "confidence interval"?

Generally, confidence intervals are used in statistical analysis to provide an estimate of the amount of error involved in a data sample. In the context of NCLB, a confidence interval may be used to determine whether a school's performance is "significantly" below the AYP target. Maryland has chosen to apply this statistical methodology to ensure that fair and valid AYP determinations are made based on the performance of very small groups of students.

### 8:46. Are individual students counted in more than one subgroup?

Yes. Maryland requested a waiver, later withdrawn, to limit the application of student's failure to make AYP to multiple student subgroups.

### 8:47. How does Maryland use the confidence interval in conjunction with the "N of 5" subgroup size?

MSDE requested and received federal approval to apply a confidence interval analysis to subgroup results to account for the relatively more statistically relevant results of very small groups of students. MSDE employs the confidence interval to determine whether the failure of a subgroup of students to make AYP, which in Maryland can be a group of as few as five students, is statistically significant enough to warrant reporting as a subgroup result. In this way, Maryland has achieved a very high rate of assessment and use of assessment data to direct instruction, while limiting the identification of schools as not making AYP based on the performance of very small numbers of students.

**8:48. Is student performance the only factor that determines making AYP?**

No. In addition to achieving levels of proficiency in reading/language arts and mathematics, school systems must attain a 95 percent participation rate on the assessments, and select at least one additional, measurable factor, such as attendance and/or graduation rate.

**8:49. What are the other academic indicators required in Maryland?**

The attendance rate is the other academic indicator for both elementary and middle schools; and the graduation rate is the other indicator for high schools.

**8:50. How is the attendance rate determined in Maryland?**

The average daily attendance rate is used to reflect the percentage of students present in school for at least half the average school day during the school year. Under NCLB, subgroups within schools, individual schools, each school system, and the state are expected to achieve a 94 percent rate to meet a satisfactory standard. For purposes of AYP this standard represents the goal for 2013-2014. Intermediate goals and annual objectives are calculated based on a linear progression from the starting point to the achievement of 94 percent for all students. The attendance rate is met if the annual target is met or the attendance improves from the previous year by at least one tenth of one percent. Schools, school systems, and the state will be accountable for satisfaction of an ultimate attendance rate of 94 percent by school year 2013-2014.

**8:51. How is the graduation rate determined in Maryland?**

Graduation rate is the other academic indicator for high schools. MSDE has chosen to determine the high school graduation rate by using the National Center for Education Statistics synthetic graduation rate formula. Students who graduate on time with general education development (GED) degrees or other certificates not aligned with state standards are not included in the formula calculation.

**8:52. What is a graduation rate based on a "four-year cohort"?**

Maryland's General Assembly enacted a new law in 2006 to require a transition to a new method of calculating high school graduation rates by 2010. The new law requires MSDE and local boards of education to begin immediately to collect and maintain data to calculate a graduation rate for each graduating class using a methodology that tracks cohorts of students as they enter ninth grade and measures the percentage who graduate with a regular high school diploma within four years (Md. Code Ann., Ed. Art. § 7-203.2).

## 8:53. How does a school, school system, or state make AYP?

Consistent with NCLB, a school, LEA, or state is said to make adequate yearly progress under the following conditions as set forth in the *State Workbook*:

1. The percentage of students in the aggregate meets or exceeds the annual measurable objective for the other academic indicators (attendance and/or graduation rate).

2. The percentage of students in the aggregate achieving at the proficient level separately for reading and mathematics meets or exceeds the annual measurable objectives.

3. The participation rate for the academic assessments in reading and mathematics, set separately both in the aggregate and for each subgroup, is 95 percent or greater.

4. The percentage of students in each subgroup achieving at the proficient level separately for reading and mathematics meets or exceeds the annual measurable objective. Or, for any subgroup failing to meet the annual measurable objective, the percentage of students achieving below the proficient level decreases by 10 percent provided that the subgroup meets or exceeds the annual measurable objective for the applicable other academic indicator of attendance or graduation rate (safe harbor).

## 8:54. What is the "safe harbor" under NCLB?

The state, school districts, schools, and each subgroup of students must reach the performance targets for increasing proficiency in reading and math to make AYP. However, there is an exception to this requirement. The state, school districts and schools may make AYP if each subgroup that fails to reach its proficiency performance targets reduces its percentage of students not meeting standards by 10 percent of the previous year's percentage, plus the subgroup must meet the attendance rate or graduation rate targets.

## 8:55. Are other student assessments required by the federal or state government or the local school system?

Yes. NCLB requires states to administer the National Assessment of Educational Progress (NAEP), which is a student assessment in reading and mathematics that predates NCLB. When NCLB was enacted, Maryland and most other states already administered the NAEP. NCLB requires that all states administer the NAEP in odd numbered years.

## 8:56. Do NAEP results impact making AYP?

No. Unlike the MSA, which is a criterion-referenced test intended to reflect student achievement of Maryland's adopted standards, the NAEP is norm-referenced and intended to provide comparative student achievement scores for the purpose of tracking student performance among the states.

## 8:57. Does NCLB mandate any federally adopted national student assessment(s)?

No. In fact, the Act specifically prohibits the use of federal funding under the Act to "develop, pilot test, field test, implement, administer, or distribute any federally sponsored national test in reading, mathematics, or any other subject, unless specifically and explicitly authorized by law" (20 U.S.C. § 6311).

## 8:58. What are the High School Assessments?

Maryland's State Board of Education has adopted regulations establishing the High School Assessments (HSAs), which include four mandatory student assessments in English, algebra/data analysis, government, and biology (COMAR 13A.03.02.07). Beginning with the 2001-2002 school year, all students are required to take the HSAs, with results included on the student's permanent report card. Beginning with the graduating class of 2009, a passing score on each HSA, or a minimum combined score, is required to receive a state diploma. Students take the HSAs following completion of the respective course, including the completion of high school level courses by middle school students. For example, most students now take algebra and the algebra/data analysis HSA in the eighth grade.

## 8:59. Are the High School Assessments mandated by NCLB?

The four High School Assessments required under Maryland state regulations include the two high school level assessments required by NCLB. NCLB's mandated statewide student assessments in mathematics and reading include annual assessments in each of grades 3 through 8 and at least once during grades 10 through 12 (20 U.S.C. § 6311(b)(3)(C)). Maryland refers generally to NCLB-mandated tests as the Maryland State Assessments (MSAs), with the exception of the high school level tests in reading (English 2) and math (Algebra), which are referred to as High School Assessments (HSAs). These two HSAs therefore serve two purposes: as components of the federal accountability requirements under NCLB, and as components of the state diploma requirements adopted by the State Board of Education in regulation.

Beginning in the 2007-2008 school year, NCLB requires the addition of an annual assessment in science at least once in the grade spans 3 through 5 and 6 through 9, and at least once in grades 10 through 12 (20 U.S.C. § 6311(b)(3)(C)(v)(II)). The biology HSA will satisfy the NCLB requirement for a grade 10 science assessment.

## Accountability Sanctions

### 8:60. What happens if a school does not make AYP?

NCLB mandates a prescriptive series of classifications and state educational agency (SEA)-implemented responses to the failure of a school to make AYP in consecutive school years. The stated objective of NCLB's progressive sanctions against low-performing schools is to ensure that all students reach the state's proficient level in reading, mathematics, and science by the 2013-2014 school year.

A school not making AYP for two consecutive years is identified as a school in improvement. Importantly, NCLB includes a provision that captures the two years of school performance prior to the 2002 enactment of NCLB; performance measured not in terms of AYP but under the State accountability system in place at the time, *i.e.*, local reconstitution status (20 U.S.C. § 6316(c)(3)).

If a school continues to fail to make AYP for two years under improvement status, the school is identified as a school in corrective action. Similarly, one additional year (five total) of persistent low-performance results in the status as a school identified for restructuring. The implications of NCLB's mandated strategies and sanctions range from school improvement plans to alternative governance arrangements such as management under contract by an private management company. Maryland has adopted school improvement regulations in accordance with NCLB (COMAR 13A.01.04.07). For additional information see *LEA and School Improvement Non Regulatory Guidance*, USDE (revised, July 21, 2006).

### 8:61. What is a school in improvement?

A school not making AYP for two consecutive years is identified as a school in improvement. NCLB requires that annually by July 1, each local school system shall identify for school improvement each elementary or secondary school that has not made AYP in reading, in mathematics, or as applicable, in the attendance rate or in the graduation rate for two consecutive years. For each school in improvement, the LEA must, within 3 months or sooner after identification, develop a 2-year school improvement plan for the school (20 U.S.C. § 6316(c)(7)).

## 8:62. What is a school improvement plan?

A school improvement plan is the plan that a school must develop to correct the pattern of two consecutive years of failure to make AYP. Maryland regulations (COMAR 13A.01.04.07A) reflect federal requirements that the plan must:

- Focus on strengthening core academic subjects;

- Incorporate strategies based on scientifically based research that will strengthen core academic subjects;

- Include funding for high quality professional development; and

- Have specific measurable objectives for each student subgroup.

## 8:63. What is the LEA's role in implementing the school improvement plan?

NCLB and Maryland regulations require that to assist the school in implementing the plan, the LEA must:

- Establish a peer review process to assist with review of the plan;

- Promptly review the plan;

- Work with the schools as necessary; and

- Approve the school plan if the plan meets the requirements of all applicable federal and state laws and regulations.

In addition, the local school system must provide a school identified for improvement with technical assistance grounded in scientifically based research that includes the following:

- Assistance in analyzing data from the state assessment system, and other examples of student work, to:

    (i)   Identify and develop solutions to problems in instruction;

    (ii)  Increase parental involvement;

    (iii) Improve professional development; and

    (iv)  Implement the school plan;

- Assistance in identifying and implementing professional development and instructional strategies and methods that have proved effective, through scientifically based research, in addressing the specific instructional issues that caused the local school system to identify the school for improvement; and

- Assistance in analyzing and revising the school's budget so that the school allocates its resources more effectively to the activities most likely to increase student academic achievement and remove the school from school improvement status (COMAR 13A.01.04.07A).

## 8:64. What is a school in corrective action?

A school in improvement that continues to fail to make AYP for two years is identified as a school in corrective action. For a school in corrective action, the school system must continue to provide technical assistance in accordance with the school improvement regulations, and take at least one of the following corrective actions:

- Replace the school staff who are relevant to the failure to make adequate yearly progress;

- Institute and fully implement a new curriculum, including providing high qualify professional development for all staff who are relevant to the failure to make AYP, that is based on scientifically based research and offers substantial promise of improving educational achievement for low-achieving students and enabling the school to make AYP;

- Significantly decrease management authority at the school level;

- Appoint an outside expert to advise the school on its progress toward making AYP based on its school plan;

- Extend the length of the school year or school day for the school; or

- Restructure the internal organizational structure of the school (COMAR 13A.01.04.07B).

## 8:65. What is a school in restructuring?

The local school system must identify a school for restructuring if after 1 full year of corrective action the school does not make AYP in reading, in mathematics, or as applicable, in the attendance rate or in the graduation rate. For a school identified for restructuring, the local school system is required to prepare a plan for alternative governance and implement the alternative governance arrangement not later than the beginning of the next school year.

The school system must implement one of the following alternative governance arrangements consistent with State law and as approved by the State Superintendent of Schools and the State Board:

- Reopening the school as a public charter school consistent with the requirements of State law and regulation;

- Replacing all or most of the school staff including the principal who are relevant to the failure to make AYP;

- Entering into a contract with an entity, such as a private management company, with a demonstrated record of effectiveness, to operate the public school; or

- Any other major restructuring of the school's governance arrangement that makes fundamental reform such as significant changes in the school's staffing and governance to improve academic achievement in the school and that has substantial promise of enabling the school to make AYP (COMAR 13A.01.04.07C).

### 8:66. What is the process for identifying and approving the designation of a school?

The school, through its principal and/or parents, may contest the school's status through a local review process. The local school system makes a final decision and forwards it to the state education agency for review and approval.

### 8:67. How does a school contest its identification as a school in improvement, corrective action, or restructuring?

In accordance with NCLB, Maryland regulations provide that before identifying a school for school improvement, corrective action, or restructuring, a local school system shall provide the school with an opportunity to review the school-level data, including academic assessment data, on which the proposed identification is based.

If the principal of a school that a local school system proposes to identify for school improvement, corrective action, or restructuring believes, or a majority of the parents of the students enrolled in the school believe, that the proposed identification is in error for statistically significant reasons, the principal may provide supporting evidence to the local school system. The local school system shall consider the evidence presented by the school before making a final determination.

### 8:68. How does the local school system make its final decision?

The local school system must provide the school 30 days for the opportunity to review the data on which the proposed identification is based before making public its determination of the status of the school.

### 8:69. Is the LEA's decision final?

No. The local school system must submit its final determination regarding a school's status to the MSDE for its review and approval.

## 8:70. Do the accountability sanctions apply to all public schools?

No. Only those schools receiving funds under Title I of the No Child Left Behind Act must comply with all applicable state and federal requirements for schools identified for improvement, corrective action, and restructuring.

## 8:71. How does the NCLB provision reflecting 2 years of school performance prior to the Act becoming law impact Maryland schools?

In Maryland, schools previously identified for improvement, corrective action, or reconstitution (term used prior to NCLB's "restructuring") are classified under COMAR 13A.01.04.04E as follows:

- A school in the first or second year of school improvement under Title I on January 8, 2002, shall be treated by the local school system as a school in the first or second year of school improvement for the 2002-2003 school year;

- A school in the first or second year under local reconstitution on January 8, 2002, that is not also a school under Title I, shall be treated as a school in the first or second year of school improvement for the 2002-2003 school year;

- A school in school improvement under Title I for 3 or more consecutive school years preceding January 8, 2002, shall be treated by the local school system as a school under corrective action for the 2002-2003 school year;

- A school under local reconstitution for 3 or more consecutive school years preceding January 8, 2002, that is not also a school under Title I, shall be treated by the local school system as a school under corrective action for the 2002-2003 school year; and.

- Any school that was in corrective action on January 8, 2002, shall be treated by the local school system as a school requiring restructuring for the 2003-2004 school year.

## 8:72. Can a school system, or LEA, be placed in improvement, corrective action or restructuring?

Yes. Maryland regulations, in accordance with NCLB, describe the requirements for placing a local school system in improvement or corrective action (COMAR 13A.01.04.08).

The State Board, upon the recommendation of the State Superintendent of Schools or upon its own motion, must identify for improvement any local school system that for 2 consecutive years fails to make AYP in reading, in mathematics, or as applicable, in the attendance rate or in the graduation rate.

### 8:73. What are the requirements for a school system in improvement?

Within 3 months of identification, state regulations (COMAR 13A.01.04.08A) require the local school system to revise applicable components of the school system master plan to:

(a) Incorporate scientifically based research strategies that strengthen the core academic program in the schools in the system;

(b) Identify actions that have the likelihood of improving student achievement to meet the State's proficiency standards;

(c) Address professional development needs of staff in schools not making AYP;

(d) Include specific measurable achievement goals and targets for each of the subgroups of students;

(e) Address the fundamental teaching and learning needs in schools and specific academic problems of low-achieving schools;

(f) Incorporate as appropriate activities before school, after school, during the summer, and during an extended school year;

(g) Specify the responsibilities of the local school system under the plan; and

(h) Include strategies to promote effective parental involvement in the school.

### 8:74. May a school system appeal the State's decision to place the system in improvement?

Yes. Before identifying a local school system for improvement, the State Board shall provide the local school system with an opportunity to review the data on which the proposed identification is based and give the local school system an opportunity to provide supporting evidence if the system believes that the proposed identification is in error for statistically significant reasons.

In addition, the State Board must promptly provide parents of each student enrolled in the schools served by the local school system identified for improvement notice, the results of the review, the reasons for identification of the school system for improvement, and how parents can participate in upgrading the quality of the local school system.

## 8:75. What sanctions may the State impose on a system in improvement?

For a local school system identified for corrective action, pursuant to COMAR 13A.01.04.08B(3), the State Board and the State Superintendent of Schools must continue to make available technical assistance and shall take at least one of the following corrective actions:

(a) Defer, reduce, or redirect State and federal programmatic and administrative funds including per pupil funding;

(b) Order the local school system to institute and fully implement a new curriculum aligned with the voluntary State curriculum that is based on State and local academic content and achievement standards, including high quality professional development based on scientifically based research;

(c) Order the local school system to replace school principals and executive officers who are relevant to the failure to make AYP with qualified personnel approved by the State Board and the State Superintendent of Schools;

(d) Remove particular schools from the direct control of the local school board and establish alternative arrangements for public governance and supervision of such schools;

(e) Order a reorganization of the local school system as approved by the State Board and the State Superintendent of Schools that groups specified schools under the direct supervision of an executive officer approved by the State Superintendent of Schools who reports directly to the local school superintendent or chief executive officer;

(f) Through court proceeding, appoint a receiver or trustee to administer the affairs of the local school system in place of the superintendent and school board; or

(g) With legislative authorization, abolish or restructure the local school system.

## 8:76. How does a school system return to the status of not being "in improvement"?

If a local school system makes AYP for 2 consecutive years beginning after the date of identification, the State Board must change the classification of the school system and may not identify the local school system for improvement or for corrective action for the succeeding school year (COMAR 13A.01.04.08B(6)).

# State Accountability

### 8:77. What is the State Accountability Plan?

Sections 9302 and 9303 of the Elementary and Secondary Education Act (ESEA), as amended by the No Child Left Behind Act of 2001 (NCLB), provide to states the option of applying for and reporting on multiple ESEA programs through a single consolidated application and report.

State accountability plans must include all public schools and school systems in the State; hold all public schools to the same performance standards; report information in a timely manner through newly mandated local and state report cards; and must include performance-based sanctions and rewards. Maryland's accountability plan is the *Consolidated State Application Accountability Workbook* (revised May 2006). The plan is available on the USDE website at: *http://www.ed.gov/admins/lead/account/stateplans03/index.html.*

The introduction to Maryland's *Consolidated State Performance Report*, March 2006, describes the state education agency's reporting function as follows: "Although a central, practical purpose of the Consolidated State Application and Report is to reduce "red tape" and burden on States, the Consolidated State Application and Report are also intended to have the important purpose of encouraging the integration of State, local, and ESEA programs in comprehensive planning and service delivery and enhancing the likelihood that the State will coordinate planning and service delivery across multiple State and local programs. The combined goal of all educational agencies—State, local, and federal—is a more coherent, well-integrated educational plan that will result in improved teaching and learning."

Maryland's most recent performance report was for the 2005-2006 school year, and is available on the MSDE website at: *http://www.marylandpublicschools.org/ MSDE/programs/esea.*

### 8:78. Has Maryland requested and/or received any waivers?

Yes. MSDE has requested, and received approval from USDE for, several waivers regarding the calculation of adequate yearly progress (AYP) based on and involving issues such as the timing of the mathematics assessments, approval for alternative assessments for students with disabilities, the required participation rate for limited English proficient students, and the graduation rate methodology. Several other waiver requests are pending.

# Parental Involvement

### 8:79. What is a parental involvement plan?

NCLB requires that each school served under Title I jointly develop with and distribute to parents of participating children a written parental involvement policy agreed on by the parents that describes the requirements of NCLB Sections 1118(c) through (f). MSDE must ensure that all Title I schools in all local school systems receiving Title I funds have written school parental involvement policies developed with parents of participating children (20 U.S.C. § 6318).

### 8:80. Are schools and school systems required to inform parents of a school's status under NCLB?

Yes. NCLB (20 U.S.C. § 6311(h)) requires the local school system to promptly notify parents of each student enrolled in an elementary school or a secondary school identified for school improvement, for correction action, or for restructuring that the school has been so identified. The notice must include:

- An explanation of what the identification means, and how the school compares in terms of academic achievement to other elementary schools or secondary schools served by the LEA and the SEA involved;

- The reason for the identification;

- An explanation of what the school identified for school improvement is doing to address the problem of low achievement;

- An explanation of what the LEA or SEA is doing to help the school address the achievement problem;

- An explanation of how the parents can become involved in addressing the academic issues that caused the school to be identified for school improvement; and

- An explanation of the parents' option to transfer their child to another public school with transportation provided by the agency when required, or to obtain supplemental educational services for the child.

Title I regulations requires that the explanation of the parents' option to transfer their child to another public school include, among other things, information on the academic achievement of the school or schools to which the child may transfer (34 C.F.R. § 200.37).

**8:81. What does NCLB require be included in the school, school system, and State report card?**

NCLB requires the following components, or data elements, in the State Report Card (20 U.S.C. § 6311(h)):

- Information, in the aggregate, on student achievement at each proficiency level on the State academic assessments (disaggregated by race, ethnicity, gender, disability status, migrant status, English proficiency, and status as economically disadvantaged, except that such disaggregation shall not be required in a case in which the number of students in a category is insufficient to yield statistically reliable information or the results would reveal personally identifiable information about an individual student;

- Information that provides a comparison between the actual achievement levels of each student subgroup and the State's annual measurable objectives for each such group of students on each of the academic assessments;

- The percentage of students not tested (disaggregated by the student subgroups), except that such disaggregation shall not be required in a case in which the number of students in a category is insufficient to yield statistically reliable information or the results would reveal personally identifiable information about an individual student;

- The most recent 2-year trend in student achievement in each subject area, and for each grade level, for the required assessments;

- Aggregate information on any other indicators used by the State to determine the adequate yearly progress of students in achieving State academic achievement standards disaggregated by student subgroups;

- Graduation rates for secondary school students disaggregated by student subgroups;

- Information on the performance of local educational agencies in the State regarding making adequate yearly progress, including the number and names of each school identified for school improvement under section 1116; and

- The professional qualifications of teachers in the State, the percentage of such teachers teaching with emergency or provisional credentials, and the percentage of classes in the State not taught by highly qualified teachers, in the aggregate and disaggregated by high-poverty compared to low-poverty schools which (for this purpose) means schools in the top quartile of poverty and the bottom quartile of poverty in the State.

# School Choice

### 8:82. What steps may a parent take on behalf of their child who attends a school failing to make AYP?

Local school systems receiving funds under Title I are required to make choice available to all students in qualifying schools. An LEA must provide any student attending a school that is in improvement, corrective action, or in restructuring, with the opportunity to transfer to another school within the school system (see *Public School Choice Non-Regulatory Guidance*, "*Choice Guidance*," USDE, February 2004; 20 U.S.C. § 6316). The USDE *Choice Guidance* is the primary source of the following questions through **8:88**.

### 8:83. Can parents choose between multiple schools when deciding whether to transfer their child?

Yes. School systems must provide at least two options of schools from which students may choose. The receiving schools must be making AYP (not in improvement, corrective action, or restructuring) and may not be persistently dangerous schools (20 U.S.C. § 6316(b)).

### 8:84. Must the school system provide transportation to the transferring student(s)?

Yes. The local school system is responsible for paying all or a portion of the transportation necessary for students to attend their new schools. A LEA may use Title I funds, as well as other allowable Federal, State, local, and private resources, to pay for the transportation required to implement the Title I school choice requirements (20 U.S.C. § 6316(b)).

The transportation mandate is subject to certain limitations. For example, if the funds available are insufficient to provide transportation to each student who requests a transfer, the local school system must give priority to the lowest-achieving students from low-income families. However, school systems must still offer the opportunity to transfer to all students (*Choice Guidance*, p. 7).

### 8:85. How may Title I funds be applied to transportation costs?

NCLB establishes a "joint funding mechanism" for choice-related transportation and supplemental educational services. Unless a lesser amount is needed to meet demand for choice-related transportation and to satisfy all requests for supplemental educational services, an LEA must spend an amount equal to 20 percent of its Title I, Part A allocation on: (1) choice-related transportation; (2) supplemental educational services; or (3) a combination of (1) and (2).

The 20 percent must be calculated before the LEA takes any reservations "off the top" of its Title I, Part A allocation for parental involvement, private school equitable participation, or other purposes (*Choice Guidance*, p. 22).

### 8:86. Is the identification of receiving schools limited by school capacity?

A local school system may not use the lack of available excess capacity for additional students at potential receiving schools to deny students the option to transfer. However, capacity may be a factor in identifying receiving schools.

### 8:87. If the school from which a student transferred later makes AYP, must the student return?

No. A student who transfers to another public school under the NCLB choice provision may remain at the receiving school through completion of the highest grade offered at that school even if the sending school is no longer in improvement.

### 8:88. May all students attending a school in improvement transfer to another school(s)?

Yes. All students enrolled in a Title I school identified for improvement, corrective action, or restructuring are eligible to transfer. The only exception is when there is no other school within the district to which students could transfer (20 U.S.C. § 6316(b)(1)(E); 34 C.F.R. § 200.44(a) (2003)).

## Supplemental Education Services

### 8:89. What are supplemental educational services (SES)?

Supplemental education services are additional educational opportunities for academic instruction designed to increase the academic performance of students attending consistently low-performing schools. These services can include tutoring, remediation and other educational interventions, and must be provided outside of the regular school day. Supplemental services must be of a high quality, research based, and specifically designed to increase the academic achievement of eligible students on the state assessment required by NCLB (20 U.S.C. § 6316(b)(5)(B); see USDE's *Supplemental Educational Services Non-Regulatory Guidance*, "*SES Guidance*", June 13, 2005). The USDE *SES Guidance* is the primary source of the following questions through **8:107**.

### 8:90. Which students are eligible to receive supplemental services?

Eligible students are all students from low-income families, based on Free and Reduced-Price Meal eligibility, who attend Title I schools that are at least in their second year of school improvement, or in corrective action or restructuring. Therefore, the criterion is not either the economic status of the student or the student's performance, but rather the combination of the school's Title I status and the economic status of the student.

### 8:91. Are all students attending a qualifying school eligible to receive supplemental services?

No. But the services are not limited to those students whose scores resulted in the school's improvement status, but to all students from low-income families (34 C.F.R. § 200.45(b)). If the approved providers do not have the capacity to serve all of the eligible students in a school system, the system must apply fair and equitable procedures for serving students (20 U.S.C. § 6316(e)(2)(C)). If the school system does not have sufficient funds to pay for supplemental services for all eligible students, the system must give priority to the low-achieving students (34 C.F.R. § 200.45(d)).

### 8:92. Who decides which students will access the services of a specific SES provider?

The parent of the eligible student.

### 8:93. How are parents informed of the option to access supplemental services?

A local school system must provide annual notice to the parents of students attending a qualifying school (in its second year in improvement, or corrective action or restructuring) regarding the availability of supplemental services and contact information for approved providers (20 U.S.C. § 6316(b)(6)(F)).

### 8:94. Who are the SES providers and how are they selected or approved?

Supplemental services must be provided by a state approved provider with a demonstrated record of effectiveness (20 U.S.C. § 6316(e)). SES providers may include non-profit entities, for-profit entities, local educational agencies, public schools, public charter schools, private schools, public or private institutions of higher education, and faith-based organizations.

All providers must meet the same eligibility criteria and must undergo the same state selection process. A provider must (1) have a demonstrated record of effectiveness in increasing student academic achievement; (2) document that its instructional strategies are of high quality, based upon research, and designed to increase student academic achievement; (3) provide supplemental educational services that are consistent with the instructional program of the LEA and State academic content standards; (4) be financially sound; and (5) abide by all applicable Federal, State, and local health, safety, and civil rights laws.

Entities that cannot serve as providers include (1) public schools identified as in need of improvement, restructuring or corrective action; and (2) LEAs identified as in need of improvement (although schools within such an LEA that are making adequate yearly progress could be providers).

### 8:95. Is there any cost to parents for supplemental services?

No. School systems negotiate contracts with SES providers and payments for services are drawn from the school system's Title I allocation, a portion of which is retained by the state education agency for this purpose.

### 8:96. May a local school system provide supplemental services?

Yes. Unless the school system itself has been identified for improvement, it may apply to the State for approval to serve as a provider, based on the same criteria as other applicants.

### 8:97. Must SES providers comply with the same "highly qualified teacher" requirements as public schools?

No. Educators, instructors, or tutors working for a supplemental service provider are not subject to the educational or professional certification requirements for other public school teachers and paraprofessionals.

### 8:98. May SES providers be religious organizations or provide services in churches or parochial schools?

Yes. Supplemental service providers may be public, private, or faith-based institutions (20 U.S.C. § 6316 (e)(12).

### 8:99. Who selects the SES provider for a student?

Parents may select any provider from the state-approved list. While the school or local educational agency may make recommendations, parents are not required to accept such recommendations.

## 8:100. When must supplemental services be offered?

Schools that are identified as in need of improvement for two or more years or subject to corrective action prior to the enactment of No Child Left Behind (*i.e.,* before January 8, 2002) must offer supplemental educational services.

## 8:101. What are the State Educational Agency (SEA) responsibilities regarding SES providers?

The Maryland State Department of Education (MSDE) must: (1) Consult with parents, teachers, local school systems, and interested members of the public to identify a wide array of providers so that parents can have a wide variety of choices; (2) Provide annual notices of the requirement to provide services and the process for obtaining approval to be a provider; (3) Develop and apply objective criteria in the selection of potential providers; (4) Maintain an updated list of approved providers; and (5) Develop, implement, and publicly report on standards and techniques for monitoring service quality and effectiveness of providers.

## 8:102. What are local school system responsibilities regarding SES providers?

Local school systems must: (1) Notify parents about the availability of services; (2) Help parents chose a provider, if such help is requested; (3) Determine which students should receive services when all students cannot be served; (4) Enter into an agreement with a provider selected by parents of an eligible student; (5) Assist the SEA in identifying potential providers within the LEA; (6) Provide information to the SEA so the SEA can monitor the quality and effectiveness of the services offered by providers; and (7) Protect the privacy rights of students who receive supplemental educational services.

## 8:103. What are the responsibilities of the SES provider?

Entities that agree to become supplemental services providers must: (1) Set specific achievement goals for the student, which must be developed in consultation with the student's parents; (2) Provide a description of how the student's progress will be measured and how the student's parents and teachers will be regularly informed of that progress; (3) Establish a timetable for improving the student's achievement; (4) Agree to terminate services if student progress goals are not met; (5) Agree to not disclose to the public the identity of any student eligible for or receiving supplemental educational services without the written permission of the student's parents; and (6) Agree that services will be provided consistent with applicable civil rights laws.

**8:104. How are supplemental education services funded?**

NCLB requires that the local school system spend up to an amount equal to 20 percent of its Title I, Part A allocation, before any reservations, on: (1) choice-related transportation; (2) supplemental educational services; or (3) a combination of (1) and (2).

**8:105. Must all of the funding for supplemental services come from Title I funds?**

No. The statutory phrase "an amount equal to" means that the funds required to pay the costs of choice-related transportation and supplemental educational services need not come from Title I allocations, but may be provided from other Federal, State, local, and private sources. However, the amount must be equal to 20 percent of the school system's Title I, Part A allocation.

**8:106. In addition to Title I, what other federal funds may be used to pay for supplemental services?**

Local school systems may use (1) funds from Title V, Local Innovative Education Program; and (2) funds transferred to Title I from other federal education programs, including funds from:

- Title II, Part A, Improving Teacher Quality State Grants;

- Title II, Part D, Educational Technology State Grants;

- Title IV, Part A, Safe and Drug-Free Schools and Communities State Grants; and

- Title V, Part A, State Grants for Innovative Programs.

**8:107. Must the local educational agency pay for or provide transportation to and from service providers?**

No. While the local school system may provide transportation, it is not required to do so.

## "Persistently Dangerous" Schools

**8:108. What is a "persistently dangerous" school as defined by NCLB?**

The Act requires that school systems permit students who attend a "persistently dangerous" school, as defined by the State, to transfer to another public school not identified as "persistently dangerous" (20 U.S.C. § 7912; see the U.S. Department of Education's *Unsafe School Choice Option Non-Regulatory Guidance "USCO Guidance"*, May 2004). The USDE *USCO Guidance* is the primary source for the following questions through **8:118**.

### 8:109. How has Maryland defined a "persistently dangerous" school?

Maryland's State Board has defined "persistently dangerous school" to mean a school in which each year for 3 consecutive school years, the total number of student suspensions for more than 10 days or expulsions for any of the following offenses equals 2½ percent or more of the total number of students enrolled in the school: arson or fire; drugs; explosives; firearms; other guns; other weapons; physical attack on a student; physical attack on a school system employee or other adult; and sexual assault (COMAR 13A.08.01.18).

Federal guidance criticizes the prevalence of approaches like Maryland's, stating that "Many current State definitions utilize suspension and expulsion data, which measure disciplinary responses to an incident. We urge SEAs to use data that relate to incidents (numbers of offenses) even when an offender is not apprehended and subsequently disciplined" (*USCO Guidance*, p.8).

### 8:110. How and when are parents informed if their child's school is "persistently dangerous"?

NCLB, and Maryland regulations, require local school systems to notify in a timely manner the parents of each student attending the school that the State has identified the school as persistently dangerous; and of the opportunity for school transfer as set forth in COMAR 13A.08.01.20. However, the first notice to parents is required at least one year prior to the designation as "persistently dangerous", when the school is placed on probationary status following the first two consecutive years of meeting the threshold of suspensions and expulsions for certain offenses.

Another source of information for parents is the SEA, which is required by NCLB to maintain a current list of all "persistently dangerous" schools in the State.

### 8:111. What is probation for being a "dangerous" school and what does it involve?

The State Board of Education places on probationary status any school having each year for a period of 2 consecutive school years, the total number of student suspensions for more than 10 days or expulsions for any of the offenses set forth in COMAR 13A.08.01.18B(4) equal to 2½ percent or more of the total number of students enrolled in the school.

Local school systems are required to notify in a timely manner the parents of each student attending the school that the State has placed the school on probationary status and the superintendent/CEO shall submit a corrective action plan to the State Superintendent of Schools within 30 days of being notified by the State Board of Education that a school in the jurisdiction of the school system is on probationary status. During the probationary status the school shall implement in a timely manner strategies to reduce the commission of the listed offenses.

### 8:112. What are the consequences for a school designated as "persistently dangerous"?

If a school has been designated a persistently dangerous school, the school shall retain that designation for at least 1 full school year. Each year that a school remains identified as persistently dangerous, the local school superintendent/CEO shall submit a corrective action plan to the State Superintendent within 30 days of being notified by the State that the status of the school as persistently dangerous has not changed. The State Board shall remove a school's designation as a persistently dangerous school if the school no longer meets the requirements (COMAR 13A.08.01.19).

### 8:113. What options are available to parents of students attending a "persistently dangerous" school?

NCLB requires local school systems to adopt "unsafe school transfer policies" that allow a student attending a public school to transfer to a safe public school within the school system if the student attends a persistently dangerous public elementary or secondary school.

The local school system must effectuate a requested student transfer in a timely manner. To the extent possible, the school system must allow a student to transfer to a school that is making adequate yearly progress and has not been identified as a school in improvement, corrective action, or restructuring (COMAR 13A.08.01.20).

### 8:114. Does a student ever have a right to transfer from a school even not designated as "persistently dangerous"?

Yes. The same right to transfer that applies to all students attending a "persistently dangerous" school applies to any student who is a victim of a violent criminal offense during the regular school day or while attending a school sponsored event in or on the grounds of a public elementary or secondary school that the student attends. The victim's right to transfer in a timely manner is contingent on the conviction, or adjudication of delinquency, of the perpetrator of the violent criminal offense. In Maryland, "violent criminal offense" is defined by cross-reference to § 14-101 of the Criminal Law Article and includes assault in the first degree, sexual assault in the first or second degree, abduction, arson, manslaughter, murder, rape, and robbery, among others (COMAR 13A.08.01.18B(7)).

### 8:115. What is "timely implementation" of a requested student transfer?

NCLB does not define or prescribe a timeline for effectuating transfers. However, the *USCO Guidance* provides that "an example of timely notification to parents or guardians is within ten school days from the time that the LEA learns that the school has been identified as persistently dangerous".

In addition, local school systems must offer students who attend persistently dangerous schools the opportunity to transfer to a safe school at least 14 calendar days before the start of the school year. Similarly, students who are victims of violent criminal offenses while at school or on school grounds have the opportunity to transfer to a safe school beginning at the start of the following school year (*USCO Guidance*, citing the Notice of Final Deadlines published in the June 16, 2003 *Federal Register*).

### 8:116. May all students attending a "persistently dangerous" school transfer to another school?

Yes. NCLB establishes an unqualified right to any requested student transfer based on the school's designation as "persistently dangerous." Maryland regulations reflect this mandate, requiring that "Each local school system shall allow a student attending a public elementary school or secondary school to attend a safe public elementary or secondary school if the student attends a persistently dangerous public elementary or secondary school" (COMAR 13A.08.01.20A).

### 8:117. Does NCLB effect whether a student who is a victim of a crime may transfer to another school?

Yes. NCLB requires that local school systems give students the opportunity to transfer to another public school if the State has identified their school as persistently dangerous, or if they have been a victim of violent crime on school property.

**8:118. Does NCLB change any requirements regarding notice to parents of crimes committed in or near schools?**

NCLB's school safety provisions are generally limited to the requirements outlined above regarding facilitating parental choice to transfer students to "safer" public school alternatives than the "dangerous" school of origin. However, the Act requires state education agencies to collect school safety related data and report it to the U.S. Department of Education per the Uniform Management and Information Reporting Systems (UMIRS) requirements under NCLB. The UMIRS provisions require States to collect the following data:

- truancy rates;

- the frequency, seriousness, and incidence of violence and drug-related offenses resulting in suspensions and expulsions in elementary and secondary schools in the State;

- the types of curricula, programs, and services provided by the State's chief executive officer, the State educational agency, local educational agencies, and other recipients of funds under the Safe and Drug-Free Schools and Communities Act (SDFSCA) State Grants Program; and

- incidence and prevalence, age of onset, perception of health risk, and perception of social disapproval of drug use and violence by youth in schools and communities.

The *USCO Guidance* emphasizes that these are only minimum collection and reporting requirements and stipulates that "the information that responds to the first two bullets above must be collected on a school-by-school basis, and information that responds to all four bullets must be made available to the public".

# NCLB Teacher Qualifications

**8:119. Does NCLB impose new qualification standards for teachers?**

Yes. NCLB imposes new requirements on school systems receiving Title I funds, most notably the requirement that all teachers must be "highly qualified" (20 U.S.C. § 6319(a)).

**8:120. What is a "highly qualified" teacher?**

Generally, NCLB defines a highly qualified teacher as a teacher who holds at least a bachelor's degree and who has satisfied other requirements such as full state certification and competency in the core academic subject area being taught. The definition of "highly qualified" teacher therefore depends largely on the state's licensing or certification requirements. In addition, the definition is specific to elementary, middle, high school, and special education teachers.

### 8:121. When did the "highly qualified" teacher requirement become effective?

One of the most striking mandates of NCLB when it was signed in early 2002 was the immediate requirement that all new teachers hired after the beginning of 2002-2003 school year must be highly qualified if teaching in programs supported with Title I funds (20 U.S.C. § 6319(a)).

Currently, school systems are striving to comply with the broader mandate that all teachers in the school system must be highly qualified by the end of the 2005-2006 school year (20 U.S.C. § 6319(a)(3)). This mandate extends to all teachers of core academic subjects, including those hired before 2002 who were excluded from the initial requirement.

### 8:122. Are new and experienced teachers held to the same "highly qualified" standard?

No. NCLB allows for differentiated standards for veteran and new teachers.

### 8:123. What defines a "highly qualified" elementary school teacher who is new to the profession?

NCLB defines a "highly qualified" elementary school teacher who is new to the profession as a teacher who:

- has obtained full State certification or has passed the State licensing examination;
- holds a license to teach in the State;
- has not had certification or licensure requirements waived on an emergency, temporary, or provisional basis;
- holds at least a bachelor's degree; and
- has demonstrated by passing a rigorous State test sufficient subject knowledge and teaching skills in reading, writing, mathematics, and other areas of the basic elementary curriculum (20 U.S.C. § 7801(23)).

### 8:124. What defines a "highly qualified" middle or secondary school teacher who is new?

NCLB defines a "highly qualified" middle or secondary school teacher who is new to the profession as a teacher who:

- has obtained full State certification or has passed the State licensing examination;

- holds a license to teach in the State;

- has not had certification or licensure requirements waived on an emergency, temporary, or provisional basis;

- holds at least a bachelor's degree; and

- has demonstrated a high level of competency in each of the subjects taught by passing a rigorous State test in each subject area being taught as well as successful completion of an academic major, graduate degree, or advanced certification or credentialing in each subject being taught (20 U.S.C. § 7801(23)).

### 8:125. What defines a "highly qualified" elementary, middle or high school teacher who is not new?

In addition to the basic requirements for new elementary school teachers, described in Question **8:123** above, experienced teachers in elementary, middle, and high schools must demonstrate competency in all of the academic subject areas in which they teach, based on satisfying the "high objective uniform State standard of evaluation" or "HOUSSE" adopted by the State (20 U.S.C. § 7801(23)). Note that the requirement for a degree or major in the subject area being taught that applies to new middle and high school teachers does not apply to experienced teachers.

### 8:126. What is a "HOUSSE"?

The "high objective uniform State standard of evaluation" or "HOUSSE" required by NCLB must be:

- set by the State for both grade appropriate academic subject area knowledge and teaching skills;

- aligned with challenging State academic content and student achievement standards;

- developed in consultation with core content specialists, teachers, principals, and administrators;

- designed to provide objective, coherent information about the teacher's core content knowledge in the academic areas in which he or she teaches;

- applied uniformly to all teachers in the same academic subject area and grade level throughout the State;

- based on factors in addition to the number of years the teacher has taught in a particular subject area; and

- made available to the public (20 U.S.C. § 7801).

## 8:127. How does Maryland define a "highly qualified" teacher?

Maryland has adopted a "highly qualified" teacher standard, including its own "HOUSSE", that includes the following components as outlined in *Achieving "Highly Qualified" Status Under No Child Left Behind (NCLB): A Guide for Maryland Teachers*, MSDE, March 2005. A teacher assigned to a core academic subject area must either:

- Hold a bachelor's degree or higher from a regionally accredited institution of higher education; and

- Hold a valid Maryland Advanced Professional Certificate (APC) or hold National Board Certification (NBC) in the core subject he or she is teaching;

OR

- Hold a bachelor's degree or higher from a regionally accredited institution of higher education, and

- Hold a valid Maryland Standard Professional Certificate (SPC) or Resident Teacher Certificate (RTC), and

- Have passed the applicable state content test(s) in each of the core subjects in which he or she is assigned and/or have completed an academic major or equivalent in each of the core subject for which he or she is assigned; and

- Have passed a state pedagogy test if the teacher is new to the profession of teaching early childhood or elementary school;

OR

- Achieve 100 points or more on the Maryland "HOUSSE" rubrics, and

- Teach in an assignment for which the teacher holds a certificate.

## 8:128. How does Maryland define "core academic subject areas"?

In Maryland, core academic subject areas include:

- Art, Music, Dance, and Theatre;

- Early Childhood;

- Elementary;

- English;

- Foreign Languages;

- Mathematics;

- Reading and Language Arts;

- Science: Biology, Chemistry, Earth/Space, Physical Science, Physics; and

- Social Studies: Civics and Government, History, Geography, Economics (COMAR 13A.01.04.02B(4)).

### 8:129. Are Special Education or English for Speakers of Other Languages (ESOL) defined as core subject areas?

No, however Special Education and ESOL teachers must be highly qualified in every core academic subject area for which they teach, plan and implement instruction, and assess student performance.

### 8:130. Do different "HOUSSE" standards apply to different types of teachers?

Yes. The "HOUSSE" for Early Childhood or Elementary Education provides that if a teacher holds a valid Advanced Professional Certificate (APC) in elementary or early childhood or a National Board Certificate (NBC) in early childhood generalist or middle childhood generalist and is teaching in that core subject area, the teacher has obtained the 100 points necessary to be highly qualified.

Similarly, the "HOUSSE" for Secondary or pre-K through 12 (Art, Music, Dance, & Theatre) teachers provides the APC and/or NBC option for teachers holding a valid APC or an NBC for middle, secondary, or pre-K through 12 (art, music, dance, & theatre) and teaching in that core subject.

### 8:131. Is the definition of "highly qualified" different for a special education teacher?

Yes. Maryland has adopted a "HOUSSE" for teachers of students with special needs who are teaching a core academic subject and who hold one or more of the following endorsements: Generic Special Education (birth–grade 3, grades 1–8, grades 6–12), Special Education K–12, Severely and Profoundly Disabled (Handicapped); Visually Impaired; Hearing Impaired. Again, a teacher may be automatically defined as highly qualified under the "HOUSSE" rubric (100 points) if the teacher holds an APC in Severely & Profoundly Disabled (SPD), and is teaching in an SPD assignment and/or holds an NBC as an Exceptional Needs Specialist.

## 8:132. What information must school systems provide to parents regarding teacher qualifications?

At the beginning of each school year, school systems must provide notice to all parents of students attending schools receiving Title I funds of their rights to request and receive information regarding their child's teacher's qualifications (20 U.S.C. § 6311(h)(6)(A)). Information that may be requested includes:

- whether the teacher has met State qualifications and licensing requirements for the grade levels and subject areas being taught;

- whether the teacher is teaching under a waiver as an emergency, temporary, or provisional teacher;

- the bachelor's degree major and other education and certification background information; and

- the qualification of any paraprofessional providing services to the child.

## 8:133. Does the "highly qualified" standard impact substitute teachers?

Not directly, but the school system must notify the parents of any child who has been taught by a teacher who is not highly qualified for four or more consecutive weeks, which may effect the assignment of long-term substitute teachers (20 U.S.C. § 6311(h)(6)(B)(ii)).

## 8:134. Does the "highly qualified" standard impact paraprofessionals?

Yes. In addition to the highly qualified teacher standard, NCLB requires states to adopt and enforce qualification standards for paraprofessionals working in programs receiving Title I funds (20 U.S.C. 6319(f)). These paraprofessionals must have completed at least two years of study at an institution of higher education; obtained an associate's degree or higher; and met the state's standard of quality as evidenced by a state or local academic assessment. The assessment must require the paraprofessional to demonstrate a basic knowledge and the ability to assist in the instruction of reading, writing, and mathematics, or early education readiness in these subject areas (20 U.S.C. § 6391(c)-(f)).

**8:135. Does NCLB or the "highly qualified" mandate impact collective bargaining agreements?**

The NCLB sets deadlines for all teachers to be "highly qualified" based either on academic and certification requirements or on the HOUSSE standards adopted in each state for veteran teachers. Thus NCLB has potentially significant implications for school systems and their tenured teachers who may not satisfy these standards by the deadline. The interrelationship between NCLB and collective bargaining agreements was addressed in an early policy letter from then U.S. Secretary of Education Rod Paige following passage of NCLB (Dear Colleague Letter of Rod Paige, USDE Secretary, June 14, 2002). In the letter, he observed:

> The NCLBA provides that nothing in Section 1116 (academic assessment and local education agency and school improvement) shall be construed to alter or otherwise affect the rights, remedies, and procedures afforded school and school district employees under federal, state, or local laws or under the terms of collective bargaining agreements, memoranda of understanding, or other agreements between such employees and their employers. Section 1116 does not operate to invalidate employee protections that exist under current law and collective bargaining and similar labor agreements. However, it does not exempt state education agencies, local education agencies, and schools from compliance with Title I based on prospective collective bargaining or similar agreements or changes in state or local law. State and local education authorities, as well as state legislatures and local governing boards, need to ensure that changes in state and local laws are consistent with Title I requirements and that any changes to collective bargaining agreements or new agreements are also consistent with Title I.

# Homeless Students

**8:136. Has NCLB changed requirements for educating homeless students?**

NCLB amended the McKinney-Vento Homeless Assistance Act of 1987. The amendments include new requirements intended to ensure that that homeless children have equal access to enrollment in public schools and the same educational programs and services provided to other students (42 U.S.C. §§ 11431 and 11432(g)(4)). Required services include transportation, education (including special education, limited English proficiency and gifted and talented programs), and school nutrition programs (42 U.S.C. § 11432(e)(3)).

## 8:137. How does NCLB define a homeless student?

NCLB defines as homeless those children and youths who lack a fixed, regular, and adequate nighttime residence and includes:

- Children and youths who are sharing the housing of other persons due to loss of housing, economic hardship, or a similar reason; are living in motels, hotels, trailer parks, or camping grounds due to the lack of alternative adequate accommodations; are living in emergency or transitional shelters; are abandoned in hospitals; or are awaiting foster care placement;

- Children and youths who have a primary nighttime residence that is a public or private place not designed for or ordinarily used as a regular sleeping accommodation for human beings (within the meaning of section 11302 (a)(2)(C) of this title);

- Children and youths who are living in cars, parks, public spaces, abandoned buildings, substandard housing, bus or train stations, or similar settings; and

- Migratory children (as such term is defined in section 6399 of title 20) who qualify as homeless for the purposes of this part because the children are living in circumstances described above (42 U.S.C. § 11434(a)(2)(A)).

## 8:138. What is a "school of origin"?

The school attended by the student when he or she was most recently permanently housed or at which the student was most recently enrolled (42 U.S.C. § 11432(g)(3)(G)).

## 8:139. What rights do homeless students have under NCLB?

Homeless students generally have the right to immediate enrollment, the option to continue to attend the school of origin which they attended prior to becoming homeless, and the assistance of a local liaison employed by the school system and assigned to ensure homeless students receive appropriate educational services from the school system (42 U.S.C. §§ 11432(g)(1)(J)(iii), 11432(g)(3)(C)(iii), and § 11432(g)(3)(G)).

## 8:140. Must transportation be provided to homeless students?

Yes. At the request of a parent/guardian or liaison, transportation must be provided for a homeless student to and from the school of origin if the homeless student continues to live in the same school system as the school of origin. If the homeless student now resides in a different school system than the school of origin, the two school systems must negotiate to share transportation costs to and from the school of origin (42 U.S.C. § 11432(g)(1)(J)(iii)).

### 8:141. What is a homeless liaison?

NCLB requires each school system to designate a liaison for homeless children. The liaison is responsible for ensuring that homeless children are identified, enroll, and receive all appropriate educational services (42 U.S.C. 11432(g)(1)(J)(ii)).

### 8:142. May a school system delay enrolling a homeless student due to failure to provide required student records?

No. A homeless student who cannot produce the requested student records must be enrolled immediately and until any dispute regarding the enrollment is resolved (42 U.S.C. § 11432(g)(3)(C)(i)).

### 8:143. How are disputes resolved regarding the homeless student's school assignment?

School systems must ensure that the student/parent/guardian is provided with a written explanation of the school system's decision regarding enrollment as well as notice of the right to appeal the decision through the local school system's dispute resolution/appeals process (42 U.S.C. § 11432(g)(3)(E)(i)).

## Other NCLB Provisions of Note

### 8:144. How does NCLB impact military recruiting in public schools?

The Act requires all school systems to provide, upon request by a military recruiter or institution of higher education, access to secondary school students' names, addresses, and telephone numbers (20 U.S.C. § 7908(a)(1)). A secondary school student or the parent of the student may request that the student's name, address, and telephone listing not be released without prior written parental consent, and the local educational agency or private school shall notify parents of the option to make such a request (20 U.S.C. § 7908(a)(2)). NCLB also requires that military recruiters have the same access to students as provided to other prospective employers or post-secondary educational institutions (20 U.S.C. § 7908(a)(3)).

## 8:145. How does NCLB impact the activities of the Boy Scouts of America?

The Act includes a provision, section 901, referred to as the "Boy Scouts of America Equal Access Act" (20 U.S.C. § 7905). This section became effective on January 8, 2002, and requires that no public school, LEA or SEA that provides an opportunity for one or more outside youth or community groups to meet on school premises or in school facilities before or after school hours shall deny equal access or a fair opportunity to meet to, or discriminate against, any group officially affiliated with the Boy Scouts of America, or any other youth group listed in Title 36 of the United States Code as a patriotic society, including Big Brothers Big Sisters, Boys and Girls Clubs of America, Girl Scouts of the U.S.A. and Little League Baseball, Inc. (see the final regulations issued in March, 2006, at 34 C.F.R. Parts 75, 76, and 108).

## 8:146. How does NCLB affect school prayer?

The Act requires the federal Secretary of Education to provide guidance on constitutionally protected prayer in public schools by September 1, 2002 and biannually thereafter (20 U.S.C. § 7904(a)). The Act further requires each SEA to establish the procedures by which LEAs will certify that they have no policies that prevent or otherwise deny participation in constitutionally protected prayer as set forth in the guidance. Each LEA was required to file an initial certification by March 15, 2003, and file subsequent certifications by October 1 of each year. The guidance, issued on February 7, 2003, addresses practices such as graduation ceremonies and moments of silence. The guidance has been criticized for generalizing about unsettled legal issues, such as whether a school is responsible for the content of a guest speaker's religious remarks (see Thomas Hutton and Lisa Soronen, *Sins of Omission: Federal Prayer Guidance May Cause More Headaches for Schools*, inside School Law (Spring 2003)).

## 8:147. How does NCLB effect the issue of gun safety?

The Gun-Free Schools Act (GFSA) was reauthorized by the No Child Left Behind (NCLB) Act of 2001 (Public Law 107-110), as Section 4141 of the Elementary and Secondary Education Act of 1965 (ESEA). Generally, the GFSA requires LEAs to have an expulsion policy consistent with the required state law to be eligible to receive ESEA funds; and appropriate enforcement provisions relating to the possession of a firearm on school premises.

Changes made to the GFSA include a clarification to require that the existing one-year expulsion requirement in each state's law include students who are determined to have possessed a firearm at school. In addition, the GFSA was amended to provide that the GFSA does not apply to a firearm that is lawfully stored inside a locked vehicle on school property, or if it is for activities approved and authorized by the local educational agency (LEA), so long as the LEA adopts appropriate safeguards to ensure student safety (see *Guidance Concerning State and Local Responsibilities Under the Gun-Free Schools Act*, USDE; available at *http://www.ed.gov/programs/dvpformula/gfsaguid03.doc*).

# 9. Tort, Liability and Insurance Issues

### 9:1. What is a tort?

The Latin word "tortus" means twisted, and that is an apt description for the kinds of wrongful civil behaviors that result in tort law cases. Both individuals and entities are accountable in monetary damages for the consequences of their unreasonable conduct, which results in harm to another individual. There are two primary categories of torts that apply in the education setting, negligence and intentional torts (see **9:26**). Torts are civil (money damages) versus criminal (jail/fines) actions and are based on state law in most cases.

Lawsuits against school systems and educators have been on the rise for quite some time. One of several possible reasons for the increase in litigation includes the belief that school systems have the ability to pay large damage awards, or have "deep pockets", to use the colloquialism. We also seem to live in times when it is rare for anything to be considered as accident, mishap, or misfortune, without the attempt to find fault, and liability for damages, against someone.

## Negligence

### 9:2. What is negligence?

Negligence occurs when a duty to protect another from a reasonably foreseeable risk of harm is breached by action or inaction and results in injury. There are four elements that all must exist in order for negligence to be actionable, and they are:

1. Duty—An individual has a duty to protect another from risks of harm that are apparent.

2. Breach—The duty to protect must be breached by a failure to exercise the appropriate standard of care.

3. Causation—There must be a proximate causal relationship between the breach of duty and the injury that occurs.

4. Injury—There must be an actual injury suffered in which there are provable damages.

### 9:3. What is the nature of the duty owed in negligence claims?

In the school setting, there are numerous situations where the risk of harm to students from foreseeable dangers creates a duty on the part of school personnel to provide for the safety of their charges. If the risk of harm in a specific set of circumstances could not reasonably have been anticipated, then no duty to protect arises. On the other hand, the level of duty to protect increases as the level of danger posed by the activity increases. For example, there is a higher duty to protect from harm owed by school personnel to a student in a science lab or on a field trip than in history or math class. While individuals do not generally have an affirmative obligation to render aid to persons that are at risk of harm, school personnel do have an affirmative duty to assist a student under their authority.

In the case of *Eisel v. Board of Education of Montgomery County*, 324 Md. 376 (1991), the Maryland Court of Appeals found that a school counselor had a duty to warn the parents of a student that died as a result of a murder-suicide pact. Others informed the counselor that the junior high student had made suicidal statements, but the student denied making suicide threats when questioned by the school counselor, and no report was made to administrators or the parents. The Court held that the counselor had a duty to the student and breached that duty by the failure to warn the parents, and they therefore had no opportunity to intervene. The Court noted that a simple phone call to the parents would have satisfied the counselor's duty, and recognized the value of erring on the side of caution in the school setting, particularly when the potential harm is great.

### 9:4. How is duty breached under the standard of care in negligence claims?

When a duty to protect from harm exists, school personnel must conduct themselves according to the appropriate standard of care for any specific situation. A breach of duty can arise from failing to act when duty requires action, and this is called nonfeasance. A breach of duty can also arise from the taking of action that is inappropriate, and this is called misfeasance. The level of care that is required for students will vary according to age, maturity, mental capacity, and experience level of the students, as well as, the nature of the activity and the surroundings in which the activity occurs. For example, students in primary grades require a higher standard of care than students in secondary grades, and students playing on a playground require a higher level of care than students seated in the library. School personnel are generally held to the standard of a reasonable and prudent person acting under similar circumstances. This hypothetical reasonable and prudent person by which school personnel are measured, is a legal fiction who possesses the following attributes:

- The person's actual physical attributes;
- The intellect, problem-solving ability, and disposition of a normal person;
- The awareness, memory, and experience level of a normal person; and
- Any actual superior knowledge and abilities possessed by the person.

This is an attempt to establish an objective standard for evaluating the actions or inactions of school personnel. Finally, the legal status of the injured person has a bearing on the appropriate standard of care that is applied to a specific situation. An invitee that is invited to be present on school premises is owed an affirmative duty to be protected from foreseeable harm. A licensee that asks to be present on school premises is only owed a duty to be warned of known hazards. A trespasser is owed no duty except that they not be willfully and wantonly injured, although a trespassing child would be owed a somewhat higher standard of care.

## 9:5. How is proximate causation established in negligence claims?

There must be a direct causal connection between the breach of duty and the injury sustained in order for negligence to exist. The behavior that leads to the harm must continue to actively cause a chain of events that naturally and inexorably lead to injury, without intervening and superseding causes. If some act that contributed to producing the harm intervenes in a substantial way after the initial breach of duty, then negligence may not be found in regard to the initial, but ultimately insignificant, behavior. For example, if a school employee negligently allowed a vehicle into an area that was closed to vehicular traffic during the school day to provide safety to students walking to and from portable classrooms, and if the driver of said vehicle subsequently collided with one of the portable classrooms due to inattentiveness while answering a cell phone, then the negligence of the driver could constitute an intervening and superseding cause of the harm to the facility and obviate the initial negligent act.

## 9:6. How is injury determined in negligence claims?

There must also be proven and demonstrable injury in order for a resultant recovery in a cause of action for negligence. The actual injury that is demonstrated may be to the person or the property of the individual asserting the negligence claim. Perhaps the simplest way to consider the requirement of injury in order to establish negligence is found in an old basketball adage, "No harm, no foul".

In the educational setting, where school system staff have a responsibility for the well being of students, it is important to note that reasonable assistance provided to an injured student is protected from liability by the "Good Samaritan" laws. School personnel specially trained to provide emergency care are immune from civil liability for any damages resulting from such care, unless they exhibit gross negligence (Md. Code Ann., Cts. & Jud. Proc. Art. § 5-309(a)(b)). Likewise, non-trained school personnel are also immune from civil liability when providing emergency medical assistance if it is provided in a reasonably prudent manner (Md. Code Ann., Cts. & Jud. Proc. Art. § 5-309(c)). Finally, a physician who provides voluntary uncompensated medical services to a public school sports program is not liable for damages resulting from the services, provided that there is no willful or wanton misconduct, gross negligence, or intentionally tortuous conduct (Md. Code Ann., Cts. & Jud. Proc. Art. § 5-309.1).

### 9:7. How does negligence most commonly occur in the school setting?

The majority of negligence cases in the education arena (other than school bus accidents) involve claims of failure to adequately supervise students, failure to adequately train and instruct students, or finally, failure to adequately maintain facilities and equipment. The most common backdrops for negligence actions to arise in the education setting are in contact sports and other athletics, dangerous activities such as some experiments in science labs, and in off campus situations such as field trips.

### 9:8. How does supervision relate to negligence?

The level of supervision required of educators varies to some extent, depending on whether school is in session. There is typically no duty of supervision owed before a student arrives at the bus stop or at school in the morning, and the duty to supervise likewise ceases when students depart from school or from the bus. If it is known that students gather at school at just before or just after official school hours, then a duty to provide some degree of supervision likely arises. During the actual school day, supervision must be afforded to the degree that a reasonable and prudent administrator would provide. Educators must also provide supervision during non-instructional times during the school day including lunch, recess, and during the time between classes. Consideration must be given to the age, experience, maturity, and mental capacity of the students; the number of students involved; the nature of the activity and the physical environment in which the activity takes place in determining the appropriate standard of supervision to be provided.

"Parents do not send their children to school to be returned to them maimed because of the absence of proper supervision or the abandonment of supervision" (*Segerman v. Jones*, 256 Md. 109 (1969)). In another recent case dealing with the duty of schools to supervise their students, an appellate court in Arizona found that a school district was not liable for injuries sustained by a motorist that was involved in an accident caused by a high school student that had left campus for lunch in violation of school district policy. The injured motorist unsuccessfully argued that the school had a duty to supervise the student in order to keep him off the road during the school day, and that the breach of that duty caused her injuries (*Collette v. Tolleson Unified School District*, 54 P.3d 828 (Ariz. Ct. App. 2002)). The New Jersey Supreme Court in the case of *Frugis v. Bracigliano*, 177 NJ 250 (2003), found that the Elmwood Park School District was negligent in their duty to supervise its students, and was liable for a principal's molestation of children. During his eight-year tenure the principal repeatedly obstructed the view into the window in his office and was observed by staff members to touch male students in a sexually suggestive manner; the Court found that the district ignored signs of the principal's misconduct and failed to implement and train staff members on proper reporting procedures.

### 9:9. How does instruction relate to negligence?

Proper instruction is required to permit students to participate in any specific activity conducted within the school setting in a manner that is safe for all. Training students to participate safely in a variety of sports, in the use of power equipment, and in the correct methodology for carrying out science experiments are all obvious areas where a failure to instruct properly could lead to injury and negligence claims.

### 9:10. How does school maintenance relate to negligence?

It is incumbent on school systems to regularly inspect and maintain safe conditions with respect to their facilities and equipment. Schedules for inspections, repairs, and required replacements should be established and followed with an eye toward the safety of students, visitors, and employees alike. In the case of *King v. Northeast Security, Inc.*, 790 N.E.2d 474 (Ind. 2003), the Indiana Supreme Court found that both the Metropolitan School District of Washington Township and the security firm that they hired were liable for negligence in failing to provide exterior security on school grounds where a student was attacked and brutally beaten by four other students in the school parking lot.

### 9:11. How does documentation relate to negligence?

Schools need to have policies and regulations that support the maintenance of a safe environment for all students. It is also important for such maintenance records to be kept as documentation of the safety steps taken by school systems. Any necessary medical screening of students to maximize safety must be carried out and records maintained to facilitate student safety. Any required permission slips and other parental waiver forms must be secured and maintained to ensure and document notification of the parents and guardians of each student. Retaining any tests of competency and contracts regarding conduct standards or safety rules signed by students is particularly important with respect to student participation in more hazardous activities such as use of power equipment and science laboratory use.

### 9:12. How does emergency management planning relate to negligence?

School systems need to be prepared for emergency situations in advance in order to provide for the greatest possible safety for their students, employees, and visitors. In addition to the establishment of plans and procedures to manage emergency situations, school system staff, students, and even volunteers must be adequately and regularly trained to respond properly when faced with potentially harmful scenarios. Communication and coordination are also essential to appropriate school system response in emergencies, along with the availability of equipment required to render aid as needed.

### 9:13. Must tort claims be brought within a certain time period to be actionable?

Failure to file suit with a statutorily set period of time from the date of an occurrence may cause a tort action to be barred by the statute of limitations. The general statute of limitations in Maryland that is applicable to negligence cases and most tort actions is three years from the date of the injury (Md. Code Ann., Cts. & Jud. Proc. Art. § 5-101). In libel and slander cases, as well as assault cases, there is a shorter statute of limitations of one year from the happening of the defamation or assault (Md. Code Ann., Cts. & Jud. Proc. Art. § 5-105). It is also important to note that when the injury is to a minor, as is often the case in a school setting, the statute of limitations extends to their reaching the age of majority, which is eighteen years old in Maryland.

### 9:14. Are there defenses to claims of negligence?

Yes, there are several defenses in addition to the statute of limitations. Potentially available defenses to claims of negligence brought against school systems and educators include: sovereign immunity, contributory negligence, voluntary assumption of risk, and waiver.

### 9:15. What is the defense of sovereign immunity?

The doctrine of sovereign immunity has its roots in English common law where the King was infallible and thus could not be sued without his express permission. For well over a century, the doctrine has been applied in this country to assert that government agencies are immune from claims of negligence, unless the privilege is modified or eliminated by the state legislature or courts. The primary rationale for retaining this antiquated limitation on liability is to protect school funds because they are for the benefit of all citizens, and that their diversion to pay damage awards may act to damage public education.

In Maryland, limited sovereign immunity has been established by statute. First of all, each county board is required to carry a comprehensive liability insurance policy with coverage limits of $100,000 for each occurrence (Md. Code Ann., Ed. Art. § 4-105).

Second, a defense of sovereign immunity for all amounts in excess of such insurance coverage is then provided for county boards, county board members, local school system employees, and school volunteers, provided that they are acting within the scope of their authority, without malice and gross negligence. Board members are also immune from civil liability when acting in their discretionary capacity, which is generally defined as exercising the judgment that is conferred upon them by law. Finally, any judgment for tort damages against a board member, school system employee, or school volunteer is to be levied against the county board only and not individually against the board member, school system employee, or school volunteer (Md. Code Ann., Cts. & Jud. Proc. Art. § 5-518).

## 9:16. What is the defense of contributory negligence?

Another defense to negligence that is more than a century old is the defense of contributory negligence. In Maryland, contributory negligence acts to completely bar any monetary recovery of damages by an individual whose actions contributed in any substantive way to the injuries that they suffered. Maryland is one of less than five states that have maintained the strict contributory negligence defense. In most other states, some version of comparative negligence exists, which typically limits recovery by the percentage of fault attributable to the victim of the negligent behavior, instead of the total bar to recovery of contributory negligence. This defense may not be available in the school setting against young students that may be found to lack the capacity to be held accountable for actions that would be contributorily negligent for someone older. The General Assembly, in its 2007 legislative session, once again rejected a bill that would have changed Maryland to a comparative negligence state.

## 9:17. What is the defense of voluntary assumption of risk?

When an individual voluntarily consents to participate in a school related activity that poses known and inherent risks of injury, the defense of voluntary assumption of the risk may arise. The basis for this defense is that the student and their parents understood and accepted the danger associated with an activity such as contact sports, where the defense most frequently arises. It should be noted that it can not always be presumed that every participant fully appreciates the dangers inherent in athletic activities, as their age, experience, and maturity may make them less informed. Voluntary assumption of the risk also does not permit an educator to avoid liability for failures to provide proper instruction, supervision, facilities, or safety equipment in order to protect student from foreseeable harm.

In *Hammond v. Board of Education of Carroll County*, 100 Md. App. 60 (1994), the Maryland Court of Special Appeals found that the doctrine of assumption of risk precluded the negligence claim for severe injuries suffered by the first female high school football player in county history. The sixteen year-old student and her father signed a permission form which states, "we do our very best to avoid accidents, but we realize that in the normal course of events, some occur." In addition, the student submitted a required doctor's certificate, which stated that she was physically able to play football, among other sports. During her first scrimmage against another team, she was carrying the ball and was tackled, sustaining injuries that resulted in extended hospitalization and the removal of her spleen and part of her pancreas. The student and her family complained that the school system was negligent in failing to properly warn them of potential risks of injury inherent in football. The Court dismissed the negligence claim on the basis of assumption of risk, noting, "No prospective player need be told that a participant in the game of football may sustain injury. That fact is self-evident…"

### 9:18. What is the defense of waiver?

It is common practice to require the parents of students to execute consent forms for participation in extracurricular activities, which contain language that would waive the ability to hold a school system liable in the event of an injury. Such waivers are not always effective in releasing the school system from liability for their acts of negligence, as a matter of public policy. In the case of *Sharon v. City of Newton*, 769 N.E.2d 738 (2002), the Massachusetts Supreme Court dismissed the negligence claim of a high school cheerleader who was seriously injured as a result of a waiver signed by her parent releasing the city school district from liability for any injury suffered from participation in the program. Even though the print was fine, and in legal language rather than plain English, the Court found that the release was clearly labeled and written, and did not violate public policy. Some other courts have found such releases to be ineffective waivers based upon public policy considerations. For some insight into the Maryland position on such waivers, see the case of *Hammond v. Board of Education of Carroll County*, 100 Md. App. 60 (1994), more fully described in **9:17** above.

### 9:19. What is personal liability for negligence?

Outside of the school setting, an individual whose negligent behavior causes the harm to occur is personally liable for the resulting damages. This would apply to a teacher, administrator or board member alike, although they would be defended by the school system and would fall within the modified sovereign immunity set forth in **9:15** above, provided that the individual was acting within the scope of their authority at the time of the occurrence.

## 9:20. What is vicarious liability for negligence?

The school system that employs the individual whose negligent behavior causes the harm to occur is vicariously liable for the resulting damages. The doctrine of respondeat superior establishes that the employer-employee or master-servant relationship makes the employer responsible for the negligent actions of an employee that is acting within the scope of their employment duties, and as a result there arises transference of liability to the employer. An employee is not found to be acting within the scope of his or her employment when they substantially deviate from their assigned duties for personal reasons.

Section 4-104 of the Education Article provides that a county board may employ and pay for counsel to represent the board or its employees in legal matters affecting the board, as a valid educational expense. Counsel may not be provided where a school employee was acting outside of the scope of his employment duties, or was acting with malice.

An example of a situation where vicarious liability will not be found, because the employee was acting outside the scope of employment, is in the area of sexual abuse. It should be noted though that the school system may be liable in its own right for negligent hiring, negligent failure to provide a safe environment for student, or based on a Title IX action for sexual discrimination. In the recent case of *Montgomery County Board of Education v. Horace Mann*, 154 Md. App. 502 (2003), the Maryland Court of Special Appeals held that the county school system had a duty to defend a teacher in a civil suit accusing the teacher of child abuse. While the Court agreed that the charges, if true, would be outside the scope of the teacher's employment and would not be covered by the school system's insurance, they nevertheless held that the teacher's denial of the charges created an obligation to provide a defense. When the school system refused to provide a defense after their investigation, the insurance carrier for the teachers union stepped in to provide a defense (the case was settled) and the Montgomery County Board of Education was required to reimburse the costs of defense by the Court on other grounds.

In the case of *Matta v. Board of Education of Prince George's County*, 552 A.2d 1340 (1989), the Maryland Court of Special Appeals had to decide whether the school board owed a defense and insurance coverage to a teacher in a suit by a female student against the teacher for inappropriate sexual conduct. Because the conduct of the teacher was alleged to be malicious rather than merely negligent, and because the alleged acts were unauthorized and outside the scope of the teacher's employment, the court determined that the claim was not covered by insurance and that the teacher was not entitled to a defense under Section 4-104 of the Education Article.

### 9:21. What is premises liability for negligence?

Premises liability arises when a hazardous condition or defect in the physical plant or equipment of the school system poses an unreasonable risk of harm to someone present. The status of the individual suffering an injury also has a bearing on the school's duty to protect them from harm while on the school system premises. An individual on school grounds may be an invitee, a licensee, or a trespasser, each of which is entitled to a decreasing degree of care that the school must exercise in order to ensure their safety while on the premises. An invitee is someone invited to the premises such as a teacher or student, and is owed the highest degree of care, namely, an affirmative duty to protect them from harm. A licensee is a guest at the premises such as a parent, and is only owed a duty to be warned of any known dangers. A trespasser has no right or permission to be on the premises, and is only owed the duty to refrain from willfully and wantonly causing them injury. It should be noted that a trespasser who is a child, not an unusual occurrence in the school setting, is owed a higher duty of care than is an adult trespasser.

### 9:22. What constitutes negligent hiring?

In the event that a school system failed to exercise proper care in screening applicants for employment within the school system, or ignored information that an individual posed a potential danger to students or staff, then the school system could be liable in tort for negligent hiring and consequently for the direct harm caused by such negligent hiring (*Doe v. Durtschi*, 716 P.2d 1238 (1968)).

### 9:23. What constitutes negligent provision of references and recommendations?

From a liability standpoint, negligence in providing references and recommendations is essentially the flip side of the negligent hiring covered in **9:22**. This is a developing area of the law, and as yet, there are no Maryland cases on point. It has been held in other jurisdictions that an individual or school system that provides factually false information, or fails to provide information regarding a former employee known to pose a potential threat to students or staff, may be held liable for the harm directly caused by such reference, recommendation, or failure to advise under a theory of negligent or intentional misrepresentation.

In the leading case of *Randi W. v. Muroc Joint Unified School District*, 60 Cal. Rptr. 2nd 263 (1997), an action against a school district for negligent misrepresentation was upheld by the California Supreme Court, where a former employee was unreservedly recommended for employment in another district without disclosure of known prior complaints alleging sexual misconduct. The Court in *Muroc* stated:

> … the writer of a letter of recommendation owes to prospective employers and third persons a duty not to misrepresent the facts in describing the qualifications and character of a former employee, if making these misrepresentations would present a substantial, foreseeable risk of physical injury to the prospective employer or third persons.

A final potential cause of action in such a situation is fraud, which was described by the Maryland Court of Special Appeals in the case of *Lubore v. RPM Associates,* 109 Md. App. 312 (1996), where it was held:

> One who conceals facts that materially qualify affirmative representations may be liable for fraud. Furthermore, concealment may amount to fraud where it is effected by misleading and deceptive talk, acts, or conduct, or is accompanied by misrepresentations, or where, in addition to a party's silence, there is a statement, word, or act on his part, which tends affirmatively to the suppression of the truth, or to a covering up or disguising of the truth, or to a withdrawal or distraction of a party's attention to the real facts.

It is significant to note that in Maryland, there is a common law qualified immunity for character references for employees that acts to defeat an action for defamation (*Bagwell v. Peninsula Regional Medical Center,* 106 Md. App. 470 (1995)). Furthermore, Maryland statutory law also provides for the existence of a qualified privilege for employment references made in good faith (Md. Code Ann., Cts. & Jud. Proc. Art. § 5-423). Under such qualified immunity, an action for defamation can only prevail if the false statement was made with actual malice, that is, with knowledge of falsity or reckless disregard for the truth of the statement made (*Marchesi v. Franchino,* 283 Md. 131 (1978)).

### 9:24. What is gross negligence?

Consider the setting of an elementary school field trip to a local park with a lake to study the ecology of the area. In this context, an example of teacher negligence would be for the teacher to get involved watching birds in the trees and thus fail to keep track of the students, while a student suffers an injury that would have been preventable with reasonable care. On the other hand, an example of gross negligence in the same setting would be for the teacher to purposely sit on a bench with back turned away from the students while listening to loud music on an

I-Pod, while a student suffers an injury that would have been preventable with reasonable care.

### 9:25. Is educational malpractice an actionable tort?

No, educational malpractice has been resolved in Maryland by the case of *Hunter v. Board of Education of Montgomery County*, 292 Md. 481 (1982). The Maryland Court of Appeals found a number of problems with this attempt to collect monetary damages for the alleged failure of the school system to properly educate the student involved. Initially, the Court recognized that there might be physical, neurological, emotional, cultural, or environmental factors that had a significant effect on the educational shortcomings of this or any other student. The Court also noted the difficulty in identifying an appropriate standard of care to apply, along with the inherent complexity in establishing a direct causal connection between the conduct of the school system and the injury claimed. The Court declared its agreement with prior out-of-state opinions, which did not recognize educational malpractice as a valid cause of action, stating,

> We find ourselves in substantial agreement with the reasoning employed by the [California and New York] courts, for an award of money damages, in our view, represents a singularly inappropriate remedy for asserted errors in the educational process. The misgivings expressed in these cases concerning the establishment of legal cause and the inherent immeasurability of damages … Moreover, to allow petitioners' asserted negligence claims to proceed would in effect position the courts of this State as overseers of both the day-to-day operation of our educational process as well as the formulation of its governing policies. This responsibility we are loathe to impose on our courts. Such matters have been properly entrusted by the General Assembly to the State Department of Education and the local school boards who are invested with authority over them.

Given the current high standards of academic accountability, high stakes testing for earning a diploma, and the NCLB expectation that all students will be on grade level by 2014, it is likely that the question of educational malpractice will be revisited in Maryland and elsewhere in the years to come.

## Intentional Torts

### 9:26. What is an intentional tort?

In **9:1** it was noted that a tort is wrongful civil (not criminal) behavior. An intentional tort is a deliberate action that results in harm to another. The action may not have specifically intended to cause harm, but a consequence must have been intended by the action, and injury results from the intended consequence. An example is that someone conveys a suspicion that an acquaintance is guilty of misconduct at work (even though the suspicion is untrue). If that statement was overheard by another person that thereafter caused the acquaintance to lose their job, then an action for slander may result in the award of damages to the wronged person. The statement that was originally shared may have been intended as harmless gossip, but an actionable intentional tort resulting in actual injury has occurred nonetheless. In the event that the consequence from the intentional act becomes one that is unlikely to have occurred, then in some instances the tort may fall into the negligence category, even though it started with an intentional action. With the exception of defamation, intentional torts are generally not covered by insurance policies.

### 9:27. What is an assault?

First and foremost, an assault is a threatened battery. The action must generate genuine apprehension or fear that injury is to be imminently inflicted by someone with the apparent ability to carry out such harm. Examples of assault would include the brandishing of a knife or the pointing of a gun. It is not necessary that any actual contact occur in order for the intentional tort of assault to be actionable. If a kindergarten age girl threatens to punch out the principal, and there is no fear or apprehension of injury, then no assault has occurred. If a high school student (without a weapon in hand) threatens to hurt someone the next day, then no assault has occurred because the threat is not imminent enough. Likewise, assault usually cannot occur over the telephone or via e-mail, because there is no present ability to carry out the threat from a remote location.

### 9:28. What is a battery?

First and foremost, a battery is a most typically a completed assault. Unlike assault, in a battery the harmful or offensive contact must actually occur in order to be actionable. It is possible to commit battery against a person without first having assaulted them. For instance, if a student threw a rock at another student who ducked to avoid being struck, and the rock were to strike a third student in the back, the student who ducked was assaulted without suffering a battery, and the student who was hit in the back suffered a battery without being assaulted. Historically, in the school setting, the largest number of battery claims resulted from the infliction of corporal punishment. Corporal punishment is not allowed under Maryland law (Md. Code Ann., Ed. Art. § 7-306), but there are still a handful of states that continue to permit the practice. Self-defense is a valid defense to a battery claim, but the only force that can be used in self-defense is that which is reasonably required for self-protection, and no more. It is also important to note that school staff may in good faith use the reasonable force required when acting in defense of others, such as when breaking up a fight between students (Md. Code Ann., Ed. Art. § 7-307).

### 9:29. What is false imprisonment?

First of all, it is not actual imprisonment, but occurs when someone is wrongly detained against his or her will in some enclosed location. Being placed in a closet, room or vehicle could constitute false imprisonment if it involved wrongful detention by physical means or verbal order without the freedom to leave. Valid school discipline actions do not constitute false imprisonment, even if involuntary detention is imposed. On the other hand, discipline actions that go too far and involve the use of physical restraints may very well rise to the level of actionable false imprisonment.

A recent District of Columbia case resulted in the suspension of a teacher and a suit for false imprisonment from the family of a student who was disciplined by being tied to a chair with masking tape (Justin Blum, "5-Day Penalty for Teacher Who Taped Boy to Chair," *Washington Post*, Tuesday, July 23, 2002, p. B2). In the case of *Peters v. Rome City School District*, 188 A.D.2d 1015 (2002), a New York appellate court upheld a jury verdict of $75,000 awarded as a result of the school district's excessive use of a time-out room, that was to be a last resort for the student's behavior problem, pursuant to an individualized education plan (IEP). The facts supporting a finding of false imprisonment included being confined in the small, unfurnished, and unventilated room for sometimes in excess of one hour on 75 occasions during a six-month period. While the room was kept unlocked, a staff person would hold the door closed if the student attempted to leave, and the student injured his hands in attempts to leave the room.

### 9:30. What is intentional infliction of emotional distress?

This is a relatively new and fairly rare area of tort law that involves mental rather than physical injury. Only the most severe sort of emotional distress is actionable, and even then the wrongful behavior that gives rise to this tort must be flagrant, outrageous, extreme, beyond human dignity, and totally intolerable within civilized society. The behavior typically must also be prolonged or continuing in nature, rather than a single incident, such as stalking or ongoing sexual abuse and harassment.

# Defamation

### 9:31. What is defamation?

Communication that causes injury to the reputation of another person is defamation. Typically, the defamatory statement involves suggestion of dishonorable actions, dishonesty, or immorality. When the defamatory communication is verbal it is slander, and when it is written it is libel. In either case, false statements made to third persons that injure someone's good name and subject them to ridicule or contempt are defamatory in nature, and actionable unless a valid defense exists. Defamation does not always result from direct accusation, and can also arise from inference, insinuation, or innuendo. It is also important to note that the person being defamed must be readily identifiable, that is, to state that some unspecified teacher (in a school with dozens of teachers) has been falsifying educational records, would not constitute defamation because there is no recognized target of the accusation. If, on the other hand, the same statement was made about a male teacher on the second floor, and there is only one male teacher on the second floor, then an action for defamation may be viable. Likewise, a statement that all teachers falsify educational records would not be actionable because no individually identifiable teacher has been defamed. The free speech rights of the person issuing the questionable communication must always be balanced against the rights of the individual that is the object of the potential defamation to protect their good name from wrongful attack. In order to be successful, a basic action for defamation in Maryland must hold an individual up to public scorn, hatred, contempt, or ridicule; must be premised upon a false statement; and must result in the suffering of actual losses (*Peroutka v. Steng,* 116 Md. App. 301 (1997)).

### 9:32. What type of defamation is slander?

Slander is typically spoken defamation, but may also take the form of gestures or other non-written forms of communication.

### 9:33. What type of defamation is libel?

Libel typically takes the form of the written word, but also may result from being broadcast by television, radio or via the internet.

### 9:34. What is publication in defamation?

In order for defamation to occur, the statement must be made to a third party. Defamation cannot occur solely as a result of fictitious communication that is only conveyed to the falsely portrayed person. Someone else must receive the false communication or no actionable defamation will stand. It is also important to note that the publication must not be made by the victims of the defamation themselves, or the necessary element of publication will not be present. That is, the person committing the defamation must be responsible for the publication in order to be liable for damages, and additional third persons may also be liable for any republication of the defamatory communication.

### 9:35. What is injury to reputation in defamation?

In order for defamation to occur, the falsely portrayed person must actually have their reputation harmed by the untrue statement. In other words, if the false portrayal is not believed by those to whom it is published, then there is no actual injury to reputation and thus, no defamation. Furthermore, the injury required must go beyond insult and hurt feelings; there must be the real prospect of actual loss, such as the loss of a promotion at work.

### 9:36. What is the difference between public and private figures in defamation?

The nature of the potentially defamatory communication must be more extreme in order to be actionable in the case of a public figure. A private figure only needs to prove that a false publication was made to a third person, and that as a result injury to their reputation occurred. Public figures, on the other hand, must prove that the false publication was made either with actual malice or reckless disregard for the truth (*New York Times v. Sullivan*, 376 U.S. 254 (1964)). In the case of a private figure, a defamatory communication is presumed to be false, and the maker bears the burden of proving the truth of the statement. On the other hand, in the case of a public figure, a defamatory communication is presumed to be true, and the public figure bears the burden of proving its falsity. Public figures include persons in the public eye such as public officials, celebrities, and professional athletes. In the school setting, courts have generally found teachers to be private figures, but administrators and coaches have not infrequently been found to be public figures, depending on their level of authority and how high their profile is within the community.

A principal has been found to be a public figure in Maryland in the case of *Kapiloff v. Dunn*, 27 Md. App. 514 (1975). Superintendents and members of county boards of education are likely to be considered as public figures as well. In a recent decision, the West Virginia Supreme Court of Appeals in *Wilson v. The Daily Gazette Company*, No. 31045 (W. Va. June 13, 2003), ruled that a high school athlete is not a public figure and was free to bring a defamation action against a local newspaper as a result of their printing a rumor that the student had exposed himself in front of the losing team's fans after his school won a state basketball championship. The newspaper claimed that the student was a public figure because of his athletic accomplishments, but the Court found that his name only came to the attention of the public in any significant way when the newspaper reported the defamatory rumor.

### 9:37. Are defenses to defamation available?

Yes, a communication that might otherwise be defamatory can be defended if the statement is truthful, or is an opinion rather than a fact, or is subject to a privilege. In addition to these specific defenses, the failure to prove any required element of defamation, such as publication or injury, will also result in a successful defense of a claim for defamation.

### 9:38. How is the veracity of statements a defense in defamation?

In the education arena, generally speaking, truth is an absolute defense to a defamation claim. Assuming that statements are not taken out of context, or that important facts have not been omitted, or that some other deliberate misrepresentation has not occurred, then communications that are true do not create actionable defamation claims.

### 9:39. How is opinion versus fact a defense in defamation?

Most opinions do not easily lend themselves to being proven to be true or false, and are thus more likely to qualify as constitutionally protected free speech that communicates a person's general viewpoint, particularly when issues of public concern are involved. For example, to state that a teacher is bad with children is likely to be viewed as an expression of subjective opinion; it is not easily proven true or false, and thus is probably not defamatory. On the contrary, to state that a teacher is an abuser of children is clearly an expression of fact; it can be proven true or false, and would likely give rise to an action for defamation. Finally, couching a factual accusation in the guise of an opinion will not protect the speech from being defamatory in nature. For example, to qualify the above statement by adding "it is my opinion" that a teacher is an abuser of children, does not alter it from being a factual statement that would support a defamation claim.

### 9:40. How is privilege a defense in defamation?

A privilege may be absolute or qualified, depending on the circumstances, although qualified privilege is far more common in the education arena. If a statement is absolutely privileged, then it cannot be the basis for a defamation action, such as statements made on the witness stand in a court proceeding (*Korb v. Kowaleviocz*, 285 Md. 699 (1979)). There are a few cases from other jurisdictions that have held that statements of board members made during a board meeting are entitled to an absolute privilege, provided that the board members are acting within the scope of their duties as board members. A qualified privilege is one where the protection from a defamation claim is conditioned upon the statement being made in good faith and with reasonable justification, with the proper motive, in the proper manner, and at the proper time. An example of a statement protected by qualified privilege would be when a guidance counselor makes comments to a student's parents about concerns over potential drug use by the student.

Furthermore, Maryland law also provides for the existence of a qualified privilege for employment references made in good faith (Md. Code Ann., Cts. & Jud. Proc. Art. § 5-423). It was affirmed in *Bagwell v. Peninsula Regional Medical Center*, 106 Md. App. 470 (1995), that Maryland common law provides a qualified privilege for employers that provide character references for employees. The Court in *Bagwell* stated, "When a statement enjoys a qualified privilege, the privilege defeats an action for defamation." Furthermore, Maryland law also provides for the existence of a qualified privilege for employment references made in good faith (Md. Code Ann., Cts. & Jud. Proc. Art. § 5-423). Under such qualified immunity, an action for defamation can only prevail if the false statement was made with actual malice, that is, with knowledge of falsity or reckless disregard for the truth of the statement made (*Marchesi v. Franchino,* 283 Md. 131 (1978)).

# Miscellaneous

### 9:41. What are compensatory damages?

Compensatory damages are a monetary award that makes someone injured by a tort, whole to the extent possible. Specific examples would include lost wages, medical bills (past and prospective), lost value of property, and pain and suffering.

### 9:42. What are punitive damages?

Punitive damages are designed, in the most extreme cases, to punish the wrongdoer monetarily so that they will not commit the tortuous act again.

### 9:43. Are there other legal defenses against liability?

In Maryland, accidental injuries to employees which arise out of and in the course of employment, even when the result of negligence, are subject to coverage under the workers compensation laws of the state. The law provides that this workers compensation coverage is the sole remedy for Maryland employees, including school system staff, for on the job injuries, and acts as a bar to negligence claims for most workplace injuries.

### 9:44. What liability exists under 42 U.S.C. § 1983?

Section 1983 is part of the Civil Rights Act of 1871, and was originally passed to enforce the anti-slavery provisions of the Thirteenth, Fourteenth and Fifteenth Amendments to the U.S. Constitution. Specifically, the statute states:

> Every person who, under the color of any statute, ordinance regulation, custom, or usage, of any State ... subjects, or causes to be subjected, any citizen of the United States or other person within the jurisdiction thereof to the deprivation of any rights, privileges, or immunities secured by the Constitution and laws, shall be liable to the party injured in an action at law, suit in equity, or other proper proceeding for redress...

The Supreme Court in *Wood v. Strickland*, 420 U.S. 308 (1975), and three years later in *Carey v. Piphus*, 435 U.S. 247 (1978), applied Section 1983 for the first times against school boards in the cases of students that were denied due process by local boards of education prior to their expulsion in discipline matters, finding that the injury to the students resulted from official board policy or established practice. Section 1983 imposes personal liability on those held liable for violating individual rights provided by the U.S. Constitution and federal laws, if they are deliberately indifferent to such rights and fail to demonstrate good faith. The majority of Section 1983 claims seem to involve either due process concerns regarding students and staff or free expression concerns involving school system policies or established practices. The Supreme Court, in *Morse v. Frederick*, 551 U.S. ___ (2007), unanimously agreed that the administrator deserved qualified immunity from personal liability for the discipline meted out to a student who displayed a banner with the message "Bong Hits 4 Jesus". The Ninth Circuit Court of Appeals decision that the administrator was subject to personal liability because there was a clear violation of the student's free speech rights was reversed.

Section 1983 does not create any new rights, but instead provides a vehicle to seek damages, consisting of compensatory damages and attorney's fees, for the violation of existing federal rights by public entities such as county boards of education or their individual members. County boards may also have vicarious liability for the unlawful violation of federal rights by school system employees that have final policymaking authority by law or as a matter of established school system practice. A recent Third Circuit case ruled that a Section 1983 claim is not allowed for issues arising under IDEA or Section 504 of the Rehabilitation Act because those statutes effectively supplant the remedies under Section 1983 (*A.W. v. The Jersey City Public Schools*, No. 05-2553 (3rd Cir. May 24, 2007)).

Finally, there are a number of defenses to Section 1983 claims, including: asserting that the charged employee lacked final policymaking authority, asserting that the action complained of was not based upon school system policy or established practice, asserting that the action complained of was reasonable and not deliberately indifferent, and asserting that the injury complained of was not caused by the violation of some federally protected right.

### 9:45. What liability exists under Title IX?

Title IX of the 1972 Education Amendments (20 U.S.C. § 1681(a)) provides protection for victims of sexual discrimination, stating in part,

> No person in the United States shall, on the basis of sex, be excluded from participation in, be denied the benefits of, or be subject to discrimination under any education program or activity receiving Federal financial assistance, ...

The Supreme Court of the United States by a unanimous ruling in *Franklin v. Gwinnett County Schools*, 503 U.S. 60 (1992), held that claims for monetary damages may be brought in cases of intentional sexual harassment. Cases since that date have established that Title IX claims can be made for teacher-to-student and student-to-student sexual harassment and that in order for the school district to be liable, the complaining student must prove that school officials acted with deliberate indifference to the teacher misconduct. To demonstrate such deliberate indifference, the school district's response, to a plainly credible report of sexual harassment that systematically deprives the victim of access to educational opportunities, must be shown to be clearly unreasonable in light of known circumstances.

And in more recent decision, the United States Supreme Court in *Jackson v. Birmingham Board of Education*, 125 U.S. 1497 (2005), found that a coach that advocated for equal funding, equal access to sport facilities and equipment based upon Title IX shortcomings for his girls team, was able to bring a Title IX action for the retaliation that he suffered.

# 10. Student Attendance, Instruction, and Records

## Student Attendance

### 10:1. May states compel student enrollment and attendance at a public school?

Yes. States may compel school attendance, a mandate that may be satisfied by attendance at a public or nonpublic school (*Pierce v. Society of Sisters*, 268 U.S. 510, 535 (1925)). States derive this authority not from the federal Constitution but rather from state constitutions which place on the respective state legislatures the duty to establish a system of public education for all children.

### 10:2. Does the federal government have a role in promoting school attendance?

The federal No Child Left Behind Act imposes myriad new accountability provisions on public schools, including the identification of "participation rates" of at least 95 percent of all students on annual standardized tests, and state and local school system accountability for average daily attendance rates in grades 1-12 and yearly high school graduation rates. These federal policy initiatives have generated local and state efforts to assess student attendance policies.

Another way in which federal law impacts student attendance is the conditioning of federal temporary assistance for needy families (TANF) or welfare assistance on school attendance. To be eligible for federal TANF payments and related state assistance, a minor must be enrolled full-time in a school or secondary school program providing the same level of vocational or technical training.

### 10:3. Where are Maryland's laws and regulations regarding student attendance found?

In statute, § 7-301 of the Education Article establishes the state's compulsory attendance law. In accordance with § 7-301, the Maryland State Board of Education has adopted regulations outlining rules and procedures regarding attendance, age of entry, lawful and unlawful absences and other student attendance issues (COMAR 13A.08.01.-.20).

School systems are required to operate schools which are open for pupil attendance for at least 180 actual school days or a minimum of 1,080 school hours during a 10-month period, and open a minimum of 3 hours during each school day (Md. Code Ann., Ed. Art. § 7-103).

## 10:4. How is compulsory school attendance defined?

In Maryland, a child who is 5 through 15 years of age must attend public school regularly unless the child is otherwise receiving regular, thorough instruction at an alternative setting, *e.g.* a private or home school (Md. Code Ann., Ed. Art. § 7-301). In recent years, the state legislature has repeatedly considered and rejected proposed legislation to raise the compulsory attendance age from 15 to 16 or 17. In 2006, the General Assembly created a taskforce to study the fiscal and policy impacts of raising the compulsory attendance age from 15 to 17.

## 10:5. Is pre-kindergarten or kindergarten subject to compulsory attendance?

Kindergarten attendance is required for all children in the state for the school year prior to entering first grade unless the child is "otherwise receiving regular, thorough instruction in the skills and studies usually taught in a kindergarten program in a public school" (Md. Code Ann., Ed. Art. § 7-301(a)(3)). The statute provides an exemption from mandatory kindergarten attendance, requiring a written request to the local superintendent that verifies that the child is enrolled full-time in a licensed child care center, full-time in a registered family day care home, or part-time in a Head Start program (Md. Code Ann., Ed. Art. § 7-301(f)). The age of entry requirement for kindergarten in Maryland, beginning with the 2006-2007 school year and each school year thereafter, provides that a child be 5 years old or older on September 1 of the school year in which the child applies for entrance (COMAR 13A.08.01.02B).

Pre-kindergarten, although subject to a state mandate that it be available to all eligible, economically disadvantaged, four-year olds, is not subject to any compulsory attendance requirement. The age of entry requirement for pre-kindergarten in Maryland, beginning with the 2005-2006 school year and each school year thereafter, provides that a child be 4 years old or older on September 1 of the school year in which the child applies for entrance (COMAR 13A.08.01.02A).

## 10:6. How do schools and school systems collect and report student attendance information?

Statute prescribes that daily student attendance records must be kept for each student in accordance with regulations adopted by the State Board of Education and the Maryland Student Records System Manual (MSRM) which is incorporated in the regulations by reference (COMAR 13A.08.02.01). For a more detailed discussion of student records, see **10:78** through **10:114**.

## 10:7. Does compulsory attendance apply to all children?

The compulsory attendance statute applies to all children ages 5 through 15 and includes "any child who has a mental, emotional, or physical handicap" (Md. Code Ann., Ed. Art. § 7-301(d)(1)). However, compulsory attendance for a child who has a mental, emotional, or physical handicap is qualified in that it does not apply to a child "whose mental, emotional, or physical condition makes his instruction detrimental to his progress; or whose presence in school presents a danger of serious physical harm to others" (Md. Code Ann., Ed. Art. § 7-301(d)(2)).

## 10:8. How does the school system determine exceptions based on health and safety reasons?

Based on the advice of the school principal, supervisor, pupil personnel supervisor, or visiting teacher and with the written recommendation of a licensed physician or a State Department of Education certified or licensed psychologist, the local superintendent may:

- Make other appropriate provisions for the free education of any student excepted from attendance under paragraph (2) of this subsection; or

- Permit the parents or guardians of that student to withdraw him from public school, for as long as the attendance of the child in a public school would be detrimental to his progress or his presence in school would present a danger of serious physical harm to others (Md. Code Ann., Ed. Art. § 7-302(d)(3)).

Even in cases of students being withdrawn from school under the circumstances outlined above, it is the responsibility of the local board of education to "make other appropriate provisions for the education of the child" (Md. Code Ann., Ed. Art. § 7-302(d)(4)).

## 10:9. May a pregnant student be excluded from the school setting?

No. State regulations provide that each local school system is responsible for educating all students including pregnant girls, married or unmarried. Regulations protect the attendance rights of pregnant students 16 years old or older by allowing the student to remain in the regular school program and prohibiting the school from involuntarily excluding the student from any part of the program. Regulations also accommodate pregnant students under compulsory school age, by allowing the student to voluntarily withdraw from school, contingent on the development of an "appropriate educational program" for the student (COMAR 13A.08.01.06).

## 10:10. What other health issues may affect school attendance?

Courts have generally upheld the constitutionality of immunization requirements as a condition for school attendance (*Zucht v. King*, 260 U.S. 174 (1922), and *Jacobson v. Massachusetts*, 197 U.S. 11 (1905)). For example, Maryland's definition of an enrolled student for purposes of calculating state aid refers specifically to a student who is a bona fide resident of Maryland and who has age appropriate immunizations (COMAR 13A.02.06.03).

## 10:11. Must schools enroll children with acquired immune deficiency syndrome (AIDS) or other communicable diseases?

Yes. Courts have generally held that public schools must enroll students with AIDS, hepatitis B, and other health conditions upon certification from medical professionals that the condition poses minimal threat of exposure to others in the school setting (*Doe v. Dolton Elementary School District No.148*, 694 F. Supp. 440 (N.D. Ill. 1998); *New York Association for Retarded Children v. Carey*, 621 F.2d. 644 (2d Cir. 1979)).

## 10:12. Are schools required to report and investigate student absences?

Yes. School principals or head administrators of all public and private schools are required to report immediately to the county superintendent, or supervisor of pupil personnel, the name of each child enrolled in a school who has been absent without lawful excuse. The school system is required to conduct an investigation in response to such notice (Md. Code Ann., Ed. Art. §§ 7-302(a) and (b)).

## 10:13. How is compulsory school attendance enforced?

An individual who has legal custody of a child aged 5 to 15 and fails to see that the child attends school is guilty of a misdemeanor. Penalties include a fine not to exceed $50 per day of unlawful absence or imprisonment not to exceed 10 days, or both. For a second or subsequent conviction the penalty is a fine not to exceed $100 per day of unlawful absence or imprisonment not to exceed 30 days, or both (Md. Code Ann., Ed. Art. § 7-301(e)(2)).

In addition, the law prohibits any person to "induce or attempt to induce a child to absent himself unlawfully from school or employ or harbor any child who is absent unlawfully from school while school is in session". A violator of this provision is guilty of a misdemeanor and on conviction is subject to a fine not to exceed $500 or imprisonment not to exceed 30 days, or both (Md. Code Ann., Ed. Art. § 7-301(e)(1)).

However, the overarching intent of the statute is to strongly encourage school attendance, as evidenced by the provision authorizing the court to "suspend the fine or the prison sentence and establish terms and conditions which would promote the child's attendance" (Md. Code Ann., Ed. Art. § 7-301 (e)(3)).

## 10:14. Does Maryland provide any specific exceptions to compulsory attendance?

Yes. For example, a child who is 5 years old may be exempted from mandatory school attendance for 1 year if the child's parent or guardian files a written request with the local school system asking that the child's attendance be delayed due to the child's level of maturity (Md. Code Ann., Ed. Art. § 7-301(a)(2)).

## 10:15. Are there other exceptions to mandatory school attendance requirements?

Yes. States may exempt married students, or students who have obtained employment certificates. In addition, courts recognize an exemption based on bona fide religious beliefs, most notably exempting Amish students who have completed the eighth grade (*Wisconsin v. Yoder*, 406 U.S. 205 (1972)).

## 10:16. May a state condition a student's driver's license on school attendance?

Yes. Many states have enacted legislation to encourage high school attendance by restricting access to the state's driver's license to persons under the age of 18 based on regular school attendance (*Means v. Sideropilis*, 401 S.E.2d 447 (W. Va. 1990)). For example, Florida's statute conditions the state's driver's license on public or private school enrollment and further restricts the license by requiring schools to report to the state's motor vehicles department instances of 15 or more unexcused absences in a 90-day period for all students over age 14. Maryland statute authorizes courts to rescind driving privileges for juvenile violators of certain criminal statutes but does not impose any penalty on a student for truancy, only on the student's parent or guardian.

In 2007, Maryland's General Assembly enacted legislation which prohibits the Motor Vehicle Administration from issuing a learner's instructional permit to an applicant under the age of 16 if the applicant's school attendance record indicates more than 10 unexcused absences during the prior school semester (Senate Bill 519/House Bill 571, Chapters 562/563, 2007 Laws of Maryland).

## 10:17. What are lawful causes of absence in Maryland?

State regulations (COMAR 13A.08.01.03) define "lawful absences" to include the following:

- Death in the immediate family; based on the locally adopted definition of immediate family;

- Illness of the student; requiring the parent or guardian to provide a physician's certificate to the principal or pupil personnel worker;

- Court summons;

- Hazardous weather conditions; based on conditions determined to endanger the health or safety of the student in transit to or from school;

- Observances of religious holidays;

- State emergencies;

- Student suspension;

- Lack of authorized transportation; and

- Other emergencies or circumstances which in the judgment of the superintendent provide a "good and sufficient cause for absence from school".

## 10:18. What are unlawful causes of absence in Maryland?

State regulations define "unlawful absences" to include a student's absence for any portion of the day for any reason other than those defined as lawful absences, and may constitute truancy.

## 10:19. How are "days absent" counted and recorded?

The Maryland Student Records System Manual (MSRM, 2007, Section C), as recently amended by the State Board of Education, outlines the manner in which students are counted present or absent, as follows:

"Students Scheduled for a Full Day"

A student is counted present for a full day if the student is in attendance four hours or more of the school day. A student is counted as present for ½ day if in attendance for at least two hours of the school day, but less than four hours.

"Students Scheduled for a Partial Day"

A student scheduled for less than a full day is to be counted present based on the amount of time he/she is scheduled. Example:

A student scheduled for a two hour block of time will be counted present for a full day if the student is in attendance for that entire block of time. If the student is absent for that entire block of time, the student will be counted as absent for a full day. A student scheduled for a two hour block of time will be counted present for ½ day if the student is in attendance for one hour.

## 10:20. May a local school system modify the state's student attendance requirements?

Each local school system must adopt a student attendance policy which includes reasons for lawful and unlawful absences as defined under COMAR 13A.08.01.03 and .04. State regulations further provide that school systems "may add specified criteria for unlawful absences" (COMAR 13A.08.01.04B(1)).

## 10:21. Are local boards of education required to adopt student attendance policies?

Yes. Each local board must adopt a policy, pursuant to COMAR 13A.08.01.05, that includes the following components:

- General statement of purpose;
- Standards for regular attendance;
- Attendance monitoring procedures that include recordkeeping in accordance with State requirements;
- Definitions of lawful and unlawful absences, and tardiness;
- Procedures to verify absences and tardiness;
- Intervention strategies for absenteeism;
- A referral process to pupil services, including case management of chronic attendance cases;
- Penalties for failure to meet regular attendance standards;
- Make-up work requirements;
- A reward process to encourage regular school attendance; and
- An appeals process, including specific due process procedures, for appealing local attendance violation decisions.

# Residency and Enrollment

## 10:22. What is required to enroll a child in a public school?

State law and regulations do not address the standards and procedures that local boards may develop to ensure proof of residency, custody, and other information necessary for a child's enrollment and school assignment. Local school systems in Maryland typically require, particularly for first time enrollments, the following information and types of verification:

- Age—birth certificate, passport/visa, hospital certificate, family bible, church certificate, parent's affidavit, other legal or notarized identification

- Identity—photo identification, drivers' license, permanent resident alien card, naturalization papers, birth certificate, court order, separation or divorce decree

- Residency—property tax bill (home owners), lease (renters)

- Physical examination and immunization—Maryland Department of Health and Mental Hygiene Immunization Form 896

## 10:23. Who determines the location of a school and its attendance area?

The local board of education is authorized to "establish a public school if, in its judgment, it is advisable" (Md. Code Ann., Ed. Art. §§ 4-109(a)). The local board, with the advice of the local superintendent, determines the geographical attendance area for each school in its jurisdiction (Md. Code Ann., Ed. Art. §§ 4-110(c)).

## 10:24. Does a child have a right to attend a particular school?

No. Maryland's highest court has ruled that "[a]bsent a claim of deprivation of equal educational opportunity or unconstitutional discrimination because of race or religion, there is no right or privilege to attend a particular school" (*Bernstein v. Board of Education of Prince Georges County*, 245 Md. 464, 472 (1966)). Other examples of State Board decisions pertaining to student transfers include: *Dennis v. Board of Education of Montgomery County*, 7 Op. MSBE 953 (1998) (desire to participate in particular courses does not constitute unique hardship sufficient to override utilization concerns); *Marshall v. Board of Education of Howard County*, 7 Op. MSBE 596 (1997) (no entitlement to attend four-year communications program offered at Mount Hebron); *Slater v. Board of Education of Montgomery County*, 6 Op. MSBE 365 (1992) (denial of transfer to school alleged to better serve student's abilities and welfare); *Williams v. Board of Education of Montgomery County*, 5 Op. MSBE 507 (1990) (denial of transfer to program offering advanced German); *Sklar v. Board of Education of Montgomery County*, 5

Op. MSBE 443 (1989) (denial of request to attend school offering four years of Latin, note taking/study skills course, and piano).

### 10:25. What is the State Board of Education's standard of review of challenges to school boundaries?

The State Board of Education has held that a local board's determination of the geographic attendance areas of schools, and the decision whether or not to conduct a boundary study, are policy making or quasi-legislative functions (*Elprin v. Howard County Board of Education*, 57 Md. App. 458, 463 (1984)). Therefore, the standard of review that the State Board applies in such cases is that the Board will not substitute its judgment for that of the local board unless the decision is shown to be arbitrary, unreasonable, or illegal.

### 10:26. What are the criteria for allowing student transfers within a school system?

Generally, a school system's policies and procedures will not allow a student to transfer between schools except in cases of a demonstrated hardship or other exception as defined in the local policy. For example, a local school system generally will not grant a transfer request based on the perceived superiority of one school over another, but may allow a transfer based on a specific program of instruction, medical reasons, twelfth grade completion, or transition from middle to high school.

### 10:27. What is the State Board of Education's standard of review regarding student transfer decisions?

The standard of review that the State Board applies in reviewing a student transfer decision is that the Board will not substitute its judgment for that of the local board unless the decision is shown to be arbitrary, unreasonable, or illegal (*Breads v. Board of Education of Montgomery County*, 7 Op. MSBE 507 (1997)).

### 10:28. What factors may a local board consider in a student transfer request?

The State Board has noted that student transfer decisions require balancing county-wide considerations with those of the student and family (*Marbach v. Board of Education of Montgomery County*, 6 Op. MSBE 351 (1992)). The State Board has identified factors such as "socio-economic level, building utilization, enrollment levels, and the educational program needs of the individual student" as legally permissible and proper subjects of consideration in weighing the impact of a request for a student to transfer from his or her home school to some other school of choice (*Slater v. Board of Education of Montgomery County*, 6 Op. MSBE 365 (1992)).

### 10:29. May local boards enter into agreements to create shared schools?

Yes. Section 4-121 of the Education Article allows, but does not require, two local boards of education to enter into a mutual agreement to establish a "jointly attended school" near the boundary of adjoining counties and may waive tuition from the students from outside the "receiving county" in which the school is located. The "sending" county must compensate the "receiving" county for the local per pupil expense for each student and state aid will be paid to the receiving county (Md. Code Ann., Ed. Art. § 4-121(c) and (d)).

# Kinship Care

### 10:30. What is an "out-of-county living arrangement"?

Maryland statute provides for the public education of children placed by a state agency in a facility, or a relative's home, in a county other than the county in which the child's parents or guardian reside. Such children are referred to as living in an "out-of-county living arrangement."

If the child is placed in a relative's home, the living arrangement is referred to as "formal" kinship care. In either case, the law provides for a per pupil funding arrangement between the "sending" county of the parent's residence and the "receiving" county in which the child is placed. The government agency's placement of the child in a facility, or the home of a relative, establishes the residency of the child for purposes of enrollment in the local school system.

### 10:31. What is meant by "formal" kinship care?

Maryland's Department of Human Resources administers a "formal" kinship care program "designed to preserve families by accommodating the needs of the children ... and prevention of the need for out-of-home placement" for children who have been committed to a local department because of abuse, neglect, dependency, or abandonment; and placed by the local department with kinship parents or kinship caregivers (COMAR 07.02.09.01).

Formal "kinship care" is defined as continuous 24-hour care and supportive services provided for a minor child placed by a child placement agency in the home of a relative related by blood or marriage within the fifth degree of consanguinity or affinity as cited in subdivision B(11) of this regulation. Kinship care includes the services provided by local agencies to the kinship care providers "to assure that the placement promotes the child's physical, emotional, and intellectual growth and well-being" (COMAR 07.02.09.02B(12)).

### 10:32. How is "kinship" defined?

Department of Human Resources' regulations pertaining to the formal kinship care program define "kin" as follows:

- "Kin" means an individual related by blood or marriage within the fifth degree of consanguinity or affinity, as defined in the Estates and Trusts Article, § 1-203, Annotated Code of Maryland, to a child who is in the care, custody, or guardianship of a local department;

- Includes a great-great-great grandparent, great-great aunt or uncle, great-great niece or nephew, and second cousin (child of a first cousin); and

- Includes other individuals who make up the family support system, such as relatives beyond the fifth degree of consanguinity or affinity, godparents, friends of the family, and other adults who have a strong kinship bond with the child (COMAR 07.02.09.02B(11)).

### 10:33. What is meant by "informal kinship care"?

Informal kinship care is defined as a living arrangement in which a relative of a child, who is not in the care, custody, or guardianship of the local department of social services, provides for the care and custody of the child due to a serious family hardship (Md. Code Ann., Ed. Art. § 7-101(c)(1)(ii)).

The impetus for the legislation establishing the "informal" as opposed to "formal" kinship care arrangement was the desire of grandparents and other relatives who had not acquired legal custody of a child to, nonetheless, enroll the child in a school system other than the system in which the parent or legal guardian is domiciled. The rights to enroll and make education decisions on behalf of the child, in the absence of legal custody or guardianship, are limited to certain relatives and conditioned on verification of a "serious family hardship" giving rise to the kinship care arrangement.

### 10:34. Must a school system recognize an informal care arrangement?

Yes. A local superintendent must allow a child who is a resident of Maryland to enroll in and attend a public school in a county other than the county in which the child is domiciled, based on the domicile of the child's parent or legal guardian, if the child lives with a relative who can verify the informal kinship care arrangement though a sworn affidavit (Md. Code Ann., Ed. Art. § 7-101(c)(2)(i)).

**10:35. How does the informal kinship care statute define "relative"?**

"Relatives" recognized under this statute include adults related to a child by blood or marriage within the fifth degree of consanguinity (Md. Code Ann., Ed. Art. § 7-101(c)(1)(iii)).

**10:36. How is "serious family hardship" defined?**

Statute specifies six categories of serious family hardships, including:

1. Death of a parent or legal guardian of the child;

2. Serious illness of a parent or legal guardian of the child;

3. Drug addiction of a parent or legal guardian of the child;

4. Incarceration of a parent or legal guardian of the child;

5. Abandonment by a parent or legal guardian of the child; or

6. Assignment of a parent or legal guardian of a child to active military duty (Md. Code Ann., Ed. Art. § 7-101(c)(1)(iv)).

**10:37. What must be included in the sworn affidavit verifying the informal kinship care arrangement?**

The affidavit, in the form provided in the statute, must include:

- The name and date of birth of the child;

- The name and address of the child's parent or legal guardian;

- The name and address of the relative providing informal kinship care;

- The date the relative assumed informal kinship care;

- The nature of the serious family hardship and why it resulted in informal kinship care;

- The kinship relation to the child of the relative providing informal kinship care;

- The name and address of the school the child previously attended;

- Notice that the county superintendent may verify the facts given by the relative providing informal kinship care in the affidavit and conduct an audit of the case after the child has been enrolled in the county public school system;

- Notice that if fraud or misrepresentation is discovered during an audit, the county superintendent shall remove the child from the county public school system roll; and

- Notice that any person who willfully makes a material misrepresentation in the affidavit shall be subject to a penalty payable to the county for three times the pro rata share of tuition for the time the child fraudulently attends a public school in the county (Md. Code Ann., Ed. Art. § 7-101(c)(3)).

## 10:38. When may an affidavit be filed and enrollment commence?

The school system must allow a child to attend school based on the filing of the affidavit (Md. Code Ann., Ed. Art. § 7-101(c)(2)). The affidavit may be filed at any time during the school year (Md. Code Ann., Ed. Art. § 7-101(c )(7)(i)). However, annually, the affidavit must be filed at least two weeks prior to the start of the school year (Md. Code Ann., Ed. Art. § 7-101(c )(7)(ii)).

## 10:39. Must an affidavit be notarized?

No. The statute requires only the signature of the relative attesting to the informal kinship care relationship and identified family hardship.

## 10:40. What types of documentation may be requested to support the affidavit?

Examples of verification of the serious family hardship(s) may include the following:

- Death—copy of the death certificate or other proof;
- Serious illness—copy of doctor's report, note, or other proof;
- Drug addiction—documentation from a doctor or treatment provider, or other proof;
- Incarceration—documentation from the legal system or detention facility, or other proof;
- Abandonment—notarized statements from legal guardians, documentation from the court or department of social services, or other proof;
- Assignment to military duty—copy of military orders or other proof.

## 10:41. Does the affidavit of serious family hardship require the unavailability of both parents?

No. The affidavit is limited in scope to identifying a hardship of any one parent or guardian. The affidavit does include the name and address of all parents and/or legal guardians and allows the superintendent to verify the affidavit by contacting these persons. However, if the affidavit is valid with regard to one parent, the circumstances of the other parent are not relevant to the school system's obligation to accept the affidavit and continue to enroll the child.

### 10:42. What rights regarding education decisions or records extend to a person providing informal kinship care?

The key objective of the statute is to facilitate the immediate enrollment of a child to a school outside their "home" jurisdiction and in proximity to the residence of their care-giving relative. In this way, this statute conveys the right to make an important decision regarding a child's education to a non-parent and non-legal guardian.

The statute is less than clear on the scope and relationship of the informal kinship care-giver's rights to make education decisions as relating to the rights of the biological parent's or legal guardian's. Section 7-101(c)(8) of the Education Article provides that "the relative providing informal kinship care shall make the full range of educational decisions for the child", whereas Section 7-101(c)(10) reserves the right of the parent or legal guardian to "have final decision making authority regarding the educational needs of the child."

### 10:43. What happens if a change occurs in the kinship care relationship or family hardship?

If a change occurs in the care arrangement or regarding the serious family hardship of the child's parent or guardian, the relative providing the kinship care must notify the school system in writing within 30 days (Md. Code Ann., Ed. Art. § 7-101(c)(6)).

### 10:44. Is the school system bound by the initial decision to enroll the student based on the affidavit?

No. The county superintendent may verify the facts contained in the affidavit and conduct an audit on a case-by-case basis after the child has been enrolled in the county public school system. If the county superintendent discovers fraud or misrepresentation, the child may be removed from the county public school system roll (Md. Code Ann., Ed. Art. § 7-101(c)(4)(viii)).

### 10:45. Is there a penalty for fraud regarding the affidavit?

Yes. The statute imposes a penalty on "any person who willfully makes a material misrepresentation in the affidavit" of payment to the school system of an amount equal to three times the pro rata share of tuition that would apply to the period of time the child attended school under the fraudulent affidavit (Md. Code Ann., Ed. Art. § 7-101(c)(4)(x)).

# Custody

### 10:46. How do custody issues impact school system operations and decisions?

Custody issues arise in the school setting when school administrators are asked to determine whether a parent, guardian or other person has rights to make routine or major education decisions, or who has access to a student's records. In addition, school administrators may be requested to testify in court regarding a custody dispute.

### 10:47. How does a child's education relate to the court's decision regarding custody?

Courts, in deciding a child custody dispute, consider factors including potential disruption of the child's social and school life, in addition to many other factors such as the capacity of the parents to communicate, fitness of the parents, preference of the child, geographic proximity of parents, financial status of the parents, among others (*Taylor v. Taylor*, 508 A.2d 964 (Md. 1986)). In light of the importance of the role that the child's preference, the physical location of the child's school, and the experiences of school employees with the parties to the custody dispute may play in the custody determination, school officials can be requested, or receive court subpoenas, to make statements or appear in court regarding a custody proceeding.

### 10:48. How does a school system determine custody?

Generally, in the absence of any court order to the contrary, parents are presumed to be the natural guardians of their children. Parents are jointly and severally liable for the support, care, nurturing, welfare, and education of their children. Neither parent is presumed to have a right to custody or decision-making that is superior to the other parent in the absence of a court order, or a valid written parenting, separation, mediation, or property settlement agreement. Any unclear language in such documents may be reviewed by the central office. With regard to access to student records, schools must presume that both parents of the student have authority to view student records (COMAR 13A.08.02.29).

## 10:49. Does knowledge of separation or divorce require any verification or action by the school system?

Separation alone, in the absence of a court order or legally binding agreement, does not alter custody or the joint and several responsibilities of both parents. Neither parent may be presumed to have a superior right to custody in the absence of a court order or legally binding instrument.

A divorce may involve a legally binding custody decision that vests sole custody with one parent, and divests the rights of the other parent to custody, visitation, and the authority to make education decisions on behalf of the child. Again, in the absence of a court order to the contrary, the school system may presume that parents who are divorced, separated, or otherwise living apart, retain permission to inspect and review student records (COMAR 13A.08.02.30).

## 10:50. How do school officials confirm that a court order is in effect?

School administrators may request the court order and deny access to any non-parent or guardian in the absence of such an order. Generally, the court orders are stamped with an official seal "true copy test" by the clerk of the court. School administrators should also note that a Maryland order takes precedence over the order of another state, unless formally enrolled in Maryland. Different types of court orders require the attention of school administrators; court orders may be pendente lite/temporary (while the litigation is pending) or permanent; and orders may also be *ex parte* (only one side heard from) orders which will have an expiration date and no validity beyond that date. Importantly, written signed statements, or notarized statements, or powers of attorney, or similar documents (other than kinship care affidavits) are not sufficient to transfer authority and control over a child's education.

If there is any question or doubt as to whether the non-physical legal custodian may make specific decisions, or if one parent asks for input that the other parent contests, then ask the parties for clarification as to their legal status. If the terms of the court's order are unclear, or disputed by the parent, the school administrator should consult the school system's central office for guidance.

## 10:51. What is meant by "legal custody"?

"Legal custody" refers to the rights and obligations to make long range decisions on behalf of a minor child, such as decisions involving the child's education, special education, health care, and general welfare. In circumstances when only one parent is awarded legal custody, the other parent becomes a non-custodial parent.

"Joint legal custody" refers to a situation in which both parents have equal authority to make decisions, and neither parent's rights are superior to the other. If both parents continue to share legal custody, both parents have the same rights to make major life decisions on behalf of the child. Therefore, on major decisions, both parties have equal rights and equal input, and school officials should treat the parents as if they are still married (*i.e.*, advise them to work out their disagreement and inform the school when they do agree). Usually, even when parents are awarded joint legal custody, one parent is awarded sole or primary physical custody.

## 10:52. What is meant by "physical custody"?

"Physical custody" refers to a parent's right and obligation to provide a home for the child and to make day-to-day decisions during the time the child is with the parent having such custody.

"Joint or shared physical custody" often involves the custody by one parent during the school year and by the other during summer vacation months, or may involve custody based on the division between weekdays and weekends, or between days and nights.

The parent who is awarded physical custody has the sole right to make day-to-day, non-major life decisions regarding the child during the times of the physical custody. For example, major life decisions to be made jointly by the parents include where the child is to be enrolled at school, whether the child needs special education, and whether the child should be held back. However, decisions regarding what the child wears to school, what the child eats for lunch, who picks up the child from school, whether the child can go on a field trip, etc., are all day-to-day non-major life decisions that should be made solely by the parent who has been awarded primary physical custody.

In this light, school administrators should defer solely to the primary physical custodian on day-to-day decisions if there is disagreement between the joint legal custodians.

Courts may assign physical custody according to very specific times of the year, days of the week, and hours of the day, *e.g.*, "mother gets physical custody from Sunday 8:00 p.m. through Friday 5:00 p.m., from August 15th through June 30th, and father gets physical custody at all other times". Recognizing that specified times may be inconvenient or confusing for the school to follow, school officials should request clarification from the parents, or ask that they provide a workable schedule to the school. The general rule is that upon the end of the school day the child returns to the location where he or she came from that morning, absent a court order or agreement to the contrary.

### 10:53. What rights are preserved by a noncustodial parent?

Non-custodial parents generally continue to have access to their child's education records and reports, including report cards, disciplinary notices, and special education notices. This includes any mailings home to the parents, but the school may require the non-custodial parent to pay a reasonable fee for the copying and mailing of the information (or otherwise file a notarized statement that he or she is unable to pay). That fee may either be paid up front, or the non-custodial parent may sign an agreement to reimburse the school for the mailings at the end of the school year. Some schools require the parent to provide self-addressed stamped envelopes. Each school system is required to develop a policy and procedures regarding the access of non-custodial parents to student records (COMAR 13A.08.02.30G).

Similarly, non-custodial parents generally retain rights to attend school activities such as parent-teacher conferences, back-to-school nights, concerts, plays, and sporting events, volunteer in class, and chaperone school trips. Importantly, the non-custodial parent's rights to receive information and to attend meetings relating to their child's education is "informational only" and does not extend to the decision-making prerogative reserved to the custodial parent.

### 10:54. May one parent prohibit the other from access to the school premises?

In a "custodial/non-custodial" situation, the custodial parent may deny the non-custodial parent the right to be in contact with, see, or speak with the child. For example, the custodial parent may demand that the school deny access by the other parent to meet the child in private, remove the child from the school premises, or have any contact with the child. However, in the absence of a specific court order these limitations would not bar the non-custodial parent from the same access to activities as other parents, including contact with their child during these activities (see **10:53**). In addition, the custodial parent may produce a court order denying the non-custodial parent access to student records (COMAR 13A.08.02.30F).

### 10:55. What rights do third-party family members have in the educational process?

Generally, absent a court order, third parties such as grandparents, other relatives, or attorneys and other advocates, do not have any rights to make education decisions on behalf of a child. School officials have the right to demand proof, in the form of a copy of the court order, if requested by a third party to recognize their right to make education decisions on behalf of a student.

An exception to this general rule, enacted by Maryland's legislature in 2002, is the affidavit of a serious family hardship to evidence an "informal kinship care" arrangement which allows certain relatives to enroll and make education decisions on behalf of a child (see **10:33** through **10:45**).

### 10:56. What rights do foster parents, court-appointed guardians, or court-appointed attorneys have?

The rights of foster parents or court-appointed guardians will be stipulated in the court's custody or guardianship decree or order. Importantly, unless special education decisions are specified in the court's order, the right to make special education decisions remains the prerogative of the biological parent.

## Homeless Students

### 10:57. Where are the laws and regulations regarding the education of homeless students found?

Maryland has adopted detailed regulations regarding "Programs for Homeless Children", in accordance with the federal McKinney-Vento Homeless Assistance Act as amended by the No Child Left Behind Act of 2001 (COMAR 13A.05.09)). For more information on these federal laws pertaining to homeless students, see **8:136** through **8:143**.

### 10:58. What is meant by "homeless student"?

Maryland regulations (COMAR 13A.05.09.02B(3)(a) and (b)) define a homeless student as a child or youth who lacks a fixed, regular, or adequate nighttime place of residence, including:

- Children and youth who are sharing the housing of other persons due to loss of housing, economic hardship, or a similar reason, are living in motels, hotels, trailer parks, or camping grounds due to lack of alternative adequate accommodations, are living in emergency or transitional shelters (also referred to as transitional housing), are abandoned in hospitals, or are awaiting foster care placement;

- Children and youth who have a primary nighttime residence that is a public or private place not designed for or ordinarily used as a regular sleeping accommodation for individuals;

- Children and youth who are living in cars, parks, public spaces, abandoned buildings, substandard housing, bus or train stations, or similar settings; and

- Migratory children, as defined in § 6399 of Title 20, who qualify as homeless for the purposes of the McKinney-Vento Act and this chapter because the children are living in circumstances as described in COMAR 13A.05.09.02.B(3)(b)(i)-(iii).

### 10:59. What is the general purpose of the homeless education requirements?

Regulations require that school systems provide homeless children and youth with access to the education and other services that they need to ensure that they have an opportunity to meet the same challenging State student academic achievement standards to which all students are held. Further, homeless children and youth, while receiving a free public education, may not be segregated in a separate school or in a separate program within a school, based on their status as homeless. Homeless children and youth shall be educated as part of a school regular academic program (COMAR 13A.05.09.01).

### 10:60. What must be included in local school system homeless education policies and programs?

Each local school system in Maryland is required to designate a homeless education coordinator and develop policies to eliminate barriers to the enrollment, retention, and success in school of homeless students, including provisions addressing the following:

- Transportation issues;

- Enrollment delays caused by residency requirements;

- Lack of available records normally required for enrollment such as birth certificates, previous school records, immunization records, medical records, proof of residency, or other documentation;

- Guardianship issues;

- Uniform or dress code requirements; and

- Opportunities to meet the same challenging State student academic achievement standards to which all students are held (COMAR 13A.05.09.03A(1)).

### 10:61. What is the role of the homeless education coordinator?

The homeless education coordinator is responsible for:

- Ensuring that homeless children and youth are identified by school personnel, are enrolled in, and have a full and equal opportunity to succeed in schools of that local school system;

- Coordinating the referrals of homeless children to health care, dental care, mental health services, and other appropriate services;

- Expediting school placement decisions;

- Monitoring programs and projects to ensure their compliance with applicable statutory and regulatory requirements, if the local school system receives funds under the McKinney Act;

- Informing parents or guardians of homeless children and youth of the educational and related opportunities available to their children, ensuring that they are provided with meaningful opportunities to participate in the education of their children;

- Developing and implementing a program to train school personnel on the educational rights of homeless children and youth, policies and procedures to identify and serve homeless children and youth, and on the special needs of homeless children and youth;

- Ensuring that enrollment disputes are mediated according to the local school system's appeal process consistent with state regulations (COMAR 13A.05.09.03A(5)).

**10:62. What is the state's role in administering the homeless education program?**

The Maryland State Department of Education (MSDE) is required to oversee and verify the program by:

- Collecting and providing local school systems with monthly information on the number of homeless students reported by shelters, to validate the accuracy of information reported to the Department, and correlate information collected by local school systems;

- Coordinating and collaborating with educators, including child development and preschool program personnel, providers of services to homeless and runaway children and youth and homeless families, local school system homeless education coordinators, and community organizations and groups representing homeless children and youth and their families;

- Facilitating coordination of services to homeless students with other State agencies;

- Administering the federal McKinney-Vento Act grant program;

- Preparing and submitting reports to the federal government in accordance with the requirements of the McKinney-Vento Act; and

- Providing the technical assistance and other support necessary to assist local school systems coordinators to ensure local school system compliance (COMAR 13A.05.09.03B).

### 10:63. How does the school system make a school placement decision regarding a homeless student?

Local school systems are required to establish student placement procedures regarding homeless students in a manner that is in the child's best interest and which should, if possible, continue the child's enrollment in the school of origin for the duration of homelessness (COMAR 13A.05.09.04). Regulations provide, however, that the school system decision is qualified "unless contrary to the wishes of the child's or youth's parent or guardian" (COMAR 13A.05.09.04B). Guidance from the Maryland State Department of Education (MSDE) describes the options available to homeless students to continue at their school of origin, transfer to a school nearest the temporary shelter, attend the same school as other students in the attendance area in which the homeless child is living, or be sent to a school other than that requested by the parent or guardian.

The school selected in accordance with this process is mandated to "immediately enroll the homeless child or youth, even if the child or youth is unable to produce records normally required for enrollment, such as previous academic records, medical records, proof of residency, or other documentation" (COMAR 13A.05.09.05).

### 10:64. May the school system investigate the claim of homeless status?

Yes. For example, the State Board of Education recently upheld a local board's decision to deny a student's enrollment at a particular high school following an investigation by school personnel of the student's homeless status. The homeless status had been attested to by the parent in a notarized letter, but was investigated in response to statements by the student. The State Board applied the standard of review for local board policy decisions which considers the board's decision as prima facie correct (*Joyce N. v. Prince George's County Board of Education*, MSBE Op. No. 07-24 (2007)).

### 10:65. What factors are considered in determining the best interest of a homeless student?

State regulations (COMAR 13A.05.09.04B(2)), in accordance with federal requirements, identify the following factors:

- The student's age;

- The school which the student's siblings attend;

- The student's experiences at the school of origin;

- The student's academic needs;

- The student's emotional needs;

- Any other special needs of the family;

- Continuity of instruction;

- Length of stay in the shelter;

- The likely location of the family's future permanent housing;

- Time remaining in the school year;

- Distance of commute and the impact it may have on the student's education and other student-centered, transportation-related factors; and

- The safety of the child.

### 10:66. May the parent or guardian of a homeless student appeal the school selection?

Yes. If the local school system sends the child or youth to a school other than the school of origin or a school requested by the parent or guardian, the school system must provide a written explanation to the homeless child's or youth's parent or guardian regarding the right to appeal (COMAR 13A.05.09.04B(3)).

## Home and Hospital Instruction

### 10:67. When must a public school system provide instruction to a student unable to attend school?

Maryland regulations establish the minimum requirements for the provision of instructional services to public school students who are unable to participate in regular school enrollment due to physical or emotional condition (COMAR 13A.03.05.01A). These regulations pertain to instruction outside the school setting that is referred to as "home and hospital teaching."

### 10:68. How does the school system determine or verify a student's physical or emotional condition?

School systems must determine the "initial service need" for instruction in a home or hospital setting by obtaining verification of the student's physical condition by a licensed physician, or verification of the student's emotional condition by a certified school psychologist, or licensed psychologist or psychiatrist. "Physical condition" includes drug and alcohol dependency. The statement of verification must include the statement that the student's condition prevents the student from participating in the school of enrollment (COMAR 13A.03.05.04).

### 10:69. In what setting may home and hospital instruction be provided?

Instructional services may be provided in the student's home, medical institution, or therapeutic treatment center licensed by the state (COMAR 13A.03.05.03A(2)).

### 10:70. Is home and hospital instruction limited to continuous long-term situations?

No. School systems may be required to provide concurrent instructional services to students whose physical condition requires the student to be absent on an intermittent basis. Regulations specify conditions including but not limited to kidney failure, cancer, asthma, cystic fibrosis, and sickle cell anemia (COMAR 13A.03.05.01C).

### 10:71. Who determines the manner in which home and hospital instruction is provided?

The school system, in consultation with the student, and the student's parent, guardian, psychologist, and physician, as appropriate.

### 10:72. What is the minimum amount of instructional time required for home and hospital instruction?

The minimum length of the instructional program that a school system must provide is six hours per week for students in a full-time program, 3 hours per week for half-time instruction.

### 10:73. Is home and hospital instruction subject to a time limitation?

Continuation of services beyond 60 calendar days requires a reverification of the initial service need. The school system, parent, or guardian may request a review of the student's service need following the initial verification.

## 10:74. When must a school system begin providing home and hospital instruction following notification?

The school system must begin to provide home and hospital instruction "as soon as possible, but not later than 10 school calendar days following notification to the school system of the student's inability to the school of regular enrollment, and receipt of the verification of the student's physical or emotional condition" (COMAR 13A.03.05.03).

## 10:75. What teacher qualifications apply to a person providing home and hospital instruction?

Beginning in July 2001, home and hospital instruction is required to be provided by a person possessing a minimum of a bachelor's degree. However, a "grandfather" provision exempts individuals demonstrating satisfactory home and hospital instruction before July 1, 2001 (COMAR 13A.03.05.03B(2)). Home and hospital instruction may be provided by a school system employee, by contract with another provider, or by contract with another school system.

## 10:76. What impact does special education have on home and hospital instruction?

The school system must develop a student's home and hospital instructional program in accordance with the Individuals with Disabilities Education Act, Americans with Disabilities Act, and § 504 of the Rehabilitation Act of 1973 (COMAR 13A.03.05.01B).

## 10:77. What records must be kept for students receiving home or hospital instruction?

School systems must record a student receiving home and hospital instruction as present, or absent, based on the student's availability for scheduled instructional services (COMAR 13A.03.05.03D).

# Student Records

## 10:78. Where are the laws and regulations pertaining to student records found?

In accordance with Section 2-205(o) of the Education Article, State regulations establish Maryland law regarding student records, incorporating by reference the Maryland Student Records System Manual (MSRM) (COMAR 13A.08.02.01-.31). The Manual states that all student records are to be maintained in accordance with state regulation; the Family Educational Rights and Privacy Act, 20 U.S.C. § 1232g, and its implementing regulations, 34 C.F.R. pt. 99; the Individuals with Disabilities Education Act, 20 U.S.C. § 1400 *et seq.*, and its implementing regulations, 34 C.F.R. §§ 300.561-300.576; and the No Child Left Behind Act of 2001 (Maryland Student Records System Manual, 2007, "MSRM", p. A-2).

In addition, the Maryland Public Information Act (Md. Code Ann., St. Gov't Art. § 10-611-630) is intended to grant the public a broad right of access to public records, including student records (see **10:85** and **10:86**).

Most recently, the Supreme Court approved changes to the Federal Rules of Civil Procedure regarding the discovery of electronic data during litigation in federal court; changes which significantly impact the day-to-day management of school and student records (FRCP 26(b)(1)).

### 10:79. What is the Maryland Student Records Manual?

Maryland regulations require each school system to have a system of information on enrollment, attendance, promotion, and other relevant student records data. The MSRM is updated annually and provides detailed instructions and sample forms to assist local school systems in the maintenance and reporting of student information.

### 10:80. What is a Student Record Card?

The Maryland Student Records Manual outlines the information required to be maintained for each student. The Manual describes the use of student record cards as not required except for card 7, the record of student withdrawal or transfer. However, the information, or data elements, contained in the manual's sample cards must be maintained for each student. The data elements include personal data and school attendance data (SR Card 1); annual student performance data, data summary pre-kindergarten-8 (SR Card 2); annual secondary school performance & data summary 9-12 (SR Card 3); high school assessment data (SR 3B); state mandated and local school system testing (SR Card 4); health screening (SR Card 5); and the student withdrawal/transfer record (SR Card 7) (MSRM, 2007, p. B-1).

### 10:81. What is the "student specific identifier"?

For several years, Maryland has been developing a unique student identifier and a longitudinal database to maintain and provide access to a single repository of all student record data elements for all students. The 2007 Student Records Manual requires local school systems to assign a unique identifier for each student enrolled (MSRM, 2007, p. B-2). The number can be any combination of letters and numbers but should be no more than 10 characters in length. The Manual emphasizes that if a student transfers to another school within the jurisdiction, the student identifier must remain the same. The state database is scheduled to be operational by the 2007-2008 school year.

## 10:82. What does the Maryland Student Records Manual require of local school systems?

The Manual outlines the following delegated responsibilities of local school systems:

- Developing and implementing procedures to ensure that data is collected and records maintained accurately in accordance with the guidelines set forth in the manual.

- Maintaining the confidentiality of these records.

- Complying with the records retention and disposition procedures outlined in the manual (MSRM, 2007, p. A-2).

## 10:83. What document retention requirements apply to student records?

The Maryland Records Manual references the Records Retention and Disposition Manual for Public School Systems of Maryland, and establishes minimum standards for the retention of student records (MSRM, 2007, Section F). The Manual prohibits the local school system from destroying any student record for which there is outstanding request to inspect and review under COMAR 13A.08.02.13.

The Manual specifies retention periods for types of documents as follows:

| STATE MINIMUM STANDARDS FOR RETENTION OF STUDENT RECORDS | |
|---|---|
| **Obsolete Student Records Cards:**<br><br>- Achievement and Attendance Record<br>- Permanent Record, Elementary School<br>- Other Pupil Records Prior to 1957<br>- Personal and Family Information<br>- Performance Information | Permanent |

| Current Student Records Cards:<br>• Personal Data | Permanent* |
|---|---|
| • Annual School Performance Data<br>• Summary, Grade Levels Prek.-8 | Student-Age 21 |
| • Secondary School Performance<br>• Data Summary, Grade Levels 9-12 | Permanent* |
| • Supplemental<br>• High School Assessment Performance Summary<br>• Test Information<br>• Health Screening, Examinations and Evaluations<br>• Immunization Records<br>• Blood Lead Certificate | Student-Age 21 |
| • Maryland Student Transfer Record | 3 Years |
| • Discipline Records | Graduation or Completion of High School Program or Age 21 |
| • Statewide Educational Interview Form | 1 Year |
| • Information Required for Students with Disabilities<br>• Individualized Education Programs (IEP)<br>• Special Service Information Systems (SSIS) Form<br>• Assessment Reports<br>• IEP Team Meeting Summary Sheets and Notes<br>• Medical Assistance Records | 6 Years |
| * Transfer periodically to the State Archives. | |

## 10:84. What responsibilities for student records are delegated to school principals?

The Maryland Student Records Manual describes the responsibilities of the school principal to include the following:

- Each principal is responsible for collecting, maintaining, and using the student record in accordance with the guidelines set forth in the manual and those developed by his/her central office.

- Each principal is responsible for adhering to the records retention and disposition procedures outlined in Section F of the manual and those procedures developed by his/her central office.

- Principals should acquaint themselves with the student records system, provide leadership to their staff on its implementation, and periodically check the system's operation.

- Each principal is responsible for maintaining the confidentiality of student records (MSRM, 2007, p A-1).

The MSRM further states that "[t]he responsibility of the principal for collecting, maintaining, and using the student record information cannot be overstated. Principals should acquaint themselves with the system, provide leadership to their staff in its implementation, and carefully check the system's operation periodically" (MSRM, 2007, p. B-1).

## 10:85. How does the Maryland Public Information Act apply to student records?

Generally, the Public Information Act (Md. Code Ann., St. Gov't Art. § 10-611-630) is intended to grant the public a broad right of access to records that are in the possession of State and local government agencies. However, the Act under §§ 10-616(k)(1)-(3) provides specific limitations on access to student records:

(1) Subject to paragraphs (2) and (3) of this subsection, a custodian shall deny inspection of a school district record about the home address, home phone number, biography, family, physiology, religion, academic achievement, or physical or mental ability of a student.

(2) A custodian shall permit inspection by:

    (i)  the person in interest; or

    (ii) an elected or appointed official who supervises the student.

(3) (i) A custodian may permit inspection of the home address or home phone number of a student of a public school by:

    1.  an organization of parents, teachers, students, or former students, or any combination of those groups, of the school;

    2.  an organization or force of the military;

3. a person engaged by a school or board of education to confirm a home address or home phone number;

4. a representative of a community college in the State; or

5. the Maryland Higher Education Commission.

(ii) The Commission or a person, organization, or community college that obtains information under this paragraph may not:

## 10:86. How does the Maryland Public Information Act relate to other state and federal laws?

The Maryland Public Information Act Manual (10th ed., January 2007) does not specifically cross-reference the federal Family Educational Rights and Privacy Act (FERPA) or corresponding state regulations adopted by the State Board of Education. However, the PIA manual includes the following advice::

> Under [State Government Article] §10-616, the custodian must deny the inspection of certain specified records. However, any of these records may be available for inspection if "otherwise provided by law." SG §10-616(a). Thus, if another source of law allows access, then an exception in SG §10-616 does not control. See 79 Opinions of the Attorney General 366 (1994) (although personnel records and other information regarding employees in Baltimore City School System would otherwise be nondisclosable, disclosure was authorized by virtue of a federal district court order).

> The converse is also true. [State Government Article] §10-616 may allow access to records but "other law" may deny access. For example, names, addresses, and phone numbers of students may be disclosed to an organization such as a PTA under SG §10-616(k). However, the Family Educational Rights and Privacy Act of 1974, the "Buckley Amendment," 20 U.S.C. §1232g, is "other law" that supersedes the [Maryland Public Information Act].

# The Family Educational Rights and Privacy Act

### 10:87. What is the Family Educational Rights and Privacy Act?

The Family Educational Rights and Privacy Act (FERPA), was first enacted in 1974, and includes definitions, procedures, and standards for maintaining and providing access to student records (20 U.S.C. § 1232g; 34 C.F.R. pt. 99). Maryland has adopted comprehensive regulations in accordance with FERPA (COMAR 13A.08.02). Courts have found that FERPA is intended to provide access to parents and eligible students to their educational records, and to protect the privacy of students by limiting the transfer of educational records without the consent of the student's parents (*United States v. Miami University*, 294 F.3d 797 (6th Cir. 2002); *Belanger v. Nashua*, 856 F. Supp.40 (D. N.H. 1994)).

### 10:88. How does FERPA define "education records"?

FERPA, and Maryland regulations, define "education records" to mean those records, files, documents, and other materials which:

- Contain information directly related to a student; and
- Are maintained by an education agency or institution or by a person acting for such an agency or institution (20 U.S.C. § 1232g(a)(4)(A); COMAR 13A.08.02.03C).

### 10:89. How broadly does FERPA define "records"?

Under FERPA, "records" include "any information recorded in any way, including handwriting, print, computer media, video or audio tape, film, microfilm, and microfiche" (34 C.F.R. § 99.3).

### 10:90. What records are excluded from the FERPA definition?

FERPA designates four categories of records as excluded from the FERPA definition and requirements. Three of these types of excluded records apply to student records, including: sole possession records, law enforcement records, and personnel records (20 U.S.C. § 1232g(a)(4)(B)).

### 10:91. What is meant by "sole possession" records?

FERPA defines "sole possession" records as records of instructional, supervisory or administrative personnel in the sole possession of the person who made the record and which are not accessible or revealed to any other person except a substitute for the person who made the record (20 U.S.C. § 1232g(a)(4)(B)(i); COMAR 13A.08.02.03C(3)(a)).

### 10:92. How are law enforcement records defined?

Law enforcement records are records created by a law enforcement unit and kept by the unit for law enforcement purposes (20 U.S.C. § 1232g(a)(4)(B)(ii); COMAR 13A.08.02.03C(3)(b)).

## 10:93. What are "personnel records" under FERPA?

Personnel records are defined by FERPA to include records pertaining to a person who is employed by an education institution and who is not a student (20 U.S.C. § 1232g(a)(4)(B)(iii)). Personnel records must be made and maintained in the normal course of business and relate exclusively to the person's capacity as an employee. Again, such records are not education records under FERPA or state regulations (COMAR 13A.08.02.03C(3)(c)).

## 10:94. Is statistical information not identifying individual students an "educational record" under FERPA?

Courts have found that statistical information that does not identify individual students but which does identify student disciplinary actions by school, does not constitute an education record under FERPA (*Hardin County Schools v. Foster*, 40 S.W.3d 865 (Ky. 2001)).

## 10:95. How does FERPA define "student" for purposes of education records?

FERPA defines a "student" to include "any person with respect to whom an educational agency or institution maintains education records or personally identifiable information" (20 U.S.C. § 1232g(a)(6)). The Act pertains to records of students who are or have been in attendance at the education institution, in contrast with records of applicants not attending the school (*Tarka v. Franklin*, 891 F.2d 102 (5th Cir. 1989)).

## 10:96. Does FERPA apply to the records of former students?

Yes. The FERPA definition includes students who are or *have been* in attendance at the school. However, former students are not extended the same rights to notice or the opportunity to opt out of the release of student directory information as current students (34 C.F.R. § 99.37).

## 10:97. How does Maryland define the records of former students?

Maryland regulations exclude the following information from the definition of student records:

- Records on a student who is 18 years old or older, or is attending an institution of postsecondary education, that are:

    (i)   Made or maintained by a physician, psychiatrist, psychologist, or other recognized professional or paraprofessional acting in the professional's or paraprofessional's professional capacity or assisting in a paraprofessional capacity,

(ii) Made, maintained, or used only in connection with treatment of the student, and

(iii) Disclosed only to individuals providing the treatment; or

- Records that only contain information about an individual after the individual is no longer a student at that agency or institution (COMAR 13A.08.02.03C(3)(d) and (e)).

## 10:98. What is meant by "maintaining" records under FERPA?

In a case involving the question of whether peer-graded papers were education records, the U.S. Supreme Court opined that "[t]he word "maintain" suggests FERPA records will be kept in a filing cabinet in a records room at the school or on a permanent secure database" (*Owasso Independent School District v. Falvo*, 534 U.S. 426 (2002)). The Court concluded that only records contained in some type of centralized system can be "education records" under FERPA. In Maryland, each school system is required to maintain a "system of information" on students in accordance with the regulations and Maryland Student Records Manual (COMAR 13A.08.02.28).

Courts have similarly held that a teacher's letter referring to a student's abilities which was not kept in the student's file was not an education record under FERPA (*Olsson v. Indiana University Board of Trustees*, 571 N.E.2d 585 (Ind. Ct. App. 1991)). Maryland regulations provide that the term "records" does not include "an education department employee's personal notes which are not made available to another person" (COMAR 13A.08.02.04C).

## 10:99. For whom does FERPA create rights?

FERPA creates rights for parents and eligible students (20 U.S.C. § 1232g(a)(4)(1)(A); eligible students are students who have reached 18 years of age (34 C.F.R. § 99.3). Maryland regulations clarify that the status of the eligible student as a dependent of the student's parents does not affect the student's rights (COMAR 13A.08.02.08B). The parents' rights are terminated and transfer to the student when the student reaches the age of 18 (20 U.S.C. § 1232g(d); 34 C.F.R. § 99.3).

## 10:100. Is the school system required to notify parents of their rights under FERPA?

Yes. Local education agencies (LEAs) must annually notify parents and eligible students of their rights under FERPA (34 C.F.R. § 99.7). The annual notification must also include the following:

- The procedure to inspect and review education records;

- The procedure to request amendment of education records;

- A specification of criteria for determining who constitutes a school official and what constitutes a legitimate educational interest if the agency or institution discloses or intends to disclose personally identifiable information to school officials without consent; and

- The right of parents to file a complaint with the Family Policy Compliance Office (FPCO) in the Department (A model FERPA notification for LEAs is available from the U.S. Department of Education's Family Policy Compliance Office: *www.ed.gov/offices/OM/fpco*).

## 10:101. How does FERPA define "parent"?

FERPA defines a "parent" as including a natural parent, a guardian, or an individual acting as a parent in the absence of a parent or guardian (34 C.F.R. § 99.4). FERPA rights extend to both parents unless the school has received evidence that a court order, state statute, or legally binding document relating to actions such as divorce, separation, or child custody, has revoked those rights (34 C.F.R. § 99.4).

## 10:102. How does FERPA define "consent"?

Consent by a parent or eligible student must be in writing, dated, and include the reason for requesting the release of the student record and to whom the information will be released (20 U.S.C. §§ 1232g(b)(2)(A)).

## 10:103. Can a school be required to release a student record to a student who is not an eligible student?

Yes. Upon the request of a parent, a school must provide a copy of the student's record to the student (34 C.F.R. § 99.30(c)(2)).

## 10:104. How are student disciplinary records treated under FERPA?

The No Child Left Behind Act required states and school systems to adopt procedures by January 8, 2004, to facilitate the transfer of disciplinary records, with respect to suspension or expulsion, to another public or private school in which a student is enrolled or seeks to enroll (20 U.S.C. § 7165).

Maryland regulations define "student records" as including "records concerning disciplinary actions taken against students" (COMAR 13A.08.02.03C(2)(a)). Maryland's highest court has held that records of and pertaining to parking tickets issued to student athletes were not "education records" under FERPA, but that the Act was intended to "keep private those aspects of a student's educational life that relate to academic matters or status as a student" (*Kirwan v. The Diamondback*, 352 Md. 74 (1998)). The court interpreted the statute as "not intended to preclude the release of any record simply because the record contained the name of the student." The court concluded that a contrary interpretation would allow schools to "refuse to release information about criminal behavior on campus if students were involved, claiming that this information constituted education records, thus keeping important information from other students, their parents, and the public."

Other courts have interpreted the Act differently, concluding that student disciplinary records are protected education records under FERPA (*United States v. Miami University*, 294 F.3d 797, 812 (6th Cir. 2002)). The Court found that Miami University violated FERPA by releasing student disciplinary records and personally identifiable information contained therein to third parties without student or parental consent. The Court permanently enjoined the University from releasing student disciplinary records or any "personally identifiable information" contained therein, as defined in FERPA and its corresponding regulations, except as otherwise expressly permitted under FERPA.

## 10:105. How are student harassment and bullying reports treated?

In 2007, the Maryland General Assembly enacted legislation defining information included in a victim of harassment or intimidation report form as confidential and prohibiting such information from being made part of a student's permanent educational record. The new law provides that the information in the forms may only be disclosed under the federal Family Education Rights and Privacy Act (FERPA) or as necessary to meet the reporting requirements associated with the forms (House Bill 383, Chapter 398, 2007 Laws of Maryland). The law is intended to promote increased reporting of bullying and harassment incidents by ensuring that the reports are not included in the victim's permanent student record.

### 10:106. What constitutes a "policy or practice" of releasing information?

Courts have found that whether a school has a "policy or practice" of releasing student information protected by FERPA without the requisite consent must be determined on a case-by-case basis. A solitary incident of releasing student information may, therefore, not constitute a violation of FERPA if it is not established that the school has a "policy or practice" of doing so. For example, courts have found that the single occurrence of releasing class rosters, including student social security numbers, was an isolated incident not determined to qualify as a "policy or practice" (*Krebs v. Rutgers*, 797 F. Supp. 1246 (D. N.J. 1992)).

### 10:107. Does FERPA permit the release of any student information without parental consent?

Yes. FERPA, and Maryland's corollary regulations, permits the release of "directory information" without consent (20 U.S.C. § 1232g(b)(1); COMAR 13A.08.02.25). The local school system may release directory information without consent only after providing public notice of the pertinent categories of information (20 U.S.C. § 1232g(a)(5)(B)).

### 10:108. What is "directory information"?

In accordance with FERPA, Maryland regulations (COMAR 13A.08.02.03B(2)) provide that a local school system may designate as directory information certain types of information contained in the student record "which would not generally be considered harmful or an invasion of privacy if disclosed", and may include the following:

(a)  The student's name;

(b)  Address;

(c)  Telephone listing;

(d)  Electronic mail address;

(e)  Photograph;

(f)  Grade level;

(g)  Enrollment status, for example, undergraduate or graduate, full-time or part-time;

(h)  Date and place of birth;

(i)  Major field of study;

(j)  Participation in officially recognized activities and sports;

(k)  Weight and height of members of athletic teams;

(l)   Dates of attendance;

(m)  Degrees and awards received;

(n)   The most recent educational agency or institution attended by the student; and

(o)   Other similar information, as defined by the local school system.

Maryland's State Board has noted that "[o]nce designated as directory information, there are fewer restraints on the disclosure of the information provided that the school system meets certain requirements, and provided that a student's parent has not objected to the designation of the information with regard to his/her child". The State Board noted that the COMAR provisions regarding student directory information (COMAR 13A.08.02.25) must be read in conjunction with the Maryland public records law, section 10-616(k) of the State Government Article, which places further limits on the disclosure of certain directory information (see footnote 3, *Williams v. New Baltimore City Board of School Commissioners*, MSBE Op. No. 01-23 (2001)).

## 10:109. Are there other circumstances in which education records may be released without consent?

Yes. FERPA excludes the following circumstances from its general prohibition of the release education records without the consent of the parents or eligible student:

**Audits and Evaluations:** Education records may be released without parental consent to state education authorities, and federal authorities such as the U.S. Department of Education, U.S. Attorney General, and the Comptroller General of the United States (20 U.S.C. §§ 1232g(b)(1)(C) and g(b)(3)). These governmental entities must maintain the privacy of the education records by preventing the release of any personally identifiable information, and must destroy such information when no longer required for the audit or evaluation (20 U.S.C. § 1232g(b)(3)).

**Testing, Instruction and Accreditation:** FERPA allows for the release of student information to "organizations conducting studies for, or on behalf of, educational agencies or institutions for the purpose of developing, validating, or administering predictive tests, administering student aid programs, and improving instruction" (20 U.S.C. § 1232g(b)(1)(F)). Similarly, FERPA allows information to be released without consent to organizations carrying out an accrediting function (20 U.S.C. § 1232g(b)(1)(G)).

**Financial Aid:** FERPA specifically excludes the release of student records "in connection with a student's application for, or receipt of, financial aid" (20 U.S.C. § 1232g(b)(1)(D)).

**Subpoenas:** FERPA provides that schools may release student records to a person or entity identified in a subpoena from a federal grand jury or other subpoena issued for law enforcement purposes. Further, based on a showing of good cause, the court may order the school to not inform the parent, student, or any person of the request or of the information requested (20 U.S.C. §§ 1232g(b)(1)(J)(i) and (ii)). By contrast, schools may release student records in response to subpoenas or judicial orders in circumstances other than those described above, but only after providing the requisite notice and opportunity to object to the parents or eligible student (20 U.S.C. § 1232g(b)(2)(B)).

**Emergencies:** FERPA provides for the release of student records if such information is necessary to protect the health or safety of a student or other persons (20 U.S.C. § 1232g(b)(1)(I)).

### 10:110. Does the U.S.A. Patriot Act affect the disclosure of student records?

The U.S.A. Patriot Act amended FERPA (20 U.S.C. § 1232g(j)) to permit schools to disclose, without the consent or knowledge of the parent, "personally identifiable information from the student's education records to the Attorney General of the united States or his designee in response to an *ex parte* order in connection with the investigation or prosecution of [specified] terrorism crimes" (USA PATRIOT Act, P.L. 107-56 (2001)). In addition, the Act provides that the Immigration and Naturalization Service (INS) must require students attending an education institution under an F-1 visa to sign a form which contains a broad consent provision allowing the disclosure of personally identifiable information to the INS for the purpose of determining immigration status, and provides that this form should be included in the student's education record.

### 10:111. What is the status of video images under FERPA?

Video recordings which become a part of a student's education record must be maintained in accordance with established education record procedures governing access, review and release of education records. However, FERPA does not specifically reference the type of video images of students and staff which are routinely recorded in the school and school bus setting in a manner not intended to enter an individual student's education record. In this context, video images raise a complex set of questions regarding the school system's recording, maintaining, and disclosing images which typically depict multiple students.

For example, a parent may request a copy of a video containing images of their child and other children, *e.g.*, video of a fight on a school bus. The school system must determine whether the video is an education record, whether it is an education record for each student depicted in the video, or is a student record but only for those students directly involved in the activity under scrutiny, *e.g.*, the fight.

Again, FERPA and Maryland regulations define an "education record" as including files, documents, and other materials which contain information directly related to a student and which are maintained by the school (20 U.S.C. § 1232g(a)(4)(A); COMAR 13A.08.02.03C). Based on a determination that the video is an education record, the school system must consider whether it is required to obtain consent from each student depicted, and whether to redact images of students not providing consent.

Interestingly, a cursory survey of school and university policies indicates the practice of including video or electronic images of students under the definition of "directory information" which are not education records and may be disclosed without prior consent. A threshold question to consider regarding directory information is the condition that such information "would not generally be considered harmful or an invasion of privacy if disclosed" (COMAR 13A.08.02.03B(2)).

In a January 2007 letter to USDE's Family Policy Compliance Office (FPCO), the National School Boards Association requested, but has not yet received, clarification on these and other questions raised by school systems regarding FERPA's regulation of video images.

## 10:112. What records of requests for student records must be maintained?

Schools are required to keep records of all requests from individuals, agencies, and organizations which have requested student education records. FERPA dictates that the record of requests "indicate specifically the legitimate interest that each such person, agency, or organization" had in obtaining the student information. Further, FERPA limits disclosure of the "record of access" to "parents, to the school official and his assistants who are responsible for the custody of such records and persons or organizations authorized [for audit and evaluation purposes under 20 U.S.C. § 1232g(b)(1)(C)]" (20 U.S.C. §§ 1232g(b)(4)(A)).

## 10:113. What rights does FERPA provide to parents to modify information in their child's record?

A parent may request that the school amend their child's education record to correct information that is inaccurate, misleading, or in violation of the student's rights of privacy. The school must make a decision regarding the request within a reasonable amount of time, and inform the parent of the decision and the parent's right to a hearing (34 C.F.R. §§ 99.20(a) and (b); COMAR 13A.08.02.14).

## 10:114. How is a FERPA hearing seeking a change in the student record conducted?

The hearing is conducted by a school administrator who does not have an interest in the outcome. If after the hearing the administrator determines that the contested information in the record is in fact misleading or inaccurate, the school must amend the record and inform the parent of the amendment in writing. If the school decides that the information is not misleading or inaccurate, the school shall inform the parent of their right to place in the record a statement contesting the information (COMAR 13A.08.02.15-.16).

## 10:115. How is FERPA enforced?

FERPA provides for a formal complaint procedure which permits persons to file complaints of alleged violations of the law with a federal agency. The federal agency conducts the investigation and, if a violation is found, may identify steps the school must take to comply with the law. If voluntary compliance is not undertaken, the federal government may withhold federal funding and/or compel compliance.

FERPA states in pertinent part that "[n]o funds shall be made available under any applicable program to any educational agency or institution which has a policy or practice of permitting the release of education records (or personally identifiable information contained therein other than directory information, as defined in paragraph (5) of subsection (a) of this section) of students without the written consent of their parents" (20 U.S.C. §§ 1232g(b)(1)). However, courts have emphasized that FERPA is not a law which prohibits disclosure of educational records, but is a provision which imposes a penalty for the disclosure of educational records (*Student Bar Association v. Byrd*, 293 N.C. 594, 239 S.E.2d 415 (N.C.1977), cited in *Norwood v. Slammons*, 788 F. Supp. 1020 (W.D. Ark. 1991)). FERPA provides for the penalty of withholding federal funds otherwise available to an educational institution which has a policy or practice of permitting the release of educational records.

## 10:116. Who may assert a violation of FERPA?

FERPA creates rights only for students and their parents (20 U.S.C. § 1232g(a)(1)(A); 34 C.F.R. § 99.3). Courts have held that FERPA does not create rights for prospective students (*Norwood v. Slammons*, 788 F. Supp. 1020 (W.D. Ark. 1991)).

## 10:117. Does FERPA create a private right of action?

No. In *Gonzaga University v. Doe*, the U.S. Supreme Count held that FERPA does not create a private right of action to enforce its provisions. Aside from the administrative enforcement mechanism set forth in the Act, the statute does not create personal rights which are enforceable. Accordingly, a private individual cannot file suit to recover monetary damages for a violation of the statute (*Gonzaga University v. Doe*, 536 U.S. 273 (2002)).

## 10:118. Does FERPA create a student/teacher privilege?

No. FERPA is intended to ensure that records are maintained and disclosed in a manner that complies with applicable law, rather than as a bar to disclosure. For example, FERPA permits disclosure of student records pursuant to subpoenas or court orders (20 U.S.C. §§ 1232g(b)(1)(J), 1232g(b)(2)). The Act goes so far as to authorize a court, based on a showing of good cause, to order the school to not inform the parent, student, or any person of the request for the student's records or of the information requested (20 U.S.C. §§ 1232g(b)(1)(J). Maryland's highest court concluded that FERPA and Maryland regulations concerning the disclosure of student records do not exclude a student's education records, including the notes of a guidance counselor, from discovery in litigation (*Zaal v. Maryland*, 326 Md. 54 (1992)).

## 10:119. May a teacher be penalized for violating FERPA?

In *Williams v. New Baltimore City Board of School Commissioners*, MSBE Op. No. 01-23 (2001), the State Board upheld the termination of a teacher on the grounds that she obtained confidential student information without authorization or consent and used it in violation of FERPA and Maryland's corollary regulations. The teacher used student information to send letters to parents with erroneous information regarding the presence of lead in the school's drinking water.

## 10:120: How does FERPA treat the records of students dually enrolled in secondary and postsecondary schools?

Generally, FERPA allows for the exchange of student records between schools under the provision allowing for the "disclosure of student records to officials of another school, school system, or institution of postsecondary education where the student seeks or intends to enroll" (34 C.F.R. § 99.31(a)(2)). USDE's Family Policy Compliance Office (FPCO) advises that in a situation where a student is enrolled in both a high school and a postsecondary institution, the two schools may exchange information on that student.

Regarding parent access to records, if the student is under 18, the parents still retain the rights under FERPA at the high school and may inspect and review any records sent by the postsecondary institution to the high school. In addition, if the student is a dependent for income tax purposes, even if over 18, the postsecondary institution may disclose any education records to a student's parents (34 C.F.R. § 99.31(a)(8)).

# The Protection of Pupil Rights Amendment

### 10:121. What is the Protection of Pupil Rights Amendment?

The Protection of Pupil Rights Amendment (PPRA) was enacted as an amendment to FERPA in 1994, and provides parents rights to notification and the opportunity to remove their child from participation in surveys administered to students and other activities designed to gather information on sensitive subjects (see 20 U.S.C. § 1232h; 34 C.F.R. Part 98). Unlike FERPA, PPRA does not apply to postsecondary institutions, nor does it apply to surveys administered in accordance with the Individuals with Disabilities Education Act (IDEA).

### 10:122. What specific types of surveys and activities are subject to the PPRA?

PPRA identifies surveys and other activities that gather information on the following topics:

- Political affiliations or beliefs of students or parents;
- Mental or psychological condition of the student or parents;
- Sexual behaviors and attitudes;
- Illegal, anti-social, demeaning, or self-incriminating behavior;
- Critical appraisals of family members;
- Legally recognized privileged relationships with lawyers, clergy, or physician;
- Religious practices; and
- Income (20 U.S.C. § 1232h(b)).

### 10:123. Does PPRA require school systems to adopt specific policies?

Yes. PPRA requires schools to adopt policies regarding:

- The right of parents to inspect, upon request, a survey created by a third party before it is distributed to students;

- Arrangements to protect student privacy in the event of the administration of a survey regarding one or more of the topics listed in Question **10:122**;

- The right of parents to inspect, upon request, any instructional material used as part of the school curriculum;

- Administration of physical examinations or screenings of students;

- The collection, disclosure, or use of personal information collected from students for marketing purposes; and

- The right to inspect, upon request, any instrument used in the collection of personal information for marketing or sales purposes before the instrument is distributed to students (20 U.S.C. § 1232h (c)).

## 10:124. What types of student surveys are conducted in Maryland?

The Maryland State Department of Education (MSDE), in conjunction with the Department of Mental Health and Hygiene (DHMH), conducts several surveys of student behavior. The Maryland Adolescent Survey (MAS) is administered biannually by MSDE to assess the nature and extent of substance abuse among adolescents in grades 6, 8, 10 and 12. The survey supports program planning and evaluation by collecting information on students' behavior, knowledge, and attitudes regarding drug use.

DHMH administers the Youth Risk Behavior Surveillance System Survey (YRBSS), which was developed by the Centers for Disease Control (CDC) in 1990 to survey samples of high school students to monitor priority health risk behaviors that contribute to the leading causes of death, disability, and social problems, including: tobacco use, dietary behaviors, physical activity, alcohol and drug use, sexual behaviors, and behaviors that contribute to unintentional injuries and violence. In addition, the Youth Tobacco Survey (YTS) is administered biannually by DHMH and MSDE.

State and local education officials continue to address concerns with the subject matters being surveyed and the role of active or passive parental consent to their child's participation in these surveys. In 2007, legislation was enacted directing MSDE and DHMH to establish a workgroup to address the burden that multiple youth health risk surveys place on public schools, a process that is expected to result in a Memorandum of Understanding between the two agencies (Senate Bill 9, Chapter 306, 2007 Laws of Maryland).

**10:125. Are there federal laws other than FERPA and PPRA regarding student records?**

Yes. For example, the No Child Left Behind Act of 2001 (NCLB) includes a provision, not amending FERPA, that relates to the disclosure of personally identifiable information from students' education records. NCLB requires that each State have "a procedure in place to facilitate the transfer of disciplinary records, with respect to a suspension or expulsion, by local educational agencies to any private or public elementary school or secondary school for any student who is enrolled or seeks, intends, or is instructed to enroll, on a full- or part-time basis, in the school" no later than January 8, 2004 (34 C.F.R. §§ 99.7 and 99.34(a)(ii)). The U.S. Department of Education's Family Policy Compliance Office (FPCO) advises that local school systems should include a notice in their annual notification of rights under FERPA that they forward education records to other schools that have requested the records and in which the student seeks or intends to enroll (*Letter of LeRoy Rooker*, FPCO (February 7, 2003)).

Another example is the mandate under NCLB to provide military recruiters the same access to secondary school students as provided to postsecondary institutions or to prospective employers; and to provide students' names, addresses, and telephone listings to military recruiters, when requested, unless a parent has opted out of providing such information (Section 9528 of the ESEA, 20 U.S.C. § 7908, as amended by the NCLB, and 10 U.S.C. § 503, as amended by § 544 of the National Defense Authorization Act for Fiscal Year 2002 (Pub. Law No. 107-107)).

# 11. Student Discipline/Search and Seizure

### 11:1. What is the legal basis for application of student discipline, and search and seizure in Maryland?

These areas of Maryland school law are governed by the U.S. Constitution, the Annotated Code of Maryland, the Code of Maryland Regulations (COMAR), and by county board of education policy and regulations.

### 11:2. What provisions of the U.S. Constitution govern student discipline and search and seizure?

The Fourth Amendment to the U.S. Constitution governs the area of student searches and seizures in the school setting, and the Fourteenth Amendment controls with regard to the provision of due process of law in meting out student discipline.

### 11:3. How does the Fourth Amendment pertain to student search and seizure?

The Fourth Amendment to the U.S. Constitution provides:

> The right of the people to be secure in their persons, houses, papers, and effects, against unreasonable searches and seizures, shall not be violated, and no Warrants shall issue, but upon probable cause, supported by Oath or affirmation, and particularly describing the place to be searched, and the persons or things to be seized.

While the Fourth Amendment does apply to schools (through the Fourteenth Amendment), the legality of a search of a student depends on the reasonableness, under all of the circumstances, of the search. In the school setting, a series of legal challenges to school searches and seizures began in the early 1970's and continued until the Supreme Court clarified this area of the law in 1985 in the landmark case of *New Jersey v. T.L.O.*, 469 U.S. 325 (1985), which is more fully discussed in **11:41** through **11:45**.

### 11:4. How does the Fourteenth Amendment pertain to student discipline?

The Fourteenth Amendment to the U.S. Constitution provides in pertinent part:

> All persons born or naturalized in the United States, and subject to the jurisdiction thereof, are citizens of the United States and of the State wherein they reside.... nor shall any State deprive any person of life, liberty, or property without due process of law...

In another landmark case the Supreme Court determined the parameters of constitutional due process for a school suspension of ten days or less in the case of *Goss v. Lopez*, 419 U.S. 565 (1975), where the Court held:

> Among other things, the State is constrained to recognize a student's legitimate entitlement to a public education as a property interest which is protected by the Due Process Clause and which may not be taken away for misconduct without adherence to the minimum procedures required by that Clause.... We do not believe that school authorities must be totally free from notice and hearing requirements if their schools are to operate with acceptable efficiency.... The Clause requires at least these rudimentary precautions against unfair or mistaken findings of misconduct and arbitrary exclusion from school.

Thus, basic constitutional due process, in the case of a short-term suspension, requires three elements:

1. A notice of the offense being charged;

2. An opportunity for the student to refute the charge; and

3. An explanation of the evidence supporting the charge.

Unlike criminal proceedings where due process requires a separation between the authority that brings charges against an individual and the authority that makes the judgment in the case after a fair hearing. School authorities in student disciplinary proceedings can both lay blame on a student and mete out discipline to the student. The exception to this rule is the case where the student can show that the administrator possessed a pre-existing hostility or bias rendering them legally incapable of acting as an impartial decision maker (*Newsome v. Batavia Local School District*, 842 F.2d 920 (6th Cir. 1988)).

In general, as the length of the exclusion from school grows as in a long-term suspension or expulsion, the required scope of constitutional due process grows as well. In such cases, increased due process is required, to protect the student's property interest in attendance, and includes such safeguards as:

- Written notice of the charges;

- A full evidentiary hearing (after time to prepare) before an impartial decision maker;

- A right to legal counsel or adult representation;

- An opportunity to present witnesses and evidence;

- An opportunity to cross-examine witnesses (except students); and

- The creation of a written record for appeal purposes.

## 11:5. Are school systems free to establish conduct policies and regulations?

Yes, local boards of education are permitted significant discretion in the establishment, implementation, and interpretation of the conduct policies and regulations that they adopt to facilitate the school's educational mission, vision, and goals and for the protection of the learning environment. The Supreme Court in *Wood v. Strickland*, 420 U.S. 308 (1975), affirmed this basic premise stating:

> It is not the role of the federal courts to set aside decisions of school administrators which the court may view as lacking a basis in wisdom and compassion.... The system of public education that has evolved in this Nation relies necessarily upon the discretion and judgment of school administrators and school board members, ...

Despite that discretion, school systems must nonetheless be careful to ensure that their conduct policies and regulations are clear and unambiguous; well publicized; enforced consistently and without discrimination; respective of student constitutional rights; accompanied by appropriate procedural safeguards; designed to advance the school's educational mission, vision, and goals; protective of the learning environment; and not arbitrary, illegal, or unreasonable.

The State Board of Education, pursuant to Md. Code Ann., Ed. Art. § 7-306(b), is to establish a state code of discipline for all public schools, including standards of conduct and consequences for violations of the standards. In addition, each county board is directed to provide appropriate student discipline by Md. Code Ann., Ed. Art. § 7-306(c), wherein it states that:

> (1) Subject to the provisions of subsections (a) and (b) of this section, each county board shall adopt regulations designed to create and maintain within the schools under its jurisdiction the atmosphere of order and discipline necessary for effective learning.

> (2) The regulations adopted by a county board under this subsection:

> (i) Shall provide for educational and behavioral interventions, counseling, and student and parent conferencing; and

> (ii) Shall provide alternative programs, which may include in-school suspension, suspension, expulsion, or other disciplinary measures that are deemed appropriate.

Maryland State Board of Education Regulations provide for county board authority as well in COMAR 13A.08.01.11A, wherein it states, "Each local board of education shall adopt a set of regulations designed to maintain an environment of order and discipline necessary for effective learning. These regulations should provide for counseling and standards for appropriate disciplinary measures, and may permit suspension or expulsion."

## 11:6. Do schools serve in an "in loco parentis" capacity?

"In loco parentis" is a Latin phrase meaning to be in the place of or position of parents. This phrase basically means that while a student is in the custody of a school, the school has the authority and duty to act as a parent. In exercising this duty of the school, many decisions can be made that are outside the normal purview of the school setting. The rationale for exercising such control over students has to do with the school's charge to educate and the importance of preventing interference with the educational process. The Supreme Court in the case of *Vernonia School District v. Acton*, 515 U.S. 646 (1995), upheld the drug testing of student athletes and affirmed the doctrine of "in loco parentis" holding:

> The first factor to be considered is the nature of the privacy interest upon which the search here at issue intrudes. The Fourth Amendment does not protect all subjective expectations of privacy, but only those that society recognizes as "legitimate." … Central, in our view, to the present case is the fact that the subjects of the Policy are (1) children, who (2) have been committed to the temporary custody of the State as schoolmaster.

## 11:7. Must students be given "Miranda rights" before they are questioned?

No, a student is not entitled to a *Miranda* warning before being questioned by school authorities. In the case of *Boynton v. Casey*, 543 F. Supp. 995 (D. Me. 1982), a student that was suspected of using marijuana was questioned by school administrators, and not by police officers. He was not informed of a right to refuse to answer the questions, and he was not allowed to have his parents present during the questioning. He was suspended from school after admission of marijuana use and the court held that he was not entitled to a *Miranda* warning under the Supreme Court's holding in *Miranda v. Arizona*, 384 U.S. 436 (1966).

## 11:8. May students be questioned without their parents in disciplinary matters?

Yes, school personnel generally may question students in disciplinary matters without first notifying their parents or having their parents present during any such questioning (*Boynton v. Casey*, 543 F. Supp. 995 (D. Me. 1982)).

## 11:9. May students be subjected to school discipline and criminal charges for the same acts?

Yes, the prohibition against double jeopardy does not protect students from both school discipline and criminal prosecution. While adults outside the school setting normally are protected from being tried twice for the same offense, courts have rejected the claim that the prohibition against double jeopardy is violated when a student is faced with both school disciplinary and criminal punishments arising from the same acts (*Payne v. Board of Regents of University of Texas System*, 355 F. Supp 199 (W.D. Tex. 1972), *aff'd*, 474 F.2d 1397 (5th Cir. 1973)). In addition, school officials are sometimes required to report delinquent acts to law enforcement authorities pursuant to COMAR 13A.08.01.15A and B, which states:

A.  Delinquent acts are offenses committed by a person who is under 18 years old which would be a crime if committed by an adult. School officials shall promptly report to the responsible law enforcement agencies all delinquent acts coming to their attention whether occurring on or away from the school premises which involve students attending the particular school.

B.  Delinquent acts do not include conduct which has been traditionally treated as a matter of discipline to be handled administratively by the particular school, except that all conduct of a serious nature should be promptly reported to the parents or guardians concerned.

## 11:10. What are the primary types of student discipline?

Punishments in school discipline matters may range from an in-school suspension or detention to a minor loss of privileges that may be imposed without the ordinary due process safeguards. The next level of student discipline involves the exclusion of the student from school either on a short-term or long-term basis by suspension, or for an extended period or permanently by an expulsion, or by referral to an alternative educational program. As the severity of the punishment increases, the amount of constitutional due process that is required increases as well. Md. Code Ann., Ed. Art. § 7-304.1, establishes a Positive Behavioral Interventions and Support Program for schools with unusually high suspension rates. When suspensions or expulsions reach significant numbers within a specific school, then the possibility arises pursuant to NCLB for the school to be placed on probationary status and ultimately to be designated as persistently dangerous (COMAR 13A.08.01.19). See **Chapter 8** for in-depth consideration of this issue.

## 11:11. What is a suspension?

A suspension is the removal of a student from the school setting on either a short-term or long-term basis. In the case of *Goss v. Lopez*, 419 U.S. 565 (1975), the Supreme Court declined to additionally formalize the suspension process, noting:

Our schools are vast and complex. Some modicum of discipline and
order is essential if the educational function is to be performed.

Events calling for discipline are frequent occurrences and sometimes require immediate, effective action. Suspension is considered not only to be a necessary tool to maintain order but a valuable educational device.

The State Board of Education in COMAR defines various suspensions including; 13A.08.01.11B(3), "'Extended suspension' means the temporary exclusion of a student from school for a specified period of time longer than 10 school days for disciplinary reasons by the local superintendent or the local superintendent's designated representative", 13A.08.01.11B(4), "'In-school suspension' means the exclusion within the school building of a student from the student's regular education program for up to but not more than 10 school days for disciplinary reasons by the school principal", and 13A.08.01.11B(6), "'Short-term suspension' means the exclusion of a student from school for up to but not more than 10 school days for disciplinary reasons by the principal."

Md. Code Ann., Ed. Art. § 7-305 sets forth the primary provisions that govern suspensions and expulsions in Maryland school systems.

### 11:12. Who makes suspension decisions?

In Maryland, school principals have the authority to suspend students for improper conduct for periods of ten days or less. Suspensions of longer than ten days are within the authority of the county superintendent or their designee (upon the written recommendation of the school principal) (COMAR 13A.08.01.11C(1)-(3) and Md. Code Ann., Ed. Art. § 7-305(a)–(c)).

### 11:13. What are the procedures that are required for a suspension?

Under the holding of *Goss v. Lopez*, 419 U.S. 565 (1975), basic constitutional due process, in the case of a short-term suspension, requires three elements:

1. A notice of the offense being charged;

2. An opportunity for the student to refute the charge; and

3. An explanation of the evidence supporting the charge.

There is no need for delay between the time notice is given and the time of the imposition of the penalty. The school administrator may informally discuss the suspected misconduct with the student immediately after it has occurred.

The State Board of Education sets forth the Maryland procedure in COMAR 13A.08.01.11B(2) stating:

(2) Suspension for Not More Than 10 Days.

(a) In accordance with the rules and regulations of the local board, each principal of a public school may suspend for cause, for not more than 10 school days, any student in the school who is under the direction of the principal.

(b) The student or the student's parent or guardian promptly shall be given a conference with the principal and any other appropriate personnel during the suspension period.

(c) At or before the conference, the student shall receive oral or written notice of the charges against him or her. If the student denies the charges, the student has the right to an explanation of the evidence supporting the charges and an opportunity to present the student's side of the story.

(d) A student whose presence in school poses a continuing danger to persons or property or an ongoing threat of disrupting the academic process may be removed immediately from school, if the notice and conference required by this subsection is provided as soon as possible.

(e) If the principal finds that an extended suspension or expulsion is warranted, the principal immediately shall report the matter in writing to the local superintendent.

Md. Code Ann., Ed. Art. § 7-305(a) also details the proper procedures to follow in the event of the imposition of a short-term suspension.

## 11:14. What is an expulsion?

An expulsion is generally the removal of a student from the school setting on either a long-term or permanent basis. The State Board of Education in COMAR 13A.08.01.11C(2) states, ""Expulsion" means, at a minimum, the removal of the student from the student's regular school program and may be further defined by a local board of education."

## 11:15. Who makes expulsion decisions?

In Maryland, expulsions are within the authority of the county superintendent or their designated representative (upon the written recommendation of the school principal) (COMAR 13A.08.01.11C(3) and Md. Code Ann., Ed. Art. § 7-305(b)).

## 11:16. What are the procedures that are required for an expulsion?

In general, in the case of an expulsion, the required scope of constitutional due process grows. In such cases, increased due process has been held to include such safeguards as:

- Written notice of the charges;

- A full evidentiary hearing (after time to prepare) before an impartial decision maker;

- A right to legal counsel or adult representation;

- An opportunity to present witnesses and evidence;

- An opportunity to cross-examine witnesses (except students); and

- The creation of a written record for appeal purposes.

The State Board of Education sets forth the Maryland procedure in COMAR 13A.08.01.11C(3) stating:

(3) Suspension for More than 10 Days or Expulsion.

(a) At the request of a principal, a local superintendent or the designated representative may suspend a student for more than 10 school days or expel the student.

(b) Upon receipt of a written report from a principal requesting an extended suspension or expulsion, the local superintendent or designated representative promptly shall make a thorough investigation of the matter.

(c) If after the investigation the local superintendent or designated representative finds that a longer suspension or expulsion is warranted, the superintendent or designated representative promptly shall arrange a conference with the student and the student's parent or guardian.

(d) If after the conference the local superintendent or designated representative finds that a suspension of more than 10 school days or expulsion is warranted, the student or the student's parent or guardian may:

(i) Appeal to the local board within 10 days after the determination;

(ii) Be heard before the local board or its designated committee; and

(iii) Bring counsel and witnesses to the hearing.

(e) Unless a public hearing is requested by the parent or guardian of the student, a hearing shall be held out of the presence of all individuals except those whose presence is considered necessary or desirable by the board.

(f) The appeal to the local board does not stay the decision of the county superintendent.

(g) The decision of the local board is final.

Md. Code Ann., Ed. Art. § 7-305(c) also details the proper procedures to follow in the event of the imposition of a long-term suspension or expulsion.

## 11:17. Are educational services provided during a suspension or an expulsion?

Yes and no. In Maryland, students are normally permitted to make up work and tests missed during the period of a suspension, but not during the period of an expulsion.

## 11:18. May conditions be placed on a student's return to school after discipline?

Yes, the local school system may place reasonable conditions on a student's return to school after discipline, particularly following a long-term suspension or expulsion. An example of such a condition would be the requirement of successful completion of counseling or an anger management program. Md. Code Ann., Ed. Art. § 7-310 provides for the development and dissemination, by each county board of education, of a community resources list with the name and contact information of local and statewide providers of services to students and families in need of such assistance.

## 11:19. What are academic sanctions and when may they be applied?

An academic sanction involves an academic consequence (*i.e.* lowering of grade) for non-academic conduct (*i.e.* excessive tardiness). An example of academic sanctions would be the denial of credit for courses taken when a student is excessively absent from school in violation of county board of education policies and regulations. It is clear that the potential for the imposition of any such sanctions must be accompanied by notice to students that academic sanctions will result from certain behavior. Md. Code Ann., Ed. Art. § 7-301(b) directs the county superintendent, school principal, or an individual authorized by them to excuse a student for lawful absences, but otherwise school attendance is compulsory.

## 11:20. What are disciplinary transfers?

A disciplinary transfer involves the moving of a student from one school setting to another for a conduct related violation unrelated to normal pupil assignment standards. An example of a disciplinary transfer would be to move the perpetrator of student-on-student violence (upon return from suspension or expulsion) to a different school for the physical protection and peace of mind of the victims of the student perpetrator's improper actions. While such disciplinary actions are allowed, they must be accompanied by appropriate due process because of the significant impact on the student being transferred. In the case of *Everett v. Marcase*, 426 F. Supp. 397 (E.D. Pa. 1977), the federal district court found that a student's interest in a disciplinary transfer was significant and worthy of more than minimal due process, stating:

> To transfer a pupil during a school year from a familiar school to a strange and possibly more distant school would be a terrifying experience for many children of normal sensibilities. I think it not melodramatic to suggest the genuine danger of physical harm being intentionally inflicted upon a transferred pupil who may be required to pass through different and strange neighborhoods on the way to and from the transferee school.

The Maryland State Board of Education in the case of *Muise-Magruder v. Montgomery County Board of Education*, MSBE Op. No. 03-20 (2003), upheld the local board's decision to transfer a student returning from expulsion to a different school because of the direct effect on maintaining school order and safety, despite the student's desire to return to his former school.

## 11:21. What are alternative educational programs?

An alternative educational program is a separate educational setting designed to address the specific needs of disruptive youth with the ultimate goal of re-entering students into the regular educational program. Md. Code Ann., Ed. Art. § 7-304, requires each county board of education, "to provide a continuum model of prevention and intervention activities and programs that encourage and promote positive behavior and reduce disruption." County boards are authorized to establish joint use facilities for disruptive youth, and are required to submit an annual report to the State Board of Education detailing the operation of all county alternative educational programs. In addition to county board of education facilities for disruptive students, Md. Code Ann., Ed. Art. § 7-305.1, directs the State Board of Education to establish as needed, in partnership with the state juvenile court system, a juvenile services alternative education program. In the Maryland case of *Aziz Barimani v. Montgomery County Board of Education*, MSBE Op. No. 00-30 (2000), the State Board of Education upheld the right of a school system to assign a student under discipline to an alternative educational program despite the disagreement of the student and his parents, and a request by the student and parents to be assigned to another comprehensive high school instead.

### 11:22. What is extracurricular discipline?

Extracurricular discipline involves an extracurricular consequence (*i.e.* suspension from a team for a set number of games) for conduct that may of may not be related to the extracurricular activity itself (*i.e.* improper conduct during a game or a pre-season hazing incident). An example of extracurricular discipline is that some policies and regulations of county boards of education provide that the off-campus violation of certain illegal substance prohibitions will result in the loss of in-school extracurricular privileges. The Maryland State Board of Education has upheld the imposition of school discipline for the violation of such policies on several occasions (*Pickett v. Montgomery County Board of Education*, MSBE Op. No. 98-45 (1998), and *Farver v. Carroll County Board of Education*, MSBE Op. No. 99-42 (1999)). In the case of *Sachs v. Howard County Board of Education*, MSBE Op. No. 03-16 (2003), the State Board of Education upheld the exclusion of a student from participating in an extracurricular activity, namely cheerleading, as a result of the student's failure to meet the grade requirements for participation.

### 11:23. What is corporal punishment and does it still exist in schools?

In the case of *Ingraham v. Wright*, 430 U.S. 651 (1977), the Supreme Court held that corporal punishment in school does not violate the Eighth Amendment prohibition against "*cruel and unusual punishment*". While corporal punishment (spanking) still exists in a handful of states, the practice is illegal in the State of Maryland. Md. Code Ann., Ed. Art. § 7-306(a), states, "Corporal punishment prohibited.—Notwithstanding any bylaw, rule, or regulation made or approved by the State Board, a principal, vice principal, or other employee may not administer corporal punishment to discipline a student in a public school in the State." In addition, the Maryland State Board of Education in COMAR 13A.08.01.11E provides, "Corporal punishment may not be used to discipline a student in a public school in the State."

### 11:24. May students be disciplined for offensive speech?

Speech that is obscene, vulgar, inflammatory, or defamatory is not entitled to constitutional protection, and thus is subject to appropriate school discipline. In *Bethel School District No. 403 v. Fraser*, 478 U.S. 675 (1986), the Supreme Court held that a student's vulgar and obscene speech was not entitled to constitutional protection and stated:

We hold that petitioner School District acted entirely within its permissible authority in imposing sanctions upon Fraser in response to his offensively lewd and indecent speech. ... The First Amendment does not prevent the school officials from determining that to permit a vulgar and lewd speech such as respondent's would undermine the school's basic educational mission. ... Accordingly, it was perfectly appropriate for the school to disassociate itself to make the point to the pupils that vulgar speech and lewd conduct is wholly inconsistent with the "fundamental values" of public school education.

In *Morse v. Frederick*, 551 U.S. ___ (2007), the Supreme Court considered whether discipline could be meted out to a student who displayed a banner with the message "Bong Hits 4 Jesus". The Court reversed the Ninth Circuit Court of Appeals, which had held that such discipline was a clear violation of the student's free speech rights (see **11:63**).

### 11:25. May students be disciplined for bullying or hazing?

Yes, since the Supreme Court decision in *Chaplinsky v. New Hampshire*, 315 U.S. 568 (1942), it has been clear that "fighting words" are not protected speech under the First Amendment. Student expression rights have also been limited when the expression mocks, demeans, or ridicules other persons or groups (*Nitzberg v. Parks*, 525 F.2d 378 (4th Cir. 1975)). In the Maryland case of *Mace v. Board of Education of Harford County*, MSBE Op. No. 01-15 (2001), the State Board of Education upheld the 20-day suspension of a student for wearing what resembled a Ku Klux Klan hood while another student unfurled a Confederate flag. Another Maryland case saw the State Board of Education uphold a suspension of a student for hazing of younger players in a school sports setting (*Junaid Ali v. Howard County Board of Education*, MSBE Op. No. 00-15 (2000)).

A statewide reporting requirement for incidents of harassment or intimidation against students has been established during the period from July 1, 2005 through June 30, 2009, pursuant to Md. Code Ann., Ed. Art. § 7-424. It is also a crime in Maryland to harass, in certain manners, another person because of their "race, color, religious beliefs, sexual orientation, or national origin" under Md. Code Ann., Crim. Law Art. § 10-304. The hazing of students is likewise a criminal offense pursuant to Md. Code Ann., Crim. Law Art. § 3-607.

### 11:26. May students be disciplined for improper on-campus computer use?

Yes, schools are free to adopt Acceptable Use Policies and regulations with regard to student in-school computer use. Schools may require students and their parents to agree to multiple limitations and restrictions on student use of school system computers, in order to be allowed the use of the equipment, and appropriate disciplinary actions may be taken with respect to violations of such policies and regulations. In *Craciunescu v. Montgomery County Board of Education*, MSBE Op. No. 00-36 (2000), the Maryland State Board of Education upheld the suspension of a student for materially disrupting the school environment by using the school's computer and network to view inappropriate websites and download data on how to build bombs.

### 11:27. May students be disciplined for improper off-campus computer use?

Possibly, courts have been divided regarding the level of control that schools may exercise with respect to student out-of-school Internet expression. In the case of *J.S. ex rel. H.S. v. Bethlehem Area School District*, 569 A.2d 638 (Pa. 2002), the Pennsylvania Supreme Court held that a student's online depictions of a decapitated teacher and solicitation of donations to have the teacher killed amounted to a material disruption and warranted expulsion. On the other hand, discipline for student blogs that merely consist of criticism of their schools or their teachers usually does not withstand First Amendment scrutiny. In *Beussink v. Woodland School District*, 30 F. Supp. 2d 1175 (E.D. Mo. 1998), a federal judge in Missouri found that a student's blog containing vulgar criticism of his school was not a material disruption and could not be the basis for discipline, stating:

> In order for the State in the person of school officials to justify prohibition of a particular expression of opinion, it must be able to show that its action was caused by something more than a mere desire to avoid the discomfort and unpleasantness that always accompany an unpopular viewpoint. Certainly where there is no finding and no showing that engaging in the forbidden conduct would 'materially and substantially interfere with the requirements of appropriate discipline in the operation of the school,' the prohibition can not be sustained.

Two cases came before the Maryland State Board of Education on appeal in 2000; both upheld decisions by the Montgomery County Board of Education to discipline students for websites created off school grounds that nonetheless were found to create a substantial disruption and a material interference with school activities. In the first case, a student created an unofficial website for his high school class of 2001, in which a message board was set up that featured numerous death threats and obscene statements toward other students (*Aziz Barimani v. Montgomery County Board of Education*, MSBE Op. No. 00-30 (2000)). In the second case, the website asked students to rate certain female classmates on specific (and lewd) sexual traits, and the female students affected suffered significant indignity and embarrassment (*Tommy Kuka v. Montgomery County Board of Education*, MSBE Op. No. 00-51 (2000)).

**11:28. May students be disciplined for other off-campus behavior?**

Yes, various off-campus violent criminal behaviors may result in the imposition of school discipline when necessary to protect the educational environment of the school and the safety of the students and staff. In addition, some extracurricular policies provide that the off-campus violation of certain illegal substance prohibitions will, in addition, result in the loss of school extracurricular privileges. A recent decision of the Maryland State Board of Education, in the case of *Martin & Deluca v. Howard County Board of Education*, MSBE Op. No. 04-09 (2004), upheld the removal of a student from extracurricular activities for 70 days as a result of on-campus alcohol possession in violation of county policy. If students are arrested for certain reportable offenses defined in Md. Code Ann., Ed. Art. § 7-303, typically crimes of violence or gang related offenses, then the local superintendent is required to be notified of the arrest and such charges within 24 hours in order that they can "maintain a safe and secure school environment for students and school personnel." In the case of *Muise-Magruder v. Montgomery County Board of Education*, MSBE Op. No. 03-11 (2003), the State Board of Education upheld the expulsion of a student for a serious racially motivated assault after school hours in a nearby shopping center parking lot.

**11:29. May students be disciplined for bringing weapons onto school property?**

Yes, in addition to local county policies banning the possession of weapons on school property, the federal Gun Free Schools Act of 1994, 20 United States Code, Chapter 70, § 8921 also applies. Maryland complied with the federal law by adopting COMAR 13A.08.01.12-1, which contains regulations promulgated by the State Board of Education, and Md. Code Ann., Ed. Art. § 7-305, which provides:

(e) Bringing a firearm onto school property.—

(1) In this subsection, "firearm" means a firearm as defined in 18 U.S.C. § 921.

(2) Except as provided in paragraph (3) of this subsection, if the county superintendent or the superintendent's designated representative finds that a student has brought a firearm onto school property, the student shall be expelled for a minimum of 1 year.

(3) The county superintendent may specify, on a case by case basis, a shorter period of expulsion or an alternative educational setting, if alternative educational settings have been approved by the county board, for a student who has brought a firearm onto school property.

Additionally, state law further makes it a crime to have a deadly weapon of any kind on school property, under Md. Code Ann., Crim. Law Art. § 4-102, with the following exceptions:

(a) Exceptions.—This section does not apply to:

(1) a law enforcement officer in the regular course of the officer's duty;

(2) a person hired by a county board of education specifically for the purpose of guarding public school property;

(3) a person engaged in organized shooting activity for educational purposes; or

(4) a person who, with a written invitation from the school principal, displays or engages in a historical demonstration using a weapon or a replica of a weapon for educational purposes.

In the case of *Morton v. Prince George's County Board of Education*, MSBE Op. No. 05-39 (2005), the State Board of Education upheld the expulsion of a student for the use of pepper spray on another student in violation of the weapons policy.

## 11:30. May students be disciplined for drug, alcohol and tobacco use?

Yes, students may be disciplined for the possession of illegal or merely banned substances by county board of education policies and regulations. Md. Code Ann., Ed. Art. § 4-124, designates Maryland schools as "drug free school zones" under Md. Code Ann., Crim. Law Art. § 5-627, which makes it a criminal offense to possess controlled dangerous substances within 1,000 feet of any county school system property. It is also a criminal offense to possess nonprescription steroids or human growth hormones at school gymnasiums under Md. Code Ann., Crim. Law Art. § 5-710. It should be noted that Md. Code Ann., Ed. Art. § 7-412, provides that if "a student seeks information to overcome any form of drug abuse", such "observation or conclusion derived from the statement is not admissible against the student in any proceeding." In addition, an alcohol abuse prevention program is established for Maryland schools pursuant to Md. Code Ann., Ed. Art. § 7-413. Finally, COMAR 13A.08.01.08 sets forth specific regulations from the State Board of Education in regard to the school use of alcohol, tobacco, and other drugs. A recent decision of the Maryland State Board of Education in the case of *Smoot v. Charles County Board of Education*, MSBE Op. No. 03-27 (2003), upheld the expulsion of a student for possession of marijuana on school grounds. Similarly, the State Board upheld a 45-day suspension and the loss of extracurricular privileges, for the current semester and following semester, imposed on a student that brought alcohol onto a school bus and distributed it to another student (*Ashtianie v. Howard County Board of Education*, MSBE Op. No. 05-20 (2005)).

### 11:31. May students be disciplined for use of electronic communication devices?

Yes, in 2003, Md. Code Ann., Ed. Art. § 26-104, entitled, "Possession of portable pager on public school property", was repealed, with the legislative proviso that "it is the intent of the General Assembly that local education agencies, working with the State Department of Education, develop their own local policies regarding the use of portable pagers and cellular telephones on public school property and, … county boards of education are free to either exclude or restrict the in-school use of electronic communication devices, and may discipline student for the violation of such policies and regulations." County boards of education are currently dealing with a growing number and variety of electronic communication devices and the myriad of privacy and academic integrity issues that their usage raise, as county boards seek to promote technology education while protecting the learning environment for the benefit of all students and school system staff. A recent decision of the Maryland State Board of Education, in the case of *Berry v. Calvert County Board of Education*, MSBE Op. No. 05-28 (2005), upheld the suspension of a student for use of a cell phone during the school day in violation of county policy.

### 11:32. May students be disciplined for behavior on the bus or at the bus stop?

Yes, the bus trip to and from school and the immediate area of the bus stop are extensions of the school setting in Maryland, and normal school disciplinary policies and regulations apply fully. A recent decision of the Maryland State Board of Education, in the case of *Ashtianie v. Howard County Board of Education*, MSBE Op. No. 05-20 (2005), upheld the suspension of a student for possession of alcohol and distribution of alcohol to another student on the school bus in violation of county policy.

### 11:33. May students be disciplined for assault on school staff?

Yes, school violence affects teachers as well as students. On average, in each year from 1995 to 1999, about 3 out of every 1,000 teachers were the victims of serious violent crime at school. Source: U.S. Department of Justice, Bureau of Justice Statistics, National Crime Victimization Survey, 1995 to 1999. A recent decision of the Maryland State Board of Education, in the case of *Lynn v. Anne Arundel County Board of Education*, MSBE Op. No. 04-20 (2004), upheld the expulsion of a student that threatened to leave a teacher "lying on the floor bleeding". Other recent State Board opinions affirmed the disciplining of students for pushing a teacher and causing her to cut her arm (*Johnson v. Baltimore City Board of School Commissioners*, MSBE Op. No. 03-19 (2003); and for hitting a teacher in the head with a piece of ice wrapped in a paper towel (*Saunders v. Charles County Board of Education*, MSBE Op. No. 04-12 (2004)).

## 11:34. May students be disciplined for damage to school property?

Yes, a student may not only be disciplined for wrongfully damaging school property, but may be required to make restitution for the resulting financial loss. The State Board of Education in COMAR 13A.08.01.11D, states:

> Restitution. Unless the student is referred to the Department of Juvenile Justice, if a student violates a State or local law or regulation and during or as a result of the commission of that violation damaged, destroyed, or substantially decreased the value of school property or property of another that was on school property at the time of the violation, as part of a conference on the matter with the student, the student's parent or guardian, and other appropriate individual, the principal shall require the student or the student's parent or guardian to make restitution. The restitution may be made in the form of monetary restitution not to exceed the lesser of the fair market value of the property, or $2,500, or by the student's assignment to a school work project, or both.

It is also a criminal offense in Maryland pursuant to Md. Code Ann., Crim. Law Art. § 10-305, to deface, damage or destroy a school building "if there is evidence that exhibits animosity against a person or group, because of the race, color, religious beliefs, sexual orientation, or national origin of that person or group."

## 11:35. What are zero tolerance policies?

Generally a zero-tolerance policy is one, which imposes a mandatory minimum penalty for a designated offense, without regard for any circumstances and without the normal availability for the decision maker to exercise discretion. These policies became popular as a "get tough" measure within the last decade, and have resulted in numerous illogical results. A Fourth Circuit case, *Ratner v. Loudoun County Pub. Schools*, 16 Fed. Appx. 140 (4th Cir. 2001), stands as one of the most absurd examples of the danger of removing common sense from the discipline equation; in it a student was given a nearly four month suspension from school (for possession of a weapon) after he took possession of a knife from a suicidal classmate in an undisputed attempt to save a life. The Fourth Circuit Court in *Ratner* reluctantly upheld the zero tolerance policy, but in a concurring opinion, Senior Circuit Judge Hamilton spoke for the Court saying:

There is no doubt that this zero-tolerance/automatic suspension policy, and others like it adopted by school officials throughout our nation, were adopted in large response to the tragic school shootings that have plagued our nation's schools over the past several years. Also, no doubt exists that in adopting these zero-tolerance/automatic suspension policies, school officials had the noble intention of protecting the health and safety of our nation's school children and those adults charged with the profound responsibility of educating them. However, as the oft repeated old English maxim recognizes, "the road to hell is paved with good intentions." The panic over school violence and the intent to stop it has caused school officials to jettison the common sense idea that a person's punishment should fit his crime in favor of a single harsh punishment, namely, mandatory school suspension. Such a policy has stripped away judgment and discretion on the part of those administering it; refuting the well-established precept that judgment is the better part of wisdom.

In the case of *Saling v. Montgomery County Board of Education*, MSBE Op. No. 03-33 (2003), the State Board of Education upheld the exclusion of a student from participation in graduation exercises because of possession of drug paraphernalia on school grounds in violation of a zero tolerance policy.

### 11:36. Are there differences in the discipline of students with disabilities?

Yes, under the Individuals with Disabilities Education Act (IDEA), there are many restrictions, considerations, and procedures that schools must follow when attempting to discipline students with special needs. See **Chapter 15** for in-depth consideration of this issue.

### 11:37. On what basis may students appeal the application of discipline?

Students who are suspended for more than 10 school days or are expelled have appeal rights as set forth in Md. Code Ann., Ed. Art. § 7-305(c)(5)-(8), which provides:

> (5) If after the conference the county superintendent or the county superintendent's designated representative finds that a suspension of more than 10 school days or expulsion is warranted, the student or the student's parent or guardian may:
>
> > (i) Appeal to the county board within 10 days after the determination;

(ii) Be heard before the county board, its designated committee, or a hearing examiner, in accordance with the procedures established under § 6-203 of this article; and

(iii) Bring counsel and witnesses to the hearing.

(6) Unless a public hearing is requested by the parent or guardian of the student, a hearing shall be held out of the presence of all individuals except those whose presence is considered necessary or desirable by the board.

(7) The appeal to the county board does not stay the decision of the county superintendent.

(8) The decision of the county board is final.

Similar provisions regarding student appeal rights are set forth in COMAR 13A.08.01.11.

Students suspended for not more than 10 school days have also been found by the State Board of Education in *Junaid Ali v. Howard County Board of Education*, MSBE Op. No. 00-15 (2000), and *Black v. Carroll County Board of Education*, MSBE Op. No. 02-24 (2002), to have a right to appeal such a suspension, although on a more informal basis (*i.e.* without an evidentiary hearing, etc.) pursuant to Md. Code Ann., Ed. Art. § 4-205(c)(3), which provides:

(3) A decision of a county superintendent may be appealed to the county board if taken in writing within 30 days after the decision of the county superintendent. The decision may be further appealed to the State Board if taken in writing within 30 days after the decision of the county board.

## 11:38. What is the process for the return to school of a suspended or expelled student?

Notification to teachers and other appropriate school personnel is required prior to the return of a student to school, following a suspension or expulsion, pursuant to Md. Code Ann., Ed. Art. § 7-305(d)(4), which states:

(4) (i) If a student has been suspended or expelled, the principal or a designee of the principal may not return the student to the classroom without conferring with the teacher who referred the student to the principal, if the student was referred by a teacher, other teachers as appropriate, other appropriate school personnel, the student, and the student's parent or guardian.

(ii) If the disruptive behavior results in action less than suspension, the principal or a designee of the principal shall confer with the teacher who referred the student to the principal prior to returning the student to that teacher's classroom.

Similar provisions regarding students returning to school after suspension or expulsion are set forth in COMAR 13A.08.01.11C(5)-(6).

### 11:39. What is a student search and seizure?

A search of a student is an examination of a student's person or property with the intent of discovering concealed contraband, the possession of which is prohibited by state law, or policy or regulation of the county board. A seizure is the act of taking possession of the discovered contraband.

### 11:40. Who may conduct a search and seizure of student possessions?

A principal, assistant principal or school security guard has the authority to make a reasonable search of a student pursuant to Md. Code Ann., Ed. Art. § 7-308(a), which states:

> (a) Authority to search student.—A principal, assistant principal, or school security guard of a public school may make a reasonable search of a student on the school premises or on a school-sponsored trip if the searcher has a reasonable belief that the student has in the student's possession an item, the possession of which is a criminal offense under the laws of this State or a violation of any other State law or a rule or regulation of the county board.

Note that Md. Code Ann., Ed. Art. § 7-308(b) permits a teacher who is designated and trained to conduct reasonable searches only on school-sponsored trips. It is also important to recognize that any student search must be made in the presence of a third party, to serve as a witness, according to Md. Code Ann., Ed. Art. § 7-308(c). Similar provisions regarding student searches and seizures are set forth in COMAR 13A.08.01.14E-F.

### 11:41. Is a warrant required for student searches and seizures?

No, school officials are not required to obtain a warrant from a judge, before searching a student's possessions or person. While the Fourth Amendment does apply to schools (through the Fourteenth Amendment), the legality of a search of a student depends on the reasonableness, under all of the circumstances, of the search. In *New Jersey v. T.L.O.*, 469 U.S. 325 (1985), the Supreme Court held:

> How, then, should we strike the balance between the schoolchild's legitimate expectations of privacy and the school's equally legitimate need to maintain an environment in which learning can

take place? It is evident that the school setting requires some easing of the restrictions to which searches by public authorities are ordinarily subject. The warrant requirement, in particular, is unsuited to the school environment: requiring a teacher to obtain a warrant before searching a child suspected of an infraction of school rules (or of the criminal law) would unduly interfere with the maintenance of the swift and informal disciplinary procedures needed in the schools. Just as we have in other cases dispensed with the warrant requirement ... we hold today that school officials need not obtain a warrant before searching a student who is under their authority.

## 11:42. Is probable cause required for student searches and seizures?

No, school administrators are not required to produce evidence of probable cause before searching a student's possessions or person. School administrators need have only a reasonable suspicion, which is a less rigorous standard than that of probable cause, in order to conduct a legal search. In *New Jersey v. T.L.O.*, 469 U.S. 325 (1985), the Supreme Court held:

The school setting also requires some modification of the level of suspicion of illicit activity needed to justify a search. Ordinarily, a search—even one that may permissibly be carried out without a warrant—must be based upon "probable cause" to believe that a violation of the law has occurred.... However, "probable cause" is not an irreducible requirement of a valid search. The fundamental command of the Fourth Amendment is that searches and seizures be reasonable, and although "both the concept of probable cause and the requirement of a warrant bear on the reasonableness of a search, ... in certain limited circumstances neither is required.... We join the majority of courts that have examined this issue in concluding that the accommodation of the privacy interests of schoolchildren with the substantial need of teachers and administrators for freedom to maintain order in the schools does not require strict adherence to the requirement that searches be based on probable cause to believe that the subject of the search has violated or is violating the law. Rather, the legality of a search of a student should depend simply on the reasonableness, under all the circumstances, of the search.

## 11:43. What is the legal standard for school searches and seizures?

The standard was established by the Supreme Court in *New Jersey v. T.L.O.*, 469 U.S. 325 (1985), where it was held:

> Determining the reasonableness of any search involves a twofold inquiry: first, one must consider "whether the ... action was justified at its inception;" second, one must determine whether the search as actually conducted "was reasonably related in scope to the circumstances which justified the interference in the first place."

Thus, two questions must be posed in determining if a student search is valid, they are:

1. Was the search justified at its inception?

2. Was the scope of the search reasonable?

In Maryland, the standard for searches is more restrictive under Md. Code Ann., Ed. Art. § 7-308(a), which requires that an appropriate school official have a reasonable basis to believe that the student is in current possession of contraband which violates Maryland criminal or civil laws or local board of education rules or regulations. Maryland school officials may not conduct searches for evidence that would support a finding that the student previously (although no longer) is in possession of such contraband.

## 11:44. When is a search justified at its inception?

The standard was established by the Supreme Court in *New Jersey v. T.L.O.*, 469 U.S. 325 (1985), where it was held:

> Under ordinary circumstances, a search of a student by a teacher or other school official will be "justified at its inception" when there are reasonable grounds for suspecting that the search will turn up evidence that the student has violated or is violating either the law or the rules of the school.

It is important to note the discovery of contraband is largely irrelevant to the determination of whether a search was justified at its inception. A search that was based upon reasonable grounds will be upheld even if no contraband is found, and conversely, the finding of contraband will not validate a search that lacked reasonable grounds at its inception. In *Jacobs v. Board of Education of Prince George's County*, MSBE Op. No. 88-7 (1988), the State Board of Education found that a reasonable basis to initiate a search existed when a report was received from a parent/teacher that he understood that a student was in possession of a knife on school grounds and when the student in question was called to the office, he was observed attempting to leave the school instead.

## 11:45. When is a search reasonable in scope?

The standard was established by the Supreme Court in *New Jersey v. T.L.O.*, 469 U.S. 325 (1985), where it was held:

> Such a search will be permissible in its scope when the measures adopted are reasonably related to the objectives of the search and not excessively intrusive in light of the age and sex of the student and the nature of the infraction.

For example, a much more intrusive search would be reasonable if there were reasonable grounds to believe that a student possessed a weapon in school. On the other hand, a far less intrusive search might be all that was reasonable when searching a student for a cigarette. Strip searches of students, for example, are very nearly always found to be unreasonable in scope. In the case of *Doe v. Renfrow*, 631 F.2d 91 (7th Cir. 1980), a strip search of a thirteen-year-old girl, after she was sniffed by a police dog, was found to be totally unreasonable, and the Seventh Circuit opinion stated:

> It does not require a constitutional scholar to conclude that a nude search of a thirteen year-old child is an invasion of constitutional rights of some magnitude. More than that; it is a violation of any known principle of human decency. Apart from any constitutional readings and rulings, simple common sense would indicate that the conduct of the school officials in permitting such a nude search was not only unlawful but outrageous.... We suggest as strongly as possible that the conduct herein described exceeded the "bounds of reason by two and a half country miles."

## 11:46. What are the primary types of student searches?

The most frequent areas of searches in the school setting are lockers, purses and backpacks, automobiles, and items of student clothing.

## 11:47. Is individualized suspicion required to search a student?

Yes, in order to search a student in school, an administrator must have some degree of individualized suspicion before searching any particular student for contraband. Additionally, a search of large groups of students has been held unreasonable, the same holds true for the search of an individual student without specific knowledge of rules violations by that particular student (*Kuehn v. Reston School District No. 403*, 103 Wash. 2d 594 (1985)).

## 11:48. What is a random search?

A random search is one which is conducted without any individualized suspicion, and in a broad and random manner. Examples of random searches may include searches of student lockers, use of drug sniffing dogs, student drug tests, and the use of metal detectors.

## 11:49. What is a consensual search?

If a student, with the capacity to refuse, consents to a search of his or her property or person, then an administrator may validly search without being subject to the various constitutional and statutory constraints set forth elsewhere herein. Consent could be defined as a student knowing that they can say no to a search, and still saying yes. It would be advisable for administrators to always request consent to any proposed search, as any potential subsequent objections are removed, with the exception of capacity questions.

## 11:50. How is a student's expectation of privacy determined?

The level of student expectation of privacy in the area of the search ranges across a spectrum where student lockers have the lowest expectation of privacy, and items of student clothing being worn by the student have the highest expectation of privacy. Purses, backpacks, and automobiles fall somewhere in between the two extremes as far as a student's entitlement to an expectation of privacy.

## 11:51. What is the basis for searches of student lockers?

A principal, assistant principal or school security guard has the authority to make a search of student lockers pursuant to Md. Code Ann., Ed. Art. § 7-308(d), which states:

> (d) Authority to search school.—
>
> (1) A principal, assistant principal, or school security guard of a public school may make a search of the physical plant of the school and its appurtenances including the lockers of students.
>
> (2) The right of the school official to search the locker shall be announced or published previously in the school.

Essentially, the proper school authorities for any reason or for no particular reason may search lockers. The normal requirements for reasonable grounds and individualized suspicion do not apply in the case of school lockers, which are seen as a part of the school facility under the direct and continuing control of school officials.

### 11:52. What is the basis for searches of student backpacks and purses?

Student backpacks and purses have a higher student expectation of privacy than that which exists for student lockers. This is a logical distinction between a portion of the school facility (lockers) and the personal property and effects of students. In order to conduct such a search, reasonable grounds and an individualized suspicion must exist (see **11:43** and **11:47**).

### 11:53. What is the basis for searches of student automobiles?

Student automobiles also have a higher student expectation of privacy than that which exists for student lockers. This is also a logical distinction between a portion of the school facility (lockers) and the vehicles, which are the property of the student or their parent. In order to conduct such a search, reasonable grounds and an individualized suspicion must exist (see **11:43** and **11:47**). In the case of *Mace v. Carroll County Board of Education*, MSBE Op. No. 88-01 (1988), the State Board of Education upheld the expulsion of a student for a gun that was in plain view in the front seat of the student's vehicle.

### 11:54. What is the basis for searches of student clothing and persons?

A student's clothing and person have a higher student expectation of privacy than that which exists for student lockers, purses and backpacks and automobiles. Even so, pat downs and other searches of student outerwear, pockets and shoes are generally permissible provided that the *TLO* standard has been met (see **11:43**). Strip searches are never a preferred option, and in the rare case when justified, require well-founded suspicion of infractions of the most serious nature, such as weapons or possibly drugs. While it has been held patently unreasonable to strip search a class of seventh grade girls to recover four dollars and fifty cents (*Oliver v. McLung*, 919 F. Supp. 1206 (N.D. Ind. 1995)), in light of the frequency of drug use in schools, courts have given school officials some degree of latitude in employing strip searches for drugs. The Eleventh Circuit has stated that it is "axiomatic that a strip search represents a serious intrusion upon personal rights" (*Justice v. City of Peachtree City*, 961 F.2d 188 (11th Cir. 1992)). The Seventh Circuit has gone so far as to find strip searches to be "demeaning, dehumanizing, undignified, humiliating, terrifying, unpleasant, embarrassing, repulsive, signifying degradation and submission" (*Mary Beth G. v. City of Chicago*, 723 F.2d 1263 (7th Cir. 1983)).

The best decision regarding a possible strip search would almost certainly be not to proceed.

## 11:55. Does the "exclusionary rule" apply to student searches?

Possibly, in the landmark Supreme Court case of *New Jersey v. T.L.O.*, 469 U.S. 325 (1985), the court addressed the issue of the exclusionary rule, but did not make a definitive decision. The *T.L.O.* Court stated:

> In holding that the search of T.L.O.'s purse did not violate the Fourth Amendment, we do not implicitly determine that the exclusionary rule applies to the fruits of unlawful searches conducted by school authorities. The question whether evidence should be excluded from a criminal proceeding involves two discrete inquiries: whether the evidence was seized in violation of the Fourth Amendment, and whether the exclusionary rule is the appropriate remedy for the violation. Neither question is logically antecedent to the other, for a negative answer to either question is sufficient to dispose of the case. Thus, our determination that the search at issue in this case did not violate the Fourth Amendment implies no particular resolution of the question of the applicability of the exclusionary rule.

## 11:56. May schools require random drug tests of students?

The Supreme Court initially held that random drug testing of high school athletes was constitutional where there was evidence that student athletes were significantly involved in an existing drug problem in the school (*Vernonia School District 47J v. Acton*, 515 U.S. 646 (1995)). In the subsequent case of *Board of Education of Independent School District No. 92 of Pottawatomie County v. Lindsay Earls*, 536 U.S. 822 (2002), the Supreme Court upheld a local school policy requiring students engaging in any extracurricular activities to take a drug test before participating and to submit to random urine testing while participating. The case was brought by a student-member of the choir, marching band, academic team and National Honor Society, and the Court held that students can be required to undergo random suspicionless drug testing as a condition of their participation in all extracurricular activities, reasoning that those who participate can take leadership roles in the school community and serve as an example to other students. In 1995, a Maryland State Department of Education Task Force recommended against adopting a student drug testing program based upon the expected high cost and limited benefit, as well as, numerous legal and privacy concerns. Breath tests to determine student alcohol use are becoming more frequent nationally, and have been used without judicial challenge in some Maryland schools prior to admittance to extracurricular events. The planned use of drug or alcohol test results may have a significant bearing on the exposure to potential legal challenges. Presumably, such tests would be less objectionable if used for exposing the need to provide help to certain students, as opposed to their use in disciplinary or criminal actions.

### 11:57. May schools make use of metal detectors?

Yes, the use of metal detectors to discover knives, guns and other weapons has been upheld by the courts that have considered the matter, on the reasoning that random metal detector searches may be necessary to keep schools safe (*People v. Pruitt*, 662 N.E.2d 540 (Ill. App. Dist. 1996)). While they are not commonly used in Maryland, nearly one-half of the largest urban districts are now using metal detectors on a routine basis.

### 11:58. May schools make use of drug sniffing dogs?

The Supreme Court in a non-school case generally upheld the use of canines for sniffing items for the location of drugs as not constituting an invalid search, based upon a finding that no expectation of privacy extends to the airspace around an item and that this "public smell" is the equivalent of contraband being found in "plain sight" (*United States v. Place*, 462 U.S. 696 (1983)). In the Fifth Circuit case of *Horton v. Goose Creek Indep. School Dist.* 690 F.2d 470 (5th Cir. 1982), the use of drug sniffing dogs in schools for lockers and automobiles was upheld as improving the ability for authorities to detect an odor, in the same way that a flashlight enhances the ability to see in the dark. On the other hand, the court found that the sniffing of students did constitute a search, which would require individualized suspicion. The Maryland Attorney General issued an opinion in response to several questions posed about the use of drug sniffing dogs by law enforcement authorities in the Carroll County School System, and opined that "the use of drug-detecting dogs to sniff around lockers does not constitute a search" and "if a dog's actions single out a particular locker, a search warrant must be obtained before the inside of a locker may be searched." The opinion noted that school officials, on the other hand, are not required to secure a warrant when searching lockers under their existing legal authority (Op. Att'y Gen. No. 65-186 (1980).

### 11:59. How do school and police interact regarding student arrests?

Police needing to arrest students are directed to do so away from school premises whenever possible, but procedures dealing with arrests of students on school premises are set forth in COMAR 13A.08.01.12:

A. When possible and appropriate, arrest by police should be made during nonschool hours and away from the school premises.

B. When an arrest on school premises during the school hours is necessary, the responsible school official shall ascertain the facts from the arresting officer which will enable the school official to fully advise the parent or guardians and other school officials of the nature of the charge, the identity of the arresting officer, and the location of the student.

C. When an arrest has taken place on school premises or during school hours, every effort shall be made by school officials to inform the parent or guardians immediately and thereafter promptly to advise the local superintendent of schools.

D. Arrest on school premises during school hours shall be effectuated in such a manner as to avoid both embarrassment to the student being arrested and jeopardizing the safety and welfare of other students.

E. School officials may not permit questioning of a student under arrest on the school premises and shall request the arresting officer to remove the student from the premises as soon as practicable after the arrest is made.

## 11:60. How do school and police interact regarding student questioning?

Likewise, police questioning that is permitted on school premises, including investigations of suspected child abuse or neglect is controlled by COMAR 13A.08.01.13:

A. Police investigations involving the questioning of students may not be permitted on school premises unless in connection with a crime committed on the premises or in connection with an investigation which, if not immediately permitted, would compromise the success of that investigation or endanger the lives or safety of the students or other persons, provided, however, that a school official should be present throughout that questioning.

B. A local school system shall permit personnel from a local department of social services or a police officer to question a student on school premises during the school day in an investigation involving suspected child neglect or suspected child abuse under Family Law Article, Title 5, Subtitle 7, Annotated Code of Maryland. The following apply:

(1) The local superintendent or the superintendent's designee shall determine, after consultation with the individual from the local department of social services or the police officer, whether a school official shall be present during the questioning of a student pursuant to this section.

(2) Records and reports concerning child abuse or neglect are confidential, and unauthorized disclosure is a criminal offense under Article 88A, § 6(b), Annotated Code of Maryland.

C. Except as provided in §D of this regulation, whenever investigative questioning of students is permitted on the premises, the school official shall promptly advise the parent or guardians and the local superintendent's office of the nature of the investigation and such other details as may be required.

D. School officials are not required to notify parents or guardians of investigations on school premises involving suspected child neglect and suspected child abuse under Family Law Article, Title 5, Subtitle 7, Annotated Code of Maryland.

E. In the absence of an arrest, school officials may not authorize the removal of a student from school for the purpose of investigative questioning without the consent of the parent or guardians, except as provided below:

(1) A student may be removed from school premises if that student is a suspected victim of child abuse or neglect and the local department of social services has guardianship of the child or a court order to remove the child;

(2) The Superintendent or the Superintendent's designee shall ensure that prompt notification of a student's removal from school under this section is made to the student's parent or guardians.

## 11:61. How do school and police interact regarding student searches?

Police searches on school premises require a warrant, and are generally restricted to prevent imminent danger to students. COMAR 13A.08.01.14 sets forth the procedures for any such searches:

D. Police officers shall conduct searches of students and the school premises in accordance with their established policies and procedures.

E. A school official may not conduct a search of the person of a student at the request of a police officer unless a search warrant has been issued authorizing the search.

F. Every effort shall be made to conduct searches in a manner which will minimize disruption of the normal school routine and minimize embarrassment to students affected.

## 11:62. How do school and police interact regarding student offenses?

Finally, school officials have an obligation to report delinquent acts by students, including acts that would be a crime if committed by an adult, to law enforcement agencies according to COMAR 13A.08.01.15:

A. Delinquent acts are offenses committed by a person who is under 18 years old which would be crimes if committed by an adult. School officials shall promptly report to the responsible law enforcement agencies all delinquent acts coming to their attention whether occurring on or away from the school premises which involve students attending the particular school.

B. Delinquent acts do not include conduct which has been traditionally treated as a matter of discipline to be handled administratively by the particular school, except that all conduct of a serious nature should be promptly reported to the parent or guardians concerned.

## 11:63. What remedies are available to students subjected to unlawful discipline?

Available remedies include clearing or expunging the student's discipline records of the alleged offense, restoration of grades and transcripts, illegally seized evidence may be suppressed, and under some circumstances, the awarding of monetary damages has been allowed. In the case of *Carey v. Piphus*, 435 U.S. 247 (1978), the Supreme Court found that only nominal damages (not to exceed one dollar) could be awarded for a procedural violation of student due process where no other injury was attributable, as opposed to a more significant substantive due process violation. The Supreme Court, in *Morse v. Frederick*, 551 U.S. ___ (2007), unanimously agreed that the administrator deserved qualified immunity from personal liability for the discipline meted out to a student who displayed a banner with the message "Bong Hits 4 Jesus". The Ninth Circuit Court of Appeals decision that the administrator was subject to personal liability because there was a clear violation of the student's free speech rights was reversed.

# 12. Student Speech, Press and Dress

### 12:1. What is the constitutional basis for expression rights in the school setting?

The vast majority of school expression rights arise by virtue of the First Amendment to the U.S. Constitution. In the case of *Keyishian v. Board of Regents*, 385 U.S. 589 (1967), the Supreme Court struck down a law that was designed to require loyalty oaths in order to keep "subversive" individuals out of teaching, and in its holding the High Court spoke of the importance of free expression within the school setting, as they stated:

> Our Nation is deeply committed to safeguarding academic freedom, which is of transcendent value to all of us and not merely to the teachers concerned. That freedom is therefore a special concern of the First Amendment, which does not tolerate laws that cast a pall of orthodoxy over the classroom. "The vigilant protection of constitutional freedoms is nowhere more vital than in the community of American schools."… The classroom is peculiarly the "marketplace of ideas." The Nation's future depends upon leaders trained through wide exposure to that robust exchange of ideas which discovers truth "out of a multitude of tongues, [rather] than through any kind of authoritative selection."… Teachers and students must always remain free to inquire, to study and to evaluate, to gain new maturity and understanding; otherwise our civilization will stagnate and die.

The right of free expression is among the most protected rights in the history of this country, and it is beyond question that students do not "shed their constitutional rights to freedom of speech or expression at the schoolhouse gate" (*Tinker v. Des Moines Independent Community School District*, 393 U.S. 503 (1969)). *Tinker* is probably the most quoted freedom of expression case, where the Court upheld the student right to wear black armbands in protest of the Vietnam War.

### 12:2. How does the First Amendment apply to student expression rights?

The First Amendment to the U.S. Constitution is part of the Bill of Rights, which is comprised of the first ten constitutional amendments, and it states in pertinent part:

> Congress shall make no law ... abridging the freedom of speech, or of the press; or the right of the people peaceably to assemble, and to petition the government for a redress of grievances.

While it is true that students do possess First Amendment rights, it is also true that student expression rights in the school setting are not the same that adults possess in other settings (*Bethel School District No. 403 v. Fraser*, 478 U.S. 675 (1986)). The *Bethel* case upheld the suspension of a high school student who repeatedly used inappropriate sexual metaphors in a student assembly speech. For the first time in two decades, the Supreme Court recently considered the extent of student free speech rights and the authority of school administrators to discipline students for disruptive expression in the case of *Morse v. Frederick*, 551 U.S. ___ (2007), where a group of students displayed a banner that read "Bong Hits 4 Jesus" across the street from their high school during a school sponsored viewing of the passage of the Olympic Torch Relay. In finding for the school administrator's right to control speech advocating or celebrating illegal drug use, the Court held,

> School principals have a difficult job, and a vitally important one. When Frederick suddenly and unexpectedly unfurled his banner, Morse had to decide to act—or not act—on the spot. It was reasonable for her to conclude that the banner promoted illegal drug use—in violation of established school policy—and that failing to act would send a powerful message to the students in her charge, including Frederick, about how serious the school was about the dangers of illegal drug use. The First Amendment does not require schools to tolerate at school events student expression that contributes to those dangers.

## 12:3. How does the Fourteenth Amendment apply to student expression rights?

A valid question is how the First Amendment that starts with the phrase, "Congress shall make no law", applies to Maryland public schools that are under the control of county and state boards of education? The Supreme Court, in *Gitlow v. New York,* 268 U.S. 652 (1925), held that the Fourteenth Amendment makes the liberties granted under the Bill of Rights applicable to the states. Thus, the first ten amendments, which were specifically directed at Congress and the federal government, have made the states, and thus local school systems, equally responsible to protect the freedoms found in the First Amendment and the remainder of the first ten amendments.

## 12:4. What student speech is not constitutionally protected?

Speech that is obscene, vulgar, inflammatory, or defamatory is not entitled to constitutional protection. Thus, not all expression is considered as speech protected by the First Amendment. In *Bethel School District No. 403 v. Fraser*, 478 U.S. 675 (1986), the Supreme Court held that a student's vulgar and obscene speech was not entitled to constitutional protection and stated:

> We hold that petitioner School District acted entirely within its permissible authority in imposing sanctions upon Fraser in response to his offensively lewd and indecent speech. Unlike the sanctions imposed on the students wearing armbands in Tinker, the penalties imposed in this case were unrelated to any political viewpoint. The First Amendment does not prevent the school officials from determining that to permit a vulgar and lewd speech such as respondent's would undermine the school's basic educational mission. A high school assembly or classroom is no place for a sexually explicit monologue directed towards an unsuspecting audience of teenage students. Accordingly, it was perfectly appropriate for the school to disassociate itself to make the point to the pupils that vulgar speech and lewd conduct is wholly inconsistent with the "fundamental values" of public school education. Justice Black, dissenting in Tinker, made a point that is especially relevant in this case: "I wish therefore, ... to disclaim any purpose ... to hold that the Federal Constitution compels the teachers, parents, and elected school officials to surrender control of the American public school system to public school students."

## 12:5. What is constitutionally protected student speech?

Freedom of speech is a fundamental right of all Americans, and when speech is being placed under restrictions by schools, a determination of the validity of such restrictions must be made. Constitutionally protected student speech should satisfy a two-part test set forth in *Spence v. Washington*, 418 U.S. 405 (1974), which reversed a criminal conviction for displaying an American flag upside down with a peace symbol taped thereto. In applying the *Spence* test to determine whether student speech is constitutionally protected, the following questions would be posed:

1. Did the student intend to convey a particularized message?

2. Is the particularized message one that a reasonable observer would understand?

This principle was affirmed by a federal court in New Mexico in the case of *Bivens v. Albuquerque Public Schools*, 899 F. Supp. 556 (D. N.M. 1995), where a school district was permitted to ban the wearing of sagging pants, despite the student's claim of first amendment freedom of expression, further noting, "not every defiant act by a high school student is constitutionally protected speech."

### 12:6. What is school sponsored speech?

School sponsored speech is student expression that is promoted by the school and appears to represent the school, and the school is thus empowered to exercise greater control based upon legitimate pedagogical concerns to protect the educational environment and to ensure that such school related expression is consistent with the educational mission, vision, and goals of the school. In *Hazelwood School District v. Kuhlmeier*, 484 U.S. 260 (1988), the Supreme Court, in a case where the principal, claiming an invasion of student privacy, removed a school newspaper article which interviewed students on the subject of student pregnancy and birth control, defined school sponsored speech as "expressive activities that students, parents, and members of the public might reasonably perceive to bear the imprimatur of the school." In *Hazelwood,* the Court noted that the school may properly limit "speech that is, for example, ungrammatical, poorly written, inadequately researched, biased or prejudiced, vulgar or profane, or unsuitable for immature audiences" and further held "the standard articulated in Tinker for determining when a school may punish student expression need not also be the standard for determining when a school may refuse to lend its name and resources to the dissemination of student expression." Also in the *Hazelwood* decision, the Court enumerated six "intent factors" which help to determine the type of forum (see **12:9**, **12:10**, and **12:11**) that has been created; they are:

1. Whether the students produced the newspaper as part of the school curriculum;

2. Whether credits and grades were received by the students for the course;

3. Whether a faculty member provided oversight to the newspaper's production;

4. Whether the school ceased treating the newspaper as a curricular activity;

5. The extent of prior control exercised by the advisor and school administrator; and

6. The applicable written policy provisions of the local board of education.

## 12:7. What is personal expression?

Personal expression is generally given the highest level or constitutional protection and consists of student speech that conveys personal ideological views. Those ideological views are not school sponsored and do not give the appearance of being sanctioned by the school, thus the views expressed merely happen to be expressed at school and must be tolerated. In the *Tinker v. Des Moines Independent School District*, 393 U.S. 503 (1969), the Supreme Court upheld the right of students to wear black arm bands to protest the Vietnam War, and held:

> In our system, state-operated schools may not be enclaves of totalitarianism. School officials do not possess absolute authority over their students. Students in school as well as out of school are "persons" under our Constitution. They are possessed of fundamental rights which the State must respect, just as they themselves must respect their obligations to the State. In our system, students may not be regarded as closed-circuit recipients of only that which the State chooses to communicate. They may not be confined to the expression of those sentiments that are officially approved. In the absence of a specific showing of constitutionally valid reasons to regulate their speech, students are entitled to freedom of expression of their views.

## 12:8. What is commercial expression?

Commercial speech is not entitled to the same level of constitutional protection that is provided to expression that conveys a particular point of view. Schools that have banned advertisements of products or services that are illegal for student use, potentially harmful to students, or are beyond the maturity level of the students have been generally upheld, including alcohol, drug paraphernalia, and firearms. In the case of *Planned Parenthood v. Clark County School District*, 887 F.2d 935 (9th Cir. 1989), it was determined that the refusal to allow family planning advertisements was not a First Amendment violation because school newspapers are nonpublic forums, and that it was reasonable to exclude the advertisements because of a belief by the school that they would be controversial and would distract the student body from their educational goals. In the case of *Williams v Spencer*, 622 F.2d 1200 (4th Cir. 1980) the Fourth Circuit Court of Appeals held that a public school administrator had the authority to ban distribution of an underground newspaper on school grounds because of the inclusion of an advertisement for a "head shop" selling drug paraphernalia, based on a belief that the contents of the publication would endanger the health and safety of the students.

## 12:9. What is a public/open forum?

The classic example of a public or open forum is the courthouse square where all are welcome to gather and freely express any and all ideological viewpoints. In the case of *Hague v. CIO*, 37 U.S. 496 (1939), the Supreme Court spoke about the importance of the historical public forum noting:

> Wherever the title of streets and parks may rest, they have immemorially been held in trust for the use of the public and, time out of mind, have been used for purposes of assembly, communicating thoughts between citizens, and discussing public questions. Such use of the streets and public places has, from ancient times, been a part of the privileges, immunities, rights, and liberties of citizens. The privilege of a citizen of the United States to use the streets and parks for communication of views on national questions may be regulated in the interest of all; it is not absolute, but relative, and must be exercised in subordination to the general comfort and convenience, and in consonance with peace and good order; but it must not, in the guise of regulation, be abridged or denied.

In the case of *Perry Education Association v. Perry Local Educator's Association*, 460 U.S. 37 (1983), the Supreme Court in discussing a public forum before contrasting it with a nonpublic forum such as a public school, stated:

> In places which by long tradition or by government fiat have been devoted to assembly and debate, the rights of the State to limit expressive activity are sharply circumscribed. ... In these quintessential public forums, the government may not prohibit all communicative activity. For the State to enforce a content-based exclusion it must show that its regulation is necessary to serve a compelling state interest and that it is narrowly drawn to achieve that end. ... The State may also enforce regulations of the time, place, and manner of expression which are content-neutral, are narrowly tailored to serve a significant government interest, and leave open ample alternative channels of communication.

## 12:10. What is a nonpublic/closed forum?

Public schools exist for the purpose of educating students, not to provide a public forum for ideological expression, and thus public schools are nonpublic or closed forums where the school has significant latitude in guarding the school environment from expression that is not consistent with its educational purpose. In the case of *Perry Education Association v. Perry Local Educator's Association*,

460 U.S. 37 (1983), the Supreme Court in discussing a school nonpublic forum, stated:

> Public property which is not by tradition or designation a forum for public communication is governed by different standards. We have recognized that the "First Amendment does not guarantee access to property simply because it is owned or controlled by the government."… In addition to time, place, and manner regulations, the State may reserve the forum for its intended purposes, communicative or otherwise, as long as the regulation on speech is reasonable and not an effort to suppress expression merely because public officials oppose the speaker's view. As we have stated on several occasions, "[t]he State, no less than a private owner of property, has power to preserve the property under its control for the use to which it is lawfully dedicated."… Implicit in the concept of the nonpublic forum is the right to make distinctions in access on the basis of subject matter and speaker identity. These distinctions may be impermissible in a public forum but are inherent and inescapable in the process of limiting a nonpublic forum to activities compatible with the intended purpose of the property. The touchstone for evaluating these distinctions is whether they are reasonable in light of the purpose which the forum at issue serves.

### 12:11. What is a limited public/open forum?

Schools may chose to create a limited public or open forum that expands the normal range of permissible expression to identified groups, usually students, during non-instructional time for expressive activities that are not directly related to the course of study offered by the school. Limited public or open forums are most often governed by the Equal Access Act (20 U.S.C. §§ 4071-74), which is covered in detail in **Chapter 13**.

In the case of student publications that fail to meet the six *Hazelwood* "intent factors" set forth in **12:6** above, it is typical to find that the intent was to create a limited public forum, and thus, only reasonable time, place, and manner restrictions and content controls that are narrowly drawn to effectuate a compelling state interest, are permissible (*Kincaid v. Gibson*, 236 F.3d 342 (6th Cir. 2001)).

### 12:12. May a school exercise control over student speech in the school setting?

Yes, schools may exercise control over student personal speech in the school setting for a number of reasons, but certainly not in all cases. Among the reasons that schools may validly curtail student expression are: when a material and substantial disruption is created; when the rights of others are invaded; when the speech is vulgar, lewd, obscene, or plainly offensive; when the speech is school-sponsored; or when the school is acting on legitimate pedagogical concerns. In addition, schools may also establish time, place and manner restrictions under certain conditions.

## 12:13. What is a material and substantial disruption?

In the case of *Tinker v. Des Moines Independent School District*, 393 U.S. 503 (1969), the Supreme Court upheld the right of students to wear black arm bands to protest the Vietnam War, because no showing of disruption was made, but the Court also held:

> [C]onduct by the student, in class or out of it, which for any reason whether it stems from time, place, or type of behavior—materially disrupts classwork or involves substantial disorder or invasion of the rights of others is, of course, not immunized by the constitutional guarantee of freedom of speech.

Contrast the case of *Guzick v. Drebus*, 305 F. Supp. 472 (N.D. Ohio 1969), where a district court upheld school officials' total ban on buttons and insignia of all type, regardless of the message, unless related to a school activity. The school had seen actual racial disturbances for several years and students were wearing buttons with messages that exacerbated the racial tensions, for example, "White is Right" and "Say It Loud, Black and Proud". The court found that the policy was not overly broad simply because it precluded a student antiwar button which was not offensive, because the school applied the policy uniformly and fairly, and it was reasonably related to the prevention of disruption. The court believed that if the school allowed students to wear some buttons but not others additional disruption within the school would likely occur.

In order for a school to prohibit student expression based upon a stated disruption concern, the school must be able to demonstrate that it can reasonably forecast the occurrence of substantial disruption. In a case where students were prohibited from wearing a button with the word "scab" to protest replacement teachers during a legal teacher strike, the Ninth Circuit Court of Appeals found such prohibition unconstitutional. The Court in *Chandler v. McMinnville School District*, 978 F.2d 524 (9th Cir. 1992), stated "The passive expression of a viewpoint in the form of a button worn on one's clothing is certainly not in the class of those activities which inherently distract students and break down the regimentation of the classroom."

## 12:14. What is speech that is vulgar, lewd, obscene, or plainly offensive?

The most significant case regarding this area of speech is the *Bethel* case set forth in **12:4**, the actual text of Fraser's banned speech being:

> I know a man who is firm—he's firm in his pants, he's firm in his shirt, his character is firm—but most ... of all, his belief in you, the students of Bethel, is firm. Jeff Kuhlman is a man who takes his point and pounds it in. If necessary, he'll take an issue and nail it to the wall. He doesn't attack things in spurts—he drives hard, pushing and pushing until finally—he succeeds. Jeff is a man who will go to the very end—even the climax, for each and every one of you. So vote for Jeff for A. S. B. vice-president—he'll never come between you and the best our high school can be.

In another more recent case, *Pyle v. South Hadley School Committee*, 861 F. Supp. 157 (D. Mass. 1994), the court held that school board policy could prohibit student attire which displayed obscene, profane or lewd pictures. Students filed suit against the school district for adopting a dress code which banned T-shirts with messages reading: "Coed Naked Band: Do It To The Rhythm," and other slogans such as "See Dick Drink. See Dick Drive. See Dick Die. Don't be a Dick." The court upheld the entitlement of the school board to ban the T-shirts as vulgar and inconsistent with the school's educational mission. Literally hundreds of different T-shirts that are to some degree sexually suggestive are appearing on teens and pre-teens in schools, causing administrators to make difficult case by case decisions.

## 12:15. What are legitimate pedagogical concerns?

In *Hazelwood School District v. Kuhlmeier*, 484 U.S. 260 (1988), the Supreme Court, in a case where the principal, claiming an invasion of student privacy, removed a school newspaper article which interviewed students on the subject of student pregnancy and birth control, stated, "we hold that educators do not offend the First Amendment by exercising editorial control over the style and content of student speech in school-sponsored expressive activities so long as their actions are reasonably related to legitimate pedagogical concerns." The Court in *Hazelwood* gave examples of the sort of legitimate pedagogical concerns that would justify censorship by a school, noting "A school must also retain the authority to refuse to sponsor student speech that might reasonably be perceived to advocate drug or alcohol use, irresponsible sex, or conduct otherwise inconsistent with the shared values of a civilized social order, or to associate the school with any position other than neutrality on matters of political controversy."

## 12:16. What does it mean for speech to invade the rights of others?

Defamation is speech that invades the rights of others, a detailed explanation of the topic of defamatory speech is found at **9:31** through **9:40**. Harassing speech is another kind of unprotected speech that invades the rights of others and it is discussed in **12:24**.

## 12:17. What are time, place and manner restrictions?

Schools may nearly always control the time, place and manner in which student expression is presented, provided that the conditions are content neutral and equitably applied. The Supreme Court in the case of *Heffron v. International Society for Krishna Consciousness*, 452 U.S. 640 (1981), found constitutionally legitimate a restriction that limited distribution of materials to an assigned location, using valid time, place, and manner criteria. Since the rule was applied equally to all groups wanting to solicit at the fairgrounds, not making restrictions based on the content of a group's message, and because the state had an important interest in protecting the safety and convenience of the fair's patrons, the restrictions were held to be legitimate. The Court found that allowing all religious, nonreligious, and commercial groups to move about the grounds distributing literature and soliciting funds would result in widespread disorder and be potentially dangerous to the fair's visitors.

In the school setting, it has been similarly held that reasonable administrative regulations as to time, place, and manner of distribution of student expression may be set, provided that they are narrowly drawn to promote the orderly conduct of school activities and are not designed to stifle expression (*Shanley v. Northeast ISD*, 462 F.2d 960 (5th Cir. 1972)).

## 12:18. What is viewpoint discrimination?

Viewpoint discrimination occurs when schools act to prevent or punish speech that conveys an unpopular or unpleasant message, rather than basing the decision to exclude student expression on valid pedagogical concerns or upon some other constitutionally recognized grounds. The federal circuits are split on the legal question as to what degree, under the *Hazelwood* case, educators are afforded discretion to prohibit student speech which they find to be inconsistent with legitimate educational or pedagogical concerns, regardless of viewpoint neutrality.

## 12:19. What is prior restraint?

Efforts by schools or school districts to exercise control over student speech before it has occurred is generally frowned upon by the courts, but the same courts are much more open to the imposition of discipline when student expression has gone too far. In the case of *Fujishima v. Board of Education*, 460 F.2d 1355 (7th Cir. 1972), a rule that required approval of the district superintendent before publications could be distributed in schools was found to be unconstitutional prior restraint in violation of the First Amendment, although it was noted that schools could impose time, place, and manner restrictions, and punish students who violated those rules. A Fourth Circuit case found that a school's requirement of prior permission of the principal for the distribution of any printed materials by students was constitutionally invalid because of the lack of any criteria for determining whether to grant or deny permission, and the absence of an established speedy review process after the principal's decision in order to provide procedural safeguards (*Quarterman v. Byrd*, 453 F.2d 54 (1971)).

### 12:20. Do school policies have a bearing on student expression?

Yes, policies that are narrowly tailored and not overbroad may validly act to control student expression, provided that the policy is tied to genuine pedagogical concerns and does not constitute improper viewpoint discrimination (*San Antonio Independent School District v. Rodriguez*, 411 U.S. 1 (1973)). In *Shanley v. Northeast ISD*, 462 F.2d 960 (5th Cir. 1972), there are five criteria set forth to determine whether a policy requiring prior review of written materials is sufficiently narrowly drawn to be constitutionally valid, they are:

1. Contains clear and specific criteria for prohibited expression that will inform a reasonably intelligent student as to what may or may not be written.

2. Contains clear and specific means for submission of proposed written materials to administration.

3. Contains a reasonably brief time period for an administrative decision.

4. Contains clear and reasonable appeal procedure.

5. Contains a reasonably brief time period for the appeal to be decided.

### 12:21. May a school establish a student dress code?

Yes, although the Supreme Court has not ruled on the constitutionality of dress codes in relation to the First Amendment rights of students. Typically, personal appearance and clothing may qualify for constitutional protection under the First Amendment if it conveys a religious or political message. It is generally not sufficient justification for a student to object to a dress code on the basis that it does not allow the expression of individuality. The Sixth Circuit Court of Appeals issued a ruling regarding a Kentucky high school's dress code in *Castorina v. Madison County School Board*, 246 F.3d 536 (6th Cir. 2001). The court highlighted several criteria that are crucial in determining whether school dress code interferes with student's constitutional rights, including:

1. If the school policy appears to be viewpoint specific as in *Tinker*, the courts will apply a higher level of scrutiny to the proposed regulation;

2. School districts will be allowed more discretion in prohibiting the clothing that is obscene, vulgar or worn in a manner that disrupts school activity or causes unrest during the school day; and

3. If the student dress could be considered to be "school-sponsored," the school district will be allowed more discretion in prohibiting the clothing when the restrictions are reasonably related to legitimate pedagogical concerns.

### 12:22. May a school exercise control over student attire?

Yes, but not in all cases (see **12:12**). In the case of *Wallace v. Ford*, 346 F. Supp. 156 (E. Dist. Ark. 1972), the court found that it was appropriate for schools to prohibit suggestive or immodest clothing in school. However, in *Newsom v. Albemarle County School Board*, 354 F.3d 249 (4th Cir. 2003), the Fourth Circuit Court of Appeals found against the school board, preventing it from enforcing a portion of its dress code against a student who had been ordered not to wear a shirt depicting men holding firearms superimposed on the letters, "NRA" positioned above the phrase, "Shooting Sports Camp". The court found the dress code, which prohibited, "messages that relate to ... weapons," was overly broad because it burdened too much expression protected by the First Amendment. The court noted that the school board failed to produce any evidence that clothing worn by students containing messages related to weapons had caused substantial disruption to school operations or interfered with the rights of others.

### 12:23. May a school exercise control over suspected gang attire?

Yes. In the case of *Jenglin v. San Jacinto Unified School District*, 872 F. Supp. 1459 (C.D. Cal. 1993), an anti-gang dress code was upheld which prohibited professional sports team clothing that was used as a gang symbol, finding that it did not offend the Constitution because of the real threat of violence created by the gang presence. If a school district can't demonstrate that a gang problem exists, the justification for such a rule will not hold up to constitutional scrutiny. In *Olesen v. Board of Education of School District No. 228*, 676 F. Supp. 820 (N.D. Ill. 1987), students challenged the constitutionality of an anti-gang rule prohibiting the wearing of earrings by male students. The court upheld the policy finding that it did not violate the student's right to free speech and expression, because the only message conveyed was in regard to the student's individuality, which was not protected by the First Amendment. The court was not troubled by a policy allowing females to wear earrings while not allowing males to wear earrings because the gender-based classification was substantially related to the legitimate educational objective of discouraging gang membership and activities.

### 12:24. May a school exercise control over harassing speech and symbols?

Possibly, since the Supreme Court decision in *Chaplinsky v. New Hampshire*, 315 U.S. 568 (1942), it has been clear that "fighting words" are not protected speech under the First Amendment. Student expression rights have also been limited when the expression mocks, demeans, or ridicules other persons or groups (*Nitzberg v. Parks*, 525 F.2d 378 (4th Cir. 1975)). In the case of *Wisconsin v. Mitchell*, 508 U.S. 476 (1993), the High Court in upholding a law that increased criminal penalties when an aggravated battery resulted from the harm caused by expression of bias toward the victim, found:

> To be sure, our cases reject the view that an apparently limitless variety of conduct can be labeled "speech" whenever the person engaging in the conduct intends thereby to express an idea.... Thus, a physical assault is not by any stretch of the imagination expressive conduct protected by the First Amendment ... Violence or other types of potentially expressive activities that produce special harms distinct from their communicative impact ... are entitled to no constitutional protection ... The First Amendment does not protect violence.

On the other hand, when only speech is involved, rather than expression that causes harm to occur, the Supreme Court in *R.A.V. v. St. Paul*, 505 U.S. 377 (1992), struck down a conviction for allegedly burning a cross in the yard of a black family in the middle of the night. The prosecution was based on a local ordinance which provided that "whoever places on public property a symbol, object, appellation characterization or graffiti, including but not limited to, a burning cross or Nazi swastika, which one knows or has reasonable grounds to know arouses anger, alarm or resentment in others on the basis of race, color, creed, religion or gender commits disorderly conduct and shall be guilty of a misdemeanor." The Court found that the ordinance, on its face, violated the First Amendment because the law was impermissibly content-based. They held that even when the government is attempting to regulate a supposedly "unprotected" category; it may not do so in a content-based manner, noting that there were ample content-neutral options.

### 12:25. May a school exercise control over Confederate flag attire?

Possibly, the wearing of Confederate flag attire has generated much controversy and a number of conflicting cases nationwide. In the case of *West v.*

*Derby Unified School District No. 260*, 206 F.3d 1258 (2000), the Tenth Circuit Court of Appeals upheld the suspension of a middle school student for drawing a confederate flag and displaying it in school, the court gave the following rationale for its finding:

> [S]chool officials in Derby had evidence from which they could reasonably conclude that possession and display of Confederate flag images, when unconnected with any legitimate educational purpose, would likely lead to a material and substantial disruption of school discipline. The district experienced a series of racial incidents.... some of which were related to the Confederate flag. The fact that a full-fledged brawl had not yet broken out over the Confederate flag does not mean that the district was required to sit and wait for one.... In this case, the district had a reasonable basis for forecasting disruption from display of such items at school, and its prohibition was therefore permissible.... it was not limited to prohibiting and punishing conduct only after it caused a disturbance.

### 12:26. May a school exercise control over speech regarding sexual orientation?

Possibly, schools have recently been faced with a growing number of disputes regarding student expression in support of or in opposition to homosexuality. Many students participate in a "Day of Silence" in April to protest discrimination against homosexuals, and schools have been divided over how to handle student silence during instructional time. An openly lesbian teen was disciplined for wearing a T-shirt with the message "Barbie is a Lesbian". On the other side of the dilemma, students have participated in a "Day of Truth" to counter the "Day of Silence" and have been disciplined for wearing T-shirts with the messages "Homosexuality is Shameful" and "Be Happy, Not Gay". Another student was disciplined for using the phrase "That's so gay" and complained that in current teen culture the meaning of the phrase is "That's so stupid" and not about sexual orientation. All of these disputes have resulted in litigation, and several are working their way up through the court system. It is unclear whether such statements of beliefs can be controlled as harassing expression when not directed at any specific individual and absent disruption of the educational environment.

### 12:27. May a school exercise control over the wearing of headgear?

Yes. In the case of *Isaacs v. Board of Education of Howard County*, 40 F. Supp.2d 335 (D. Md. 1999), a student wore a multicolored headwrap to school and was found to be in violation the school's "no hats" policy. The student asserted that her primary motivation in wearing the headwrap was to celebrate her African-

American and Jamaican heritage. The Court found that the school system's interest in banning "hats" was compelling for the following reasons:

1. Hats can cause conflict and "horseplay" in the school hallways;

2. Hats can obscure a view of students wearing them and may cause signs of substance abuse or health problems to be missed;

3. Hats can block other student's view of the board;

4. Hats can facilitate the hiding of contraband; and

5. Hats foster a less respectful and focused climate for learning.

The Court in *Isaacs* further noted that the policy was not adopted to limit student expression, and that other means of expressing the student's cultural heritage remained available. The Court also had no trouble finding the policy content-neutral despite the fact that religiously required headgear was allowed under the policy.

### 12:28. May a school exercise control over student hairstyle and grooming?

No, not in Maryland or the Fourth Circuit, although most other circuits have permitted schools to control hairstyle and grooming, at least to some extent. The Fourth Circuit Court of Appeals overturned a school district policy banning long hair on males, in the case of *Massie v. Henry*, 455 F.2d 779 (4th Cir. 1972), and in its decision stated:

> Whether the right of a male to wear long hair and to have long or fulsome side burns is a constitutionally protected right is a question which has given birth to a rash of recent litigation resulting in conflicting adjudications. And if the right is recognized as a constitutionally protected one, there is a similar lack of agreement as to its precise nature, that is, the chapter and verse of the Constitution which protects it. Unquestionably, the issue is current because there is abroad a trend for the male to dress himself more extravagantly both in the nature, cut and color of his clothing and the quantity and mode of his facial and tonsorial adornment. The shift in fashion has been more warmly embraced by the young, … With respect to hair, this is no more than a harkening back to the fashion of earlier years. For example, many of the founding fathers, as well as General Grant and General Lee, wore their hair (either real or false) in a style comparable to that adopted by plaintiffs. Although there exists no depiction of Jesus Christ, either reputedly or historically accurate, He has always been shown with hair at least the length of that of plaintiffs. If the validity and enforcement of the

regulation in issue is sustained, it follows that none of these persons would have been permitted to attend Tuscola Senior High School.

### 12:29. May a school require the wearing of uniforms?

Possibly. The first public school in this country known to have adopted the wearing of uniforms was Cherry Hill Elementary in Baltimore, Maryland, in 1987. Presently, no state legislature or state department of education mandates the use of student uniforms. Currently, more than twenty states, including Maryland, have passed laws or state regulations authorizing districts or schools to require uniforms. In the Maryland case of *John and Mary Mattingly v. Prince George's County Board of Education*, MSBE Op. No. 04-10 (2004), the Maryland State Board of Education upheld a decision of the county board which involuntarily transferred a student from an elementary school with a mandatory school uniform policy to another elementary school that did not require the wearing of a school uniform. The student being transferred for failure to comply with the mandatory uniform policy made the rather unique but unsuccessful argument that a belief in Druidism provided a constitutionally protected religious exception from complying with the uniform policy.

The U.S. Court of Appeals for the Fifth Circuit in the case of *Canady v. Bossier Parish School Board*, 240 F.3d 437 (5th Cir. 2001), upheld the constitutionality of a mandatory public school uniform policy in a Louisiana school district with a goal of "improving the educational process" in a manner that was "viewpoint-neutral." The Court further stated "the school board's uniform policy will pass constitutional scrutiny if it furthers an important or substantial government interest; if the interest is unrelated to the suppression of student expression; and if the incidental restrictions on First Amendment activities are no more than is necessary to facilitate that interest." The Court found that the resulting reduction in disciplinary problems constituted an important and substantial government interest and noted that students were still free to express themselves through other mediums during the school day.

### 12:30. May a school exercise control over student walkouts, boycotts, etc?

Yes, schools may discipline students that engage in walkout and boycotts, as those types of activities are harmful to the educational mission of a school, because students do not learn when they do not participate in the instructional program, and such activities are harmful to the learning environment (*Tate v. Board of Education*, 453 F.2d 975 (8th Cir. 1972)). In *Dodd v Rambis*, 535 F. Supp. 23 (S.D. Ind. 1981), a United States District Court upheld the suspension of students for distributing a leaflet promoting a student walkout. In ruling for the school system, the court was persuaded that because there had been a prior walkout of students, the actions regarding the leaflet distribution were appropriate because of the relationship between the distribution of leaflets and possible material disruption of school activities.

## 12:31. May a school exercise control over school newspapers and publications?

Yes, under the decision in *Hazelwood School District v. Kuhlmeier*, 484 U.S. 260 (1988), The Supreme Court upheld a school principal's action to remove two articles from the student newspaper. One article described students' experience with pregnancy and the other discussed the impact of divorce on specific students at the school. The principal believed that the stories could identify the students and thus pose privacy concerns, and that references to sexual activity and birth control were age inappropriate for a number of the younger students. The Supreme Court held that where a school sponsors an expressive activity that students and others may reasonably perceive to represent the school's views the school's ability to control student speech is much greater than in the *Tinker* case. Applying the "reasonable relation" test, the Court found that the principal acted reasonably, based on the facts possessed by the principal. The exclusion of the articles was reasonably related to the school objectives of defending privacy interests, protecting young students from age inappropriate materials, and teaching journalistic evenhandedness.

In *Gambino v Fairfax County School Board*, 564 F.2d 157 (4th Cir. 1977), the Fourth Circuit Court of Appeals heard a Virginia case involving a high school principal's decision to not allow the publishing of certain portions of a student's article in the school newspaper. The principal agreed to publish data from a student survey regarding attitudes toward birth control, but was not willing to include contraceptive information. The student editors demanded that the entire article be published. In finding in favor of the students, the Court noted the lack of several of the six intent factors set forth in *Hazelwood* (see **12:6**) and accordingly found that the student publication had developed into a "public forum" for student opinions over time and thus was no longer susceptible to school content regulation.

## 12:32. May a school exercise control over underground publications?

Possibly. An underground newspaper is a student publication that is not affiliated with the school and is published apart from any school class and without school materials or assistance. A school may not exercise the same level of control allowable for school-sponsored publications, but some controls may be valid. After the Supreme Court decision in *Hazelwood* (see **12:6**), underground newspapers became even more popular, in an attempt by students to avoid the greater ability to censor granted to administrators with respect to school sponsored publications. In

*Fujishima v. Board of Education*, 460 F.2d 1355 (7th Cir. 1972), three students were suspended for distributing underground leaflets without prior district approval. The rule that required approval of the district superintendent before publications could be distributed in schools was found to be unconstitutional, although it was noted that schools could impose time, place, and manner restrictions, and punish students who violated those rules. However, the school board would have to inform students of any rules regarding time, place and manner of distribution and it could not require the students to apply for approval of time, place and manner each time they wished to distribute something.

### 12:33. May a school exercise control over student in-school computer use?

Yes, schools are free to adopt "Acceptable Use Policies" with regard to student in-school computer use. Schools may require students and their parents to agree to multiple limitations and restrictions on student use of school system computers in order to be allowed the use of the equipment. School districts are increasingly blocking student access to social networking websites such as MySpace and Facebook.

### 12:34. May a school exercise control over student out-of-school Internet expression?

Possibly. Courts have been divided regarding the level of control that schools may exercise with respect to student out-of-school Internet expression. In the case of *J.S. ex rel. H.S. v. Bethlehem Area School District*, 569 A.2d 638 (Pa. 2002), the Pennsylvania Supreme Court held that a student's online depictions of a decapitated teacher and solicitation of donations to have the teacher killed amounted to a material disruption and warranted expulsion. On the other hand, discipline for student blogs that merely consist of criticism of their schools or their teachers usually does not withstand First Amendment scrutiny. In *Beussink v. Woodland School District*, 30 F. Supp. 2d 1175 (E.D. Mo. 1998), a federal judge in Missouri found that a student's blog containing vulgar criticism of his school was not a material disruption and could not be the basis for discipline, stating:

> In order for the State in the person of school officials to justify prohibition of a particular expression of opinion, it must be able to show that its action was caused by something more than a mere desire to avoid the discomfort and unpleasantness that always accompany an unpopular viewpoint. Certainly where there is no finding and no showing that engaging in the forbidden conduct would "materially and substantially interfere with the requirements of appropriate discipline in the operation of the school," the prohibition can not be sustained.

Two cases came before the Maryland State Board of Education on appeal in 2000, both upheld decisions by the Montgomery County Board of Education to discipline students for websites created off school grounds that nonetheless were found to create a substantial disruption and a material interference with school activities. In the first case, a student created an unofficial website for his high school class of 2001 in which a message board was set up that featured numerous death threats and obscene statements toward other students (*Aziz Barimani v. Montgomery County Board of Education*, MSBE Op. No. 00-30 (2000)). In the second case, the website asked students to rate certain female classmates on specific (and lewd) sexual traits, and the females students affected suffered significant indignity and embarrassment (*Tommy Kuka v. Montgomery County Board of Education*, MSBE Op. No. 00-51 (2000)). The line between online speech that is harassing, threatening or disruptive and that which is merely offensive and thus not subject to school control is unclear, and will be played out in schools and courts for years to come.

## 12:35. May a school exercise control over the books available in the school library?

Possibly. In the case of *Board of Education v. Pico*, 457 U.S. 853 (1982), the Supreme Court considered a First Amendment claim by students who objected to the local board of education's removal of certain books from the school library because the board found the content to be objectionable. The Court in *Pico* overturned the local board decision to remove the books and found in favor of the students, stating:

> For as this case is presented to us, it does not involve textbooks, or indeed any books that Island Trees students would be required to read. Respondents do not seek in this Court to impose limitations upon their school Board's discretion to prescribe the curricula of the Island Trees schools. On the contrary, the only books at issue in this case are library books, books that by their nature are optional rather than required reading. Our adjudication of the present case thus does not intrude into the classroom, or into the compulsory courses taught there. Furthermore, even as to library books, the action before us does not involve the acquisition of books. Respondents have not sought to compel their school Board to add to the school library shelves any books that students desire to read. Rather, the only action challenged in this case is the removal from school libraries of books originally placed there by the school authorities, or without objection from them.

## 12:36. May a school exercise control over student rights to assemble?

Possibly. *Lawrence University Bicentennial Commission v. City of Appleton*, 409 F. Supp. 1319 (E.D. Wis. 1976), is a case involving a group of students who applied for permission to rent a high school gym to host a public lecture by Angela Davis. Their application was denied by the Board of Education, as the school policy stated that school buildings were not to be used for religious or political activities unless the activity was nonpartisan or nondenominational. The student group claimed to meet the standards set by the board, which had previously allowed the League of Women Voters and political candidates to use the facility. There was also no basis presented to find that the proposed lecture would result in disruption. The Federal District Court directed that the student group be allowed to use the high school gym for the lecture and found that the political and religious prohibition in the policy was invalid, noting that the school was regulating speech improperly on the basis of content. The decision held that when a school opens its doors to some groups, it is limited in its ability to restrict access to groups whose views it might not share.

# 13. Church/State Relations and Equal Access Act

### 13:1. What provisions of the U.S. Constitution govern church/state relations?

The vast majority of school church/state relations cases arise by virtue of the First Amendment to the U.S. Constitution which is specifically limited in its application to Congress. The Supreme Court, in *Gitlow v. New York,* 268 U.S. 652 (1925), held that the Fourteenth Amendment makes the liberties granted under the Bill of Rights applicable to the states. Thus, the first ten amendments, which were specifically directed at Congress and the federal government, have made the states, and thus local school systems, equally responsible to protect the freedoms found in the First Amendment and the remainder of the first ten amendments.

### 13:2. How does the First Amendment pertain to church/state relations?

The First Amendment to the U.S. Constitution is part of the Bill of Rights, which is comprised of the first ten constitutional amendments, and it states in pertinent part:

> Congress shall make no law respecting an establishment of religion, or prohibiting the free exercise thereof...

There are two separate portions of the First Amendment dealing with church/state matters which are known as the Establishment Clause and the Free Exercise Clause, and it should be noted that these two clauses are often in seeming conflict with each other in the school setting. Administrators considering First Amendment religious matters should take care to attempt to view any such issue through the lens of both the Establishment Clause and the Free Exercise Clause prior to making a decision that may have significant legal ramifications.

### 13:3. What is the Establishment Clause and what is its purpose?

The Establishment Clause provides, "Congress shall make no law respecting an establishment of religion". Obviously, schools are not in the business of establishing religions, but the purpose of the Establishment Clause exists to prohibit schools and their staff members from favoring a religion in their policies, regulations, or practices. Furthermore, schools and their staff members must avoid actions that would in any way proselytize or seek to convert the students under their charge. In the case of *Everson v. Board of Education*, 330 U.S. 1 (1947), the Supreme Court in upholding a New Jersey law which allowed reimbursements of money to parents who sent their children to private school on buses operated by the public transportation system, held:

The "establishment of religion" clause of the First Amendment means at least this: Neither a state nor the Federal Government can set up a church. Neither can pass laws which aid one religion, aid all religions, or prefer one religion over another. Neither can force nor influence a person to go to or to remain away from church against his will or force him to profess a belief or disbelief in any religion. No person can be punished for entertaining or professing religious beliefs or disbeliefs, for church attendance or non-attendance. No tax in any amount, large or small, can be levied to support any religious activities or institutions, whatever they may be called, or whatever form they may adopt to teach or practice religion. Neither a state nor the Federal Government can, openly or secretly, participate in the affairs of any religious organizations or groups and vice versa. In the words of Jefferson, the clause against establishment of religion by law was intended to erect "a wall of separation between church and State."

It is important for school administrators to remember that the Establishment Clause is applicable to the school and its teachers and administrators but does not prevent students from expressing religious viewpoints in an appropriate manner.

### 13:4. How is a violation of the Establishment Clause identified?

In what is probably the most prominent Supreme Court religion case, a tripartite (three part) test was adopted in a case where Pennsylvania and Rhode Island state statutes provided for direct aid to parochial schools, restricting that the money only be spent for secular instruction (*Lemon v. Kurtzman*, 403 U.S. 602 (1971)). The *Lemon* test continues to be the primary method used by the courts for determining whether an Establishment Clause violation has occurred, but there has been broad dissatisfaction with the test and several competing alternatives have been proposed. In fact in the case of *Lamb's Chapel v. Center Moriches Union Free School District*, 508 U.S. 384 (1993), Justice Scalia, in a concurring opinion stated, "Like some ghoul in a late-night horror movie that repeatedly sits up in its grave and shuffles abroad, after being repeatedly killed and buried, *Lemon* stalks our Establishment Clause jurisprudence once again, frightening the little children and school attorneys…"

One alternative to *Lemon* is a coercion test, where the government action would be invalidated if it directly or indirectly coerced the profession of a religion. The coercion test was described by the Supreme Court, in a case which found that a school's invitation of a clergy member to give a graduation invocation was prohibited, in *Lee v. Weisman*, 505 U.S. 577 (1992), by the following language:

The principle that government may accommodate the free exercise of religion does not supersede the fundamental limitations imposed by the Establishment Clause, which guarantees at a minimum that a government may not coerce anyone to support or participate in religion or its exercise, or otherwise act in a way which "establishes a [state] religion or religious faith, or tends to do so."

A second stricter alternative test is an endorsement test where the government action would be invalidated if it had the purpose of endorsing religion. Justice O'Connor described the endorsement test in a concurring opinion in the case of *County of Allegheny v. American Civil Liberties Union*, 492 U.S. 573 (1989), which prohibited several public religious displays in the city of Pittsburgh, stating:

> As a theoretical matter, the endorsement test captures the essential command of the Establishment Clause, namely, that government must not make a person's religious beliefs relevant to his or her standing in the political community by conveying a message "that religion or a particular religious belief is favored or preferred."

## 13:5. What is the *Lemon* Test?

In the case of *Lemon v. Kurtzman*, 403 U.S. 602 (1971), two state laws from Rhode Island and Pennsylvania were being challenged based upon their provision of financial aid to sectarian schools. In finding that the Establishment Clause was violated in both cases, the Supreme Court crafted the three criteria that became known as the *Lemon* Test, finding:

> First, the statute must have a secular legislative purpose; second, its principal or primary effect must be one that neither advances or inhibits religion; finally, the statute must not foster an excessive government entanglement with religion.

The three prongs of the *Lemon* test as applied to schools are thus:

1. Does the school's action have a secular (or non-religious) purpose?

2. Does it have a primary effect that neither advances nor inhibits religion?

3. Does it foster an excessive entanglement of government with religion?

## 13:6. What does it mean to have a secular purpose?

The "secular purpose" test first appeared in the case of *Abington v. Schemmp*, 374 U.S. 203 (1963), which involved a Pennsylvania Statute requiring that ten Bible verses be read in public schools, and a Maryland law (from the famous Madalyn Murray O'Hair case) allowing for daily Bible reading and the recitation of the Lord's Prayer in public schools. The Court found that neither program had a secular purpose. Under the "secular purpose" test which was later to become the first prong of the *Lemon* test, the Supreme Court found that each of the laws violated the Establishment Clause. An example of a school action based on religious grounds yet with a valid secular purpose is the closing of schools for religious holidays because of the resulting negative impact on the learning environment when significant numbers of students and staff are absent.

### 13:7. What does it mean to have a primary effect that neither advances nor inhibits religion?

The "primary effect" test also first appeared in the case of *Abington v. Schemmp*, 374 U.S. 203 (1963), which involved a Pennsylvania Statute requiring that ten Bible verses be read in public schools, and a Maryland law allowing for daily Bible reading and the recitation of the Lord's Prayer in public schools. The Court under the "primary effect" test, that was later to become the second prong of the *Lemon* test, found that both challenged laws had the primary effect of advancing religion in violation of the Establishment Clause. An example of a school action based on religious grounds yet with a valid primary effect that neither advances nor inhibits religion is the closing of schools for religious holidays because of resulting negative impact on the learning environment when significant numbers of students and staff are absent.

### 13:8. What does it mean to foster an excessive entanglement of government with religion?

The third and final prong of the *Lemon* test was first set forth in the *Lemon* case itself. In the case of *Lemon v. Kurtzman*, 403 U.S. 602 (1971), two state laws from Rhode Island and Pennsylvania were being challenged based upon their provision of financial aid to sectarian schools. In addition to citing the previously recognized "secular purpose" test and "primary effect" test, the Court in *Lemon* added a third test, that no excessive entanglement of government and religion exist, and found that the test was violated by the challenged laws. A more recent example of applying the "excessive entanglement" test is found in the case of *Board of Education of Kiryas Joel v. Grumet*, 512 U.S. 687 (1994), where the Supreme Court considered a New York law which created a special school district comprised solely of a Hasidim Jewish Village. The Board of Education of that district operated only a special education school, and the rest of the school-age children attended a publicly funded religious school. The Court held that one of the primary principles of the Establishment Clause is that the "government should not prefer one religion to another, or religion to irreligion." The law was found to excessively entangle government with religion by its establishment of a grant to run a public school based upon purely religious tenants and resulting in a "purposeful and forbidden fusion of government and religious function."

Later in *Agostini v. Felton*, 521 U.S. 203 (1997), the Supreme Court reversed a previous decision and upheld a New York City program that sent public school teachers into parochial schools to provide remedial education to disadvantaged children. The Court discussed the excessive entanglement prong of the *Lemon* test and stated:

> Regardless of how we have characterized the issue, however, the factors we use to assess whether an entanglement is "excessive" are similar to the factors we use to examine "effect." That is, to assess entanglement, we have looked to "the character and purposes of the institutions that are benefited, the nature of the aid that the State provides, and the resulting relationship between the government and religious authority." … Not all entanglements, of course, have the effect of advancing or inhibiting religion. Interaction between church and state is inevitable…and we have always tolerated some level of involvement between the two. Entanglement must be "excessive" before it runs afoul of the Establishment Clause.

## 13:9. What is the Coercion Test?

One possible alternative to the *Lemon* test is a coercion test where the government action would be invalidated if it directly or indirectly coerced the profession of a religion. The coercion test was described by the Supreme Court in a case which found that a school's invitation of a clergy member to give a graduation invocation was prohibited under the Establishment Clause, *Lee v. Weisman*, 505 U.S. 577 (1992). The Court held:

> The principle that government may accommodate the free exercise of religion does not supersede the fundamental limitations imposed by the Establishment Clause, which guarantees at a minimum that a government may not coerce anyone to support or participate in religion or its exercise, or otherwise act in a way which "establishes a [state] religion or religious faith, or tends to do so."

This test was proposed by Justice Kennedy in his dissent in the case of *County of Allegheny v. American Civil Liberties Union*, 492 U.S. 573 (1989), which prohibited several public religious displays in the city of Pittsburgh, and essentially suggests that a law can be constitutional even if it recognizes or accommodates a religion, as long as its demonstration of support does not appear to coerce individuals to support or participate in a religion. Thus under the coercion test the government action does not violate the Establishment Clause unless it provides direct aid to religion in a way that would tend to establish a state church, or coerces people to support or participate in religion against their will.

### 13:10. What is the Endorsement Test?

A second less permissive alternative to the *Lemon* test is an endorsement test where the government action would be invalidated if it had the purpose of endorsing religion. Justice O'Connor described the endorsement test in a concurring opinion in the case of *County of Allegheny v. American Civil Liberties Union*, 492 U.S. 573 (1989), which prohibited several public religious displays in the city of Pittsburgh, stating:

> As a theoretical matter, the endorsement test captures the essential command of the Establishment Clause, namely, that government must not make a person's religious beliefs relevant to his or her standing in the political community by conveying a message "that religion or a particular religious belief is favored or preferred."

Justice O'Connor in the case of *Lynch v. Donnelly*, 465 U.S. 668 (1984), involving a Rhode Island public Christmas display, created this test which would find an Establishment Clause violation if a law favors one religion over another in a way that makes some people feel like outsiders and others feel like insiders. The endorsement test asks whether a particular government action amounts to an endorsement of religion. The endorsement test has occasionally been subsumed into the first two prongs of the *Lemon* test by asking if the challenged government action has the purpose or effect of advancing or endorsing religion. The endorsement test is most often applied in situations where the government is engaged in communicative activities, and challenges such as religious symbols on government property may be considered in light of this test.

### 13:11. What is the Free Exercise Clause and what is its purpose?

The Free Exercise Clause found in the First Amendment provides, "Congress shall make no law respecting an establishment of religion, or prohibiting the free exercise thereof…" Applicable to states and therefore schools by virtue of the Fourteenth Amendment, the Free Exercise Clause in the school setting essentially states that schools shall take no action prohibiting the free exercise of religion by their students or staff. Although the language sounds absolute, the courts have placed some limits on the free exercise of religion. For example, courts would not hold that the First Amendment protects the right to miss an excessive number of school days, such as every Friday, even if some religion required it (*Commonwealth v. Bey*, 70 A.2d 693 (Pa. Super. Ct. 1950)). The Supreme Court has interpreted this clause to mean that the freedom to hold religious beliefs is absolute, but the freedom to act out those beliefs is not (*Cantwell v. State of Connecticut*, 310 U.S. 296 (1940)). School-related free exercise questions usually arise when a student or staff member's obligation to comply with secular purposed school policies conflicts with that student or staff member's religious beliefs or practices. If a school policy specifically singled out a specific religion or particular religious practice, it would almost certainly violate the Free Exercise Clause. The most challenging Free Exercise controversies arise when a school policy is both generally applicable and religiously neutral but yet has the accidental or unintentional consequence of hindering a particular religious practice or belief.

Under Maryland law, it is a crime to interfere with an individual's Free Exercise rights under certain specific conditions. Md. Code Ann., Crim. Law Art., § 10-303, provides:

> § 10-303. Obstructing exercise of religious belief.
>
> A person may not, by force or threat of force, obstruct or attempt to obstruct another in the free exercise of that person's religious beliefs.

The Free Exercise Clause was applied in *Wisconsin v. Yoder*, 406 U.S. 205 (1972), where Wisconsin's compulsory school-attendance law required Amish children to attend public or private school until reaching age 16, but the Amish declined to comply on religious grounds, and the Supreme Court held, "A regulation neutral on its face may, in its application, nonetheless offend the constitutional requirement for governmental neutrality if it unduly burdens the free exercise of religion." In the *Yoder* case, the Amish religious belief, when coupled with an alternative structured vocational program, was found to outweigh the state's interest in universal education.

### 13:12. How is a violation of the Free Exercise Clause identified?

The case of *Sherbert v. Verner*, 374 U.S. 398 (1963), considered the Free Exercise complaint of a Seventh-day Adventist practitioner who was dismissed by her South Carolina employer because she would not work on Saturday, the Sabbath Day of her faith. When she was unable to obtain other employment as a result of her religious principles which prohibited Saturday work, she filed a claim for unemployment compensation benefits and was denied because of her refusal to work on Saturday. In considering the question presented in *Sherbert*, the Supreme Court found a violation of the Free Exercise Clause, holding:

> Plainly enough, appellant's conscientious objection to Saturday work constitutes no conduct prompted by religious principles of a kind within the reach of state legislation. If, therefore, the decision of the South Carolina Supreme Court is to withstand appellant's constitutional challenge, it must be either because her disqualification as a beneficiary represents no infringement by the State of her constitutional rights of free exercise, or because any incidental burden on the free exercise of appellant's religion may be justified by a "compelling state interest in the regulation of a subject within the State's constitutional power to regulate...." We turn first

to the question whether the disqualification for benefits imposes any burden on the free exercise of appellant's religion. We think it is clear that it does. The ruling forces her to choose between following the precepts of her religion and forfeiting benefits, on the one hand, and abandoning one of the precepts of her religion in order to accept work, on the other hand. Governmental imposition of such a choice puts the same kind of burden upon the free exercise of religion as would a fine imposed against appellant for her Saturday worship.

The relevant questions to determine whether a Free Exercise violation exists in the school setting are thus:

1.  Does the school's action substantially burden religion either by forcing adherence to a rule that violates sincerely held religious beliefs or prohibiting conduct which is religiously required?

2.  If the school's action does substantially burden religion, then is there a compelling state interest which requires the school's action?

3.  Is the compelling state interest, which is burdening religion, being implemented by the least burdensome means possible, and is a reasonable alternative or accommodation which would meet that important state interest available?

### 13:13. What does it mean to substantially burden religion?

Under *Sherbert*, governmental actions may substantially burden religion either by forcing adherence to a rule that violates sincerely held religious beliefs or prohibiting conduct which is religiously required.

### 13:14. What does it mean to force adherence to a rule that violates sincerely held religious beliefs?

The facts of the *Sherbert* case are a good example of government action that substantially burdens religion by forcing adherence to a rule that violates sincerely held religious beliefs in violation of the Free Exercise Clause. In *Sherbert,* a Seventh-day Adventist practitioner was dismissed by her South Carolina employer because she would not work on Saturday, the Sabbath Day of her faith. When she was unable to obtain other employment as a result of her religious principles which prohibited Saturday work, she filed a claim for unemployment compensation benefits and was denied because of her refusal to work on Saturday.

## 13:15. What does it mean to prohibit conduct which is religiously required?

The case of *Church of the Lukumi Babalu Aye v. City of Hialeah*, 508 U.S. 520 (1993), is a good example of government action that prohibits conduct which is religiously required in violation of the Free Exercise Clause. The case involved a challenge to a local law which prohibited the sacrifice of animals as part of religious rituals, and was specifically targeted at the Church of the Lukumi Babalu Aye. The Supreme Court struck down the law which was not neutral or of general application and therefore was subject to the most exacting constitutional scrutiny. A law that restricts religious practice must advance an important state interest and must be narrowly tailored in pursuit of such interests. The Free Exercise Clause requires the government to exercise religious tolerance and ensure that the only reasons for imposing burdensome laws and regulations are secular.

## 13:16. What is a compelling state interest for Free Exercise Clause purposes?

In the case of *Frank v. State*, 604 P.2d 1068 (1979), the Supreme Court of Alaska considered an appeal of a criminal conviction of an Alaskan native who killed a moose out of season for the purpose of securing meat religiously required to be used in a funeral ceremony and with unlawful transportation of the game illegally taken. In overturning the criminal conviction because the state interest in regulating hunting was insufficient, under the circumstances, to overcome Free Exercise rights, the Court in *Frank*, stated:

> No value has a higher place in our constitutional system of government than that of religious freedom. The freedom to believe is protected absolutely. The freedom to act on one's religious beliefs is also protected, but such protection may be overcome by compelling state interests. ... A law imposing criminal or other penalties on the performance of acts which conscience compels, pressures the underlying beliefs and infringes to that extent the freedom to believe. Because of the close relationship between conduct and belief and because of the high value we assign to religious beliefs, religiously impelled actions can be forbidden only where they pose "some substantial threat to public safety, peace or order," ... Having established that protected religious conduct is involved, we turn next to an evaluation of the competing state interest. There can be no question but that there is a very strong state interest underlying hunting restrictions. It is not enough, however, simply to conclude that there is a compelling state interest in maintaining a healthy moose population. The question is whether that interest, or any other, will suffer if an exemption is granted to accommodate the religious practice at issue.... "Justifications

founded only on fear and apprehension are insufficient to overcome rights asserted under the First Amendment."

### 13:17. What is a reasonable alternative or accommodation that meets a compelling state interest?

An example of a reasonable alternative or accommodation which would meet a compelling state interest and yet uphold Free Exercise rights would be a student who had religious reasons for refusing a required school immunization. The school would have a sufficiently compelling state interest in protecting the health and safety of all students and staff to force compliance despite a sincere religious objection. If though, an alternative oral medication that was proven effective was available, but not widely enough available for regular use, Free Exercise rights would require the school to allow the alternative means of compliance which would meet the state health interest and preserve religious freedom.

### 13:18. What is the Religious Freedom Restoration Act of 1993 (RFRA) and how does it apply?

A concern by Congress that Free Exercise rights were being eroded by Supreme Court decisions led to the passage of the Religious Freedom Restoration Act of 1993 (RFRA), 107 Stat. 1488, 42 U.S.C. § 2000bb *et seq.* The law was declared to be unconstitutional with respect to the states, but is applicable to the federal government. The RFRA provides in pertinent part:

(a) Findings: The Congress finds that—

(1) the framers of the Constitution, recognizing free exercise of religion as an unalienable right, secured its protection in the First Amendment to the Constitution;

(2) laws 'neutral' toward religion may burden religious exercise as surely as laws intended to interfere with religious exercise;

(3) governments should not substantially burden religious exercise without compelling justification;

(4) in Employment Division v. Smith, 494 U.S. 872 (1990) the Supreme Court virtually eliminated the requirement that the government justify burdens on religious exercise imposed by laws neutral toward religion; and

(5) the compelling interest test as set forth in prior Federal court rulings is a workable test for striking sensible balances

between religious liberty and competing prior governmental interests.

(b) Purposes: The purposes of this Act are—

(1) to restore the compelling interest test as set forth in Sherbert v. Verner, 374 U.S. 398 (1963) and Wisconsin v. Yoder, 406 U.S. 205 (1972) and to guarantee its application in all cases where free exercise of religion is substantially burdened; and

(2) to provide a claim or defense to persons whose religious exercise is substantially burdened by government.

### SEC. 3. FREE EXERCISE OF RELIGION PROTECTED.

(a) In General: Government shall not substantially burden a person's exercise of religion even if the burden results from a rule of general applicability, except as provided in subsection (b).

(b) Exception: Government may substantially burden a person's exercise of religion only if it demonstrates that application of the burden to the person—

(1) is in furtherance of a compelling governmental interest; and

(2) is the least restrictive means of furthering that compelling governmental interest.

In the case of *City of Boerne v. Flores*, 521 U.S. 507 (1997), a decision by local zoning authorities to deny a church a building permit was challenged under the Religious Freedom Restoration Act of 1993 (RFRA). The local government questioned the constitutional authority of Congress to enact RFRA. The Supreme Court concluded that the statute exceeds Congress' power and declared it unconstitutional as far as its applicability to the states. Thus while RFRA no longer applies to the states, it is still applicable to the federal government and its actions.

### 13:19. Does the Maryland Constitution govern religion in any way?

Yes, Article 36 of the Declaration of Rights of the Maryland Constitution provides:

That as it is the duty of every man to worship God in such manner as he thinks most acceptable to Him, all persons are equally entitled to protection in their religious liberty; wherefore, no person ought by any law to be molested in his person or estate, on account of his religious persuasion, or profession, or for his religious practice, unless, under the color of religion, he shall disturb the good order, peace or safety of the State, or shall infringe the laws of morality, or injure others in their natural, civil or religious rights; nor ought any person to be compelled to frequent, or maintain, or contribute, unless on contract, to maintain, any place of worship, or any ministry; nor shall any person, otherwise competent, be deemed incompetent as a witness, or juror, on account of his religious belief, provided, he believes in the existence of God, and that under His dispensation such person will be held morally accountable for his acts, and be rewarded or punished therefor either in this world or in the world to come.

Nothing shall prohibit or require the making reference to belief in, reliance upon, or invoking the aid of God or a Supreme Being in any governmental or public document, proceeding, activity, ceremony, school, institution, or place.

Nothing in this article shall constitute an establishment of religion.

### 13:20. What are the primary areas of church/state conflict in the school setting?

There are numerous church/state issues that arise with some degree of regularity in the school setting, including matters pertaining to: school prayer; religious holidays; distribution of religious materials; religious dress and expression; calendar issues; and curriculum issues. These and other areas of conflict will be discussed in the balance of this chapter.

### 13:21. What about school prayer in general?

Conflicts about prayer in school under various forms and in various circumstances have been a major source of continuing litigation over a period of more that four decades, and continue as a major source of conflict to this day. In the case of *Engel v. Vitale*, 370 U.S. 421 (1962), the Supreme Court considered an action by the New York Board of Regents which composed the following prayer for daily morning recitation in public schools, "Almighty God, we acknowledge our dependence upon Thee, and we beg Thy blessings upon us, our parents, our teachers and our country." The Supreme Court in *Engel v. Vitale* held that:

> [T]he constitutional prohibition against laws respecting an establishment of religion must at least mean that in this country it is not part of the business of government to compose official prayers for any group of the American people, to recite as a part of a religious program carried on by government.

The U.S. Department of Education in 2003 issued a document entitled Guidance on Constitutionally Protected Prayer in Public Elementary and

Secondary Schools, which was produced as a result of a provision in the No Child Left Behind Act of 2001 (NCLB). Each state is required to secure from each local school system an annual certification that they have no policies that prevent or otherwise deny participation in constitutionally protected prayer as set forth in the guidance.

A current issue that is the subject of much debate in Maryland and nationally is requests by Muslim students either for a place within the school for required daily prayers or to be released from school in order to participate in required prayers. Most school systems are attempting to accommodate these requests if it can be done reasonably and without extensive loss of instructional time, but there are not as yet reliable court precedents to provide guidance.

### 13:22. What about periods of silent meditation or prayer?

A daily period of silent meditation is allowed but not required in Maryland by Md. Code Ann., Ed. Art. § 7-104, which provides as follows:

> (a) Silent meditation.—Principals and teachers in each public elementary and secondary school in this State may require all students to be present and participate in opening exercises on each morning of a school day and to meditate silently for approximately 1 minute.

> (b) Praying or reading holy scripture permitted.—During this period, a student or teacher may read the holy scripture or pray.

The Supreme Court in the case of *Wallace v. Jaffree*, 472 U.S. 38 (1985), considered a series of three successive Alabama laws concerning school prayer and a moment of silence; the laws were overturned by the Court because of the very clearly stated legislative intent to return prayer to the classrooms of the state. The purposes of the laws were religious in nature and as such constituted a violation of the Establishment Clause. The Fourth Circuit in a Virginia case upheld that state's moment of silence law which also included voluntary prayer in the case of *Brown v. Gilmore*, 258 F.3d 265 (4th Cir. 2001), which like the Maryland law had no such legislative history of an overtly religious purpose.

### 13:23. What about prayer at graduation ceremonies?

Prayer at a school graduation ceremony violates the Establishment Clause because the primary effect is to advance religion. In the case of *Lee v. Weisman*, 505 U.S. 577 (1992), the Supreme Court found that allowing principals to invite members of the clergy to give invocations and benedictions at middle and high school graduations in the Providence (RI) School Commission was unconstitutional. Because of the practical and symbolic significance of the ceremony, for all intents and purposes, its attendance became an "obligatory" state controlled religious exercise. Even if students were the ones to invite the member of the clergy to the graduation ceremony, the school would still be allowing the prayer to be included, and would be unconstitutional according to the Maryland Attorney General in Opinion of the Attorney General No. 93-050. The same constitutional prohibition would occur if students were allowed to choose a classmate to give a graduation prayer, according to the case of *Jones v. Clear Creek Independent School District*, 977 F.2d 963 (5th Cir. 1992).

In the case of *Lassonde v. Pleasanton Unified School District*, 320 F.3d 979 (9th Cir. 2003), the administrator's decision to censor the sectarian and proselytizing portions of a student high school graduation speech was found to be necessary to avoid a conflict with the Establishment Clause. On the other hand, students may choose to participate in a separate, non-school sponsored baccalaureate service performed by clergy members and which include prayer and other religious accoutrements. A recent challenge was made to the practice of holding some Montgomery County graduation ceremonies in local churches because of the need to accommodate large crowds and the inability of the schools in question to afford the cost of larger public venues. The school system resolved the dispute by agreeing to absorb the cost of the more expensive public facilities in order to avoid parent legal challenges and the even higher cost of defending a lawsuit.

### 13:24. What about prayer at extracurricular events?

Prayer at school sponsored events usually violates the Establishment Clause because it appears to represent the viewpoint of the school, and it is impermissible for schools to advance or favor any religion. In the case of *Jager v. Douglas County School District*, 862 F.2d 824 (11th Cir. 1989), the 11th Circuit Court let stand a lower ruling which found that pre-game invocations by coaches at high school football games were unconstitutional, and the "coach's prayer" prohibition is probably the most widely occurring Establishment Clause violation to this day. In *Santa Fe Independent School District v. Doe*, 530 U.S. 290 (2000), the Supreme Court issued its most recent decision on the subject of prayer at school sponsored extracurricular events. The Texas case involved a policy which permitted, but did not require, student-initiated and student-led prayer at all the home football games, and which authorized two student elections, the first to determine whether "invocations" should be delivered at games, and the second to select the student spokesperson to deliver them. In finding that the policy violated the Establishment Clause, the Court stated:

> The majoritarian process implemented by the District guarantees, by definition, that minority candidates will never prevail and that their views will be effectively silenced.... Moreover, the District has

failed to divorce itself from the invocations' religious content. The policy involves both perceived and actual endorsement of religion, ... declaring that the student elections take place because the District "has chosen to permit" student-delivered invocations, ... and that it must be consistent with the policy's goals, which include "solemniz[ing] the event." A religious message is the most obvious method of solemnizing an event. Indeed, the only type of message expressly endorsed in the policy is an "invocation," a term which primarily describes an appeal for divine assistance and, as used in the past at Santa Fe High School, has always entailed a focused religious message.

### 13:25. What about religious holiday displays and observances in general?

Such displays may be permissible under certain circumstances; it must be clear that the school is not endorsing any religion and that the purpose for such displays and observances is cultural or historic rather than religious. The Eighth Circuit considered a challenge to a school system policy which permitted religious holiday displays and observances for their cultural value in the case of *Florey v. Sioux Falls School District*, 619 F.2d 1311 (8th Cir. 1980). In upholding the district policy the Court in *Florey* held:

> Thus, although the rules permit the schools to observe holidays that have both a secular and a religious basis, we need not conclude that the School Board acted with unconstitutional motives. To the contrary, we agree with the district court's finding that the School Board did not adopt the policy statement and rules for the purpose of advancing or inhibiting religion.... Hence, the *study* of religion is not forbidden "when presented objectively as part of a secular program of education." ... We view the term "study" to include more than mere classroom instruction; public performance may be a legitimate part of secular study. This does not mean, of course, that religious ceremonies can be performed in the public schools under the guise of "study." It does mean, however, that when the primary purpose served by a given school activity is secular, that activity is not made unconstitutional by the inclusion of some religious content.... Since all programs and materials authorized by the rules must deal with the secular or cultural basis or heritage of the holidays and since the materials must be presented in a prudent and objective manner and symbols used as a teaching aid, the advancement of a "secular program of education," and not of religion, is the primary effect of the rules.... Rather than entangling

the schools in religion, the rules provide the means to ensure that the district steers clear of religious exercises.

The Supreme Court recently denied consideration of an appeal in a holiday display case from the Second Circuit Court of Appeals. In *Skoros v. City of New York*, 437 F.3d 1 (2d Cir. 2006), the opinion began with the wry observation, "No holiday season is complete, at least for the courts, without one or more First Amendment challenges to public holiday displays". The holiday display policy challenged prohibited the display of a nativity scene to symbolize Christmas, while permitting the display of a menorah, and star and crescent to symbolize Chanukah and Ramadan, respectively. The *Skoros* Court found that the promotion of understanding and tolerance of diverse religious and cultural perspectives served a valid secular purpose under the *Lemon* test, and the policy was therefore upheld.

### 13:26. What about concerts in conjunction with religious holidays?

It is without dispute that a large percentage of the existing pool of available chorale music is religious in origin. Schools that perform chorale music should be careful to maintain a balance between sacred and secular music in the formation of any program of performance. As with the previous question, the case of *Florey v. Sioux Falls School District*, 619 F.2d 1311 (8th Cir. 1980), considered concerts and other performances in conjunction with religious holidays and found them to be valid under the school system's policy, stating, "We view the term 'study' to include more than mere classroom instruction; public performance may be a legitimate part of secular study. This does not mean, of course, that religious ceremonies can be performed in the public schools under the guise of 'study'." One of the footnotes to the *Florey* decision specifically addresses some of the important educational considerations of concerts, noting:

> The singing of "Christmas carols" appears to be a primary focal point of appellants' objections to the rules.... Today, carols are sung with regularity on public and commercial television and are played on public address systems in offices, manufacturing plants and retail stores in every city and village.... Many carols have a religious theme; some do not. As in the centuries gone by, some persons object to the singing of carols with a religious basis in any place but the church or home because they feel that to do so debases religion; others have the same objection but because they feel it enhances religion. We take no part in this argument, it being entirely clear to us that carols have achieved a cultural significance that justifies their being sung in the public schools of Sioux Falls, South Dakota, if done in accordance with the policy and rules adopted by that school district.

## 13:27. What about in-school teaching concerning religion in general?

This has been a difficult area for public schools since the case of *McCollum v. Board of Education*, 333 U.S. 203 (1948), where the Supreme Court struck down an Illinois state curriculum plan which offered religious instruction to all public school students. Those students not wishing to participate were reassigned to study halls or similar activities. The Court believed that the plan created a situation where students were forced to either participate in religious instruction or risk being ostracized by teachers and peers and it thus violated the Establishment Clause. Schools may, for example, study the Bible from a literary or historic context; furthermore, discussing the religious significance does not constitute prohibited teaching of a religion or religious proselytizing. Affirming this basic premise, the Supreme Court in *Abington v. Schemmp*, 374 U.S. 203 (1963), stated:

> In addition, it might well be said that one's education is not complete without a study of comparative religion or the history of religion and its relationship to the advancement of civilization. It certainly may be said that the Bible is worthy of study for its literary and historic qualities. Nothing we have said here indicates that such study of the Bible or of religion, when presented objectively as part of a secular program of education, may not be effected consistently with the First Amendment.

## 13:28. What about a teacher sharing their own personal religious views?

Generally speaking, there are serious Establishment Clause problems with teachers sharing their own personal religious views with students because they are representatives of the school and because they are in a position of power, influence and authority over students that are a captive audience in school, where they are present to receive an education. On the other hand, the 8th Circuit Court of Appeals in *Wigg v. Sioux Falls School District*, 382 F.3d 807 (8th Cir. 2004), found that a teacher's leading of an after-school religious club was protected, despite the school district's ban on her participation, because teacher's involvement constituted private speech and thus did not cause the school to violate the Establishment Clause. In any event, there is nothing to prohibit one teacher from sharing his or her own personal religious beliefs with another teacher, because they would not have the same hierarchical relationship with one another as between student and teacher.

## 13:29. What about a student sharing their own personal religious views?

Students are free to share their personal religious views in the school setting, provided that it takes place during non-instructional time and does not cause a disruption to the school learning environment. Like other protected expressive student speech, administrators are always free to impose reasonable time, place and manner restrictions. In addition, in Maryland, there is an Opinion of the Attorney General No. 93-050, that upholds the Free Exercise rights of a student to carry a Bible or possess other religious materials in the school setting. A First Amendment suit is currently pending against a Prince George's county administrator and middle school in the U.S. District Court of Maryland based on an allegation that a student was ordered to cease reading her Bible at school during her lunch period.

### 13:30. What about a student expressing their religious views in school assignments?

The acceptability of students expressing religious views in the context of school assignments depends in large part on the specific requirements of the assignment in question in order to avoid charges of viewpoint discrimination. For example, an assignment requiring the writing of an essay about an admired individual and the reasons that they are admired could be properly fulfilled by an essay about a student's pastor and the religious reasons why they are admired. On the other hand, the same essay about the admired pastor could not properly fulfill a writing assignment about the effects of gravity, because it would not be in accordance with the specific guidelines and instructions provided. In the event that it is determined that an overtly religious student presentation is to be displayed, then the posting of a disclaimer from the school may help to avoid an Establishment Clause challenge. A new Texas law purports to require schools to accept religious submittals of students without any potential penalty for the religious nature of the design or purpose of the assignment submitted.

### 13:31. What about the distribution of religious or other materials at school in general?

Schools are closed or nonpublic forums in general, and as such may exercise significant control over materials that are distributed on school grounds. If though, a school opens its forum to some degree and allows the distribution of other non-curricular materials by way of normal school channels, then the exclusion of religious materials solely because of their religious content could constitute improper viewpoint discrimination.

### 13:32. What about the distribution of religious or other materials by students?

Students are also generally free to distribute materials expressing their personal religious views in the school setting, provided that it takes place during non-instructional time and does not cause a disruption to the school learning environment. Like other protected expressive student speech, administrators are always free to impose reasonable time, place and manner restrictions (*Hedges v.*

*Wauconda*, 9 F.3d 1383 (11th Cir. 1993)). In *Raker v. Frederick County Public Schools*, 470 F. Supp. 2d 634 (W.D. Va. 2007), a rule which limited student distribution of non-school material to either before or after the school day was found to be unreasonable and overbroad and it thus violated the student's First Amendment rights. Likewise, a preliminary injunction was issued preventing school administrators from enforcing a rule which banned students from distributing materials in the hallways between classes (*M.A.L. v. Kinsland*, No. 07-10391 (E.D. Mich. Jan. 30, 2007)). Finally, it was ruled constitutionally impermissible to require prior approval before the distribution of a student's statement of personal religious beliefs during non-instructional time (*M.B. v. Liverpool Central School District*, No. 04-1255 (N.D. N.Y. March 29, 2007)).

### 13:33. What about the distribution of religious or other materials by teachers and schools?

Generally speaking, there are serious Establishment Clause problems with teachers and schools sharing religious materials with students because they are seen to represent the views of the school, and because they are in a position of influence and authority over students that are present in school to receive an education.

### 13:34. What about the distribution of religious or other materials by outsiders?

Schools are closed or nonpublic forums in general, and as such may exercise significant control over materials that are distributed on school grounds, particularly by outside groups. If though, a school opens its forum to some degree and allows some outside groups to distribute materials by way of normal school channels, then the exclusion of religious materials solely because of their religious content would likely constitute improper viewpoint discrimination (*Child Evangelism Fellowship of Maryland v. Montgomery County*, 373 F.3d 589 (4th Cir. 2004)). A challenge to Montgomery County's revised policy on distribution of materials by the same group resulted in the policy being once again struck down as the Fourth Circuit found that the revised policy, "utterly fails to provide adequate protection for viewpoint neutrality ..." and "[b]ecause the policy offers no protection against the discriminatory exercise of MCPS's discretion, it creates too great a risk of viewpoint discrimination to survive constitutional scrutiny" (*Child Evangelism Fellowship v. Montgomery County Public Schools*, 457 F. 3d 376 (4th Cir. 2006)). In the case of *Peck v. Upshur County Board of Education*, 155 F.3d 274 (4th Cir. 1998), the Court held that a school policy which prevented an outside group, the Gideons, from going into public school classrooms and handing out Bibles was reasonable and constitutional.

## 13:35. What about the wearing of religious garb by students?

In order for a school to ban the wearing of religious clothing by students, in the face of Free Exercise rights, then the school would be required to show some compelling state interest, with no availability of a reasonable, less restrictive alternative, for the ban to be upheld.

## 13:36. What about the wearing of religious garb by teachers?

The issue that a school would face in prohibiting teachers from wearing religious garb is the teacher's Free Exercise rights in opposition to the school's requirement to remain religiously neutral and to avoid influencing or proselytizing students. Existing cases have gone in both directions, and the determination would likely rest on factors such as the overt nature of the religious garb and the age of the students being taught. For example, a small cross on a necklace would likely be protected, but a shirt with a large cross and the words, "Jesus saves" would probably not be protected. Similarly, elementary students would be more easily influenced by a teacher's religious garb than a high school student. On the other hand, a clearly required item such as a Jewish yarmulke would be acceptable under any circumstance.

## 13:37. What about religious messages on bricks and tiles?

A number of legal challenges have arisen in recent years over the practice of fundraising schemes that involve the sale of messages on brick pavers or wall tiles that become a permanent part of the school facility. If inadequate or no restrictions are placed on the messages, then schools have found themselves either defending their decision to exclude religious messages or explaining their failure to exclude religious messages. The good news for schools is that the forum will only become open if the school fails to issue specific and content neutral guidelines for this school-sponsored speech prior to the start of such sale of messages. For example, a school is perfectly within its rights to limit such messages to certain specified and pre-approved language such as the student's name and years of attendance or statements of school spirit.

## 13:38. What about religious holidays and school calendars in general?

There are a number of current controversies over religious holidays on school calendars. More religions are requesting that their religious holidays be reflected on the school calendar, even if those holidays are not days on which school will be closed. Some school systems have attempted to include as wide a range of religious holidays as possible on their calendars, aiming to be inclusive, while other school systems have gone in the opposite direction and have endeavored to totally secularize their calendars. As with most religious controversies, neither approach to modifying the traditional school calendar has met with widespread enthusiasm.

### 13:39. What about the closing of school for religious holidays?

The closing of schools for religious holidays, because of the effect on students and staff attendance if a significant number were absent, and the resulting negative impact on the learning environment, is also an example of a school action involving a religious matter that is not invalidated because it has a secular purpose (attendance) and its primary effect is to increase school attendance rather than to advance or inhibit religion. In Maryland, all school systems are closed for major Christian holidays as a matter of state law (Md. Code Ann., Ed. Art. § 7-103), less than half of the state's school systems currently close for the two highest Jewish holy days, and those that do close, make the decision based on student and teacher absence projections. In several Maryland school systems, there are currently individuals advocating for schools to close on the high holy days of other religions, and school systems should base such school closing decisions on pre-established standards of expected attendance projections in order to avoid Establishment Clause challenges for appearing to favor one religion over another.

### 13:40. What about student and teacher absences for religious holidays?

Student and teacher absences for religious holidays are normally allowed without penalty pursuant to the rights granted under the Free Exercise Clause. The accommodation, by the school, of student and teacher religious beliefs does not constitute either advancement of religion or cause excessive entanglement and thus does not violate the Establishment Clause. COMAR 13A.08.01.03F, makes the observance of a religious holiday a legally excused absence for a Maryland student. Clearly though, if an excessive number of absences were involved and the delivery of education was compromised, then the school would have a compelling interest that could overcome the student's Free Exercise rights.

With respect to employees, Title VII of the Civil Rights Act of 1964 prohibits religious discrimination, and would require a school to make reasonable accommodations for absence for religious holidays unless there is an undue hardship on the school. The school would have the ability to determine the maximum number of such absences and whether or not the teachers are paid for religious holiday absences, subject to county board policy and the negotiated agreement in place in that county.

## 13:41. What about student exemption from curriculum requirements for religious reasons?

Students may be excused from any portion of the curriculum on health and sex education that is found by the parents to be religiously, or otherwise, objectionable, according to COMAR 13A.04.18.03, and advanced elective courses covering such subjects require advance parental consent. Students may be excused from HIV/AIDS curriculum pursuant to COMAR 13A.04.18.04. Other curricular materials that are found to be objectionable by a parent are generally not avoidable by their child simply as a result of such objection, whether on religious or other grounds.

## 13:42. What about teacher objections to curriculum for religious reasons?

Generally speaking, teachers are required to teach the curriculum, and are not authorized to modify the materials to be taught as a result of their personal religious beliefs. The school's compelling interest in maintaining a suitable curriculum for the benefit of its students overcomes the Free Exercise rights of a teacher with religious objections.

## 13:43. What about parent challenges to curriculum for religious reasons?

The Sixth Circuit in *Mozert v. Hawkins County Public Schools*, 827 F.2d 1058 (11th Cir. 1987), considered a challenge that a requirement that all students in grades one through eight use a prescribed set of reading textbooks, forced the student-plaintiffs to read school books which teach or inculcate values in violation of their religious beliefs and convictions, constituting a clear violation of their rights to the free exercise of religion protected by the First and Fourteenth Amendments to the United States Constitution. In overruling the challenge to the district's curriculum, the *Mozert* Court held:

> The requirement that students read the assigned materials and attend reading classes, in the absence of a showing that this participation entailed affirmation or denial of a religious belief, or performance or non-performance of a religious exercise or practice, does not place an unconstitutional burden on the students' free exercise of religion.

Curriculum issues continue to generate controversy including recent trends to create biblical literature elective courses and yoga education, both of which have caused Establishment Clause challenges in numerous states.

## 13:44. What about the teaching of creationism or intelligent design?

In the case of *Edwards v. Aguillard*, 482 U.S. 578 (1987), the Supreme Court struck down a Louisiana Law which prohibited the teaching of evolution unless creationism was also taught. The Court found a clear Establishment Clause violation because the law advanced a religious doctrine by providing that a certain subject, evolution, would never be taught unless a religious perspective of that subject, creationism, was presented simultaneously. More recently, in the case of *Kitzmiller v. Dover Area School District*, 400 F. Supp. 2d 707 (M.D. Pa. 2005), the school board's direction to teach intelligent design drew a judicial finding that the required teaching of intelligent design as an alternative to evolution constitutes a clear violation of the Establishment Clause. In addressing the national attention garnered by the case, the Court noted:

> Those who disagree with our holding will likely mark it as the product of an activist judge. If so, they will have erred as this is manifestly not an activist Court. Rather, this case came to us as the result of the activism of an ill-informed faction on a school board, aided by a national public interest law firm eager to find a constitutional test case on intelligent design, who in combination drove the Board to adopt an imprudent and ultimately unconstitutional policy. The breathtaking inanity of the Board's decision is evident when considered against the factual backdrop which has now been fully revealed through this trial. The students, parents, and teachers of the Dover Area School District deserved better than to be dragged into this legal maelstrom, with its resulting utter waste of monetary and personal resources.

## 13:45. What about disclaimers concerning the teaching of evolution?

There continue to be challenges to the teaching of evolution, in *Epperson v. Arkansas*, 393 U.S. 97 (1968), the Supreme Court struck down an Arkansas law making it illegal to teach evolution in the public schools. The Court held that prohibiting the teaching of evolution actually had the effect of advancing a particular religion's beliefs and so violated the secular purpose test. The case of *Selman v. Cobb County School District*, 390 F. Supp. 2d 1286 (N.D. Ga. 2005), is currently pending after a remand, in the State of Georgia regarding the constitutional validity of a disclaimer sticker about evolution that was required to be placed on science textbooks by the local school district policy. The contested disclaimer, which was initially found by the federal court to be an Establishment Clause violation, stated:

> This textbook contains material on evolution. Evolution is a theory, not a fact, regarding the origin of living things. This material should

be approached with an open mind, studied carefully, and critically considered.

### 13:46. What about the pledge to the flag and the phrase "under God"?

Pursuant to Md. Code Ann., Ed. Art. § 7-105, the display of the U.S. flag and the recitation of the pledge of allegiance, specifically including the phrase "under God" are legally required for each public school classroom in the State of Maryland, although an exception is made for any student or teacher that wishes to be excused from participation. The Supreme Court in *Elk Grove Village Unified School District v. Newdow*, 542 U.S. 1 (2004), overturned a Ninth Circuit ban on the pledge to the flag because Mr. Newdow lacked standing to bring the case, on behalf of his daughter, as a non-custodial parent. A similar challenge to the pledge in the school setting, because of the "under God" phrase, was heard by the Seventh Circuit in the Illinois case of *Sherman v. Community Consolidated School District*, 980 F.2d 437 (7th Cir. 1992), where the court upheld the pledge on the basis that the phrase "under God" constituted "ceremonial deism" and not a true Establishment Clause violation.

### 13:47. What about the posting of the ten commandments?

The Supreme Court in *Stone v. Graham*, 449 U.S. 39 (1980), invalidated a Kentucky law which called for the placement of the Ten Commandments in all public school classrooms, despite the fact that funding was to come from private sources and despite a disclaimer which appeared at the bottom of the display asserting that the Ten Commandments had a secular purpose as they were the basis of Western Civilization and the Common Law of the United States. The *Stone* Court held:

> The pre-eminent purpose for posting the Ten Commandments on schoolroom walls is plainly religious in nature. The Ten Commandments are undeniably a sacred text in the Jewish and Christian faiths, and no legislative recitation of a supposed secular purpose can blind us to that fact. The Commandments do not confine themselves to arguably secular matters, such as honoring one's parents, killing or murder, adultery, stealing, false witness, and covetousness.... Rather, the first part of the Commandments concerns the religious duties of believers: worshipping the Lord God alone, avoiding idolatry, not using the Lord's name in vain, and observing the Sabbath Day.

### 13:48. What about the use by schools of faith-based organizations?

The Supreme Court considered a similar question in the case of *Bowen v. Kendrick*, 487 U.S. 589 (1988), upholding the constitutionality of the federal Adolescent Family Life Act which provides federal grant funds to public and private organizations on issues concerning sexual activity of adolescents, teen pregnancy, family planning and abortion. Specifically challenged was a provision of the law which required grant applicants to describe how they will involve religious organizations in the provision of services. The Court found that the law did not have the principle purpose or effect of advancing religion and that it was not a violation of the Establishment Clause for a religious organization to participate in the state program even when certain religious goals were furthered.

### 13:49. What is the Equal Access Act and how does it apply to schools?

The meeting of religious clubs in school facilities pursuant to their rights under the Equal Access Act could create the appearance of school endorsement of religion in violation of the Establishment Clause. School administrators must clearly indicate that the school is not sponsoring, endorsing or promoting any such non-curriculum student groups by issuing disclaimers or otherwise. It should also be noted that teachers at the school may not establish, endorse, lead or participate in student religious meetings under the Equal Access Act, but may be assigned to supervise such meetings. Those from outside the school also may not conduct, direct or regularly attend meetings of such student groups, but they may occasionally attend if invited by the students and if the school does not prohibit all outside visitors. The Equal Access Act is found at 20 U.S.C. § 4071, Title 20, Education, Chapter 52, Education For Economic Security, Subchapter VIII, Equal Access.

In *Board of Education v. Mergens*, 496 U.S. 226 (1990), the Supreme Court considered the appeal of students at a public high school who asked for permission to start a religious club to meet during non-instructional time. The school board denied permission under a belief that it would violate the Establishment Clause, and the students claimed a violation of the Equal Access Act. The Court found that the school's denial did violate the Equal Access Act because the school allowed other extracurricular groups, including chess, student government, and social service groups, to meet during non-instructional time. The Court upheld the constitutionality of the Equal Access Act and reasoned that high school students were mature enough to understand that the school was not specifically endorsing the religious activity.

**13:50. What is a federally funded secondary school under the Equal Access Act?**

A secondary school is defined by state statute, and in Maryland it means a high school consisting of grades 9 through 12. While there is not a definitive federal court ruling, it appears that the Equal Access Act probably does not apply to middle schools.

**13:51. What is a non-curriculum related student group under the Equal Access Act?**

A non-curriculum related student group under the Equal Access Act refers to those student groups whose activities are not directly related to the course of studies offered by the public secondary school. Student groups that are directly related to the subject matter of courses offered by the secondary school do not fall within the non-curricular category and thus would be considered curricular. Thus, if the group is not part of the school curriculum, for example, the chess club, which is not a class, as opposed to the band, which is a class, then it cannot be discriminated against based upon religious, political or philosophical content in the degree of access provided. The Act states:

> (a) Restriction of limited open forum on basis of religious, political, philosophical, or other speech content prohibited. It shall be unlawful for any public secondary school which receives Federal financial assistance and which has a limited open forum to deny equal access or a fair opportunity to, or discriminate against, any students who wish to conduct a meeting within that limited open forum on the basis of the religious, political, philosophical, or other content of the speech at such meetings.

**13:52. What is a limited open forum under the Equal Access Act?**

If a public secondary school allows any voluntary student led, non-curricular groups to meet on school grounds during non-instructional time, then a limited open forum is created and all such groups must be allowed. Non-instructional time under the Equal Access Act consists of any time available before classroom instruction begins or after classroom instruction ends. Non-instructional time also includes an activity period or lunch period during which instruction does not occur and during which other groups are allowed to meet. The Act (20 U.S.C. § 4071) provides:

> (b) "Limited open forum" defined. A public secondary school has a limited open forum whenever such school grants an offering to

or opportunity for one or more noncurriculum related student groups to meet on school premises during noninstructional time.

### 13:53. What is the definition of equal access under the Equal Access Act?

Under the terms of the Act, equal access or fair opportunity means that the same degree of school access, for example, announcements of meetings, which are provided to any student group within a limited open forum, must be provided to all similarly situated student groups. School administrators have the right to observe meetings to ensure order and discipline on school grounds, and may deny access to groups, which materially and substantially interfere with the educational mission of the school. School administrators may also establish reasonable time, place and manner restrictions for such meetings, provided that the limitations are uniform and nondiscriminatory. School administrators also have the ability to terminate the limited open forum by prohibiting all non-curriculum related student groups from meeting on school grounds, thus ending any obligations under the Equal Access Act. The Act (20 U.S.C. § 4071) itself provides:

(c) Fair opportunity criteria. Schools shall be deemed to offer a fair opportunity to students who wish to conduct a meeting within its limited open forum if such school uniformly provides that—

(1) the meeting is voluntary and student-initiated;

(2) there is no sponsorship of the meeting by the school, the government, or its agents or employees;

(3) employees or agents of the school or government are present at religious meetings only in a nonparticipatory capacity;

(4) the meeting does not materially and substantially interfere with the orderly conduct of educational activities within the school; and

(5) nonschool persons may not direct, conduct, control, or regularly attend activities of student groups....

(f) Authority of schools with respect to order, discipline, well-being, and attendance concerns. Nothing in this subchapter shall be construed to limit the authority of the school, its agents or employees, to maintain order and discipline on school premises, to protect the well-being of students and faculty, and to assure that attendance of students at meetings is voluntary.

## 13:54. What about gay-straight alliance clubs under the Equal Access Act?

The formation of gay-straight alliance (GSA) clubs under the Equal Access Act has generated significant controversy during recent years. Most cases have supported the Equal Access Act's application to such clubs, and have required school administrators to approve their existence provided that all criteria for the application of the Act are met. A recent example is the case of *Gay-Straight Alliance of Okeechobee High School v. School Board of Okeechobee County*, 2007 U.S. Dist. LEXIS 25729 (S.D. Fla. Apr. 6, 2007), where the court ordered the recognition of the GSA club despite the school district's unproven assertion that it is a "sex-based club" that would be contrary to the well-being of students and would cause disruption of the educational environment. On the other hand, in a similar dispute at a Texas high school, a refusal to recognize a GSA club was upheld because that particular club's website was found to contain links to sexually explicit materials (*Caudillo v. Lubbock Independent School District*, 311 F. Supp. 2d 550 (N.D. Tex. 2004)). Finally, in a new twist, the State of Utah, in what is generally perceived as a direct response to the growth of GSA clubs, recently passed a law requiring all student clubs to: maintain the boundaries of socially appropriate behavior; establish mandatory parental consent to join a student club; and to submit all written club materials to the school principal for review by the administrator and parents of the student club members.

## 13:55. What about access to schools by community religious groups?

In *Lamb's Chapel v. Center Moriches Union Free School District*, 508 U.S. 384 (1993), the Supreme Court upheld the complaint of a religious organization which was denied permission to show a religious film at a public school during a time when the facility was not being used for school purposes. The school district had a policy of allowing certain uses during non-school hours, and specifically excluded the use of the building for religious purposes. The Court held that the school policy favored non-religious over religious viewpoints and therefore violated the First Amendment. The Court went on to hold that use of school property to show the religious film was not a violation of the Establishment Clause because it was not scheduled during school hours or sponsored by the school and because the film was open to the public. The Court found that the school board policy had, in effect, created an open or public forum.

In the case of *Child Evangelism Fellowship v. Anderson School District*, 457 F. 3d 376 (4th Cir. 2006), it was held that the charging of a facilities usage fee could not be based upon administrative discretion without constituting impermissible viewpoint discrimination. It would still apparently be possible to base such fees on a policy which is viewpoint-neutral.

## 13:56. What about county boards of education opening meetings with prayer?

While it did not deal with a school board, a recent Fourth Circuit case out of South Carolina, considered a challenge to the practice of opening meetings of local government bodies with prayer. In the case of *Wynne v. Town of Great Falls, South Carolina*, 376 F.3d 292 (4th Cir. 2004), the practice of opening the city council meeting with prayer was struck down because of the overtly sectarian and proselytizing nature of the prayer. In a decision that would be applicable to county boards of education in Maryland, the Court in *Wynne* held:

> Public officials' brief invocations of the Almighty before engaging in public business have always ... been part of our nation's history. The Town Council of Great Falls remains free to engage in such invocations prior to council meetings. The opportunity to do so may provide a source of strength to believers, and a time of quiet reflection for all.... This opportunity does not, however, provide the Town Council, or any other legislative body, license to advance its own religious views in preference to all others, as the Town Council did here.

In a subsequent Fourth Circuit case, the Court upheld the decision of the Chesterfield County (Virginia) Board of Supervisors to exclude the request of a Wiccan practitioner to be added to the otherwise broadly inclusive list of clergy that provided non-sectarian invocations at the meetings of the Board of Supervisors (*Cynthia Simpson v. Chesterfield County Board of Supervisors*, 2005 U.S. App. LEXIS 6156 (4th Cir.)).

# 14. Student Classifications and Diversity Issues

### 14:1. What does the Constitution say about classifying people?

The Fourteenth Amendment to the United States Constitution says, in part, that "No State shall make or enforce any law which shall ... deny to any person within its jurisdiction the equal protection of the laws." This provision is commonly referred to as the Equal Protection Clause. While Maryland's Constitution does not have a similar provision, Maryland's highest court has determined that Article 24 of the Maryland Constitution's Declaration of Rights embodies the same concept (*Renko v. McLean*, 346 Md. 464, 697 A.2d 477 (1997)).

The Constitution does not require things that are different to be treated as though they are the same, but when a governmental body, including a school board, draws a distinction among people and treats them differently based on some characteristic, such as race or ethnicity, gender, or wealth, it must justify that decision or the classification will be deemed to violate Equal Protection.

### 14:2. How do the courts determine if a classification is justifiable?

Courts use three different tests to determine if a challenged classification is legal. The most difficult test to meet is the "strict scrutiny" test. The second test called the intermediate or "heightened scrutiny" test is somewhat more easily satisfied. The third, and most easily satisfied, standard of review is the traditional or "rational basis" test. Each is applied to particular kinds of classifications. These tests assist the courts in drawing the line between permissible and impermissible classifications.

### 14:3. What is "strict scrutiny" and when it is applied?

"Strict scrutiny" is a test applied by courts when reviewing a classification that involves a "suspect class" of persons or a "fundamental right." To be found constitutional, the court must find that the classification serves a compelling state interest and that the means chosen are necessary or "narrowly tailored" to achieve the goal. This judicial standard of review is designed to test the "importance and the sincerity of the reasons advanced by the governmental decisionmaker" for the classification (*Grutter v. Bollinger*, 539 U.S. 306, 327 (2003)).

### 14:4. What is a "suspect class" to which "strict scrutiny" applies?

The name of this group may be misleading. It is not the class of persons that is suspect, but rather the motives of the government (school board) in creating the classification that are suspect. Given the history of the United States, it is fair to say that perhaps the most *suspect* classifications are those based on race and classifications based on race are presumptively invalid (*Personnel Administrator of Massachusetts v. Feeney*, 442 U.S. 256, 272 (1979)). The special status of race as a suspect class derives in part from the Fourteenth Amendment itself which was ratified in 1868 during the Post-Civil War Reconstruction Period. [Maryland, together with other border states and southern states, initially rejected the Amendment on March 23, 1867. It was approved on April 4, 1959.]

Other *suspect* classifications to which strict scrutiny will be applied include those based on ethnicity, nationality or alienage, and religious affiliation.

### 14:5. What are "fundamental rights" to which "strict scrutiny" applies?

While no court case specifically defines this term, fundamental rights have been described as those that touch on the "sensitive and important area of human rights" or those involving "one of the basic civil rights of man" (*Reynolds v. Sims*, 377 U.S. 533, 562 (1964)). "Fundamental rights" have also been described as those rights that are explicitly or implicitly guaranteed by the Constitution. Fundamental rights include, for example, the right to procreate (implicit constitutional right to privacy), the right to vote, and the right to interstate travel.

### 14:6. Is education a "fundamental right?"

In 1973, the United States Supreme Court declined to apply "strict scrutiny" to a case challenging the way Texas funded public education. The case alleged that students were treated differently because school districts with a wealthier tax base had more revenue and, therefore, had more money to fund local schools than poorer areas, resulting in a two-tier, unequal educational system. The Supreme Court found no violation of the Equal Protection Clause (*San Antonio Independent School District v. Rodriguez*, 411 U.S. 1 (1973)).

The Supreme Court said that, even though a public education is an important societal goal, the right to an education is not mentioned in the U.S. Constitution and, therefore, was not a "fundamental right" to which strict scrutiny applied.

The right to an education *is* found in the Maryland Constitution. Article VIII, Section 1, of the Maryland Constitution provides: "The General Assembly ... shall by Law establish throughout the State a thorough and efficient System of Free Public Schools; and shall provide by taxation, or otherwise, for their maintenance." The highest court in Maryland, however, rejected a challenge to the State's system of financing education, similar to that brought against Texas, because it found that the right to an education was not a fundamental right, despite the inclusion of a right to a public education in the Maryland Constitution. "The right to an adequate education in Maryland is no more fundamental than the right to personal security, to fire protection, to welfare subsidies, to health care or like vital governmental services" and, therefore, strict scrutiny did not apply. The court also declined to find that wealth or the lack of wealth constituted a suspect class to which strict scrutiny would apply. (*Hornbeck v. Somerset County Board of Education*, 295 Md. 597 (1983)).

### 14:7. What is "heightened scrutiny" and when is it applied?

Heightened or intermediate review requires the government to show that the classification serves an *important* governmental objective and that the means chosen are *substantially* related to achieving the objective. "Heightened scrutiny" has been applied to classifications based on gender (*Craig v. Boren*, 429 U.S. 190 (1976)). Although not a traditional "suspect class," heightened scrutiny appears to have developed because the courts recognized that discrimination based on gender also had long, historical roots where women (and men) were subject to stereotyped distinctions similar to those based on race (*Frontiero v. Richardson*, 411 U.S. 677 (1973)). Courts have noted that sex, like race and national origin, is an immutable characteristic that is determined solely by one's birth, without relation to ability or other individual talents or skills.

### 14:8. What is the "rational basis" test and when is it applied?

Most classifications created by governmental bodies are subject to the traditional, "rational basis" test. It is the easiest standard to satisfy. In these cases, the court will presume that the classification is lawful and the program, policy, or decision will be upheld if the facts show any "reasonable relationship" to a "legitimate governmental interest." As a result, a classification will be upheld unless it is patently arbitrary. The rational basis test is applied to the overwhelming number of classifications, including those based on wealth.

### 14:9. Are there other laws that set legal parameters for classifications of people?

The United States Congress and the Maryland General Assembly each have passed a number of laws that impact the government's ability to adopt programs or make decisions that impact classes of individuals differently. Some examples are: Title VI of the Civil Rights Act of 1964, Title IX of the Education Amendments of 1972, the Age Discrimination Act of 1975, § 504 of the Rehabilitation Act of 1973, the 1990 Americans With Disabilities Act, the Boy Scouts of America Equal Access Act, the Equal Educational Opportunities Act of 1974, and Article 49B of the Annotated Code of Maryland. These laws, passed at different times, overlap with each other and with protections provided by the U.S. Constitution or Maryland's State Constitution.

### 14:10. What is Title VI of the Civil Rights Act of 1964 and what does it do?

Title VI of the Civil Rights Act of 1964 (42 U.S.C. § 2000d) prohibits discrimination based on race, color, religion or national origin: "... no person in the United States shall, on the ground of race, color, or national origin, be excluded from participation in, be denied the benefits of, or be otherwise subjected to discrimination under any program or activity receiving Federal financial assistance from the Department of Education." The nondiscriminating requirement is attached to the acceptance of Federal funding, but it provides the same protections as the U.S. Constitution. For that reason, it is common to see court cases which allege violation of the Equal Protection Clause of the U.S. Constitution and Title VI of the Civil Rights Act of 1964.

In *Lau v. Nichols*, 414 U.S. 563 (1974), for example, the U.S. Supreme Court found that Title VI required school districts to provide a meaningful opportunity for students with limited English proficiency to participate in educational programs. The Office for Civil Rights, within the U.S. Department of Education, has taken the position that Title VI is violated if programs for limited English proficiency students are not designed to teach them English as soon as possible, if students are excluded from effective participation in school because of their English skill level or are mis-assigned to special education classes because of their lack of English skills.

### 14:11. What is the Equal Educational Opportunities Act of 1974 and what does it do?

The Equal Educational Opportunities Act of 1974 (20 U.S.C. § 1703) prohibits denial of equal educational opportunity based on race, color, sex, or national origin by segregation or failure to remove vestiges of a dual system, school assignment or transfer of students and failure to overcome language barriers to access education. The law states that no State is to deny equal educational opportunity to an individual on account of his or her race, color, sex, or national origin, by:

    (a) the deliberate segregation by an educational agency of students on the basis of race, color, or national origin among or within schools;

    (b) the failure of an educational agency which has formerly practiced such deliberate segregation to take affirmative steps ... to remove the vestiges of a dual school system;

    (c) the assignment by an educational agency of a student to a school, other than the one closest to his or her place of residence within the school district in which he or she resides, if the assignment results in a greater degree of segregation of students on the basis of race, color, sex, or national origin among the schools of such agency than would result if such student were assigned to the school closest to his or her place of residence within the school district of such agency providing the appropriate grade level and type of education for such student;

(d) discrimination by an educational agency on the basis of race, color, or national origin in the employment, employment conditions, or assignment to schools of its faculty or staff, with some exceptions listed in the law;

(e) the transfer by an educational agency, whether voluntary or otherwise, of a student from one school to another if the purpose and effect of such transfer is to increase segregation of students on the basis of race, color, or national origin among the schools of such agency; or

(f) the failure by an educational agency to take appropriate action to overcome language barriers that impede equal participation by its students in its instructional programs.

### 14:12. What is Title IX of the Education Amendments of 1972 and what does it do?

Title IX (20 U.S.C. § 1681) prohibits sex discrimination by educational institutions in the operation of their programs and services. Title IX states that: "No person in the United States shall, on the basis of sex, be excluded from participation in, be denied the benefits of, or be subjected to discrimination under any education program or activity receiving Federal financial assistance." This law is credited, most particularly, with increasing opportunities for women in athletic programs at public schools and post-secondary institutions. More recently, Title IX's prohibition against sex discrimination has been the basis of court cases and administrative enforcement efforts dealing with sexual harassment.

In *Davis v. Monroe County Board of Education*, 526 U.S. 629 (1999), the U.S. Supreme Court found that a school's deliberate indifference to a teacher's sexual harassment of a student violated Title IX. Similarly, a school's deliberate indifference to sexual harassment of a student by another student, if sufficiently severe, can constitute discrimination on the basis of sex in violation of Title IX.

### 14:13. What is the Americans With Disabilities Act and what does it do?

The 1990 Americans With Disabilities Act (42 U.S.C. § 12131) prohibits discrimination on the basis of disability. The law prohibits discrimination against a qualified individual with a disability because of the disability in regard to job application procedures, the hiring, advancement, or discharge of employees, employee compensation, job training, and other terms, conditions, and privileges of employment. An individual with a disability is someone who has a physical or mental impairment that substantially limits one or more of the major life activities, has a record of such an impairment or is regarded as having such an impairment. The ADA requires a school district to provide "reasonable accommodation." "Reasonable accommodation" can include modification to facilities used by employees to make them readily accessible to and usable by individuals with disabilities. It can also include job restructuring or part-time or modified work schedules. It includes provision of qualified readers or interpreters and other similar accommodations.

### 14:14. What is Article 49B of the Annotated Code of Maryland and what does it do?

This Maryland state law (Md. Code Ann., Art. 49B § 16) prohibits employment discrimination (and housing discrimination) based on an "individual's race, color, religion, sex, age, national origin, marital status, sexual orientation, genetic information, or disability unrelated in nature and extent so as to reasonably preclude the performance of the employment, or because of the individual's refusal to submit to a genetic test or make available the results of a genetic test."

### 14:15. Can a school board be held liable for a neutral policy if it impacts groups unequally?

There are two theories of liability for civil rights violations: intentional discrimination and disparate impact. School board policies, programs, or decisions that intentionally disadvantage a protected group are illegal. However, it is also possible to violate the civil rights of protected groups if an otherwise neutral policy disproportionately impacts members of these groups.

To assess disparate impact cases, courts use a three-part analysis. First, it will look at whether the individual is a member of the class of persons protected by the law and whether the individual was denied some benefit or right (a *prima facie* case). The court will then look at whether the governmental entity had some legitimate, nondiscriminatory reason for its decision. Lastly, it will look at whether the reasons offered by the government were mere pretext. Pretext can be shown by articulated reasons that had no basis in fact or were not the true reason for the decision or were insufficient to justify the action (*McDonnell Douglas Corp. v. Green*, 411 U.S. 792 (1973); *Manzer v. Diamond Shamrock Chemicals Co.*, 29 F.3d 1078 (6th Cir. 1994)). This type of analysis is often referred as the *McDonnell Douglas* test.

Unlike intentional discrimination, disparate impact is not always accepted as proof of conduct violating a person's civil rights. For example, in *Alexander v. Sandoval*, 532 U.S. 275 (2001), the U.S. Supreme Court held that Title VI of the Civil Rights Act of 1964 (which prohibits discrimination on the basis of race, color, or national origin) applied to intentional discrimination only and that an otherwise neutral policy did not violate the law because groups were impacted differently. In that case, the Alabama Department of Public Safety had a policy of administering driver's license examinations in English only. The law was challenged on the basis that, while not overtly discriminating, the policy had the effect of disadvantaging applicants based on national origin. Note that the Equal Education Opportunities Act of 1974 specifically prohibits states from denying equal education opportunity by failing to take actions to overcome language barriers that impede equal participation of students in instructional programs (20 U.S.C. § 1703).

## 14:16. Can a school board classify students based on race or ethnicity?

Distinctions based on race/ethnicity are considered suspect and are presumed to be invalid (*Personnel Administrator of Massachusetts v. Feeney*, 442 U.S. 256 (1979)). In order to overcome this presumption of invalidity, the school board must produce strong justification for establishing a classification based on race/ethnicity.

Courts test the justification for a racial/ethnic classification by asking whether the program, policy, or decision based on race/ethnicity serves a "compelling state interest" and whether the program, policy, or decision is "narrowly tailored" to meet that interest (see **14:3**).

Of course, *Brown v. Board of Education*, 347 U.S. 483 (1954), invalidated America's dual system of education based on race, finding it violated the Equal Protection Clause. Prior to the *Brown* decision, students in many states were admitted to or assigned to schools based on their race.

The U.S. Supreme Court had wrestled with the question of whether racial classifications violated the Equal Protection Clause and had determined that the classification was constitutional if the separate systems were equal. In *Plessy v. Ferguson*, 163 U.S. 537 (1896), the Supreme Court specifically considered and rejected the notion, accepted in *Brown*, that separate was inherently unequal.

> When the government ... has secured to each of its citizens equal rights before the law, and equal opportunities for improvement and progress, it has accomplished the end for which it was organized, and performed all of the functions respecting social advantages with which it is endowed. Legislation is powerless to eradicate racial instincts, or to abolish distinctions based upon physical differences, and the attempt to do so can only result in accentuating the

difficulties of the present situation. If the civil and political rights of both races be equal, one cannot be inferior to the other civilly or politically. If one race be inferior to the other socially, the constitution of the United States cannot put them upon the same plane.

The *Brown* decision rejected *Plessy* specifically and completely. It rejected its factual predicate and its legal conclusions. The Supreme Court in *Brown* cited, with approval, the challenged Kansas court decision:

> Segregation of white and colored children in public schools has a detrimental effect upon the colored children. The impact is greater when it has the sanction of the law; for the policy of separating the races is usually interpreted as denoting the inferiority of the Negro group. A sense of inferiority affects the motivation of a child to learn. Segregation with the sanction of law, therefore, has a tendency to (retard) the educational and mental development of Negro children and to deprive them of some of the benefits they would receive in a racial(ly) integrated school system.

### 14:17. Is desegregation a sufficient reason for making racial distinction?

School districts under court order to desegregate in order to remedy past *de jure* segregation (segregation by law) must take race into consideration and desegregation is a compelling state interest. School districts under court order to desegregate have considerable leeway in fashioning programs and policies that consider race.

There are no school districts in Maryland that are currently under court order to desegregate. In Maryland, only Prince George's County was ordered by a federal court to desegregate. Sylvester Vaughns led a group of parents who sued the Board of Education in 1971 for failing to dismantle Maryland's previous dual system of education. The federal judge ordered development of a desegregation plan using bussing. Busing in some form for purposes of desegregation remained a part of education in Prince George's County until 1998 when the court approved an agreement to end busing. The federal judge who approved the agreement was quoted in a local newspaper as calling the agreement "a fitting denouement to one of the most serious dramas of modern America."

**14:18. Is the desire to promote integration or diversity a sufficient reason for making racial distinctions?**

It can be, but a school policy that takes race or ethnicity into consideration to promote a diverse student enrollment in a school or program will have a difficult time surviving "strict scrutiny."

**14:19. Can the promotion of diversity support consideration of race in the Higher Education setting?**

The U.S. Supreme Court has determined that promoting diversity, including race/ethnic diversity, is a compelling state interest that satisfies the first prong of the "strict scrutiny" test. The University of Michigan Law School has an admissions policy that seeks to achieve a diverse student body by looking at academic ability and "soft variables," such as the enthusiasm of recommendations, quality of undergraduate institution, difficulty of course work, applicant's essay and contribution to the overall diversity of the law school (*Grutter v. Bollinger*, 539 U.S. 306 (2003)). There was special reference to the need to enroll a "critical mass" of under-represented minority students identified as African-American, Hispanic and Native-American students. The Supreme Court was persuaded that benefits, which included promoting cross-racial understanding, helping to break down racial stereotypes and gain a better understanding of different races, and better preparing students to work in an increasingly diverse workforce and society, constituted a compelling state interest. In addition, the Supreme Court found that engaging in an individualized, "holistic" review of the applications, giving serious consideration to all of the ways an applicant could contribute to a diverse educational environment satisfied the "narrow tailored" prong of strict scrutiny. Consideration of race-neutral alternatives which might have achieved the goal is one aspect of determining if a policy is "narrow tailored." In *Grutter*, race-neutral alternatives such as a lottery or decreasing emphasis on GPA and LSAT scores were considered but rejected because they would affect the academic quality and experience of all admitted students.

**14:20. Can the promotion of diversity support consideration of race in the K-12 setting?**

On June 28, 2007, the U.S. Supreme Court, in a 5-4 decision, overturned student assignment plans in Seattle, Washington, and in Jefferson County, Kentucky, that were designed to promote diversity. The question before the Court was "whether a public school that had not operated legally segregated schools or has been found to be unitary may choose to classify students by race and rely upon that classification in making school assignments." The "swing vote" was that of Justice Kennedy who agreed with the majority that the school districts' plans were not "narrowly tailored," but specifically acknowledged that "[d]iversity, depending on its meaning and definition, is a compelling educational goal a school district may pursue" (*Parents Involved in Community Schools v. Seattle School District No. 1*, 551 U.S. ___ (2007); decided together with *Meredith, Custodial Parent and Next Friend of McDonald v. Jefferson County Board of Education et al.*).

The Seattle, Washington, school board adopted an open choice student assignment plan to "end de facto segregation in the schools and provide all of the District's students with access to diverse and equal educational opportunities." Rising 9th grade students select the high school they wish to attend and, whenever possible, the student is assigned to his or her first choice. When too many students select the same school, students are assigned in the following order of priority: (1) siblings who are attending the requested school, (2) race, (3) distance from student's home to the school, and (4) lottery. The race-based factor is used if the school, after placement of siblings, is racially imbalanced. If a school is more than 55 percent or less than 25 percent white, it is considered imbalanced. The percentages are based on the overall white student population in the school district which is 40 percent. The allowable range is plus or minus 15 percent of that demographic. The percentage of white student enrollment is constantly monitored so that the race criterion can turn off and on depending on how the percentage is affected by students as they are placed.

Jefferson County Public Schools has a different program and is in a different historical posture. For 25 years, Jefferson County Public Schools was under a court order to desegregate. It was released from judicial supervision in 2000. At that time, the school district chose voluntarily to maintain its integrated status by use of a "managed choice plan that include[d] broad racial guidelines." The Jefferson County Public School program is more complicated and involves consideration of more acceptance/assignment criteria than the Seattle plan, but it, too, sets percentage goals. The program aims to attain or retain at each school a Black enrollment of at least 15 percent and not more than 50 percent.

The federal circuit courts in the Washington and Kentucky cases both recognized the educational benefits of racial diversity in public schools. Expert testimony in the cases, accepted by the courts, reported the following educational benefits for students attending racially diverse schools: improved critical thinking skills (the ability to both understand and challenge views that are different from one's own), improved race relations, reduction of prejudicial attitudes, improved academic performance, appreciation for the country's diverse heritage, and better preparation for working in diverse workplaces and training of the nation's future leaders. The Kentucky court also cited approvingly the school board's belief that school integration benefits the system as a whole "by creating a system of roughly equal components, not one urban system and another suburban system, not one rich and another poor, not one Black and another White." The Washington court discussed the school board's interest in the "flip side" of the benefits of an integrated educational experience—avoiding racially isolated schools. It cited research that has found that racially isolated schools are characterized by high poverty, lower average test scores, lower levels of student achievement, fewer advanced courses, and less qualified teachers.

The Washington court found the plan to be narrowly tailored, in part because it did not set aside any fixed number of slots for white or nonwhite students and used race only as a "tiebreaker" when a school was oversubscribed. It noted that the number would vary from year to year and was necessary to avoid student assignments that replicated Seattle's segregated housing patterns. The Kentucky court said the school board's plan there "fit" the intended objective because it did not unduly harm other students because all schools have similar funding, offer similar academic programs, and have the same range of students. It did not see any race-neutral alternative that would accomplish the school board's compelling objective.

Contrary to the findings of the lower appellate courts, however, the U.S. Supreme Court found that, given the small number of assignments affected by the two plans, the schools failed to prove that the desired end could not have been achieved through different, race-neutral, means. "Those entrusted with directing our public schools can bring to bear the creativity of experts, parents, administrators, and other concerned citizens to find a way to achieve the compelling interests they face without resorting to widespread governmental allocation of benefits and burdens on the basis of racial classifications." (J. Kennedy, concurring.)

## 14:21. Can race be considered by school districts in ways that do not involve assignment of students?

The U.S. Supreme Court's decision in the Seattle, Washington, and Jefferson County, Kentucky, cases specifically stated that school districts could use "strategic site selection" for new schools, the drawing of attendance boundaries, targeted recruiting of students and faculty, and allocation of resources for special programs to pursue the goal of bringing together students of diverse backgrounds and races.

## 14:22. Can a school board classify students based on gender?

Gender-based classifications usually face heightened judicial scrutiny (see **14:7**). In *United States v. Virginia*, 518 U.S. 515 (1996), the United States Supreme Court found no "exceedingly persuasive justification" for excluding all women from VMI (Virginia Military Institute), a public institution of higher learning.

In Maryland, however, gender-based classifications are required to meet the higher "strict scrutiny" standard (*Murphy v. Edmonds*, 325 Md. 342 (1992)). This is because, in 1978, Maryland ratified the Equal Rights Amendment to the Maryland Constitution's Declaration of Rights (Article 46). The Amendment states: "Equality of rights under the law shall not be abridged or denied because of sex." By adopting the Equal Rights Amendment, Maryland made distinctions based on gender "suspect" and, therefore, subject to "strict scrutiny."

### 14:23. Must schools have an equal number of teams for boys and girls?

Title IX (20 U.S.C. § 1681) applies to clubs and to intramural and interscholastic athletic programs. In enforcing this law, the U.S. Department of Education's Office for Civil Rights looks for "substantial proportionality" and school districts "are not required to offer the same sports or even the same number of sports to men and women ... [but schools] are required to provide equal opportunity to participate and to equally effectively accommodate the athletic interests and abilities of men and women." Title IX Athletics Investigator's Manual, Office for Civil Rights, Department of Education (1990).

The Office for Civil Rights uses a tripartite test to help it evaluate substantial proportionality. First, it looks first at whether there is a statistical disparity between the numbers of males and females participating in sports. If there is a statistical disparity, then the Office for Civil Rights will look at whether the educational institution can show a history and continuing practice of expanding program opportunity demonstrably responsive to developing interest and abilities of members of the gender that is under-represented or, if it cannot show program expansion, whether the educational institution can demonstrate that the interests and abilities of the under-represented group have been fully and effectively accommodated by the present program. This sometimes involves actual surveys of the under-represented group to ascertain any unmet interest.

The case of *Horner v. Kentucky High School Athletic Association*, 43 F.3d 265 (5th Cir. 1994), provides an illustration. The Kentucky High School Athletic Association, which had a men's fast-pitch baseball team, failed to offer a fast-pitch softball team for female students. Two surveys revealed that only 9 percent and 17 percent, respectively, of the females surveyed were interested in a fast-pitch softball team for women. Furthermore, female students were not prohibited from trying out for the "men's" team. The federal court concluded that plaintiffs had failed to show that the needs and abilities of female students were not being adequately accommodated.

Gender equity can also involve scrutiny of equipment and supplies, practice times and game schedules, travel accommodations, coaching assignments and compensation, locker room facilities, and publicity.

## 14:24. Are single-sex schools or single-sex classes lawful?

Title IX of the Education Amendments of 1972 prohibits sex discrimination in education programs or activities (see **14:12**). This Federal law states: "No person in the United States, on the basis of sex, can be excluded from participation in, be denied the benefits of, or be subjected to discrimination under any education program or activity receiving Federal financial assistance" (20 U.S.C. § 1681). There are several exceptions, including father-son and mother-daughter activities so long as each sex has comparable activities.

On January 8, 2002, the President signed into law the No Child Left Behind Act of 2001 (NCLB). NCLB included a provision that encouraged "innovative" programs, including single-sex classes. The U.S. Department of Education was directed to develop guidelines for schools to use in establishing single-sex schools and classes within 120 days of the enactment. Draft guidance was developed and circulated for comment on March 9, 2004, with comments to be received by April 23, 2004. Final regulations were released on October 24, 2006.

The regulations permit a school system to offer single-sex *classes* under certain conditions. The school system will be required to identify an important governmental interest, such as improving academic achievement or offering a diverse range of educational opportunities for students, pursuant to a school district policy, that might also include charter schools, magnet schools and the like.

The school district must also offer a substantially equal single-sex or coeducational class to the other sex. A non-exhaustive list of factors that will be considered in determining whether a "substantially equal" class is offered to the other sex includes quality, range, and content of curriculum and other services provided; the quality and availability of books, instructional materials, and technology; the faculty and staff; geographic accessibility; the quality, accessibility, and availability of facilities and resources, and intangible features, such as reputation of faculty.

It would not necessarily have to offer a substantially equal single-sex class in the same subject for the other sex. If, for example, parents and students showed keen interest in a single-sex chemistry class for girls and boys expressed no interest in a single-sex chemistry class, the school could offer the class so long as a comparable coeducational chemistry class was also offered.

The regulations require a school district to conduct evaluations of their single-sex classes at least once every two years to ensure compliance with regulatory requirements.

### 14:25. Can a school district classify students on the basis of socio-economic status?

Wealth, or lack of wealth (poverty), is not a "suspect class." Consequently, classifications based on socio-economic status (SES) will be upheld by the courts if the classification bears any rational relationship to a legitimate governmental interest. Some experts note that socio-economic integration is more significant than racial integration because motivated students and active parents track more by class than by race and these are significant factors influencing academic success of students. A 1988 National Education Longitudinal Study found that middle-income parents are four times more likely than low-income parents to be PTA members and twice as likely to have contacted their children's school about academic matters.

Several school districts, including most notably the San Francisco Unified School District, began to use socio-economic status, among other factors, in student assignment decisions. San Francisco is a good illustration of the evolution of desegregation efforts in public schools since *Brown v. Board of Education*, 347 U.S. 483 (1954).

In 1978, the National Association for the Advancement of Colored People (NAACP) and a group of black parents filed a class action lawsuit against the school district alleging the failure to desegregate the schools. After litigating various issues, the parties submitted a consent decree which was approved by the court on May 20, 1983. The decree contained guidelines to prevent any racial or ethnic group from exceeding 45 percent of the student body at any regular school or 40 percent at any "alternative" school. The decree was modified on November 5, 1993, following receipt of a report from a court-appointed investigative team that found the goal of desegregation largely to have been achieved, but noting the persistence of an achievement gap between black and Hispanic students and other students.

On July 11, 1994, suit was filed against the school district on behalf of schoolchildren of Chinese descent alleging that the 45/40 percent ethnic distribution requirement constituted race discrimination. On the first day of trial, February 16, 1999, the parties submitted a settlement agreement which was accepted because the demographics of the school district had changed and the judge believed that the race-based student-assignment plan was no longer necessary or constitutional. The settlement eliminated the race/ethnic based student assignment plan. The plan was amended on July 11, 2001, and, among other things, contained a new student assignment plan based on (1) the school attended by siblings, (2) any special learning needs, and (3) a "diversity index" which took into account socio-economic status, academic achievement, English-language learner status, mother's educational background, academic performance history, language spoken at home, and geographic area. The decree, by agreement, was to terminate on December 31, 2005.

As the deadline for termination of the 1999/2001 settlement approached, the school district and others asked that the consent decree be extended 18 months. In an opinion dated November 8, 2005, the judge refused to extend the decree, ending over 20 years of court-supervised desegregation in San Francisco. The judge said: "The consent decree itself has lasted almost twice as long as the period of Reconstruction following the Civil War." The judge's refusal to extend the decree was based on failure of the plan to maintain desegregated schools and persistence of the achievement gap. In 1997-1998, only one school had a student body that was more than 50 percent of one race, but by 2005, one in three schools were resegregated and the academic achievement gap was greatest in these schools. The court expressed disappointment in the failure of the diversity index to maintain desegregated schools, but did not find that the resegregation was a "vestige" of past discrimination and so the decree was ended.

## 14:26. Can a school district classify students based on age?

Age traditionally has not been considered a suspect class and, therefore, classifications based on age will be upheld under the U.S. Constitution so long as there is some rationale for drawing the distinction. There is an Age Discrimination in Employment Act (ADEA) which was adopted by Congress and signed into law in 1967. It provides special protection for individuals who are 40 years of age or older from employment discrimination based on age. The so-called *McDonnell Douglas* test (see **14:15**) is used by courts to determine whether an individual has been discriminated against in violation of the ADEA. Maryland also has a law that prohibits discrimination based on age but, unlike the federal ADEA, it does not define any age.

School districts typically draw a number of distinctions based on age. For example, the Education Article of the Annotated Code of Maryland defines those who have access to a free public education by residency and by age. "All individuals who are 5 years old or older and under 21 shall be admitted free of charge for the public schools of this State" (Md. Code Ann., Ed. Art. § 7-101). Maryland has defined this provision to mean that a student must be at least 5 years old on or before September 1 in the year in which the child applies for entrance. The rationale for the age requirements and limits presumably is based on the maturity level of children and their readiness for school work and discipline on the one end (5 years old) and on the other end the time it should take a student to complete the required program of studies (21 years old).

**14:27. Can a school district classify students based on ability?**

Grouping students by ability, sometimes referred to as "tracking," is constitutional so long as it is not a subterfuge for discrimination based on race/ethnicity or nationality. In *Lau v. Nichols*, 414 U.S. 563 (1974) (see **14:10**), the United States Supreme Court said that "any ability grouping or tracking system employed by a school system to deal with the special language skill needs of a national origin-minority group must be designed to meet such language skill needs as soon as possible and must not operate as an educational dead end of permanent track."

Sometimes ability grouping in subject matter/content areas results in classes that are racially/ethnically imbalanced. While this fact alone does not constitute unlawful discrimination, it will often trigger a legal challenge. Courts will defer to the educational judgment of a school, but will also examine the motivation for the program and how evenhandedly the program is administered. "[A]s a general rule, school systems are free to employ ability grouping, even when such a policy has a segregative effect, so long, of course, as such a practice is genuinely motivated by educational concerns and not discriminatory motives" (*Holton v. City of Thomasville School District*, 425 F.3d 1325 (2005), quoting *Castaneda v. Pickard*, 648 F.2d 994 (5th Cir. 1981)).

# 15. Education of Students with Disabilities

### 15:1. What are the Maryland and Federal laws governing the education of students with disabilities?

The federal Individuals with Disabilities Education Act (IDEA), 20 U.S.C. §§ 1400-1487, was amended in 2004 by the Individuals with Disabilities Education Improvement Act (IDEIA or IDEA 2004) (collectively referred to as IDEA). Regulations for the amended law (34 C.F.R. Part 300) were promulgated in 2006. IDEA requires that eligible disabled students receive special education and related services if they are between the ages of 3 and 21, meet the definition of one or more of the categories of disabilities specified in the IDEA and be in need of special education and related services as a result of the disability or disabilities. Services are also provided to eligible children, ages birth through age 3 under either Parts B or C of IDEA. In the three decades since IDEA was passed, the number of students identified to receive services has doubled to a point where more than 10% of all students nationwide are identified as special education students. The cost to educate special education students is on average double the cost per pupil of general education students and the federal government currently provides less than half of the federal share called for under IDEA; the target funding level being 40% of the cost of special education services.

A student who does not meet the definition of an eligible disabled student under IDEA may qualify as a student eligible for services under two other federal statutes; Section 504 of the Rehabilitation Act of 1973, as amended ("Section 504"), or the Americans with Disabilities Act, 42 U.S.C. § 12101 *et seq.* ("ADA"). All IDEA eligible students qualify under Section 504. Students with only temporary illnesses, such as a broken arm or leg, do not qualify under Section 504.

Title 8 of the Education Article to the Annotated Code of Maryland requires the State of Maryland and each local school system to make a free appropriate public education available to each child with a disability who resides in Maryland (Md. Code Ann., Ed. Art. § 8-403). State regulations are found in COMAR 13A.05.01. Maryland's special education laws and regulations duplicate federal laws in most instances.

### 15:2. Who is a child with a disability under the Individuals With Disabilities Education Improvement Act of 2004?

A student must have one or more of the following disabilities to qualify: mental retardation, hearing impairments (including deafness), speech or language impairments, visual impairments (including blindness), emotional disturbance, orthopedic impairments, autism, traumatic brain injury, other health impairments,

411

(*i.e.*, asthma, attention deficit hyperactivity disorder, diabetes, epilepsy, a heart condition, Tourette syndrome), specific learning disabilities, deaf-blindness, or multiple disabilities. This is an exhaustive list, which means if a disability is not in the above list, the student does not qualify under IDEA. In addition to the disability, the student must require special education in order to receive related services.

If the determinant factor is a lack of appropriate instruction in reading, including the essential components of reading instruction, the student may not be considered eligible. The "essential components of reading instruction" means: explicit and systematic instruction in phonemic awareness, phonics, vocabulary development, reading fluency, including oral reading skills, and reading comprehension strategies." This definition is found in the federal No Child Left Behind Act (NCLB), 20 U.S.C. § 6368(3) (see IDEA, 20 U.S.C. § 1414(b)(5)(A)).

In Maryland, if a student requires speech and language services, the student qualifies as a student with a disability (COMAR 13A.05.01.03).

Being intellectually gifted does not qualify a student under IDEA as giftedness is not considered a legal disability, but a gifted student may be eligible under IDEA if he has one or more of the above disabilities. For instance, a gifted student may be learning disabled. In a recent case, the First Circuit Court of Appeals held that a student with Asperger's Syndrome was a qualified individual with a disability even though her academic performance was excellent (*Mr. I, et al. v. Maine Admin. Dist. No. 55*, No. 06-1368/1422 (1st Cir. Mar. 5, 2007)). Many students with Asperger's Syndrome who have good academic performance nevertheless require speech and language services due to poor communications and pragmatic language skills.

### 15:3. What is special education and can it only be provided by a special educator?

Special education means the provision of a Free Appropriate Public Education (FAPE) specially designed instruction to meet the unique needs of a disabled student. It includes instruction in the classroom, in the home, in hospitals and institutions, and elsewhere. It is free to the parents. Specially designed instruction means the adaptation of content, methodology, or delivery of instruction to address the unique needs of a disabled student to ensure access to the general curriculum, so the student can meet the educational standards that apply to each student in the school system (COMAR 13A.05.01.03.B.(63)).

Special education does not need to be provided by a special educator. Depending on the service to be rendered, it can be provided by multiple individuals including but not limited to: a special educator, regular educator, reading teacher, instructional assistant, related service provider or assistant. The question is whether the service is being provided, not who is providing it. No law requires that only a special educator can provide a particular service.

## 15:4. What is a Free Appropriate Public Education (FAPE)?

FAPE describes the education that is legally required to be provided to students identified to receive services under IDEA. First of all, the education services are to be offered to the student "free" of charge. In a recent California case a school district paid more than $100,000.00 to the parents of a special education student to refund the cost of gifts that were found to have been given by the parents to special educators in order to secure various parent-requested special education services for their child. The determination of what is an "appropriate" education under IDEA is decided on a case-by-case basis. In *Board of Education of the Hendrick Hudson Central School District v. Rowley*, 458 U.S. 176 (1982), the Supreme Court identified a two-part analysis in determining FAPE: (1) Has the school system complied with IDEA's procedures, and (2) Is the individualized educational program developed through these procedures reasonably calculated to enable the child to receive educational benefit? While the cost of education services provided under IDEA is paid for with "public" funds, they are occasionally provided in private school settings when the Individualized Education Program (IEP) can only be provided in such a private setting.

## 15:5. What is an Individualized Education Program (IEP)?

An Individualized Educational Program (IEP) is an educational plan designed for the unique needs of each special education student and is formed by parents, teachers, administrators, related services personnel, and age appropriate students working together. An IEP is a legally binding document and constitutes the foundation for the educational services provided to every student with a disability. It must include academic and functional annual goals, and benchmarks or short-term instructional objectives.

## 15:6. Do goals and objectives need to be measurable?

Yes, the IEP must include measurable academic and functional annual goals, as well as benchmarks or short-term instructional objectives. The team must insure that the goals and objectives enable the student to be involved in and make progress in the general curriculum (COMAR.13A.05.01.09).

### 15:7. How is eligibility for special education and related services determined?

Eligibility for special education and related services is determined by the individualized education program (IEP) team and other qualified professionals.

The first step in the eligibility determination is to evaluate the student. Either the parent of the child, the State, or school system personnel may initiate a request for an initial evaluation to determine if the child is a child with a disability (20 U.S.C. § 1414(a)(1)(B)). The Child Find requirements of IDEA require the school system to identify, locate, and evaluate all children with disabilities residing in the jurisdiction. This includes students in private schools in each jurisdiction, even if they live in another county or State. Those children who are highly mobile, such as migrant and homeless children, are subject to Child Find requirements (20 U.S.C. § 1412(a); 34 C.F.R. § 300.111).

### 15:8. What constitutes an evaluation under IDEA?

Evaluations include information provided by the parents, current classroom-based assessments, local or state assessments, classroom-based observations, and observations by teachers and related service providers. The purpose of the evaluation is to determine whether the child is a child with a disability, the educational needs of the child, the Present Levels Of Performance (PLOP), whether the child needs special education and related services, and whether any additions or modifications to the special education and related services are needed to enable the child to meet the measurable annual goals set out in the child's IEP and to participate as appropriate in the general curriculum (20 U.S.C. § 1414(c)(1)(B)). Private evaluations provided by the parents must be considered by the IEP team. To be considered is not the same thing as being accepted verbatim, as the private evaluator may be looking at the student from a clinical or medical model, as opposed to an educational model and may not be as familiar with the student as the teachers who see him every school day.

An evaluation is not the same thing as a screening. Screenings include basic tests or procedures used for all children in a school, grade, or class, such as the Maryland State Assessments, and parental consent is not required for screenings (20 U.S.C. § 1414(a)(1)(E)). Evaluations require parental consent and include individual assessments of the student.

### 15:9. When must the evaluations be conducted?

Initial evaluations must take place within 60 days of receiving signed parental consent for the evaluation. The 60-day deadline does not apply if the parent fails or refuses to produce the child for the evaluation or if the child enrolls in the school system after the 60 days began in the sending/prior school system. In the latter case, the receiving/new school system must work towards a prompt completion of the evaluation and the parent and school system need to agree to a specific time when the evaluation will be completed (20 U.S.C. § 141414(a)(1)(C)(ii)(I)).

An evaluation is not required before the termination of a child's eligibility due to graduation from secondary school with a regular diploma or due to exceeding the age of 21. However, in the above cases, a Summary of Performance must be provided which describes the child's academic achievement and functional performance as well as recommendations as to how to assist the student in meeting his postsecondary goals (20 U.S.C. § 1414(c)(5)).

## 15:10. How is a student to be evaluated?

After a student has been referred to the IEP team by the parent or someone in the school system, the team must determine:

- Is the child a student with a disability?

- What are the present levels of performance (PLOP)?

- What are the child's educational needs?

- What information does the IEP team need to develop an IEP that enables the student to be involved in and progress in the general curriculum?

- What are the special education and related services needed by the student?

To make these decisions, the team should use a variety of assessment tools and strategies. It should gather relevant functional, cognitive, developmental, behavioral, and physical information, academic information, and information provided by the parent, as well as printed tests and observations. It should look at current classroom-based assessments, including State and county-wide assessments and observations. The assessment should be in all areas related to the suspected disability such as academic performance, communication, general intelligence, health, hearing, motor abilities, social, emotional, and behavioral status. The team should not use a single procedure or assessment to determine if the student has a disability or the appropriate educational program for the student. If the assessment was not administered under standard conditions, the assessment document must state how it varied from standard administration procedures (20 U.S.C. § 1414(a); COMAR 13A.05.01.06).

If the suspected disability is a learning disability, someone other than the teacher must observe the student and the learning environment, including the regular classroom setting, to document academic performance and behavior in the area of difficulty (COMAR 13A.05.01.05.B.(4)).

Evaluations must be conducted before the team develops an initial IEP. Parents should be provided with the IEP team evaluation decision. IDEA "does not establish a timeline for providing a copy of the evaluation report or the documentation of determination of eligibility to the parents...." (71 Fed. Reg. 46645).

The team should ask whether the determinant factor is a lack of appropriate instruction in reading, including the essential components of reading instruction (phonemic awareness, phonics, vocabulary development, reading fluency—including oral reading skills, and reading comprehension strategies).

A screening by a teacher or specialist to determine appropriate instructional strategies for curriculum implementation is not an evaluation for which parental consent is required (20 U.S.C. § 1414(a)(1)(E)).

### 15:11. What is the timeline to evaluate or re-evaluate the student?

In cases involving an initial evaluation, the IEP team has 60 days to conduct an assessment from the date of receiving parental consent or 90 days after the IEP team receives a written referral (20 U.S.C. § 1414(a)(1)(C); COMAR 13A.05.01.06.A.(1)). Then, the team has 30 days following review of the assessment to develop the initial IEP. The only exceptions occur (1) when the student moves into another county after the parents provide consent for assessment (the parent and the new county need to agree to a specific time when the evaluation will be completed) and (2) when the parent refuses to produce the child for the evaluation (COMAR 13A.05.01.06.A.(2)).

Re-evaluations need occur only once a year, unless the school system and parents agree otherwise. The IEP team must re-evaluate at least once every 3 years, unless the child needs a more frequent timetable. In a re-evaluation, the team is determining whether the child is still a qualified special education child with a disability, the present levels of academic achievement and needs, and whether the IEP needs any additions or modifications (20 U.S.C. § 14149(a)(1)(E); COMAR 13A.05.01.06.E).

### 15:12. What if a parent refuses to provide consent or revokes consent for an evaluation or a reevaluation?

The school system should consider filing for mediation and a due process hearing because the evaluation process is for the benefit of the child. Team members should consider the parents' reason for refusing consent or revoking consent. The reason may be justifiable, or it may indicate a parental concern with exposing certain physical, emotional, or familial problems of the child. But if the school-based members of the IEP team believe that the evaluation is essential for determining the needs of the child, strong consideration should be given to filing a request for mediation and/or a due process hearing.

### 15:13. What should happen if a parent requests a publicly-funded Independent Educational Evaluation (IEE)?

Parents have the right to obtain an IEE of their child. An IEE is an evaluation conducted by a qualified examiner not employed by the school system. Upon request for an IEE, the school system must provide information about where the IEE may be obtained and the criteria for IEEs. A parent may ask the school system to pay for the IEE if the parent disagrees with an evaluation obtained by the school system. In such case, the school system must either pay for the IEE or file a request for a due process hearing. The school system cannot refuse to pay and then fail to file for a due process hearing. In the hearing, the school system must show that (1) the parent's IEE did not meet the school system's criteria, or (2) that the school system's evaluation is appropriate. Should the school system prevail, the parent may still obtain an IEE, but not at school system expense.

The school system may ask why the parent wants an IEE or why the parent objects to the school system's evaluation, but may not require the parent to respond; nor may the school system unreasonably delay either providing the IEE or filing for a due process hearing.

Any IEE obtained by the parent must be considered by the school system and presented at any due process hearing. To consider an IEE only means that the IEP team reviews and discusses the IEE results; it does not mean that the IEP team must comply with the recommendations of the IEE (20 U.S.C. § 1414; 34 C.F.R. § 300.502(c)).

### 15:14. Is an IEP a contract?

No, the IEP is not a contract as there is no offer, acceptance, or consideration. But it is a statement of special education services to be provided to a student in order for the student to receive a FAPE. The special education services identified in the IEP must be provided. An IEP document states the student's present levels of academic and functional performance, and states how the disability affects the student's involvement and progress in the general curriculum. It states measurable academic and functional annual goals, including benchmarks or short-term instructional objectives that relate to the student's needs that result from the disability to help the student to be involved in and make progress in the general curriculum. The IEP identifies the special education and related services and supplementary aids and services based on peer-reviewed research to the extent practicable that are necessary for the student to make progress towards his or her goals. This includes the staffing support, program modifications or supports for school personnel. It includes the individual accommodations that are needed to measure the student's academic achievement and functional performance on Statewide or district-wide assessments (20 U.S.C. § 1412(a)(16)(A)).

No school system or employee is to be held accountable if the student does not achieve the progress projected in the annual goals or objectives. But the school system and personnel must make a good faith effort to assist the child to achieve the goals and objectives (COMAR 13A.05.01.09). However, just because a student does not make progress on a component of an IEP for two school quarters has not been shown as enough to indicate that the IEP is inadequate (*Alexis v. Board of Education for Baltimore County Public Schools*, 286 F. Supp. 2d 551 (D. Md. 2003)).

Sometimes, the school system will commit a procedural error and not strictly comply with the technical standards of the IDEA. But if the student continues to make educational progress despite the procedural error, that does not invalidate the IEP (*Gadsby by Gadsby v. Grasmick*, 109 F.3d 940, 956 (4th Cir. 1997)).

### 15:15. Does the IEP have to be implemented?

Yes, the IEP must be implemented as soon as possible. In *Board of Education of Montgomery County v. Brett Y*, No. 97-1939, 1998 WL 390553 (4th Cir. 1998), the Court stated that "as soon as possible" does not mean "immediately" or "immediately, most of the time." Once an IEP is signed, it must be implemented in whole. In those cases where the IEP is not an initial IEP, but is not signed by the parent, the IEP must still be implemented. Parental signature is only required for the initial IEP (34 C.F.R. § 323).

If an educator or parent does not agree with an existing IEP, the only recourse is to hold a new IEP meeting or to file for mediation and/or a due process hearing. In the meantime, the IEP must be implemented. The IEP cannot be ignored. Should the educators implementing the IEP find that the IEP is not appropriate, a new IEP meeting should be scheduled.

### 15:16. If a student transfers into a school in Maryland from another school system, does the receiving school system need to implement the existing IEP?

If a student, within the same academic year, transfers to a new school (the "receiving school"), but had an IEP in the sending school located in Maryland, the receiving school must provide the child with FAPE, which includes comparable services to those received in the sending school, in consultation with the parents. These services must continue to be provided until the IEP team adopts the prior IEP or develops a new IEP. If the student came from outside of Maryland within the same academic year, the receiving school must also provide FAPE, which includes comparable services to those provided in the sending school, in consultation with the parents, until an evaluation is conducted and a new IEP is developed (20 U.S.C. § 2014(d)(2)(C)(i)(I); COMAR 13A.05.01.09.E.)

The receiving school should obtain the student's school records from the sending school. The sending school should take reasonable steps to promptly provide the records (20 U.S.C. § 2014(d)(2)(C)(ii)).

### 15:17. How does the IEP team determine if the student is receiving a free, appropriate, public education ("FAPE")?

The first part of the analysis focuses on whether the procedures of IDEA have been followed, such as timely evaluations. The second part of the analysis is the focus of most due process hearings—the issue of receipt of educational benefit, or FAPE. Receipt of FAPE does not require the best possible education, but "some educational benefit." The issue is never whether an alternative private school is better than the public school, or even appropriate, but whether the public school has offered an appropriate program. The team may examine various factors, such as whether the student is achieving passing marks and advancing from grade to grade. The team may look at the report card, work samples, and classroom performance. "IDEA does not require a program that would maximize a student's potential, but instead simply a program that is appropriate" (*A.B. ex rel. D.B. v. Lawson*, 354 F.3d 315 (4th Cir. 2004)). The school system need only provide a "basic floor of opportunity." There is no maximization standard in Maryland. "IDEA's FAPE standards are far more modest than to require that a child excel or thrive. The requirement is satisfied when the state provides the disabled child with 'personalized instruction with sufficient support services to permit the child to benefit educationally from the instruction.' " (*Board of Education of the Hendrick Hudson Central School District v. Rowley*, 458 U.S. 176 (1982); *MM ex rel. DM v. School District of Greenville County*, 303 F.3d 523 (4th Cir. 2002); *Hartmann by Hartmann v. Loudoun County Board of Education*, 118 F.3d 996 (4th Cir. 1997); *Lawson*).

IEP teams may be provided with private reports that contend that a child needs certain services or accommodations or modifications that the child's teachers do not believe are necessary in order to provide a FAPE. "(I)n evaluating whether the IEP proposed by the local school board for a disabled child provides a FAPE, deference may be given to trained educators over psychologists or other 'experts,' and the child's teachers are especially helpful in the development of an appropriate IEP." (*King v. Board of Education of Allegany County*, 999 F. Supp. 750 (D. Md. 1998)). Some private evaluators provide worthwhile information to the IEP team whereas others base their reports on erroneously reported historical information and/or make clinical-medical recommendations.

**15:18. What is an accommodation or modification?**

An accommodation is a practice or procedure that provides a disabled student equitable access during instruction and assessments in the areas of presentation, response, setting and scheduling. A modification is a practice that changes, lowers, or alters learning expectations. The United States Department of Education issued *Standards and Assessments: Non-regulatory Guidance* on March 10, 2003, which grouped accommodations into four (4) categories: (1) Presentation, such as repeat directions, read aloud, larger bubbles on test answer sheets; (2) Response, such as marking answers in a book, the use of reference aids; (3) Setting, such as the use of a study carrel, special lighting, separate room; and (4) Timing/scheduling, such as extended time and frequent breaks. Care should be taken by the IEP team not to oversubscribe to accommodations that are not necessary for a particular student to receive FAPE. Each one should be separately considered.

**15:19. What are the responsibilities of the IEP team?**

The IEP team, including the parents, is responsible for identifying and evaluating students with disabilities, developing, reviewing, or revising an IEP for a student with a disability, and determining the placement of a child with a disability in the least restrictive environment (COMAR 13A.05.01.03; 34 C.F.R. § 300.305). Once a child is identified as eligible under IDEA, the IEP team must meet at least once a year to review the IEP to determine whether the annual goals are being achieved, to revise the IEP and as appropriate, to address any lack of expected progress towards the annual goals and in the general curriculum, the results of any re-evaluations, information provided by the parents, and the child's anticipated needs (34 C.F.R. Part 300, App. A, No. 20).

The IEP team develops the IEP at IEP meetings that are held for any of the above purposes. Decisions of the IEP team do not have to be unanimous; the IEP team strives for consensus. There is no voting at the IEP team meeting. The school system has the ultimate responsibility to ensure that the IEP includes the services needed for a child to receive FAPE. When there is no unanimity in a decision, the school system must send the parents Prior Written Notice of the proposals or refusals or both, regarding the child's educational program (34 C.F.R. Part 300, App. A, No. 9).

**15:20. Do notes need to be taken during the IEP team meeting?**

There is no requirement for notes or minutes. However, the parents are entitled to receive written notice each time the IEP team proposes or refuses to initiate or change the identification, evaluation educational program, or educational placement of a child, or the provision of FAPE to a child. The notice can be placed on a form called Prior Written Notice and/or the notice can be included or enhanced in the notes or minutes of a meeting. The Prior Written Notice and/or other notes of the meeting may be sent via electronic mail if the school system makes such an option available and the parent agrees. The Prior Written Notice should (1) describe the action(s) proposed or refused at the meeting; (2) explain why the school system proposed or refused the actions; (3) describe other options considered and why they were rejected; (4) describe each evaluation procedure, test, record, or report used as a basis for the proposed or refused actions; (5) describe other relevant factors; (6) advise parents of their procedural safeguards (which is done by giving the parents a copy of *Procedural Safeguards – Parental Rights*). At a minimum, the booklet, which is written by the Maryland State Department of Education, must be provided to parents upon the initial referral or parental request for evaluation, upon request by a parent, or upon the filing by the parent of a complaint. Otherwise, the booklet needs only to be provided to the parent once per year. The booklet may be placed upon the school system's Internet website (20 U.S.C. § 1415(d)). (A good practice is to provide a copy to the parents at each IEP team meeting.); and (7) provide sources for the parents to contact to obtain assistance in understanding IDEA (which can be done by giving out a list of attorneys and advocates). Parents may inspect and review all of the student's records relating to the identification, evaluation, educational placement, and provisions of FAPE (COMAR 13A.05.01.10). Upon request, test protocols may be made available for inspection and review, but not copying due to the copyright laws.

### 15:21. Does the IEP team meeting need to be taped?

Neither State nor federal law requires that IEP team meetings be audio-taped or video-taped. Each school system may require, prohibit, limit or otherwise regulate the use of recording devices at IEP team meetings. However, should there be a policy, it must provide for exceptions if the parent needs to tape to ensure his/her understanding of the IEP or the IEP process. Any tape made by the school system becomes an "educational record" under the federal Family Educational Rights and Privacy Act (FERPA) (34 C.F.R. Part 300, App. A, No. 21). The school system is not required to produce a transcript of a tape made at an IEP team meeting. Even if a parent is allowed to tape an IEP team meeting, such permission does not extend to taping parent-teacher conferences or telephone conversations. Any taping must be conducted consistent with Maryland's wiretapping laws, which require knowledge of the person being taped. There is no right under Maryland or federal laws to allow a parent or classroom observer to audio-tape or video-tape classroom instruction and doing so would likely violate the privacy rights of the other children in the classroom.

There have been occasions at IEP team meetings that parents and their advocates have taped the meeting without the knowledge of the school-based team members. The parents should be advised that the taping was illegal and cannot be used. Ideally, the tape should be destroyed if it was made illegally. Sanctions can be taken against attorneys who knowingly tape an IEP meeting in violation of the wiretapping laws.

### 15:22. Who are the required members of the IEP team?

The IEP team should include the parents of the student, not less than one special education teacher or not less than one special education provider of the student, a representative of the school system who is qualified to provide, or supervise the provision of specially designed instruction for the student and who is knowledgeable about the general curriculum and the available resources of the school system, an individual who can interpret the instructional implications of evaluation results, and the student, if appropriate. Either the parents or the school system may invite others, who have knowledge or special expertise regarding the student. The team must also include not less than one regular educator of the student if the student is or may be participating in the regular education environment. But if the student does not have a general education teacher or is younger than school age, the team must include someone qualified to teach a child of that age. When the student is age 14 or older, the student should be invited to the IEP team meeting, along with a representative of any other agency that is likely to be responsible for providing or paying for transition services (COMAR 13A.05.01.07). If the student attends a private school, the private school should be invited to participate in the IEP team meeting (34 C.F.R. § 300.325).

### 15:23. Who is considered a parent under IDEA?

A parent under IDEA is the biological or adoptive parent, a guardian, a person acting as a parent of a student (*i.e.*, grandparent, stepparent or other relative with whom the child lives), an individual who is legally responsible for the child's welfare, or a foster parent with whom the child lives, if the foster parent has been granted limited guardianship for educational decision-making purposes by the court or a properly appointed surrogate parent (COMAR 13A.05.01.B.(52)).

### 15:24. Do all of the members of the IEP team need to attend the IEP meeting?

Team members do not have to attend if the parent and school system agree that attendance is not necessary because the member's area of the curriculum or related services is not being modified or discussed. Team members should attend the meeting if the meeting involves a modification to the IEP or discussion of the member's area of the curriculum or related service. Under IDEA 2004, to be excused when the meeting involves a modification to the IEP or discussion of the member's area of the curriculum or related service, the member must submit a written summary of input into the development of the IEP prior to the meeting and there must be agreement by the parent and school system in writing as to the excusal (20 U.S.C. § 1414(d)(1)(C)).

### 15:25. How often does an IEP team meeting need to be held?

Meetings must be held periodically, but not less than annually, to review and revise the IEP. Meetings must be held within 30 days of conducting an evaluation for the purpose of developing the IEP (COMAR 13A.05.01.08). In cases where the student is being reevaluated, the IEP team must meet within 90 days of the IEP team meeting after the team determines that additional data is needed, the parents notified, and parental consent requested. The team must annually consider whether Extended School Year (ESY) services must be provided to the student (COMAR 13A.05.01.08.B.(2)).

An IEP meeting does not include informal or unscheduled conversations between staff regarding methodologies or lesson plans. A meeting does not include staff meetings to develop or respond to a parental proposal (34 C.F.R. § 500).

### 15:26. How much notice needs to be provided to parents to hold an IEP team meeting, whether it is for an annual review or for disciplinary reasons?

Ten (10) calendar days notice of a meeting must be given unless an expedited meeting is held to address discipline, determine the placement of a child with a disability who is not currently receiving special education services, or to meet urgent needs of the student to ensure the provision of FAPE. Should the parent advise that he/she did not receive the ten (10) day notice of the IEP team meeting, the parent should be asked if he/she wants to reschedule the meeting or sign a ten-day notice waiver.

### 15:27. Does the parent need to consent to the IEP?

The parent only needs to consent to the initial (first) IEP. Without consent, the school system may not provide special education and related services to the disabled student. The school system may not initiate due process (mediations or due process hearings) to try to obtain consent for an initial IEP. However, if consent is not provided for the initial IEP, the school system is not liable for failure to provide a FAPE and is not required to reconvene subsequent IEP meetings or develop IEPs (20 U.S.C. § 1414(a)(1)(D)(ii); COMAR 13A.05.01.13.B). Therefore, the student does not receive the benefits of IDEA and may be disciplined as any regular education student without the need for the development of a functional behavioral assessment (FBA) and behavioral intervention plan

(BIP) and the school system may change the placement of the student without compliance with IDEA's due process procedures.

Once consent is given for the initial IEP, consent is not required for any subsequent IEP. If a parent disagrees with a subsequent IEP, the parent must file for mediation or a due process hearing to stop the implementation of any subsequent IEP (COMAR 13A.05.01.13.B; 20 U.S.C. § 1414(a)(1)(D)(ii)).

If a parent declines consent for a particular service, that parental decision cannot be used to deny the student the other services recommended by the IEP team.

### 15:28. Do both parents have to sign the IEP?

Only one parent needs to sign the initial IEP. Occasionally, one parent may consent to the IEP and the other may refuse to consent. Under that circumstance, if the IEP is an initial IEP, the IEP may be implemented. If the IEP is not an initial IEP, but one parent provided consent, the IEP may also be initiated. If neither parent signs the IEP and it is not an initial IEP, the IEP may be implemented. The parent who has not provided consent may always challenge the IEP by filing for mediation or a due process hearing.

School systems frequently confront disputes between parents. It is important for the IEP team to keep the child's interests first and foremost. Towards this end, it is good practice for members of the IEP team to decline to meet with counsel for either parent unless the team member has been subpoenaed.

### 15:29. What do you do if a parent keeps canceling IEP team meetings?

The school system should keep careful records on the cancellations. If the meeting is repeatedly cancelled by or on behalf of the parents, the school system should write to the parents and advise that the meeting will be held without their presence; confirm that the parents are important members of the IEP team, but that the meeting must be held; and that the parents may participate by telephone if they cannot be at the meeting in person. There is no magic number of cancelled meetings that should result in the school system sending this letter as each case is different. However, it is reasonable to assume that if three (3) meetings are cancelled, the school system should follow the above instructions and hold the meeting even if the parents cannot be present. If the parents disagree with decisions made at the IEP team meeting at which they were not present, the school system may offer to hold another meeting. However, in the interim, the team should implement the IEP unless, of course, the team was dealing with an initial IEP where parental consent is required.

## 15:30. How does the IEP team determine the "placement of a child"?

The IEP team is required to place a child in the Least Restrictive Environment (LRE) where the goals and objectives of the IEP may be implemented. Special education is a service for a child, rather than a place. Placement decisions must be made at the IEP team meeting after the IEP is developed. The Fourth Circuit has opined that the IEP team is to compare benefits in the regular classroom to benefits in a segregated classroom and ask if the services in a segregated classroom can be feasibly provided in the regular classroom (*Devries by Deblay v. Fairfax County School Board,* 882 F.2d 876 (4th Cir. 1989)). The placement does not have to be the best. Even if a student is thriving in a private special education school, all the school system need show is that the student can garner some benefit in the public school placement (*A.B. ex rel. D.B. v. Lawson,* 354 F.3d 315 (4th Cir. 2004); 34 C.F.R. §§ 300.114, 116).

## 15:31. What is the Least Restrictive Environment (LRE)?

The Least Restrictive Environment (LRE) means that in making placement decisions, the IEP team must place children with disabilities, to the maximum extent appropriate, with children who are not disabled. Team members should ask whether the services can feasibly be provided in a non-segregated setting (*Hanson v. Smith,* 212 F. Supp. 2d 474 (D. Md. 2002) (the requirement to "maximize" is only applied in Maryland to placement of the disabled child in the LRE; the word "maximize" is not used elsewhere in federal or State law with regards to special education)). Special classes, separate schooling, or other removal of children with disabilities from the regular educational environment occurs only when the nature or severity of the disability of a child is such that education in regular classes with the use of supplementary aids and services cannot be achieved satisfactorily (20 U.S.C. § 1412(a)(5)(A); *Hartmann by Hartmann v. Loudoun County Board of Education,* 118 F.3d 996 (4th Cir. 1997)).

## 15:32. What is inclusion and mainstreaming?

While inclusion and mainstreaming are sometimes used as interchangeable terms in special education today, there are subtle but important historical differences. Mainstreaming has referred to the selective placement of special education students in some general education classes. Inclusion, on the other hand, usually indicates a commitment to place special education students in the school and classes that they would otherwise attend, to the maximum extent appropriate and beneficial. Inclusion brings support services to the student rather than bringing the student to the support services as might have been done with mainstreaming.

No matter what term is used, the student is to be educated with regular education peers to the maximum extent possible. In fact, this is the one time that the word "maximum" should be used in special education. There are myriad ways for a student with special education needs to receive special education services while being educated with nondisabled peers, all of which are determined by the IEP team. The student may receive special education support through co-teaching by a regular educator and special educator in the regular education classroom. Services may be provided by just the regular education teacher in the regular education classroom. Services may be provided by an instructional assistant who provides one-on-one support or is simply available to assist the student in the classroom. A student can receive therapy in the classroom with pull-out therapy as needed, or may receive just pull-out therapy. A student may receive individual therapy in the classroom or in a group setting. Some students receive educational services in a room separate from their regular education peers by just the special education teacher, but are placed in regular education classes as they are ready, with the opportunity to be pulled out if they are not receiving benefit in their regular education classes.

Neither inclusion or mainstreaming is required if the student will not receive educational benefit, if the marginal benefit received by the child is significantly outweighed by the benefits which could feasibly be obtained only in a separate instructional setting, or if the student is disruptive in the regular setting (*Doe v. Arlington County School Board*, 41 F. Supp. 2d 599 (E.D. Va. 1999)). Inclusion or mainstreaming is not required for every disabled child (*Devries by Deblay v. Fairfax County School Board*, 882 F.2d 876 (4th Cir. 1989)).

The issue of the obligation of the school system to provide a continuum of services is one of the most heavily litigated in special education, as it includes the argument often made by parents that a child cannot receive a FAPE if the child has any interaction with nondisabled peers contrary to the intent of IDEA.

### 15:33. What is a continuum of services?

This means that a school system must provide all services necessary for a child to receive a FAPE. The continuum of services includes instruction in regular education, instruction in special education pull-out classes, instruction in the home when a student is physically or emotionally ill and cannot attend school and receiving Home and Hospital Instruction pursuant to COMAR 13A.03.05.01, instruction in State facilities, and instruction in private schools when the public schools cannot provide the FAPE in a public facility. Supplementary aids and services, such as speech and language therapy, transportation, and nursing services, must be provided to the student if necessary for the student to receive a FAPE. School systems do not have to offer the same special education services in all schools but are allowed to centralize services, which is often done when the services are low frequency, such as when an interpreter is needed (*Barnett by*

*Barnett v. Fairfax County School Board*, 927 F.2d 146 (4th Cir. 1991); 34 C.F.R. § 300.115).

## 15:34. What are Extended School Year (ESY) services?

Some students need Extended School Year (ESY) services in order to receive a FAPE. Each state makes its own decisions on the standards for determining eligibility for ESY services. In Maryland, ESY eligibility must be determined annually. The IEP team must consider seven factors:

1. Whether the IEP includes annual goals related to critical life skills.

2. Whether it is likely the child will suffer a substantial regression of critical life skills caused by the normal school break in the regular school year and fail to recover those lost skills in a reasonable time.

3. The child's degree of progress towards mastery of IEP goals related to critical life skills.

4. The presence of emerging skills or breakthrough opportunities.

5. Whether the child has interfering behaviors.

6. The nature and severity of the disability.

7. The existence of special circumstances.

Assuming at least one factor exists, the IEP team next must determine whether the benefits the student gains during the regular school year will be significantly jeopardized if the student is not provided with ESY services during a normal break in the regular school year (COMAR 13A.05.01.08.B.(2); 34 C.F.R. § 300.106; 64 Fed. Reg. 12406, 12576 (1999); *Procedural Safeguards – Parental Rights*, Maryland State Department of Education (July 2005)). The "significantly jeopardized" language was the standard used by the Fourth Circuit Court of Appeals in *MM ex rel. DM v. School District of Greenville County*, 303 F.3d 523 (4th Cir. 2002). Even if one of the above seven factors exists, unless the benefits the student gains during the school year will be significantly jeopardized without ESY services, the services are not required.

Note that "regression and recoupment" is not the only factor the IEP team must consider. Moreover, the Fourth Circuit noted in *MM* that all students, disabled or not, may regress to some extent during lengthy breaks from school.

Additionally, parentally placed private school students are not entitled to ESY services.

## 15:35. When does the IEP team need to review ESY eligibility and the determination of needed services?

ESY eligibility needs to be reviewed annually and early enough in the school year to allow the parents time to file for mediation and/or a due process hearing if the parent disagrees with the ESY eligibility determination or the provision of ESY services (*Reusch v. Fountain*, 872 F. Supp. 1421 (D. Md. 1994)).

## 15:36. What are related services?

Related services means transportation and such developmental, corrective and other supportive services as may be required to assist a student with a disability to benefit from special education. COMAR provides a non-exhaustive list: speech language pathology (although a speech language impairment alone may qualify a student for services), interpreting services, psychological services, physical therapy, occupational therapy, recreation, therapeutic recreation, early identification and assessment of disabilities, counseling, rehabilitation counseling, orientation and mobility services, medical services for diagnostic or evaluation purposes, school health services, nursing services, social work services in school, and parent counseling and training. Not included in the definition are medical devices that are surgically implanted or the replacement of such a device (20 U.S.C. § 1401(26); COMAR 13A.05.01.03.B.(58)). Related services also include the early identification and assessment of disabling conditions in children (20 U.S.C. § 1401(26)). Related services must be provided to the student if written into the IEP, so long as the student is not absent. If a student is absent due to illness and qualifies for Home and Hospital Instruction, the IEP team must meet to develop a Home and Hospital Instruction IEP. When the student returns to school, the IEP team should meet again to review the student's program.

## 15:37. What medical services need to be provided to a student with a disability?

Medical services are defined as those services provided by a physician which determine a child's medically related disability that results in the child's need for special education and related services (20 U.S.C. § 1401(26); 34 C.F.R. § 300.34). Physician services that are for treatment are not a related service (*Laughlin III v. Central Bucks School District*, No. 91-7333, 1994 WL 8114 (E.D. Pa. 1994)). Therapeutic services that must be performed by a psychiatrist are not related services. But if the IEP team determines that the child may have ADHD which may be impacting the child's ability to receive an education and that a medical diagnosis is required, that diagnostic service would need to be provided by the school system.

Health care services by a registered nurse may need to be provided to a student as a related service if the health care services are needed in order for the student to attend school. If a physician and not a nurse must provide the services, they are not considered related services that must be provided by the school system. For instance, clean intermittent catheterization is not an excluded medical service as it does not have to be performed by a physician (*Irving Independent School District v. Tatro*, 468 U.S. 883 (1984)).

A related service does not include a medical device that is surgically implanted, or the replacement of such a device (20 U.S.C. § 1401(26); 34 C.F.R. § 300(b)).

The issue of health-care related services has become a greater issue as more critically ill children are surviving infancy and are entitled to services as medically fragile students who need round-the-clock or intensive care, but not by physicians. In *Cedar Rapids Community School District v. Garrett F. ex rel. Charlene F.*, 526 U.S. 66 (1999), the Supreme Court explained that even if the child needs constant services, such as a child with a ventilator dependency, so long as the services do not have to be provided by a physician, the health related services are a required related service under IDEA. A school system which needs to provide school health services should insist on receiving a written protocol by the physician and should not depend on a parental report for determining the services to be provided. The parent should provide a written release for the school system to communicate with the student's physicians and other health care providers.

### 15:38. Are health care services choices available to parents?

Parents may be concerned with the qualifications of the provider of the health care services. Maryland's Nurse Practice Act will provide guidance in this area. In many cases, the services can be provided by a licensed practical nurse and not by a registered nurse. Sometimes, the parents will prefer that their registered nurse provide the services in the school instead of having a school-provided nurse provide the service, even if they are utilizing their own private insurance for this purpose. Whether or not to allow the parents to bring in their own private duty nurse is within the sole discretion of the school system. Should the school system allow the parents to use their own nurse, the school system should require that the parents' nurse comply with any requirements set forth by the school system, such as keeping the school nurse advised of the student's health, medical needs, and medications. In such a case, the school system must inform the parents that they are not required to use their own insurance because the school system is required to provide the related service at no cost to the parents. This notice should be put in writing. The parents may still choose to access their own insurance. The school system may not require parents to sign up for Medicaid or to incur an out-of-pocket expense such as the payment of a deductible or co-pay amount. The school system may not use a child's benefits under a public insurance program if the use will decrease the available lifetime coverage or any other insured benefit or result in the family paying for services that would otherwise be covered by the public insurance program and that are required for the child outside of school. The school system should not use a child's public health benefits if the result would be to increase premiums, lead to the discontinuation of insurance or risk loss of eligibility for home and community-based waivers (34 C.F.R. § 300.154(d)).

## 15:39. What is an interpreting service?

An interpreting service is a service for a student who is deaf or hard of hearing. It includes oral transliteration services, cued language transliteration services, sign language transliteration and interpreting services, transcription services, including Communication Access Real-Time Translation (CART), C-Print, and TypeWell, as well as special interpreting services for students who are deaf-blind (COMAR 13A.05.01.03.B.(36)). If a student requires these services to receive a FAPE, the services must be identified on the IEP. The local school system must also "ensure that hearing aids or the external components of surgically implanted medical devices worn in school by students with hearing impairments are functioning properly" (COMAR 13A.05.01.08.A.(11)). Mapping services, which involve the programming of the speech processor following a cochlear implant, are not required (300 C.F.R. 113).

## 15:40. What is assistive technology?

An IEP team must consider whether a student requires assistive technology or assistive technology services to benefit from his education. Assistive technology is an item, piece of equipment, or product system, whether acquired commercially or off the shelf, modified, or customized, that is used to increase, maintain, or improve the functional capabilities of a student with a disability (20 U.S.C. § 1401(1); COMAR 13A.05.01.03.B.(4)). Assistive technology devices do not include medical devices that are surgically implanted nor does the term include the replacement of such a device (20 U.S.C.§ 1401(1)). Assistive technology services are services that directly assist a disabled student in the selection, acquisition, or use of an assistive technology device, such as an assistive technology evaluation, purchasing or leasing a device, selecting, designing, fitting, customizing, adapting, applying, maintaining, repairing, or replacing the devices, and providing training or technical assistance for the disabled student or his family.

If a student needs a computer at home in order to receive FAPE, it must be provided by the school system (*Letter to Anonymous*, 29 IDELR 1089 (OSEP 1997)). But in such case, the parents are responsible for damage due to inappropriate use or care (*i.e.*, losing the computer or leaving it outside in the rain), while the school system is responsible for reasonable repairs and maintaining the computer (*Letter to Anonymous*, 21 IDELR 1057 (OSEP 1994)).

Cost may be a factor in deciding what type of assistive technology device to provide to the student, with the proviso that the device selected must be appropriate to meet the student's needs. For instance, the most expensive laptop need not be purchased even if it is the best, as the Supreme Court said in 1982 in *Rowley* that "maximization" is not a requirement of IDEA.

### 15:41. Do student with disabilities have a right to supplementary aids and services for extracurricular activities?

Participation in extracurricular activities is a privilege and not a right. However, if a student is participating in extracurricular activities, the school system must give the student an equal opportunity to participate and the IEP must include a statement of supplementary aids and services necessary for participation in extracurricular and other nonacademic activities (20 U.S.C. § 1414(d)(1)(A)(i)(IV); COMAR 13A.05.01.03.B.(79)). It is more of a Section 504 accessibility issue than it is a requirement to provide nonacademic services and extracurricular activities to students with disabilities. If a student needs supplementary aids and services to participate in a program offered by the public school system, then those supplementary aids and services must be provided for extracurricular activities and field trips.

### 15:42. What are the school system's responsibilities when a child eligible for special education services is placed on Home and Hospital Instruction?

The IEP team does not place the child at home or in a hospital if the child is too ill to attend school. This is not an IEP team responsibility. The obligation to develop an IEP for a student on Home and Hospital Instruction is only triggered when the student meets the stringent requirements for placement in a home or hospital (COMAR 13A.03.05). The regulations provide that the student must have a physical or emotional condition, verified by a licensed physician, psychologist, or psychiatrist, that prevents the student from attending school (COMAR 13A.03.05.04.A). It is the responsibility of the school system, not the IEP team, to review the need for home and hospital services sixty (60) calendar days after the initial determination of eligibility, or sooner at the request of the parent, guardian or local school system, and re-verify the service need if home and hospital services are continued beyond 60 calendar days. The Maryland State Department of Education, by memorandum dated December 3, 2001, opined that home and hospital services are not appropriate for students awaiting enrollment in an alternative program. MSDE stated that "the local school system must provide services in a school-based program (such as a self-contained classroom) while the student is awaiting an appropriate placement. The student may require increased supports (such as additional staffing) as determined by the IEP team while awaiting placement" (COMAR 13A.03.05.10.C.(5)). However, as each student's needs must be evaluated individually, it is possible that there will exist a situation where the IEP team determines that the home is the appropriate place to deliver services pending placement in an alternative program. Such decision is subject to review in a due process hearing.

The school system must convene an IEP team meeting to develop a Home and Hospital IEP. The team will determine what special education and related services the child is able to receive while on Home and Hospital Instruction, including a determination of hours of instruction required to provide the student with a FAPE. When the student returns to school, another IEP team meeting must be convened to develop another IEP (COMAR 13A.05.01.10.C.(6)).

### 15:43. What are the obligations of the local public school system to a student who attends a private school?

Private school students are only entitled to receive a Service Plan, not an IEP (34 C.F.R. § 300.132). The Service Plan is a written statement that describes the special education and related services, including the location of the services and transportation (COMAR 13A.05.01.B.(69)). The Service Plan is developed in meetings initiated and conducted to develop, review, and revise the service plan (COMAR 13A.05.01.16.B). The obligations to a private school student are far more limited than the obligations to a public school student. The private school student has no "individual right to receive some or all of the special education and related services the child would receive if enrolled in a public school" (34 C.F.R. § 300.137). The special education services that are available for eligible private school students are those services identified by the local school system after an annual consultation with private school representatives and representatives of parents (34 C.F.R. § 300.134; COMAR 13A.05.01.16.B).

After the consultation, a local school system may determine that private school students may only receive speech and language services and the monies to be spent on all of the eligible private school students limited to the expenditure of a specified percentage of Federal Part B funds. The cost of transportation may be included in the calculation of funds (71 Fed. Reg. 46,596-46, 597 (2006); COMAR 13A.05.01.16.B). While additional funds may be spent, they do not have to be spent and due to the failure of the Federal government to adequately fund IDEA, the amount of money available is very small (34 C.F.R. § 300.133). As a result, some disabled private school students will not receive any services. Due process procedures are not applicable to the provision of services to private school students, except for allegations regarding Child Find (34 C.F.R. § 300.140(b)). The Comments note that the school system in which the private school of the student is located is responsible for conducting Child Find, including an individual evaluation for a child with a disability enrolled by the parents (71 Fed. Reg.46,592 (2006)). Parents may opt out of Child Find (300 C.F.R. § 300(e)(4)). Significantly, the Comments provide, "If the parent makes clear his or her intention to keep the child enrolled in the private elementary school or secondary school located in another LEA, the LEA where the child resides need not make FAPE available to the child" (71 Fed. Reg. 46,593).

The Supreme Court has agreed to decide a case to determine whether a child with disabilities that has been parentally placed in a private school is entitled to tuition reimbursement when the school district has offered FAPE but the child has never been enrolled in public school. The case is made more interesting because the student's father is the multi-millionaire co-founder of MTV and former CEO of Viacom, Inc., and is suing the funding-strapped New York City school district (*Board of Education of the City School District of the City of New York v. Tom F.*, Docket No. 06-637).

### 15:44. What are the requirements for transition services?

Transition services help the student in the planning of the transition to the post-secondary world, whether oriented towards work, training, schooling, or just living as independently as possible. While IDEA 2004 requires transition planning for students turning age 16, Maryland retained the requirement for transition planning to begin at age 14 (COMAR 13A.05.01.09.A.(3)). Participants in the IEP team meeting when transition services are discussed include a representative of any other agency likely to be responsible for providing or paying for transition services, but only with the consent of the student's parent or the student if the student has reached the age of majority. If the participating agency does not attend the meetings, the school system must take other steps to obtain the involvement of the agency in the planning and provision of transition services (COMAR 13A.05.01.07.A.(3)). The IEP must address "appropriate measurable postsecondary goals, based upon age-appropriate transition assessments relating to training, education, employment, and where appropriate, independent living skills" (34 C.F.R. § 300.320(b)(1)). Transition services are result oriented, based on the student's individual needs, and may include instruction, related services, community experiences, the development of employment and other post-secondary living objectives. For some students, transition planning will include planning for post-secondary activities in the area of daily living skills and a functional vocational evaluation (COMAR 13A.05.01.03.B.(80)). If appropriate, the IEP must provide a statement of the participating agency's responsibilities or linkages, or both, before the student leaves the secondary school setting (COMAR 13A.05.01.09.A.(3)).

**15:45. What occurs when a special education student turns age 18?**

Under COMAR 13A.08.02.08, which is Maryland's equivalent of FERPA, "if a student is 18 years old or older, the (student records) rights accorded to and the consent required of the parent or guardian of the student shall thereafter only be accorded to and required of the eligible student." However, under IDEA and COMAR, in most cases the parents will retain special education due process rights. This is because the special education rights only transfer to the student if the student has not been adjudged incompetent under Section 8-412.1(a) of the Education Article and there is documentation that:

- The parents are unavailable or unknown. In such case, the student must request that parental rights be transferred to the student in lieu of a surrogate parent,

- Despite attempts by the school system to involve the parents, the parents have refused to participate in the special education process,

- The parents affirmatively rejected participation in the special education process,

- The parents are unable to participate in the special education process due to prolonged hospitalization, institutionalization, or serious illness or infirmity of one or both parents and the parents have consented to the transfer of rights to the student,

- There exist extraordinary circumstances beyond parental control that precludes the parents' participation in the special education process and the parents have consented to the transfer of rights to the student, or

- The student does not live with the parents and is not in the care or custody of a public agency.

In cases where the parents do not consent to the transfer of rights to the 18-year-old student, and the student has not been adjudged incompetent, either the parents or the student may file for due process for a decision on whether the rights should transfer. In the typical case where parents have been involved in the IEP process, it is likely that the parents' rights will continue.

**15:46. Is the discipline of special education students different from the discipline of their non-disabled peers?**

Yes. There are a number of significant limitations under IDEA for the provision of discipline to students with disabilities that do not apply to discipline of their non-disabled peers. During the congressional reauthorization of IDEA in 2004, probably the most hotly debated and controversial topic was the discipline of special education students and the result was some loosening of the discipline limitations effecting public schools. State regulations include a separate chapter entitled, "Discipline of Students with Disabilities" (COMAR 13A.08.03.02.01-.11), which includes provisions on change of placement, parental notification, whether the behavior is a manifestation of the student's disability, and rights to appeal.

## 15:47. What is a change in placement for disabled students in terms of discipline?

Disabled students may be removed from their current educational placement without the provision of educational services for not more than 10 consecutive school days for any violation of school rules to the same extent as non-disabled students (*Honig v. Doe,* 484 U.S. 305 (1988)). If a disciplinary action exceeds 10 consecutive school days, it is considered a change in placement. Short term disciplinary actions (fewer than 10 school days) that cumulatively add up to more than 10 school days may also constitute a change in placement if the removal is part of a pattern. The team needs to examine the length of each removal, total time of the removals in one school year, and the proximity of the removals to each other. If a removal is determined to be a change in placement, certain IDEA protections are triggered, including a requirement to make a manifestation determination. In cases when removals amount to more than 10 school days in a school year, school personnel must determine the extent of services needed to enable the student to progress in the general curriculum and toward the IEP goals. If the removal is not a change in placement, the student may be removed from the current placement, but services must be provided "to enable the child to participate in the general education curriculum, although in another setting, and to progress toward meeting the goals set out in the child's IEP" (20 U.S.C. § 1415(k)(1)(B); COMAR 13A.08.03.05).

According to the Supreme Court in *Honig,* in-school disciplinary procedures such as the use of study carrels, time-out, detention, or the restriction of privileges do not constitute a change in placement.

Whether a bus suspension is a change in placement depends on whether the bus transportation is part of the student's IEP. If it is not a part of the student's IEP, it is the parents' obligation to get the student to school, as with any regular education student. But, the school system should examine whether the behavior on the bus is similar to behavior in a classroom that is addressed in an IEP. Additionally, the team may need to determine whether the bus behavior should be addressed in the IEP or behavioral intervention plan (64 Fed. Reg., No. 48 12619 (1999)).

### 15:48. How is the manifestation determination made?

When the disciplinary action will result in a change in placement, the IEP team must review all relevant information in the student's file, including teacher observations, and information from the parents to determine:

1.  Was the student's conduct caused by or did it have a direct and substantial relationship to the student's disability?

2.  Was the student's conduct the direct result of the school system's failure to implement the IEP?

If either answer is "yes," the conduct is considered to have been a manifestation of the student's disability. If so, the IEP team must:

1.  Conduct a functional behavioral assessment (FBA);

2.  Implement a behavior intervention plan (BIP);

3.  If a BIP already exists, review the BIP and modify it, if necessary;

4.  Return the student to his placement, unless the parents agree otherwise with the school system as part of the BIP, unless the student was removed to an interim alternative educational setting (IAES) for drugs, weapons, or serious bodily injury (20 U.S.C. § 1415(k)(1)(E) and (F)).

### 15:49. What rules apply to students who are disciplined for drugs, weapons, or serious bodily injury offenses?

Disabled students may be removed to an interim alternative educational setting (IAES) for up to 45 school days for the offenses listed below. This removal is not considered a change in placement and it is inconsequential if the behavior was a manifestation of the student's disability, if the student:

1.  Carries or possesses a weapon at school or a school function;

2.  Knowingly possesses, uses, sells or solicits the sale of illegal drugs while at school or a school function;

3.  Inflicted serious bodily injury upon another person at school, on school premises or at a school function (20 U.S.C. § 1415(k)(1)(G)). Serious bodily injury means an injury that results in a substantial risk of death, extreme physical pain, protracted and obvious disfigurement, or protracted loss or impairment of the function of a bodily member, organ, or mental faculty (COMAR 13A.08.03.02).

Therefore, even if the student carried or possessed a weapon at school or at a school function, and these actions were the direct and substantial result of the student's disability, the student may still be removed to the IAES for up to 45 school days. Should the IEP team also determine that the student requires a change in placement because the student is dangerous to himself or others and if the parent disagrees with the proposal of the IEP team, the school system may seek injunctive relief in the local circuit court or the United States District Court.

Law enforcement authorities should always be contacted and a report made in cases where the student has engaged in conduct which may result in placement in an IAES for the above reasons.

## 15:50. What is a Functional Behavioral Assessment (FBA) and a Behavioral Intervention Plan (BIP)?

FBAs were first required in IDEA 1997, are also required in IDEA 2004, and required in COMAR, but never defined. IDEA 2004, 20 U.S.C. § 1415(k)(1)(D)(ii), provides that if an eligible disabled student is removed from his placement, the student shall "receive, as appropriate, a functional behavioral assessment, behavioral intervention services and modifications that are designed to address the behavior violation so that it does not recur." The comments to the current federal regulations provide that "IEP teams need to be able to address the various situational, environmental and behavioral circumstances raised in individual cases." In some situations, parental consent is required before conducting the FBA. Other times, it may consist of a review of existing data (64 Fed. Reg. 12620 (March 12, 1999)). The FBA gives the IEP team an opportunity to search for the reason the student misbehaved. Best practice is to conduct a FBA prior to removing a student for more than ten (10) days.

The BIP is developed based on the information gained by the IEP team with the FBA. If a BIP already exists, the IEP team is required to review the plan and modify it, if necessary, to address the student's problem behavior.

## 15:51. If it is determined that the student's behavior was not a manifestation of his disability, what disciplinary action may be taken?

In cases where the IEP team determines that the student's misbehavior was not a manifestation of his disability, the school may use the same regular disciplinary rules and procedures that it uses with non-disabled students. If the student's removal is for more than 10 school days, then FAPE must be provided. However, the FAPE may be provided in an interim alternative educational setting (IAES). These services in the IAES must allow the student "to continue to participate in the general education curriculum, although in another setting, and to progress toward meeting the goals set out in the child's IEP." The student is also entitled to receive a functional behavioral assessment, behavioral intervention services and modifications to address the behavior violation so that it does not recur (20 U.S.C. § 1415(k)(1)(D)(ii)).

The manifestation decision may be appealed by the parent. In such case, the Office of Administrative Hearings will hold an expedited hearing, which means that the hearing will be held within twenty (20) school days from the date of the hearing request. The decision of the administrative law judge must be rendered within ten (10) school days after the hearing. Contrary to prior law, the disciplinary setting (the interim alternative educational placement) is the stay-put placement until the administrative law judge decides the issue or until the expiration of the disciplinary period (20 U.S.C. § 1415(k)(4)).

### 15:52. May a disabled student be expelled?

Yes. Generally, a student with a disability cannot be suspended for more than 10 school days if his misconduct was caused by, or was related to, his disability. However, under limited circumstances, a disabled student may be expelled whether or not the misconduct is a manifestation of his disability. For example, where the misconduct involves the disabled student: (a) bringing a weapon or drugs to school; (b) inflicting serious bodily injury on another person; or (c) otherwise posing a danger to himself of others, expulsion of the disabled student may be warranted. Whenever a disabled student is excluded from his educational setting for more than 10 school days, his removal is subject to special rules and limitations (COMAR 13A.08.03.03.B). But, "school personnel may consider any unique circumstances on a case-by-case basis" when determining whether a change of placement is appropriate for a disabled student who violates a code of conduct (COMAR 13A.08.03.03.B.(2)). The school district must continue to provide educational services for IDEA-eligible students with disabilities who have been expelled or suspended for more than 10 school days (*Honig v. Doe*, 484 U.S. 305 (1988); COMAR 13A.08.03.06.C).

### 15:53. May a dangerous disabled student be removed from the public school setting?

Yes. Notwithstanding the fact that local educational agencies are generally prohibited from expelling or suspending disabled students for more than 10 consecutive (and, in limited circumstances, 10 cumulative) school days under the IDEA, disabled students who are regarded as "dangerous" may be removed from the public school setting. 20 U.S.C. § 1415(k)(1)(G)(i)–(iii) sets forth specific instances pursuant to which educationally disabled students are subject to removal and placement in an interim alternative educational setting (IAES). Where removal of a disabled student is warranted for any of these circumstances, the IEP team determines the location of the IAES (20 U.S.C. § 1415(k)(2); COMAR 13A.08.03.06.B). The IAES must be designed to enable the disabled student to:

1. Progress in the general curriculum;

2.  Receive the services and modifications included in the student's IEP;

3.  Meet the goals of the IEP; and

4.  Receive services and modifications designed to address the behavior to prevent its recurrence. The placement in an IAES may be made notwithstanding the relationship of the misconduct to the student's disability. Thus, the local educational agency may remove a student to an IAES for not more than 45 school days if the disabled student:

    a.  Carries or possesses a weapon to or at school, on school premises, or to or at a school function under the jurisdiction of a State or local educational agency;

    b.  Knowingly possesses or uses illegal drugs, or sells or solicits the sale of a controlled substance, while at school, on school premises, or at a school function under the jurisdiction of the State or local educational agency; or

    c.  Has inflicted serious bodily injury upon another person while at school, on school premises, or at a school function under the jurisdiction of a State or local educational agency.

## 15:54. How is a due process hearing requested and what are the responsibilities of the school system?

In June 2005, the Maryland State Department of Education (MSDE) issued its most recent version of the *Maryland Guidelines for Special Education Mediations and Due Process Hearings* ("*Guidelines*"). The *Guidelines* were established in an effort to provide parents of special needs students and representatives of local educational agencies specific detail with regard to the request for and conduct of hearings and mediations under IDEA 2004, and accompanying State laws and regulations. As noted in the *Guidelines*, "[t]hese processes provide a forum to resolve disputes concerning the identification, evaluation, placement, or provision of a free appropriate public education (FAPE) to students with disabilities when a public agency and parents are unable to resolve the disagreement" (*Guidelines*, p. 1).

In accordance with the *Guidelines*, either a parent or a public agency may initiate (*i.e.*, request) a special education due process hearing by making a written request, except that a public agency may not initiate a request for hearing concerning a parent's refusal to provide consent for the initial provision of special education services. Said request must be filed within two years after a violation of the IDEA and/or accompanying State law is alleged to have occurred (*Guidelines*, p. 1; 20 U.S.C. § 1415(f)(3)(C)).

Pursuant to the *Guidelines*, whenever a parent files a request for a special education due process hearing, it is mandatory that the public agency carry out the following responsibilities:

1.  Document the date of receipt as the date on which the request was postmarked, hand delivered, or transmitted by facsimile (COMAR 28.02.01.03.D);

2.  Provide the parent with a copy of the procedural safeguards document, notwithstanding the statutory requirement that said document be provided to parent upon the first occurrence of the filing of a due process hearing request;

3.  Within 10 days of receipt of a parent's request for due process hearing, provide the parent with prior written notice regarding the issues in the request if the public agency has not already done so;

4.  Within 10 days of receipt of a parent's request for due process hearing, respond in writing to the parent, specifically addressing the issues outlined in the request,

5.  Convene a resolution session within 15 days of receipt of a parent's request for due process hearing, except under limited circumstances. Where both parties agree, in writing, not to conduct a resolution session or agree to use mediation through the Maryland State Office of Administrative Hearings (OAH), the public agency is not required to convene a resolution session.

6.  Forward to the OAH a completed Notice of Outcome of Resolution Session and a completed Transmittal Form within the following timelines:

    Non-expedited hearings—four (4) business days following the conclusion of the resolution session, or one (1) business day following the signed waiver of the resolution session;

    Expedited hearings—one (1) business day following receipt of a request for due process hearing. Expedited hearings are formal proceedings for educationally disabled students who have been removed from school for disciplinary reasons or for students not enrolled and attending school. Additionally, the MSDE has explicitly stated that, "[i]f, at the time of the due process hearing request, the student who is the subject of the hearing is not enrolled and attending an educational program, or whose placement has been changed due to disciplinary actions, expedited hearing schedules shall apply" (COMAR 13A.05.01.15.C.(8) and (9)) (*Guidelines*, pp. 2-3; see also COMAR 13A.05.01.15.C.(3)).

## 15:55. What is a resolution session?

A resolution session is a process established for the purpose of providing the parties to a special education dispute "an opportunity to resolve the disagreement in an efficient and effective manner so that a due process hearing can be avoided" (*Guidelines*, p. 3, § 3). For purposes of scheduling, the public agency must convene a resolution session within 15 days of receiving a parent's request for a due process hearing, or 15 days from the date that the public agency notifies the parent that it will request a due process hearing, except where both parties agree in writing not to conduct a resolution session or agree to use mediation through the OAH to attempt to resolve the dispute.

If a resolution session proves unfruitful, a due process hearing may then be held. Unless an attorney accompanies the parent to a resolution session, the public agency may not include an attorney in the resolution session. The public agency is required to include "a representative of the public agency who has decision-making authority" at every resolution session (*Guidelines*, p. 3, § 3).

If the parties resolve the dispute pursuant to a resolution session, each is required to execute a legally binding agreement. The parents must execute the agreement on behalf of the disabled student, and the public agency is required to have the agreement executed by a "representative of the public agency who has the authority to bind the public agency" (*Guidelines*, p. 3, § 3).

## 15:56. What is mediation?

Mediation is a closed, voluntary confidential proceeding conducted by a qualified mediator who is randomly selected from a list of eligible mediators maintained by the OAH (*Guidelines*, p. 4, § 4). Either party to a dispute may request mediation at any time, whether or not a formal request for a special education due process hearing has been made. Additionally, either party has a right to be accompanied and advised by counsel during the mediation process.

As mediations are "closed" proceedings, discussions that occur during mediation may not be used in a subsequent due process hearing or civil proceeding. Should the parties participating in mediation resolve the dispute through this process, a legally binding, written agreement is crafted and executed by the parties and is subject to enforceability in any State court of competent jurisdiction or in a District Court of the United States. The OAH convenes the special education mediation session at a time and place that is reasonably convenient to the parties and in accordance with the law. If a special education due process hearing is requested simultaneous to a request for mediation, the OAH is required to make reasonable efforts to schedule a mediation session within 20 calendar days of its receipt of the written request. While mediation is voluntary, it may not be used to deny or delay any party's rights under federal or State law (*Guidelines*, p. 4, § 4; see also COMAR 13A.05.01.15.B).

### 15:57. What is the stay-put placement of the student during the pendency of the hearing process?

During the pendency of any due process hearing, the student must remain in his or her current educational placement, unless the public agency and the parent agree otherwise (*Guidelines*, p. 6; COMAR 13A.05.01.15.C.(16)(a)).

The "stay-put" or status quo provision of the IDEA was established in an effort to maintain continuity and the stability of a student's educational placement during the pendency of a dispute over the student's special education identification, evaluation, placement, or provision of a FAPE. Specifically, during the pendency of any administrative or judicial proceedings regarding a complaint under 34 C.F.R. § 300.511, unless the State or local educational agency and the parents of the disabled student otherwise agree, the student involved in the complaint must remain in his or her current educational setting (34 C.F.R. § 300.518).

As the IDEA's stay-put provision serves as a self-effectuating or automatic injunction, a court order need not be obtained. Moreover, the stay-put provision imposes an obligation on school districts only, not parents.

### 15:58. Who has the burden of proof in a due process hearing?

The party initiating the action, whether the parents of a disabled student or the school district, bears the burden of proof in an administrative special education due process hearing (*Schaffer ex rel. Schaffer v. Weast*, 546 U.S. 49 (2005) (holding that "the burden of persuasion in an administrative hearing challenging an IEP is properly placed upon the party seeking relief, whether that is the disabled [student] or the school district")).

### 15:59. May attorney's fees be awarded in special education disputes?

IDEA 2004 added provisions dealing with assessing attorney's fees in an effort to eliminate frivolous litigation against school systems. Under IDEA 2004, reasonable attorney's fees may be awarded by a United States District Court to any of the following:

1.  A prevailing parent who is the parent of the child with a disability;

2.  To the school system or Maryland State Department of Education against the parents' attorney if the complaint filed was frivolous, unreasonable, or without foundation.

3. To the school system or Maryland State Department of Education against the parents' attorney if the attorney continued to litigate after the litigation clearly became frivolous, unreasonable or without foundation.

4. To the school system or Maryland State Department of Education against the attorney or the parents if the parents' complaint or subsequent cause of action was presented for any improper purpose, such as to harass, to cause unnecessary delay, or to needlessly increase the cost of litigation (20 U.S.C. § 1415(i)(3)(B)).

The Ninth Circuit recently ruled that the entering of a settlement agreement that was not court approved did not qualify the parents as prevailing parties that are entitled to attorneys' fees (*P.N. v. Seattle School District No. 1*, No. 04-36141 (9th Cir. Amended Opinion Jan. 29, 2007)).

### 15:60. Is there a statute of limitations in special education due process hearings?

Under IDEA 2004, there is a two (2) year statute of limitations for special education cases. This means that the school system is not responsible for acts occurring more than two (2) years before the request for due process was filed, so long as the parent knew or should have known of the basis for the complaint. If the school system withheld information from the parent it was required to provide or intentionally misled the parent to believe that the disputed issue was resolved, then the two (2) year limitations period may be extended on a case-by-case basis. Should the parent file a hearing request because the parent was dissatisfied with a proposed IEP or placement, in most cases the two (2) year statute of limitations would apply. This change in the law reflects the concern of school systems that without the restricted time period, they were being required to respond to stale complaints, long after employees had transferred or resigned. The prior law was also prejudicial to school systems whose employees educate hundreds of students and who need speedy resolution of special education disputes. The new law still provides an adequate opportunity for parents to file claims and is consistent with *MM ex rel. DM v. School District of Greenville County*, 303 F.3d 523 (4th Cir. 2002), in which the Court explained that parents cannot claim continuing violations when they failed to seek due process for IEPs for each separate school year at the appropriate time. The two (2) year statute of limitations is included in the *Procedural Safeguards – Parental Rights* booklet, which makes it especially important to provide the booklet to parents at each IEP team meeting.

### 15.61. When may an appeal be filed in federal court?

Under Maryland statute, within 120 calendar days of the issuance of the hearing decision, any party to the hearing may file an appeal from a final decision of the Office of Administrative Hearings to the federal District Court for Maryland or to the circuit court for the county in which the child resides (Md. Code Ann., Ed. Art. § 8-413(j)). This 120-day time period replaces the prior 180 days, and reflects a compromise following the amendment of the federal IDEA to allow states to adopt a time period of not less than 90 days.

### 15:62. Can a non-attorney parent represent themselves in IDEA matters in federal courts?

Yes. The Supreme Court in *Winkelman v. Parma City School District*, 550 U.S. ___ (2007), ruled that non-attorney parents can litigate IDEA disputes in federal courts. The Court found that the parents have an independent and enforceable legal right to seek the entitlement to a FAPE for their child.

### 15:63. May expert witness fees be awarded in special education disputes?

No. The Supreme Court in *Arlington Central School District Board of Education v. Murphy*, 548 U.S. ___ (2006), ruled that IDEA does not require school districts to reimburse parents for expert witness fees even when the parent prevails in a special education dispute. The Court found that IDEA's specific provision for the awarding of attorney's fees does not make the school district responsible for other costs incurred by the prevailing parent absent specific statutory language and notice.

### 15:64. What are Parts A, B, C, and D of IDEA and how do they apply?

Part A of IDEA defines important terms used in the law. Part B of IDEA provides funding for services for students with disabilities and sets forth the rules and regulations that states must follow to receive those funds. Part C of IDEA contains the Early Intervention Program for Infants and Toddlers with disabilities. Finally, Part D of IDEA establishes grants to develop information and research for early intervention systems to address the unique needs of children with disabilities.

### 15:65. What is Section 504 of the Rehabilitation Act of 1973 and how does it apply?

Section 504 of the Rehabilitation Act of 1973 is a federal statute that protects qualified individuals from discrimination, from entities receiving federal funding, based upon their disability. Under Section 504 an individual with a disability is someone with a physical or mental impairment which substantially limits one or more major life activities. A student may only be covered under Section 504 if the disability substantially interferes with a major life activity including learning, caring for one's self, walking, seeing, hearing, speaking, breathing, working, or performing manual tasks. Section 504 requires that students have equal access to educational opportunity and that the school system make reasonable accommodations for individuals with disabilities to allow them to have access to and participate with their non-disabled peers in school programs. Section 504 is a nondiscrimination law in contrast to IDEA, which creates an affirmative obligation to provide special education and related services to eligible students (29 U.S.C. § 794(a)).

### 15:66. If a child with a disability does not qualify for special education, does that mean that the child qualifies for a Section 504 Plan?

The student only qualifies for a Section 504 Plan if he has a record of having, is regarded as having, or has a physical or mental impairment that significantly interferes with one of life's major activities (34 C.F.R. § 104.3(j)). A major life activity includes "functions such as caring for one's self, performing manual tasks, walking, seeing, hearing, speaking, breathing, learning and working" (34 C.F.R. § 104.3(j)(2)(ii)).

Attention Deficit Disorder/Attention Deficit Hyperactivity Disorder (ADD/ADHD) is not identified as a disabling condition under IDEA. However, a student with ADD/ADHD may qualify under the "Other Health Impaired" category if the ADD/ADHD limits the student's alertness and adversely impacts his educational performance. Some students with ADD/ADHD are affected in such a way as to qualify as emotionally disturbed under IDEA. If a student with ADD/ADHD does not qualify under IDEA, the educators should examine whether the student qualifies under Section 504. Not every student with ADD/ADHD qualifies under IDEA or Section 504. The ADD/ADHD must be severe enough to substantially impair a major life activity and this must be determined on a case-by-case basis (*Jefferson Parish (LA) Public Schools*, 16 IDELR 755 (OCR 1989)).

### 15:67. What are the basic requirements of Section 504 in connection with providing educational services?

The Supreme Court has held that when looking at the Section 504 definition of a qualified individual with a disability, the focus should be on whether the disability significantly interferes with a major life function. So, should a student have ADD/ADHD, but the ADD/ADHD does not substantially interfere, for instance, with the ability to learn, that student may not be eligible under Section 504. The Supreme Court has also held that "if a person is taking measures to correct for, or mitigate, a physical or mental impairment," such as wearing glasses or a hearing aide, that person may not be substantially limited (*Sutton v. United Air Lines*, 527 U.S. 471 (1999)). In *Albertson's v. Kirkingburg*, 527 U.S. 555 (1999), the Court stressed that a "mere difference" in ability does not amount to a "substantial limitation." Therefore, if the student's glasses, hearing aids, or medication corrects or mitigates a physical or mental impairment, the student may not be eligible under Section 504.

The school system may not require that a student be medicated. But should educators have reason to believe that a parent is failing to give the student prescribed medication, or is experimenting with the medication, a referral should be made to the local Department of Social Services for possible neglect, consistent with Section 5-704 of the Family Law Article of the Annotated Code of Maryland.

### 15.68. Are special education students required to participate in federal or state mandated student assessments?

Yes. The IDEA regulations issued in 2006 add a reference to the No Child Left Behind Act (NCLB) and clarify that all children with disabilities are included in all general state and district-wide assessment programs, including assessments described in NCLB (34 C.F.R. Part 300). The regulations allow for appropriate accommodations and alternate assessments where necessary and as indicated in the student's IEP. For a detailed discussion of student assessments required under NCLB, see **Chapter 8**.

States and local school systems may develop and implement guidelines for providing alternate assessments, provided that the standards:

- Are aligned with the state's challenging academic content standards and challenging student academic achievement standards; and

- If the state has adopted alternate academic achievement standards permitted under the regulations promulgated to carry out NCLB, must measure the achievement of children with disabilities against those standards.

### 15.69. Has Maryland adopted any alternate assessment standards or procedures for disabled students?

In accordance with NCLB, Maryland requires students with disabilities in grades 3-8 and 10 to participate in either the Maryland School Assessment (MSA) or the Alternative Maryland School Assessment (Alt-MSA). The decision for which assessment is appropriate for an individual student is made by each student's IEP team. For additional information, see the Alt-MSA, Alternative Maryland School Assessment Handbook, MSDE, (2007).

In addition to federally mandated assessments, Maryland is implementing a High School Assessment (HSA) program that will require passage of four high school assessments in order to graduate, beginning with the graduating class of

2009. A state workgroup is developing recommendations regarding the alternative assessments and/or alternate graduation requirements for disabled students, students with 504 plans, and limited English proficiency students.

## 15:70. What is the Americans with Disabilities Act and how does it apply?

The Americans with Disabilities Act (ADA) is a federal statute that prohibits discrimination on the basis of an individual's disability, and Title II of the Act makes it applicable to public schools (42 U.S.C. § 12101 *et seq.*). In the education setting, the ADA requires the provision of reasonable accommodations for disabled students such as building new facilities in an accessible fashion, altering existing facilities to provide accessibility, redesigning educational equipment for use by the disabled, providing needed aides, and providing tests and other written materials in alternative formats.

## 15:71. How do the "service animal" provisions of ADA apply to public schools?

Recent disputes have occurred in Maryland and other states over the request of students with disabilities to bring animals to school with them as an accommodation. While each case is decided on a case-by-case basis, the request for a service animal in school may be refused if the animal is not needed for the student to receive a FAPE. Some educators have concerns regarding disruption in the classroom setting, allergies of fellow-students and staff, and sanitary issues, among others.

The Americans with Disabilities Act (ADA) includes a definition of "service animal" under Title III, which does not apply to public schools (*DeBoard v. Board of Education of Ferguson-Florissant School District*, 123 F.3d 1102 (8th Cir. 1997)). Title II of the Act, which does apply to public schools, is silent on the issue. Therefore, service animal cases involving students are brought under Section 504 of the Rehabilitation Act of 1973.

The U.S. Department of Education, Office of Civil Rights, is responsible for oversight of Section 504 and has issued guidance on the use of service animals in public schools (*Letter to Goodling* (17 IDELR 1027 (OCR 1991)), stating that "if not allowing a student to bring a service dog into the classroom would effectively deny the student the opportunity, or an equal opportunity, to participate in or benefit from the education program [of a recipient of Federal financial assistance], then the recipient school would be in violation of Section 504 [of the Rehabilitation Act of 1973] and its implementing regulation."

Most recently, Maryland amended its service animal statute to replace references to "service dogs" with references to "service animals" to conform to the

Americans with Disabilities Act (ADA), which defines "service animal" as any guide dog, signal dog, or other animal individually trained to do work or perform tasks for the benefit of an individual with a disability.

# 16. Public Charter Schools and Public School Alternatives

### 16:1. Where are the laws and regulations governing charter schools in Maryland found?

The Charter School Act of 2003 established Title 9 of the Education Article of the Maryland Annotated Code, referred to as the "Maryland Public Charter School Program" (Chapter 358, 2003 Session Laws of Maryland). Title 9 contains all of the State's statutory definitions and requirements regarding public charter schools in Maryland (Md. Code Ann., Ed. Art. §§ 9-101 to 110). Following passage of the Act, the State Board has not adopted regulations regarding the Charter School Program, but has issued formal opinions responding to appeals from charter applicants, and issued orders in response to petitions for waivers. The Charter School Act requires each local school system to adopt a charter school policy and school systems have also adopted regulations and procedures. As required by the Charter School Act, the State Board approved the *Maryland Public Charter Schools Model Policy and Resource Guide* (*"Resource Guide"*), to provide a model policy and compile relevant state and federal laws and regulations.

In addition to these State and local actions, federal laws, regulations, and guidance also apply to public charter schools. The federal role includes providing charter school planning and implementation grants through the Charter School Program (CSP) to be awarded by state education agencies. In addition, the No Child Left Behind Act identifies public charter schools as one of the alternative governance models that must be selected by a local school board for a consistently low-performing, restructured school.

## Charter Schools Generally

### 16:2. How does Maryland law define a "charter school"?

A charter school in Maryland is a pubic elementary or secondary school authorized to operate in accordance with Title 9 of the Education Article and the terms of the contract, or charter agreement, between a private entity and a local board of education or, in limited circumstances, the State Board of Education. Title 9 defines a charter school as a public school that:

1. Is nonsectarian in all its programs, policies, and operations;

2. Is a school to which parents choose to send their children;

3. Is open to all students on a space available basis and admits students on a lottery basis if more students apply than can be accommodated;

4.  Is a new public school or a conversion of an existing public school;

5.  Provides a program of elementary or secondary education or both;

6.  Operates in pursuit of a specific set of educational objectives;

7.  Is tuition free;

8.  Is subject to Federal and State laws prohibiting discrimination;

9.  Is in compliance with all applicable health and safety laws;

10. Is in compliance with § 9-107 of this title;

11. Operates under the supervision of the public chartering authority from which its charter is granted and in accordance with its charter and, except as provided in § 9-106, the provisions of law and regulation governing other public schools;

12. Requires students to be physically present on school premises for a period of time substantially similar to that which other public school students spend on school premises; and

13. Is created in accordance with this title and the appropriate county board policy (Md. Code Ann., Ed. Art. § 9-102).

Charter schools in Maryland are required to comply with all local, state, federal laws governing other public schools, unless a waiver has been granted by the local board or State Board (Md. Code Ann., Ed. Art. § 9-106(a)).

## 16:3. What is a charter?

A "charter", or charter agreement, is a formal agreement or contract entered into by a chartering authority and an eligible applicant. A charter requires a public charter school to comply with all state and local laws, regulations and policies governing other public schools unless specifically waived.

## 16:4. What is a chartering authority?

A chartering authority, or charter authorizer, is the entity responsible for receiving, reviewing and approving or denying applications to open a public charter school. In Maryland, the local board of education is the primary public chartering authority for granting a charter (Md. Code Ann., Ed. Art. § 9-103(a)). The State Board of Education is the secondary public chartering authority for granting a charter in its appeal review capacity or as the public chartering authority for a restructured school (Md. Code Ann., Ed. Art. § 9-103(b)).

## 16:5. What is the purpose of charter schools in Maryland?

The first provision of the Charter School Act of 2003 states, "There is a Maryland public charter school program. The general purpose of the program is to establish an alternative means within the existing public school system in order to provide innovative learning opportunities and creative educational approaches to improve the education of students" (Md. Code Ann., Ed. Art. § 9-101).

# Application and Review

## 16:6. What is a charter application?

The application to establish a public charter school is the mechanism through which an eligible applicant proposes a plan to a chartering authority to establish and operate a charter school in accordance with federal, state, and local laws, regulations, and policies.

## 16:7. What should a charter application include?

According to the *Maryland Public Charter Schools Model Policy and Resource Guide*, which was first adopted by the State Board in 2003 and revised in 2005, applications shall include, but not be limited to, the following components:

- A statement of intent to comply with applicable federal, state, and local laws and regulations and this policy.

- The applicant's vision of public charter school expectations and mission. The primary mission must remain focused on student academic achievement.

- A description of any special or unique educational focus to be implemented.

- Strategies for developing and delivering educational programs including curriculum, staffing patterns and grade levels.

- Specific educational results including student academic outcomes and how they will be measured.

- Specific plans for meeting or exceeding current accountability provisions of the local school system and state law and regulations.

- Student admission procedures.

- A facilities plan that describes the type of facilities, possible location, and the characteristics of the facility that will be needed to ensure the appropriate implementation of the proposed education program. The plan should also include the requirements to ensure accessibility consistent with the Americans with Disabilities Act. Final charter approval would be contingent upon the acquisition of the appropriate facilities consistent with the facilities plan.

- A defined management and administrative structure that will be in place for the public charter school.

- The proposed duration of the Charter Agreement which provides legal accountability for the operation of the public charter school.

- Demonstration of financial solvency for the duration of the Charter Agreement and accountability for the use of funds and resources as addressed in the budget section of the charter school application.

- A plan which provides programmatic accountability for the length of the Charter Agreement.

- Specific waivers of local, state and federal requirements needed to implement the proposed education program.

- A plan for providing needed school support services such as transportation, custodial and maintenance, health services, and food services.

- A description of the type and extent to which there is sufficient community support for the proposed public charter school must be submitted.

### 16:8. What is the timeline for the chartering authority's review and decision regarding the charter application?

Generally, the local board of education is required to review a charter application and render a decision within 120 days of receipt of the application. The statute does not refer to any specific dates or references to the school year or fiscal year, thereby creating an open, or rolling, application process throughout the calendar year. Some local boards have adopted local policies that allow for rolling applications while others provide annual deadlines.

The State Board has opined that local boards may not defer accepting or reviewing applications or defer the establishment of a charter school generally until a future date (*City Neighbors Charter School v. Baltimore City Board of School Commissioners*, MSBE Op. No. 04-38 (2004)). Specifically, a local board is prohibited from imposing a two-year delay between the approval of a charter application and the opening of the charter school (*Chesapeake Public Charter School v. St. Mary's County Board of Education*, MSBE Op. No. 05-23 (2005)).

For restructured schools, the local board must expedite its review and decision on the application to convert one of these schools to a charter school. The board must review the application and render its decision within 30 days of receipt of the application. The board may apply to the State Board for an extension of up to 15 days. If the local board does not render a decision by the deadline, the State Board may, but us not required to, become the chartering authority for the restructured school.

## 16:9. What are restructured schools and why are they treated differently?

The No Child Left Behind Act (NCLB) requires States to develop academic performance goals for students, schools, and school systems, and requires state and local school systems to use alternative strategies to improve student performance, including the conversion, or restructuring, of low-performing schools to public charter schools. NCLB defines a restructured school as a consistently low performing school that fails to meet adequate yearly progress (AYP) for five consecutive years and which must be restructured by the local school system in one of the following ways:

1. Reopen the school as a public charter school;

2. Replace all or most of the school staff, which may include the principal, who are relevant to the school's failure to make AYP;

3. Enter into a contract with an entity, such as a private management company, with a demonstrated record of effectiveness, to operate the school as a public school;

4. Turn the operation of the school over to the state education agency, if permitted under State law and agreed to by the State; or

5. Any other major restructuring of a school's governance agreement.

Maryland's State Board of Education has codified the federal requirements for schools in improvement, corrective action, and restructuring under COMAR 13A.01.04.07. In addition, COMAR 13A.01.04.08 outlines the State's options for restructuring a school system, including altering the governance structure of individual schools within the system. See **Chapter 8** for more information regarding restructured schools and Maryland's implementation of its school improvement program in accordance with the federal No Child Left Behind Act.

## 16:10. Must a school system review and decide on all charter applications?

Upon receipt of a charter application from an eligible applicant, the local school board must review the application and render a decision within 120 days. The statute does not provide a timeline following approval of the application by which the charter agreement must be finalized. However, the State Board determined that the charter agreement must be completed within 30 calendar days of approving the application (*City Neighbors Charter School v. Baltimore City Board of Education*, MSBE Op. No. 05-17 (2005)).

### 16:11. Is there a cap or limit on how many charter schools may be applied for or approved in a school system or the State?

No. There is no statutory cap on the number of charter school applications that may be submitted or approved for a school year or overall. The State Board has clarified that a local school system may not adopt an arbitrary cap on the number of charters that may be granted, and therefore may not limit the number of applications or reviews (*City Neighbors Charter School v. Baltimore City Board of School Commissioners*, MSBE Op. No. 04-38 (2004)).

### 16:12. Is there an application fee for charter schools?

No. A local school system may not charge a fee to submit an application to start a public charter school.

### 16:13. Who is eligible to apply to establish a charter school?

An application to establish, or found, a public charter school may be submitted to a local board of education by:

- a parent/guardian of a student who attends a school in the county/city;
- a nonsectarian nonprofit entity;
- a nonsectarian institution of higher education in the State;
- staff of a public school; or
- any combination of these individuals or groups (Md. Code Ann., Ed. Art. § 9-104).

### 16:14. Who is not eligible to apply to establish a charter school?

In addition to the limitations imposed by the definition of eligible applicants in § 9-104, creating the negative implication that sectarian entities may not apply, the statute also specifically prohibits a chartering authority to grant a charter to a private, parochial, or home school (Md. Code Ann., Ed. Art. § 9-104(a)(3)).

### 16:15. Must a school system provide technical assistance to a charter school applicant?

No. the State Board has determined that the Charter School Act does not require the local school system to provide technical assistance to an applicant (*Dr. Ben Carson Charter School, et al. v. Harford County Board of Education*, MSBE Op. No. 05-21 (2005); *Columbia Public Charter School v. Howard County Board of Education*, MSBE Op. No. 05-31 (2005)). In practice, some school systems do voluntarily provide technical assistance to applicants.

### 16:16. How are charter school applications reviewed?

The Charter School Act establishes timelines but not standards of review or criteria for the local board's review and decision on the merits of the application. According to the State Board adopted *Model Policy Statement Concerning Public Charter Schools* ("*Model Policy*"), the review of a charter school application is the responsibility of the local board: "It is the chartering authority's responsibility to review and approve or disapprove an application based on standards established by the chartering authority consistent with the state law authorizing public charter schools." (*Model Policy*, p. 18).

### 16:17. How does a local school system evaluate a charter application to determine approval or denial?

The Charter School Act requires each local board to develop a charter school policy that shall include, in part, guidelines and procedures regarding the evaluation of public charter schools. The State Board has elaborated on this provision in opinions responding to challenges of the evaluation used by local boards to support the decision to deny a charter application.

For example, the State Board has directed that, "If a numerical rating scale is used to evaluate an application, the local board must provide an analytical key that describes with specificity what is necessary or adequate to achieve each point on the scale" (*Potomac Charter School v. Prince George's County Board of Education*, MSBE Op. No. 05-08 (2005)). However, the State Board has clarified that there is no legal requirement that a local school system use a numeric scale in its evaluation process (*Chesapeake Public Charter School v. St. Mary's County Board of Education*, MSBE Op. No. 05-23 (2005)).

### 16:18. How are recommendations to approve or deny a charter application developed and presented to the local board?

The State Board has determined that it is "beneficial to the local board, the charter applicant, and the general public for the local superintendent to make a recommendation with supporting rationale for approval or denial of a charter application. We therefore direct each local superintendent from now forward to provide to the local board a detailed recommendation for approval or denial of a charter school application" (*Chesapeake Public Charter School v. St. Mary's County Board of Education*, MSBE Op. No. 05-23 (2005)).

### 16:19. Must a local board issue a written decision approving or denying a charter application?

No. However, the local board must provide an explanation or rationale for its decision, and if the rationale is presented orally then it must be presented at a public meeting (*Chesapeake Public Charter School v. St. Mary's County Board of Education*, MSBE Op. No. 05-23 (2005)).

### 16:20. Are public hearings required for the review of a charter school application?

No. The State Board has rejected arguments by applicants that a local board should have held a hearing in order to provide an opportunity for the applicant to respond to concerns that aspects of the application were lacking or incomplete. The Board noted that "there is no legal requirement that a charter school applicant be afforded a hearing prior to a decision on the merits of the application" (*Potomac Charter School v. Prince George's County Board of Education*, MSBE Op. No. 05-08 (2005)).

### 16:21. Is approving an application the same as granting a charter?

No. The State Board has defined a "two-step chartering system approach" that distinguishes the charter application from the charter agreement. The Board first adopted this approach in its *Model Policy and Resource Guide* and has since reiterated its endorsement of this approach in several charter school opinions. According to the State Board, "The first step consists of the application development, submission, and review process" and then, "After the application has been approved, the second step is the completion of a charter agreement which is a legally binding contract that explains in detail the responsibilities of all parties involved in the operation of the charter school." (*City Neighbors Charter School v. Baltimore City Board of Education*, MSBE Op. No. 05-17 (2005)).

## 16:22. May a church or other religious organization apply to found a charter school?

No. A church is prohibited from applying because the law limits eligible applicants to "nonsectarian" nonprofit entities. This prohibition should be distinguished from the allowance in some state charter school programs for applications from sectarian organizations agreeing to provide nonsectarian education.

## 16:23. May a charter be granted to a private, parochial, or home school?

No. Public chartering authorities are prohibited from granting a charter to a private school, parochial school, or home school (Md. Code Ann., Ed. Art. § 9-104). In addition, regarding home schools, the list of criteria defining charter schools in Maryland requires charter school students to be "physically present on school premises for a period of time substantially similar to that which other public school students spend on school premises" (Md. Code Ann., Ed. Art. § 9-102).

## 16:24. May a charter be granted to establish a "cyber" or "virtual" charter school?

The Charter School Act requires "students to be physically present on school premises for a period of time substantially similar to that which other public school students spend on school premises" (Md. Code Ann., Ed. Art. § 9-102). This provision is the only statutory guidance for a chartering authority regarding applications to create "cyber" or "virtual" charter schools in Maryland. However, such schools typically do not own or operate "school premises" which students attend, but rather rely significantly, or exclusively, on instruction of individual students in separate locations via remote access to internet-based educational programs.

# Application Denials and Appeals

## 16:25. May an applicant appeal the denial of its application?

Yes. The applicant may appeal the local board's decision to deny its application to the State Board in accordance with Section 4-205(c) of the Education Article. The Charter School Act requires the State Board to render a decision within 120 days of the filing of the appeal (Md. Code Ann., Ed. Art. § 9-104(b)(2)). If the State Board reverses the local board decision, the State Board may direct the local board to grant a charter and shall mediate between the local board and charter applicant to implement the charter.

**16:26. What standard of review does the State Board apply in charter school cases?**

The State Board defers to the local board's decision in accordance with the same standard of review it applies in other cases involving a local policy or a controversy and dispute regarding the rules and regulations of the local board. The local board decision "shall be considered *prima facie* correct, and the State Board may not substitute its judgment for that of the local board unless the State Board finds the local board decision is arbitrary, unreasonable, or illegal" (*Potomac Charter School v. Prince George's County Board of Education*, MSBE Op. No. 05-08 (2005)).

A decision is considered arbitrary and unreasonable if it is "contrary to sound educational policy or if a reasoning mind could have reasonably reached" the decision (see COMAR 13A.01.05.05B(1) & (2)). A decision is illegal if it is unconstitutional; exceeds statutory or jurisdictional boundaries; misconstrued the law; results from the unlawful procedures; is an abuse of discretion or is affected by errors of law (see COMAR 13A.01.05C).

Charter applicants have argued on appeal that the standard of review should be *de novo* based on the provision of Section 9-103(b) granting the State Board secondary chartering authority for the granting of a charter acting in its appeal review capacity or as the public chartering authority for a restructured school. The State Board has rejected the argument that it is required to exercise its independent judgment in reviewing an appeal of a local board's denial of a charter application (*Potomac Charter School v. Prince George's County Board of Education*, MSBE Op. No. 05-08 (2005)).

**16:27. Is the "unreasonable, arbitrary, or illegal" standard of review always applied in charter school cases?**

No. The State Board applies a different standard of review when it is interpreting provisions of the Education Article, including Title 9. This standard of review is restated by the State Board in *City Neighbors Charter School v. Baltimore City Board of Education*, MSBE Op. No. 05-17 (2005), as follows:

> Regarding interpretation of law, § 2-205(e) of the Education Article provides that the State Board ... shall explain the true intent and meaning of the provisions of the Education Article that pertain to public schools and public school systems in Maryland and the rules and regulations adopted by the State Board. By regulation found at COMAR 13A.01.05.05E, the standard of review that the State Board applies when it is interpreting schools laws and regulations is that: *The State Board shall exercise its independent judgment on the*

*record before it in the explanation and interpretation of the public school laws and State Board regulations.* (Emphasis added.)

## 16:28. Does the State Board become the chartering authority following its reversal of a local board's decision to deny an application?

No. The Charter School Act defines the State Board's secondary chartering authority as including either the granting of a charter on appeal, or "as the public chartering authority for a restructured school" (Md. Code Ann., Ed. Art. § 9-103(b)). Therefore, following a reversal on appeal and the State Board's order to the local board to grant a charter, the local board retains chartering authority and the State Board's role is to mediate the approval and implementation of a charter agreement.

# Waivers

## 16:29. What provisions of law and regulation governing other public schools may be waived for a charter school?

The Charter School Act provides that public charter schools "shall comply with the provisions of law and regulation governing other public schools" and that a waiver of those requirements "may be sought through an appeal to the State Board" (Md. Code Ann., Ed. Art. § 9-106(a) and (b)). However, rather than providing a list of requirements that may be waived, the Charter School Act contains a specific list of types of requirements that may not be waived.

A waiver may not be granted from provisions of law or regulation relating to:

(1) audit requirements;

(2) the measurement of student academic achievement, including all assessments required for other public schools and other assessments mutually agreed upon by the public chartering authority and the school; and

(3) the health, safety, or civil rights of a student or an employee of the charter school" (Md. Code Ann., Ed. Art. § 9-106(c)).

Following passage of the Act, the State Board asserted that it has the authority to grant waivers of provisions of Title 9, the Charter School Act, because these provisions are not specifically excluded in the section cited above. Maryland's highest court has rejected this argument, holding that provisions of the Charter School Act, Title 9 of the Education Article, are not subject to waiver (*Patterson Park Public Charter School, Inc., et al. v. The Baltimore Teachers Union,*

*American Federation of Teachers Local 340, AFL-CIO, et al., No. 99*, September Term, 2006).

### 16:30. What are the audit requirements that may not be waived?

Public school systems are subject to the following audit requirements under Section 5-109 of the Education Article:

> (a) Each county board shall provide for an annual audit of its financial transactions and accounts.

> (b) (1) The audit shall be made by a certified public accountant or a partnership of certified public accountants who are:

>> (i) Licensed by the State Board of Public Accountancy; and

>> (ii) Approved by the State Superintendent.

> (2) The audit shall be made in accordance with the standards and regulations adopted by the State Board.

The state regulations implementing Section 5-109 also implement the Single Audit Act of 1984; the Single Audit Act Amendments of 1996; and the Office of Management and Budget Circular A-133, "Audits of States, Local Governments, and Non-Profit Organizations", which requires State, local governments, and nonprofit organizations to provide for an annual audit of federal awards (COMAR 13A.02.07.01). In addition, no waivers may be granted from any local audit requirements.

### 16:31. What are the laws and regulations relating to "the measurement of student academic achievement, including all assessments required for other public schools" that may not be waived?

Maryland measures academic progress of public school students, schools, and school systems each year by administering the Maryland School Assessment (MSA), the Alternate Maryland School Assessment for students with disabilities (Alt-MSA), and the Maryland High School Assessments (HSAs). Maryland's assessment program is governed by the State Board through regulations contained in the Code of Maryland Regulations (COMAR), and administered by MSDE.

## 16:32. What are laws and regulations relating to "the health, safety, or civil rights of a student or an employee of the charter school" that may not be waived?

The Charter School Act provides no further guidance on these broad categories of laws that may not be waived. For example, Maryland state laws and regulations regarding the health of a student or employee may include, but are not limited to, student immunizations, vision and hearing screenings, smoke-free workplace requirements, school nutrition standards, and standards for the delivery of services by school nurses, school-based health centers, and others.

Laws relating to the safety of students or employees may include school facility standards, transportation standards, occupational health and safety standards, playground equipment standards, and standards for asbestos, lead, pesticides, drinking water and indoor air quality. In addition, school safety provisions may include procedures ranging from student discipline to emergency responses.

Federal laws, and any corresponding state laws, relating to civil rights of students or employees may include, but are not limited to, the Civil Rights Act of 1964 (see **Chapter 6**), the Individuals with Disabilities Education Act (see **Chapter 15**), the Americans with Disabilities Act (see **Chapter 5**), the Rehabilitation Act of 1973 (see **Chapter 15**), the Age Discrimination in Employment Act (see **Chapter 6**), and the Equal Access Act (see **Chapter 13**).

## 16:33. What is the process for requesting a waiver?

The only guidance provided in Title 9 is that a waiver may be sought through an appeal to the State Board (Md. Code Ann., Ed. Art. § 9-106(b)). The law does not specifically grant local boards the authority to grant waivers from local school system rules, regulations or policies, nor does it specify the process by which a charter applicant, approved charter school, or school system, may request waivers from State laws and regulations.

The State Board directed that requests to modify local board policies and procedures shall be submitted to the extent practicable with the charter school application and resolved by the parties during the application review period (*Patterson Park Public School, Inc. v. Baltimore City Board of School Commissioners*, MSBE Op. No. 05-19 (2005)).

In practice, providing that waivers from state law and regulation "may be sought through an appeal to the State Board" has resulted in a new process by which charter schools may petition the State Board to issue an order granting a requested waiver.

**16:34. What type of waivers have been requested?**

In July 2005, the State Board issued ten orders responding to waiver requests from charter schools located in Baltimore City. The State Board responded to waiver requests regarding certification, collective bargaining, hiring authority, enrollment, food services, procurement, school calendar, and curriculum. The following questions address the State Board's decisions on each of these issues.

# Enrollment/Admissions

**16:35. How is the enrollment of students in the charter school determined?**

Generally, charter schools may recruit students, reserve enrollment for a limited number of students whose parents are founders of the charter school, and use a random lottery for enrollment of students if applications exceed available space. The Charter School Act defines a charter school, in part, as "a school to which parents choose to send their children" and which is "open to all students on a space available basis and admits students on a lottery basis if more students apply than can be accommodated" (Md. Code Ann., Ed. Art. § 9-102). The Act does not include provisions regarding recruiting and marketing, enrolling founders' children, or procedures for conducting enrollment lotteries.

Most recently, the State Board denied a charter school applicant's request for a waiver of the open, lottery-based, admission requirement to give admission priority to "children with Montessori experience" (*Piscataway Creek Montessori Communities, Inc. v. Prince George's County Board of Education*, MSBE Op. No. 07-21 (2007)). The State Board concluded that not only would such a preference violate Maryland's statutory open enrollment requirement, but also would violate the federal requirements for receipt of federal charter school funds (*Non-Regulatory Guidance,* Title V, Part B, Charter Schools Program, USDE, July 2004).

**16:36. Can founders' children constitute the majority, or all, of the students enrolled in a charter school?**

Charter schools receiving federal grant funds through the Charter School Program (CSP) must comply with federal non-regulatory guidance (CSP Guidance) that imposes limitations on exemptions from the lottery, including an exemption for "children of a charter school's founders (so long as the total number of students allowed under this exemption constitutes only a small percentage of the school's total enrollment)" (*Non-Regulatory Guidance*, Title V, Part B, Charter Schools Program, USDE, July 2004). The "small percentage" referred to in the Guidance is not further defined.

**16:37. What other federal standards apply to charter school enrollment and admissions?**

Federal CSP Guidance addresses enrollment issues including the use of weighted lotteries, exempting categories of students from the lottery, and using gender-based lotteries. Again, this Guidance controls only those charter schools receiving federal grant funds through the Charter School Program (CSP). To determine whether a charter school is subject to the CSP Guidance, contact MSDE, which administers the CSP in Maryland.

The CSP Guidance also lists the following federal statutory or regulatory requirements with which charter schools must comply in order to be eligible for federal grants:

- Part B of the Individuals with Disabilities Education Act;

- Federal civil rights laws, including, but not limited to, Title VI of the Civil Rights Act of 1964;

- Section 504 of the Rehabilitation Act of 1973; and

- Title II of the Americans with Disabilities Act of 1990.

**16:38. May a charter school use a weighted lottery in favor of certain categories of students?**

Yes. A charter school that receives funds under the federal CSP program may weight its lottery in favor of students seeking to change schools under the Title I public school choice provisions.

**16:39. Do the federal CSP enrollment guidelines apply to charter schools conducting a lottery for the next year, in which no federal CSP funds will be received?**

A charter school receiving its final year of CSP funds may select students for the next school year, when the school will not be receiving CSP funds, without using a lottery.

**16:40. Can enrollment criteria be related to a special focus or mission of the charter school?**

The Charter School Act provides that a charter school "operates in pursuit of a specific set of educational objectives" but does not address the use of preferential recruiting or admissions policies intended to enroll a "specific set" of students. Similarly, according to the federal CSP Guidance, NCLB "does not specifically prohibit charter schools from setting minimum qualifications for determining who is eligible to enroll in a charter school and, thus, to be included in the lottery." The Guidance further provides, "a charter school funded under the CSP may set minimum qualifications for admission only to the extent that such qualifications are: (a) consistent with the statutory purposes of the CSP; (b) reasonably necessary to achieve the educational mission of the charter school; and (c) consistent with civil rights laws and Part B of the Individuals with Disabilities Education Act. CSP grantees should consider using program funds to assist "educationally disadvantaged" and other students to achieve to challenging State content and performance standards" (*Non-Regulatory Guidance*, Title V, Part B, Charter Schools Program, USDE, July 2004).

### 16:41. May a local board of education approve a charter school which will operate in another school system?

No. The application must be submitted to the local board in the jurisdiction in which the charter school would operate (Md. Code Ann., Ed. Art. § 9-104(a)(1)).

### 16:42. May a charter school in one jurisdiction enroll students residing outside the school system?

In accordance with local policy, a school system may permit the enrollment of a student residing in another jurisdiction, typically conditioned on the payment of tuition and provision of student transportation. Therefore, a charter school could enroll non-resident students in accordance with local policy and the charter agreement.

### 16:43. May a charter school limit enrollment to one gender to create an "all boys" or "all girls" charter school?

The answer to this question is unclear. Maryland's Charter School Act provides that a charter school may operate "in pursuit of a specific set of educational objectives" but also requires that a charter school must be "open to all students" (Md. Code Ann., Ed. Art. §§ 9-102(3) and (6)).

Federal Charter School Program (CSP) guidance states that a charter school "may not create separate lottery pools for male and female students, even if the intent is to ensure that it has a reasonably equal gender balance." The CSP guidance recommends that, "A school seeking to achieve greater gender balance should do so by targeting additional recruitment efforts toward male or female students" (*Non-Regulatory Guidance*, Title V, Part B, Charter Schools Program, USDE, July 2004).

In addition, recently revised federal regulations under Title IX may have implications for single-sex charter schools. In December 2006, final regulations were issued under Title IX, the Education Amendments of 1972 (20 U.S.C. § 1681), to expand the authority of school districts to offer single-sex schools that offer "substantially equal" opportunities to students of the other sex in a single-sex school or a coeducational school. In addition, a school includes a "school within a school," which means an administratively separate school located within another school (34 C.F.R. § 106.34(c)).

## Educational Program

### 16:44. May a charter school focus on a particular subject area, such as fine arts, or science?

Yes. The Charter School Act defines a charter school, in part, as a school that "operates in pursuit of a specific set of educational objectives" (Md. Code Ann., Ed. Art. § 9-102(6)). In addition, such schools are consistent with the Act's stated intent, "to establish an alternative means within the existing public school system in order to provide innovative learning opportunities and creative educational approaches to improve the education of students" (Md. Code Ann., Ed. Art. § 9-101).

### 16:45. Are charter schools allowed to develop their own curriculum?

The State Board has responded to this question in a response to a waiver request, requiring that "The curriculum and courses of study for [a charter school] shall be aligned with the Maryland Voluntary Curriculum and governed by the terms of the approved charter agreement with the [local school system]." (*Inner Harbor East Academy*, MSBE Order (July 29, 2005)). This direction provides considerable discretion to the local board to approve a charter school-specific curriculum that remains consistent with the broader framework of the state curriculum. However, a waiver from the requirement to align a charter school's curriculum with the voluntary state curriculum would require a waiver from the State Board.

### 16:46. Are charter schools subject to meeting adequate yearly progress (AYP)?

Yes, charter schools, like all public schools within Maryland, are subject to state laws and regulations adopted in accordance with the NCLB's Title I accountability requirements. State charter school laws determine the entity responsible for overseeing charter school accountability for Title I purposes. In Maryland, local school systems in their role as primary charter authorizers are responsible for charter school accountability.

**16:47. May a charter school have a longer school day or week than other public schools?**

Yes. However, the State Board has clarified that a waiver of the school day or week may require amendments to the locally adopted collective bargaining agreement, which would require the approval of the local board. Similarly, the State Board determined that a change in the opening date would require local board approval (*City Neighbors Charter School*, MSBE Order (July 29, 2005)).

## Management/Operations

**16:48. Who or what manages a charter school?**

The Charter School Act delegates this question to the terms of the charter agreement entered into between the eligible applicant and local board. Management control may be delegated in the charter agreement to the applicant, which may include an individual or group including the staff of a public school, parents, nonsectarian nonprofit entity; nonsectarian institution of higher education, or any combination of these individuals or groups. In Maryland, charter schools are not independent Local Education Agencies (LEAs), as in some other states and, therefore local boards retain relatively more authority over charter schools.

**16:49. Must a charter school comply with food service requirements for other public schools?**

The State Board considered this question and directed MSDE staff to establish a panel of charter school representatives, local school system staff, and MSDE staff to develop procedures for the delivery of food services by charter schools for the 2007-2008 school year. The State Board will permit a charter school to apply for a waiver to deliver food services consistent with the newly developed procedures.

**16:50. Must a charter school follow procurement laws applying to other public schools?**

Yes. The State Board, in *City Neighbors Charter School*, MSBE Order (July 29, 2005), opined that a charter school:

> … must adhere to all State and local laws and regulations governing the expenditure of public monies and adhere to conditions specified in the [school's] charter agreement; submit to the [local board of education] alternative procurement policies and procedures preferably modeled on the standards adopted by Maryland non-profit entities; submit to [the local school system] a budget prior to each contract year specifying how public monies will be expended;

proposed procurements that exceed $15,000 must be submitted for approval to the [local board of education] prior to purchase; procurements may not be artificially divided into increments below $15,000 to avoid the [local board] approval requirement; [the charter school] must submit quarterly statements to [the local board] that provide a full accounting of funds; and the year-end audit of [the charter school] must include a full accounting of funds.

### 16:51. Must a school system provide student transportation for charter school students?

The Charter School Act does not require local boards to provide transportation services to charter school students, thus requiring the local board and applicant to resolve this issue in the charter agreement. The guidance adopted by the State Board reflects this view, intending that the application include a "plan for providing needed school support services such as transportation, custodial and maintenance, health services, and food services" (*Model Policy*, p. 14).

### 16:52. Must a school system provide insurance to a charter school?

The Charter School Act does not require local boards to provide insurance for charter schools. The types of insurance to consider include property, commercial liability, business auto, workers' compensation, excess liability, educators legal, governance/operators liability, and "claims made" liability insurance.

## Special Education

### 16:53. Are charter schools required to comply with the special education laws applicable to other public schools?

Yes. Not only are charter schools required to comply with special education requirements applicable to other public schools, but Maryland's Charter School Act also includes several provisions imposing additional special education requirements on charter authorizers, operators, and state education officials. The law ensures that charter schools may not be created to avoid special education requirements applicable to other public schools. Charter authorizers must inform applicants of the respective responsibilities of the school system and charter school regarding students with disabilities. The law further requires the chartering authority to inform the approved charter operator of their special education related responsibilities.

The Maryland State Department of Education (MSDE) recently issued comprehensive guidance regarding special education services in charter schools

(*Special Education in Charter Schools: A Resource Primer for the State of Maryland*, MSBE, August 2006). The *Resource Primer* states:

> Charter Schools are public schools, and as such are required to comply with federal and state special education laws and regulations. A local board of education shall ensure that the authorizing process for a public charter school and the application address the roles and responsibilities of the local school system and the operators of the public charter school consistent with the 2004 Individuals with Disabilities Education Act (IDEA) Amendments and its regulations, and the Code of Maryland Regulations (COMAR) 13A.05.01: Provision of a Free Appropriate Public Education and COMAR 13A.05.02: Administration of Services for Students with Disabilities.

### 16:54. What are the special education laws with which public schools, including charter schools, must comply?

Several major federal laws, and accompanying regulations, impose requirements on the conduct of all public schools, including: the Individuals with Disabilities Education Act (IDEA) of 2004; the Elementary and Secondary Education Act (ESEA), reauthorized as the No Child Left Behind Act (NCLB); Section 504 of the Rehabilitation Act; the Americans with Disabilities Act (ADA); and the Family Educational Rights and Privacy Act (FERPA).

### 16:55. Who is responsible for ensuring compliance with Special Education requirements?

The Charter School Act requires the Maryland State Department of Education (MSDE) to provide technical assistance to charter schools to help them comply with the federal special education laws (Md. Code Ann., Ed. Art. § 9-107). However, federal law requires charter authorizers to be accountable for a charter school's compliance with federal requirements; and local boards are the primary chartering authority in Maryland.

### 16:56. Do students with disabilities have a federally protected right to attend charter schools?

Yes. Section 504 of the federal Rehabilitation Act specifically prohibits discrimination solely on the basis of disability to public and private programs and activities that receive federal financial assistance. Children who attend charter schools are covered by these civil rights laws in the same way as children in any other public school.

## 16:57. May a waiver be granted from Special Education requirements?

While charter schools must comply with all federal laws and regulations, just as any other public school in the State, a waiver may be requested from State or local requirements that exceed the federal requirements.

## 16:58. Must a charter school facility be accessible to students with disabilities?

Yes. The Americans with Disabilities Act (ADA) and Section 504 of the Rehabilitation Act of 1973 impose the same accessibility requirements on all public schools.

# Personnel/Employment

## 16:59. Who is the employer of the teachers and other staff working in the charter school?

The Charter School Act cross-references the Education Article's definitions of "public school employer" to mean a county board of education or Baltimore City Board of School Commissioners; and defines "employees of a public charter school" by cross-referencing the statutory definitions of public school employees under §§ 6-401(d) and (e) and 6-501(f) and (g) (Md. Code Ann., Ed. Art. § 9-108(a)). Therefore, the local board is the employer, and the employees are defined as either certificated professionals or noncertificated individuals employed for at least 9 months a year on a full-time basis by a public school employer (Md. Code Ann., Ed. Art. §§ 6-401(d) and 6-501(f)). For a detailed consideration of employment issues, see **Chapters 6** and **7**.

## 16:60. How are charter school teachers and other staff hired or assigned?

The Charter School Act does not affect the superintendent's authority to hire teachers and other staff and to transfer staff between schools. However, the State Board has allowed a charter school to "recruit and select all staff subject to the final approval of the [superintendent/CEO], and where required by statute, subject to the final approval of the [local board]" (*City Neighbors Charter School*, MSBE Order (July 29, 2005)).

## 16:61. Must a charter school teacher be certified and/or highly qualified under NCLB?

NCLB allows States to exempt charter school teachers from the state teacher certification requirements and yet be defined as "high qualified". Maryland's Charter School Act does not grant this exception, requiring that "a member of the professional staff of a public charter school shall hold the appropriate Maryland certification" (Md. Code Ann., Ed. Art. § 9-105). The State Board qualified this certification requirement to provide an exception for a position for which no certification requirements presently exist, such as a karate teacher (*City Neighbors Charter School*, MSBE Order (July 29, 2005)). For more detailed coverage of NCLB teacher requirements, see **Chapter 8**.

### 16:62. Are charter school employees included in the collective bargaining agreement?

Yes, generally. Title 9 confers to charter school employees "the rights granted under Title 6, Subtitles 4 and 5, of the Education Article". These sections define all certificated and noncertificated employees as members of their respective bargaining units, to be represented by an employee organization for purposes of collective bargaining (Md. Code Ann., Ed. Art. § 9-108(a)). (See **Chapter 7**.)

*The Maryland Public Charter Schools Model Policy and Resource Guide* (*"Guide"*) further explains that charter school employees "are in the bargaining unit(s) with other public school employees in similar job classifications and are entitled to the salaries, benefits and working conditions in the existing negotiated agreement for their job classification." In addition, the *Guide* reiterates that the "superintendent retains the authority to assign and transfer educators as the needs of the system require and as negotiated in the Charter Agreement."

The State Board granted a limited exception to the general rule that charter school employees must be included in a bargaining unit, by ruling that:

> With the exception of positions not currently offered by [the local school system] such as that of a karate teacher, all employees of [the charter school] are public school employees subject to the applicable collective bargaining provisions unless modifications are negotiated under Educ. Section 9-108(b).

(*City Neighbors Charter School*, MSBE Order (July 29, 2005)).

### 16:63. Can the existing collective bargaining agreement be amended with respect to the operation of a charter school?

Yes. The Charter School Act provides that "the employee organization and the public charter school may mutually agree to negotiate amendments to the existing agreement to address the needs of the particular public charter school" (Md. Code Ann., Ed. Art. § 9-108(b)). These agreements are subject to local school board approval.

This process is intended to facilitate amendments to agreements already in effect at the time of the charter approval. This provision of Title 9 does not limit the board and employee organization parameters for bargaining provisions specific to a charter school in the regular course of negotiating the terms of a new annual or multi-year agreement.

### 16:64. May the State Board grant a waiver from the requirement that a charter school's employees are subject to collective bargaining requirements for other public school employees?

No. Maryland's highest court recently held that provisions of the Charter School Act, including § 9-108, which defines the bargaining rights of charter school employees, are not subject to waiver (*Patterson Park Public Charter School, Inc., et al. v. The Baltimore Teachers Union, American Federation of Teachers Local 340, AFL-CIO, et al., No. 99*, September Term, 2006). The Charter School Act, in Sections 9-108(a)(1) and (2), defines charter school employees as public school employees and Section 9-108(a)(3) provides that charter school employees "shall have the rights granted under Title 6, Subtitles 4 and 5 of this article." Title 6 confers collective bargaining rights to all certificated and non-certificated public school employees. In addition to these provisions applying collective bargaining requirements to charter school employees, § 9-108(b) prescribes the method for amending an existing bargaining agreement with respect to the operation of a specific charter school.

The State Board indicated in opinions issued in 2005 that it would accept waiver requests regarding the status of charter school employees as members of the bargaining unit and regarding certification requirements (*Patterson Park Public School, Inc. v. Baltimore City Board of School Commissioners*, MSBE Op. No. 05-19 (2005)). State legislators and teachers unions argued that this statutory interpretation is contrary to legislative intent that the waivers may be granted only from "provisions of law and regulation governing other public schools", and that the Charter School Act's provisions are, by definition, not applicable to other public schools and therefore may not be waived. Agreeing with this argument, in *Patterson* the Court of Appeals stated "[t]o conclude otherwise would lead to the absurd result that all of Title 9's provisions could be waived, rendering the entire Title nugatory, a result that conflicts with the canons of statutory interpretation."

## Facilities

### 16:65. Must charter schools comply with facility requirements for other public schools?

Yes. Charter school facilities are subject to the review and approval of the State Superintendent. As public schools, the purchase or construction of charter schools are subject to the requirements under Section 2-303(f) of the Education Article, which provide, in part, that:

> (1) Subject to the bylaws, rules, and regulations of the State Board, the State Superintendent shall approve or disapprove each:

>> (i) Proposal for the purchase or sale of any ground, school site, or building;

>> (ii) Plan or specification for the remodeling of a school building if the remodeling costs more than $350,000;

>> (iii) Plan or specification for the construction of a new school building; and

>> (iv) Change order that costs more than $25,000 for the remodeling, restoration, or construction of a school building."

### 16:66. Are rented or leased charter school facilities subject to State approval?

Yes. MSDE issued a memorandum on March 1, 2005 outlining the process for local and State review and approval of rented or leased private or publicly-owned real property by a school system, or by a charter school, for use as a public school building. MSDE cited Section 4-115(b) of the Education Article as relevant statutory authority. The memorandum provides that:

1. Requests for approval shall be in writing from the local school system or, for charter schools, from the local school system chartering authority.

2. The local school system shall inspect and approve the site for use as a public school prior to submission of the request for approval to the State Superintendent.

3. The local school system or charter school shall obtain all approvals required by the fire marshal and other State and local agencies prior to submission of the request for approval to the State Superintendent.

4. The Maryland State Department of Education may inspect the site and may require review by other State agencies as a part of its evaluation of the lease.

5. The State Superintendent shall approve or disapprove all applicable leases in writing.

6. If the State Superintendent disapproves a lease, the Superintendent shall state the reasons for disapproval in writing.

## 16:67. Is the charter applicant's failure to secure a facility a sufficient basis to deny an application?

The State Board has opined that "failure to [identify an acceptable facility] may constitute a justifiable basis for denial of the application" (*Chesapeake Public Charter School v. St. Mary's County Board of Education*, MSBE Op. No. 05-23 (2005)).

## 16:68. May charter schools use the facilities of a religious organization?

A charter school may use the facilities of a religious organization to the same extent that other public schools may use these facilities. For example, a charter school may lease space from a church or other religious organization as long as the charter school remains non-sectarian in its programs and operations (*Non-Regulatory Guidance*, Charter School Program, Title V, Part B, USDE, July 2004).

# Finance

## 16:69. May a charter school charge tuition?

No. The Charter School Act defines a charter school, in part, as a public school that is "tuition free" (Md. Code Ann., Ed. Art. § 9-102(a)(7)). The *Model Policy,* approved by the State Board, provides that students domiciled in [the jurisdiction] will be eligible for admittance without tuition charge. Students not domiciled in [the jurisdiction] will be eligible for admittance without tuition charge only as allowed by the school system for other non-domiciled students attending other schools in the school system. In addition, the *Model Policy* states that "No eligible non-tuition-paying student may be denied admittance in the public charter school in order to accept a tuition-paying student" (see *Model Policy*, p.10).

## 16:70. How is a charter school funded?

The Charter School Act requires a local board to "disburse to a public charter school an amount of county, state, and federal money for elementary, middle, and secondary students that is commensurate with the amount disbursed to other public schools in the local jurisdiction" (Md. Code Ann., Ed. Art. § 9-109(a)). The Act also allows the State Board or local board to give surplus educational materials, supplies, furniture, and other equipment to a public charter school (Md. Code Ann., Ed. Art. § 9-109(b)). Other sources of funding could include private donations, or additional local, state, or federal funding.

**16:71. How is "commensurate with the amount disbursed to other public schools" defined?**

In three opinions issued in 2005, the State Board defined "commensurate" and "disbursed" according to the American Heritage Dictionary definitions, finding that "commensurate" means "of the same size, extent, or duration; corresponding in size or degree, proportionate", and "disbursed" means "paid out; expended as from a fund." The State Board concluded from the plain meaning of the terms that the General Assembly "intended that a public charter school receive federal, State, and local funding in an amount proportionate to the amount of funds expended for elementary, middle, and secondary level students in the other public schools in the same system" (*City Neighbors Charter School v. Baltimore City Board of Education*, MSBE Op. No. 05-17 (2005)).

**16:72. How is the "amount proportionate to the amount expended" for students calculated?**

The State Board acknowledged that Maryland has no "statewide formula or methodology that determines how local school systems fund their schools" and decided to "divide the total annual operating budget and each of the major category appropriations by the annual September 30 enrollment count of the school system for the previous year to calculate the average per pupil funding overall and per major category" (*City Neighbors Charter School v. Baltimore City Board of Education*, MSBE Op. No. 05-17 (2005)).

**16:73. Must the school system disburse this total per pupil amount to a charter school?**

The State Board revised its initial three funding decisions, including *City Neighbors* cited above, by reducing the total per pupil amount by 2 percent to reflect the costs to the school system to perform central office functions including data collection and reporting. This adjusted average per pupil amount is then multiplied by the student enrollment of the charter school to determine the total amount of funding for the charter school.

From this total amount, the charter school must reimburse the school system for costs including the salaries, local retirement contributions, and other fringe benefit costs for the public school employees working in the charter school. Similarly, the charter school must reimburse the school system for any regular services or supplies that it requests the system to provide.

In *Monocacy Montessori Communities, Inc. v. Frederick County Board of Education*, MSBE Op. No. 06-17 (2006), the State Board clarified that it had not intended to impose "such a rigid approach to determining commensurate funding" as a formula that must be applied "without deviation." Rather, the State Board is applying a standard of whether the amount of money a local school system is providing to a charter school corresponds to the "bottom line amount of money" determined by the State Board's formula.

### 16:74. Has the State Board's funding approach been challenged in court?

The State Board opinions defining commensurate funding were appealed to the circuit courts of Baltimore City and Prince George's County. The Baltimore City circuit court indicated that the State Board's reasoning was flawed, but decided the funding issue was moot (*Baltimore City Board of School Commissioners v. City Neighbors Charter School, et al.*, Case No. 24-C-05-005406 (2005)). The Prince George's County circuit court concluded that the State Board acted arbitrarily and capriciously in established a funding formula not prescribed by statute or supported by the record, and that the Board engaged in improper rulemaking by establishing a funding formula applicable to other school systems and charter school applicants without adhering to proper procedures for the issuance of regulations under the Maryland Administrative Procedures Act (*Board of Education of Prince George's County v. Lincoln Public Charter School, Inc.*, CAL05-10496 (November 10, 2005)).

The Maryland Court of Special Appeals heard the appeals arising from these circuit court decisions and affirmed the State Board's funding decision, finding that the State Board has the authority to determine the definition of commensurate funding, that it did so reasonably, and that the State Board may order a local board to correct any underfunding of a charter school. (*Baltimore City Board of School Commissioners v. City Neighbors Charter School, et al.*, September Term 2005, No. 1598).

In April 2007, Maryland's highest court, the Court of Appeals, heard oral arguments in the appeals it granted from the Court of Special Appeals decisions (*Baltimore City Board of School Commissioners v. City Neighbors Charter School, et al.*, No. 100, September Term, 2006; and *Board of Education of Prince George's County v. Lincoln Public Charter School, Inc.*, No. 121, September Term, 2006).

### 16:75. How are services for students eligible for special services under federal programs such as Title I or IDEA funded under this formula?

The State Board concluded that "with the exception of a student with disabilities for whom the IEP designates a non public school placement, we find that an average per pupil amount derived from the total annual system operating budget is sufficient for the charter to deliver the services for which the school's students are eligible." The charter school may choose whether to directly provide special services to eligible students or to have the school system provide the services. If the charter school chooses to not provide the services, it must reimburse the school system the proportionate cost of the services.

The Board recognized that funding restrictions in the two major federal programs, special education and Title I, would require adjustments by the charter school to comply with laws and regulations under these programs. The Board attached guidance documents to its funding decisions to further explain "Steps to Include Title I Funding for Charter Schools", "Special Education and Charter Schools", and "Use of Average per Pupil Funding and Central Office Support" (*City Neighbors Charter School v. Baltimore City Board of Education*, MSBE Op. No. 05-17 (2005)).

### 16:76. Does the federal government provide funding to support charter schools?

Yes. The federal Public Charter School (CSP) program, operated by the U.S. Department of Education, provides grants to State Education Agencies, including MSDE, to award to charter schools and applicants (20 U.S.C. §§ 8061–8067).

### 16:77. What grants are available to charter applicants and operators?

A total of $400,000 in federal grants may be awarded to a new charter school through the pre-planning, planning, and implementation phases. Pre-planning grants of up to $10,000 are available to charter applicants prior to receiving approval of a charter school agreement by a local school system. Pre-planning grants may be used for activities to facilitate the writing of a charter school proposal, such as hiring consultants, developing objectives, facility planning, professional development, and administrative costs.

Two planning and design grants of up $50,000 each are available to support the further design of the educational program, accountability tools, professional development, and community outreach. Planning and design grant funding will only be dispersed upon the charter school application being approved by the local board.

Two implementation grants of $100,000 each are available to approved charter operators to acquire necessary equipment, educational supplies and materials; acquire or develop curriculum materials; and to support other initial operational costs.

# Reporting

### 16:78. What must charter schools report to the local school system?

Title 9 requires each local board to develop a public charter school policy that includes guidelines and procedures regarding reporting requirements (Md. Code Ann., Ed. Art. § 9-109(a)).

### 16:79. What must the local school board report to the State Board?

Local boards are not subject to any state reporting requirements specific to charter schools that do not apply to all other public schools.

### 16:80. What does the State Board report to the General Assembly?

The Charter School Act requires the following:

> [O]n or before October 1, 2006, based on information gathered from each local board of education, the Board of School Commissioners of Baltimore City, and the public, the State Board of Education shall submit to the General Assembly, in accordance with § 2-1246 of the State Government Article, a report including an evaluation of the public charter school program. The report shall address the advisability of the continuation, modification, expansion, or termination of the program.

(See uncodified Section 3, Public Charter School Act of 2003, Chapter 358, Laws of Maryland (2003).)

# Evaluation

### 16:81. Who evaluates charter schools?

The local board must develop a public charter school policy that includes guidelines and procedures regarding the evaluation of public charter schools; revocation of a charter; reporting requirements; and financial, programmatic, or compliance audits (Md. Code Ann., Ed. Art. § 9-109(a)).

### 16:82. Under what conditions may the local school board revoke a charter?

Maryland statute does not prescribe any criteria or provide any guidance regarding the local board's authority to revoke a charter, other than the statutory requirement to develop and submit to the State Board the local policy, procedures, and guidelines for revocation of a charter (Md. Code Ann., Ed. Art. § 9-109(a)).

## Conflict of Interests

### 16:83. Are charter school personnel subject to the conflict of interest laws, regulations, and policies applying to other public school employees?

Notwithstanding any local or state waiver, charter schools "shall comply with the provisions of law and regulation governing other public schools" (Md. Code Ann., Ed. Art. § 9-106(a)).

### 16:84. Are federal Charter School Program grant recipients subject to any other "conflict of interest" requirements?

Yes. Federal guidance (34 C.F.R. §§ 74.42–74.44) provides that CSP grantees must comply with federal procurement standards in order to avoid a "conflict of interest" when purchasing equipment or services. The federal guidelines state:

> When using Federal funds to enter into a contract for equipment or services, a charter school must comply with the procurement standards set forth in the Department's regulations at 34 CFR 74.40-74.48. Those standards require Federal grant recipients to develop written procurement procedures and to conduct all procurement transactions in a manner to provide, to the maximum extent possible, open and free competition. No employee, officer, or agent of the charter school may participate in the selection, award, or administration of any contract supported by Federal funds if a real or apparent conflict of interest exists.

## Renewal and Revocation

### 16:85. How long can a charter school contract be renewed?

The Charter School Act does not place any limitations on the duration of a charter agreement or the timing or terms of the local school system's review and/or renewal of the charter. Therefore, the terms and conditions for renewal would be subject to the charter agreement.

### 16:86. For what reasons may a charter be revoked?

In the absence of statutory provisions, any State Board review of a local board's renewal or revocation decision would be reviewed under the "unreasonably, arbitrary, or illegal" standard applied in all cases involving a local policy or a controversy and dispute regarding the rules and regulations of the local board.

# Nonpublic Schools

### 16:87. What authority does the State's education system have with regard to nonpublic schools?

The responsibilities of State and local education agencies extend beyond the 24 local school districts to the many nonpublic schools and education programs operating in the State. In addition to the more than 860,000 public school students, thousands of children in the State attend private and parochial schools, or are home schooled by a parent or guardian. To a significant degree, State standards also apply to the operation of these schools and to home instruction.

### 16:88. What is a nonpublic school?

Generally, in addition to Maryland's system of public schools, children may attend privately operated schools or educational programs in accordance with laws and regulations administered by the Maryland State Department of Education. These nonpublic educational options include certified nonpublic schools, church exempt schools, and home instruction.

In addition, local school systems must place a student with a disability who needs special education and related services that cannot be provided in a public school, in an appropriate nonpublic educational program (Md. Code Ann., Ed. Art. § 8-406).

### 16:89. Does the State of Maryland oversee the operation of nonpublic schools?

Yes. MSDE administers Maryland's legal requirements pertaining to nonpublic schools. All nonpublic educational programs must hold a Certificate of Approval issued by the State Board of Education, with one major exception. Nonpublic schools that are operated by a bona fide church organization may register the school with MSDE as a church exempt school under the exemption provision in state law.

### 16:90. Must all nonpublic schools or programs be approved by MSDE?

No. However, every nonpublic school must either be approved or registered with MSDE as church-exempt.

### 16:91. May any nonpublic entity refer to itself as a "school"?

No. An entity may not use of the terms "preschool", "school", "institute", or "academy" or "words of like meaning, in such manner as to connote the offering of a high school, junior-high or middle school, elementary school, kindergarten, nursery school, or any combination thereof" unless the entity holds the appropriate MSDE certification or is church-exempt (COMAR 13A.09.01).

### 16:92. Do private schools receive any direct State funded education aid?

The annual State budget bill has, for several years, appropriated limited funds to support nonpublic school purchases of textbooks, computer hardware and software, and other electronically delivered learning materials.

### 16:93. Does the State have any record-keeping requirements for nonpublic schools?

Yes. MSDE maintains and issues secondary school transcripts for students who attended nonpublic secondary schools that have closed.

## Church-Exempt Schools

### 16:94. What is a "church-exempt" school?

Nonpublic schools that are governed and operated by a bona fide church organization may be exempt from holding a Certificate of Approval from the State Board of Education and the educational standards adopted under COMAR 13A.09.09 (Md. Code Ann., Ed. Art. § 2-206).

### 16:95. Is a church-exempt school required to comply with any approval or licensure requirements?

A church-exempt school is exempt from all State education regulations other than the requirement to register with MSDE as a church-exempt school. However, a church-exempt school is not exempt from the various laws applicable to other schools, such as local zoning ordinances, health department regulations, fire safety regulations, asbestos regulations, criminal background checks, child abuse and neglect reporting law, and child care licensing requirements.

### 16:96. What educational standards must a church-exempt school meet?

A church-exempt school operates its educational program in accordance with standards that are established by the governing church.

**16:97. Does attendance in a school that does not hold a Certificate of Approval or is not registered as church-exempt meet the compulsory school attendance law (Age 5 through 16)?**

A school that does not hold a Certificate of Approval or that is not registered as church-exempt is not operating in compliance with Maryland law. Attendance in such a school, therefore, may not meet the compulsory school attendance requirement.

# Home Instruction

**16:98. What is home-schooling or home instruction?**

Home instruction is instruction provided in accordance with State laws and regulations that is provided by parents or guardians to a child not enrolled in a public or nonpublic school (see COMAR 13A.10.01).

**16:99. Is home instruction supervised?**

Yes. Home instruction must be supervised, and a parent may choose to have the home instruction supervised by the local school system, a certified nonpublic school, or an education program operated by a bona fide church organization that is registered with the MSDE.

**16:100. What is the local school system's role in supervising home instruction?**

Regulations require each local school system to establish a procedure to be used by the superintendent to determine if a child participating in a home instruction program is receiving regular, thorough instruction during the school year in the studies usually taught in the public schools to children of the same age (COMAR 13A.10.01.01).

**16:101. What is a parent's role?**

If a parent/guardian chooses home schooling under the supervision of the local school system, the parent/guardian is required to comply with three requirements:

- Initially sign a statement consenting to the pertinent provisions of State regulation;

- Maintain a comprehensive portfolio of materials that demonstrates the child's progress; and

- Permit a local school system representative to review the portfolio, discuss the education program, and observe instruction (COMAR 13A.10.01).

## 16:102. Are there any curricular requirements for home instruction?

Regulations (COMAR 13A.10.01.01) require that a home instruction program shall:

(1) Provide regular, thorough instruction in the studies usually taught in the public schools to children of the same age;

(2) Include instruction in English, mathematics, science, social studies, art, music, health, and physical education; and

(3) Take place on a regular basis during the school year and be of sufficient duration to implement the instruction program.

## 16:103. May a local school system impose any additional requirements for home instruction?

No. State regulations, COMAR 13A.10.01F, prohibit additional requirements beyond those stated in the regulations.

## 16:104. Must a home-schooled student participate in State assessments, such as the MSAs or HSAs?

No. However, at the request of the parent/guardian, a student receiving home instruction may participate in these assessments in the school the child is eligible to attend (COMAR 13A.10.02).

## 16:105. May a home-schooled student participate in public school activities?

No. Public schools are not statutorily authorized to allow home-schooled students to participate in extracurricular activities and academic programs at public schools. Legislation has been introduced in recent years, but not enacted, that would have authorized a public school to allow a home-schooled student to participate in extracurricular activities and the academic programs offered at the public school.

## 16:106. What is the nonpublic school's role in supervising home instruction?

State regulations, COMAR 13A.10.01.05, allow a parent or guardian to provide home instruction offered through correspondence courses under the supervision of a non public school. The regulations require that supervision by the nonpublic school must include, at a minimum, all of the following components: (1) textbooks, lesson materials, and other instructional materials or equipment designed to be used independently by the student at a site other than a school; and (2) assignment of a school-based teacher to assist the parent/guardian in using the correspondence courses and to assist the student by issuing progress reports, marking papers, and grading tests.

## 16:107. What is the religious organization's role in supervising home instruction?

State regulations, COMAR 13A.10.01.05, allow a parent or guardian to provide home instruction offered through correspondence courses under the supervision of a bona fide church organization. The regulations require that the supervision must include, at a minimum, all of the following components: (1) pre-enrollment conferences with parents/guardians; (2) textbooks, lesson materials, and other instructional materials or equipment designed to be used independently by the student at a site other than a school; (3) annual visits by supervisory personnel to the site where the student is receiving instruction; and (4) conferences with parents/guardians at appropriate intervals during the period of enrollment.

## 16:108. Are home schooled students entitled to receive special education services?

Children with disabilities who are home schooled do not have an individual entitlement to special education services. Federal special education law, the Individuals with Disabilities Education Act (IDEA), requires local school systems to make special education services available to students in public and private schools, but this requirement does not extend to students who are home-schooled.

However, IDEA does require that local school systems identify and evaluate all children in the district who are in need of special education and related services. See **Chapter 15** for a detailed discussion of this IDEA "Child Find" requirement.

# TABLE OF CASES

## A

## B

## C

# D

# E

Lawrence University Bicentennial Commission v. City of Appleton, 409 F. Supp. 1319 (E.D. Wis. 1976) – 12:36

Ledbetter v. Goodyear Tire & Rubber Co., Inc., ___ U.S. ___ (2007) – 6:72

Lee v. Weisman, 505 U.S. 577 (1992) – 13:4, 13:9, 13:23

Lee v. York County School Division, 484 F.3d 687 (4th Cir. 2007) – 7:52

Lemon v. Kurtzman, 403 U.S. 602 (1971) – 13:4, 13:5, 13:8, 13:25

Livers v. Charles County Board of Education, 6 Op. MSBE 407 (1992), *aff'd*, 101 Md. App. 160, *cert. denied*, 336 Md. 594 (1994) – 6:18, 6:35, 7:1, 7:9, 7:23

Lubore v. RPM Associates, 109 Md. App. 312 (1996) – 9:23

Lynch v. Donnelly, 465 U.S. 668 (1984) – 13:10

Lynn v. Anne Arundel County Board of Education, MSBE Op. No. 04-20 (2004) – 2:42, 11:33

# M

M.A.L. v. Kinsland, No. 07-10391 (E.D. Mich. Jan. 30, 2007) – 13:32

M.B. v. Liverpool Central School District, No. 04-1255 (N.D. N.Y. March 29, 2007) – 13:32

Mace v. Board of Education of Harford County, MSBE Op. No. 01-15 (2001) – 11:25

Mace v. Carroll County Board of Education, MSBE Op. No. 88-01 (1988) – 11:53

Makovi v. Sherwin-Williams Co., 316 Md. 603 (1989) – 7:32

Manzer v. Diamond Shamrock Chemicals Co., 29 F.3d 1078 (6th Cir. 1994) – 14:15

Marbach v. Board of Education of Montgomery County, 6 Op. MSBE 351 (1992) – 10:28

Marchesi v. Franchino, 283 Md. 131 (1978) – 9:23, 9:40

Marshall v. Board of Education of Howard County, 7 Op. MSBE 596 (1997) – 10:24

Martin & Deluca v. Howard County Board of Education, MSBE Op. No. 04-09 (2004) – 11:28

Mary Beth G. v. City of Chicago, 723 F.2d 1263 (7th Cir. 1983) – 11:54

Massie v. Henry, 455 F.2d 779 (4th Cir. 1972) – 12:28

Matta v. Board of Education of Prince George's County, 552 A.2d 1340 (1989) – 9:20

Mayer v. Monroe County Community School Corporation, 474 F.3d 477 (7th Cir. 2007) – 7:52

McCarthy v. Board of Education of Anne Arundel County, 280 Md. 634 (1977) – 2:9, 4:59

# Q

United States v. Virginia, 518 U.S. 515 (1996) – 14:22

## V

Venter v. Howard County Board of Education, MSBE Op. No. 05-22 (2005) – 7:21

Vernonia School District 47J v. Acton, 515 U.S. 646 (1995) – 11:6, 11:56

## W

Wallace v. Ford, 346 F. Supp. 156 (E. Dist. Ark. 1972) – 12:22

Wallace v. Jaffree, 472 U.S. 38 (1985) – 13:22

Washington County Education Classified Employees Association v. Board of Education of Washington County, 97 Md. App. 397 (1993) – 6:32, 6:67

Waters v. Churchill, 511 U.S. 661 (1994) – 7:52

West v. Derby Unified School District No. 260, 206 F.3d 1258 (2000) – 12:25

Wigg v. Sioux Falls School District, 382 F.3d 807 (8th Cir. 2004) – 13:28

Wiggins v. Board of School Commissioners of Baltimore City, MSBE Op. No. 04-44 (2004) – 7:5

Wiley v. School Commissioners, 51 Md. 401 (1879) – 2:33

Williams v. Board of Education of Montgomery County, 5 Op. MSBE 507 (1990) – 10:24

Williams v. New Baltimore City Board of School Commissioners, MSBE Op. No. 01-23 (2001) – 10:108, 10:119

Wilson v. Board of Education, 234 Md. 561 (1964) – 2:34

Wilson v. The Daily Gazette Company, No. 31045 (W. Va. June 13, 2003) – 9:36

Winkelman v. Parma City School District, 550 U.S. ___ (2007) – 15:62

Wisconsin v. Mitchell, 508 U.S. 476 (1993) – 12:24

Wisconsin v. Yoder, 406 U.S. 205 (1972) – 10:15, 13:11, 13:18

Wood v. Strickland, 420 U.S. 308 (1975) – 9:44, 11:5

Worton Creek Marina, LLC v. Claggett, 381 Md. 499 (2004) – 2:9

Wynne v. Town of Great Falls, South Carolina, 376 F.3d 292 (4th Cir. 2004) – 13:56

## Z

Zaal v. Maryland, 326 Md. 54 (1992) – 10:118

Zeitschel v. Board of Education, 274 Md. 69 (1975) – 2:34

# USER'S GUIDE TO THE INDEX

This index contains treatment of the material compiled in *Maryland School Law Deskbook*, 2007 – 2008 School Year Edition. The references in the index are to question numbers.

Two basic rules for using this index are:

1. *Consult the most pertinent subject.* For example, if you were looking in an evidence book for information about prayer in schools, you would start with PRAYER IN SCHOOLS rather than broader headings like NCLB or RELIGION. The broader headings may also exist, but to find the material more quickly, look for the specific subject first.

2. *Cross references.* Pay close attention to and make full use of the index cross references. An index cross reference directs the index user to go to another part of the index to find treatment. This serves to keep indexes to a manageable size by reducing repetition of treatment under different headings.

The index benefits from customer suggestions. Especially helpful are popular names or legal terms specific to your profession or area of practice. We are grateful for your assistance in the ongoing improvement of the index.

To contact the indexers, you may use either of the following methods:

- Contact the indexers via a toll-free number, 1-800-897-7922, for assistance in locating material within the index, or to make comments or suggestions.

- Contact the indexers by e-mail to *lng-cho-indexing@lexisnexis.com*.

For issues not directly related to the index, such as ordering or other customer service information, you may contact Customer Service via a toll-free number, 1-800-833-9844, or by toll-free fax at 1-800-828-8341.

# INDEX

# Notes

# Notes

# Notes

# Notes

# Notes

# Notes

# Notes

# Notes

# Notes

**Notes**

# Notes

# Notes

# Notes

# Notes

**Notes**

# We invite your comments on this publication

*Send us your feedback and receive a discount\* on your next purchase. Complete and fax or mail this form to:*

FAX: 434-972-7531, attention Custom Legal Publications

MAIL: LexisNexis, CLP-Rm 440, 701 East Water Street, Charlottesville, VA 22902

PUBLICATION TITLE: _____ Product #: _____

| Please rate the following features: | Quality: High ———> Low | | | | | Importance to you: High ———> Low | | | | |
|---|---|---|---|---|---|---|---|---|---|---|
| Timeliness of publication | 5 | 4 | 3 | 2 | 1 | 5 | 4 | 3 | 2 | 1 |
| Content | 5 | 4 | 3 | 2 | 1 | 5 | 4 | 3 | 2 | 1 |
| Index | 5 | 4 | 3 | 2 | 1 | 5 | 4 | 3 | 2 | 1 |
| CD-ROM (if applicable) | 5 | 4 | 3 | 2 | 1 | 5 | 4 | 3 | 2 | 1 |
| Price | low $ | fair $ | | high $ | | 5 | 4 | 3 | 2 | 1 |

I would like to see the following **additional statutes** included: _____
_____
_____
_____

I would like to see the following **additional index entries** included: _____
_____
_____
_____

I would find this publication more useful with the following **change(s)**: _____
_____
_____
_____
_____

❏ **YES, please send my discount\*:**          Date: ___ / ___ / _____

Name _____ Job Title _____
Organization _____
Address _____
_____

Phone _____ Email _____

May we contact you to follow up on your comments . . . . . . . . . . . . . . . . . . . . . . . . . ❏ YES   ❏ NO

I am interested in receiving email on LexisNexis special offers and products. . . . . . ❏ YES   ❏ NO

\* You will receive a discount code limited to one use.